Introduction

The world of LightWave 3D is so powerful that it has brought extinct creatures to life and has sunk mighty "unsinkable" ships. As an owner of LightWave, you now have this power in your hands. Mastering such power is a massive challenge that will require a lot of time and mental energy. Luckily, you'll find this book—*Light-Wave Applied, Version 6.5 & 7*—a strong guide to conquering this challenge.

LightWave Applied, Version 6.5 & 7 is unlike any other book or manual you've stumbled across. That is because *LightWave Applied, Version 6.5 & 7* is based on the notion that people learn best from hands-on projects. Therefore, instead of a list of button descriptions and quick tips, this book takes you into the world of actual model building and animation—a world where you create an awesome environment of hands-on projects.

The tutorials in *LightWave Applied, Version 6.5 & 7* are some of the most in-depth tutorials ever written for any book—some containing hundreds of steps and images. Luckily, you'll find this book easy to follow because each tutorial is divided into a step-by-step process. The novice and advanced applications in Tutorials 3 through 11 may be intimidating for those entering the 3D community with LightWave 3D. This is the reason for Tutorial 1, which gives those just starting out some of the basic knowledge, advice, and beginner instructions needed to overcome the "intimidation factor."

Though Tutorials 1 through 10 were written for LightWave 6.5, we have found them to work equally well in LightWave 7. In addition, Tutorial 11 is completely about LightWave 7.

It is our sincere hope that every page will be a great benefit in advancing your work and career, as that was the reason for writing the book.

AUTHOR COMMITMENT

Each author of *LightWave Applied, Version 6.5 & 7* is very responsive to questions from readers. That is why the authors have set up a forum in the reader-only bonus area of the website where you can ask questions pertaining to any of the tutorials in this book. You can access the forums by going into the reader bonus area at http://www.advanstarbooks.com/lightwave/.

SPECIAL THANKS AND ACKNOWLEDGMENTS

The authors wish to express their thanks for the support of family and friends during the writing of this book. The authors also thank Danell Durica, the book manager, for her persistence, patience, and all around great management skills. Her ability to manage such huge projects is quite impressive.

In addition, the authors express a special thank you to Lachina Publishing Services for its excellent services in putting the book together. A big thank you to the Epic Software Group for the CD and to Willie Lloyd for the cartoons. Finally, the authors acknowledge NewTek and the LightWave 3D community, particularly for the dreams and visions each user strives for to reach their ultimate success. Here's to you!

ABOUT THE AUTHORS

Dave Jerrard, from Valencia, California, is a Hollywood special effects artist whose work has been seen on TV shows like "Roughnecks: Starship Troopers Chronicles." For three years, Dave Jerrard served as the lead tutorial writer for NewTekniques magazine, specializing in Hollywood special effects using LightWave 3D. Jerrard's last book was *LightWave 3D Applied—Version 5.6*, which was so successful that many universities started using the book as an animation teaching tool.

LightWave™ Applied
Version 6.5 & 7

Dave Jerrard
Joe Tracy
Jennifer Hachigian
Epic Software Group

ADVANSTAR
COMMUNICATIONS

Cleveland, Ohio

Printed in the United States of America

10 9 8 7 6 5 4 3 2 1

ISBN 0-929870-59-X

Library of Congress Card Number 2001086087

Published by Advanstar Communications Inc.

Advanstar Communications is a worldwide business information company that publishes magazines, directories, and books, produces expositions and conferences, provides a wide range of marketing services, and maintains numerous Websites.

For additional information on any Advanstar product or for a complete catalog of published books, please write to: Advanstar Customer Service, 131 West 1st Street, Duluth, Minnesota, 55802 USA; or call 1-800-598-6008; or visit www.advanstar.com.

To purchase additional copies of *LightWave Applied, Version 6.5 & 7*, please call 1-800-598-6008; outside the U.S. call 218-723-9180; on-line at www.advanstarbooks.com/lightwave/. Price per copy is $49.95; call for quantity discounts.

ATTENTION PUBLISHERS, TEACHERS, SEMINAR LEADERS, ORGANIZATIONS, COLLEGES AND UNIVERSITIES: Quantity discounts are available on bulk purchases of this book for sales promotions, educational purposes, or premiums. For more information, please call 1-800-598-6008 or outside the U.S. at 218-723-9180.

Publisher/Product Manager: Danell M. Durica
Cover Design and CD-ROM: Epic Software Group, Inc., The Woodlands, Texas
Interior Design: Lachina Publishing Services, Inc., Cleveland, Ohio
Cartoons: Willie Lloyd, Fort Meyers, Florida

LightWave ™ is a trademark of NewTek, Inc.

About the LightWave™ Applied 6.5 & 7 CD-ROM and Cartoons

THE CD-ROM

By working the tutorial projects in LightWave Applied, Version 6.5 & 7, you will gain practical, hands-on experience and learn many secrets of the pros. The CD-ROM, produced by the animation wizards at the Epic Software Group, contains an animated intro, along with content from the book showcased in an easy-to-use interactive menu. Here you will find dozens of LightWave 3D Gallery samples and even the full version of the latest LightWave demo reel. You are just a few clicks away from bonus tutorials, Web links, and eye candy designed to educate and inspire all who wish to gain mastery of the world of LightWave 3D.

The CD-ROM is easy to use. Just pop it into your CD-ROM drive and follow the instructions/menu. For more detailed information about using the CD-ROM, check out the *LightWave Applied* Website at http://www.advanstarbooks.com/lightwave. We believe that you'll find this free CD alone to be worth the price of the entire book. Enjoy!

THE CARTOONS

The cartoons that begin each tutorial were created by Willie Lloyd, a long-time LightWave 3D artist. Lloyd has done a lot of LightWave 3D work for television affiliate stations (mostly Warner Brothers) across the United States. In his free time, Lloyd does humorous LightWave sketches.

Contents

Joe Tracy, from Santa Barbara, California, was the founding editor and associate publisher of *NewTekniques* magazine, which is recognized as the #1 magazine for LightWave 3D artists and animators. Tracy spent four years as a high school computer animation teacher and has written three books including *Web Marketing Applied*. In addition, he was one of the authors of *LightWave 3D Applied—Version 5.6*.

Epic Software Group, located in The Woodlands, Texas, was founded by Victor F. Cherubini, current company President, in 1990 to create a dynamic computer based multimedia presentations company. The group he assembled creates 3D graphics and animations that are interactive, unique, and highly memorable. These presentations are used in CD-ROM's, video productions, and on the Internet.

Jennifer Hachigian, from southern California, is a visual effects artist. She runs the Celshader.com Website. Hachigian earned her bachelor's degree in computer science from Michigan State University, with a cognate in studio art. Her interests include anime, comic books, manga, martial arts, video games, cool computer hardware, as well as writing and drawing a small-press comic book called *"Lore."*

1

Introduction to LightWave 6.5

Joe Tracy

OVERVIEW

Many people who buy LightWave 3D as their first introduction into the 3D world find the program too intimidating to use. Some of these people resell the program to a friend while others let it sit on a shelf and collect dust.

The purpose of this tutorial is to take those of you who are beginners in the world of LightWave 3D and introduce you to some introductory techniques that will help you overcome that intimidation and open the door to a broader experience. If you are already gifted in LightWave 3D you'll want to move on to the next tutorial, which begins the more advanced step-by-step tutorials. If this is your first experience into the world of 3D, then read on! The majority of our time in this tutorial will be spent in Modeler, which for many is the more difficult of the two (Modeler and Layout) to learn.

In this tutorial you will use:

- Many basic features and buttons in Modeler
- Many basic features and buttons in Layout

What you will need:

- LightWave 3D 6.5 or 7.0
- A couple of free hours

What you will learn:

- Three things your computer needs to enhance Modeler/Layout
- The general interface structure of Modeler
- How to create and surface objects
- Uses of the Boolean command
- How to use Layers
- How to create multiple surfaces on one object
- How to create 3D text
- How to cut, paste, and set the Perspective view
- How to change surfaces in Modeler and Layout
- How to create keyframes
- How to create a lens flare
- How to use background images
- How to move and rotate objects
- X, Y, Z, and H, P, B

THE POWER OF LIGHTWAVE

NewTek's LightWave 6.5 is a very powerful program. Like versions before it, LightWave gives everyone the opportunity to create stunning animated productions without selling their home. Lead LightWave programmers Allen Hastings and Stuart Ferguson, along with their team of senior programmers, are to thank for giving the power to the people when it comes to 3D animation.

Since NewTek was founded in 1985, it has empowered users, through products like LightWave, to make their visions a reality. Suddenly creating your own *Star Wars* effects is very much achievable. Yet to do that, you must first learn the program and overcome the intimidation factor.

The Intimidation Factor

First-time users of LightWave may be hit with what I call "the intimidation factor." There are so many buttons, options, and "foreign commands" in LightWave that it is easy for a first-time user to become intimidated.

One of the authors of the last *LightWave 3D Applied* book was Scott Wheeler. Wheeler is well known for the excellent LightWave effects he created for shows like *Space: Above and Beyond, The X-Files, Buffy the Vampire Slayer,* and *From the Earth to the Moon.* Yet he was once in the exact position you are in today. Wheeler best explains his situation in the April 1997 issue of *NewTekniques* magazine. He had just been hired as a cable employee in Danvers, Massachusetts: "Soon after I arrived, we got a Video Toaster and I began playing with the Switcher, CG, and ToasterPaint," Wheeler says. "Occasionally I would hit the 3D button [which loads Light-Wave] by accident and scream in horror at the alien nature of the module." But one day, he decided to dive right in and experiment.

Wheeler wasn't alone; this intimidation factor usually hits new users when they open up LightWave for the first time and see numerous buttons with words they've never heard of, such as Lathe, Boolean, Dithered Motion Blur, Edge Z Scale, Pivot Point, Rail Extrude, and Numeric Knife Parameters.

Like Wheeler, you will find it important to commit to diving in and learning LightWave without fear of becoming intimidated. "Slowly, I began exploring more with the 3D button and eventually got to the point where I was making logo openings for shows we produced," says Wheeler. As Wheeler discovered, and so will you, *the more you experiment the more fun it becomes.*

It is important to note that Wheeler didn't become a LightWave expert overnight. Rather, over a period of years he molded his skills with LightWave until he eventually became a premier Hollywood artist creating award-winning special effects!

This tutorial is aimed at beginners and will provide you with an easy step-by-step start to using LightWave and to learning what several of the commands represent. This tutorial will cover very basic concepts and controls that will leave you feeling more comfortable to experiment on your own. After completing this tutorial, you will be able to tackle the more advanced tutorials (Tutorials 2–9), which are presented in the same easy-to-follow step-by-step format.

Getting Started

LightWave 6.5 is a free upgrade for users of LightWave 6.0. The upgrade contains new time-saving features, bug fixes, and several new additions such as an integrated particles system and new HyperVoxel nodes.

It is imperative that you upgrade to 6.5 if you are using 6.0, particularly if you are using LightWave on the Macintosh. Many Macintosh users reported a vast number of bugs with LightWave 6.0 that made it nearly impossible to use the program. The LightWave 6.5 upgrade has resolved these issues for the Macintosh along with many issues that plagued the Windows version.

If you are using LightWave 6.0 you must upgrade before proceeding in order to properly use the tutorials throughout this book. To upgrade, go to http://www.newtek.com/products/lightwave/downloads_main.html and click the appropriate link (Windows or Macintosh) to begin your download process.

System Requirements

If you are using LightWave for Windows, NewTek recommends the following minimum system requirements:

1. Windows NT 4.0 with Service Pack 6a or higher

2. 64 MB of RAM or more

3. PII 266 MHz processor or higher

4. 32 MB or higher video display card that supports the OpenGL standard

In addition, NewTek has a number of security measures in place to make sure you are a licensed user. One of these requirements is a dongle (or "Hardware Key," as it is sometimes called) that connects to your computer's parallel port (for Windows) or ADB port (for Macintosh). Make sure your computer is turned off before inserting the dongle.

The second security measure is requiring you to obtain a *permanent license key* number in order to use the program beyond 14 days. For every day you don't have a key, you will receive a reminder (Figure 1-1) until your 14 days are up. Then the program simply won't load, giving you an error message that you must obtain a permanent license key to proceed.

FIGURE 1-1

Here are the steps you need to follow to obtain your permanent license key:

STEP 1: When you install LightWave 6.0 (or 6.5) you will be given an Internal Dongle ID #. Write this number down.

STEP 2: Write down your serial number, which is located on the back of the CD case that contains your LightWave 6.0 (or 6.5) CD-ROM.

STEP 3: Call NewTek Customer Service at 1-800-862-7837. Let them know that you need a permanent license key number. The representative will ask for your Internal Dongle ID # and your serial number. After you provide this information to the representative, he or she will give you your permanent license key number. Write this number down and repeat it back to the representative to make sure it is correct. If you are using a Mac, have the representative assist you with "installing" the permanent license key number. If you are using Windows, then continue to the next step.

STEP 4: From your computer desktop, double-click the My Computer icon.

STEP 5: Double-click the local drive (usually Drive C:) icon.

STEP 6: Double-click the LightWave folder.

STEP 7: Double-click the Programs folder.

STEP 8: Double-click the Lightwave_support folder.

STEP 9: Find the License icon, then double-click it. If you are asked what program to use to open it, choose Notebook.

STEP 10: When the file opens, you'll see a number. Delete the number and replace it with your permanent license key number that the NewTek representative provided for you. Choose File, then Save. Close the Notebook window.

Congratulations! You are now registered and almost ready to begin exploring the power of LightWave. But first, there are three important things you should have to simplify your life in the computer animation world.

Three Things to Simplify Your Life

Before you start using LightWave, you should strongly consider obtaining three key things that will simplify your life while using the program:

1. *RAM.* RAM is cheap and makes a major difference in the amount of resources and memory you have when operating LightWave 6.5. I very strongly recommend that you have at least 128 MB of RAM installed in your computer. While a minimum of 128 MB of RAM is well above the program's requirements, it is necessary when you consider the relative low cost of RAM and the amount of frustration that extra RAM will save you from enduring. Many aspects of LightWave 6.5 heavily depend on RAM,

and the more RAM you have, the more smoothly the program will run. If you can afford it, purchase even more than 128 MB of RAM.

2. *OpenGL card.* You must have an OpenGL card installed in your computer to properly use LightWave 6.5. Most graphics cards (including many preinstalled cards) are OpenGL compatible. But you must be sure before proceeding. So what is the best card for you to own? Not only is that question very debatable, but the results change regularly as new cards are introduced. Luckily, we have prepared a special bonus Web site for *Light-Wave Applied* readers; one part of the Web site contains links to dozens of OpenGL Web sites (such as http://www.opengl .org/) and articles that compare OpenGL cards. To access the bonus area, go to http://www.advanstarbooks.com/lightwave/ and click "Access LightWave Applied Bonus Area."

3. *Updates.* Check NewTek's Web site (http://www.newtek.com/) regularly to see if any bug fixes or updates have been recently released. As of this writing, the direct URL to NewTek's LightWave Support page is http://www.newtek.com/support /psupport/ lightwave.html. If this changes, it will be updated in the LightWave Applied bonus area.

Time to Play!

Now that all the formalities are out of the way, let's have some fun. This tutorial has been set up to explain some beginning process techniques to you in the most simplistic form possible. Once you've mastered these techniques, you should feel confident to begin experimenting on your own and to try the more advanced tutorials in Tutorials 2–9 to increase your knowledge. In addition, the Light-Wave Applied bonus area contains links to what I consider good starting points for LightWave newbies. Also, be sure to check out the bonus links on the CD-ROM that came with this book.

Keep in mind when going through this tutorial that there are dozens of ways to accomplish the same task in LightWave. Therefore, experimentation is extremely important.

There are two main parts of LightWave. The first is called Modeler and the second is called Layout. Modeler is where you create objects and Layout is where you animate objects. You'll notice when going to open LightWave that you have two choices—an icon named LightWave and an icon named Modeler. Clicking the LightWave icon opens Layout (NewTek should simply call it "Layout" to help avoid confusion).

Clicking the Modeler icon opens Modeler. You can easily switch between Modeler and Layout by simply pressing F12. So if you're in Modeler and want to move to Layout, pressing F12 instantly takes you to Layout while still keeping Modeler open in the background. And speaking of Modeler . . .

MODELER SIMPLIFIED

Our journey into the world of LightWave begins with Modeler. In its most basic form, Modeler represents two ideas:

1. Shapes make objects.

2. Points are dots and polygons are the connection of the dots.

You might be surprised to learn that some of the most detailed 3D objects you see in videos and on television are simply shapes that have been manipulated into objects. Remember when you were a kid playing with Legos? You would take the shaped Lego pieces and connect them to make some inventive and cool creations. Or perhaps you played with clay; you would roll the clay into a big circle then begin shaping it into another object. Both of these are examples of Modeler simplified!

A Look at the Interface Windows

When you first enter Modeler, your screen should look like Figure 1-2. The workspace is divided into four "windows" (or screens). Three of the windows are for you to work in; the fourth window (top right) is where you view the results of your work. The window defaults for LightWave Modeler are as follows:

1. The upper-left window is the Top view.

2. The lower-left window is the Back view.

3. The lower-right window is the Left view.

4. The upper-right window is the Perspective view.

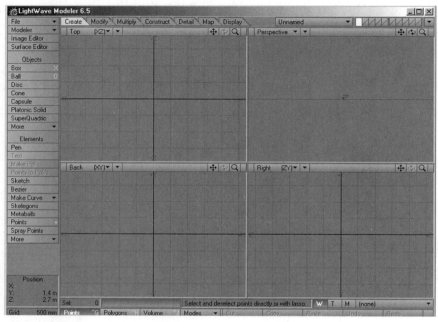

FIGURE 1-2

You'll work within the first three windows and view the results of your work within the Perspective view window. See Figure 1-3 to easily identify the four windows.

When working with LightWave Modeler, you'll notice that NewTek has provided many customized options to help you work more efficiently. While working with four windows is a standard in the 3D industry, NewTek realizes that users have different preferences. With that in mind, Modeler now provides users with an array of display options for your windows. The default (Figure 1-3) is called the Quad view. But you may find something other than the Quad view more suitable to your needs. Here's how to change the default:

STEP 1: On the main toolbar under the File button is another button named Modeler. Use your mouse pointer to point to the Modeler button, then click and hold the mouse button. More options will appear. From these choose Options, then Display Options (Figure 1-4) and release the mouse button. The Display Options panel will open (Figure 1-5). (*Note:* In the future you can bring this panel up quickly by simply pressing D).

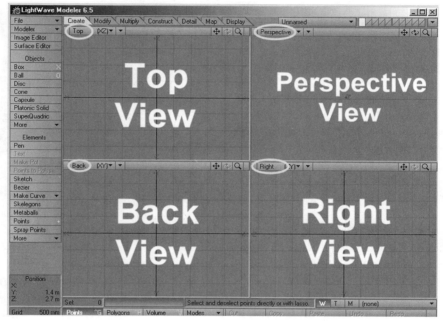

FIGURE 1-3

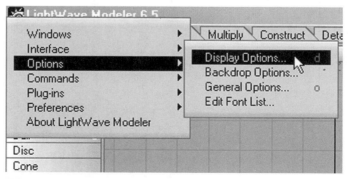

FIGURE 1-4

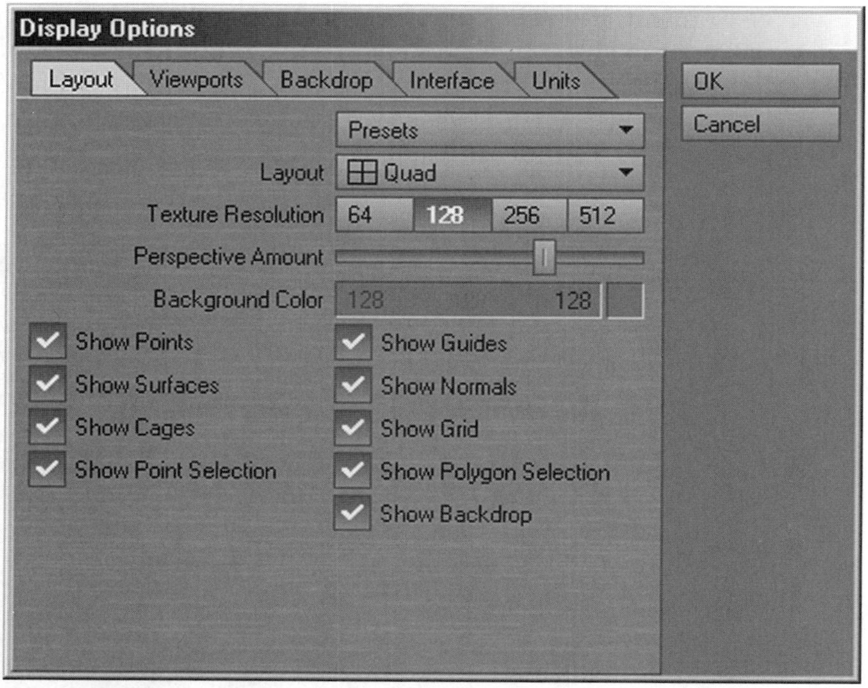

FIGURE 1-5

STEP 2: In the Display Options panel you'll see that *Quad* appears on the menu to the right of the word *Layout*. Point to this menu, then click and hold to see more options. From these options, choose 2 Left, 1 Right (Figure 1-6). Click OK to close the Display Options panel.

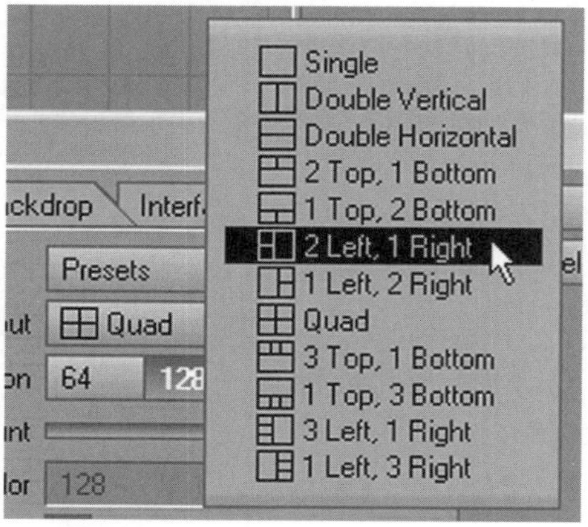

FIGURE 1-6

As you can see in Figure 1-7, Modeler has changed to reflect the new Layout option. You can choose from the 12 options shown in Figure 1-6 when working in Modeler.

For the purposes of this tutorial, you'll want to revert to Quad view. Press D to open the Display Options panel and change the Layout option back to Quad. Click OK.

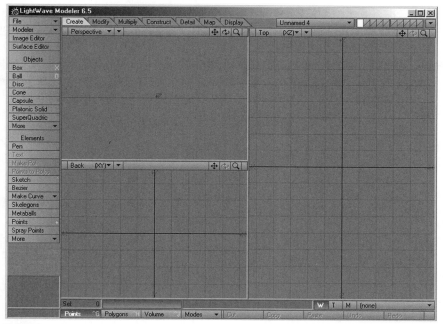

FIGURE 1-7

Tip: Enlarge Viewing Area

When working with a window, if you want that window to temporarily fill the screen, move your pointer to the screen you want to enlarge, then press 0 on your keyboard's numeric keypad (usually located on the right side of your keyboard). This will instantly enlarge that window to fill the screen. To return to your regular display, press 0 again. This very cool new feature will save you a lot of time when trying to focus on important details.

Toolbars and Tabs

Another new aspect of LightWave 6.5 Modeler is the small tool-bars that appear above each window view with commands that help you view your object. The first part of the toolbar lists the current view (see circled items in Figure 1-3). Notice the black down arrow immediately to the right of the view name. This indicates that this button has more options.

Point to the word *Top* in the Top view window, then click and hold. As you can see in Figure 1-8, a list of new view options appears. The options are (none), Top, Bottom, Back, Front, Right, Left, Perspective, and UV Texture. This makes it easy to customize the window views for maximum efficiency. For the purpose of this tutorial, leave the defaults as shown in Figure 1-3.

FIGURE 1-8

The button immediately to the right of the view type is the View/Rendering Style, which allows you to select options for viewing your object: Wireframe, Sketch, Smooth Shade, and so on. Most of the time you'll be working in Wireframe mode. To the right of this are three smaller icons, which, in order, stand for Pan, Rotate (which works only in Perspective view), and Zoom. Point to these buttons, then click and drag to achieve the desired viewing.

Tip: Quickly Zooming In and Out

Press the period key on your keyboard to zoom in on an object (all windows will zoom in accordingly) and press the comma key to zoom out (all windows will zoom out accordingly). To zoom in greater increments, hold down the Shift key while pressing the comma or period key.

At the top of the Modeler window, different tabs provide different toolbars to aid you in your work. LightWave 6.5 has the following default tabs: Create, Modify, Multiply, Construct, Detail, Map, and Display (see Figure 1-9). Each tab has its own main toolbar that appears vertically down the left side of the Modeler window.

LightWave 6.5 Modeler allows you to create and customize your own tabs. This is good for quickly accessing the commands you use most frequently or for adding commands that you have

| Create | Modify | Multiply | Construct | Detail | Map | Display |

FIGURE 1-9

mastered. It is also a great tool for LightWave teachers, who can customize the interface to show only what they want students to initially see (which helps simplify the intimidation factor).

Let's take a moment to create a custom tab.

Creating Custom Tabs

Here are the steps you need to create your own custom tabs:

STEP 1: On the main toolbar, point to the Modeler button, then click and hold to see more options. Choose Interface, then Edit Menu Layout (Figure 1-10). The Configure Menus panel will open (Figure 1-11).

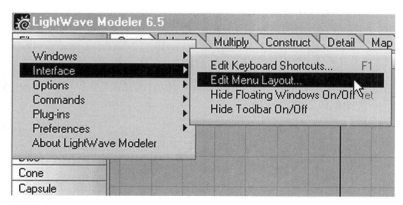

FIGURE 1-10

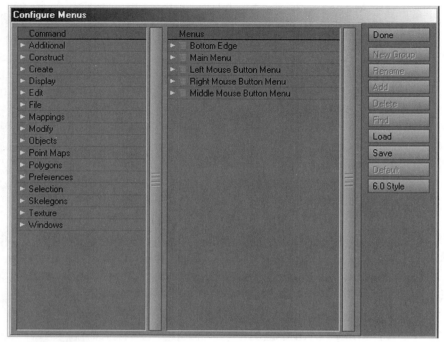

FIGURE 1-11

The Configure Menus panel consists of three windows. The first is the Command window, the second is the Menus window, and the third contains the command buttons for the panel.

STEP 2: In the Menus window, click the little white arrow to the left of Main Menu so that the arrow points down and shows the submenu (Figure 1-12). (*Note:* Your panel may already show the submenu under Main Menu.)

The submenu items under Main Menu coincide with the Modeler tabs (Figure 1-9). We will create a new custom tab here.

STEP 3: In the submenu, click Display once so that it is highlighted (Figure 1-13).

STEP 4: In the third window of this panel, click the New Group button (just under the Done button). This will create a new item under Display on the submenu called New Group (Figure 1-14).

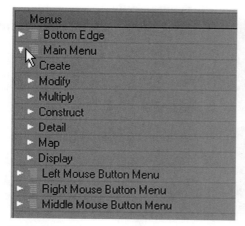

FIGURE 1-12

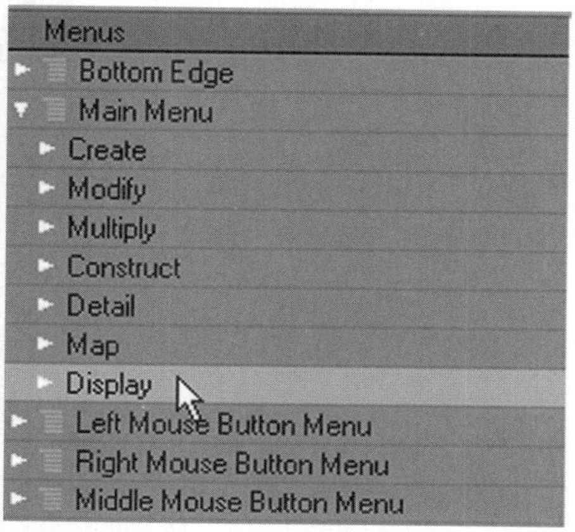

FIGURE 1-13

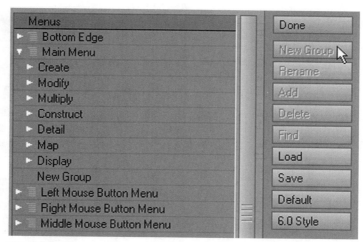

FIGURE 1-14

STEP 5: In the submenu, click New Group to highlight it (Figure 1-15). In the third window of the panel, click the Rename button to open the Rename Group panel (Figure 1-16). In the Rename Group panel type *LWA* (which stands for *LightWave Applied*). Click OK. In the Configure Menus panel, click the Done button to return to the Modeler window.

FIGURE 1-15

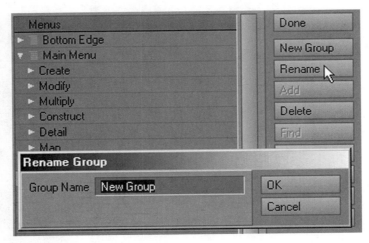

FIGURE 1-16

Look at your tab at the top of Modeler and you'll see a new tab that says LWA (Figure 1-17). Of course, this new tab does us little good until we add some buttons to it. Notice that when the LWA tab is highlighted, there are no buttons on the main toolbar because we haven't added any yet. That will soon change.

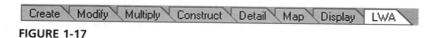

FIGURE 1-17

STEP 6: You need to open the Configure Menus panel the same way we did in Step 1. But to first do that, you need to click one of the other tabs (such as Create) so that you have a toolbar on the left side!

The first window in the Configure Menus panel (Command) simply provides the commands that you can move into your new submenu (LWA). You find a command, then drag it over to LWA and drop it in. It's that simple. Let's try it.

STEP 7: From the Command window, click the little white arrow to the left of Edit so that the arrow points down and shows the submenu. The first submenu item will be Copy. Point to the word *Copy* and drag it to LWA in the Menus window. Position it (while still holding the mouse button) until a bold line appears just under LWA (Figure 1-18). Now release the mouse button.

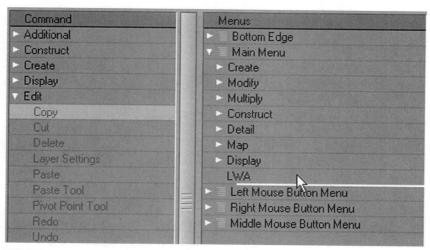

FIGURE 1-18

You have added your first option for your new LWA tab (Figure 1-19). Now whenever you click the LWA tab, the Copy button will be available on the main toolbar. As you learn Modeler, you can put your most-used commands on this tab to keep from switching between tabs while working.

FIGURE 1-19

Now that you know how to create tabs, you can delete this one since we don't need it for the rest of these tutorials. There are two ways to delete it. The first is to select it, then click the Delete button in the third window. The second is to simply click the Default button in the third panel, which resets the menus to the original default LightWave 6.5 settings. You may notice the 6.0 Style button under the Default button. If you have been using LightWave 6.0 and prefer the menu setup it used, then you can click this button and instantly have LightWave 6.5 mimic the 6.0 defaults for you.

Note: After you delete a tab, Modeler will default to another tab and show it selected, but the menu to the left is still blank. Simply click the same tab, or click another tab and then come back to it, to see the menu.

Understanding Objects and Layers

The way that objects and layers are handled in LightWave 6.5 is vastly different from how they were handled in LightWave 5.6. So different, in fact, that it may take some getting used to. But once you understand the concepts and reasoning, the move to this format will make sense.

Look at Figure 1-20. This is part of the toolbar in the upper-right corner of Modeler. When you load an object into Modeler, the name of the object will appear on the Current Object menu (Figure 1-21). You can use this menu to easily choose from the various objects you have loaded. Let's quickly try this out:

FIGURE 1-20

FIGURE 1-21

STEP 1: On the main toolbar, point to the File button, then click and hold to see more options. Choose Load Object (Figure 1-22) to open the Load Object panel (Figure 1-23), which should automatically default to your Objects folder.

FIGURE 1-22

Load Object			? ✕

Look in: Objects

Animals	Holiday	TextureExamples
Apparel	Household	Tools
Aviation	Human	Toys
Characters	Landscape	Tutorial
Computer	Logos	Vehicles
Electronics	Marine	VideoFX
Flags	Misc	Weapons
Food	Music	Weather
Furniture	Robots	
Games	Space	
Geography	Sports	

History
Desktop
My Documents
My Computer
My Network Pl...

File name: Open

Files of type: Objects   Cancel

FIGURE 1-23

STEP 2: Double-click the Weapons folder. Now click Sword, then click the Open button. This will load the sword into Modeler and the Current Object area will now show the name Sword, letting you know that the Sword object is currently the active object.

When an object loads into Modeler, you sometimes won't be able to see it because of the perspective it loaded (either too big or too small). This problem is easily solved:

STEP 3: Click the Display tab to bring up the Display toolbar on the left side.

STEP 4: On the main toolbar, click the Fit Selected button to properly display the sword in all screens (Figure 1-24).

Now let's load a second object into this screen.

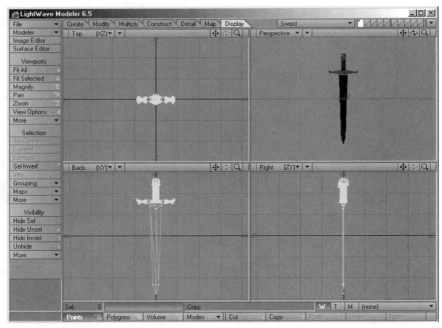

FIGURE 1-24

STEP 5: To quickly load another object, simply press L to open the Load Object panel. This is quicker than going to the File button and choosing Load Object.

Because LightWave is smart, it will remember the last folder you were in when you loaded an object and will thus default to the Weapons folder. However, in this case we don't want to load a weapon. We want to load a different object.

STEP 6: In the Load Object panel, click the icon of a folder with an arrow (Figure 1-25) to go up one level, thus returning to the Objects folder. Now double-click the Games folder, then double-click the ChessPieces folder. Click DarkKing, then the Open button. The piece will likely look very small, so go to the main toolbar and click the Fit Selected button as you did in Steps 3 and 4.

FIGURE 1-25

You'll now notice that your chess piece is showing but the sword is nowhere to be seen. It's there, but just "invisible" at the moment.

STEP 7: Use the Current Object menu to choose the object you want to work with. Point to the Current Object menu, then click and hold to see the objects you currently have loaded (only two at the moment). Move the pointer to Sword (Figure 1-26) and release the mouse button. Now the sword is displayed.

FIGURE 1-26

Now we're going to change gears to take working with objects a step further. Follow closely as we clear all objects in Modeler and load two new objects.

Tip: Clearing the Project

On the main toolbar, point to the File button, then click and hold to see more options. Choose Close All Objects to remove the sword and the chess piece from Modeler. Modeler is now clear for you to begin another project.

STEP 8: After clearing Modeler, press L to open the Load Object panel. Navigate back to the Objects folder, then double-click the Geography folder. Now double-click TheUnitedStates folder. Click Florida once, then click the Open button. Florida will load onto your screen. If it isn't showing, then go to the main toolbar and click the Fit Selected button as you did in Steps 3 and 4.

Tip: Fit the Object Quickly

A quick method to fit the object into your windows is to simply press A on your keyboard.

STEP 9: Open the Load Object panel again. This time choose Georgia, then click the Open button. Georgia will now load onto your screen. If you want the state to fit properly on the screen, click the Fit Selected button on the main toolbar.

As you can see, only Georgia is showing. But what if you wanted Florida to also be displayed while you were doing work on your Georgia model? That's where the Layers Browser comes in.

STEP 10: On the main toolbar, point to the Modeler button, then click and hold to see more options. Choose Windows, then Layer Browser Open/Close (Figure 1-27) to open the Layers Browser (Figure 1-28).

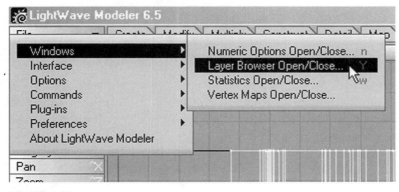

FIGURE 1-27

FIGURE 1-28

Let's take a quick moment to dissect this panel. First, across the top you'll notice columns labeled with F, B, Name, Num, and an eye icon.

F stands for Foreground, B stands for Background, Name is the name of the image, Num is the number of the layer where the object resides, and the eye icon is for Visibility—whether a layer is visible for use in Layout (layers not visible will not be loaded for use into Layout). This tool is very handy because instead of deleting work you've done you can simply hide it (by turning its visibility off) and it will still be available for you to reference in Modeler!

If you have ever worked with a program like Photoshop, you will find this type of layer display familiar. If you haven't worked with other programs that have layer options, fret not, as the basics will be covered here.

STEP 11: In the Layers Browser, click in the B column to the left of Florida. A checkmark will appear (Figure 1-29). Do not close the Layers Browser.

STEP 12: Make sure the Display tab is selected. Now click the Fit All button on the main toolbar. You will now clearly see Georgia (the Foreground object) and a black outline of Florida (the Background object). Your screen should look like Figure 1-30.

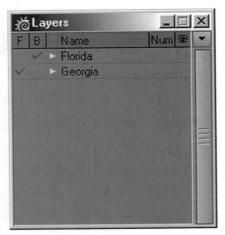

FIGURE 1-29

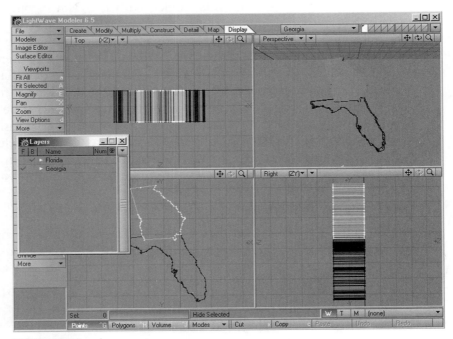

FIGURE 1-30

Because you will find yourself using the Layers Browser quite a bit, it is best to leave it open as you work. Otherwise you can quickly open it in the future by holding down the Shift key and pressing Y.

Now let's look at the layer buttons (Figure 1-31). As you can see, there are 10 layer buttons, each one divided by a diagonal line. When selected, the top part of each layer button (above the diagonal line) represents the layer displayed as Foreground; the bottom part (when selected) represents the Background. If you see a little black triangle in the upper-left corner of the layer button, it means that the layer has data in it (such as in layer 1, where we currently have two objects loaded—Florida and Georgia). Whenever a layer is displayed as Foreground, the entire layer is selected. Whenever a layer is displayed as Background, only the bottom portion is selected.

FIGURE 1-31

You can easily move an object from one layer to another. For example, let's say that you don't want Georgia to be in the same layer as Florida. The solution is to select Georgia in the Current Object menu, Cut it (by clicking the Cut button on the bottom menu), click the layer 2 button, then Paste the object (by clicking the Paste button on the bottom menu).

Tip: Selecting Multiple Layers

If you ever want to select multiple layers (or multiple Backgrounds in the Layers Browser), simply hold down the Shift key while selecting.

Note: Layers are not used for just holding objects. Layers can contain a number of elements that make up your complete Modeler project.

Let's take a quick look at a project already broken down into several layers so that you can better understand the concept behind layers.

STEP 1: From the File menu, choose Close All Objects. If you are asked to save, click Don't Save (you may be asked twice since two objects were loaded).

STEP 2: Press L to open the Load Objects panel. Navigate back to the Objects folder. Double-click the Human folder, click Hominid-Skull once, then click the Open button. Press A to bring the object into perspective.

Tip: Opening an Object Faster

Instead of clicking an object once, then clicking the Open button, you can double-click the object to open it automatically.

Notice that when the HominidSkull object opens, the first two layers are highlighted. Both layers contain important elements that make up the complete object. Your screen should look like Figure 1-32.

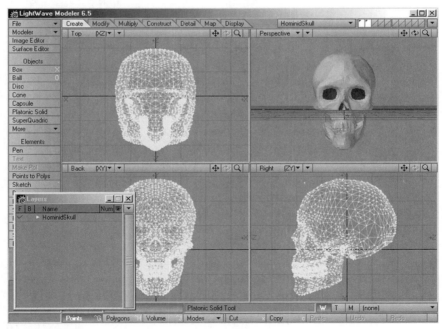

FIGURE 1-32

STEP 3: Click the layer 1 button. You'll notice that the jaw portion of the object disappears. That is because it is a separate element of the object, contained in layer 2. If you click the bottom part of the layer 2 button, a black outline of the jaw will appear. If you hold down the Shift key and click the top part of the layer 2 button, both will appear in the Foreground.

This is a good time to point out something new in the Layers Browser. Notice the small white triangle to the left of the name of the object. Click it to expand the sublistings of the object. The panel should look like Figure 1-33. It is now telling you that the Cranium portion of the object is in layer 1 and the Mandible portion of the object is in layer 2. Both will be viewable when the object is loaded into Layout. However, if I took away the dot to the right of Mandible under the eye icon and saved the object (this is an example; don't actually do it in this case), then when I loaded the saved object into Modeler, the Mandible portion wouldn't show.

FIGURE 1-33

This should give you a clear view of the importance of layers and how they work both with your object and with the object's purpose in Layout.

Working with Text

Before you can work with text in Modeler, you must first load fonts.

STEP 1: From the Modeler menu, choose Options, then Edit Font List to open the Edit Font List panel (Figure 1-34). From this panel you can load and remove any fonts that you wish to use with Modeler.

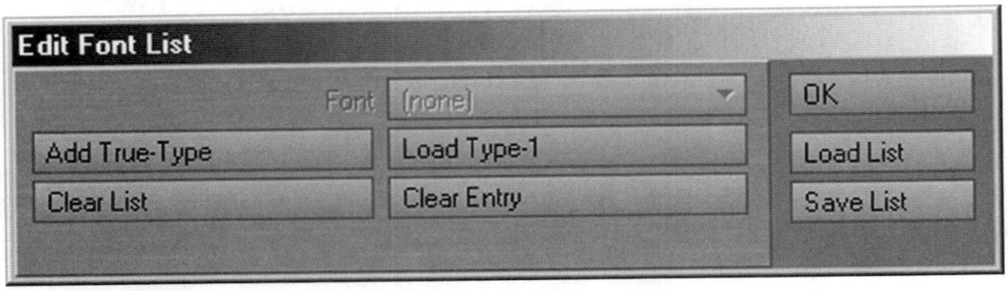

FIGURE 1-34

STEP 2: Click the Add True-Type button to open the Font panel. On the Font menu, choose Times New Roman, then click OK to close the Font panel.

In the Edit Font List panel, notice that the Times New Roman font is listed (Figure 1-35) whereas before it was unavailable. You can load more fonts if you wish; they will show up on this menu for you to choose for use in Modeler. You can also create a list of fonts you'd like to use with a particular project and save that list by using the Save List button in this panel. Likewise, you can load that list for another project by using the Load List button.

FIGURE 1-35

STEP 3: Click OK to close the Edit Font List panel.

Using Text and Surfaces

Now that we have a font loaded (Times New Roman), we are ready to experiment with a few quick text effects. Modeler makes working with text both fun and easy.

For this example we're going to create a few simple text effects based on my Digital Media FX (dFX) site at http://www .digitalmediafx.com/. Since the logo abbreviation is dFX, that's what we'll work with as our text.

STEP 1: Make sure the Create tab is selected. On the main toolbar, click the Text button.

STEP 2: Move your pointer into the lower-left window—the Back view window—and click below and left of center. A text marking (which appears as an aqua-colored L shape) will appear (Figure 1-36). Now type *dFX*. Your window should look like Figure 1-37.

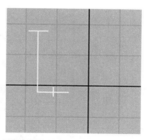

FIGURE 1-36

Tip: Deleting Text

Next time you go to use your text tool, it will default to the last text you wrote (like a stamp). Simply press Backspace to delete the letters as desired in order to type in your new text. If you want to quickly delete the whole line, hold down the Shift key and press Backspace once. The entire text will be deleted.

STEP 3: Place your text cursor anywhere within the window, then click and hold the mouse button while moving your mouse. You'll notice that the text moves with it. This allows you to easily pick up and place the text as desired. Place your text so that it is similar to Figure 1-37.

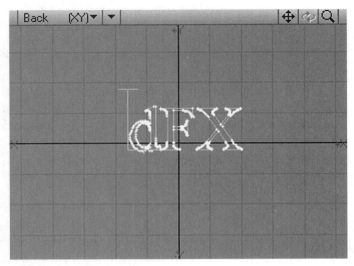

FIGURE 1-37

Congratulations! You have made your first text. From here the options are endless. You can extrude the text to give it a 3D look, bevel it, and so on. Only your imagination and effort are the limits. Let's continue on and experiment with creating a reflection of this text. First, we'll want to create a surface for our text.

Tip: Importance of Naming Surfaces

Naming the surfaces of your objects in Modeler is of the utmost importance. A surface is a predetermined area of your object to which you want to apply a texture or color. Take, for example, your eye. If you were creating an eye, you'd want three different surfaces. One would be the white part of the eye, which is called the sclera. The next surface would be the iris, and finally you would have the pupil. You'd want to give each of these a different surface name in Modeler so that you could apply separate textures to each part via the Surface Editor.

Creating Surfaces

Our goal now is to create a surface for the face of our dFX text. If you have been using LightWave 5.6 or an earlier version, you should be aware that surfacing has experienced many changes. For example, in our last book, *LightWave 3D Applied, Version 5.6,* I showed how to create a surface name for an object in Modeler, and then how to texture it in Layout. It's no longer done that way. LightWave 6.5 has a Surface Editor panel, identical in both Modeler and Layout, that allows quick and easy access to your project without jumping between Modeler and Layout. This should make life simpler as we continue our text tutorial.

STEP 4: Your dFX text should still be displayed as shown in Figure 1-37. First we need to name this surface. To do this, first click the Text button on the main toolbar again to deselect it (otherwise the program thinks you're still in text mode and doesn't allow you to use your keyboard shortcuts). Once you've deselected the Text button, press Q to open the Change Surface panel (Figure 1-38).

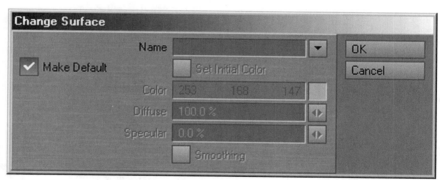

FIGURE 1-38

STEP 5: Next to Name in the Change Surface panel, type *dFX Front.* Click OK. You have given this object its own surface name: dFX Front. When we start working with the Surface Editor in a few minutes, you'll be able to adjust this surface separately from other surfaces we create.

Tip: Saving Files

From the File menu, choose Save Object As to open the Save Object As panel. Now simply navigate to the Objects folder (which is likely already the default), give your object a name, then click Save. If you need to save more than one object, choose Save All Objects As.

Using the Mirror Tools and Volume Button

In continuing with our tutorial we will create another version of our dFX logo, turn it upside down, give it a surface name, and create a reflection.

STEP 6: You should still have the word *dFX* on your screen. Click the Multiply tab. On the main toolbar, click the Mirror button.

STEP 7: Move your pointer into the lower-left window (the Back window). Place your pointer just under the word *dFX* and slightly to the left of it. Now begin dragging to the right. A mirrored version of the text will appear under the main dFX object. Align it so that it looks like Figure 1-39.

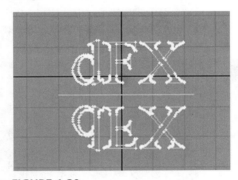

FIGURE 1-39

Congratulations on creating a mirrored version of the logo! As you can see, LightWave makes the process easy.

Now our goal is to give this upside-down dFX a different surface name from the original one. To do this, we will use the Volume button. At the bottom left of your screen are three buttons named Points, Polygons, and Volume (Figure 1-40).

FIGURE 1-40

Tip: Understanding Points and Polygons

Points and polygons are the foundation building blocks for creating 3D objects. Points are much like the dots in dot-to-dot coloring books we used to do as children. A polygon is the shape that the points make after all the dots are connected. Once a polygon is made, we can texture (color) it.

STEP 8: Click the Volume button once so that it is highlighted. Move your pointer into the lower-left window (the Back window) and, while holding down the mouse button, draw a box around the upside-down dFX part of the object. It should look like Figure 1-41. You'll learn more about the Volume button again in a few minutes.

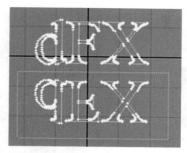

FIGURE 1-41

Tip: Undoing a Volume Mistake

If you make a mistake while drawing your Volume selection, simply right-click to remove the selection so that you can try again.

By drawing a box around the upside-down portion, you have isolated it so that you can give it a different surface name.

STEP 9: Press Q to open the Change Surface panel. Next to Name, type *dFX Reflect*. Click OK. Now click the Points button to get rid of the Volume box.

Congratulations! You have now created two separate surfaces, which allows you to give each one a different color or texture. Now it's time to master the Surface Editor panel.

The Surface Editor Panel

The Surface Editor panel allows you to easily change the surface areas of your object.

STEP 10: On the main toolbar, click the Surface Editor button (this button is always on the main toolbar) to open the Surface Editor panel (Figure 1-42). As you can see in Figure 1-42, the Surface Name section on the left side of this panel contains three surface names: Default, dFX Front, and dFX Reflect. Changing the surfaces is as easy as clicking the one you want to change, making the changes, then clicking the next one. Here's how:

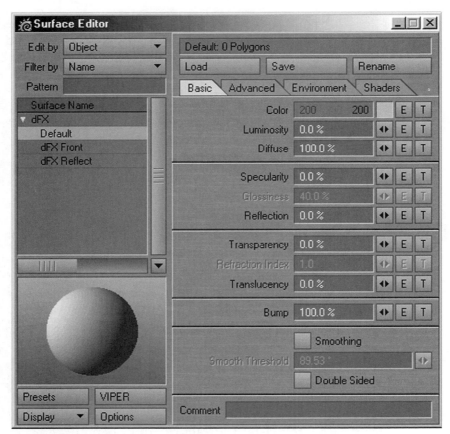

FIGURE 1-42

STEP 11: In the Surface Name area, select dFX Front, as shown in Figure 1-43. Now any changes you make in the Surface Editor will directly apply to the dFX Front surface.

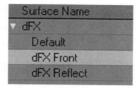

FIGURE 1-43

Let's start with something simple like making the dFX Front surface red and the dFX Reflection surface blue.

STEP 12: On the right side of the Surface Editor panel is a Color section with a color box (Figure 1-44). Click in the color box to open the Color panel. From here you can select the color you want the surface to be, or you can type in the Red, Green, and Blue values. Near the bottom right, type in a Red value of 230, a Green value of 0, and a Blue value of 0. This will give us a dark red. The panel should now look like Figure 1-45. See the CD-ROM for a color version of this image. Click OK to close the panel.

FIGURE 1-44

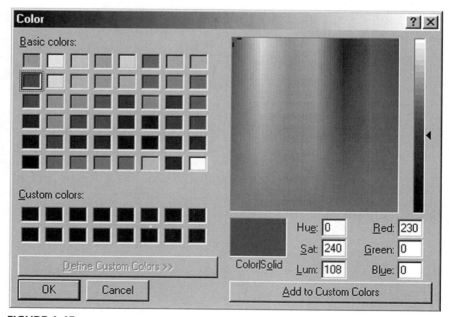

FIGURE 1-45

You can see that the sphere in the Surface Editor panel changes to the color that you set to give you an idea of what it will look like. Now let's work on the reflection.

STEP 13: In the Surface Name area, select dFX Reflect. In the Color section, click in the color box (as we did in Figure 1-44) to open the Color panel. Change the Red value to 0, the Green value to 13, and the Blue value to 176. Click OK. Now close the Surface Editor panel by clicking the Close button (the "X") in the upper-right corner.

Tip: Leaving Comments

The Surface Editor panel contains a Comment box near the bottom so that you can leave yourself or another artist comments on the specific surface. Simply select a surface and type in your comments in the Comments box.

In your Perspective window, you should now see the main dFX logo in red and its reflection in blue! If you still have the Volume box showing, simply click the Points button at the bottom of Modeler to get rid of it.

Now we need to save this object. From the File menu, choose Save Object As to open the Save Object As panel. Make sure you are in the Objects folder. Name the file *dFX* and click Save.

By now you are probably eager to see what this would look like rendered. So let's take a short trip over to Layout, where we will render this object and learn about a very cool new feature called VIPER.

A Peek at Layout, VIPER, and Surfacing

We will now render our dFX logo object in Layout (Figure 1-46) to see how it looks, and we'll also learn about a new feature called VIPER that makes surface changes very easy. From there we'll enhance the logo with a reflective texture to give the reflection more of a reflection feel.

STEP 1: In the upper-right corner of Modeler you will see a black down arrow (Figure 1-47). Point to the arrow, then click and hold to see more options. Choose Send Object to Layout (Figure 1-48). Layout will now load with your object in it!

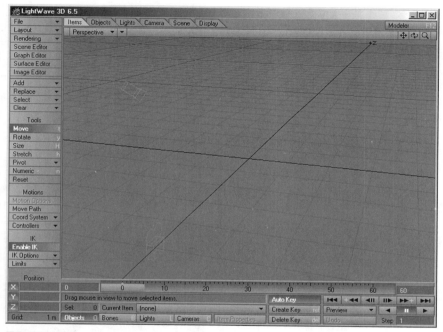

FIGURE 1-46

FIGURE 1-47

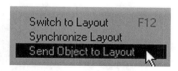

FIGURE 1-48

Tip: Dual Updating

Because your object is open in both Layout and Modeler, making changes in one will automatically change the object in the other! If you have problems with this, choose Synchronize Layout from the menu in the upper-right corner of Modeler (see Figure 1-48).

STEP 2: The main toolbar in Layout contains a Rendering button. Point to the Rendering button, then click and hold to see more options. Choose Render Current Frame. A small Render Status window will open and render the frame so that you can see what it looks like (Figure 1-49). After viewing the render, click Continue to close the window.

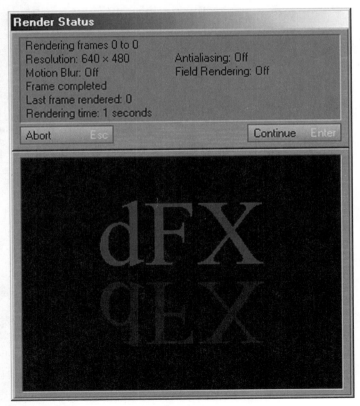

FIGURE 1-49

One of the cool aspects of Layout is a feature called VIPER (which you can use with the Surface Editor while in Layout). VIPER stands for Versatile Interactive Preview Render. (I like to refer it as Visual Interface Panel = Easier Routine.) In short, VIPER allows you to visually adjust elements of your setting, which makes it easier for you to complete your projects with the look you want.

In order to use VIPER, you must first enable it.

STEP 3: On the main toolbar of Layout, choose Rendering, then Render Options to open the Render Options panel. Select the Enable VIPER check box. On the menu next to Render Display, choose Image Viewer. Your panel should look like Figure 1-50. Close the Render Options panel by clicking the Close button in the upper-right corner.

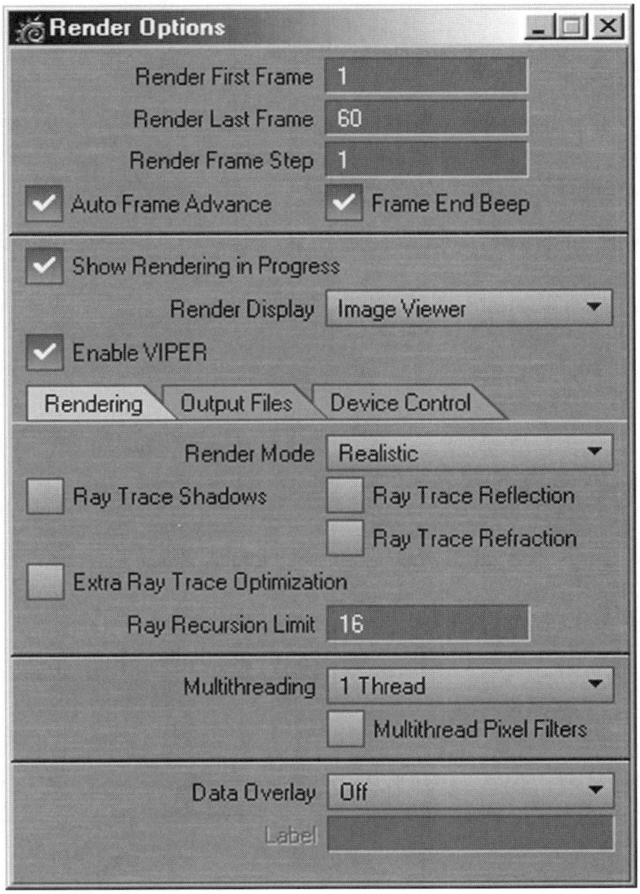

FIGURE 1-50

Sidebar: What Is Image Viewer FP under Render Display?

According to NewTek, "The FP (floating-point) version of the Image Viewer maintains the floating-point image data. Use it if you want to save files from the viewer and need the FP data. Note that it uses more memory than the regular Image Viewer."

Before checking out VIPER, let's render this object again since we've now changed the Render Display. This is an easy one-step process.

STEP 4: Press F9. Now when the object is rendered and you close the Render Status window, you will see a larger render of your object! Now let's move on to VIPER.

STEP 5: Make sure your Render Status window and the larger Render window are both closed so that you are back in Layout. On the main toolbar, click the Surface Editor button to open the Surface Editor panel.

As you can see, the surface attributes reflect the surface changes we made to our dFX object in Modeler. But now we're about to take this a step further.

STEP 6: In the lower-left section of the Surface Editor, click the VIPER button to open the VIPER: Surfaces panel. Click Render to render the dFX object.

Here's where the fun begins. First, if you ever want to change surfaces, you can click that surface in the VIPER: Surfaces panel and the change will be made in the Surface Editor. Likewise, any changes you make in the Surface Editor will be immediately updated in the VIPER: Surfaces panel so that you can immediately see the results.

STEP 7: Move the VIPER: Surfaces panel so that it is to the left of the Surface Editor, as shown in Figure 1-51. This will make it easier to work with both panels at the same time.

STEP 8: In the VIPER: Surfaces panel, click the dFX Reflect surface, as shown in Figure 1-52.

Notice that the attributes change in the Surface Editor to those of the dFX Reflect surface. That's what is so great about VIPER— it's visual. Click the area you want to work on and you're good to

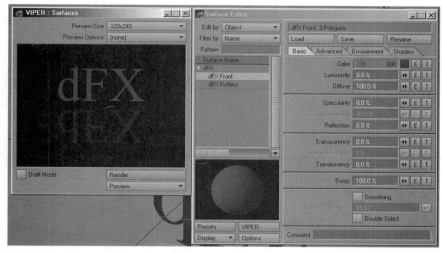

FIGURE 1-51

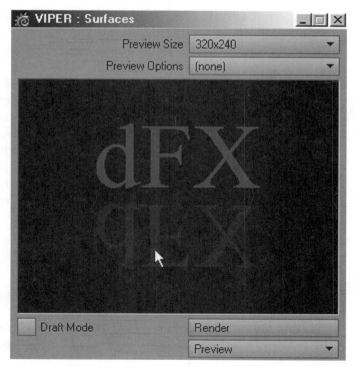

FIGURE 1-52

go. Make a change in the Surface Editor and it instantly shows up in the VIPER: Surfaces panel.

Our goal now is to apply a procedural texture to the dFX Reflect surface to give it more of a watery look.

STEP 9: In the Surface Editor, click the small T button to the right of the Color box (Figure 1-53) to open the Texture Editor for dFX Reflect Color. Change the Layer Type to Procedural Texture. You'll see an immediate update to the object in the VIPER: Surfaces panel. Change the Procedural Type to Underwater. Notice the instant change in the VIPER: Surfaces panel. Feel free to select different Procedural Types as you experiment with the best look.

FIGURE 1-53

We have just touched the surface of VIPER and the Surface Editor. In upcoming tutorials, particularly Tutorial 5, you'll learn a lot more about textures, surfacing, and VIPER.

Before moving on to a new tutorial, you need to close the Texture Editor, the VIPER: Surfaces panel, and the Surface Editor. If you want to see a rendered image of your object with the new surface/texture attributes you gave it, press F9. After viewing the render, close both screens so that you are back in Layout. In Layout, choose File, then Quit. If you are asked whether you are sure you want to quit LightWave, click Yes. You should now be back in Modeler with the dFX object loaded. In Modeler, choose File, then Close All Objects. It's up to you whether you want to save.

With Modeler now clear, it's time to learn how to create some nifty text tricks.

Nifty Text Tricks

If you have something already loaded in the Modeler screen, clear it out (choose File, then Close All Objects).

In this scenario we are going learn a variety of nifty text tricks. Keep in mind that the features you learn here are not just for text. They are for objects too.

Tip: Multiple Fonts

LightWave 6.5 is highly interactive. If you load several fonts (following the instructions given to you earlier in the "Working with Text" section), you can easily cycle through the fonts to see which you like best with your text. Simply click the Text button, type the text you want into Modeler, then press the up or down arrow keys on your keyboard to cycle through the list of loaded fonts.

Before getting into some of the tricks, such as Extrude, Bevel, Drill, and Boolean, let's first examine a method that gives you total control over your text.

STEP 1: Make sure the Create tab is selected. On the main toolbar, click the Text button.

STEP 2: Move your pointer into the lower-left window—the Back view window—and click below and left of center. A text marking (which appears as an aqua-colored L shape) will appear. Now type *dFX*.

STEP 3: On the main toolbar, choose Modeler, then Windows, then Numeric Options Open/Close. Your screen will look like Figure 1-54. From here you can see how you have total control over the text. You can change what the text says, the font, alignment, axis, scale, kerning, and even the type of corners you want it to have (sharp or buffered). Let's change the kerning. Change the Kern value from 0.0% to 5.0% and press the Tab key. We just spread the dFX letters out a little further so they aren't so close together. Now change the Center X, Y, and Z values all to 0. Next to Alignment, click Center.

STEP 4: We're done with this panel, so click the Close button in the upper-right corner. Now click the Text button on the main toolbar to deselect it (we don't want it selected anymore). Press Q to open the Change Surface panel. Next to Name, type *dFX Front*. Clear the Make Default check box. Change the color to red. Click OK. Your dFX text will now be red. Save this object as *dFX2*.

Now it's time to learn how to extrude text.

STEP 5: Click the Multiply tab. On the main toolbar, click the Extrude button. Press N to open the Numeric panel. The first button is a menu defaulted to Actions. Point to this button, then click and hold to see more options. Choose Activate to enter numeric information for this particular command.

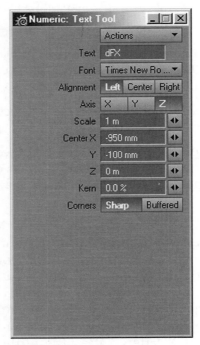

FIGURE 1-54

Tip: Numeric Panel

The Numeric panel changes depending on what command you have selected. This makes it easy for you to make your changes based on numbers. You may want to just leave your Numeric panel open as you work, as you'll find yourself using it often.

STEP 6: The Extent X, Y, and Z values should all be 0. Change the Z value to 200 mm (*Note:* make sure you type *200 mm* with two m's). Press Tab. You will see your text extrude within Modeler! Now let's change the surface using the Volume command we learned earlier.

STEP 7: Close the Numeric panel. At the bottom of Modeler, click the Volume button. Move your pointer to the Top view and click and drag to draw a box around the extruded part of the text. Now click the Volume button one more time and the box will be highlighted. Your screen should look like Figure 1-55.

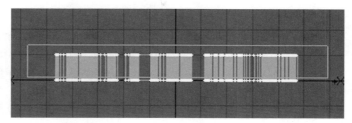

FIGURE 1-55

Tip: Understanding Include and Exclude

When you draw a box (using the Volume button) around a certain area of an object, "Include" (which is a highlighted box) selects both what is inside the box and any points and polygons immediately attached along the outside border of the box. "Exclude" (the nonhighlighted box) selects only the points and polygons on the inside of the box. These commands are especially helpful when you need to make important changes or additions while working with numerous objects or surfaces in one layer.

STEP 8: Press Q to open the Change Surface panel. Next to Name, type *dFX Side.* Change the color to dark blue. Click OK to close the panel. Now move your pointer to the Perspective window. The Perspective window toolbar contains a small button with two curved arrows. This stands for "rotate object." Point to this button, click and hold, and move your mouse to rotate the object. As it rotates, you can see that the front of the image is red and the sides are now blue (Figure 1-56). Great job!

FIGURE 1-56

Now you can apply this knowledge to a variety of projects in order to create a nice extrude and additional surfaces.

STEP 9: On the bottom menu, click the Points button to get rid of the Volume box.

The Ultracool Boolean Command

Now it's time to introduce you to my personal favorite command in Modeler—Boolean. In short, Boolean will take something in the background layer and add it to or subtract it from something in the foreground layer. Since hands-on application is the best learning model, let's get right to it! Your 3D (extruded) text should still be loaded.

STEP 1: To start, we need to make the surface colors for dFX Front and dFX Side the same. So load the Surface Editor by clicking the Surface Editor button on the main toolbar. Change both the dFX Front and dFX Side to yellow. Recall that you do this by clicking the surface name on the left side, then changing the color in the Color area on the right side. As you make the changes, they will be updated in real time in Modeler. Once you've changed both surfaces to yellow, close the Surface Editor. Your entire 3D text should be yellow.

STEP 2: Go to layer 2 by clicking the layer 2 button, as shown in Figure 1-57. Your text will seem to have disappeared. Actually, it's still in layer 1. Click the bottom part of the layer 1 button and your text will appear in an outlined (onionskin) format.

FIGURE 1-57

STEP 3: Click the Create tab, then click the Box button on the main toolbar. Your pointer will turn into a tiny white cube. Move the pointer to the Back view window and draw a box around your entire object. It should look like Figure 1-58.

STEP 4: Now move your pointer to the Right view window. Click just to the right of the blue line, but before reaching the end text, as in Figure 1-59. Now, remaining in the Right view window, do the same thing on the other side. Your Right view window should look like Figure 1-60.

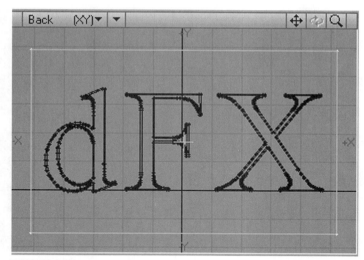

FIGURE 1-58

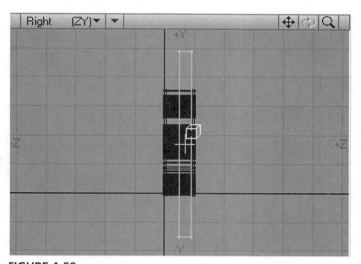

FIGURE 1-59

Note for Step 4: Your adjustment process may be slightly different. The important thing is that you achieve the same result as shown in Figure 1-60. If you have done this step right, you will see an outline of the dFX logo on your box in the Perspective window. If you don't see that outline, then make the box skinnier than shown in Figure 1-60.

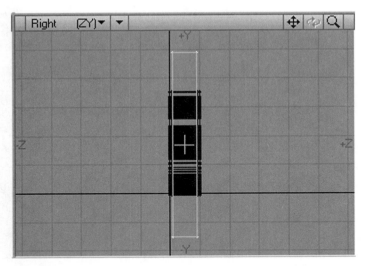

FIGURE 1-60

STEP 5: Press Q to open the Change Surface panel. Next to Name, type *box*. Change the color to light yellow and click OK. In the Perspective window you will see that you now have a yellow box.

STEP 6: Save this object as *BooleanTest*. Your Perspective window should look like Figure 1-61.

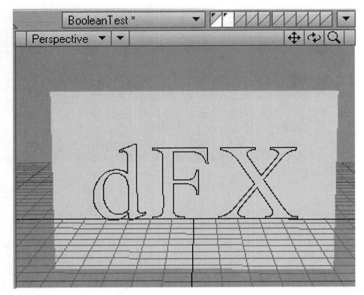

FIGURE 1-61

So far, we've created a box that is taller and wider than the dFX text but also skinnier than the dFX text. Here's where the fun begins.

STEP 7: Click the Multiply tab. On the main toolbar, click the Boolean button. The Boolean CSG panel will open. Make sure that the Subtract button is selected, then click OK. After a short period, the box you created will have a cutout of your text on it, as in Figure 1-62!

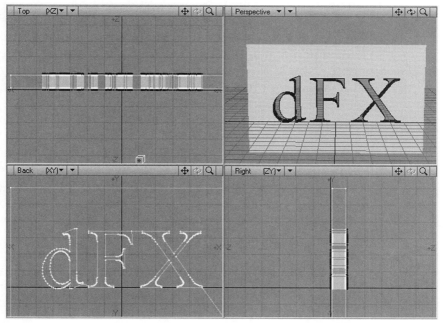

FIGURE 1-62

There are some interesting things to note about this new object. First, if you rotate in the Perspective view you will notice that the inside of the cutout is blue. This is because your dFX Side color was blue. If you reload BooleanTest and change the dFX Front and dFX Side to the same color yellow as the box, you will get a nice clean cutout.

You can have a lot of fun experimenting with the Boolean command. For example, reload BooleanTest and perform the operation again, except Add instead of Subtract. The dFX object becomes embedded in the box.

Take some time to experiment with both the Boolean command and the Solid Drill commands by reloading BooleanTest and performing the operation. You will learn a lot from it.

Now that you have tried this with text, you should experiment with objects. Load a couple of objects into Modeler (one into layer 1 and another into layer 2) and experiment with Boolean and Solid Drill. You will begin to see the endless possibilities of these commands when applied to your future projects.

When experimenting, you should be very inquisitive. For example, going back to our original BooleanTest, think to yourself, "What would happen if I made the back side of the box fatter than the text?" Now try it. As you will see, the text will go only as far into the box as you told it to. If you have a fatter back of the box, then the front will be engraved and the back will be solid.

Also, feel free to experiment with some of the other commands. For example, reload the dFX Object and experiment with Bevel. Or try this: Reload BooleanTest and click the layer 1 button (the top portion, so that both are highlighted). On the main toolbar, choose Bevel. Press N to open the Numeric panel. Choose Activate from the Actions menu. Next to Shift, type *10 mm.* Press Tab. Now click the Outer button next to Edges. As you can see, you've now created a slight bevel that gives the text a more bold look.

Through experimentation, you begin to gain a true understanding of how commands work and what the results will look like.

Now let's switch gears away from text to learn a few more Modeler commands before exploring Layout.

Making a Cube

You've learned quite a bit so far about many of the basic operations of Modeler and how those operations work. One of the things you learned was how to apply two surfaces to an object so that you can give each its own color or texture. Now we're going to go a step further and create a cube with each side having its own surface.

STEP 1: Make sure that Modeler is clear (choose File, then Close All Objects).

STEP 2: Click the Create tab. On the main toolbar, click the Box button.

STEP 3: Place your pointer in the Top view window and draw a box as in Figure 1-63.

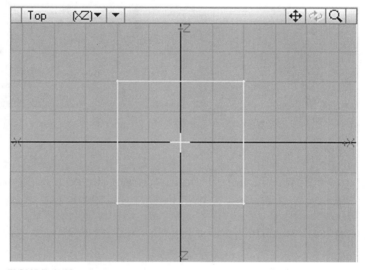

FIGURE 1-63

STEP 4: Move your pointer to the Right view window. You will see a flat blue line. Point to the middle of the line, then click and hold to drag the line up a little. Go back to the middle of the line and select it again, this time dragging it down a little. Your Right view should look like Figure 1-64.

Congratulations—you've created a cube! Use the Rotate command in the Perspective view window to better see the results. Now our task is to create a separate surface for each side of the cube.

STEP 5: On the bottom menu, click the Polygons button. The box lines will turn from blue to a faint white.

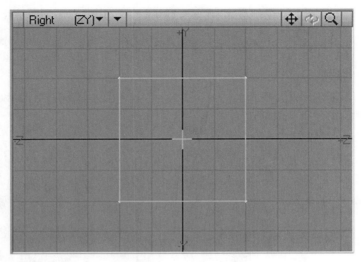

FIGURE 1-64

STEP 6: Move your pointer to the Right view window. Position the pointer just above the top part of the box, hold down the *right* mouse button, and draw an oval around the top of the box exactly like Figure 1-65. When you are done, release the mouse button and the top line will be highlighted in yellow.

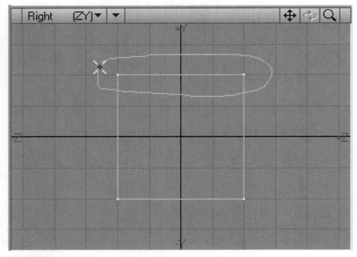

FIGURE 1-65

STEP 7: Press Q to open the Change Surface panel. Clear the Make Default check box. Next to Name, type *Side1*. Now change the color to yellow. Click OK to close the Change Surface panel.

Use the Rotate command in your Perspective view window to see that one side of your cube is now yellow.

STEP 8: Return to the Right view window and use the right mouse button again to draw an oval in the same area as before. This time the highlight will disappear. You have deselected Side1.

STEP 9: Now use the right mouse button to draw an oval around the bottom line in the Right view window, as in Figure 1-66. Release the mouse button and the bottom line will be highlighted. Press Q to open the Change Surface panel. Next to Name, type *Side2*. Now change the color to red. Click OK to close the panel.

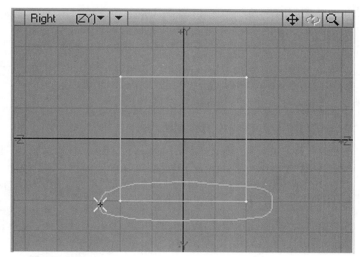

FIGURE 1-66

Use the Rotate command in the Perspective view window to see that you now have a red side of the cube opposite the yellow side.

STEP 10: Return to the Right view window. Use the right mouse button to draw another oval around the bottom line to deselect Side2.

STEP 11: Now, while still in the Right view window, draw an oval around the left side of the box as you did before (Figure 1-67).

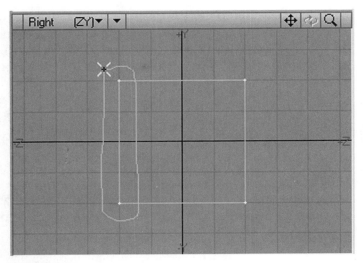

FIGURE 1-67

Press Q to open the Change Surface panel. Next to Name, type *Side3*. Now change the color to green. Click OK to close the panel. We're now halfway done surfacing our cube.

STEP 12: We are still working in the Right view window. Draw another oval around the left line to deselect Side3.

STEP 13: Now draw an oval around the right side of the box. Press Q to open the Change Surface panel. Next to Name, type *Side4*. Now change the color to pink. Click OK to close the panel. You've now finished four surfaces.

STEP 14: We are still working in the Right view window. Draw another oval around the right line to deselect Side4.

STEP 15: Now we are going to the Top view for the final two sides. In the Top view window, draw an oval around the left side of the box, as in Figure 1-68. Press Q to open the Change Surface panel. Next to Name, type *Side5*. Now change the color to dark blue. Click OK to close the panel. Only one side left!

STEP 16: In the Top view window, draw another oval around the left line to deselect Side5.

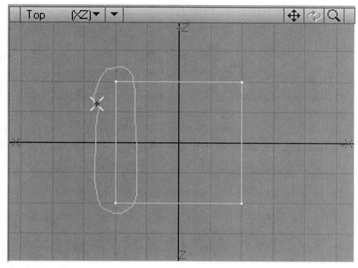

FIGURE 1-68

STEP 17: In the Top view window, draw an oval around the right side of the box. Press Q to open the Change Surface panel. Next to Name, type *Side6.* Now change the color to light blue (or aqua). Click OK to close the panel.

STEP 18: In the Top view window, draw another oval around the right line to deselect Side6.

Congratulations! You've created a cube with different surfaces for each side. Save this object as **Cube.**

Tip: Intelligent Surfacing Technique

As you begin to master Modeler, you will learn that there are many ways to accomplish a task, which will make you more appreciative of its sheer power and intelligence. For example, redo Steps 1–4 to create a cube. Now click the Polygons button (if it is already highlighted, click Points to deselect it, then Polygons to select it again). Now move your pointer to the Perspective view and click one of the sides—it automatically selects the area you need to give a surface name to! Using this method you could click, name a surface, click to deselect, rotate the cube, and repeat, getting the task done much more quickly. So why did we go through all the trouble in Steps 5–18? Because you need to learn this method for when you work with objects not as easily discernible.

Use the Rotate command in the Perspective view window to see your results. Now do some surfacing experiments on your own. On the main toolbar, click the Surface Editor button to open the Surface Editor. From here the possibilities are endless. You can even load an image! Here's a tip to get you started: Select a surface in the leftmost column, then click the T button to the right of Color. On the menu next to Image, choose Load Image. Navigate to the Logo folder and select VTJuice. Change Width Tile to Reset and Height Tile to Reset. Now click the Automatic Sizing button. Voilà—an image on one of the six sides! As you can see, there are a lot of options for you to experiment with.

Modeling a Game Piece

Now let's turn our attention to the Pen button and how to use points, polygons, Lathe, and Layers to create a simple game piece. You will also begin learning about the generic information display (bottom-left corner of Modeler), which I like to simply refer to as the Position box (a much easier and non-intimidating name). The information will show up in the box only when you put your cursor in one of the view windows.

When you finish this simple tutorial, you should have a good starting point to begin experimentation on doing your own modeling. Within minutes of completing this tutorial, you should be able to start creating your own objects, such as a wineglass.

STEP 1: Make sure that Modeler is clear (choose File, then Close All Objects). Also, make sure the Points button is selected at the bottom of Modeler.

STEP 2: For this tutorial we will be starting in layer 2, so select layer 2 from the row of layer buttons (make sure you click the top portion of the layer 2 button).

STEP 3: Click the Create tab.

STEP 4: On the main toolbar, click the Disc button. This button is different from the Ball button in that it lets you make a *flat* polygon circle.

STEP 5: Move your pointer to the Back view window. Position the pointer on the upper Y axis until the Position box (lower-left corner of Figure 1-69) reads X: 0 m, Y: 1 m. Your screen should look like Figure 1-69.

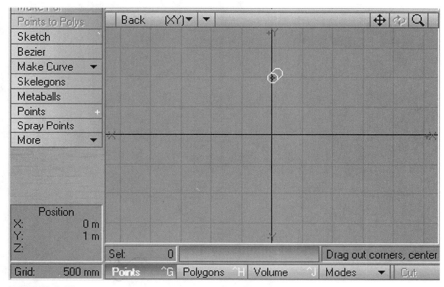

FIGURE 1-69

STEP 6: Hold down the *left* mouse button and drag down to the right until the Position box reads W: 2 m, H: 1 m (W stands for *width*; H stands for *height*). See Figure 1-70.

STEP 7: On the main toolbar, click the Pen button.

STEP 8: Select layer 1 by clicking the top part of the layer 1 button (your object will temporarily "disappear" because it is in layer 2). Now click the bottom part of the layer 2 button. The disc appears again in black, telling us it is in the background. We will use this as a template for drawing the top of the game piece. Before you proceed, your entire screen should look like Figure 1-71.

STEP 9: Move your pointer to the Back view window. Because Pen is selected, the pointer will change to a small plus sign with a small Pac-Man-like box attached to it. Press N to open the Numeric

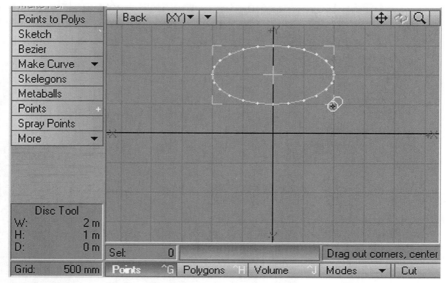

FIGURE 1-70

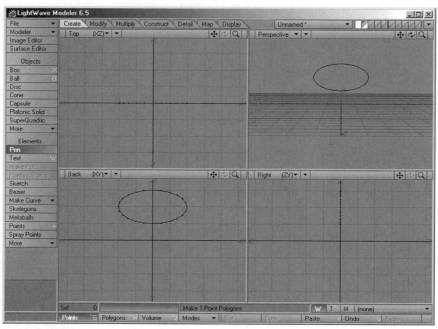

FIGURE 1-71

panel. Move it to the side and move your pointer to the Back view window. Now place your pointer on the Y axis on the black line on top of the circle (Figure 1-72). Click once. A blue target cursor will appear at that point. Now move your pointer to the Numeric panel (which activates after your first click) and click the Add Point button.

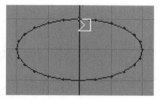

FIGURE 1-72

STEP 10: Now follow the black curve on the left side of the circle, placing Pen dots (the circle dots are a good model to follow) and then clicking Add Point so that your final result looks like Figure 1-73. You can adjust any Pen point to make the curve smoother. Once you are satisfied, click the Pen button to deselect it. Now click in the gray area above the Position box to get rid of your highlight.

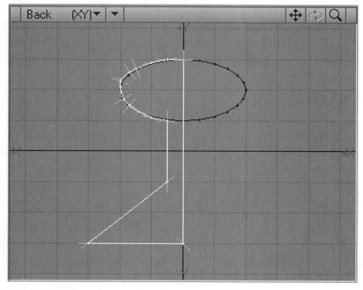

FIGURE 1-73

So far you have placed an "object" in the background to help you create this half-polygon game piece. Now we need to do a Lathe operation to make the game piece whole.

STEP 11: Click the Multiply tab. On the main toolbar, click the Lathe button. Move your Lathe tool to the Top view window and position it so that it is aligned perfectly in the middle, as in Figure 1-74. Now click once to activate the Numeric panel.

Here's where the magic happens.

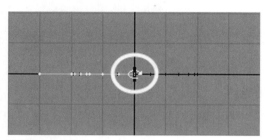

FIGURE 1-74

STEP 12: Next to Axis in the Numeric panel, click the Y button. Your entire game piece is now made!

Congratulations on creating your first nontext object—a 3D game piece. You will find the Lathe tool one of the most powerful in all of Modeler. And as with many of the other tools, the possibilities are endless. There are just a couple of more quick steps to complete it.

STEP 13: Click the top part of the layer 1 button so that the background object in layer 2 no longer shows. On the main toolbar, click the Surface Editor button to open the Surface Editor. Since we didn't give the surface a name, we are working with Default. If you wish, go ahead and give the surface a name. Now select the Smoothing and Double Sided check boxes. This gives your game piece a much better look. From here you can texture it or color it to your desire.

See Figure 1-75 for the final results of creating the game piece. If you are not pleased with the results, then repeat the process and carefully adjust each Pen point to perfection. Make the base smaller or the middle longer. Make a completely different object using this method, like a wineglass! Experiment!

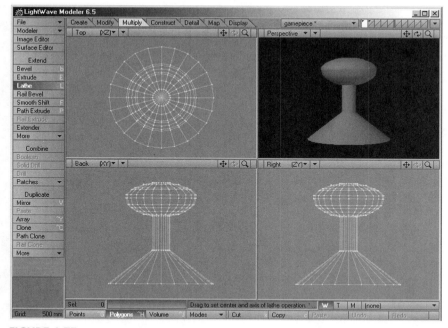

FIGURE 1-75

Continuing Your Exploration of Modeler

We have just touched a few basics of Modeler that, I hope, have given you the enthusiasm to explore further. There are a lot of tabs to select, buttons to push, and discoveries to be made! But before you get lost in the wonderful world of Modeler, let's take a quick look at LightWave's Layout.

LAYOUT SIMPLIFIED

In its simplest form, the secret to animating is to move or rotate an object and create a key. You then move or rotate the object again and create another key. That's the basic concept of animation in a nutshell—*move or rotate an object and create a key*. As you will soon discover, this process is almost as simple as it sounds.

Take a moment to load Layout (by loading LightWave 6.5). It should look like Figure 1-76. Just as in Modeler, you will see that it

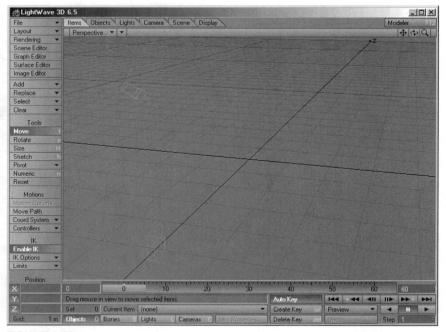

FIGURE 1-76

has tabs on the top and menus on the left. The menu on the left changes according to what tab is selected, except for the top seven buttons, which never change. Layout also has a window toolbar with the option of changing the view (the default is Perspective), moving the scene, rotating the scene, or zooming in or out on the scene.

The bottom menu in Layout contains your animation controls, as seen in Figure 1-77. This is where you'll accomplish the majority of your work, such as creating keyframes and viewing the results of your work. NewTek has done a nice job of fitting the most-used commands into this one area to help you work more efficiently.

FIGURE 1-77

Instead of defaulting to four different windows as in Modeler, Layout has one big window. But that doesn't mean you can't change it. Press D to open the Display Options panel. From here you can customize the view to your heart's desire. For the purpose of our tutorials, we'll stick with the one-window view.

Layout is like a Hollywood lot. It is a stage where you direct your objects, lights, and camera. By default, Layout automatically starts with one light and one camera set up on your stage and ready to go.

In Hollywood, filming projects are broken down into scenes. It is the same with Layout. You load your objects (actors) onto the stage and create a performance . . . a scene. So let's begin work on our first scene.

Orc in the Road

In the past you may have come across a fork in the road with some confusion as to which direction to go. But what if you came across an Orc in the road? What would you do then? For our first Layout challenge, we will be getting rid of the fork in favor of an Orc.

To set the mood for this scene, we first need a road. For our purposes, that can be achieved by loading a background image.

Loading a Background

One of the top seven buttons on the main toolbar that never change, no matter what tab you have selected, is the Image Editor button. This editor is the key to loading and managing images in Layout.

STEP 1: Click the Image Editor button to open the Image Editor panel, as seen in Figure 1-78. Now click the Load button. Navigate to your Images directory, then double-click the Landscape folder. Click **MountainHighway.iff,** then click the Open button. The image will load into the Image Editor. To see it, select **MountainHighway.iff** in the Name column of the Image Editor. The image will appear in the box under the Name column. Close the Image Editor.

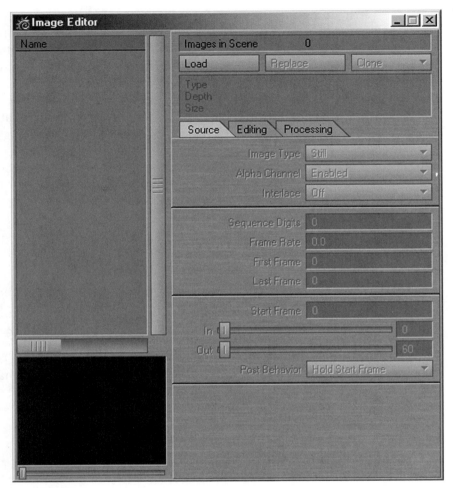

FIGURE 1-78

Tip: A Bigger View

Double-click the image name in the Name column of the Image Editor to see a bigger rendition of that image! Likewise, you can double-click the image in the box to see a bigger version of it.

Now that we have the image loaded, we need to tell Layout to display the image in the background of this scene.

STEP 2: Change your view from Perspective to Camera View. Next, click the Scene tab. Your screen should look like Figure 1-79.

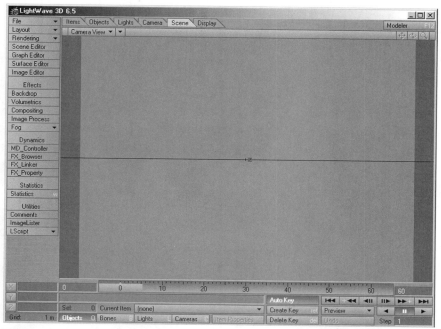

FIGURE 1-79

STEP 3: On the main toolbar, click the Compositing button. The Effects panel will open and the Compositing tab in this panel will be highlighted. On the menu next to Background Image, choose **MountainHighway.iff.** Close the panel.

Even though you can't see it, the image will now render in the background of your scene. But that does us no good, because we need to see the image. So let's set the display to show us the image.

STEP 4: Click the Display tab. Now click the Display Options button to open the Display Options panel. Near the bottom of this panel is a Camera View area. On the menu next to Camera View Background, choose Background Image. Instantly the background will now show in Layout! Before closing this panel, select the

Show Safe Areas check box. This provides a guide to the area of your scene that will be clearly viewable on a TV. Close the Display Options panel. Your screen should now look like Figure 1-80.

FIGURE 1-80

Now that we've set the mood for the scene, it is time to bring in the actor . . . the Orc.

Loading an Object

STEP 5: On the main toolbar, choose File, then Load, then Load Object. The Load Object panel will open. Navigate to the Objects folder (if you're not already there). Now double-click the Characters folder, then the Monsters folder. Click OrcLowRes, then the Open button. The Orc will load in the middle of your scene. Your screen will look like Figure 1-81.

Press F9 to render your Orc friend to see what he looks like several feet off the ground.

FIGURE 1-81

Now everyone knows that Orcs can't fly, so we need to bring this big fella, who looks like a character from *Shrek,* down to Earth and properly position him in our scene. This will require use of the Move and Rotate commands.

STEP 6: Make sure you have closed the Render panel and that you are back in Layout. Click the Items tab. In the Tools area on the main toolbar, you'll see buttons named Move and Rotate. You will use these often. If the Move button isn't selected, click it now.

Tip: Understanding Move, Rotate, and X, Y, Z

In the bottom-left corner of Layout is the Position box, which helps you track the movement and placement of your objects. When Move is selected, the Position box shows X, Y, and Z coordinates. X represents moving an item sideways (left and right). Y represents moving an item up and down. Z represents moving an item back and forth (toward you and away from you).

Notice that the X, Y, and Z in the Position box are actually buttons. The great thing about these buttons is that you can deselect the ones you don't want to use! This means that if I just want to move our Orc up and down, I can deselect the X button and Z button and the only direction Layout will allow me to move the Orc is up and down.

There is a slightly tricky aspect to using X, Y, and Z. To move items along the X and Z axis, you must hold down the *left* mouse button. To move items along the Y axis, you must hold down the *right* mouse button.

When the Rotate button is highlighted, the three buttons change to reflect H, P, and B axes. These represent your rotation angles. H (Heading) represents rotating your item to the left and right. P (Pitch) represents rotating your item up and down. B (Bank) represents rotating your item side to side (like a boat rocking side to side in the ocean). As with the X, Y, and Z axis, there is a tricky aspect to this scenario. Items rotated around H and P use the *left* mouse button, while items rotated around B use the *right* mouse button.

STEP 7: The Move button should be selected. Our goal is to move the Orc down (remember that Y represents up and down) and away from us (remember that Z represents back and forth). Click the X button in the Position box once to deselect it, since our interest is only in moving the Orc along the Y and Z axes.

STEP 8: Position your pointer over the Orc and hold down the *right* mouse button. Move the mouse downward and the Orc will follow (if you see the Orc turn into a highlighted box while moving it, don't worry—this is normal). Stop moving the Orc and release the mouse button when it looks like the Orc is standing on the road. Now hold down the *left* mouse button and move your mouse upward. The Orc will move further away from you. Make any adjustments necessary so that your scene looks like Figure 1-82.

Tip: Orc Placement

If your Orc looks too big, move it back farther (Z axis) and then down (Y axis). You can effectively decrease the size while still making it look close to the camera. Another option is to use the Size button to adjust the Orc's size).

FIGURE 1-82

Earlier I said that the secret to animating is to move or rotate an object and create a key. It's time to create that key.

STEP 9: At the bottom of the Layout window, click the Create Key button. The Create Motion Key panel will open (Figure 1-83). Since this example is a still picture (and not an animation), we will accept the Default keyframe of 0. So simply click OK.

FIGURE 1-83

Tip: Understanding Create Key

The Create Key button is one of the most important buttons in Layout because it is where you save the settings of all the moves and rotations that you make to your objects, camera, and lights throughout your animation. If you are creating a still scene, you only have to worry about creating a key at the default setting of 0. But if you were animating, you would follow the rule that 30 frames equals one second of video. Let's say that when the Orc was in the air, we clicked on Create Key and changed the default number 0 to number 1 (the first frame, where the animation begins). Now let's say that we moved the Orc into the position on the road (as outlined in the steps we've completed), clicked Create Key, and made the keyframe number 30. The result would have been a one-second animation in which the Orc would have "flown" down from the sky onto the road!

Now you may be wondering about that Auto Key button. This is an advanced feature, which basically creates keyframes for you or automatically remembers changes to keyframes you already have, depending on the settings. This is not important for beginners, so deselect it.

OK. It's a beautiful day in the country. No cars are in sight. The Orc is exercising in the middle of the road while admiring the view. What can we do to improve this scene? No, adding a car coming toward the Orc at 75 mph is not the answer! How about a sun in the sky?

STEP 10: Click the Items tab. On the main toolbar, choose Add, then Lights, then Add Distant Light to open the Light panel. Type *Sun*, then click OK.

Because you just created this light, it is automatically selected and ready to be placed.

STEP 11: Remember a few steps back when we moved the Orc? Following that same example, move this light to the upper-right corner of the screen, as shown in Figure 1-84. Create a key at frame 0, as you did in Step 9.

Now it's time to turn this light on!

STEP 12: Click the Lights tab. On the main toolbar, click the Lens Flare button. That's it! Render the scene and you'll see that the sun has been added, giving warmth to the Orc in the road who looks like he wants to hug a semi.

Figure 1-85 shows the final scene. You can do some additional experimenting with the Lens Flare settings by clicking the Flare

FIGURE 1-84

FIGURE 1-85

Options button. Feel free to do some more experimentation, like adding a car to the scene. . . or a sidekick character, like a donkey.

Tip: Making a Selection

There are two main ways to select an item in your scene to make it active. The first is to click one of the buttons at the bottom of Layout (Objects, Bones, Lights, Cameras). The second is to simply click the item within Layout. It will automatically be selected as the current item you are working on!

Learning Basic Animation in 15 Minutes

When you complete this 15-minute tutorial, you will have basic animation under your belt, with the power of experimentation increasing your skills even further. And you will still be using only three percent of Layout's total power! Be sure that you've first mastered the techniques in the preceding tutorial ("Orc in the Road"), then start your stopwatch and let's get going.

STEP 1: Load Layout. If it is already loaded, clear the scene by choosing File, then Clear Scene. On the bottom menu, make sure that Auto Key is deselected (if it is selected, click it once to deselect it).

STEP 2: Change the view from Perspective to Camera View. We are now looking through the eye of the camera, which is why we no longer see other scene elements, such as the light.

Now it's time to load an object to animate.

STEP 3: On the main toolbar, choose File, then Load, then Load Object to open the Load Object panel. Navigate to the Objects folder. Double-click the Space folder. Click LittleSpaceship once, then click Open. The spaceship will load into your scene as in Figure 1-86.

Tip: Load Objects Quickly

You can open the Load Objects panel quickly by pressing the plus key (+) on your keyboard's numeric keypad.

Press F9 to see what the back of this ship looks like. After you're done, close the render screens so that you're back in Layout.

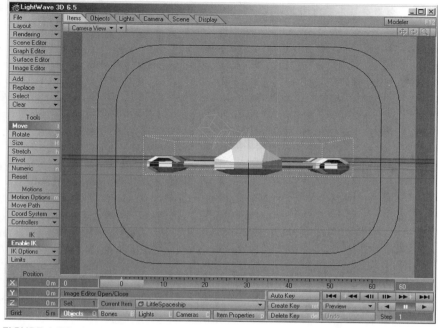

FIGURE 1-86

Our goal now is to rotate the spaceship around so that it is facing us.

STEP 4: On the main toolbar, click the Rotate button. We simply want to spin the ship around to face us. In the Position box, click the P and B buttons so that they are deselected, leaving only H selected. Position your pointer over the spaceship and hold down the *left* mouse button. Drag to the right and the spaceship (or an outline of it) will begin to move toward you. While you rotate the ship, keep an eye on the Position box until you see that H = 180 (Figure 1-87). Release the mouse button. The spaceship is now facing you.

FIGURE 1-87

Our goal now is to move the spaceship into its starting position, where we will create the first keyframe of our animation.

Tip: Rotating with Numbers

An alternative to rotating your object is to simply type in the values if you know them. For example, in Step 4 you could have typed *180.00* in the H area of the Position box to rotate the spaceship around to face you. Press Tab after typing in the number to register the change.

STEP 5: On the main toolbar, click the Move button. Click once in the X and Y boxes, leaving only Z highlighted, because we are going to move the spaceship back to a starting point where we will animate it zooming toward the camera. Place your pointer over the spaceship and hold down the mouse button. Drag up to move the ship into the distance on the Z axis. Watch your Position box again and stop when Z = 50 m (an alternative is to just type *50 m* in the Z area, then press Tab to see the change take place). Your screen should look like Figure 1-88. This is our starting point.

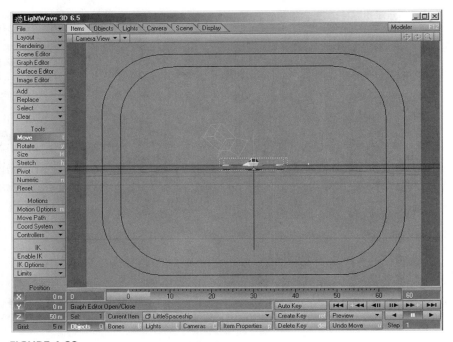

FIGURE 1-88

STEP 6: Click the Create Key button and accept the default of 0 by simply clicking OK. Now click the Create Key button again and change the 0 to 1. Click OK to close the Create Motion Key panel. The first Create Key action was simply to send Layout the starting coordinates (rotate coordinates, move coordinates, and so on). The second Create Key action for frame 1 was to set our first frame of the animation.

STEP 7: Now we want to move the spaceship toward us. Place your pointer over the spaceship and hold down the mouse button. Drag down to move the spaceship toward you. Watch the Position box until it reads Z = −6 m. This is our ending point.

STEP 8: Click the Create Key button and change the 0 to 30. Click OK. You have just told Layout to start the ship far back and bring it up close in 30 frames. Remember that in video, 30 frames equals one second. Therefore, the ship will travel from your starting point to the end point in one second. It will look like it is about to crash through your screen when it stops. Let's make a preview.

STEP 9: The first step is to properly set the preview in and out points (1 and 30). You can do this from the bottom of Layout. Look at Figure 1-89. This is the preview timeline; it defaults to 0 (at the left) to 60 (at the right). These numbers are easy to change. Change the 0 to 1 and the 60 to 30 (remember to press Tab after changing the numbers so that Layout can recognize the change).

FIGURE 1-89

STEP 10: The bottom menu of Layout contains a Preview button. Point to this button, click and hold, and choose Make Preview. Layout will automatically begin rendering the preview and then will present you with preview controls to play back your preview (Figure 1-89). Use the controls to view the results of your work so far. When you are done, click the End Preview button.

Congratulations on making your first animation! It would be mean of me, however, if I didn't show you how to render it. We'll turn it into an .mov file that you can view on your computer screen using QuickTime.

STEP 11: On the main toolbar, choose Rendering, then Render Options to open the Render Options panel. This is where you determine what frames to render, name the file, and make other important rendering decisions. Change Render First Frame to 1 and Render Last Frame to 30. Select the Auto Frame Advance check box (which allows the program to render the whole scene, rather than forcing you to click Continue after each frame is rendered). Select the Show Rendering in Progress check box. Click the Output Files tab. Select the Save Animation check box. Click the Animation File button. Navigate to the folder you want to save the file in and name the file **spacetest.mov,** then click OK to close the Save File panel. On the menu next to Type, choose QuickTime(.mov). You're set! Your panel should look like Figure 1-90.

STEP 12: Close this panel, then press F10 to render the scene and to be able to watch it as each frame is rendering! If you get a message box that says, "Warning, Auto Frame Advance is on. Turn off render display?," simply click No. If you get a panel that allows you to change defaults, simply click OK to accept the defaults. Your scene will render, saving your animation as a .mov file. After it is done, access the file on your computer to view it in Quick-Time.

Tip: Faster Rendering

Selecting the Show Rendering in Progress check box slows down your overall rendering time, but allows you to watch each frame as it is rendered. If you don't care about watching the frames as they are rendered, clear this check box to slightly speed up the process.

Congratulations on mastering the basics of animation in 15 minutes, with a couple to spare! Now you can practice rotations, space maneuvers, and laser battles. Before you know it, you'll be animating on the next *Star Trek* spin-off series!

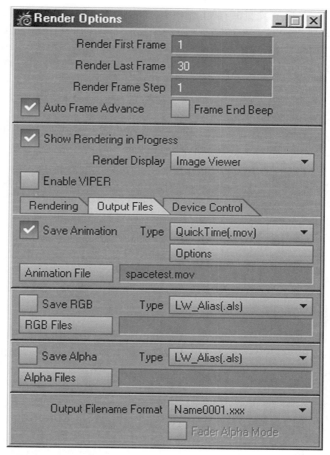

FIGURE 1-90

EXPERIMENTATION IS ESSENTIAL

To learn the full power of LightWave 6.5, you must experiment. This means that you need to set aside a 5- to 10-hour block at least once a week in which you do nothing but experiment with the different buttons in Modeler and Layout to see how changes you make affect your work. You will be amazed not only by the power you discover, but also by how much fun it is! In a matter of seconds, you may accidentally turn a circle into a vortex or a square box into a planet.

Some of the best medical discoveries of the past century were discovered by accident, and animation is no different. You'll be amazed at how you can start with one shape and end up with something inconceivably different. The power of Modeler and Layout is simply amazing, and the only way to unleash the full power is to experiment on a regular basis. Be sure to keep notes during your experiment sessions (that's how I was able to write the *Flyer Mastery Guide* book when NewTek first shipped the Flyer).

Tip: Shortcut Keys

Learn the shortcut keys! Keyboard shortcuts make your life much easier and will save you a lot of time. You can see what your keyboard shortcuts are in Layout or Modeler simply by pressing F1. You can even change them! However, that is not always advised as it may alter your ability to complete book, magazine, and online tutorials.

CONCLUSION

As stated earlier in this tutorial, there are dozens of ways to accomplish each task in Modeler and Layout. In this tutorial you have learned only one way. Find a way that best meets your needs and go with it, but always keep an open mind to other ways of accomplishing tasks.

You still have many areas to cover and explore. In this tutorial we haven't covered even one-thousandth of the possibilities that Modeler and Layout can open for you. To do so, simply from a beginning perspective, would take at least three entire books! We have only touched the tip of the iceberg with quick methods to get you up and running, while having some fun along the way (how's your Orc doing in the middle of the country desert road?).

The tutorials ahead are much more advanced and in-depth, but feel free to jump in and try them out. The Epic Software Group, Dave Jerrard, and Jen Hachigian have structured their tutorials in a step-by-step fashion that should make the task a little easier for you. I'll touch base with you again in the final tutorial of this book, which talks about building your own animation company.

You can also read my "Breaking into Hollywood" tutorial on this book's CD-ROM.

Be sure to check out the bonus area on the LightWave Applied Web site, which has links to other basic tutorials to help you master LightWave even more. The Web site is located at http://www .advanstarbooks.com/lightwave/.

2

Awesome Architecture, (LightWave 6.5 Modeler)

Epic Software Group

OVERVIEW

This tutorial aims to provide the user with the basic skills required to create the fundamental parts of an architectural visualization to be created with LightWave. In the following tutorial, we will model an office building, the landscape on which it sits, and additional objects to enrich the scene with realistic detail.

In this tutorial you will use:

■ Many of the basic modeling tools in Modeler.

What you will need:

■ A copy of LightWave.

■ A quantity of your preferred beverage.

What you will learn:

■ How to model an office building.

■ How to model a parking lot.

■ How to model a light pole.

■ How to model a fountain.

INTRODUCTION

Architecture is typically defined as "the art and science of designing and erecting buildings."* You can think of architecture as an art form we experience by walking through it and living within it. Architecture can be so powerful that one can simply look at the silhouette of a famous structure and instantly define its location. People travel the globe to experience and marvel at architectural structures created throughout history—from the Great Pyramids of Cairo to the modern skyscrapers of cities the world over.

For thousands of years, architects have used three-dimensional scale models to communicate their artistic vision and test their conceptual design. Models tell a story that everyone can understand, and the story starts the instant your eyes see the model. The story may last 15 seconds for an overview, or it may last 30 minutes for the interested viewer. The presentation power of models is the reason so many models are used effectively in sales and public relations. Yet architectural models made from materials such as clay, cardboard, and plastic can be time-consuming and expensive to construct. Physical models are not very portable, and once constructed they are not easy to change. The computer is revolutionizing the way architects visualize and present their ideas to investors and future tenants. Architectural *fly-throughs* are appealing because they show something people can relate to. Most people have a hard time understanding how to read and visualize blueprints; this technology gives them a "within the building," ever-changing perspective revealing depth, shadows, reflections, colors, and textures.

In its simplest form, visualization is the visual representation of data. A 3D architectural visualization can bring a level of detail and realism to an architectural design that is impossible to achieve with a simple physical model. To truly understand a space, one must experience it. The best way to experience it without incurring the time and expense to actually build a structure is to create it virtually. A few short years ago, the technology needed for visualizing immersive virtual environments was outside the reach of mere mortals. LightWave has really leveled the playing field for artists who have the vision, but not necessarily the bucks to dream large . . . really large!

---

*American Heritage Dictionary, 4th edition.

TUTORIAL OBJECTIVE

This tutorial was created for industry professionals such as architects, designers, illustrators, graphic artists, and serious students who wish to use the power of LightWave 6.5 to bring their visions to life. In this tutorial we will explain the basics of planning, modeling, and texture-mapping a generic architectural project. We will learn how to create buildings, landscapes, and a variety of architectural elements. In Tutorial 3, we will bring our project to life using the Layout section of LightWave. Using Layout we will show you the step-by-step process of how to light, animate, and render a 3D project from both an artistic and technical point of view. We will examine a case study example of a real-world visualization created for a major real estate developer for a project delivered early in the spring of 2001. Documenting every aspect of a project of this size could easily fill a book of its own. Our objective is to teach you enough, in this basic tutorial, to be able to apply the knowledge gained to any future architectural visualization project. Though this project is considerably simpler than the full-scale visualization that was the inspiration for this tutorial, it will do fine for our purposes.

Now, let's get started, but before we do, take a minute to ponder the words of an icon of the world of architecture—an individual who is arguably one of the most famous and influential of all architects, Frank Lloyd Wright:

> What is architecture anyway? Is it the vast collection of the various buildings, which have been built to please the varying taste of the various lords of mankind? I think not.
>
> No, I know that architecture is life; or at least it is life itself taking form and therefore it is the truest record of life as it was lived in the world yesterday, as it is lived today or ever will be lived. So architecture I know to be a Great Spirit. . . .
>
> Architecture is that great living creative spirit which from generation to generation, from age to age, proceeds, persists, creates, according to the nature of man, and his circumstances as they change. That is really architecture.
>
> —Frank Lloyd Wright, from *In the Realm of Ideas,*
> edited by Bruce Brooks Pfeiffer and Gerald Nordland

CASE STUDY

The Epic Software Group is proud to call The Woodlands, Texas, its home. Conceived more than 30 years ago by visionary George Mitchell, The Woodlands is a 27,000-acre forested master-planned community just north of Houston. It has 60,000 residents and 900 businesses, and offers a truly special lifestyle and work environment. One of the concepts Mr. Mitchell had from the start was the creation of a spectacular water park he called The Woodlands Waterway. In 1998, The Woodlands was acquired by Crescent Operating, Inc., and the new development company felt the time was right to make Mr. Mitchell's dream a reality. In the spring of 2000, construction work began on The Woodlands Waterway.

The Woodlands Waterway is a 1.25-mile transportation thoroughfare and water amenity. Although it will take several years to completely build out, it is scheduled to open in the fall of 2001. When completed, it will link 18 million square feet of offices, shopping, restaurants, entertainment, and housing. Trolleys, water taxis, and tree-lined pedestrian walkways will make navigating The Waterway fast and enjoyable.

The investment required for a project of this magnitude is enormous, even for a major development company. The key to success for The Waterway is to attract new businesses and have them make a financial commitment to a new and unproven venture. It is a catch-22 in which businesses are hesitant to sign up unless other prominent companies have previously reserved space. Building a critical mass of tenants will attract the retail and commercial traffic needed for success.

Historically, the sales agents for The Woodlands have used 3D topographical models to help prospective residents and business owners visualize the plans for future of the development. Although a physical model of The Waterway could accurately depict the locations and topography, it would fall short in delivering the drama and excitement possible with a 3D virtual fly-through.

One of the most practical uses of 3D rendering and animation is that of visualizing an architectural space. With a 3D model of a proposed building we can actually see what the space is going to look like, long before the first concrete is ever poured for the foundation. The potential tenant can use this visual information in planning for the use of the space. The architect can use it to catch potential problems before they are "cast in stone," and the real estate agent can use the information as a potent sales tool for selling or leasing space before it actually exists. The local success of regional sport stadium projects that used 3D fly-arounds convinced the development firm of the power of this new media.

The client had some experience with 3D fly-throughs, and he expressed from day one exactly what he didn't want—a CAD-like visualization that is technically accurate, but visually flat and boring. LightWave's ability to attach lifelike materials to 3D geometry enables us to accurately calculate shadows, reflections, and transparency. Additionally, radiosity allows us to model the effects of indirect lighting in architectural interiors. This technology can calculate the subtle indirect lighting effects from the physical properties of lights and materials. It seemed obvious that LightWave was the right tool to use to give our fly-through the textures, shadows, and dramatic lighting necessary to make the Hollywood-like presentation the client had envisioned.

We must address a number of considerations when preparing for this kind of animation job. Since the client is interested in giving his potential tenants or investors a sense of what the development might be like once completed, the client wants part of the project to include interiors as well as exteriors. The level of detail that the client expects is an important consideration in any animation project, particularly in an architectural visualization. In most, if not all, cases, the client's interest is to make the project look as attractive as possible to prospective tenants or investors. In some cases detailed plans are in place, which mostly dictate choices about the design of the models, placement of buildings, landscaping, and so on. In these sorts of projects the animator enjoys very little latitude. Everything is modeled from the plans and drawings created by the architects and engineers who have designed the development, and the client obviously has certain expectations that have to be met. In other situations, however, the animator has a lot more freedom in designing his or her models and animation.

In our case, the client came to us with precious little in terms of a detailed final design. The project consisted of a land development slated to stretch for 1.25 miles down a proposed "waterway," which at the time looked like an oversized drainage ditch. There were a few existing buildings and two that were under construction. For the most part, the land was undeveloped wooded property in the center of a heavily wooded planned community.

The Business End—Not So Fast . . .

Although most animators would prefer not to think about the business side of a project, before you can create an awesome 3D animation for anyone, you must first sell it to the client. Simply put, you must prove you can pull it off for the price you bid, in the time you have been allotted, and deliver the quality agreed upon.

When bidding a job, there is always the need to be both cost- and time-effective, but not let quality suffer as a result of time or budget constraints. The artist's good name and reputation is on the line. It also is important to thoroughly understand the experience level of your modelers, animators, technicians, and programmers, along with the required deadlines, before making a commitment for a completion date.

There is an art in selling 3D, and the key is to create a small sample of what is possible, and let the client's imagination do the rest. In this case, the client gave us a 2D architectural rendering that the successful architect had submitted as the winning design for the new Woodlands Waterway convention center. From this simple print rendering of the convention center, we went to work to create a tiny portion of the fly-through.

Using the techniques shown in this tutorial, we created a three-second "fly-up" of the proposed hotel. You can see this animation in the bonus content on the CD in the back of the book (**Hotel_1.mpg**). We invited several people from the client company to our studio to view the animation. In addition to the actual animation clip, we opened the convention center scene in Layout, and moved the camera real-time to show various angles. As an experienced LightWave user you may remember the excitement of first seeing and moving 3D objects in a wireframe scene. The excitement was infectious, and allowing the client to play "director" helped us seal the deal.

Script Development

Our "deliverable" in this project was not simply a 3D fly-through, but a fully interactive CD-ROM. After viewing the fly-through, viewers are offered a menu from which they can pick and choose which section of the CD they want to explore; they can also click on any of several buildings and fly into that structure.

No builder would ever take on a significant project without first having a set of plans that have been thoroughly reviewed and approved by the client. Unless you like to do a job several times over (usually for the same price you originally agreed upon), then don't get started until you have a script. Most scripts require several iterations, but it is far simpler to move text around in a Word document than to create and move objects in a 3D environment. Without a script, the project could easily have become a victim of "mission creep," in which the mission continually grows in scope and never comes to an end.

Although there was nothing magical about the format of our script, we found that breaking it into two key sections made it easy to understand. Section I is the flow chart section of the script. The flow chart is a skeletal view of the project, showing the relation of each part to the whole.

In Section II, we get into the specific details of each frame of the script. Section II is made up of two columns: Audio and Video. The Audio column describes what the voice talent will read in a recording studio and what the user will hear when playing each section of the presentation. The Video column provides the necessary information for the artists, animators, and programmers to plan the project.

Asset Collection

The planned fly-through would need to incorporate existing elements (bridges, several existing buildings, roads, and so on) and a number of proposed buildings. To make sure the scale and placement were technically accurate, we met with representatives who are responsible for the municipal aspects of The Woodlands. They provided CAD drawings, topographical maps, soil surveys, aerial photos, and several other bits and pieces of data that helped us literally understand the lay of the land.

To get further in touch with nature, we walked the 1.25-mile length of the Woodlands Waterway, photographing architectural elements, foliage, and textures we knew would later prove helpful. A trip to the top of one of the multistory buildings that was under construction helped us visualize the waterway from overhead. Then we hit on an asset that proved very helpful. The client offered us some videotape made from a helicopter flying down the waterway at three different elevations. We knew from this footage that our camera should be approximately 100 feet above the water level.

Enough talk about the Woodlands Waterway fly-through—take a minute to look at it firsthand. You'll find it on the companion CD. Windows users, click **Waterway.exe**; Macintosh users, click **Waterway.avi.**

OK—Let's Build Us an Office Building!

Finally it's time to fire up LightWave 6.5 and get started. In this tutorial we will cover the creation of the key elements in an architectural scene. You will learn how to create an office building, the surrounding landscape, and some smaller architectural elements that add detail and realism.

Let's say, hypothetically, that a client has hired your firm to create a visually exciting 3D fly-through of a proposed building that will be the centerpiece of their new corporate park project. They want to give prospective buyers the opportunity to "see" the finished project before it is actually built (or even fully designed, as in our test case). They would like the finished piece to be attractive, reasonably realistic, and as descriptive as possible, all within the confines of their ever-tightening budget. All they have at this point are a few "artist's conception" illustrations (Figure 2-1) and a general idea of the overall dimensions. There are no hard plans on how the floor plan will be laid out. Those are still on the drawing board and probably won't be finalized until someone actually buys the space and specifies how they want their part to be designed. So in this case we have a lot of artistic freedom. Unlike the case study we've been talking about, we can use our imagination for this job, and not have to go through the effort of creating a model of a building from blueprints and exact measurements. The key thing to remember is to think about what you want to accomplish beforehand and decide on a course of action based on the needs of the project. In this project we want to make a modern-style office building, constructed with steel and glass and masonry, that stands about 11 or 12 stories tall. Since our goal in this case is just to show the building in an attractive setting as it might look after it is actually built, we don't have to worry about a huge degree of detail.

FIGURE 2-1 Conceptual Drawing of office building.

STEP 1: Let's build our office building first. Load Modeler and begin by pressing . or , to zoom in or out until the Grid box at the bottom left of the Modeler window reads 5 m. Make sure the Create tab is selected. On the main toolbar, click the Box button. Press N to open the Numeric panel. We'll want our building to be impressive, so let's make it about 12 stories tall. Enter the following values:

	Low	High	Segments
X	−20 m	20 m	12
Y	3 m	33 m	10
Z	−20 m	20 m	12

Be sure to press either Enter or Tab after entering any values into an entry field in LightWave. This is essential to make the values "stick." Now click the Box button again to deselect it. Your screen should now look like Figure 2-2. These settings give us a box 40 m wide, 30 m high, and 40 m deep. This will be the basis for our modern office building.

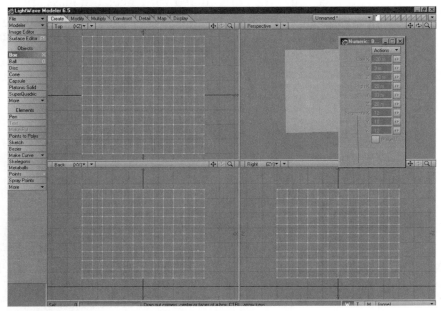

FIGURE 2-2 Numeric panel shown in top right of window.

Now, let's assign our building a surface. Click the Detail tab. Now, click the Surface button in the Polygons area (or press Q) to open the Change Surface panel. Type *building_outer* in the Name field. Then press Tab and click the color swatch to open the Color panel. Enter the following RGB color values:

Red	235
Green	215
Blue	175

This will be the base color of our building's exterior. Click OK to accept this color. (All surface attributes in LightWave are assigned to polygons based upon the surface name assigned to those polygons. So if you want to apply a different surface to a different part of your object, you must assign that part a surface name unique to the polygons that are to receive that particular surface attribute.)

STEP 2: Now we'll begin to add some features to our rather plain beginnings. Activate Polygons selection mode by clicking the Polygons button on the bottom menu (or by pressing Ctrl+H). Select the polygons that make up the top and bottom of our building by right-clicking and dragging around the polygons you wish to select (Figure 2-3). Now, click the Construct tab, choose More in the Reduce group, then Reduce-Polygons to open the Co-Planar Polygon Reduction Tool. Click OK to accept the default values. This function tests the selected polygons for a certain flatness threshold and removes the division from polygons that it determines to be co-planar (occupying the same plane). In this case, we subdivided the box to give ourselves a foundation of geometry upon which we can build the building's window walls. We want to be able to use the Bevel tool to construct the roof and ground floor of the building, so we can use the Reduce-Polygon command to get these two flat areas back to single polygons upon which we can easily use the Bevel tool.

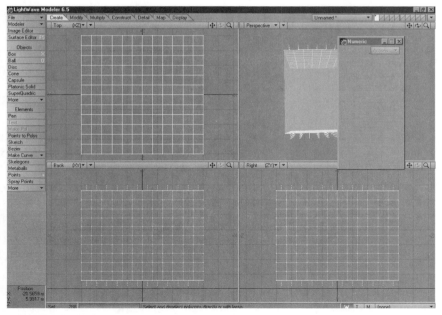

FIGURE 2-3 Reduce selected polygons with Co-Planar Polygon Reduction Tool.

Deselect the top polygon by clicking it, so that only the bottom polygon is selected. Click the Multiply tab. In the Extend area on the main toolbar, click the Bevel button (or press B). On the Actions menu in the Numeric panel, choose Reset. Now click Actions again and choose Activate.

Tip: This Reset and Activate process will soon become almost automatic for you if you use the Numeric panel a lot in your modeling. The numeric data is remembered in LightWave from one use of a particular tool to the next. Therefore, if you have already used the Bevel tool in a given session and made a bevel with an Inset value of 10 mm and a Shift value of 10 mm, the next time you activate the Numeric panel for the Bevel tool, it will automatically use the same values again. If you choose Reset on the Actions menu, the values are cleared from the fields and you can start fresh. While this may seem somewhat inconvenient to some, the upside is that you can repeat the Bevel function almost instantaneously if you need a series of similar bevels.

Enter an Inset value of 3 m and a Shift value of 0. Then click the Bevel button again to deselect it. Now click it again to activate it. Reset and Activate the Numeric panel as we did before, but this time enter an Inset value of 0 and a Shift value of 2.8 m. This will be our first floor. Click the Bevel button to deselect it, then press / to deselect the bottom polygon.

STEP 3: We are not even close to being finished with the outside of our building yet, but we can use what we have so far to create an interior for our building's outer shell. So, before we add any more detail, press C or click the Copy button on the bottom menu to make a copy of the model. Go to the next empty layer and click Paste (or press V) to create a perfect duplicate of the building. We are going to use this copy of our building's outer skin to build an inner surface for our building. We may want to render the interior of the building at some point, so it will be to our advantage to create those surfaces now.

Click the Modify tab (Shift+H), click Size in the Stretch group on the main toolbar, and press N to open the Numeric panel if it is not already open. Reset and Activate the Numeric panel. Enter a Factor value of 99%, then click Apply. Click the bottom half of the layer 1 button to put our outer shell into the background layer. Your screen should now look like Figure 2-4. We have moved the polygons in enough to give our building's outer walls some thickness. This will prevent the interior surface from occupying the same plane as the outer one and save us from the rendering problems that might have been created by overlapping polygons. Since this is going to be an interior surface, the Polygons should be facing inward; click the Detail tab and click Flip (or press F) in the Polygons area on the main toolbar.

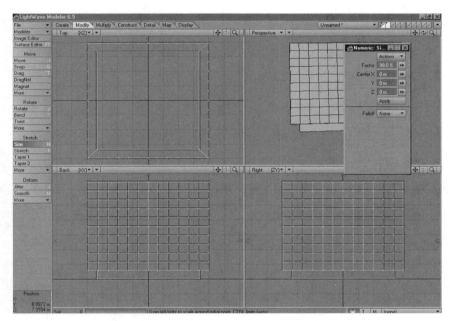

FIGURE 2-4 Outer shell of building is in the background layer.

STEP 4: Now we will give our interior surface some windows. Make certain you are in Polygons selection mode (Press Ctrl+H or scroll through the different selection modes using the spacebar). Using the right mouse button, click and drag to draw a line around the polygons that make up the subdivided portion of the walls on the sides of the top ten floors of our building. It's easiest to select one wall at a time and then add the next wall by holding down the Shift key and lassoing the next set of polygons. Be careful not to inadvertently select any of the top- or bottom-facing polygons.

Your Selection count should be 480 polygons (Figure 2-5). Click the Bevel button. Open the Numeric panel and enter an Inset value of 100 mm. Click the Bevel button again to deselect it (or click in the Modeler workspace to close the Numeric panel and press B). Press Q to open the Change Surface panel. Type *window_frame_inner* in the Name field and press Tab.

Tip: The Selection count is located just above the Points button at the lower left of the Modeler window.

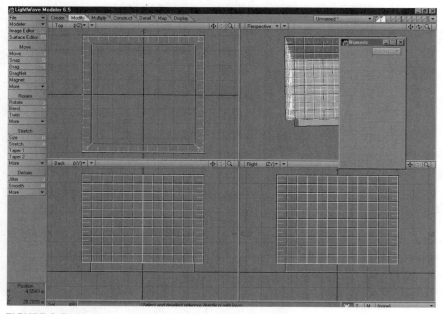

FIGURE 2-5 480 selected polygons ready for beveling.

Tip: A lot of people have missed this cool and handy feature of the LightWave 6.5 Color panel. By clicking the colored numbers and holding down the mouse button while you drag to the left or right, you can drag the values up and down, just as the old mini-slider buttons did in earlier versions of the program.

Click and drag on the Red value to set it to 145. Now set the Green and Blue values to 145 also. This gives us a neutral gray hue. Click the Bevel button. In the Numeric panel, choose Actions > Activate to apply the same bevel values again. Press Q to open the Change Surface panel, type *window_glass_inner* in the Name field, and set the following RGB values:

Red	145
Green	175
Blue	145

This gives us a nice gray-green color for our window glass surface. Now we have the interior surfaces we will need later when we take our camera into the interior of the office building. Your interior should look like Figure 2-6.

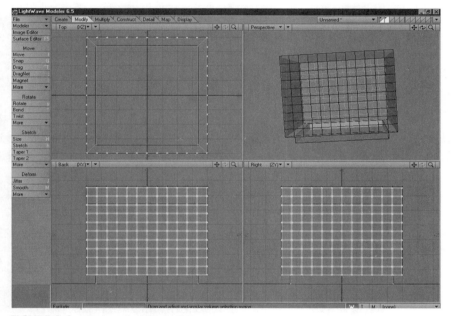

FIGURE 2-6 Interior of office building.

STEP 5: Click the layer 1 button to look at the building exterior. It has the basic shape we want, but it's pretty boring at best. The exterior walls of the top 10 floors of our building are made up of rectangular grids of quadrilateral polygons. We can use these grids now to add architectural interest to the design of our model. Let's add some balconies to some of the executive offices on the front side of the building.

Beginning in (horizontal) row 2, (vertical) columns 9 and 10, and in row 3, columns 9 and 10, select the front-facing polygons in a stair step pattern going down from right to left (Figure 2-7).

Be sure to deselect any polygons you may have selected on the back of the building (those facing the positive Z direction). We want to shift out the faces of all these polygons together in order to make a structure for our executive balconies. This is a perfect example of a situation that calls for the Smooth Shift tool. Whenever you need to shift a group of individual co-planar polygons along their surface normal (an imaginary line projected perpendicular to the surface plane) without also adding unwanted interior edge geometry, the Smooth Shift tool is the way to accomplish it.

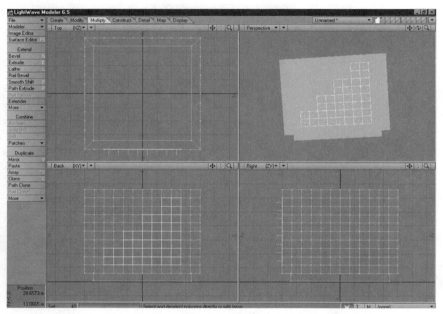

FIGURE 2-7 Stair stepped polygon selection to form balconies.

Click the Multiply tab. In the Extend area on the main toolbar, click the Smooth Shift button (or press F). Press N to open the Numeric panel. Reset and Activate the Numeric panel. Enter an Offset value of 2 m and leave the other values at the default. Now click the Smooth Shift button (or press F) again to deselect it. Click the Bevel button, press N, and Reset and Activate the Numeric panel. Enter an Inset value of 200 mm. Deselect the Bevel tool and then reselect it to begin a new bevel. We will be using this method quite a bit to add new layers of geometry to groups of polygons without resorting to Boolean functions, which can leave lots of invisible duplicate points and polygons lying around.

Reset and Activate the Numeric panel as we did before. Enter a Shift value of –2 m. That moves our polygons back to the same Z position they had before. Open the Change Surface panel and type *balcony_window_frame* in the Name field. Set all three RGB values to 145, just as we did for the inner frame. Again, click the Bevel button twice to finish the previous bevel and start a new one. This time, enter an Inset value of 100 mm and a Shift value of 0. Open the Change Surface panel and type *balcony_window_glass* in the Name field. Set the following RGB values:

Red	145
Green	175
Blue	145

Now there is a bit more interest in our building facade.

Close the Change Surface panel and the Numeric panel too, if it is still open. Click the Bevel button to deselect it, then click in the gray area on the left side of the Modeler window below the buttons to deselect the surface. Your screen should now resemble Figure 2-8.

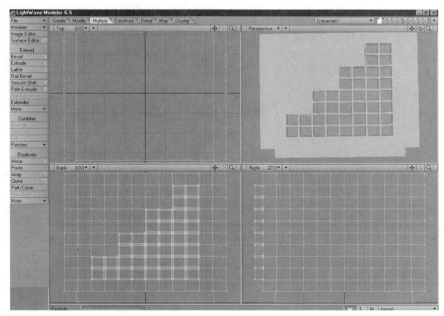

FIGURE 2-8 Beveled and extruded balcony ledges.

STEP 6: It might be a good idea to save what you have so far, just in case. I strongly advise you to develop the habit of saving often. You never know when something might go wrong, and saving all your steps will pay off many times over in the long run.

Tip: This is a good opportunity to introduce you to one of the new features of Modeler. Press the Ctrl and Shift keys simultaneously and right-click in one of the view windows. Choose File > Save Object As and then save your file as **Building.lwo.** LightWave now has many of the most useful commands mapped to the combination of Ctrl+Shift and the left, right, or center mouse button (if you have a three-button mouse). You may also customize each list by adding commands using the Edit Menu Commands panel, which is accessible by choosing Modeler > Interface >Edit Menu Commands on the main toolbar. Of course, all of these commands are also accessible in the traditional manner. But if you like to use shortcut keys and these menus, you have the option to turn off the tool menus completely, providing the greatest amount of desktop real estate for you to work in. But, for now, keep the interface in the default state so we're all on the same page.

STEP 7: Our front facade is a little more interesting now, but we probably need to add railings to the balcony so that nobody will fall off! Click the layer 3 button. This layer should still be empty. Click the bottom part of the layer 1 button to put our outer building in the background so we can use it as a guide for the positioning and scale of the railings. Click the Box button and open the Numeric panel. Enter the following values:

	Low	High	Segments
X	10.15 m	13.2 m	1
Y	7.25 m	7.35 m	1
Z	−21.8 m	−21.75 m	1

This will be the top rail for the balcony. Click the Multiply tab, then click the Mirror button on the main toolbar. Open the Numeric panel if it is not already open. Click the Y button and enter a Center Y value of 6.9 m. Leave the other values at the default. They shouldn't matter since all we are doing is mirroring the rail on the Y axis. Press Shift+A to fit the selected foreground polygons to fill all view windows.

Let's create some stiles for our rails now. Click the top part of the layer 4 button. Then click the bottom part of the layer 3 button to put the rails in the background. Click the Box button on the main toolbar and enter the following values in the Numeric panel:

	Low	High	Segments
X	10.4125 m	10.4875 m	1
Y	6.5 m	7.3 m	1
Z	−21.775 m	−21.775 m	1

As you can see from the identical entries in the Low Z and High Z fields, this box doesn't have any thickness to it, but it will do fine for our purposes. Now we need to make several more of these and space them out equally, a job made very simple by using Light-Wave's Array tool.

Click the Multiply tab, then click the Array button on the main toolbar. Open the Numeric panel and choose Rectangular array type. Enter an X Count value of 12 and leave the others at the default value of 1. Choose Manual offset type, enter an Offset X value of 220 mm, and leave the others alone. Click OK. Click the Cut button (or press X) to cut the contents of this layer to the clipboard, then click the layer 3 button (where the rails are located) and click Paste (or press V).

Now we can give our railing a surface. Press Q to open the Change Surface panel and type *balcony_railing* in the Name field. Set all three RGB values to 145. Click OK. Now let's make sure that our railing renders on both sides. Click the Surface Editor button on the main toolbar. In the Surface Name area of the Surface Editor, click the white triangle next to building to expand the list, and select the balcony_railing surface (Figure 2-9). Select the Double Sided check box. This will render both sides of our railing stiles so that their reflections will be picked up in our window glass later. Close the Surface Editor.

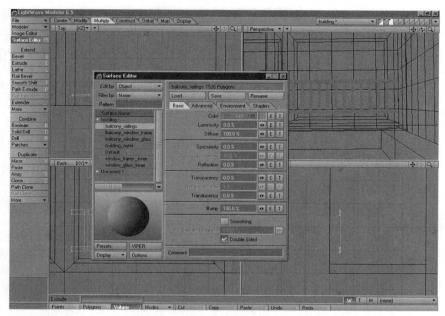

FIGURE 2-9 Select "Double Sided" for balcony_railing surface in Surface Editor.

STEP 8: Now we need a lot more railings, so click the Multiply tab, then click the Array button. In the Numeric panel, enter an X count value of 0 and enter a Y Count value of 8. Choose Manual offset type and enter an Offset Y value of 3 m. Click OK. Close the Numeric panel. Place the pointer at the left end of the bottom railing on the lowest balcony in the Back view window and press G to center the view on the pointer. Now zoom in. This is a handy way to zoom in on a certain area. Your screen should resemble Figure 2-10.

Now click the Mirror button. Click and drag to draw a vertical line on the centerline separating the last vertical row of balconies from the column just to the left (Figure 2-11). The next two vertical rows of balconies are two floors shorter, so select the railing polygons in the bottom six floors of railings, as in Figure 2-12. Press C to copy these to the clipboard, then click the Move button. Open the Numeric panel, enter an Offset X value of −6.66 m, and click Apply. This will move those railings over two rows to the left. Press the spacebar to deselect the Move tool, then press V to paste the copies back into the original position. Now there are four

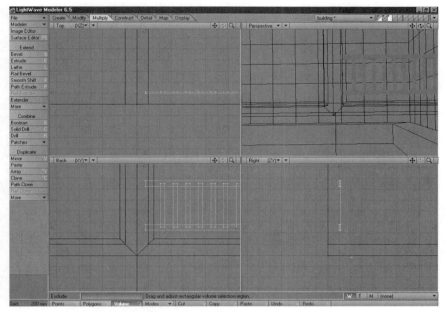

FIGURE 2-10 Viewports zoomed in on arrayed railings.

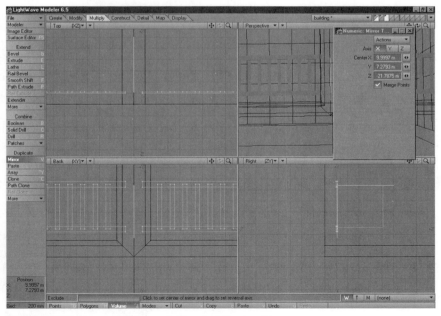

FIGURE 2-11 Draw vertical centerline to Mirror railings.

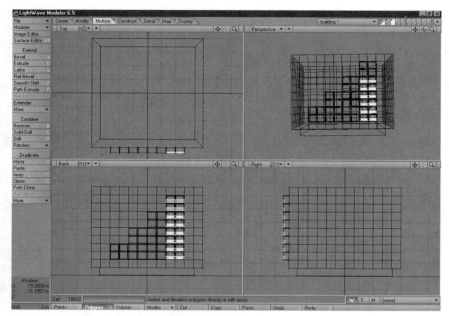

FIGURE 2-12 Selected railings for copying.

vertical rows of railings in place. Now, right-click and drag around the top two horizontal rows of your selection to deselect those railings, and copy the selection to the clipboard again. Apply the same Offset X value of −6.66 m to the remaining selection and then press V again. Now there are six rows. Deselect two more horizontal rows from the top and repeat the copy, move, and paste procedure. Your screen should now resemble Figure 2-13. Close the Numeric panel and press the spacebar to deselect the Move tool. Click in the gray area of the Modeler window to deselect the remaining polygons. Voilà! Our railings are done. Now, click the layer 1 button and save the object to protect your work.

STEP 9: Now that we've got the balconies done, we can add windows to the rest of the building's faces. Select Layer 1. Using the lasso selection method, select all the polygons on the outer left wall of our building. Make sure you don't get anything but the subdivided upper part of the building (Figure 2-14). Hold down the Shift key and lasso the back and right side polygons in a similar fashion. You should now have a Selection count of 360 polygons.

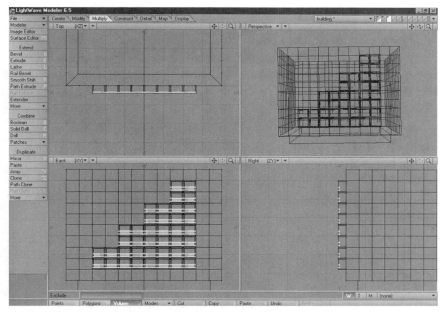

FIGURE 2-13 Completed balcony railings.

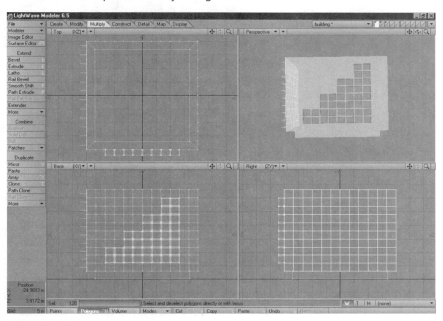

FIGURE 2-14 Selected polygons of outer left wall of building.

Tip: The Selection count is located just above the Points button at the lower left of the Modeler window (Figure 2-15).

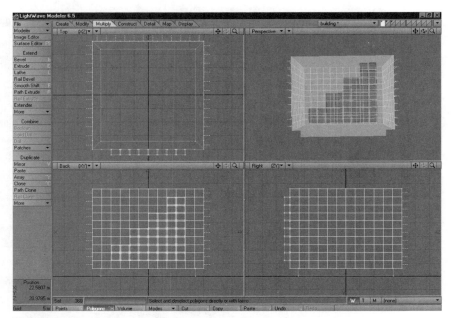

FIGURE 2-15 Selected three outer walls with a 360 polygon count.

Now for the tricky bit. Holding down the Shift key, add the front wall polygons to the selection, but not ones that make up the outer face of the balcony area. See Figure 2-16. This last selection got our front window polygons, but also took in the windows and frames from our balconies. Make sure you are in Polygons selection mode and press W to open the Statistics panel (or choose Modeler > Windows > Statistics Open\Close . . .). Near the bottom of the list in the Statistics panel, you will see an entry that says Surf: none. Click this entry to expand it. You should see the three surfaces we have created thus far. Select balcony_window_frame and then click the minus sign (−) to the left of the surface name. This subtracts the polygons with that name from those currently selected. Now click the surface name again, drag down to balcony_window_glass, and click the minus sign next to it. This will subtract the polygons named balcony_window_glass from our selection. Our Selection count should now be at 440. All we

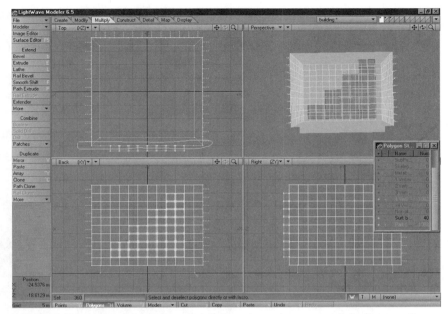

FIGURE 2-16 Holding the RMB and shift key, drag a lasso around the front wall.

have selected now are the window polygons that we haven't changed from our building texture yet.

Click the Bevel button and open the Numeric panel. Reset and Activate the Numeric panel and enter an Inset value of 100 mm. Now click in a view window to re-enter Modeler and press B twice to deselect and reselect the Bevel tool. In the Numeric panel, choose Reset. This time, enter a Shift value of −25 mm to move the selected polygons inward a bit. Open the Change Surface panel and type *building_window_frames* in the Name field. Set all three RGB values to 145, as before. Click OK.

We now have the surface for the window frames, so let's add the glass. Click the Bevel button again. This time, enter an Inset value of 100 mm and a Shift value of 0. Deselect the Bevel tool. Now, open the Change Surface panel. Type *outer_window_glass* in the Name field. Set the following color values:

Red	145
Green	175
Blue	145

Click OK to apply this surface. Now click the Bevel button again, this time entering a Shift value of −50 mm to separate the glass from the frame and add a nice shadow line. Deselect the Bevel tool and press / to deselect the surface. Zoom in (using the > key) to get a closer view of your windows. They should look like Figure 2-17.

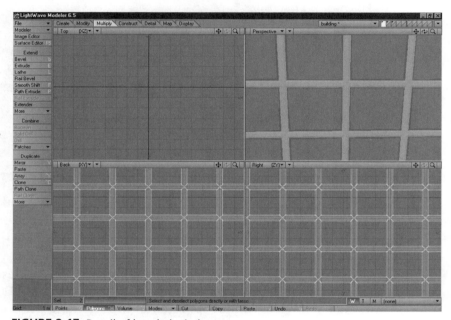

FIGURE 2-17 Detail of beveled windows.

STEP 10: Our building is really starting to take shape now! The next thing we need to address is the ground floor, which will need considerably more detail than the upper stories. First of all, we will need some doors so that we have a way to enter the building. In Polygons selection mode, click and drag laterally across the four unsubdivided polygons that make up the four walls of the bottom story of our building to select them. Take care to get all four walls and not the bottom polygon (Figure 2-18). Make certain that the Selection count indicates that you have only four polygons selected. Press X to cut them from layer 1 and then press V to paste them into the next empty layer, which should be layer 4.

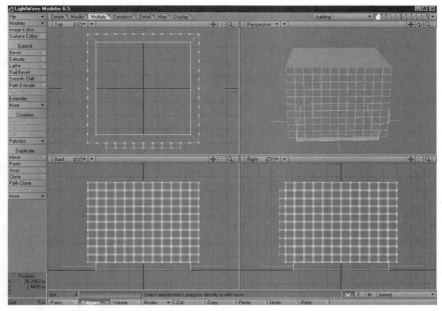

FIGURE 2-18 Bottom story with four walls selected.

STEP 11: Our walls consist of four polygons, each one 34 meters wide and 2.8 meters tall. To add some detail we first need to subdivide our geometry a little. We can accomplish this by using the Julienne command. Julienne makes regular slices in geometry along a specified axis, so it is a handy tool to use when you need more geometry to work with.

Click the Construct tab. In the Subdivide area on the main toolbar, click the Julienne button. The Julienne panel allows you to select an axis along which to subdivide and specify the number of subdivisions to perform. Select the X axis and set Divisions to 12. Click OK to perform the Julienne. There are now a number of evenly spaced polygons in layer 5. These are the polygons that Julienne used to slice up our front and back walls. You can delete these safely now.

STEP 12: As a side effect of using an even number of subdivisions, Julienne places a division at the center of our polygon, which we can use as the edge of our doors. Now our bottom story has 12 segments on the X axis. Now select the two adjacent segments at the center of the wall on both the front and back walls, as in Figure 2-19. We'll need to subdivide these even further, so click the Subdivide button (or press D). When the Subdivide Polygons panel opens, click the Faceted check box, and then click OK. This divides our center polygons in half along both the X and Y axes, so each polygon becomes four new polygons. Select the polygons just to the left of the centerline, top and bottom, on both the front and back walls. Your selection should look like Figure 2-20.

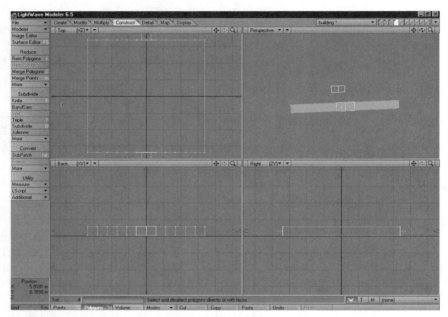

FIGURE 2-19 Selection of Julienne subdivided polygons.

Now we can get rid of the extra subdivision on the Y axis. Make sure the Construct tab is selected. In the reduce group, choose More > Reduce Polygon and accept the default settings. This command checks the selection for co-planar polygons and attempts to unify them. Essentially, we have subdivided the polygons evenly along the X and Y axes with facets. So, since we don't want the vertical division, we're using the Reduce Polygon command to remove the unneeded subdivision. Now deselect those polygons and do the same thing to the polygons just to the right side of the centerline. When you are finished, your screen should look like Figure 2-21.

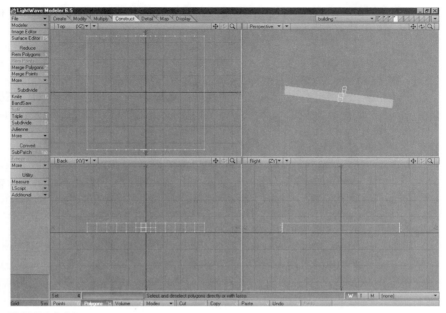

FIGURE 2-20 Selection of vertically subdivided center polygons.

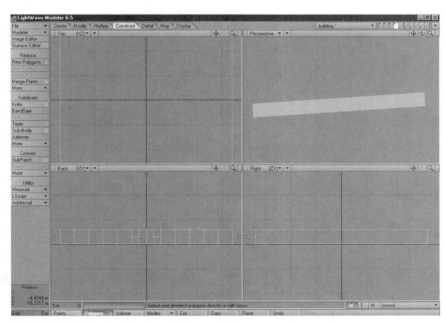

FIGURE 2-21 Result of Reduce Polygon button on co-planar polygons.

STEP 13: Now that we have the basic geometry needed for the construction of our doors, we can add some much-needed detail. Select the four polygons that we just finished creating and cut them to the clipboard. Click the next empty layer (which should be layer 5). Paste the polygons for the doors into this layer. Like most of the trim on our modern office building, these doors are to be constructed of metal and glass. So we can use the same technique we used on our window frames to create our doors.

Make sure you are in Polygons selection mode. Lasso all four of the door polygons. Open the Change Surface panel and name the new surface *door_frame*. Give it the same neutral gray color that we used before, with RGB values of 145. Now click the Bevel button and open the Numeric panel. Reset the Numeric panel and enter an Inset value of 100 mm and a Shift value of 0. That will be good for our door frames, so now we can add the glass. Open the Change Surface panel and assign the selected inner polygons the surface name *door_glass*. Give this glass the following color values:

Red	145
Green	175
Blue	145

STEP 14: At this point, our doors are connected in two pairs, one pair for the front and one pair for the back. We need to separate the doors so that we can extrude them for thickness. If we were to extrude them while they were in their current state (connected and sharing the centerline edge), we would not end up with edges between the two doors, but only face polygons and edges around the outer perimeter of the door polygons. Clear any selected polygons. In the Back view, draw a lasso around the polygons that make up the doors on the right side (Figure 2-22). Cut these into the clipboard. Go to the next empty layer and paste the polygons into it. Now lasso the polygons that make up the front door (the one that faces the negative Z axis). Click the Multiply tab, then click the Extrude button and open the Numeric panel if it isn't already open. Enter an Extent value of 100 mm on the Z axis. Now, deselect the front door and select the polygons for the back

door. For this selection, make the Extrude Extent –100 mm so that it is extruded toward the origin. Repeat this process for the two doors on the left side of the centerline.

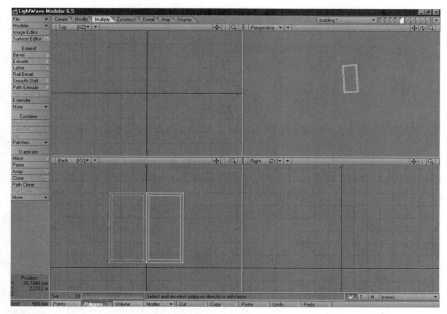

FIGURE 2-22 Right hand doors selected for extruding.

STEP 15: Now all of the doors have edges and thickness, but in order to animate them individually, we must make sure that each door occupies its own layer and has its own separate pivot point. At this point we have the two doors on the left on one layer and the two doors on the right in another. In each of these two layers, select the door at the back side (the one on the positive side of the Z axis), and cut it out of the layer it shares with the front door. Then paste each door into the next empty layer. When you are finished, you should have a single door in each of the last four occupied layers.

STEP 16: Go to the layer that contains the left front door. Press A to zoom in to the door and center it in all views. Notice that the dark grid line representing the 0 value of X runs along the right edge of the door (Figure 2-23). This is the edge of our door that will swing back and forth when the door is rotated into the open position. The pivot point for this door will therefore need to go on the other (left) edge of the door. We could adjust this in Layout, but we have a new tool in LightWave 6.5 that allows us to set the pivot point for a layer in Modeler, so we may as well use it!

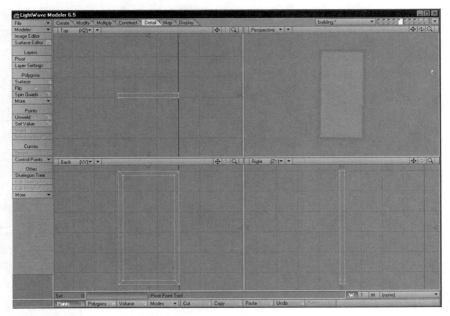

FIGURE 2-23 Close-up of left front door.

Click the Detail tab. In the Layers area on the main toolbar, click the Pivot button. In the Top view window, position the pointer near the left edge of the door, approximately in the center of the four points at the left edge of the door, and click to set the pivot point (Figure 2-24). Repeat this process for the remaining doors. Remember that the pivot points for the doors to the right of the centerline will go on the right side of the doors. When you have set the pivot points for all four doors, save the object as **building.lwo** to protect the changes we have just made.

STEP 17: The doors we've built will now rotate properly, but we still need to give them some sort of handles. Since the detail of our building is going to be largely composed of steel and glass, we can use basic tubular steel door pulls.

FIGURE 2-24 Placement of pivot point for left front door.

Select the next empty layer. Put the left front door layer into the background by clicking the bottom half of the button for the layer it occupies. We will use it as a guide for the positioning and scale of our door handle. Press A to fit the door in the background into all views. Click the Create tab, then click the Disc button and open the Numeric panel. Enter the following values:

Axis		Z
Sides		24
Segments		1
Bottom		−17.03 m
Top		−17 m
Center X		−50 mm
	Y	1.3 m
	Z	−17.015 m
Radius X		20 mm
	Y	20 mm
	Z	15 mm

Click the Disc button again to deselect it. Zoom in on the disc. In Polygons selection mode, lasso the front polygon of the disc— that is, the one facing the negative Z axis (Figure 2-25). Press F to flip this polygon. Now, click the Multiply tab, then click the Lathe button. Open the Numeric panel if it isn't already open. Reset and Activate the Numeric panel and enter the following values:

Sides	6
Axis	X
Start Angle	0
End Angle	90
Center X	−50 mm
Y	1.35 m
Z	−17.03 m
Offset	0

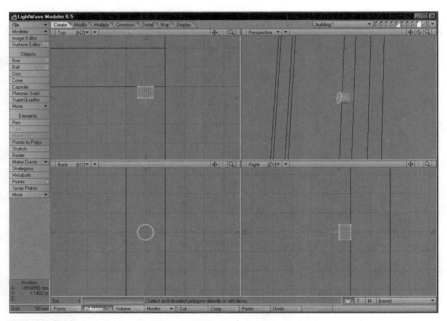

FIGURE 2-25 Newly formed disc with front polygon selected.

Deselect the Lathe button. Let's look at what we have so far. A close inspection of the object and its polygons reveals that all the polygons on the sides of our tubular form are quadrilateral—that is, they all have four sides. Therefore, the only polygons in our object that have more than four sides are the circular polygons that made up the ends of the original disc and additionally, the ones that we created with the Lathe tool when we swept out the elbow section. These polygons are superfluous because they are not going to be seen, and because they can cause unwanted results when the surface is smoothed, leaving seams cutting through sections of what should be a seamless object. So we need to get rid of the unwanted polygons.

Press A to fit the object to all views. Press W to open the Statistics panel. Make sure you are in Polygons selection mode. In the Polygon Statistics panel, click the plus sign next to >4 Vertices. This will add all the polygons on the current layer with a total number of sides greater than four to the current selection (Figure 2-26). As we can see in the Polygon Statistics panel, there are four circular polygons in our object that we don't need. Press K to remove the polygons from the selection while leaving the points.

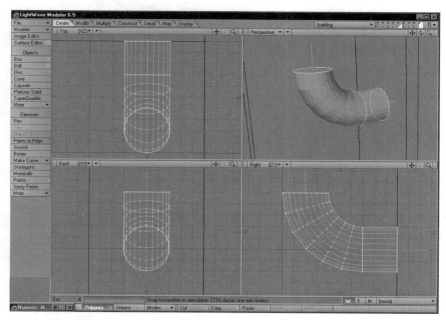

FIGURE 2-26 Selection of polygons with number of sides > 4.

Tip: The Statistics panel is great for making selections that would be difficult, if not impossible, to make using any of the direct selection methods available. Points and polygons can be isolated and selected by either surface name or point/polygon count, even if they are sharing the same space or points or edges with others.

Activate Points selection mode either by using the spacebar to quickly scroll through the different modes or by clicking the Points button on the bottom menu. Lasso the points in the top row of the elbow-shaped object we have created. Your selection should look like Figure 2-27. Click the Multiply tab, then click the Extender button to activate the Point Extender tool. At first glance it may appear as if nothing has happened. Click the Move button (or press T), open the Numeric panel, and Reset and Activate the Numeric panel. Enter an Offset Y value of 150 mm and click Apply. Deselect the selected points.

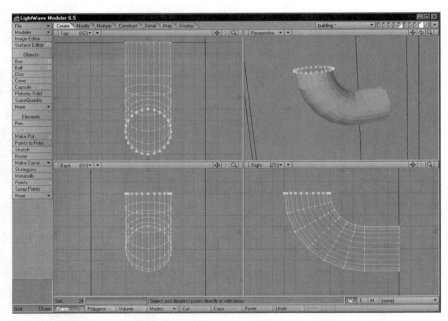

FIGURE 2-27 Elbow-shaped object with top row of points selected.

Now click the Mirror button. In the Numeric panel, enter a Center Y value of 1.5 and click the Y button. Your results should look like Figure 2-28.

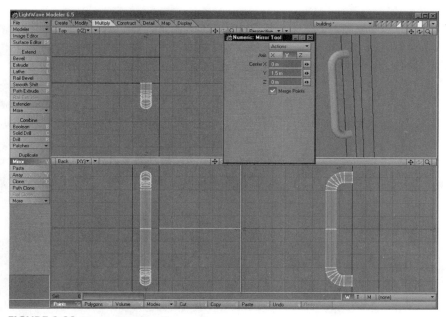

FIGURE 2-28 Front door handle.

Now click the Construct tab. In the Reduce area on the main toolbar, click the Merge Points button. This will test for and remove any points that share coordinates. Select Automatic as the Type and click OK. Open the Change Surface panel and give our new surface the name *door_handle.* Set all three RGB values to 145. Click OK to apply the surface.

Of course, since we've made one handle, there's no need to make any more. To make a handle for the right door, simply click the Mirror button again and Reset and Activate the Numeric panel. Now set the Mirror axis to X and leave all the Center fields set at 0. This will make a copy of our handle just to the right of the first one (Figure 2-29). To make a pair for the back doors, Reset the Mirror tool again, and this time set the Mirror Axis to Z. Again, all the Center values should be left at 0. Now there are four handles in this layer, so all that is left to do with them is to select the individual handles one at a time, cut them out of the current layer, and paste them into the layer containing the corresponding door.

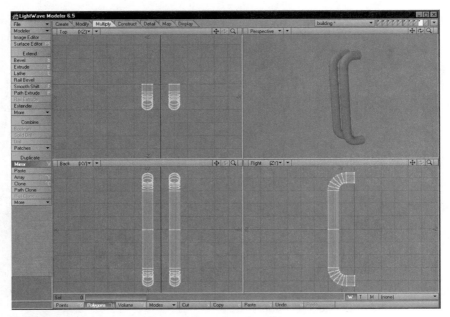

FIGURE 2-29 Placement of second front door handle.

STEP 18: Now that the doors are done, let's return our attention to the bottom floor of the building. Select layer 4 (which should be where we left the bottom floor walls) and press A to fit the object in all views. We divided the front and back facing walls earlier. Now we can do the same to the side walls. Click the Construct tab, then click the Julienne button. We'll use an odd number of subdivisions here so that we can select alternating polygons and still end up with a symmetrical pattern. Select the Z axis and set Divisions to 11. Click OK. Once again, the Julienne tool leaves some superfluous polygons in the first available empty layer. Just press the apostrophe key (') to flip layers, delete the 11 long polygons that Julienne made, and then press the apostrophe key again to return to the walls in layer 4.

STEP 19: Activate Polygons selection mode. Using Figure 2-30 as a guide, select alternating polygons of the walls. We can now add a little more architectural interest by making these wall segments into windows, much as we did for the upper stories. Press Q to open the Change Surface panel. Select the building_window_frames surface for these polygons. Click the Bevel button on the main toolbar. Open the Numeric panel and Reset the values. Enter an Inset value of 100 mm. Click the Bevel button twice to deselect and then reselect it. Reset the Numeric panel and enter a Shift value of −50 mm. This will create an edge for the frame and a nice shadow line. Deselect the Bevel button. Open the Change Surface panel, select the outer_window_glass surface, and click OK to apply. Figure 2-31 will give you an idea what each window panel should look like.

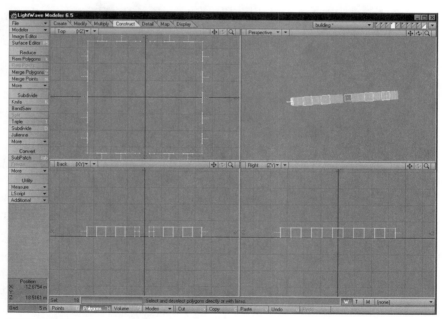

FIGURE 2-30 Alternately selected polygons of walls.

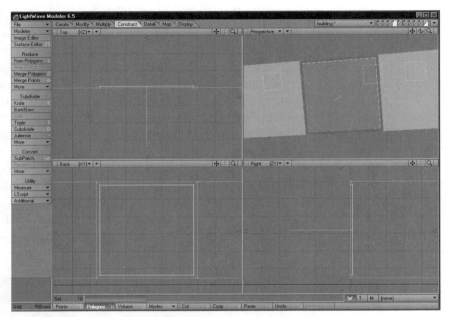

FIGURE 2-31 Detail of a window panel.

STEP 20: Deselect the selected polygons by clicking in the gray area on the left side of the Modeler window. Since we are done with the bottom floor walls, we can now return them to the rest of the building. Press X to cut the walls to the clipboard, then select layer 1, where our upper floors are waiting. Paste the walls back in by pressing V. To get rid of any superfluous geometry we may have picked up along the way, press M to merge any duplicate points. Save the object now to protect our changes thus far.

STEP 21: Let's do a little housekeeping now and reclaim a little working room. Our balcony railings can be cut from layer 3 and pasted into layer 1 with the building exterior. Leave the interior walls in layer 2. We should probably name our layers so that we will know better what each layer contains when we get into Layout later. This gives us an opportunity to explore the Layers Browser, a new feature available in LightWave 6.0 and higher.

To open the Layers Browser, choose Modeler > Windows > Layer Browser Open/Close (or press Shift+Y). This panel consists of a list of the objects open at the time. Each entry on this object list can be expanded by clicking the small white triangle to the left of the object name. Click the triangle next to the building object. Depending on how your layers are arranged, it should look something like Figure 2-32. This list can be used as an expanded, unlimited counterpart to the 10 regular layer buttons at the top right of the Modeler window. The two columns to the left of the white triangle, marked F and B, function pretty much the same way as the regular buttons do; clicking in the F column displays that layer as the foreground object, and clicking in the B column displays that layer as the background. As usual, pressing Shift while clicking enables multiple selections. Clicking in either column next to the object name selects all layers for that object and places them in the respective foreground or background mode. Clicking on the column beneath the eye icon to the right of a layer name hides that object from visibility when loaded into Layout. Notice that the layers here go beyond the usual 10; Modeler now supports a virtually unlimited number of layers. This panel is the only way to access the layers beyond 10, so it's a good idea to get used to using it. We can also name our layers in this panel, which is why we came to it in the first place, so let's do it.

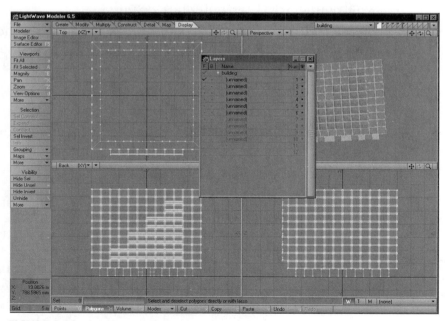

FIGURE 2-32 Layer browser revealing contents of objects.

Double-click layer 1 to open the Layer Settings panel. Type *building_outer* in the Name field. Click OK. Now click layer 2. This is where we put our building's inner walls. Name this layer *building_inner.* Notice that you can also designate a parent layer in this panel. This time, drag to the building_outer entry on the Parent list. This way, whatever transformations we make to the outer layer in Layout will also affect this layer automatically. Now go through each of the four layers containing the doors and give each a name that will remind you of its position, such as *front_left_door, back_right_door,* and so on. Save the object to protect your work.

STEP 22: Now we can add the last bits of detail to our building's outer structure. Let's finish the bottom floor first. Select layer 1. Switch to Polygons selection mode if you are not already in it. Select the single polygon that makes up the bottom of the building. Click the Bevel button and open the Numeric panel. Enter an Inset value of –3 m to bring the polygon out to the width and depth of the upper floors. Leave the other values at 0. Click the Bevel button twice to start a new bevel. Reset the Numeric panel. This time, enter a Shift value of 200 mm and an Inset value of 0. Click the Bevel button again to deselect the tool and click in the gray area to deselect the bottom polygon.

STEP 23: Now we need some columns to support the second-story cantilever. Select an empty layer and put layer 1 in the background. Click the box button and open the Numeric panel. Enter the following values:

	Low	High	Segments
X	−19.5 m	−19 m	1
Y	200 mm	3 m	1
Z	−19.5 m	−19 m	1

Press A to fit the box in all views. It should look like Figure 2-33. Now that we have created our first support column, we can use the Array tool to make copies of this column to go all the way around the first floor.

Click the Multiply tab. In the Duplicate area on the main toolbar, click the Array button. Open the Numeric panel and enter the following values:

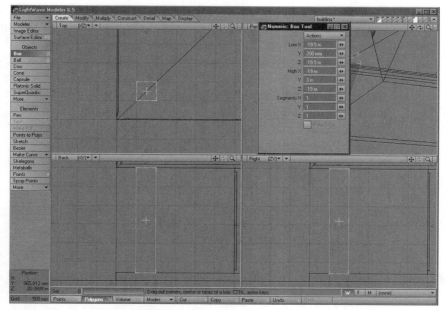

FIGURE 2-33 Fit Selected support column in viewports.

Array Type	Rectangular
X Count	9
Y Count	1
Z Count	9
Jitter X	0
Y	0
Z	0
Offset Type	Manual
Offset X	4.81 m
Y	0
Z	4.81 m

Click OK to create the array. Now use the right mouse button to lasso all the boxes that are not on the outer edge of the array.

To this selection we also need to add the two columns (one on both the front and back rows) in the center of the group on the X axis, which currently sit in front of the doors. Press the Shift key and lasso each of the two center columns in the front and back rows. Your selection should look like Figure 2-34. Press the Delete key to delete the extraneous boxes. Now we'll give these columns the same surface as our building's outer masonry. Open the Change Surface panel and select the building_outer surface. Click OK to apply the surface to our columns. Press X to cut the columns to the clipboard. Select layer 1. Paste the columns into layer 1 by pressing V. Save the object to protect our changes.

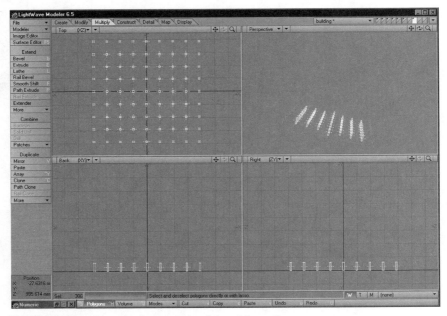

FIGURE 2-34 Selected columns to be deleted from the array.

STEP 24: Our model is really starting to shape up now. We'll add just one more detail to finish up the exterior. The one area we haven't addressed yet is the roof. Carefully select the single polygon that makes up the flat area of the building's rooftop. Check the Selection count. If you have more than one polygon selected, check around the perimeter of the roof polygon with the view zoom and move buttons (located at the top right of the view window) until you find the extra polygons and deselect them. When you have only the single top polygon selected, press Q to open the Change Surface panel. Type the new surface name *roof.* Set all three RGB values to 45 to create a dark gray, almost black hue.

Click OK to apply the surface to the roof polygon. Click the Bevel button and open the Numeric panel. Enter an Inset value of 10 m. Click the Bevel button twice to start a new bevel. This time, enter a shift value of 3 m and an Inset value of 0. Now, deselect the Bevel tool and deselect the top polygon. Select the four polygons that make up the perimeter of the box we just created on the roof. Your selection should look like Figure 2-35. Open the Change Surface panel, select the building_outer surface, and click OK to apply the surface to the polygons. Save the object to protect your work.

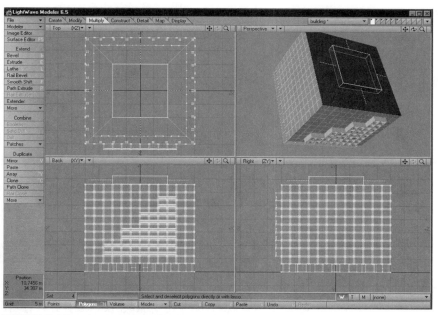

FIGURE 2-35 Selection of roof polygons for surfacing.

There now, that wasn't nearly as bad as you thought, was it? This building is simple and kind of generic-looking, but using this technique and with the help of a artist sketch or some blueprints, you can recreate just about any kind of building you may need.

STEP 25: We need to give the building we've just created a plot of land to sit on. Choose File > New Object (or press Shift+N). This is going to be a fairly simple, flat, ground plane, so we can start with a simple box shape. Click the Box button and open the Numeric panel if you need to. Reset and Activate the Numeric panel and enter the following values:

	Low	High	Segments
X	−1 km	1 km	1
Y	0	0	1
Z	−1 km	1 km	1

Click the Box button again to deselect it. This gives us more than enough room to create a setting for our building that will be attractive. Press Q to open the Change Surface panel. Name our new surface *ground* or something equally creative and descriptive. Set the following color values:

Red   100

Green   150

Blue   40

Click OK to apply. Select the polygon to see if the surface normal is pointing up. If it is pointing downward, press F to flip the polygon so it will render properly in the scene.

STEP 26: The next thing we need to address is the sky for our scene. In some scenes that don't use camera movement, it would suffice to use a sky picture as a background image. Our scene, however, is going to have the camera moving completely around our building in a big circular path, so a background image won't work. Any time you have an animated camera, avoid using a background image; the background images are mapped to the entire viewing area of the camera, so if the camera moves, the image moves with it. Any sense of camera motion is destroyed because the background view does not change with changes in camera angle, position, and so forth. In order to have a sky that stays put and behaves as a sky should behave, I like to use an inverted half sphere as a sort of a sky dome. Select the next empty layer and click the Ball button. In the Numeric panel, enter the following values:

Type		Globe
Sides		36
Segments		18
Center X		0
	Y	0
	Z	0
Radius X		1 km
	Y	1 km
	Z	1 km

Click the Ball button again to deselect it. Because this object is going to completely surround our scene, and we'll spend the entire time moving around inside the ball, we now need to flip the polygons so that the normals point inward, by pressing F. We don't need the bottom half of the sphere, since our ground plane basically cuts off the object at its equator. Lasso the polygons that make up the bottom half of the ball. Your selection should look like Figure 2-36. Press Delete to get rid of the unwanted polygons. Open the Change Surface panel and type the new surface name *sky_dome.* We'll be mapping an image to this surface later, so the color doesn't matter much. For now just enter the following values:

Red	150
Green	200
Blue	255

Select the Smoothing check box so we don't get any nasty visible facets in our sky. Save this object as **skydome.lwo.**

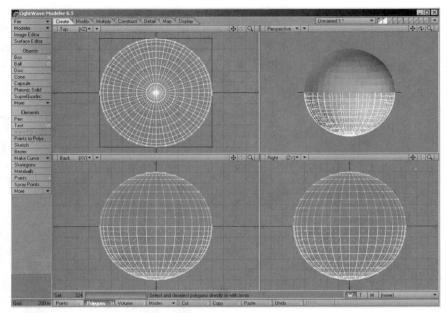

FIGURE 2-36 Skydome ball with bottom half selected for deletion.

Now we are in the home stretch. We've created our building and a basic environment to put it into, and now we need to create some detail. We need just a few more objects that will sell our image as a description of a real space where people live and work and give it a level of realism that feels believable.

Modeling a Light Pole

STEP 1: We're going to need some light poles to illuminate the parking area and lawn of the building. Launch Modeler and begin a new object. Most light poles are built on a concrete foundation block, so our foundation will basically start from that box shape. Select the Box tool, open the Numeric panel, and enter the following values:

	Low	High	Segments
X	−150 mm	150 mm	1
Y	0	500 mm	1
Z	−150 mm	150 mm	1

Deselect the Box tool. Open the Change Surface panel and type *light_pole_base* as the new surface name. Enter the following color values:

Red	255
Green	200
Blue	0

Leave the Diffuse at 100% and set the Specularity at 20%. Click OK to apply this surface to our box.

Now we need to give our box something of a taper, like the base blocks under any common light pole. Click the Modify tab and select the Taper 1 tool. Keep your eye on the Numeric panel, place the pointer in the center of the box in the Top view window, and drag in until the Taper Factor is 75%. Deselect the Taper tool. Your result should look like Figure 2-37.

STEP 2: Now we have a base, but we still need a pole. We can use the top polygon of our foundation block as a starting point for the pole object. With the right mouse button, lasso the top polygon of our tapered box. With that polygon selected, click the Bevel tool. In the Numeric panel, enter an Inset value of 50 mm and a Shift

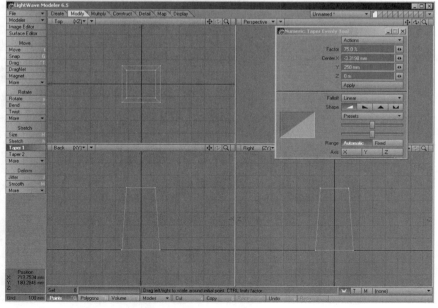

FIGURE 2-37 Result of Taper Tool on light pole box.

value of 0. Close the Numeric panel and press Q to open the Change Surface panel. Type the new surface name *light_pole* and set all three RGB values to 0 to set the color to black. Click OK to apply the surface to the inner polygon we just created.

STEP 3: Select the Bevel tool and open the Numeric panel. Enter a Shift value of 4 m and an Inset value of 0. Click the Bevel tool twice to deselect and then reselect it; this time enter a Shift value of 100 mm and leave the Inset at 0. This creates a narrow band of polygons around the top perimeter of our pole. Deselect the polygon at the very top of the pole and then select the four polygons around the outer perimeter. Be careful not to get the one on top; you just want the side polygons in the band around the top. Your selection should look like the one in Figure 2-38. Check your Selection count; if you have four polygons, select the Bevel tool, then Reset and Activate the Numeric panel. Enter a Shift value of 400 mm to bring four arms out from the center (Figure 2-39).

STEP 4: Click in the workspace, then press B twice to deselect and then reselect the Bevel tool. This time enter an Inset value of –150 mm to widen our end polygon and give us a back plate for our light fixtures. Click the Bevel tool twice, then Reset and Activate

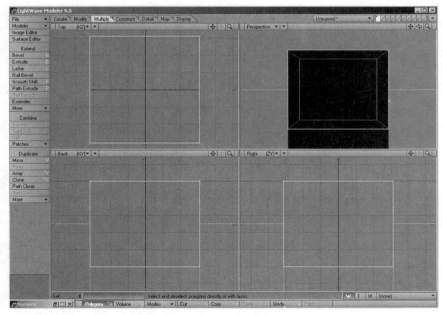

FIGURE 2-38 Top of pole with band of four polygons selected.

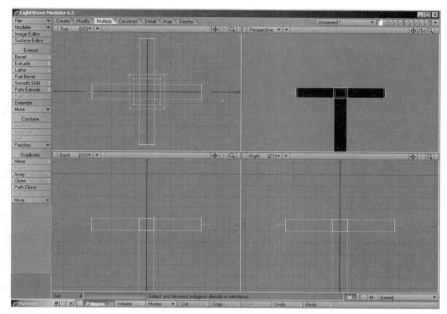

FIGURE 2-39 Beveled arms extending from pole's center.

the Numeric panel. Enter a Shift value of 1 m and an Inset value of 0 to create the boxes for our lights. Using the right mouse button, lasso all four of the selected polygons to deselect them. Our object is starting to resemble a light pole now, but the housings for the lights are a bit fat. Lasso the polygons that form the bottom downward-facing polygons at the bottom of all four of the boxes (Figure 2-40). When you have the downward-facing polygons selected, click the Move tool. Using the Ctrl key to constrain your movements, move the polygons up until they are just even with the lower polygons of the arms that come out to join into these boxes at the back.

STEP 5: While those polygons are still selected, let's give ourselves a nice white plastic diffuser cover for our lights. Press Q to bring up the Change Surface panel and type the surface name *white_panel.* Set all three RGB values to 255. Leave the Diffuse at 100% and the Specularity at 20%. Click OK to apply the texture to the surface. Now select the Bevel tool and enter a Shift value of about 40 mm. Your object should now resemble Figure 2-41. There you have a light pole that will add realistic detail to any architectural rendering. Save this object as **light_pole.lwo**.

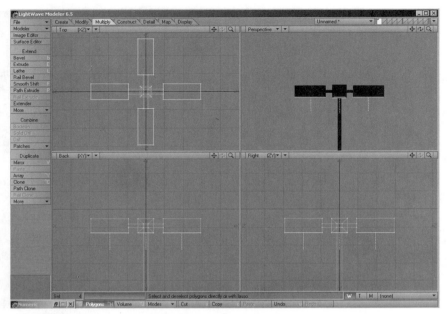

FIGURE 2-40 Light boxes with downward-facing polygons selected.

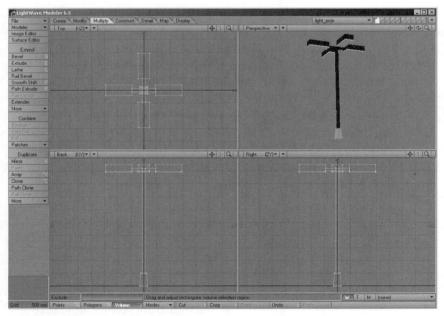

FIGURE 2-41 Result of beveling polygons denoting light panels.

Modeling a Fountain

STEP 1: Like many modern public buildings today, our office building will benefit from the addition of a water feature as part of the architecture of the surrounding landscape. Not only will this add to the unique character of the space, but it will also provide a soothing oasis and naturally attractive decorative aspect. So let's build a fountain to go in front of our building. We'll start with the foundation. Again, we begin with our most basic architectural shape, a simple box. By the very nature of architecture and especially modern construction techniques, it seems as if the box shape is the basis for almost everything you might want to model. Choose File > New Object. Select the Box tool, open the Numeric panel, and enter the following values:

	Low	High	Segments
X	−2 m	2 m	1
Y	0	50 mm	1
Z	−23 m	−21 m	1

Open the Change Surface panel and name this new surface *Foundation.* We will make this surface a grayish-white concrete color, so set all three RGB values to 230. Leave the Diffuse at 100% and set the Specularity to 0 for now. Click OK to apply the surface.

STEP 2: Select the polygon at the top of our foundation box. Your selection should look like Figure 2-42. Select the Bevel tool and open the Numeric panel. Enter an Inset value of 300 mm and leave the Shift set to 0. This polygon will be the beginning of our reflecting pool for our fountain. Open the Change Surface panel and enter the surface name *fount_basin.* We are going to give our fountain a dark marble surface later, to contrast against the lighter stone of the building. So set all three RGB values to 40. Leave the Diffuse at 100% and set the Specularity to 40%. Click OK to apply the color.

STEP 3: Select the Bevel tool and open the Numeric panel. Enter a Shift value of 500 mm and an Inset value of 0. Click the Bevel tool twice to deselect and then reselect it. This time, enter an Inset value of 150 mm and a Shift value of 0. Click the Bevel tool twice

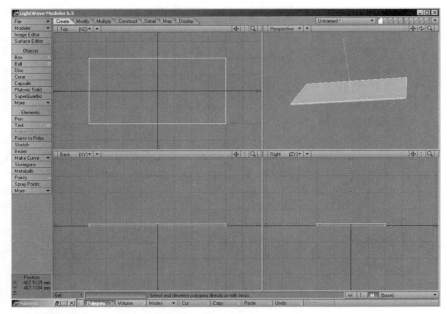

FIGURE 2-42 Foundation box with top polygon selected.

to start a new bevel. This new polygon will be the bottom surface of our reflecting pool, so we need to bevel in this time to create the basin. Reset and Activate the Numeric panel and enter a Shift value of –400 mm and an Inset value of 0. Now we have the basin for our fountain (Figure 2-43).

STEP 4: While this polygon is still selected, press C or click the Copy button on the bottom menu to copy it, select layer 2, and paste that polygon into it. Now we have a copy of the polygon at the bottom of our pool; we're going to use this for the water that will fill the basin. Open the Change Surface panel and name this surface *fountain_water.* Enter the following RGB values:

Red	0
Green	230
Blue	255

This is a nice sky-blue color, which gives us the base color for our water. Set the Diffuse at 60%, since water is highly transparent and

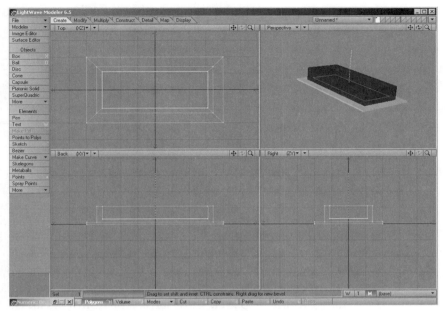

FIGURE 2-43 Fountain basin with floor polygon selected.

reflective. This means that what you see in the water's surface comes largely from its surroundings rather than from its own intrinsic attributes. Set the Specularity to a relatively high 75%, since water is very shiny due to its reflectivity. We'll talk more about this in the following tutorial, where we address more completely the surfacing of our objects. Select the Move tool and open the Numeric panel. Enter an Offset Y value of 250 mm and click Apply to bring our water level up.

STEP 5: Now we have our reflective catch basin and water, but we still need the active part of the fountain. Every good fountain has some sort of moving water feature. The one we are building is based on a real one used in the architectural project upon which this tutorial is based. That fountain had a simple spillway, on either side of an upper basin, from which the water poured in a very relaxing and simple way into the reflecting pool below. So now we will concentrate on the upper basin and the spilling water. Click the next empty layer, which should be layer 3 (you can also press 3 on the regular keyboard, not the numeric keypad). Select the Box tool and open the Numeric panel. Enter the following values:

	Low	High	Segments
X	−525 mm	525 mm	1
Y	150 mm	900 mm	1
Z	−22.275 mm	−21.725 mm	1

Now click the Box tool to deselect it.

STEP 6: Make sure you are in Polygons selection mode and select the polygon that makes up the top of this box. Then select the Bevel tool and open the Numeric panel. Enter an Inset value of 70 mm and a Shift value of 0. Click the Bevel tool twice to deselect and then reselect it. Reset and Activate the Numeric panel and enter a Shift value of –620 mm. Press C to copy this polygon, go to layer 4, and press V to paste it into that layer. We'll leave it alone for now, though. Go back to layer 3 to the box we just made, open the Change Surface panel, and select the fount_basin surface to apply that same black color to our fountain's upper basin box. Go to layer 4 and the polygon we previously left here. Open the Change Surface panel, select the fountain_water surface, and click OK. This will apply the same surface attributes that we used on the water in our reflecting pool. Select the Move tool and open the Numeric panel if it's not already open. Enter an Offset Y value of 500 mm and click Apply to bring the level of our water up on the inside of the upper fountain basin. Click the bottom part of the layer 3 button to put the basin in the background. Now your screen should resemble Figure 2-44.

STEP 7: Hold down the Shift key and click each of the four layers we've used so far. You can see that our fountain is simply a couple of concentric boxes, one nested inside the other. The way our fountain will work is that there will be two spillways cut into the upper rim of the central basin, which will allow the circulating water an avenue of escape. To accomplish this, we can use the Boolean functions in LightWave. Go to the next empty layer, which should be layer 5. Click the bottom part of the layer 3 button to put it into the background. Select the Box tool and open the Numeric panel. Enter the following values:

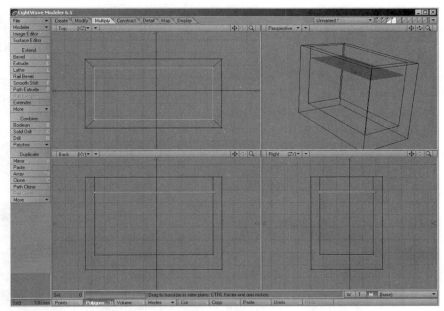

FIGURE 2-44 Water surface polygon shown with basin in background.

	Low	High	Segments
X	−750 mm	750 mm	1
Y	800 mm	1 m	1
Z	−22.07 m	−21.92 m	1

Deselect the Box tool. Press the apostrophe (') key to swap layers. Your upper fountain basin should be in the foreground layer, and the box we just created (to be used as a cutting tool) should be in the background layer. Click the multiply tab, click the Boolean button, choose Subtract in the Boolean CSG panel, and click OK. The Boolean Subtract command removes the volume of the background object from the volume of the foreground object. In this case, the box we made as a cutting tool cuts nice little grooves in our fountain basin object.

STEP 8: The problem with Boolean commands like this is that they tend to leave hidden, unnecessary geometry. The Boolean Subtract command always leaves duplicates of the points created in the process of the cutting operation. In order to get rid of these unwanted extras, you should get into the habit of performing a

Points Merge after any similar Boolean operation. To do this, simply click the Construct tab. Choose Reduce > Merge Points to open the Merge Points panel. Since the points we need to get rid of are already occupying the same space as their duplicates, we can leave the Type set to Automatic. Click OK. You should get a message telling you that 16 points were removed. Click OK to close the panel. Your screen should resemble Figure 2-45.

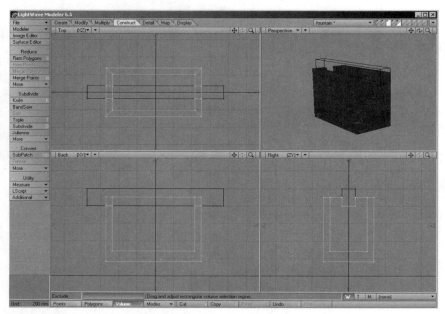

FIGURE 2-45 Boolean subtracted spillways in fountain basin.

STEP 9: Now we need to create some water to come pouring out of our grooves. Go back to layer 5 and press Delete to delete the box we just used as a cutting tool. Select the Box tool and open the Numeric panel. Enter the following values:

	Low	High	Segments
X	450 mm	1.35 m	20
Y	800 mm	850 mm	4
Z	−22.075 m	−21.92 m	5

Click the Box tool again to deselect it. Press Shift+A to fill the views with the subdivided box. This is going to make up our stream of water, so we are going to deform it quite a bit. That's why we needed the subdivisions. To make sure we don't end up with any nonplanar polygons, click the Construct button and click the Triple button (or press Shift+T) to convert all of the polygons to triangles. This way we know they are going to be planar. By definition, any three noncollinear points define a plane.

STEP 10: Now we need to bend the water down so that it looks like it is pouring out of the box. Switch to Polygons selection mode and lasso all the polygons except the first two rows on the left. Your selection should look like Figure 2-46. Click the Modify tab and select the Bend tool. In the Right view window, click at the end of the box and drag it down until the Bend Angle is 90 degrees in the information box at the bottom left of the screen. Hold down the Ctrl key to constrain your movement along the Y axis and keep the bend straight. When you have a 90-degree bend, change to the Stretch tool, in the Top view, place your pointer over that second polygon just coming out of your fountain box, and stretch the box in toward the fountain box or to the left until you get something that looks like Figure 2-47. The information box should show a Stretch value of about 40%. Now that you have a reasonable stream of water, with the same polygons selected, click the Modify tab. Select the Jitter tool, and enter the following values in the Jitter panel:

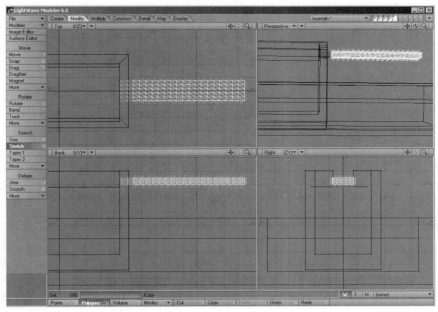

FIGURE 2-46 Subdivided and tripled box with selected polygons ready for bending.

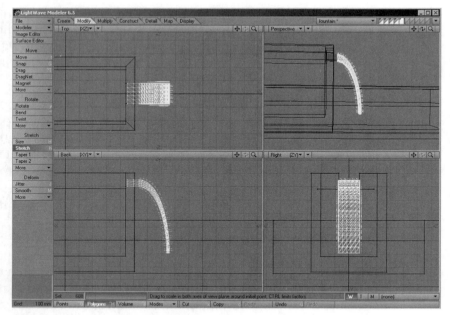

FIGURE 2-47 Resulting shape after bending and stretching water object.

Type	Gaussian
X	15 mm
Y	15 mm
Z	15 mm

Click OK. The surface is probably a little too jagged for water, so select the Smooth tool. Set the Strength at 3 and the Iterations at 1 and click OK to smooth it out a bit. This will give a nice undulating surface to our stream of water (Figure 2-48).

STEP 11: Now we have one stream of water coming out of our fountain, but we need another one for the other side. Click the Multiply tab, select the Mirror tool, place your pointer right on the Y axis in the Back view window, and drag the axis of mirroring down along the axis. This should place an identical copy of your stream of water pouring out the other side of your box. Select all five occupied layers; your screen should look like Figure 2-49. Select layer 4 and put layer 5 in the background, so that your streams are now in the background and you're looking at the

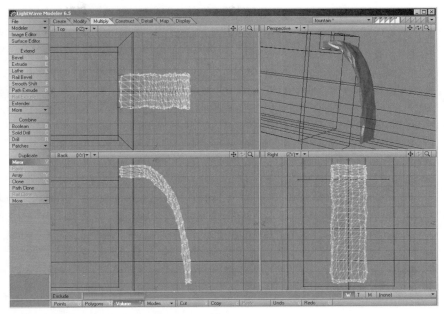

FIGURE 2-48 Water object after Smoothing.

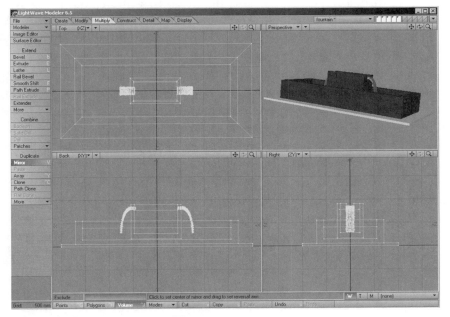

FIGURE 2-49 Composite water fountain.

small rectangular polygon that makes up the inside of your fountain box water. Move that water level straight up using the Move tool, until it is roughly flush with the tops of your two streams.

STEP 12: You should have the fountain basin in layer 1, the water from the basin in layer 2, the inner box in layer 3, the water for the inner box in layer 4, and your two streams in layer 5. Save this object as **Fountain.lwo.**

Parking Lot and Sidewalk

We've created some cool detail to dress up our building model. But the building is not the whole story in terms of visualizing a working space. To give the viewer a realistic sense of the whole building project, we must also address certain other practical issues, such as the parking area and access to it from the building's entrances. Since the parking area can often require as much space as, if not more space than, the building itself, it is an integral part of the planning process and a necessary part of any architectural model created for evaluation or design purposes. Though it may seem dull, unglamorous, and uninteresting in terms of 3D work, it is relatively painless to create and adds credibility to the scene. So, that being said, launch Modeler and begin a new object to build a parking lot for our building.

STEP 1: Select the Box tool. We'll create this lot to have basically the same footprint as the building itself. Open the Numeric panel and enter the following values:

	Low	High	Segments
X	−20 m	20 m	1
Y	0	50 mm	1
Z	26 m	66 m	1

Click the Box tool to deselect it. Open the Change Surface panel and type the surface name *parking_lot_pavement.* Set all three RGB values to 85. Click OK to apply the surface. That will be our base pavement.

STEP 2: Now we need to create some of those concrete barrier blocks that are so common in parking lots. Select the next empty layer. Once again, we begin with the Box tool. Select it and enter the following values in the Numeric panel:

	Low	*High*	*Segments*
X	−16.75 m	−15.25 m	1
Y	0	100 mm	1
Z	27.1 m	27.25 m	1

Click the Box tool again to deselect it. Now we need to fix the top of the parking block. Select the top polygon of the box. Now select the Bevel tool and open the Numeric panel. Enter an Inset value of 35 mm and a Shift value of 35 mm. Leave the other values at the default.

Deselect the Bevel tool and the selected poly and open the Change Surface panel. Type the surface name *parking_block.* Enter the following color values:

Red   200

Green   175

Blue   000

Click OK to apply the surface. Put the layer with the pavement box in the background so you can see the relationship between the block and the pavement.

STEP 3: We now need to distribute the blocks around the lot, placing one block at the center of each parking space. Let's see, cars are about 2 m across, and we need to leave about a meter on either side for door opening space. So our blocks should be spaced about 4 meters apart on center. Select the Array tool, open the Numeric panel, and set the following values:

Type   Rectangular

X Count   9

Y Count   1

Z Count   1

Jitter X   0 m

      Y   0 m

      Z   0 m

Offset Type   Manual

Offset X	4 m
Y	1 m
Z	1 m

Click OK to perform the array. Your screen should look like Figure 2-50. That gives us a nice even spacing across the lot.

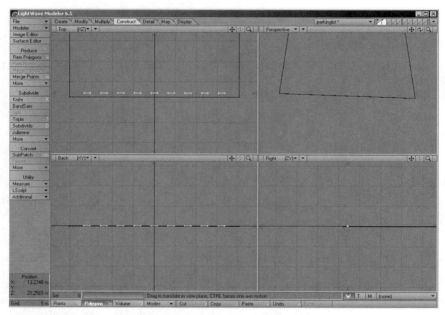

FIGURE 2-50 Concrete barrier block arrayed for parking lot.

STEP 4: Now we need to duplicate this row on the north edge of the lot. Copy the row of blocks we just made to the clipboard. Select the Move tool. Hold down the Ctrl key to constrain your movement to the Z axis and click and drag to move the row of blocks across the lot, keeping your eye on the Info box at the lower left of the Modeler window. Drag until the information box indicates a move on the Z axis of about 38 m. You may not be able to stop at exactly 18.5 by dragging, but in this case, you can afford to be a little off. Press V to paste back in the copy of the row of blocks we made before the Move operation.

STEP 5: Now there are blocks at either edge of the lot, but we still need some in the middle to add more rows of spaces to the parking area. Lasso the row of blocks we just pasted back into the layer.

Now, lasso the block at the left end of the row to deselect that block, leaving the selection of the eight remaining blocks in that row. Your selection should look like Figure 2-51. Press C to copy the selected blocks. Select the Move tool. Drag these blocks toward the positive Z direction about 18.5 m, using the Ctrl key to constrain the movement as we did before. Press V to replace the blocks we just moved. Easy, huh? Now select the row of blocks we just moved toward the center of the lot, copy them, and move them further in the positive Z direction about 1.8 m. Then paste again to replace the ones we moved. Now we have a parking lot consisting of four rows of parking spaces, with an open area on the left side where the cars might have room to travel from one lane to another. Since the blocks won't be moving (unless some careless driver runs into them), we can add them to the same layer as the pavement object, just so we won't have to worry about keeping them together later in Layout. Press X to cut the blocks out of the current layer and change to the layer where we left the pavement object. Paste the blocks into this layer. Your object should now resemble Figure 2-52. Save the object as **parkinglot.lwo.**

The Sidewalk

The final model we are going to make will be the sidewalk to go around the building and lead to the parking areas and the street. Like the parking lot we just created, the inclusion of the sidewalk might seem unimportant, but it is useful in planning pedestrian traffic handling for the building and adds a little touch of familiar reality that will make our building seem complete. Begin a new object in Modeler.

STEP 1. We will begin by creating a pad upon which we can place our fountain model. We'll place it at the center of the building's front lawn just in front of the entrance. Select the Box tool. Open the Numeric panel and enter the following values:

	Low	High	Segments
X	−3 m	3 m	4
Y	0	100 mm	1
Z	−24 m	−20 m	3

You'll notice that we've subdivided our box on the X and Z axes. As before, these subdivisions give us geometry to use as a

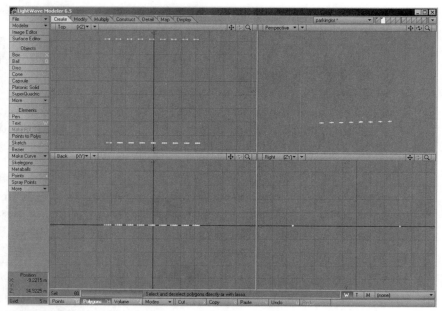

FIGURE 2-51 Selection of blocks.

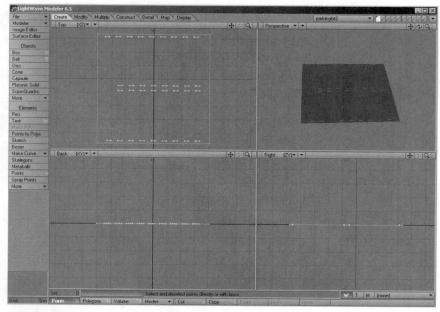

FIGURE 2-52 Final arrangement of blocks on parking lot.

starting point for extensions, which we will sweep out. Deselect the Box tool to exit the Numeric panel.

STEP 2. As shown in Figure 2-53, Select the two center polygons on the edge of the box facing the negative Z axis. Select the Smooth Shift tool and Reset and Activate the Numeric panel. Enter an Offset value of 20 m and leave the other values at the default. This will form our main front walk, going from the street to the front door. Deselect the Smooth Shift tool and click in the gray area on the left side of the Modeler window to deselect the selected polygons.

STEP 3. Now select the center polygon on both of the left and right edges of our box object (Figure 2-54). Select the Smooth Shift tool again and enter an Offset value of 17 m in the Numeric panel. This operation will move our sidewalk out to the left and right edges of the building perimeter.

STEP 4. Deselect and then reselect the Smooth Shift tool, then Reset and Activate the Numeric panel. This time enter an Offset value of 1.5 m. Once again we have created new polygons as a basis for another Smooth Shift operation. Deselect the tool and click in the gray area to deselect the selected polygons.

STEP 5. Now select the polygons on the positive Z edge of the extensions we just created (Figure 2-55). Do a Smooth Shift on these two polygons with an Offset value of 41.5 m to bring the sidewalks all the way back to the rear end of the building. Deselect the Smooth Shift tool to finish that operation and then reselect it to begin another one.

STEP 6. This time enter an Offset value of 1.5 m to create new geometry so that we add sidewalk along the X axis at the rear of the building. Drop the tool. Deselect the selected polygons.

STEP 7. Now select the inner polygons on the side edges of the square sections we just created (Figure 2-56). Select the Smooth Shift tool. Enter an Offset value of 20 m to bring the two edges together and finish the sidewalk. Deselect the tool and the selected polygons.

STEP 8. Open the Change Surface panel, enter a surface name of *sidewalk,* and set all three RGB values to 175. Click OK to apply the surface. Save the object as **sidewalk.lwo**

Now that we have our pieces and parts modeled, we can move right along to the really fun part. Now, we will venture into Layout, where we'll create our scene. We'll surface, light, and animate our way to a fabulous fly-through.

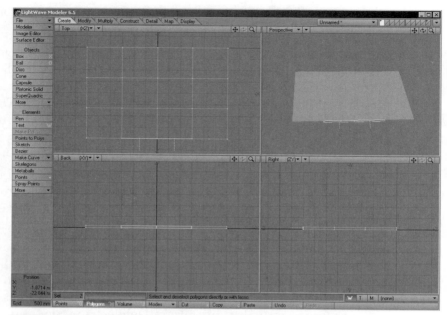

FIGURE 2-53 Selected sidewalk square polygons for Smooth Shifting.

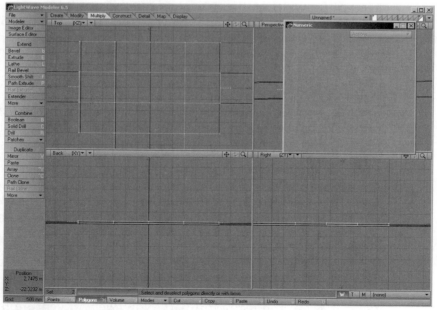

FIGURE 2-54 Selected center polygons on left and right edges.

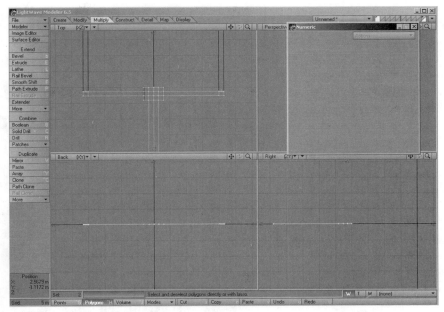

FIGURE 2-55 Selected polygons on the positive Z edge of sidewalk extensions.

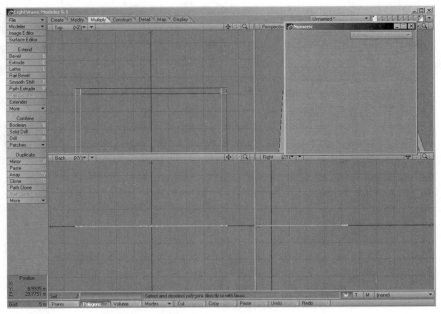

FIGURE 2-56 Sidewalk polygons selected for final Smooth Shift.

3

Fabulous Flights,
(LightWave 6.5 Layout)

Epic Software Group

OVERVIEW

In the previous tutorial, we focused mainly on the modeling aspects of our architectural fly-through. Through a series of tutorials, we learned about modeling a modern office building, along with step-by-step instructions on modeling a variety of architectural elements needed for the scene. We learned about creating scenery and produced several highly detailed but deceptively simple models that are easy to build and modify but still look good.

Now the real excitement begins. Put on your director's cap and get ready to explore the power of Layout—the LightWave environment where you light, texture, and animate your 3D world.

TUTORIAL OBJECTIVES

In Tutorial 3 we will cover three very important areas of creating an architectural fly-through: surfacing, lighting, and animation. Here is a preview of what you will learn in this tutorial:

Surfacing

- Texturing—You will learn how to use a paint/image manipulation package to create Texture and Bump maps.

- Surfacing—You will follow an in-depth tutorial on the use of the new Surface Editor in Layout to create realistic surfaces for buildings, grass, and pavement textures.

Lighting

- You will learn 3D lighting techniques, such as placement of lights, basic lighting theory, and light color.

Animation

- Camera—We will show you how the camera is used in the fly-through, with a discussion on meeting special client needs.

- Rendering—We will provide a step-by-step explanation of rendering settings.

Before we get into the details of the fly-through, we'll take a step back and once again try to get inside the head of the architect to better understand how we can represent the structures he or she envisions. Then we'll take a closer look at each of the technical elements that make a virtual fly-through come to life. It may be a good idea to review the Woodlands fly-through on the CD-ROM in the back of this book. It's in the Tutorial 3/Animations folder. Just double-click on the **waterway.mpg** file.

FROM THE ARCHITECT'S POINT OF VIEW

> The physician can bury his mistakes, but the architect can only advise his client to plant vines—so they should go as far as possible from home to build their first buildings.
>
> —Frank Lloyd Wright, from
> *New York Times Magazine,* October 4, 1953

Architecture may also be thought of as the expression of society or culture in a spatial, experiential form. Architects use physical materials such as stone, metal, wood, and glass, as well as light, to order forms and elements in three-dimensional space to create meaning. If architecture is the marking of place, the expression of a society in physical form, how can its existence be justified in a society of simulations and virtual realities? The answer may be that virtual architecture uses the metaphor of physical architecture in order to represent electronic information. At some point in the future, the profession may split into two disciplines: physical architecture and virtual architecture.

For now, let's accept the fact that architecture is a concept or idea that has both physical and virtual expressions. And just like physical architecture, virtual architecture requires careful design. Unlike the physical form, virtual architecture expresses values in electronic form, with polygons, vectors, and texture maps. Lacking physicality, it does not exist on a geographic site as traditionally understood. Rather, it is accessible via computer and human-interface technology. Although computer-generated architecture lacks many of the constraints and conditions of the physical world, it has its own set of constraints and conditions. The virtual realm does not have gravity, climate, geographic limits, site boundaries, or property lines. Yet virtual architecture does have technical constraints and limitations that affect its design. To be viewed as realistic, virtual architecture must rely on natural laws and human factors such as cognition and perception.

SURFACING

The world around us is made of objects with surface characteristics that give us visual clues about their nature. The believability of a 3D scene depends heavily on both texture and surface characteristics. When you enter a physical space and look around, the visual clues from the textures of the objects communicate information in both subtle and direct ways. The terms *shiny, dull, rough,* and *smooth* define surface characteristics. Surfacing (sometimes called *shading*) is the process of assigning values and parameters to the surfaces of objects. The art of surfacing comes down to understanding how the range of surfacing parameters interact to create imaginative or realistic effects. These values generally control the manner in which the surface interacts with light in the scene to create the object's color, specularity (highlights), reflective qualities, transparency, and (if the surface is transparent) refraction.

Tip: Be a good observer. Learn to see. Your own vision is the most important and powerful tool at your disposal as a 3D artist (or any kind of artist, for that matter). As obvious as it seems, it bears saying. Learning to observe and understand your surroundings is critical to your ability to produce believable imagery. Notice the detail in everyday things. This is extremely important in terms of surface. Even the most rudimentary model can look amazingly detailed with careful and thoughtful surfacing. Take a walk around your neighborhood and just practice noticing the myriad of textures in the world around you. Take note of the characteristics of building materials, grass, and all the things that are common to any exterior scene.

Working with good source material is critical to the success of a 3D surfacing project. Watching a wireframe object change as just the right surface texture is applied is truly an inspiring moment. And like most things artistic, getting just the right surface comes down to paying attention to detail. For an architectural fly-through, it's critical that the surfaces of the 3D objects in your scene accurately reflect their real-world counterparts. Luckily, many of the surfaces we need are relatively easy to find, either by photographing real-world examples or by using the wealth of surface images to be found in print, on the Internet, or in commercial texture libraries. Those that we can't find, we can create with a combination of image manipulation tools and LightWave.

LightWave artists can control the diffuse color of a surface on a pixel-by-pixel basis either through texture mapping or by assigning an overall color value. Texture mapping is done by applying a color bitmap image to the surface of a 3D model. A second way to apply color patterns to a 3D object is by generating *procedural tex-*

tures, which are created mathematically by LightWave when the user enters values that change a variety of characteristics such as color, turbulence, frequency, and contrast.

Procedural shaders have certain advantages over simple texture maps. A 3D artist can use a procedural shader to create both random patterns (the grain structure of a piece of granite) or regular patterns (a wallpaper pattern). With procedural shaders you can create a very believable surface on a 3D object because the pattern follows the shape of the object it is applied to. Bitmapped textures, on the other hand, are difficult to map around the surface of an irregular object. As usual, the best way to learn the advantages and disadvantages of each is by experimenting. In addition to learning by following tutorials such as this, you are encouraged to experiment with texture and the way it affects the form and reflective and transmissive properties of different surfaces.

If we were not constrained by such factors as processor speed, video resolution, data transfer rates, and time, we could make the objects in our scene look incredibly lifelike. Unfortunately, the trade-off for detail is speed. The more detail in your textures and surfaces, the longer it takes to render the needed frames, and the more horsepower it takes in terms of playback. Like most things in life, you have to give a little to get a little. For our fly-through, we'll use simple texture maps and procedurals to provide surface detail.

STEP 1: We'll begin this set of tutorials by bringing our newly created objects into Layout and surfacing them. Load Layout and it's time to begin the fun. Let's start by loading the building object into Layout. Choose File > Load > Load Object. Select the **building.lwo** file and click Open.

By default, Layout begins by displaying the scene in Perspective view. Eventually, we will end up using most of the different camera views in the process of building our scene, but for now, we will be mostly interested in surfacing our objects. Camera View is the one that will actually render our images, and since we will need to use the renders in the surfacing process, let's switch to Camera View now. On the View menu at the top left of the Perspective view window, choose Camera View. Your screen should look like Figure 3-1.

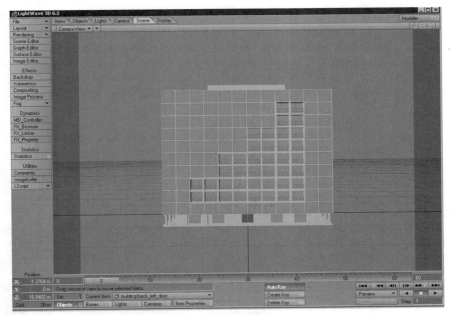

FIGURE 3-1 Camera view of loaded object **building.lwo.**

STEP 2: We are going to work with the building's outer masonry first, so let's move the camera up close and personal to the building so we can get a good view of what is going on. Select the camera as the Current Item by clicking the Cameras button on the bottom menu (or by pressing Shift+C). Make sure the Items tab is selected. Select the Move tool (if it is not already selected). Now we are going to use the numeric entry feature in Layout. Unlike Modeler, there is no Numeric panel that opens when you press N in Layout. Instead, in Layout the numeric entry fields double as the information display that reports data on whichever tool is currently selected. At the bottom left corner of the Layout window you will find the numeric entry fields. With the Move tool selected, the Position box is active, with buttons marked X, Y, and Z and a data entry field next to each one. (Notice that if you select the Rotate tool, the box is labeled Rotation and the buttons switch to

H, P, and B.) When you press N or click the Numeric button on the main toolbar, the top field is activated and highlighted and ready for entry of the appropriate value. Enter the following values:

X   0 m

Y   4 m

Z   −21 m

Hit the [key 3 times to reduce the Grid Square size to eliminate clipping the front polygons in the view.

Your view should now look like Figure 3-2. This gives us a good sample of each of the three textures we will use for our exterior surfaces.

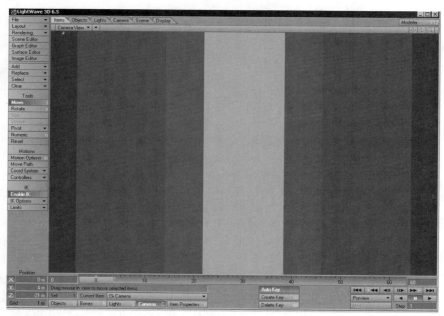

FIGURE 3-2 Repositioned camera view for close-up of exterior surfaces.

STEP 3: Even though the Surface Editor is now available to us in Modeler, I still prefer to surface in Layout, where we can use one of LightWave's most exciting new features. I am referring, of course, to VIPER. VIPER stands for Versatile Interactive Preview Render. I love to use VIPER because it has virtually flattened the learning curve on mastering surfacing in LightWave. Let's check it out.

On the main toolbar, choose Rendering > Enable VIPER On\Off to toggle the VIPER preview on. Now choose Rendering > Ray Trace Shadows to toggle that function on. We could enable Ray Trace Reflection here as well, but we don't have anything else in our scene to reflect yet, so, in the interest of speedier render times, we can leave it off for now. Now open the Surface Editor by clicking the Surface Editor button on the main toolbar. Click the VIPER button to open the VIPER: Surfaces panel. Now press F9 to quickly do a test render so that VIPER will have some data to work with. When the render is finished, close the render window, and click the Render button in the VIPER: Surfaces panel to get a preview. You will notice that although the shadows are calculated and rendered in the actual render, they are not visible in the VIPER preview. While VIPER uses the data from the render engine to calculate its previews, it does not do a complete scene evaluation, so effects that depend on raytracing are not visible in the VIPER preview. It does, however, do a wonderful job of showing changes in textures as you make them, eliminating the need to constantly do full test renders each time you make a change.

STEP 4: Our building is going to be constructed mostly of steel and glass, with a colored concrete and aggregate mixture intended to give it a more earthy, natural, and warm effect. Let's concentrate on the concrete surface first. What we're going for is the sort of tan concrete with gravel added for texture and strength. You can see examples of this material in just about any urban area, as it has been a very popular construction material for a number of years. While it shouldn't be too difficult to find a bitmap image of this kind of texture from the Internet or a texture library, this is a great opportunity to create our own surface using the powerful procedural textures available to us in LightWave.

First we will address the color aspect of our texture. When we were modeling the building we assigned our base color to the surfaces of the model. Now we can give it a texture to simulate the inclusion of darker gravel aggregate within the concrete. Select the building_outer surface from the list. Click the T (Texture) button next to the Color field in the Surface Editor to open the Color Texture Editor. Set the Layer Type to Procedural Texture. We want to achieve the look of gravel suspended in the concrete, more or less evenly distributed. The Veins texture is ideal for this kind of look.

It simulates the appearance of randomly shaped and more or less evenly distributed areas of color (our gravel) separated by a weblike network of veins (the concrete). It is commonly used for textures such as cobblestones, leaf veins, and stonework. Leave the Blending Mode and the Layer Opacity as is. Click the Procedural Type menu and select Veins. Set the following Texture Color values:

Red	185
Green	165
Blue	125

You may notice that the color we just set is approximately 20% darker than the base color of our building_outer texture. By default, this color will be applied to the veins, making them somewhat darker than the patches they separate. We want the opposite effect, with lighter veins of concrete separating darker stones. Select the Invert Layer check box to reverse the effect. Set the Coverage value to 0.0 so that the vein color will be applied only to the veins themselves. A higher Coverage value (0.5 and up) would allow the vein color to infiltrate the spaces and overtake the stone color. Similarly, we want the Ledge Level to have a sharp termination, so set the Ledge Level to 0.0 also. The Ledge Width changes the apparent depth of the raised areas, with useful values mostly falling between 0.2 and 1. Set the Ledge Width to about 0.7 to give our stones a nice protrusion.

We want our stones to resemble gravel rather than flagstones, so we need to scale this texture down a bit. Set the Scale to about 20 mm in all three dimensions.

That takes care of the color part of the surface, so now we'll move on to the Bump aspect of the texture in order to have the pebbles actually appear to protrude. We will need to use many of the same settings for this aspect as we did for the color, so let's save ourselves some typing by using the Copy feature of the Texture Editor. Click the Copy menu above the Layer Name list and select Current Layer to copy these settings to the clipboard. Now click the Use Texture button to close the Color Texture Editor. After the VIPER screen has updated itself, your screen should resemble Figure 3-3.

STEP 5: Now click the T button next to the Bump field in the Surface Editor to open the Bump Texture Editor. Click the Paste menu

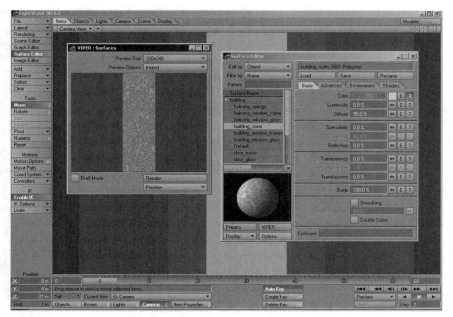

FIGURE 3-3 Gravel texture applied and shown in VIPER window.

and select Replace Current Layer to paste in the Color settings we copied. This puts in the values for the similar settings between the two textures, but a couple of settings are different from those in the Color texture. The Bump texture has no color settings, as such, because the bumps are generated according to changes in value rather than color. So the darker areas of the procedural pattern will appear to recede while the lighter ones will appear to protrude.

As you may remember, we inverted the Color texture so that the color would be applied to the spaces rather than the veins. So we need to do the same thing here so that the bump will be applied to the stones. Select the Invert Layer check box. Now set the Texture Value to 100% to give us nice clearly delineated separation between the stones and the mortar. Click the Use Texture button to close the Bump Texture Editor and return to the Surface Editor. The VIPER: Surfaces panel will update to display the surface now sporting a new 3D look (Figure 3-4). The texture is a bit harsh-looking though, so set the Bump value down to 25% or so to tone it down somewhat (Figure 3-5).

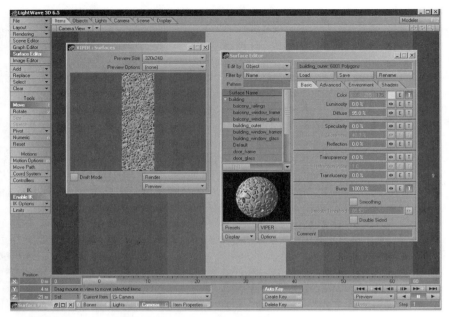

FIGURE 3-4 Bump texture added to **building_outer** surface.

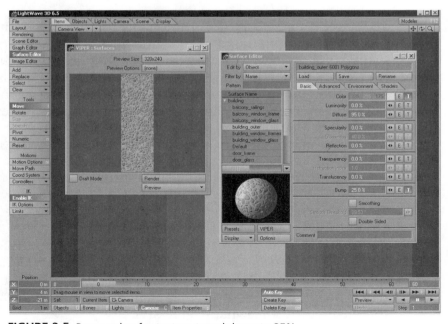

FIGURE 3-5 Bump value for texture toned down to 25%.

STEP 6: Before we go on to the next surface, let's use another one of LightWave's new features to make our life a bit easier in the future. Our building's exterior will consist of only three different surfaces, but the settings for each will be applied to two or more surface names. We could save the settings by using the Save Surface feature, but then we would have to load the surface each time we needed it. Instead, we can make a custom preset "shelf" and copy our surfaces into it for easy access when they are needed. Click the Presets button next to the VIPER button in the Surface Editor. Position your pointer in the Surface Preset window, and right-click, and choose Library > Create Library. In the Create Library panel, enter a name for the preset group. Use something descriptive, as usual, so that you'll know what it is if you come back to it later (Figure 3-6). Select the new library from the pull-down list at the top of the window. Now, double-click the surface sample preview window in the Surface Editor. This will put a copy of the building_outer surface settings into the shelf, along with a thumbnail of the sample sphere (Figure 3-7).

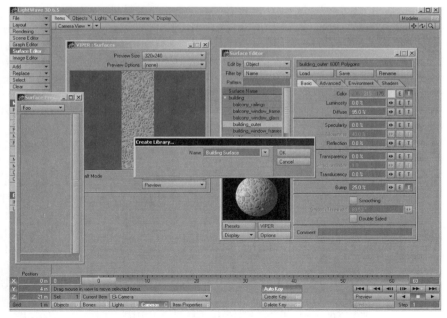

FIGURE 3-6 Enter name for preset group in the Create Library panel.

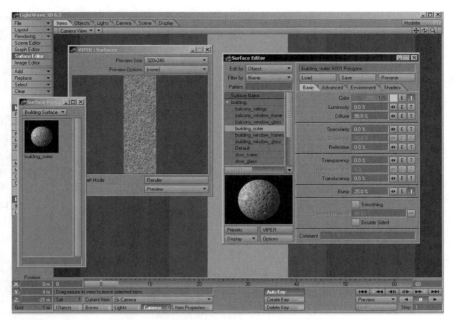

FIGURE 3-7 **Building_outer** surface added to **Building Surface** preset shelf.

STEP 7: Now let's move on to the next surface for our building model. In the VIPER: Surfaces panel, click in one of the gray areas to either side of the masonry we just created. Notice that the selected surface changes to the building_window_frames surface. This is a great feature of the VIPER preview that allows you to select the surface you want to work on quickly and visually, rather than guessing at which name you applied to what when you have a complex object. Although our object is not that complex, it's still a pretty neat feature, don't you think?

We want our window frame surface to have a shiny, brushed-metal appearance. The important thing to remember about shiny surfaces is that they tend to be somewhat reflective; therefore, they tend to pick up more of the colors of their surroundings and that is what we see when the light is returned to our eyes. So most reflective items need to have a lower diffuse value and a higher degree of reflectivity. As a general rule of thumb, the sum of the Reflection value and the Diffuse value should be roughly equal to or less than 100%. Set the Diffuse value for the window frames to about 50%. For the sake of simplicity, set the Specularity, Glossiness, and Reflection values to about 50% also. These settings will work fine, but remember to feel free to experiment with these numbers and notice how each change affects the appearance of the material.

Although we have set a Reflection value for the surface, it doesn't appear to be reflecting anything yet, partially because there is nothing else in the scene to reflect and because we haven't told Layout to trace the reflections. Even if we turn on Ray Trace Reflections, the VIPER preview won't display reflections because it doesn't use the raytracing engine to produce its previews. We can get more of a reflective feel to our surface by adding an environmental reflection map. I like to do this even when there are objects to be reflected, simply because it tends to liven up the surface somewhat and make it seem all the more shiny. Click the Environment tab in the Surface Editor. Set the Reflection Options to Ray Tracing + Spherical Map. This option maps a bitmap image onto a virtual sphere that completely encircles the object being surfaced, giving that reflective surface something to reflect. On the Reflection Map menu, choose (load image). Navigate to your LightWave Content directory and load **Reflections/Tinfoil.tga.** Click the Basic tab again. Now our window frames are starting to look like shiny metal (Figure 3-8). Double-click the surface sample sphere to add our surface to the preset shelf.

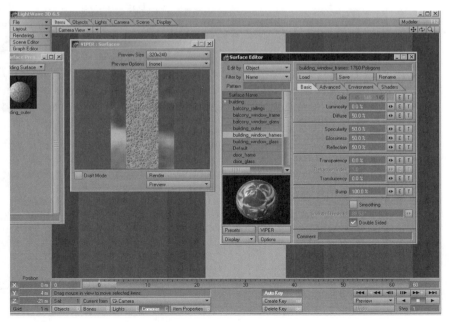

FIGURE 3-8 Reflection image map added to window frame surface.

STEP 8: Next we will create a mirrored glass surface for our building's windows. Just like the metal surface we just created, this will be a highly reflective surface that takes most of its appearance from the world around it. Click the green area next to the window frames in the VIPER: window to select the building_window_glass surface. As we did for the metal, set the Diffuse and Reflection values to about 50% each. Because glass is about as smooth and highly polished as a surface can get, it will require maximum Specularity and Glossiness values, so set them both to 100%. Normally we would give a glass surface a fairly high degree of transparency. Since this glass is fairly reflective, and because we want to mask the fact that our building is pretty much empty, we can leave the Transparency set at 0%.

If you go downtown in a large city and look at one of those steel-and-glass skyscrapers, one thing you might notice is that although the surface is flat and highly reflective, there is a good deal of variation in the reflections. Due to small variations in the placement of the glass from one pane to another, there are tiny changes in the angle of the sheets, which cause the reflections to shift and warp. We can simulate this effect by using a Bump texture to vary the angle of the reflections the raytracer produces slightly. Click the T button next to the Bump field to open the Bump Texture Editor. Set the Layer Type to Procedural Texture. Set the Procedural Type to Fractal Noise. Now set the Contrast to 0.5 so that we get a medium level of variation from dark to light. We don't need a lot of tiny detail, so set the Small Power to 0.0. We want the variation to appear to occur from pane to pane of our window glass, so set the Scale to about 3 m on each axis to avoid ending up with glass that looks too warped. Click the Use Texture button to return to the Surface Editor. Again, we don't want to warp our glass excessively, so set the Bump value to about 5%. Double-click the sample to copy the texture to the preset shelf, and we are done with the glass texture.

STEP 9: Now that we have established our three building materials, we can use the preset shelf to copy these surfaces to all of our building's surface names. In the Surface Name list, select the balcony_railings surface. Now hold down the Ctrl key, go down the list, and add balcony_window_frame, door_handle, and door_frame, and all of the similar surfaces to the selection. This is another great new feature in LightWave. Now you can make global changes to any number of surfaces at once. With all of the metallic surfaces selected, double-click the metallic sample image in the preset shelf to open the Load Confirmation panel (Figure 3-9). Click OK to apply the metallic surface to each of the selected names.

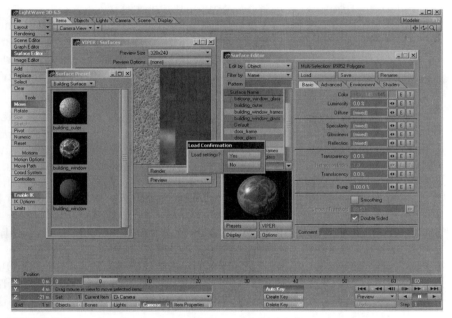

FIGURE 3-9 Load Confirmation panel for applying metallic surface.

STEP 10: Now repeat this process by selecting all the glass surfaces and applying the glass preset we made to them.

STEP 11: The only surface we haven't done anything with yet is the roofing material. Since this surface is located where the camera is unlikely to show any great detail for our fly-through, we won't spend too much effort on it. However, if you want to give it some kind of surface, just in case you decide to take the camera over it at some point in your fly-through, we can give it the same Bump texture we used on the walls of the building's exterior. Select the building_outer surface from the list. Open the Bump

Texture Editor. Copy the texture layer to the clipboard as we did before. Now, close the Bump Texture Editor and select the roof surface. Click the T button next to the Bump field and paste the Bump texture from the clipboard into the layer list. Click the Use Texture button to close the panel and that's it.

Now let's save our building object to save the textures to the object file. Press Tab to hide the Surface Editor. On the main toolbar, choose File > Save > Save All Objects.

Cool, huh? Now we have a great-looking building as the basis for our fly-through scene. But the work isn't over yet. In fact, we've only just begun to scratch the surface of creating a realistic architectural scene. Now we need to populate the scene with all that great detail that will really show off our building.

STEP 12: Now it's time to give our scene a setting. On the main toolbar, choose Add > Objects > Load Object. Open the **Skydome.lwo** object we created in the previous tutorial. We'll need to make a couple of adjustments to this object at this point. First we need to turn off shadows for this object. It wouldn't do to have shadows being cast on our sky! The skydome object consists of two layers. The first layer is the ground plane and the second layer is the actual skydome. Make certain that the layer containing the skydome is selected as the Current Item on the bottom menu. Click the Item Properties button to open the Properties panel. Click the Rendering tab to access the rendering properties. Clear the Self Shadow, Cast Shadow, and Receive Shadow check boxes to disable shadows for this object.

STEP 13: Now we need to put our camera in a position where we can better tell what's going on in our scene. Press shift + C to make the camera the Current Item. Select the Move tool if it isn't already selected and enter the following values in the numeric entry fields:

X   0

Y   15 m

Z   −100 m

Your screen should now resemble Figure 3-10.

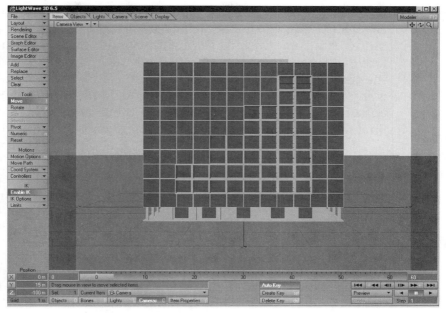

FIGURE 3-10 Repositioned camera view.

STEP 14: We'll continue by creating a grassy surface for our ground plane. In order to keep our memory and processor resources as free as possible, we'll use an image file to create a grass surface that will look pretty good while not overtaxing our system. This is one of those compromises that occurs all too often in the world of 3D graphics. Often we must consider the relative importance of detail that we include in our scenes and cut corners in order to save resources for something more important. If we tried to use actual geometry to model blades of grass, we'd soon have an unmanageable number of polygons in our scene. Besides, this is an architectural fly-through we're creating, and the building takes precedence. Click the Image Editor button to open the Image Editor panel. Click the Load button and load the **grass.iff** file from the CD-ROM that accompanies this book.

STEP 15: Open the Surface Editor. Click the white triangle next to the skydome object name to expand the surface list for the skydome object. Select the ground surface. Open the Color Texture

Editor. Leave the Layer Type set to Image Map. Set the Layer Opacity to 50%. This will apply the image to the surface, allowing some of the base color to show through to soften the effect somewhat. Leave the projection set to Planar. Click the Image menu and select the **grass.iff** image. Clear the Texture Antialiasing check box. We are going to use antialiasing to render our animation later; if we antialias the image here, it will soften the image too much in the final render. We want to project the image onto our ground plane, so set the Texture Axis to Y. Leave the Scale set to the default values. We can use these same settings for the Bump texture for our ground surface, so click the Copy menu and choose Current Surface. Now, click the Use Texture button to close the panel and return to the Surface Editor. Open the Bump Texture Editor and paste the information from the clipboard into the Current Layer. Click Use Texture.

STEP 16: Let's do a test render to see what we've got so far. Press Tab to hide the Surface Editor. On the Rendering menu, choose both Ray Trace Shadows and Ray Trace Reflections. Now select the Camera as the Current Item and open the Camera Properties panel. Set the Resolution to VGA (640 × 480). Leave the other settings at their default values. On the Antialiasing menu, choose Low. Close the Camera Properties panel. On the main toolbar, choose Rendering > Render Options. In the Render Options panel, choose Render Display > Image Viewer FP so that we have something to look at. Press F9 to perform a test render of the scene. After a few minutes of rendering time (depending on the speed of your system), your screen should look like Figure 3-11.

STEP 17: Now we should make a surface for our skydome itself. All we need here is some nice wispy clouds to give an indication of a sky and add some interest to the reflections in our mirrored windows. Press Tab to reopen the Surface Editor. Click in the sky area in the VIPER: Surfaces panel to select the skydome surface. Open the Color Texture Editor. Set the Layer Type to Procedural Texture and the Procedural Type to the ever-popular Fractal Noise.

Set the Texture Color to 255 for all three colors. Enter a Frequency value of 4. This will increase the variation in our cloud pattern. Enter a Contrast value of 2 to make the clouds really stand out from the blue of the sky color. Enter a Small Power value

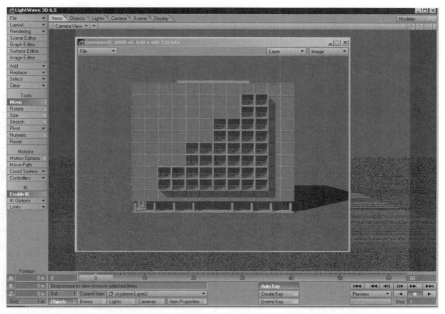

FIGURE 3-11 Test render with Ray Trace Shadows and Reflections enabled.

of 0.4 to create a smooth blend between the large and small features of our clouds. Finally, set the following Scale values:

X   350 m

Y   75 m

Z   350 m

Click the Use Texture button to accept these settings and close the Color Texture Editor.

STEP 18: Because the light from our Distant Light is directional, it tends to make the part of our skydome that is in front of the light look brighter than the back. In order to have a more realistic appearance to our sky, we need to remove the influence of the light source from the object so that it won't be shaded like our other 3D objects. Press Tab to hide the Surface Editor. Select skydome:Layer 2 as the Current Item and open the Object Properties panel. In the list at the bottom of the panel, click in the Exclude column next to the Light entry to exclude the light's influence on this object

(Figure 3-12). Now return to the Surface Editor and set a Luminosity value of about 45% for the skydome surface so that the surface will self-illuminate. Choose File > Save > Save All Objects to protect your surfacing work.

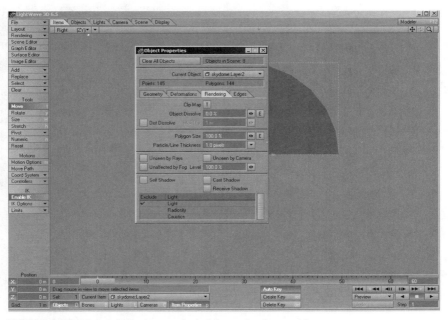

FIGURE 3-12 Light's influence excluded from sky dome object.

STEP 19: In order to protect all of the changes we have made, it's time to save our scene file as well, since the light exclusion we made in Step 18 wasn't saved in the object file. Choose File > Save > Save Scene As. Give the scene file the name **fly-through.lws**.

STEP 20: Load the **sidewalk.lwo** file we made in the last tutorial into the scene. All we need to do to this surface is add a bit of a Fractal Noise pattern to the Bump texture for this object. Leave all the settings at the default values and give it a Scale of 10 mm on all three dimensions.

STEP 21: Now load the **parkinglot.lwo** object we made in the previous tutorial into our scene. Because we modeled this item in its position relative to the building object, it will load behind the building. We'll need to change our view of the scene in order to work with this item. Hide the Texture Editor, switch from the Camera view that we've been using to the Top (XZ) view, and center your view over the **parkinglot.lwo** object. Zoom in or out until your view looks like the one in Figure 3-13.

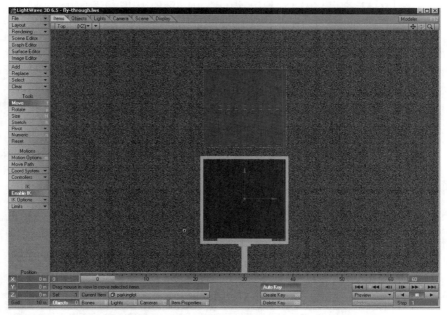

FIGURE 3-13 Top view of scene with **parkinglot.lwo** object added.

STEP 22: Open the Image Editor. Click the Load button and open the lot_stripes.iff image on the CD-ROM that came with this book. Close the Image Editor and press Tab to reopen the Surface Editor. Locate the parkinglot object in the surface list and expand the list of surfaces for that object by clicking on the white triangle next to the object name. Select the parking_lot_pavement surface. Open the Color Texture Editor. By default, the Layer Type should be set to Image Map and the Projection should be Planar. On the Image menu, select **lot_stripes.iff.** Set the Texture Axis to Y and click the Automatic Sizing button to fit the image to the object. Close the Color Texture Editor and return to the Surface Editor.

We can get even more good use out of our pebble bump texture for this surface. Select the roof texture, make a copy of the Bump texture from it, and paste it into the Bump texture for the parking_lot_pavement surface, as we did before. We can tone it down a bit, though, since most paved surfaces are rolled out fairly flat. Set the Bump value to about 20% for this surface. Click the Use Texture button and we're done with the parking lot surfacing.

STEP 23: Our parking area can accommodate only about 34 vehicles as it is, but this is actually only half of the space planned for the parking area. We can easily double the parking area by making a Clone of the object and placing it to the right side of the building, similar to the drawing supplied to us by the client. Let's do that now. Select **parkinglot.lwo** as the Current Item if it's not already selected. Choose Add > Clone Current Item. When the panel opens, leave the Number Of Clones value set to 1 and click OK. Select parkinglot (2) as the Current Item. Click the Rotate tool (or press Y, as in Modeler) and enter an H value of 90 degrees. Now the parking lot is facing forward, but it's on the wrong side of the building. Select the Move tool and enter an X value of −92 m. Choose File > Save > Save All Objects now to protect your surfacing work. Now would also be a good time to save the scene file. If you want to, press F9 to do a test render and check out what you have so far. Your results should resemble Figure 3-14.

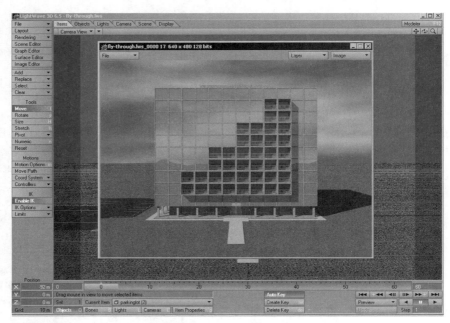

FIGURE 3-14 Test render of building with additional parking lot.

STEP 24: Now we can bring in our fountain and complete the surfaces for it. Load the **fountain.lwo** object into the scene. At this distance it's a tad tiny to work with, though, in terms of texturing. We can use one of LightWave's new features to get closer without having to relocate the camera. We can add another camera! Choose Add > Add Camera. Enter a name for the new camera in the Camera Name panel. I called mine *cu* for "close up." The new camera comes into the scene at the origin (0, 0, 0), which is inside our model. Make sure that cu is the Current Item. Select the Move tool and enter the following values:

X   0

Y   1.5 m

Z   −25 m

In the Camera View, from the cu camera, your view should look like Figure 3-15.

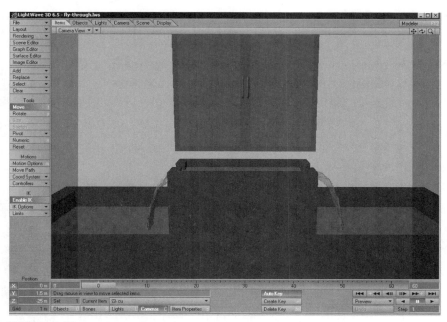

FIGURE 3-15 View from the cu camera centered on the fountain.

STEP 25: Our fountain object has three surfaces to work with: fountain_water, foundation, and fount_basin. Let's approach the water first. On the Surface Name list in the Surface Editor, click the white triangle next to the fountain object and select the fountain_water surface. Click the T button next to the Bump field. The Crumple procedural type is great for water surfaces, so set the Layer Type to Procedural Texture, set the Procedural Type to Crumple, and enter a Texture value of 35%. Enter a Frequencies value of 4, set the Small Power to 0.75, and set Scale values of 400 mm for all three dimensions. Click the Use Texture button to close the Bump Texture Editor. These settings will rough up our water surface a bit with some small detail.

Since most of the color in our water will be from reflections from the surrounding environment, and since the water in most well-kept fountains is mostly transparent, let's turn the Diffuse down to about 35%. Set the Specularity, Glossiness, and Reflection to 75%. Note that the sum of the values for Reflection and Diffuse falls near 100%.

Click the Environment tab. Now set the Reflection Options to Ray Tracing + Backdrop. Then click the Basic tab again, set the Transparency to about 75% and the Refraction Index to 1.5, and there's our water surface. We could spend a lot of time making realistic ripples in the surface, splashes around the streams of water, and even animating the water itself, but water isn't the focus of the animation we're setting up. The building is. Once again, if you want to do something like that, you are heartily encouraged to do so. Experiment to your heart's content. But for our purposes, what we have already done will suffice.

STEP 26: Select the fount_basin surface in the Surface list. Since this is going to be black marble, turn the Diffuse down to 65%. We want the surface of the marble to be highly polished, so crank the Specularity up to 100%. Likewise, set the Glossiness to 75%. Click the T button next to the Color field. Set the Layer Type to Procedural Texture; leave the Blending Mode set to Additive. Set the Layer Opacity to about 15%, because we want really dark, subtle veining in this marble. Set the Procedural Type to Marble and set the Texture Color to 175 for all three colors. Set the Frequencies at 6, Turbulence at 1, Vein Spacing at 2, and Vein Sharpness at 2.1. To size the texture, set the following Scale values:

X   500 mm

Y   100 mm

Z   100 mm

Click the Use Texture button and that should give us a nice, shiny, subtle marble with the grain running from left to right. Press F9 to do a sample render and check out your good work.

For the foundation surface, we can use the same Bump Texture we applied to our sidewalk surface. Just copy and paste the Bump texture as we did before. Now that we have the basic surfaces for our foundation, we need to save the object so that these surfaces are locked in. Click the Use Texture button and close the Surface Editor. Choose File > Save > Save All Objects, and this will save our surfaces onto our objects. Choose File > Save > Save Scene to save the scene as well, to make sure that all our recent changes are protected.

We are at that point of the process where the creativity of imagination really starts to make the sometimes tedious, technical work of modeling pay off in a big way. We now shift our focus to creating an environment that will embrace our models and make them seem to belong there. One of the goals in creating architectural models of any kind, physical or virtual, is to portray the architectural design in place, to show off how well the form and function of the design work in terms of real space—without, of course, having the real thing to look at. In order to achieve that goal, you must somehow get viewers to forget, however briefly, that what they are seeing is simply a representation created for that purpose. One way to achieve this is by adding a level of realistic detail that makes the model seem less artificial and more familiar to the viewer, more like what a person expects to see in the real world. The main goal is still simply to illustrate the form of the design, but at the same time we must find a way to make the subject seem attractive and inviting.

Up until now I've pretty much directed you step by step through the process of creating our architectural scene. From here on out, the choices get a little more subjective and open to experimentation on your part, especially in terms of arranging the more decorative detail elements of the scene. We have already placed all the major parts of the project into the scene. Our building is in place, the parking areas are situated, we have added a sky and the ground, and we even have a lovely fountain to dress up the entrance. Our scene has all the major areas of focus included, but it still seems somewhat sparse.

Press C to highlight Cameras and then Select Camera from the Current Item list.

STEP 27: Let's add some detail now to dress up our scene and make our building seem a little less sterile. Load the **lightpole.lwo** object we created in Tutorial 2. When you load the object into Layout, it will be inside the building, so let's move it out so we can see it. Select the Move tool and enter a Z value of about −30 m to place it out in front of the building. We probably want to get it out of the middle of the sidewalk, so let's enter an X value of −3 m or so. We're going to need a whole bunch of these, spread throughout the scene. Choose Add > Clone Current Item. Enter a Number Of Clones value of 19. Of course, this will put all 20 of the light poles right on top of each other; so don't panic if you don't see the copies. Select the lightpole (2) object and change its X value to 3 m, to move it across the sidewalk from the first one. Beginning with lightpole (3), move all of the remaining clones to the parking lots, nine for each lot, arranging them however you like. Figure 3-16 shows a Top view wireframe illustrating a sample placement scheme that I used.

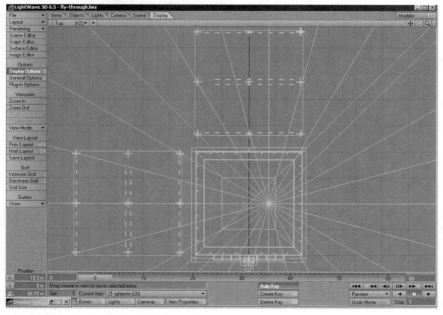

FIGURE 3-16 Top view of sample placement scheme of light poles in scene.

Tip: If you are moving objects around in Layout, and they are moving so little that it take dozens of mouse movements to get them where you want them, or if they jump out of sight as a result of a tiny nudge, you probably need to adjust the Grid Square Size. All mouse actions are scaled relative to this setting. You can change this setting at any time by pressing D to open the Display Settings panel and changing the value in the Grid Square Size field.

STEP 28: Let's move our main camera to a position where we can take in more of the action. Select the Camera as the Current Item, make sure the Move tool is selected, and set the following values:

X   −100 m

Y   5 m

Z   −140 m

Select the Rotate tool and set the following rotation values:

H   35.0

P   −3.0

B   0

Now press P to open the Camera Properties panel. Enter a Zoom Factor of 5.0. Your screen should now look like Figure 3-17. Save the scene.

STEP 29: We need some more nature in our scene to make it seem more . . . well, natural. We can use some existing objects to add detail without having to do more modeling. Our horizon is pretty flat, so let's grab an object from the content that comes with Light-Wave and adapt it to our needs here. Load the **MountainRange.lwo** object from the CD-ROM that came with this book. This object is also in the Landscape directory located in the content that came with LightWave. I have already applied our grass texture to the object from the CD-ROM, and scaled it to fit our scene.

One of the primary requirements I had to meet while creating the fly-through project that inspired this tutorial was to pay ample attention to the trees, which were a huge part of the appeal of the planned forested community that was to be the future home of the development project. Because of the sheer scope of the animation project (the fly-through encompassed a 1.25-mile trip through

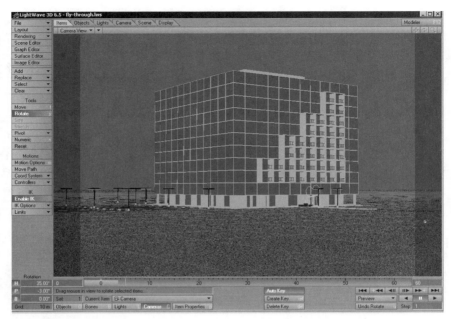

FIGURE 3-17 View from main camera repositioned to take in more action.

a heavily wooded business park), I was forced to use flat, single-polygon objects that got their shape from a photographic clip map. The downside of this was that if the camera wasn't perpendicular to the tree, it became instantly apparent that the object was two-dimensional. So then I had to use a third-party plug-in to keep the trees facing the camera at all times. Needless to say, with more than 1,000 trees in the scene, keeping all that working quickly became a logistical nightmare. Luckily the scene we are creating is much smaller, and because we are focusing on one building, and need only one small area populated, we can use real 3D trees with no plug-ins necessary.

STEP 30: Let's add some foliage to our scene. When creating outdoor scenes, I like to use a method that I learned from Dave Jerrard's excellent tree tutorial that was included in the bonus content of the CD-ROM that accompanied *LightWave 3D Applied Version 5.6*, the predecessor to this book. I have included some foliage that I have created for use in this scene on the companion CD-ROM for this book. Because the method involves the use of clip maps to create many leaves from simple polygons, we should not load the objects using the usual method. Clip map information is saved in the scene file rather than in the object file. So in order to bring these objects into our scene, we must use the Load Items From Scene command to keep the original settings. Choose File > Load > Load Items From Scene and open the **foliage.lws** file located in the Tutorial 3 directory on the companion CD-ROM. When asked if you wish to load lights from the scene, answer No. Three objects will be loaded from the scene.

The **hedgerow.lwo** object is a low row of shrubbery that you can clone and arrange as you wish. I used about ten clones of this object to create two rows of hedges that sit on either side of the sidewalk and fountain along the front edge of the building between the sidewalk and the building foundation. The **3dtree1.lwo** object consists of two layers. The trunk layer is the trunk and branches, along with a circular bed of earth. The leaves layer contains the leaves of the tree, which needed to be in a separate layer because of the clip map used to create the individual leaves out of simpler polygons.

You can create a veritable forest of different-looking trees by simply cloning, scaling, and rotating the one tree object to get different profiles. Select the 3dtree1:leaves object as the Current Item. Press M to open the Motion Options panel. Notice that the 3dtree1:trunk object is the parent of 3dtree1:leaves. If you want to scale, move, or transform the tree in any way, you must select the parent object and perform the transformation on it, and the changes will also affect the child. If you move the child, it will leave the parent and be affected by the change independently. So when you clone the tree the procedure can get a little tricky. In this case, when you clone 3dtree1:trunk the resultant object created would become 3dtree1:trunk(2) and the original would then appear in the object list as 3dtree1:trunk(1). Then, when you clone 3dtree1:leaves, the original would become 3dtree1:leaves(1) and the clone would be 3dtree1:leaves(2). Because all settings for the cloned object are copied from the original, the 3dtree1:leaves(2) object will still be parented to the 3dtree1:trunk(1) object. So, before performing any transformation on the second set of parts, the 3dtree1:leaves(2) object would need to be parented to 3dtree1:trunk(2). Whew! Clear as mud, isn't it? It's really not as bad as you might think; it just calls for a bit of careful organization and a consistent parenting scheme. If you wanted five trees in total, you would follow these steps in order:

1. Clone both layers of the tree object, making four clones for each.

2. For each clone of the leaves layer, set the parent of each clone number to the corresponding clone number of the trunk layer. The relationships would be as follows:

Parent	Child
3dtree1:trunk(1)	3dtree1:leaves(1)
3dtree1:trunk(2)	3dtree1:leaves(2)
3dtree1:trunk(3)	3dtree1:leaves(3)
3dtree1:trunk(4)	3dtree1:leaves(4)
3dtree1:trunk(5)	3dtree1:leaves(5)

3. Make desired transformations (Move, Scale, Stretch) to parent items only.

By following these steps you can make any number of trees you want, keeping in mind that these trees are fairly heavy in polygon count, so the more you add to your scene, the richer the scene will look, but the more rendering time you have in front of you. As usual, it boils down to finding a happy balance between realism and practicality. Vary the appearance of the trees as much as possible and try not to be too symmetrical or orderly in their placement. Remember, we are trying to mimic nature, and unlike the orderliness of our architecture, nature is all about chaos.

More items are included on the LightWave Applied Version 6.5 CD-ROM for use in your fly-through scene. While these extra models are certainly not required for the scene, any detail that you add will add to the overall richness of the environment. The **businessman.lwo** model is also included on the companion CD-ROM. This figure is great to add to a scene in order to give a reference of scale to your architectural scene. I've also included things such as a trashcan, a bench, and even a lobby so that you can do a fly-through into the building's interior if you'd like to. Feel free to use these models as you wish.

LIGHTING

After getting all the models situated within our fly-through scene, the next issue we turn our collective attention to is the lighting aspect of the 3D scene. In architectural renderings light can be used to manipulate space and the way you experience space. How you light your scene will have an effect on the contrast between light and shadow, how colors are perceived, and ultimately the emotional impact of the scene on the viewer. In lighting architecture for a 3D scene, it's important to be true to the architect's vision. You should try to see the building the way the architect sees it.

For me, it is easy to get excited about creating an outdoor scene because I have nature to inspire me. Take a simple walk through a forest and observe the shafts of sunlight (they are sometimes called "glories") coming through the trees. Watch how water in a stream trickles over a rock dam and how the light sparkles from the movement. There is a great deal you can learn from nature that can be applied directly to design. Sit in a secluded area of a park on a sunny day and watch the drama and intensity of light and shadows and its iridescent quality on natural and manufactured objects.

Learn to see light as a design tool, to note the composition of lighting elements in the space. Mentally note how each beautiful composition can add excitement to the overall project. LightWave can create awesome lighting effects. These techniques are a wonderful way to gain experience and knowledge about manipulating light. Pick up a good book on architectural photography and try to duplicate some of the lighting effects illustrated in the book. Build a visual reference guide by accumulating great architectural images that can be pulled from a folder and referenced when designing a project. Take note of how each element works together to form a light composition.

For our fly-through, we will be simulating the kind of light that you might experience on any given spring morning. We want our light to be bright, warm, and somewhat directional, but at the same time, we don't want our shadows to be too deep. While high-contrast lighting can be quite dramatic, our primary concern is to convey visual information, not obscure it.

Our main source of outdoor light in the real world is, of course, the sun. Because of its distance from the earth, it casts what appears to be directional light. The light rays appear to be virtually parallel and traveling all in the same direction. This is, of course, an illusion. What's more, in reality the sun is the primary source of light, but almost every other item under the sun becomes a secondary light source, as light bounces off one surface and on to the next and so on. LightWave has one of the best lighting engines around, offering a myriad of possibilities in terms of simulating real-world lighting effects. We can even use global illumination or radiosity to achieve photoreal lighting simulation, enabling us to emulate the scattering of the sun's rays.

I considered using this feature for our fly-through, but as usual, all of that power comes with a price. That price in this case would be a dramatic increase in render times. The sheer magnitude of the number of calculations needed to render the scene would have resulted in render times measured in hours per frame as opposed to minutes. When you consider that it takes 900 frames to make a 30-second animation, you can see that one would have to really want that kind of realism to make it worthwhile. Many tutorials pertaining to this feature are available on the Web, and we have included links to these Web sites on the CD-ROM that accompanies this book.

STEP 31: The default light loaded into each new scene in Light-Wave is the good old Distant Light. It is the default light type because of all the light types in LightWave; it is the only one that casts parallel rays of light, mimicking the apparent effect of sunlight traveling millions of miles to the earth. All the other light types cast light outward in multiple directions away from the source. For this reason, the Distant Light is a good choice to use for our sunlight. Also, the Distant Light casts light in a given direction infinitely, regardless of its position, so no matter where it is located, it will illuminate the scene, casting its light in the set direction. Besides, it's already here in our scene!

Press L to select Light as the item type. With the Distant Light selected as the Current Item, select the Rotate tool. Experiment with rotating the Distant Light to various angles to see how it affects the shadows in the scene. Change the setting and press F9 to perform a test render. Now, study the results of your experimentation. Notice how the form of the model is defined by its interaction with light and shadow. Good starting values for the light in our scene would be as follows:

H   58

P   55

B   0

This gives us a bright morning light with shadows that enhance the depth of image without being too long and obscuring the detail we worked hard to achieve. The problem with this light is that there is no bouncing and scattering of the rays, so the shadows are way too dark to look realistic, and areas in the shadows are poorly illuminated. Before the improvements of Radiosity rendering there was the Ambient Light feature, and we can use this tried-and-true method to simulate the global illumination effect of scattered and diffused reflected light.

Press P to open the Light Properties panel. Click the Global Illumination button and set the following Ambient Color values:

R   165

G   235

B   255

These settings will give a cool, bluish cast to our shadow areas. Enter an Ambient Intensity value of 45% to brighten up the areas cast in shadow.

Experiment with other settings and shadow colors to see what kind of effects you can achieve. The previous settings are only to get you started. The only real way to learn about how your settings affect the scene is to do a lot of tests and take note of the results.

ANIMATION

Using the Camera

Computer animation consists of many still images whose subtle changes in position, rotation, and scale, when played in rapid succession, produce the illusion of smooth motion. By simply defining a path through or around any architectural model and moving the rendering camera along that path, a virtual "walk-through" or "fly-through" can be created.

Moving a camera through a virtual space can be more complex than moving a camera through a real environment. In the physical world, we navigate an environment in three degrees of freedom. We move along the earth's surface as a plane (expressed in terms of the X and Z axis), and rotation by turning one's body around (expressed in terms of the Y axis). In the virtual realm, there can be up to six degrees of freedom to navigate through space: movement along three axes (X, Y, and Z), and rotation around these axes (heading, pitch, and bank, or H, P, and B). Movement in all six degrees of freedom allows the camera (and the viewer) the sensation of a free-floating body in space.

But just because we have all this freedom doesn't mean we can do willy-nilly aerobatics with our virtual camera. Remember, our job here is to show off our building, not to see how many barrel-rolls it takes to make our clients nauseated. In an architectural fly-through we are better served by smooth flowing motion, like the view one might have from a really smooth helicopter flight.

In the physical world, we move through the voids between solid objects. In other words, we walk from one room to another by passing through a doorway (void) between the doorjambs surrounded by the wall, ceiling, and floor (all solids). In a virtual world, the movement of the camera does not have to avoid collisions with solid objects, but may pass directly through them. We generally want to try to avoid flying the camera through solid objects in our 3D renderings, though. Nothing destroys the illusion we strive so hard to create faster than having the camera clip through a supposedly solid brick wall. Generally, it's a good rule of thumb that if a real-life camera can't do it, we shouldn't try with our virtual one. By seeming to follow the same physical laws in our virtual world that real cinematographers do in the real world, we help protect the suspension of disbelief that allows us to create our own reality and share it credibly with others.

The use of scale in a virtual environment is also an important element in a fly-through. In the physical world, scale is established by the size of elements relative to the participant. In a virtual world the viewer has no inherent size. Often models of people are included within the scene as indicators of relative scale. Scale is also indicated through the perception of velocity. The scale of the 3D environment is indicated by the rate at which one moves through it. Details of the virtual environment will also influence the perception of scale. For example, the surface of an object in the physical world can affect your sense of scale in much the same way that the size of an object does. Similarly, the detail and number of polygons rendered within a participant's field of view affects one's perception of scale virtually. Another good rule of thumb is to slow the movement of the camera when you add complexity of detail to a scene. Not only does this add weight and substance to your creation, but it also gives the viewer the opportunity to see and appreciate the detail you took such pains to produce!

So now we're about ready to begin to animate our fly-through at last. We've created our models, supplied them with realistic surfaces, arranged the scene layout, and set our lighting controls. All that remains is to make a path for our camera to follow, and set up the render so the computer can do the rest. So grab a fresh beverage and let's get cracking.

STEP 32: We will begin our scene with the camera up high, and far enough back from the building to get a shot that establishes the building as our subject matter while showing the entire site in a pleasing composition. Select the main camera as the Current Item. Select the Move tool and enter the following values:

X   −88 m

Y   60 m

Z   −98 m

Select the Rotate tool and set the following rotation values:

H   −320

P   20

B   0.0

Your screen should now look like Figure 3-18. Save the scene to protect your work.

STEP 33: Before we go any further, we need to set a length for the animation. As I previously mentioned, in order to give our animation weight and substance we need to use slow, smooth movement for our camera motion. The bad news is that this means a lot of frames will need rendering. This isn't going to be one of those instant gratification kinds of things. As I have said before, quality comes at a price, and the price in this case will be in rendering time. By default, Layout has a scene duration of 60 frames. Needless to say, we are going to need a lot more than that. At the

FIGURE 3-18 View from main camera at keyframe 0.

end of the frame slider at the lower right of the Layout interface is the frame count field. Click and drag on the number 60 in this field to highlight it and type in a value of 1000. This will give our scene a duration of roughly 33 seconds. This is much longer than most scenes you will ever animate in LightWave. Generally small bits are much easier to deal with. When doing other types of animating, I generally try to keep my shots to four seconds or shorter. This is the exception to the four-second rule. For a fly-through, I like to have one long continuous shot in order to emphasize scale and space. This longer time period will provide ample time to circle the building and will give the viewer an unobstructed view of all sides as well as the parking areas around the back and on the side of the building.

STEP 34: All of our objects have a keyframe set at frame 0 by the Auto Key feature in Layout. However, LightWave begins rendering at frame 1, not frame 0. So when the first frame is rendered, the camera is already on its way to the next keyframe location. In order to have our camera begin from a stopped position and move into action as a real camera in the physical world might, we must set a duplicate keyframe for the camera at frame 1. Click the Create Key button on the bottom menu (or press Enter) to open the Create Motion Key panel. Enter a value of 1 in the Create Key At field (Figure 3-19). Click OK to set a duplicate of keyframe 0 at frame 1 and close the Create Motion Key panel. Save the scene.

FIGURE 3-19 Create Motion Key panel.

STEP 35: In the physical world, objects do not normally go from a full stop to top speed instantaneously. Instead, inertia causes them to start to move slowly and build up velocity until they reach their top speed. In animation we have to simulate inertia through the use of ease in and ease out. This is accomplished by applying a Tension value to the keyframe at the beginning of a motion. Click the Graph Editor button to open the Graph Editor for the Camera. The Graph Editor opens with the motion channels for position and rotation listed individually in the Channel list. Click the Camera.Position.X entry to highlight it. Then hold down the Shift key and click the Camera.Rotation.B entry at the bottom of the list to select all six items on the list. Right-click and drag a selection box around all the keyframes in the first column on the left side of the motion graph (Figure 3-20). Now enter a Tension value of 1. This will cause the camera's motion curves to hug the keyframe, simulating the gradual buildup of speed that real objects are subject to. Remember to press Enter after entering the number to lock the change in. Close the Graph Editor and return to Layout.

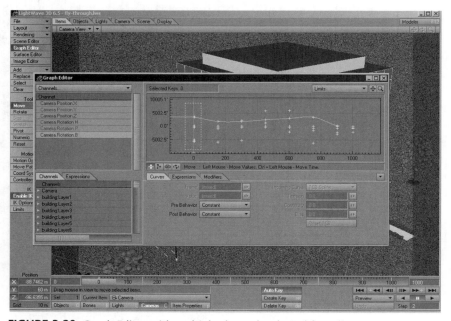

FIGURE 3-20 Graph Editor with multiple channels selected for edit.

Tip: Always use the smallest number of keyframes you can get away with in your animation. Not only will the motion be a lot smoother, but also if you need to make changes for some reason, it's always better to have to change 8 keyframes than to have to change 80.

STEP 36: Now it's simply a matter of setting keyframes to lay out the path for the camera. In order to have a smooth camera motion, we should try to use as few keyframes as possible. Also, to keep the speed constant, we'll try to keep the spacing of the keyframes in time as even as possible. Press F to open the Go To Frame panel. Enter 150 and press Enter. This will advance our position in time to frame 150 on the timeline. Alternatively, you can drag the frame slider to the right until the slider button reads 150. Select the Move tool and enter the following values:

X   −16 m

Y   30 m

Z   −102 m

Now select the Rotate tool and enter the following values:

H   −351

P   12

B   0

Press Enter twice to set a keyframe at the current frame with the entered settings. Repeat this process for each keyframe outlined in the following steps.

STEP 37: Advance to frame 300. Enter the following values for the Move tool:

X   38 m

Y   31 m

Z   −91 m

Enter the following values for the Rotate tool:

H   −386

P   11

B   0

Set a keyframe.

STEP 38: Advance to frame 450. Enter the following values for the Move tool:

X   103 m

Y   44 m

Z   22 m

Enter the following values for the Rotate tool:

    H   −451

    P   17

    B   0

Set a keyframe.

STEP 39: Advance to frame 600. Enter the following values for the Move tool:

    X   −40 m

    Y   55 m

    Z   105 m

Enter the following values for the Rotate tool:

    H   −561

    P   25

    B   0

Set a keyframe.

STEP 40: Advance to frame 750. Enter the following values for the Move tool:

    X   −109 m

    Y   62 m

    Z   −28 m

Enter the following values for the Rotate tool:

    H   −645

    P   28

    B   0

Set a keyframe.

STEP 41: Advance to frame 900. Enter the following values for the Move tool:

    X   −42 m

    Y   5 m

    Z   −50 m

Enter the following values for the Rotate tool:

H   −665

P   −7

B   0

Set a keyframe.

STEP 42: Advance to frame 1000. Enter the following values for the Move tool:

X   −10 m

Y   2 m

Z   −37 m

Enter the following values for the Rotate tool:

H   −687

P   −5

B   0

Set a keyframe.

STEP 43: Our last keyframe ends up with a close-up view of the entrance of the building. It's always a good idea to begin and end a shot with a still frame with nice composition so that if it's going to be edited together with other footage later, the editor has fewer problems to contend with. Since our camera is coming to a stop at the last keyframe, we should set an ease-in for the ending so that the camera doesn't just slam to a stop abruptly. Open the Graph Editor again and select all the channels in the list as we did in Step 35. This time, right-click and drag a box around the last column of keyframes (Figure 3-21). Again enter a Tension value of 1 to set the ease-in. Save the scene to protect all these changes.

STEP 44: Click the Preview button on the bottom menu and choose Make Preview. This may take a while, depending on your machine. When the preview has completed, click the Play button on the VCR-like buttons on the Preview Playback Control panel to see an OpenGL preview of your animation.

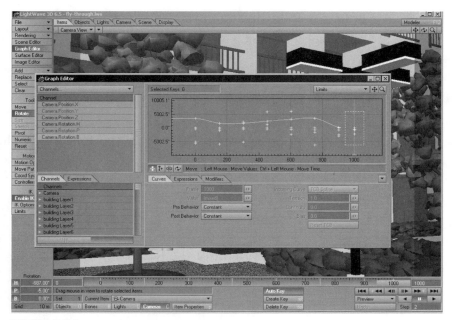

FIGURE 3-21 Last column of keyframes selected for camera in Graph Editor.

Tip: If it seems as if it's going to take a long time to generate the preview, you may want to set the frame step to 2 in the Step field at the bottom right corner of the Layout window. This will force the preview to render only every other frame of the preview, so it will take only half the time to finish calculating. It will play back at double speed, however. To get a better idea of the real speed, click on the 15 button on the right side of the Preview Playback Control panel to set the playback to run at 15 frames per second. It may seem a little jerky, but it will give you a better idea of what the final speed will look like.

Rendering

We now arrive at the final stage of the animation process for our fly-through, the final render. This is where we make all the decisions about how our final animation will be prepared for playback. Obviously, the render for output to film resolution would be different from that for a multimedia presentation that would play back in a window on the computer desktop. In the working world, we must render to a format specified by the client, based on their needs. In this case, we want to render to an animation file for playback on the computer. For Windows users, this means rendering to an .avi file for playback with Windows Media Player. For those working with LightWave on the Macintosh, the QuickTime .mov format is standard. Let's look at how we set up for rendering in LightWave.

STEP 45: Make sure the Camera is the Current Item. Press P to open the Camera Properties panel. By default, the Resolution is set to VGA (640 × 480). If you were rendering for NTSC video, you would set this to D1 (NTSC), which would output frames at a resolution of 720 × 486 pixels, the American standard for video. For our purposes, the default setting is adequate. For playback on most computers, a format of 320 × 240 is about the maximum size you can expect to play back at a smooth frame rate. So that's what resolution we want to use for our animation. Click the Resolution Multiplier menu and choose 50%. That sets our output resolution to 320 × 240. Click the Antialiasing menu and choose Low. The Antialiasing feature uses color averaging to smooth the pixelation that occurs on edges and diagonal lines in digital imagery. The important thing to remember about antialiasing is that it consumes more render time, another case of better quality = longer time. Therefore, it's good to use as low a setting as you can without sacrificing too much quality. For most video and multimedia work, the setting never really needs to exceed Enhanced Low. Close the Camera Properties panel. Save the scene.

STEP 46: Choose Rendering > Render Options to open the Render Options panel. This is where we make all the settings relating to what kind of output we are going to make, and where we want to put it. First we want to tell LightWave how much of our animation we want to render. Enter 1 in the Render First Frame field. Enter 900 in the Render Last Frame field. This is the equivalent of in and out points in video editing applications. Make certain that the Auto Frame Advance check box is selected. On the Render Display menu, choose (none). The Rendering tab should be selected by default. Render Mode should be set to Realistic. Select the Ray

Trace Shadows, Ray Trace Reflection, and Ray Trace Refraction check boxes. To speed things up a bit, also select the Extra Ray Trace Optimization check box. Set the Ray Recursion Limit to 2. The panel should look like Figure 3-22.

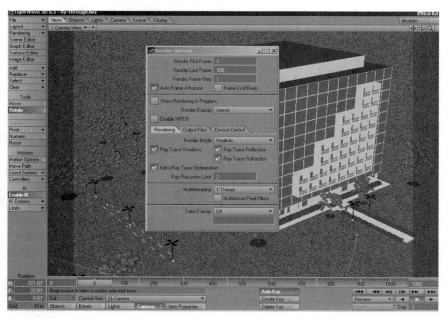

FIGURE 3-22 Render Options panel setup for final render.

Now click the Output Files tab. Select the Save Animation check box. Set the Type to the appropriate type of animation file (AVI [.avi] for Windows Media or QuickTime [.mov] for Apple Quick-Time). Click the Options button to set the compression codec and quality settings. Remember that lower quality results in smaller file size at the expense of image sharpness. Finally, click the Animation File button to open the Save File panel. Navigate to the destination where you want your animation to be saved to and enter a file name for the animation file.

OK, finally we are ready to render our animation. Close the Render Options panel and save the scene file one more time. I like to always save the file before I do a render. You never know what can happen, and it's much too late in the game to mess up now.

STEP 47: Press F10 to begin the rendering process and go away for a while. It's going to take a bit to render this file to animation. You may want to start the render just before you go to bed, because the computer is going to be busy for quite a while. However, the final result will be worth it. The scene that inspired this tutorial took nine days to render on a dual-processor graphics machine! You can find it along with a version of the animation created in this tutorial on the companion CD-ROM.

Now you're ready to create your own fly-through masterpiece. With the techniques we've covered here and your imagination, there's no limit to what you can accomplish. In the last couple of tutorials we have learned how to create an architectural fly-through animation from beginning to end, soup to nuts. All in all, it's been a pretty good day's work. Take a break while your animation renders and congratulate yourself on a job well done.

Understanding Textures, Part 1

Dave Jerrard

OVERVIEW

Aside from the actual modeling process, texturing is one of the most important parts of 3D imagery, along with lighting. Without textures, everything would be boring and flat shaded solid colors, reminiscent of the experimental CG of the early 1970s. Photorealistic imagery is extremely dependent on texturing, since real-world objects, no matter whether they're natural or machine-made to a mirror finish, all have imperfections. We're so used to seeing these imperfections, whether they're jagged cracks, rust, dust, or microscopic scratches, that their absence will immediately register in our minds as just not looking right. Texturing is also one of the main difficulties people have when they get involved with 3D, again, right up there with lighting. The importance of texturing is emphasized in LightWave 6.5 by the major overhaul the surfacing engine has gone through. Several new features have been added since previous versions, making the new Surface Editor (Figure 4-1) probably the most noticeably updated feature in LightWave 6.5. This also means that we have to look at surfacing in a slightly different way as well.

In this tutorial you will use:

- Image mapping

- Procedural textures

- Graph Editor

- VIPER

What you will need:

- Texture images included on CD

- Prebuilt objects included on CD

What you will learn:

- Basic to advanced surfacing techniques

- In-depth knowledge of how procedurals work

- How to animate textures

- Texture layer blending modes

- How to use VIPER

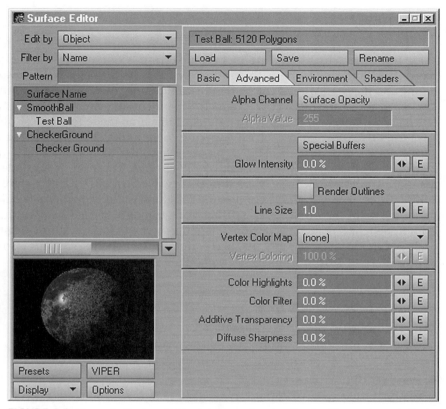

FIGURE 4-1 The main Surface Editor interface showing the familiar surface attributes and a new surface list.

To get started, we'll take a look at the changes in the Surface Editor so we can find our way around more easily. The first thing you'll notice on the main Layout screen is six tabs named Items, Objects, Lights, Camera, Scene, and Display. Clicking any of these will change the list of buttons on the main toolbar, as in Modeler. Click the Surface Editor button (Figure 4-2) and we'll get started.

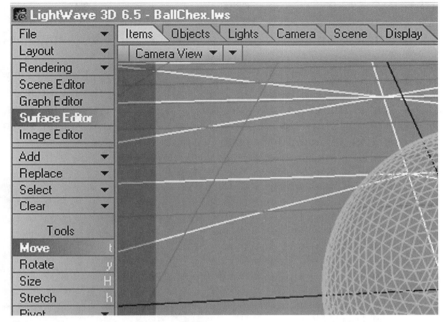

FIGURE 4-2 The location of the Surface Editor button. It's in the same place under each of the default layout tabs.

Note: Previously, in LightWave 6.0, there were only three tabs—Actions, Settings, and Extras—which are still available in LightWave 6.5. If you have these tabs visible, you can easily switch to the new LightWave 6.5 layout by clicking the Extras tab, choosing Edit Menus, then clicking the Default button in the Configure Menus panel that opens. You will also notice options for LightWave 6.0 and LightWave 5.6 style configurations as well. As you become more comfortable with LightWave 6.5, you may want to customize the menus and keyboard shortcuts. These tutorials assume that the default keyboard and menu layouts are being used. If you've modified these, we strongly recommend that you load the default setting before proceeding.

GETTING STARTED

STEP 1: Drag the Surface Editor out of the way. Unlike previous versions of LightWave, most of the windows in LightWave 6.5 can be left open while you work on other things. Figure 4-3 shows an extreme example of this. While this example may be a bit severe for most people, you may want to increase your screen resolution so you can keep a couple of often-used windows off to the side, rather than run Layout in full-screen mode.

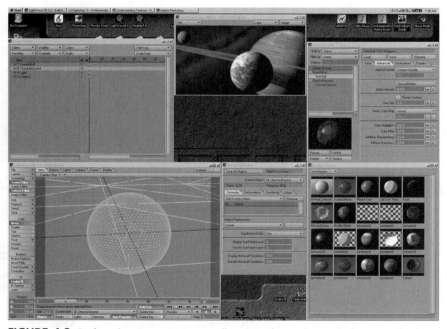

FIGURE 4-3 By keeping Layout at a smaller size, the various windows can be kept open and out of the way. This example, on a 1600x1200 desktop, shows the main Layout interface, the Scene Editor, the Surface Editor, the Surface Presets panel, and the Image Viewer.

With Surface Editor off to the side, choose File > Load Scene. Load the **BallChex.lws** scene from the CD; you'll notice that the Surface Editor now has two objects and two surfaces listed in it (Figure 4-4).

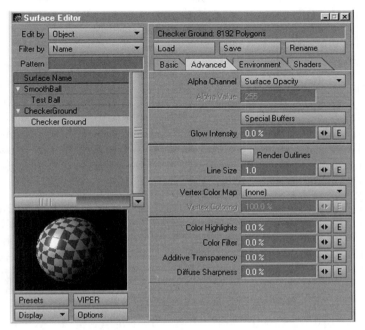

FIGURE 4-4 The new Surface Editor not only automatically updates the surface list as objects are added and removed, but can sort them by object and filter the list as well. Do you want to see only the surfaces that have a specific shader or texture applied? Just type in part of its name in the Pattern field.

Note: The Surface Editor has two methods of listing surfaces: by object or by scene. Previous versions of LightWave listed the surfaces by scene, which took into account only the surface name, allowing objects with identical surface names to overwrite previously loaded surfaces. While this might sound like a bad thing, it is occasionally very useful, which is one of the reasons the method is still available. The LightWave 6.5 default is to list them by object, which isolates one object's surfaces from another. Identical objects (multiple copies of the same object, not to be confused with objects of the same name that reside in different directories), however, will still share surfaces in the list. For these tutorials, you should make sure the Surface Editor is set to Edit by Object (top left corner).

This scene, as cliché as it is, simply consists of a ball on a checkered ground plane. Although it's very uninteresting, this scene illustrates very clearly how the various textures and attributes affect a surface, and that's what we want to learn here.

Since we'll be working mainly with textures, we're going to want to see how they look quite frequently. Test rendering can add up to a lot of time spent waiting, so LightWave 6.5 has an added feature called VIPER to both speed things up and make previewing things easier. To start using VIPER, we need to do two things: open its preview window, and feed it information about the scene.

STEP 2: First, open the VIPER window by clicking the VIPER button at the bottom left of the Surface Editor. A small VIPER window titled VIPER: Surfaces will appear. (This title will change to reflect the scene item we're working on, such as HyperVoxels or Volumetric Lights.) It will initially contain a black image, but this is because we haven't told it what to display yet. We feed it this information by simply rendering a frame, which tells VIPER where every surface and polygon is in the scene. Press F9 to do a quick render (Figure 4-5a).

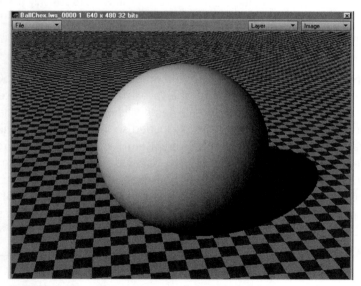

FIGURE 4-5A A frame of the BallChex scene, as displayed in LightWave's Image Viewer.

Note: While doing test renders, as we'll be doing throughout this tutorial, it's a good idea to select the Show Rendering In Progress check box in the Render Options panel. It will add a very small amount of time to the renders, but you can watch everything LightWave does and pick out problems as they happen, rather than try to figure out what went wrong from the final image. You can abort the render when you see something that needs fixing right away, rather than wait for the frame to complete, and you can find ways to optimize a scene to render faster by watching just how LightWave works. Be aware, also, that if you're rendering with multiple threads, LightWave will not draw each polygon as it's rendered, and will update the display only when a render pass has completed. To see the render as it happens, you'll need to render with a single thread.

STEP 3: When this frame is finished, click the Abort button (or press Esc) and the VIPER window will create a small version of the frame we just rendered. (If this doesn't happen automatically, click the Render button in the VIPER window.) Be aware, however, that there will be small differences between the two images. For instance, VIPER doesn't display shadows or raytraced reflections, so these will be missing from the VIPER display (Figure 4-5b). This is fine, since we're concerned with the textures and shading of surfaces and we don't need raytracing effects getting in our way.

VIPER is also more than just a nice preview device. A much-overlooked feature is its ability to instantly call up the surface settings of any object by simply clicking the surface in the image (double-clicking saves the surface as a preset). This comes in handy when you have large scenes with hundreds of surfaces. Try clicking the ground and the ball and watch the Surface Editor switch between surfaces.

Now that we have VIPER set up and running, select the Test Ball surface in the Surface Name list and we'll take a good look at the Surface Editor.

We're going to be primarily concerned with the Basic tab of this panel, since this is where most of the surfacing tools are. From here we can change the color, diffuse, reflection, and even translucency aspects of a surface. We can even animate the values of these attributes by applying an envelope to them using the E button beside each attribute. These attributes are called *texture channels;* while some of them seem similar—Reflection and Specularity, for

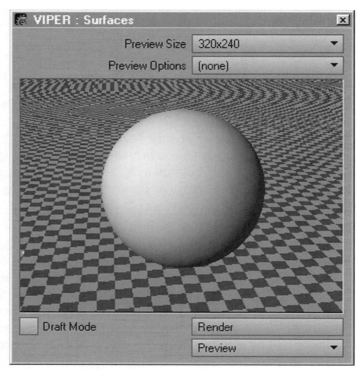

FIGURE 4-5B The same frame as seen in the VIPER preview. Note the lack of a shadow.

example—they're all actually rendered separately and then combined. In fact, you can see each channel on its own by clicking the Display button at the bottom left corner of the Surface Editor and selecting the channel you want from the list. The selected channel usually shows up as a grayscale image in the Surface Preview above the list, showing the value of the selected channel without any of the others being visible. This is extremely useful when you start working with layers of textures and you need to see how each is applied. To start off, we'll simply add some specularity to our ball to get a better understanding of how we can use VIPER.

STEP 4: Change the Specularity value to 100% and watch VIPER immediately render the change in the ball surface. Note that it doesn't actually re-render anything else in the frame, but blanks it out temporarily as the current surface is recalculated. VIPER only worries about the surface and shading information of the selected surface. With VIPER active, most of your surface experimentation will be done like this, without having to repeatedly press F9 for test renders. Play with the various surface attributes for a few minutes to get a feel for how they all affect the VIPER preview.

TEXTURES

As you have probably noticed, solid colors don't make for very realistic imagery. Luckily, LightWave provides three methods of applying textures to a surface: Image Map, Procedural Texture, and Gradient (Figure 4-6). A fourth method uses shader plug-ins, but these usually tend to be either image or procedural in nature. We'll be dealing mainly with the built-in textures here, since these are the most commonly used.

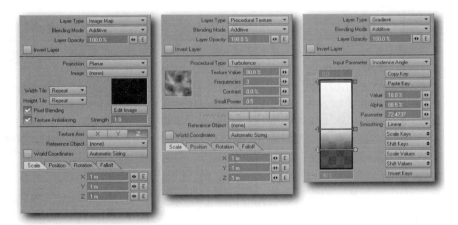

FIGURE 4-6 The Texture Editor options for each of the three texture types.

Note: Throughout these tutorials you'll see the terms *surface* and *texture* used frequently. A distinction between them should be made clear here. Surfaces are the actual polygons that will be colored. Objects can have multiple polygons and surfaces, and surfaces can be applied to multiple polygons, but polygons can have only one surface applied to each. Each surface is given a surface name to isolate it from other polygons that will be surfaced differently. Textures are part of a surface definition, and can be applied to any of the surface's various attributes, or channels. There is no limit to how many textures can be applied to a surface.

Image mapping is the simplest method of applying a texture, and is little more than taking an image and placing it on a surface. Signs, labels, tire treads, TV screens, floor tiles, and earth maps are all good examples of where images would be used in LightWave.

Procedural textures, sometimes called *fractals,* are created by mathematical formulas. The Checkerboard texture is a pattern created by a simple math formula, while textures such as Turbulence and Crumple are much more complicated. They're all three-dimensional textures, though, meaning that the texture is actually calculated throughout the X, Y, and Z axes, creating a virtual texture volume. What we see on a surface is where that volume is intersected by a polygon, in much the same way we see different patterns of wood grain depending on the angle at which we cut a piece of wood or bread. In fact, the bubbles in a loaf of bread are similar to how the dots of the Crust texture are arranged.

Gradients are a new beast altogether, and are used for more specialized effects, such as changing the color or specularity of a surface depending on the angle it's viewed from, or its distance from another object, or even based on how bumpy it is. A common gradient use would be to simulate the Fresnel effect for a water surface, to make the water more reflective toward the horizon, and less reflective when viewed straight on.

We'll be covering procedurals in detail here since these are very powerful and often misunderstood texturing methods. We'll start off with a quick look at the Grid texture.

STEP 5: Reload the **BallChex.lws** scene and select the Test Ball surface in the Surface Editor. Click the T button next to Color to open the Texture Editor (Figure 4-7). At the top right we can specify the type of texture we want to apply by clicking the Layer Type menu. By default it's set to Image Map, so click it and select Procedural Texture. The rest of the panel will change to show the Procedural Texture options, including the Procedural Type menu, already set to the Turbulence texture. Click this menu and select the Grid texture. Again, the panel will update to provide controls specific to the Grid texture. Set all three color values to 199 and set the Line Thickness to 0.1.

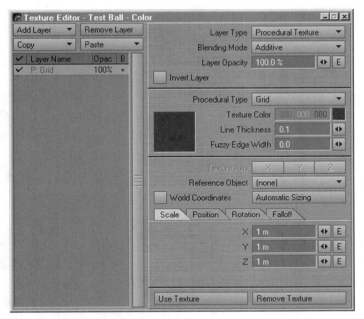

FIGURE 4-7 The Texture Editor with a Grid texture applied.

We just created a Grid texture on the ball (Figure 4-8). By default, the scale of this grid is 1 meter, so each square of the texture is a meter. The Line Thickness is relative to the texture scale, so the lines in our grid are 0.1 meter thick. If we made the texture smaller, the lines would become thinner as well. As we get further into the upcoming projects, we'll cover the relationships of the various textures and their respective settings.

Note: The grid texture can be thought of as an invisible array of cubes stretching out in all directions, with the grid lines being the spacing between the cubes. What we see on the surface is basically the shape of that array at the point where the ball intersects the texture. Try gradually moving the texture by slightly adjusting the values on the Position tab at the bottom of the panel. Figure 4-9 illustrates this 3D volumetric nature of procedurals by applying the same texture to LightWave's ground fog. Yes, these same textures can be applied to more than surfaces, which we'll get into a bit later.

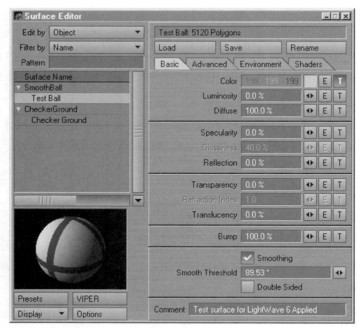

FIGURE 4-8 The ball with a grid texture applied. Since this is a 3D texture, you see only the parts that are intersected by the ball's surface. In this view, the center of the grid is at the center of the ball.

FIGURE 4-9 The same grid texture applied to both the ball and a layer of ground fog to illustrate the true 3D nature of procedurals. Note how the fog lines up exactly with the lines on the ball.

LAYERING TEXTURES

You've probably already noticed that the term *layer* has been used here and in the Texture Editor, and yes, textures can be layered. In fact, for realistic surfacing, you're very likely to be using many layers at a time. This might seem overwhelming at first (as it was in earlier versions of LightWave), but it only seems that way until you learn to concentrate on specific attributes and layers. We'll start off with a simple project involving the much-misunderstood but very powerful Marble procedural and create some lightning effects.

Project: Lightning

STEP 6: To start this project, we'll need a simple object that we'll use as our lightning bolt. Load Modeler, click the Create tab, and click the Box button on the main toolbar.

Note: As with Layout, Modeler has user-configurable menus, and LightWave 6.5 has a new default that is different from that of LightWave 6.0, as seen in Figure 4-10. These projects assume the use of the LightWave 6.5 menu configuration, so if you don't have it selected, click the Objects tab and then click the Preferences button to open the Configure Menus panel. Now click the Default button in the lower-right corner of the panel. If you've previously changed menus, you might have to hunt around for that option, which is a good reason not to mess with the menus too much. (Imagine using a custom menu configuration, only to find that you neglected to add a Configure Menus option and you wanted to change them again. . . .) If you must edit your menus, it's a good idea to simply add the tools you want to a new tab, rather than change the existing ones. This goes for Layout as well.

Drag out a box in the Back view window to a size of 5 meters tall and 1 meter wide (Figure 4-11). Alternatively, you can press N to open the Numeric panel and enter the following values:

Low X	−0.5 m
Y	0 m
Z	0 m

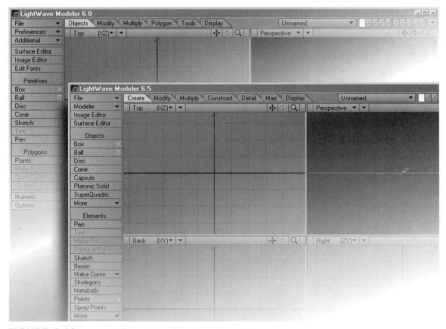

FIGURE 4-10 Some of the many menu changes between LightWave 6.0 and the new menus of LightWave 6.5.

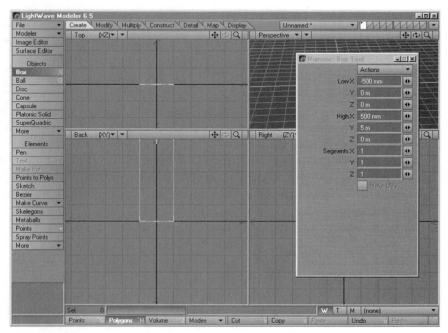

FIGURE 4-11 The numeric settings used to create our lightning bolt object.

High X	0.5 m
Y	5 m
Z	0 m
Segments X	1
Y	1
Z	1

Be sure to deactivate the Box tool by clicking the Box button again, or the Points or Polygons button at the bottom of the screen, before you click anywhere else, or you could find yourself clearing the box you just created!

Note: If you have only a single view window visible, try pressing 0 on the numeric keypad while the mouse pointer is over that window. This will toggle between the normal Quad view and a single full-sized view. If you can't see the labels, press D to open the Display Options panel and then make sure the check box for Viewport Titles on the Interface tab is selected. If none of the viewports is labeled Back, click the label on the lower-left one and choose Back from the list. (Another reason to avoid getting "configuration-happy" while following along with these tutorials.)

If you're looking at the Perspective view, you may have noticed that you can't see the box. This is simply because it's facing away from us, and by default, the polygons that LightWave uses are single-sided, meaning they're visible from only one side. This may sound like a bug, but it's intentional, and as you'll soon discover, *very* useful. We can make polygons double-sided if necessary, but for now, we'll just flip this one around. Press F (or click the Flip button on the Detail tab) and the polygon will turn to face us. Now that we have a box, let's give it a surface name.

STEP 7: Press Q to open the Change Surface panel. Type in a name and press Enter (Figure 4-12). There are a few other options, but they're very rarely used since this box's main function is to create surface names. Now that our lightning bolt has been modeled and given a surface name, we're ready to make it look like lightning.

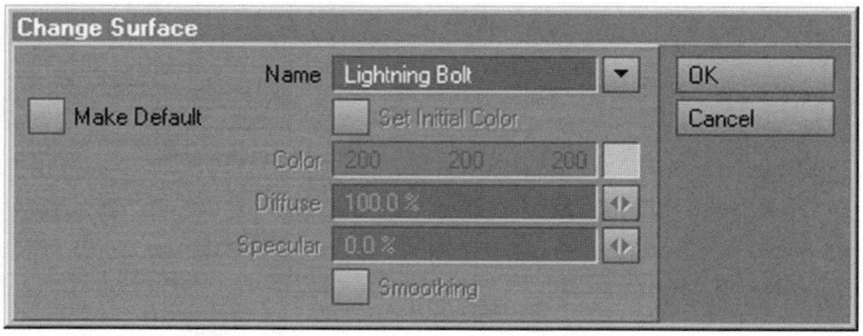

FIGURE 4-12 The Change Surface panel, where we create and name new surfaces.

Note: LightWave 6.0 added a new tool called the *Hub,* which is, at its simplest, a link between Layout and Modeler, allowing them to pass information to each other. Previously, this was possible through the use of the Get and Put (and more formerly Import and Export) commands in earlier versions of Modeler. When running, the Hub adds a Modeler button in the top left corner of the Layout screen, and allows automatic updating of objects when they're modified in one program. If you have an object in Layout and then load Modeler, the selected object will automatically be opened in Modeler, ready to edit (All other objects will also be accessible as well, via the object list in Modeler). If you modified that object at all, when you return to Layout, the modified object will automatically be loaded back into Layout. However, the object file on disk will *not* be affected unless you re-save the object from either program. Also note that this object sharing will take place only with objects that already exist on the disk. Our lightning bolt object, since we haven't saved it yet, cannot be shared yet. I recommend using the Hub for this feature and the next one I'll be covering. (By default, LightWave automatically runs the hub as it starts up. There is a special command line option to prevent the hub from running, but only advanced users should try it.)

Save this object as **LightningBolt.lwo** by choosing File > Save Objects As or by pressing Shift+S. Now we can go to Layout for the rest of this project.

STEP 8: Load Layout and load the LightningBolt object we just created by choosing File > Load > Load Object. . . . (You can also load objects by clicking the Add button on the Items tab, or by simply pressing the plus key (+).

Note: Alternatively, you can click the small triangle button in the upper-right corner of Modeler and choose Send Object to Layout, which will pass the object through the Hub and then to Layout, saving you the hassle of searching for the object on your disk.

STEP 9: Now that we have the object loaded, let's get VIPER set up. Open the Surface Editor and click the VIPER button. We don't have to worry about camera position, since LightWave automatically adjusts the camera's position to fit objects in its view when they're first loaded, *unless* you've previously created a keyframe for the camera manually. This position will work fine for our purposes for now.

Press F9 to create a test render and feed VIPER the info it needs about our lightning bolt (Figure 4-13).

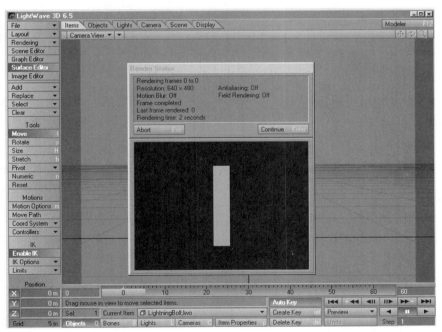

FIGURE 4-13 A quick test render to give VIPER the information it needs to do its job. From this point on, the brunt of the work will be handled through VIPER.

STEP 10: Press Esc to close the Render Status window, then move over to the VIPER window and click the Render button there. Now we can start surfacing. The first thing we want to do is create a basic shape of our lightning bolt. To do this, we'll use the Marble procedural texture, so click the T button next to the Color channel and then select Procedural Texture as the Layer Type in the Texture Editor.

Note: This is slightly different from how LightWave 6.0 worked. In Light-Wave 6.0, the same window was used for both the Surface Editor *and* the Texture Editor. This new method, while popping yet another window onto the screen, allows you to edit base values in the Surface Editor (even for other surfaces), while at the same time allowing you to change the texture settings, without having to repeatedly switch between two modes. If you click another texture button for another surface or attribute, the Texture Editor will switch to that texture, without losing the texture you had there before. It'll take a short time to get used to, but it will save a few mouse clicks during surfacing, which can really add up, allowing your mouse to live a longer life.

STEP 11: Select Marble as the Procedural Type by clicking the pop-up button, which will originally be set to Turbulence.

Note: There's really nothing special about the Turbulence texture that makes it the default texture here. The textures are simply listed alphabetically, from Brick to Wood, and then followed by a few extras that are part of a shader plug-in called Rapts.p, which is covered in detail by Marvin Landis in the LightWave 6.5 manual. Turbulence just happens to be in the center of this list, and the list is centered merely to save time. Rather than having to scroll through the entire list from Brick to get to Turbulent Noise, this method ensures that no texture is more than half a list away from the starting point. Don't feel you *have* to use Turbulence, just because it's there. It's simply a timesaving convenience. (But it is also a nice texture.)

Now before we go too much further, we should get a better understanding of how Marble works and what those numbers do. Marble is best thought of as a stack of paper on a skewer, with each sheet of paper representing a vein (Figure 4-14). The skewer represents the Texture Axis. The space between the sheets of paper is the Vein Spacing, and the base of the skewer is the texture center. Turbulence is how crinkled or flat each sheet of paper is. Frequencies is how many crinkles there are in a given area, and the Texture Scale defines the size of that area. The texture we'll see on the surface of an object is the shape of these sheets of paper at the point where they would be intersected by the object's surface, if they were placed inside it. Got that? OK, let's break that down a bit.

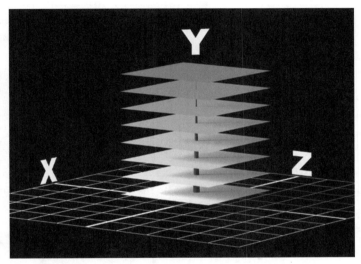

FIGURE 4-14 A 3D representation of the Marble texture, shown here as being mapped on the Y axis. Each square of the grid is 1 meter and the spacing between the sheets is 50 centimeters.

We'll start with the Texture Axis. We can map a texture along the X, Y, or Z axis, so by pointing our skewer along one of these axes, we can see which way our veins will run. If the skewer is vertical, or mapped on the Y axis, we can see that the sheets of paper will lie horizontally, as in Figure 4-14. If we mapped it along the X axis, then they would appear edge-on looking at them on the Y or Z axis, and mapping them on the Z axis will make them appear face-on on that axis, but they'd still be edge-on vertically (Figure 4-15).

The Vein Spacing is the distance between sheets. A lower number means the sheets are packed closer together and a higher number means they're farther apart (Figure 4-16).

Turbulence tells the paper how crinkled it is. A value of 1 means the paper is crinkled so much that each sheet is able to touch the sheet next to it. A value of 0 means the sheet is flat and the texture will appear to be a series of parallel lines. Basically, this is a percentage of the Vein Spacing, so a value of 2 would mean the space that the crinkles cover is double the space between the sheets (200%). This means that each sheet will crinkle enough to reach the sheet on the opposite side of an adjacent sheet. They won't actually pass through one another, since the sheets do follow a common pattern. Where one sheet pushes up, the next will bend to allow it, and so on, like a stack of damp paper (Figure 4-17).

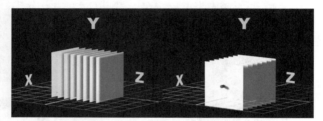

FIGURE 4-15 The same stack of paper mapped on the X axis, left, and on the Z axis, right.

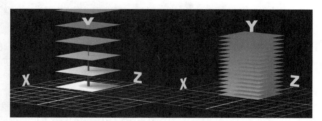

FIGURE 4-16 The same stack of paper, but with a spacing of 1 meter on the left and 25 centimeters on the right.

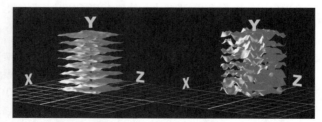

FIGURE 4-17 A 3D representation of the effects of Turbulence. The higher the value, the greater the effect. Note that the pattern is the same. Only the amplitude is increased with higher settings.

The effect of the Frequencies setting is a bit harder to grasp at first, since it's tied in with the Texture Scale. It defines the number of crinkles in a given area, which is defined by the Texture Scale. Think of the scale as a 3D grid that runs through the texture. As each sheet, or vein, of the texture passes from one section of this grid to the next, it's deformed. The frequencies basically define how many times the texture is deformed in that area. With a texture scale of 1 m, for example, the texture will be deformed, or creased once, every meter (Figure 4-18a), while a value of 8 means there will be eight deformations (Figure 4-18b). With a larger texture size, these deformations will be spaced further apart, creating smoother-flowing patterns, while a smaller size will be tighter and will create a more diffused, swirly, or even grainy appearance. The amount of turbulence will still define how much area this deformation can cover.

FIGURE 4-18A A Frequencies setting of 1 creates a very simple-looking disturbance in the paper. Note the gridlike appearance that's visible in the creases at this low setting.

FIGURE 4-18B A Frequencies setting of 8 follows the same general pattern as in Figure 5-18a, but breaks up the grid effect so it's no longer visible.

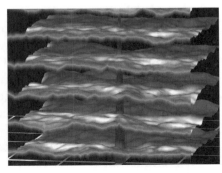

FIGURE 4-18C A 3D representation of the marble texture overlaid with the real thing, illustrating how the texture would look on a real surface. The settings used here were a Vein Spacing of 0.5 meters, a Vein Sharpness of 4, and a Frequencies setting of 8. Texture size is 1 meter and Turbulence is 0.5.

Vein Sharpness is probably the most straightforward value, next to Color, but still bears a bit of explanation. Marble veins *always* have soft or blurry edges to them, no matter how sharp you try to make them. The Vein Sharpness really controls the thickness of these blurry lines. A value of 1 will cause the blurry edge of these lines to be the same thickness as the Vein Spacing, while a value of 2 will be half. The default value of 4 is, as you might have guessed, one quarter the Vein Spacing. Values lower than 2 will actually cause the veins to overlap, so they'll tend to obscure any details below them. Higher values will make the lines thinner, with the side effect of making them appear spaced further apart as well. Generally, you'll want to stay with values between 3 and 20, since anything higher starts to fall between the pixels when you render, causing unwanted flickering in animations, or moiré problems for stills.

STEP 12: Now that we have a better understanding of how this texture works, we'll continue on with our lightning bolt. The next thing we want to do is place a marble vein on this polygon so it runs vertically down the center of it. Remembering the way the texture works in Figure 4-15, we know that we'll need to map it on the X axis, since our polygon is facing the Z axis. Click the X Axis button and the VIPER window will automatically update. We won't see much yet because the color of the texture at the moment is very similar to the base color, so go back to the Surface Editor (you won't have to close the Texture Editor for this) and change the color to black. A quick way to do this is to right-click one of the color values, which will change them from RGB values to HSV (Hue, Saturation, and Value), then drag left on the V value until it reads zero (Figure 4-19).

STEP 13: Now we have some light-colored veins running vertically down a black polygon, but they're a bit squiggly-looking. Go back to the Texture Editor and lower the Turbulence setting to 0 to straighten them out. We still have too many veins, so we need to space them out a bit. Our polygon is a meter wide, so to get a single vein to fill it, we need to use at least a meter for our vein spacing. Go back to the Texture Editor and change the Vein Spacing to 1. VIPER will once again update, but will reveal what looks like the exact opposite of what we're after (Figure 4-20).

This brings us to one last detail we need to know about Marble. The texture center is always halfway between two veins. To place a

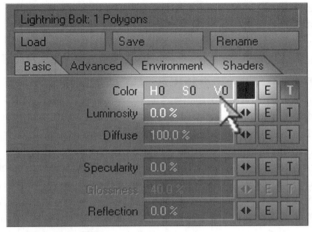

FIGURE 4-19 Right-clicking the Color values will toggle between RGB and HSV color models.

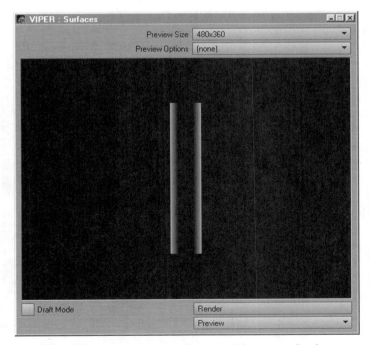

FIGURE 4-20 Since the center of the Marble texture lies between two veins, we're left with a vein running down each side of the polygon, rather than one running down the center.

vein exactly where we want it, we need to either add or subtract half of the Vein Spacing amount to the texture's Position value on the axis it's being mapped on. This will shift the veins along that axis enough that they'll appear where we want them.

STEP 14: Click the Position tab at the bottom of the Texture Editor and set the value for the X axis to 0.5 m. This will immediately adjust the texture so we now have a vein running down the center (Figure 4-21). This also pushes the adjacent veins off the edge of the polygon where they can't be seen unless we crank up the Turbulence too much again. If we do, then the veins to either side can start creeping onto the polygon and spoil the effect. To prevent this, we'll increase the Vein Spacing to 2. This will also have the effect of making the vein we want appear wider, and shifted to the side. Remember, to center a vein, we need to offset the position by half of the Vein Spacing. Since we just changed that spacing, we need to change the offset again. Increase the X axis position to 1 m, and all will be fine again.

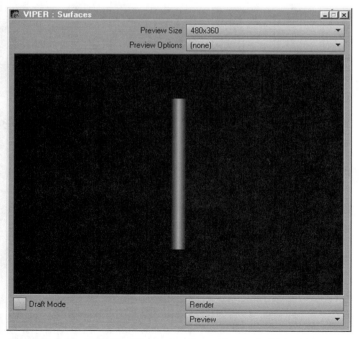

FIGURE 4-21 Adjusting the texture's position by half the Vein Spacing value aligns it correctly, so we now have a single vein running vertically down the center of our object.

Note: Changing the Vein Spacing affects not only the vein positions, but also their apparent thickness. If this is changed after the other settings are set, you'll quite likely have to adjust the Vein Sharpness to compensate. Luckily, they can both be adjusted by the same factor, so if you double the spacing, you can double the sharpness as well. Turbulence, however, will need to be adjusted the other way. Doubling the spacing would mean you'd have to cut the Turbulence by half. Since we haven't set the Vein Sharpness or Turbulence yet, we don't have to worry about it right now.

This still doesn't look like much of a lightning bolt yet, so let's start adding some detail.

STEP 15: One of the things most people know about lightning is that it's bright, so let's make this bolt luminous. Go back to the Surface Editor and increase the Luminosity to 100%. Lightning is also not affected by external light, so we can get rid of the Diffuse value while we're here as well. Drop that down to 0%.

Note: Many luminous effects that you'll tackle in LightWave will have this trait in common. Unless you want the effect to be shaded by a light source (and there will be times), a luminous surface should have no diffuse value since it's simulating a light-casting surface. Fire, for example, does not reflect light from a flashlight pointed at it. Instead, the flashlight will shine straight through it, and the only light you see coming off the flames is from the fire itself.

Also note that the Luminosity value does not actually cast light into the scene. What it does is eliminate the influence of shadowing and shading, so that in the complete absence of any external illumination, you're seeing the true colors of the surface, at an intensity specified by the Luminosity setting. If any light is falling on the surface, then it will be added to the surface, making it brighter. You can think of Luminosity as being similar to the Ambient Light in LightWave, but on a surface-by-surface basis.

The Diffuse value is sometimes treated as a brightness control for surfaces, and this causes confusion for many people. While it does seem to act like one much of the time, it's not actually adjusting the brightness of a surface. Rather, it affects the amount of diffuse, or ambient, light that hits it, much as the Specularity controls how much direct light is reflected off the surface, creating a shiny highlight. A white ball with a Diffuse level of 50% will appear gray under a 100% light. If the light is increased to 200%, the ball will again appear white, not gray as some people might think. However, if it has Color highlights applied, the surface of the ball, under normal lighting, will appear gray, but the highlights will be white. If the color of the ball is yellow, the lower Diffuse value will make it look darker, but the highlights will remain true to the actual color and appear yellow. This combination of lower diffuse Values and color highlights is important to making metallic surfaces, which we'll get to later. Dry surfaces tend to have higher Diffuse levels and lower Specularity, while the same surfaces when they're wet tend to be less diffuse and more specular. Again, we'll cover this a bit later.

STEP 16: Now that our lightning bolt is luminous, let's give it some more electric coloration. Electrical sparks, being high-energy releases, tend toward the blue end of the spectrum (fire is a lower energy form, and tends toward the red end of the spectrum), so we'll make a blue lightning bolt. (Lightning can actually appear in many colors, depending on the gases it's flowing through, but in general, people expect it to appear blue. We aim to please, sooo . . .) Go back to the Texture Editor and change the color for the marble to a light blue. RGB values of 0, 150, and 255 are a good start. This will now give us a soft, light blue line, but lightning rarely ever travels in a straight line. Increase the Turbulence to 0.1 to get a better-looking bolt (Figure 4-22).

You will notice that the texture is starting to get clipped at the sides of the polygon because it's being deformed too far. This can easily be fixed either by reducing the Turbulence or by increasing the Vein Sharpness. The brightest section down the center looks nice, so we'll leave the Turbulence alone, and just increase the Vein Sharpness to 6.

So far, it looks like a wiggly blue line. We need to make the center a bit brighter. We can do that by adding a second texture layer.

STEP 17: There's a couple ways we can add an additional layer to a surface. One is to simply create one using the Add Layer button, or we can copy an existing one and paste it in. Since we're going to just add another layer of marble to this, we can save ourselves a bit of work by just copying the settings we already have and use those. Click the Copy button in the upper-left corner of the Texture Editor and choose Current Layer. Now click Paste and choose Add to Layers. You should now have two entries in the list below those buttons, both labeled P: Marble (Figure 4-23). The P means the layer is a procedural, and it is followed by the type of proce-

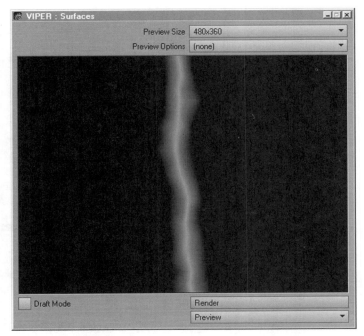

FIGURE 4-22 A closer view of the lightning bolt, now with some color and turbulence added. Note that the texture is running into the edge of the polygon in this view.

dural, Marble. They should both have a check mark beside them, indicating that both layers are active. We'll get to the other two columns later, but for now, select the top layer by clicking it. This is the one we just added, and it's going to be our "hot spot" of the lightning bolt.

STEP 18: Since this will be the layer that makes our lightning bolt brighter, we'll make it a lighter color. It doesn't need to be white, but it should be very close. Try RGB values of 255, 240, and 255 to give it a slight pink tinge for now. VIPER will still be updating as you make changes, and should now be showing a very bright, thick squiggle that's light pink in the center and a baby blue at the edge (Figure 4-24). The blue is the first layer we created showing through the second one near the edge.

Texture layers work like layers of glass, each with some kind of pattern painted on them, and then stacked on top of one another.

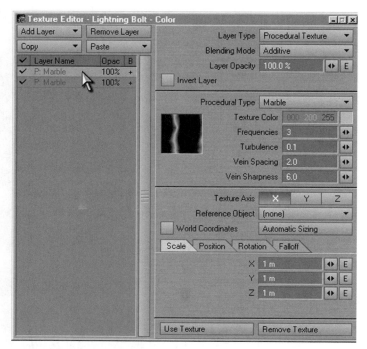

FIGURE 4-23 The newly created texture layer, added on top of the previous one, ready to be edited further.

The color we specify in the Surface Editor is the very bottom of this stack, and then each texture layer goes on top, in the same order you see them listed in the Texture Editor. In the case of Marble, each layer only has a pattern of veins, with transparent areas between them. The fuzzy edge of the veins is actually a gradient transparency, fading off to nothing on each side of each vein. The texture layer on the top of the list is the first one we see, and it's completely unobscured. However, it does obscure any textures or color below it, wherever it happens to be adding some color of its own. The center of the vein in these layers is 100% opaque, which is why we can't see the blue color of the second layer showing through the center of the top layer's vein. But near the edge, it's showing through and blending with the top layer. This is a little feature we're going to take advantage of.

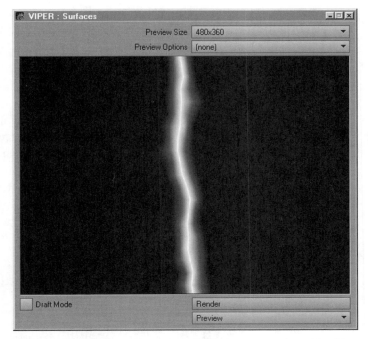

FIGURE 4-24 A second, thinner marble layer over the wider blue layer creates a nice color gradient from white-pink to light blue.

STEP 19: Since the area around the veins in a Marble layer is transparent, we can force colors from lower layers to show through these areas. If we make the top vein thinner, then we'll see more of the blue vein below. Try increasing the Vein Sharpness to 12 and watch the VIPER window. The overall vein will seem to thin out, but that's due to the fact that there's now less blending going on near the edges. The blue vein itself is still the same thickness, but the pink one is thinner. If we increase the sharpness even more, say to 15, then you'll be able to see more clearly that only the pink line is getting thinner and the blue at the edges is no longer being affected. The lighting bolt is starting to look more like lightning now.

STEP 20: The bolt's shape could use a bit of help now since it's looking a bit simple. Increase the Frequencies value to 6 and watch as VIPER draws out a more jagged-looking pink vein. The blue area also suffers the same problem, so click the second texture layer and increase its Frequencies value as well. It's a minor change, but it does break up the larger, smooth areas of gradient color, making it look a lot better. That outer color could be a bit darker though.

STEP 21: We'll add a third layer to this texture, but this time it will be used to add a darker color around the veins we already have. Since we haven't copied anything else, we will still have the first layer stored in memory, so we can just click Paste again and add a third layer. This new layer will again appear at the top of the list. Click and drag downward. A short yellow line will appear, indicating where the texture will be placed when you release the mouse button (Figure 4-25). Move down to the bottom of the list so the line appears immediately below the bottom texture, then release the mouse button.

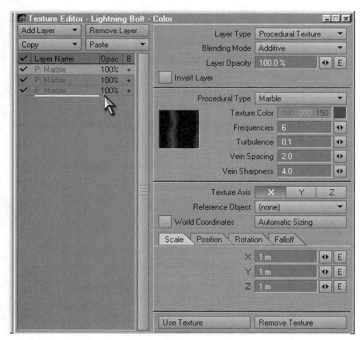

FIGURE 4-25 A yellow line indicates where the dragged layer will be moved to when the mouse button is released.

STEP 22: Now that this texture layer is positioned, change its color to a darker blue or purple. I've used RGB values of 100, 0, and 150 in the figures.

STEP 23: The next thing we need to do is to make this vein wider than the two above it. We could just specify a lower Vein Sharpness, but when we originally created the first layer, it was already getting clipped at the edges of the polygon. Instead, we'll leave it the way it is and make the other two layers thinner. Select the middle layer by clicking it and increase the Vein Sharpness to 10. At this point the bolt will be looking quite nice, but continue on to the top layer and increase its Vein Sharpness to somewhere between 20 and 30. Notice that as the Vein Sharpness values get higher, there's a less noticeable change between them. When you start working with values higher than 20, you'll save yourself some time by simply going in steps of 10 until you get a result you like. A value of 30 produces a bolt like that shown in Figure 4-26.

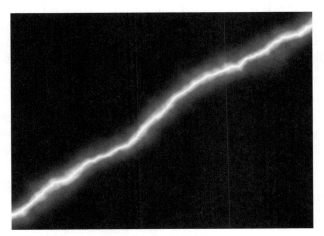

FIGURE 4-26 A finished lightning bolt.

Note: There's no real limit to how sharp you can make a vein, but when they get too thin, you will start having trouble rendering them, unless you use high amounts of antialiasing, without any Adaptive Sampling. Even then, they could still cause unwanted flickering in animations.

So, we now have a lightning bolt, but it's pretty static-looking (pun intended). We can bring it to life easily by adding some movement to the textures. If you look back at Figures 4-16 through 4-18, you'll see that the marble texture we see is only a slice of a continuous, undulating 3D texture. If we slice through that texture in a different spot, or at a different angle, we'll see a different pattern. Normally, when people think about moving a texture, they think only about moving *along* a surface, as you might do with an image of text to create a credit scroll. With images, this is pretty much all you can do with them, but procedurals can be moved *through* a surface. This will create an ever-changing, living texture.

STEP 24: Select the top texture layer in the Texture Editor and click the Position tab at the bottom. Next, click the E button next to the Z field to open the Graph Editor. Move that out of the way if it's covering the Texture Editor. We'll be using the graph to make our texture move, but rather than do the same thing three times, once for each layer, we can edit all three layers simultaneously. Click the middle layer and then click the E button next to the Z field. A new entry will be added in the Graph Editor for this layer as well. Do the same for the last layer, so you'll have three listings in the Channels section of the Graph Editor for TextureLayer. Under each will be a list of position channels, one each for the X, Y and Z positions.

STEP 25: Since we have all three layers listed in the Graph Editor, along with their position channels, we can set up a motion for them, but first we have to specify what channels we want to apply motion to. Click one of the Position.Z channels once, and then, holding down the Ctrl key, click each of the other two channels once to select them as well. Next, drag these channels up into the Channel list (Figure 4-27). Channels in this area can be edited, either in groups or individually.

STEP 26: Now that we have the channels we want, select them in the Channel list by clicking the top one and then, while holding down the Shift key, clicking the bottom one to select them all. Now that they're selected, we can modify their values all at the same time.

STEP 27: Under the graph area, click the Create Key button (it's the second button, which looks like a small key with a plus sign beside it). Now we're ready to add a second keyframe to the graph. Move the pointer up over the mark at frame 10 and click on the line. A small dot will appear with three lines of text describing it. You've just created a keyframe for three motion channels (Figure 4-28). Now we need to fine-tune it.

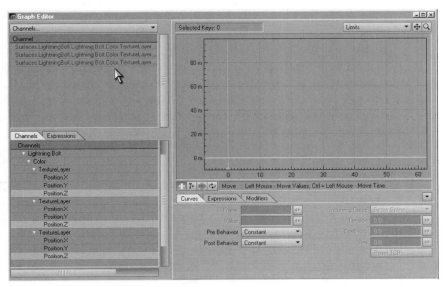

FIGURE 4-27 The Graph Editor, showing the three texture layers and their position channels.

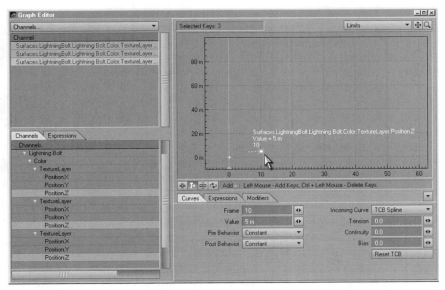

FIGURE 4-28 A keyframe is created for three selected motion channels.

STEP 28: Click the Move button (the one immediately to the left of the Create Key button) and drag the new keyframe vertically until its value is 5 m, which you'll see displayed in the second line of text that floats near it. This creates a simple 10-frame animation that moves the three texture layers 5 meters on the Z axis, *through* the polygon they're applied to. Since we're going to want the textures to keep moving for longer than 10 frames, we need to tell the graph to keep it moving after frame 10. In the section below the graph is a tab labeled Curves. Click that, if it's not already selected, and then click the Post Behavior button. Choose Linear, which will make the graph at the last keyframe continue on in a straight line at the same angle as between frames 0 and 10 (Figure 4-29). This is a fast way to give an item a motion that will go on forever, without having to place a keyframe several hundred frames away and try to figure out what the value should be there to create a smooth flowing motion.

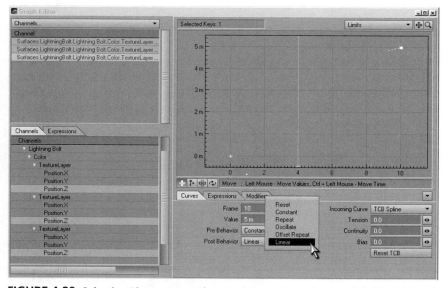

FIGURE 4-29 Selecting Linear causes the graph to continue in a straight line through the last keyframe, rather than stop there.

STEP 29: Now that we have this motion, let's see how it looks on the lightning bolt. First of all, you don't need to close the Graph Editor, but you may want to move it out of the way of the VIPER window. VIPER not only works well for previewing textures, but it can also show them animated, and that's just what we want to see now. Click the Preview button at the very bottom of the VIPER window and choose Make Preview, then sit back for a few minutes.

VIPER will generate a preview animation showing how the texture moves with the motion we gave it. This is incredibly handy for textures that have built-in motion attributes, such as the Ripples or Smoky textures. Rather than spend a long time rendering actual frames of a scene to test a texture animation, you can use VIPER to test only the surface you're concerned with. After a few minutes, press Esc to stop the preview. Since the motion goes on forever, theoretically, so could the animation. However, VIPER will preview only the range of frames that's specified on the main Layout screen, starting and ending on the frames specified on either side of the frame slider. You'll notice that as soon as you aborted, a set of VCR-style controls appeared. Click the Play button on the right (Figure 4-30) to play the animation forward. (The one on the left plays backward.)

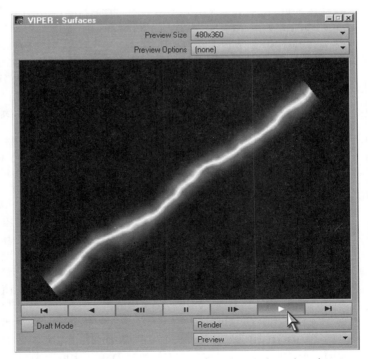

FIGURE 4-30 VIPER not only previews textures, but also plays texture animations, allowing you to fine-tune the timing of animated textures without having to render tests of your scenes.

STEP 30: The lightning bolt does bounce around pretty fast, so let's go back to the Graph Editor and slow it down. Drag the keyframe at frame 10 to a value of 1 m this time. You might want to click the Limits button at the top and choose Automatic Limits to better fit the keyframes in the window. Once this is done, go back to VIPER and generate another preview.

This time it looks much better. If you want, you can repeat Steps 25 to 30, but apply them to the Position.Y channels to have the texture also move along the length of the polygon.

STEP 31: Now that we have a working lightning bolt, there's only one more thing we need to do with it before it's ready to be used in a scene. In the main Layout window, click the Scene tab and then click the Backdrop button in the Effects area on the main toolbar. This will open the Effects panel, with the Backdrop tab active. Select the Gradient Backdrop check box, then click the Render button on the VIPER window again or press F9 to do a test render. (If the screen is getting cluttered, you can close the Graph Editor and Texture Editor. You can see why I recommend a large screen.)

You should be able to tell pretty quickly what's wrong with this (Figure 4-31). We need to make all that black area around the lightning transparent, but without affecting the marble texture itself. One way would be to use another marble texture as a transparency map, but there's another way—an easier way that works better.

STEP 32: In the Surface Editor, click the Advanced tab. Near the bottom, there's a setting labeled Additive Transparency (Figure 4-32). Set this to 100%, then click in the main Layout window and press F9. You should see the bolt shining brightly over the gradient backdrop, as in Figure 4-33.

Additive Transparency will not show up in VIPER, which is why you had to press F9 to do a test render. In previous versions of LightWave, this was simply a check box called Additive. It works the same way, except now you can control how additive the effect is. Additive Transparency simply takes the value of a point on the surface and adds that value to whatever is behind it. This results in the colors of the additive surface becoming brighter when they're in front of a lighter object or backdrop, but only if the color on the additive surface is not black. Black has RGB values of 0, 0, and 0, and any time you add 0 to a number, the number remains unchanged. Since the area around the texture was black, it simply rendered as if it were 100% transparent since it had no

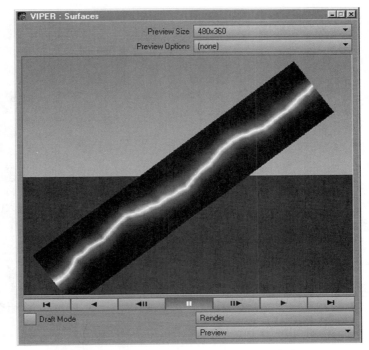

FIGURE 4-31 One last thing to fix on the lightning bolt.

value to add to the colors behind it. The rest of the texture did have some color, and this was added to the backdrop colors. You'll notice that the blues in the lightning bolt become brighter over the blue sky, but remain darker over the brown area. The blue of the lightning was being added to the blue in the sky, resulting in a brighter blue, while in the brown area, the main color being added was red, which was absent in the surface. This results in the surface looking like a normal transparency for that area. This is how a real spark or lightning bolt would act, though a real lightning bolt would be much brighter than the stuff behind it, so the effect would be very hard to distinguish, not to mention a bit on the dangerous side.

STEP 33: Save this object by choosing File > Save Current Object.

To use this bolt in a scene you would simply create an Object Dissolve envelope to have it appear for a few frames at a time. Stretching the object is perfectly fine in order to get it to fit, or you can create your own custom lightning bolt object. Feel free to experiment with the texture settings to create different looks, particularly the Scale.

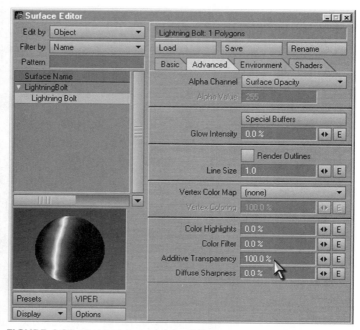

FIGURE 4-32 The location of the Additive Transparency setting.

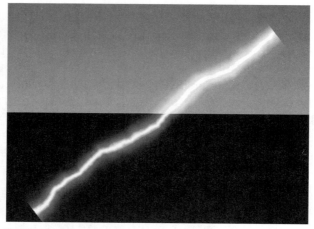

FIGURE 4-33 The finished lightning bolt. As an Additive surface, it behaves as a real spark would.

With the new Surface Editor, we get all these cool new features at the expense of having a list of recent surface previews that we had in LightWave versions 4.0 to 5.6. Now, if you change a texture, it's no longer a simple matter of clicking one of the recent previews to restore the previous settings. Sure, there is the preset shelf, but virtually no one out there will be saving presets after every little tweak they make. And if you happen to suffer a crash while surfacing, you can't just load the last surface that was saved when you rendered a preview anymore. You're stuck with whatever the settings were when you last saved the object.

But there is some salvation here. If you're running the Hub (and I strongly recommend it), you should have a couple of settings active. Double-click the Hub icon in the system tray, then double-click Options near the bottom of the panel, or right-click the system tray Hub icon and choose Options from the menu. There are two options here: Automatic Shutdown and Automatic Save. Automatic Save is the important one. When this is on, objects will be saved at regular intervals to a temporary folder called **lwhub.** In Windows, this is in the Windows Temp folder. Inside this folder, if you have the saving feature active, you will find numbered files, with a four-digit prefix followed by the filenames of the objects you've recently worked with, similar to the following:

0001.LightningBolt.lwo	1 Kb	Fri Jan 12 04:27:12 2001	LightWave Object
0001.SmoothBall.lwo	90 Kb	Thu Jan 11 03:17:32 2001	LightWave Object
0002.CheckerGround.lwo	146 Kb	Thu Jan 11 03:16:20 2001	LightWave Object
0003	258 bytes	Thu Jan 11 05:02:38 2001	
0004.LightningBolt.lwo	478 bytes	Thu Jan 11 05:24:42 2001	LightWave Object
0005	474 Kb	Thu Jan 11 05:46:44 2001	
0006.MarbleIllustration.lwo	488 Kb	Thu Jan 11 06:41:50 2001	LightWave Object

0009.MarbleIllustration.lwo	668 Kb	Thu Jan 11 18:33:10 2001	LightWave Object
0011	38 bytes	Thu Jan 11 18:58:20 2001	
0012.MarbleIllustration.lwo	1136 Kb	Thu Jan 11 20:21:34 2001	
0013.LightningBolt.lwo	930 bytes	Thu Jan 11 22:46:56 2001	LightWave Object

Automatic Save will save only files that have been modified, and only at the intervals you specify. If you select 5 minutes (Figure 4-34), then within five minutes of modifying an object, it will be saved to this folder. It will not save again until you've further modified that object, in which case it will be assigned a new four-digit prefix, and be saved again. In the example here, you can see that three different revisions of the LightningBolt object have been saved. I can't tell you how much time and aggravation this feature has saved me. If you do happen to lose a bunch of surface settings that you've been working on, simply load the last version of the object from this folder, and you'll have only a few minutes of work to redo.

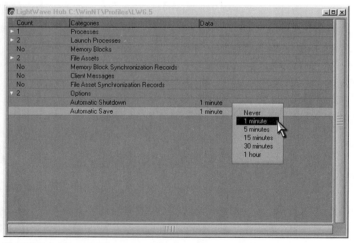

FIGURE 4-34 The Hub's main window, showing the Automatic Save and Automatic Shutdown options.

The other feature is less useful, but still good to know. Automatic Shutdown, while sounding a bit dangerous, is simply a time limit for the Hub to wait after you close Layout and Modeler before it automatically exits. Normally, once the Hub is running, it continues running until you manually quit it. That usually happens when you try to shut down Windows, only to find that the Hub is keeping Windows from shutting down because it's still present. By setting Automatic Shutdown to five minutes or so, you have enough time to reload Modeler or Layout if they should happen to vanish or you quit and realize you didn't want to quit just yet. If neither program is loaded again before this time is up, the Hub itself will exit quietly.

Now, on to the next project, again, featuring the Marble texture.

Project: Puddles

I frequently say that you can use Marble for all kinds of things, except creating marble, and this project is no exception. It excels at surfaces that have a regular, repeating pattern to them, such as stripes. Examples of this would be the lines on lined writing paper, or a texture of vertical or venetian blinds, or even the glow of fluorescent tubes in a backlit sign or ceiling lights. Or the puddles seen in Figure 4-35, which is the effect we're going to cover here. The first thing we need is a parking lot.

FIGURE 4-35 A wet parking lot, courtesy of Marble.

STEP 34: Rather than build another one (assuming you've completed Tutorials 2 and 3), we'll just use a simple stand-in parking lot for now, so load the **ParkingLot.lws** scene from the CD. This scene contains a simple parking lot object, large enough to hold over 600 cars, the '64 Thunderbird (which comes with LightWave), and a SkyTracer sky, which we won't see right away. Just ignore the car for now, since it's there only to provide a sense of scale. Once this scene is loaded, open the Surface Editor and select the Parking Lot surface. This would also be a good time to start VIPER and generate a test image for it.

Note: When loading scenes that were originally created on another computer, it's common for LightWave to complain about not being able to find some images or objects. To overcome this, either set the Content directory to point to the Content folder on the CD (the folder that contains the scenes, objects, and images folders), or manually select the files from that folder as LightWave asks for replacement files. Also, be sure to read any **readme.txt** files that appear on the CD, as there may be important changes or additional instructions you need to know about.

STEP 35: The first thing we need to do is provide this parking lot with its basic coloration. This can be done by using either an image map or a procedural texture. Of course, there's no rule saying we can't use both. We'll start off using a simple image. First, click the T button for the Color channel to open the Texture Editor. Since no texture is specified here yet, it will default to a Layer Type of Image Map, which is exactly what we want. Click the Image button, approximately halfway down the panel, and choose (load image) (Figure 4-36). In the Load Image panel, select the Concrete.jpg image from the CD.

By default, this image will be mapped on the Z axis, which means we're only going to see the very center section of it stretched across the surface of the parking lot as a series of streaks. Change the Texture Axis to Y to map the image onto the surface of the parking lot, rather than along it. Since this image, by default, is being repeated along the X and Z axes, you may notice a slight tiling effect (Figure 4-37).

This is one of the main problems with using images for large surfaces. Either you need an enormous image to fill the area with enough detail that it doesn't look blurry, or you need to use an image that will tile nicely, without leaving an obvious gridlike

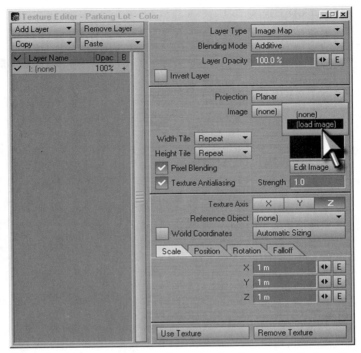

FIGURE 4-36 Selecting the option to load an image directly from the Texture Editor.

FIGURE 4-37 The parking lot surfaced with a small, 1-by-1-meter tiled image. A slight repetitive pattern can barely be seen.

effect on the surface. The preferred method is to use smaller, tiled images like this one since they're less memory-intensive. This also requires that the images have the same brightness and color along their opposing edges, so when they tile, the edges blend together. This concrete image is one such image, but although a slight tiling is still visible, it's nowhere near as bad as an image that has not been prepared correctly (Figure 4-38).

FIGURE 4-38 The same surface, but with an image less suited for tiling. A very obvious pattern can be seen here.

Note: On surfaces that will be viewed from a sharp angle, such as this parking lot, the Texture Antialiasing effect can become exaggerated and, at times, result in the texture details being completely blurred out of existence. This is especially true for surfaces that have images mapped at acute angles. This blurring of Texture Antialiasing can also be used for special effects as well, by increasing the strength to intentionally blur an image, rather than create a second, blurred version of an image in a paint program. We'll be covering this in detail a bit later.

STEP 36: There are a couple things we can do, aside from actually editing the image in a paint program. One is to resize the texture in LightWave. This will stretch the image to cover more area, resulting in fewer repetitions over the surface. This means there's less of a noticeable repeating pattern for our eyes to detect. At the bottom of the Texture Editor, change the Scale to 5 m and compare it with the previous texture (Figure 4-39).

FIGURE 4-39 The same image as in Figure 4-37, but this time with a larger scale. The gridlike pattern is much harder to distinguish now.

The second option is to use texture layering by adding a procedural over the image. Due to the nonrepetitive nature of procedurals (excluding the simpler Grid, Checkerboard, and Dots textures), these will help break up the pattern created by a tiled image. You can also layer a second tiled image, with a different size, and use Layer Opacity to blend them. This will result in two tiled patterns that overlap, but don't match, meaning that each tile on the bottom is overlapped by a different section of a tile from the upper layer than the one next to it. The result, again, is that the tiled appearance has been broken up and is less noticeable.

We're going to solve the tiling problem here using a combination of methods. First of all, since this is a parking lot, we should have some lines on it so drivers know where to park.

STEP 37: In the Texture Editor, click the Add Layer button at the top left and choose Image Map. We now have a second image layer to work with, so we need an image for it. Click the Image button, select the **ParkingLines.iff** image from the CD, and set the Texture Axis to Y. The surface will appear very dark, with some rather jaggy-looking white lines, in the VIPER preview. This is because the texture's fine lines are being displayed without the benefit of any antialiasing. (See the Tip at the end of Tutorial 5 for more information on how antialiasing works.)

You'll also notice that the texture we previously applied is now gone, completely replaced by this new image. We'll fix that in a minute, but right now, we need to get this texture sized right, since there's no way that car out there will fit in any of these spaces right now. You may have noticed that when this object was first rendered, it was composed of several smaller polygons. This was done for two reasons. The first reason is to cut down on wasted rendering, which is a frequent occurrence when rendering very large polygons mixed in with several smaller ones. LightWave renders polygons starting from the closest one and working out to the most distant one, and then renders transparent polygons afterward, working in the opposite direction. It determines the distance of a polygon based on its center, *not* the nearest point like you might expect. By using a tabletop as an example, we can see what happens. If you're sitting at a computer, you have a keyboard, mouse, and monitor, and if you're like many animators, there's probably a collection of action figures and other items scattered around as well. If you think of the stuff in front of you as 3D models, the tabletop would most likely be your largest polygon, while the keyboard and everything else is made up of much smaller ones. Now, think of yourself as the camera, and figure out which polygons are closest to you. Remember, you're going by the closest polygon *centers*, not edges, so even though the edge of the desk might be closer to you than the keyboard, its center is most likely several inches behind it. In most cases, the order would be something like this:

> Keyboard, mouse, mouse pad, coffee mug, paper scraps, CDs, desktop, more CDs, monitor, speakers, wall.

Now if LightWave were going to render these, it would render them in this order. Since the desktop is such a large polygon, though, it will render after the keyboard, but before the monitor. With shadows on, this means that the entire back half of the desk will be rendering the complete shadows of everything sitting on that area, only to have all that information covered up when the monitor renders. That's a lot of wasted rendering going on for stuff that will never be seen. Now, take the same setup, but this time, mentally divide the desktop into three smaller sections: front, middle, and back. Now our rendering order will be something like this:

> Keyboard/desktop front, mouse, mouse pad, coffee mug, desktop center, paper scraps, CDs, desktop, more CDs, monitor, desktop back, speakers, wall.

By further subdividing the surface, you can reduce the amount of rendering overlap even more. Remember, the less you have to render, the faster things will go; during an animation, an extra minute per frame can really add up.

The other reason the parking lot is subdivided is to provide some visual reference in wireframe mode for car placement. Each polygon was built the size of a parking space, making it easy to position a car in a space without going through trial and error: moving the car, test rendering, moving again, and so on. LightWave's solid 3D modes are nice, but sometimes you'll still want to use the old-fashioned wireframe modes (Figure 4-40).

STEP 38: Since we have a reference for the size of the parking spaces built right into the object, we can take the measurements we need

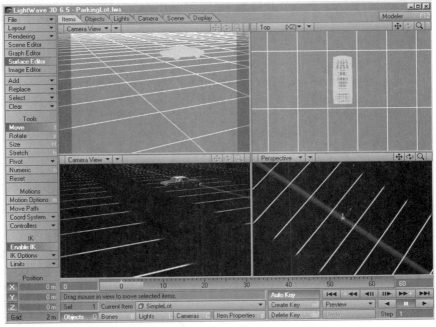

FIGURE 4-40 The edges of the polygons, when seen in wireframe mode, serve as outlines for the various parking spaces, making it easy to position a car in one.

to size the texture right from the object itself. Click the Modeler button in the upper-right corner of the main Layout window to open Modeler and load both the car and the parking lot objects into it. The object that's visible in Modeler first is the object you had selected in Layout (or the first object in the list if no object was selected). At the top of the Modeler screen, make sure you see SimpleLot listed as the active object. If not, then select it. Move the mouse over the Top view window, press 0 on the numeric keypad to toggle it to full window size, then adjust the zoom so you can easily see the individual polygons. Since all the polygons are the same size, we can measure any one of them to get the dimensions of a parking space. Click the Polygons button at the bottom of the window (or press Ctrl+H) to switch to Polygons mode, then select one of the polygons on the object. Press C to copy it, then switch to a new layer by clicking the top part of one of the empty layer buttons in the top right corner. Press P to paste the copy of that polygon into this layer.

Note: If you're using a three-button mouse, the middle button will work as a "select always" button. Normally, the left button will select Points/Polygons as long as it's held down, but as soon as you let go, it switches to deselect mode. To continue selecting, you must hold down the Shift key and start selecting again. With the middle button, you can always select, and use the left button to deselect. Certain third-party mouse drivers that add other functionality to the mouse can prevent this from working, so check the driver settings and make sure that the middle button is actually set up as a middle button and not something else.

STEP 39: Now that we've isolated a single polygon, we can measure it two ways. One is to use the Measure tool, hidden at the bottom of the Construct menu. Another way, which is a bit faster, is to use the Backdrop function in the Display Options panel. Press D to open the Display Options panel, and then click the Backdrop tab. Normally this is used to place an image in Modeler's background, for use as modeling reference, but it has a handy little function called Automatic Size, which will automatically size that image to fit the polygons in the current layer. Since we have only one polygon, the Automatic Size feature will scale the image to the same size. That size will also be displayed to the right of the Automatic Size button, providing an instant readout of the polygon's dimensions. Before you can use the function, you must first pick an image from the Image list. The two images we've already loaded into Layout will appear in this list, so just pick one (it doesn't matter which, since we're only after the dimensions of the polygon and need to activate the button to do it), then click the Automatic Size button (Figure 4-41).

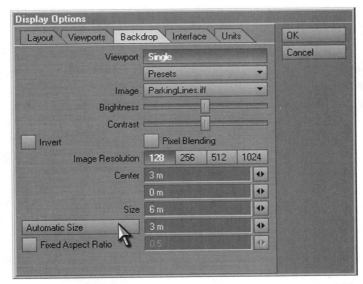

FIGURE 4-41 The Backdrop tab of the Display Options panel, which can be used to automatically get the dimensions of any polygons in the current layer.

We're not going to worry about the Center value, since we only want to know how big a parking space will be. According to the panel, they're 6 meters by 3 meters. Now that we have that information, we can go back to Layout and continue surfacing, but first, we'd better clear that layer. If we don't, then when we return to Layout, the object in Modeler, with that extra layer, will be exported back to Layout. We don't want that extra layer, so before we leave Modeler, press Delete, then switch back to the first layer. Now we're safe.

Note: You can also use the Layer's panel (Modeler > Windows > Layer Browser Open/Close . . .) to specify layers that should load or not load into Layout. However, clearing a layer this way is a cleaner way of doing things.

STEP 40: Before we can set the size of the **ParkingLines.iff** image, we need to know how it will be used. Take a look at the image itself first by opening the Image Editor. You can access the Image Editor by clicking the Edit Image button under the thumbnail of the image in the Texture Editor, or by clicking the Image Editor button on the main toolbar in Layout.

STEP 41: In the Image Editor, select the ParkingLines image by clicking it in the list. The preview at the bottom will show a distorted view of the image, stretched to fill the area. Double-click this preview to open the Image Viewer, which LightWave normally uses to display a rendered frame. This time, the Image Viewer will show a full-size version of the image in the editor.

You can see that this image looks like a large H, with a bit of space left over at the top and bottom. The H itself represents the lines around two adjoining parking spaces, while the space above and below would be the lane that leads to them. That space also happens to be half the length of the parking spaces, so the entire image is actually three spaces long (two spaces in the middle and two halves, one at each end) and one space wide. If we tile this image horizontally, we'll have two rows of parking spaces facing each other, with a small lane above and below the spaces. If we also tile it vertically, then we'll have wider lanes, with more rows of parking spaces. To get these lines to match the object, we need to size them accordingly.

STEP 42: In Modeler, we found that each polygon is 3 meters wide and 6 meters long. Go back to the Texture Editor and set the X scale for this image to 3 m. Now the image itself is actually three spaces long, and each space is 6 meters long, so that works out to 18 meters total. Enter a Z scale of 18 m, and that should do it. VIPER should now be showing you an image that looks like Figure 4-42.

Now that our lines have been painted, we can see that there's still the problem of the rest of the image covering our pavement texture with pure black. We need a way to tell LightWave that we want only the white parts of the image to be applied, not the black part. In earlier versions, we could simply activate the Alpha channel for the texture, but it's no longer there!

Well, it's still there, but hidden a bit, and much more useful than before. Texture alphas are now applied just like any other

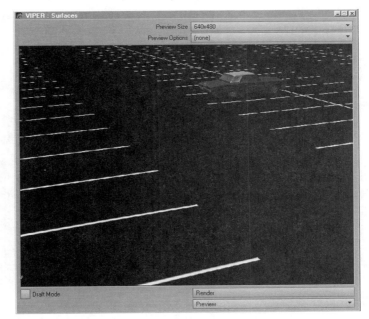

FIGURE 4-42 The parking lot now has shiny new parking spots neatly marked out.

texture, and they affect the layer immediately below them. This means that an alpha no longer has to be the same size as the texture it's affecting, nor does it even have to be the same type of texture. The next few steps will illustrate this.

STEP 43: Since we want to see only the white lines of this image, we need an alpha image that will mask them. Fortunately, we can use the same image as a mask for itself, and since we already set the image up once, we can save ourselves a bit of time by simply copying the settings from this layer to a new one. Click the Copy button and choose Current Layer. Now click Paste and choose Add To Layers. You will now have a third texture layer on top of the two we've already set up. Now, to make this an alpha, simply click the Blending Mode button to the right, and choose Alpha. That's it!

With alpha layers, the white parts of the texture reveal the layer below, while the darker parts, in effect, punch holes through it, revealing what's further down. In this case, the black parts of the top image punched holes through the second layer, revealing the texture of the bottom layer. The white lines of the second layer remain visible, and now serve as markings on the pavement (Figure 4-43).

FIGURE 4-43 Applying an alpha layer fixes the previous texture, so we're left with pristine white lines on our parking lot. Maybe just a little too pristine.

Alpha layers appear in the Texture Editor followed by an A (for Alpha) in the B (for Blending mode) column. You'll quickly learn to keep an eye on that column as you get further into surfacing, as it makes things much easier to work with when that layer list starts getting long.

Note: For an image such as this one, where we're creating some hard-edged lines, you will get better results by deactivating the Pixel Blending check box in the Texture Editor. While it works well on most images, for line art it tends to soften the lines more than you'll generally want. In Figure 4-44, you can see the results of the Pixel Blending along the edges of the line, where you can see a soft edge. This is because the lines in the image are only a few pixels thick. A larger image, with more pixels defining the lines, would reduce this blurring effect, but at the cost of more memory usage. If you turn this feature off, the edges will be very sharp again, and we could actually even use a smaller image, with lines only a single pixel in thickness, and still get good results. In fact, try replacing the **ParkingLines.iff** image with the **ParkingLines-Small.iff,** which is one-quarter the size and has single-pixel-thick lines, and test the effects of Pixel Blending with it.

FIGURE 4-44 A close-up look at a well-weathered line. At this distance, the image map for the pavement becomes blurry. The dark shadow is cast by a car.

STEP 44: OK, now that our lines are working, let's make things look a little more realistic. When's the last time you saw lines this clean in a parking lot? Let's weather them up a bit and create some wear and tear. We can apply a chipped look to them by applying a second alpha layer, and have it use a procedural texture to randomly "remove" parts of the lines. Click the Add Layer button and choose Procedural. You can use basically any procedural you want here, but for now, we'll just use the Turbulence texture.

Turbulence is very much like Fractal Noise, and it even has the same three settings. The textures are similar, but Turbulence tends to look fluffier or "smokier" at lower contrast settings than Fractal Noise does. Fractal Noise, at a lower Frequencies setting, tends to reveal a 3D gridlike artifact that matches the texture's scale, much like our Marble example in Figure 4-18a. Turbulence, while also revealing this grid artifact to a lesser extent, also reveals a much finer detailed diagonal one as its Small Power increases. Which texture you use is basically a matter of personal preference, but they are equally useful.

To make some nice hard-edged holes in our texture, increase the Contrast to around 75 or higher. Contrast can go as high as 100 for Turbulence and creates a completely sharp-edged texture. To break the texture up and add finer details, increase the Small Power to 0.8 or higher. The higher this number, the more small details will emerge. The scroll button will only allow values between −1 and 2, but values outside this range may be typed in. Finally, increase the Frequencies value to 5 or more (8 usually produces very nice results). This will add more detail to the texture. Feel free to experiment with the settings, including Scale, to come up with your own weathering effects. Try Fractal Noise, as well as some of the other procedurals, for different looks. Also, feel free to move the camera around to get a close look at the surface so far.

Now you're probably wondering how this alpha layer, being the fourth layer in the list, can affect the second layer, a layer that's not immediately below it. Well, it's actually not affecting the second layer. It's affecting the third layer, basically cutting holes in that image. What's left of that image is then applied to the second layer, effectively combining two alphas into one.

Note: The Layer Opacity can be used to further refine a procedural layer. While values between 0 and 100% basically work as expected and control the transparency of the texture, values higher than 100% may also be used. If they are, then the setting acts more like an intensity control. The higher the values, the more the texture is applied, basically supersaturating the areas already covered, thickening the edges, and adding texture to areas that were clear. Strange results can occur with values over 100% on normal additive layers, but in the case of alpha layers, the effect is to increase the area of transparency.

After a quick look at those lines, you'll notice that they're nice and sharp, but the surrounding texture looks blurry, especially when viewed up close. As mentioned earlier, this is one of the problems with using an image map for a large area. Let's get this fixed. While Fractal Noise or Turbulence are great for breaking up a surface, they don't create a convincing stone effect. Crumple, on the other hand, excels at this, and if you look at Figure 4-45a, you'll see why. Stony surfaces are generally composed of small granules, and the same is true for stonelike surfaces such as concrete, sand, and, to a slightly different extent, wood and other organic surfaces. It's this granularity that gives stone its look and feel. If we take a close look at the Crumple procedural, we can see it has a similar granularity, though its granules all tend to look like small beads all stuck together. In Figure 4-45a we can see a black crumple texture applied to a brown base color, revealing the fact that the texture actually applies the space between the "spheres" as the texture.

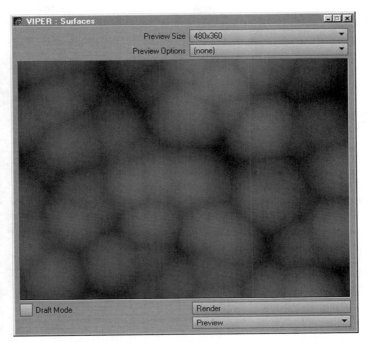

FIGURE 4-45A Magnified detail of the Crumple procedural, revealing its spherical nature. Its grainy features make it ideal for many natural surfaces, such as stone, sand, or even bubbles. Frequencies is set at 6.

Crumple also has only two settings to determine its look: Frequencies and Small Power. The Frequencies setting (formerly Number of Scales in previous versions of LightWave) determines the number of spheres it creates in a small area. The higher this number, the more spheres will be created. If you think of it as a subdivision level, you'll better understand it. With a setting of 1, you'll see a few large spheres in a small area, but if the Frequencies setting is increased, those spheres are split into more and more smaller ones. Any gaps that existed at low values will still remain, but they'll be surrounded by many more smaller spheres, slightly changing the shape, but the overall flow of the texture will remain the same. The Small Power on this texture acts like an intensity, or contrast control, and higher values increase the amount of coverage of the color the texture applies. At the default of 0.75, the texture is very slight, and with a value of 2, as in Figures 4-45a and 4-45b, it's more intense.

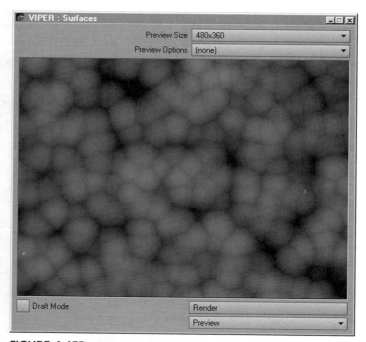

FIGURE 4-45B The same section of the texture, this time with Frequencies increased to 7. The same general pattern is present when compared with Figure 4-45a. Where there used to be large isolated spheres, there are now clumps of smaller ones. Note the matching dark area at the top and center right areas of both images.

Note: When used as a bump map, Small Power values above 1.0 tend to be too strong. Since the attribute acts as an amplifier, the higher this number, the deeper the bumps will appear. It will also make the texture appear to have more detail, since even the faintest details will be exaggerated. For a nice generic stone surface, Frequencies settings between 6 and 10 work well, with the Small Power set to 1. Bump intensity should be kept lower for best results.

After looking at this texture, we can see that it would be a good choice for adding a random graininess to our parking lot.

STEP 45: Click the Add Layer button again, and choose Procedural. Again, this will add the new layer to the top of the list. Next, click the Texture Type button to select the Crumple procedural, and give it a black color. Remember, we're using this to add some graininess to the surface, and this texture actually creates the color between the spheres of its texture, revealing the underlying layers through the spherical parts of the texture itself. Making this texture dark will create the effect of a series of tiny dark cracks in the pavement. If you're watching VIPER, you'll see that a very soft darkening has been applied to the entire surface, with subtle patches of variation. Increase the Small Power to increase this texture's contrast so we can see it easier. A value of 1 will do nicely.

You'll notice that this just darkened the entire surface a bit more, including the lines we applied earlier. What we're trying to do is fix only the pavement surface, since our lines are pretty much exactly how we want them. We need to prevent the Crumple layer from affecting those lines, and there are a couple of ways to do this. One is to use another alpha layer to mask the lines again, but this isn't really necessary. Remember, LightWave renders the layers from the top down, like sheets of painted glass. If we reordered the layers, so the lines were on top, they would naturally cover all the layers below them.

STEP 46: Click the layer we just applied in the list and drag it down so it's second from the bottom, placing it immediately above the pavement texture we first applied (Figure 4-46). VIPER should now be showing you an updated preview, showing white lines completely unobscured by the texture we just added.

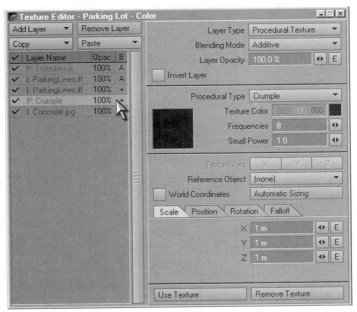

FIGURE 4-46 The new Crumple layer and its position in the layer list.

STEP 47: This is still not exactly the graininess we're after, so let's increase the Frequencies setting. A Frequencies value of 6 will get us closer to what we want, but in close views, it might still appear too much like glass beads, so let's try 7 or 8. You can go much higher, but as the Frequencies setting increases, so does the time it takes to render the surface. A value of 10 will usually be as high as you'll want to go. Anything higher starts to take an extremely long time to render, and provides very little difference in texture. Figure 4-47 shows a close view of the texture with a Frequencies setting of 8.

FIGURE 4-47 A close-up of the Crumple layer, revealing some of the pavement image below. Note that the lines are unobscured by the Crumple texture.

We're almost done with the surfacing of this parking lot. As it stands now, it's still a dry surface, but a bit flat-looking. While the texturing we added does seem to add some bumps to it, those bumps don't actually react to light like they should. A bump map, however, would.

STEP 48: Click the T button next to the Bump channel in the Surface Editor. The Texture Editor will appear to clear itself of the textures we just applied, but these have not been lost. It's just showing the list of textures that are currently applied to the Bump channel, and since we haven't applied any yet, it's empty, except for the default layer it always opens with. We're going to apply a procedural bump to the surface—again, to avoid any tiling problems—so click the Layer Type button and choose Procedural Texture. As we've already seen, Crumple is a great generic texture for simulating stony surfaces, and as we are about to find out, it's even better when used as a bump map.

STEP 49: Keeping in mind the way the texture works based on the last few steps, we have a good idea of what setting we should use to get a similar bump out of it. Set the Frequencies value to somewhere between 6 and 10, which will give us a high-quality rough surface, and increase the Small Power to 1. This will make the surface appear more jagged and detailed. A higher Small Power has the side effect of making the bumps appear too deep, so we'll now counter this by decreasing the Texture Value to around 10%. (Previously, this was labeled Bump Amplitude.)

Note: Texture Opacity, when used on bump maps, works as a second control for the amplitude of bumps. It can take values outside the normal 0–100% range, including negative numbers, just like the Texture Value setting. The main difference is that the value for Texture Opacity can be animated. We've now applied a rough, stonelike bumpiness to the entire parking lot, which will react to light direction. If you change the angle of the light, the bumps will be shaded differently, and you'll be able to see what appear to be small raised areas of pavement, as well as what appear to be slight cracks. Just the things you'd expect to see in a real parking lot.

Note: The bumps we applied are in no way affected by the alpha layers we added in the Color channel, or any layers in any other channels, for that matter. Layers affect other layers only in the channel where they're applied, with the exception of a specific gradient type, which we'll cover a bit later.

STEP 50: Now would be a good time to save the object. You might also want to save a preset for this surface, which you can access at any time through the Presets button in the lower-left corner of the Surface Editor.

Creating a preset is as easy as double-clicking the surface preview, or double-clicking the surface you want in the VIPER window. After doing so, when you look on the preset shelf, you will see a surface named Parking Lot, which is the name of the surface we've been working with (Figure 4-48). When you save a preset, it takes its name from the surface's current name. Presets can easily be renamed later if need be, by simply right-clicking them and choosing Set Name from the menu.

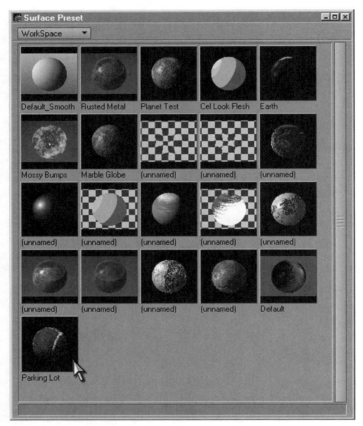

FIGURE 4-48 The preset shelf, showing the newly created Parking Lot surface.

With this surface saved, we can now continue with the project, which was to create puddles. I mentioned we were going to use Marble again, and now's the time.

Tip: One of the most important things you need as a 3D modeler/texturer is a keen sense of observation. If you have a good eye for detail, you'll be more readily able to pick out problems in a surface. With practice, you'll learn to make fairly accurate estimations of Specularity, Glossiness, and other attributes for objects you see every day. In fact, don't be surprised if you find yourself looking at something on a shelf somewhere, and thinking about it in texturing terms.

If you ever look closely at a puddle on pavement, you'll notice a few things about it. Water usually soaks into a porous surface, such as pavement, and this causes the surface to appear darker. As the surface becomes wetter, the water coating it causes light to be reflected more strongly—in essence, making the pavement shiny, or more specular. Finally, water tends to pool up in only the lowest areas, surrounded by these darker, wet regions. These pools of water are actually reflective enough to reflect images of their surroundings, much like a mirror. To create a realistic puddle in LightWave, we'll need to keep these three traits in mind.

If you think about it, we've just described three different texture regions, each successive one being a tighter version of the last, much like the lightning bolt we created earlier. Only this time, instead of layering three colors of marble over one another, we'll be applying them in different channels: Diffuse, Specularity, and Reflection.

Let's start with the wet look first, since it's going to be the widest part of the texture. In a parking lot, water will tend to be splashed and smeared in the higher traffic areas, where the lot is usually slanted to aid drainage. Rather than have water getting deep where the cars are parked, and people soaking their feet getting in to and out of their vehicles, lots are usually designed to drain this water away from parked cars. This means it usually runs down the center of the lanes between the parking spaces—or at least that's the general plan. This also means we know where we want to place our puddles on this lot.

STEP 51: If you take a good look at the lot, you'll see that it's divided into evenly spaced lanes, each separated by a double row of parking spots. When we laid those spots out, we found that the lanes were 18 meters apart (Steps 40–42). If we created a marble texture with veins spaced that same amount, we should be able to fit a vein down each lane. To start the wet texturing, we'll make the ground darker by applying the first texture to the Diffuse channel, so click the T button for Diffuse, and select Procedural as the Layer Type. Next, select the Marble texture and set the Vein Spacing to 18. To make things easier for now, drop the Turbulence to 0, so we can better see what we're doing.

By default, the texture is being mapped on the Z axis, and this means the veins are going to be running across it, along both the X and Y axes, as we learned in the previous project. In the case of our parking lot, this is just what we want. In fact, the default values already look good, creating an effect of worn traffic areas down each lane (Figure 4-49). Let's make those marks a bit wider by lowering the Vein Sharpness to 2, which will let these bands spill into the parking spaces a bit. Since this does look nice, as if vehicles have been driving along these lanes frequently, we'll keep this texture as is, and simply add a second layer for our puddles.

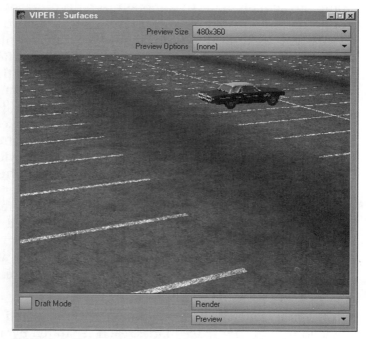

FIGURE 4-49 The default Marble texture, with veins spaced 18 meters apart, already improves the look of the parking lot.

STEP 52: We'll use this texture as a starting point for our puddles, so copy this layer and paste it using the Add To Layers command. Water rarely runs in a straight line, as you can see by looking at any natural river (Los Angeles's paved "rivers" are not exactly considered natural), so it makes sense that our puddles should waver back and forth as well. (The reason for using marble is becoming clear now.) Puddles tend to be quite dark on the bottom, due to all the grime that gets washed into them, so we'll lower the Diffuse value of this layer to around 20%.

Note: By lowering the diffuse value, we make the surface appear darker without affecting the actual colors of the textures on it. (While you could conceivably create a similar effect using the Color channel, the attempt would become maddening when other color textures are present!) If you select the Display button under the surface preview in the Surface Editor and choose Color Channel, you can see the surface colors, completely unaffected by lighting or shading. The VIPER window will also be updated, showing only the Color channel, revealing that the diffuse textures we're applying actually have no effect on color, but rather the shading that's applied to them. As we get further into texturing multiple channels, you'll find yourself using this feature more often to better see what each channel is doing.

STEP 53: With a Diffuse value that low, you should see very dark, almost black, bands going down each lane. They're still straight, so we need to add some disturbance to them. Increase the Turbulence to 0.25, which will cause the veins to waver up to 25% closer to the adjacent veins. VIPER will update with the new texture, but at this point things will be getting hard to make out. Try unchecking the first texture layer to deactivate it temporarily while we work on this second layer. (You might also want to switch the Display mode to Diffuse Channel now and then, to clearly see the texture being applied on this channel, as in Figure 4-50.)

STEP 54: This texture is just a little too wild right now. We want larger, gentler wavers in the veins, and we can create these by increasing the texture's scale. It's currently set to 1 meter, so let's double that and see how it looks. Better, but there's an obvious gridlike artifact visible. Increase the Frequencies setting to break that up a bit. A value around 8 should do nicely. Figure 4-51 shows the Diffuse channel as seen through VIPER.

STEP 55: Finally, to finish this layer, let's increase the Vein Sharpness slightly to 2.5, so it's no longer the same width as the layer below it. This will increase the "dry" area of the surface slightly, without making this vein too thin. Now it's time to create the next level of the puddles where the ground becomes shiny.

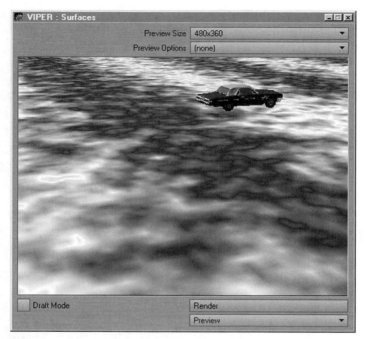

FIGURE 4-50 When viewed using only the Diffuse channel, the texture's shape becomes much easier to see.

STEP 56: You've probably guessed it already: our next layer will be applied to the Specularity channel. Since we'll be using the same basic texture setting, copy the layer we just created. Before we get ahead of ourselves, we need to be aware that Specularity and the attribute below it, Glossiness, are both closely related. Water normally has a fairly bright, tight specular highlight, while pavement has a very wide, dull one. As pavement gets wetter, it will become shinier, and the highlights will quickly become sharp. This means we should be using the same basic texture for both of these channels. And when you think about it, we're likely going to be using the same one again for Reflectivity. We've already copied the basic texture, so all we have to do is paste it into the Texture Editor for each of those other channels. Since the Texture Editor can remain open while we switch channels, this is made easier. Just click the T button for Specularity, and in the Texture Editor, click Paste and choose Replace Current Layer. Do the same for the Glossiness and Reflection channels.

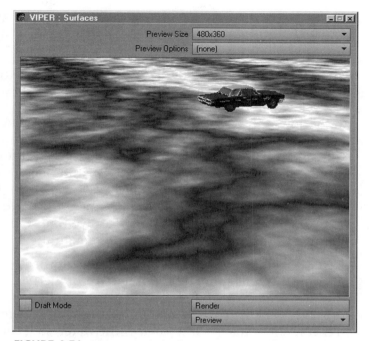

FIGURE 4-51 An increase in both texture size and frequencies adds some smoothing to the darkest parts of the veins, and gentle diffusion to the edges.

We've just added a base texture to three different channels. Now we need to tweak them slightly.

STEP 57: While we still have the Texture Editor for Reflection open, deactivate the texture in it by unchecking it in the list. This will make the other two textures easier to work with for now.

STEP 58: Go back to the Texture Editor for the Specularity channel. Since we want a gradual change from low to high Specularity on this channel, we need to specify how much Specularity to add. We also have to keep in mind that the centers of these veins will also be simulating water, so the Specularity in the centers should be high. Generally, values of 75% or higher work well for water. The rest of this texture will be fine the way it is.

STEP 59: Now that we have the texture's Specularity defined, we need to set the Specularity of the surrounding area. This is currently 0%, as you can see in the Surface Editor. Nearly every real-world surface has some amount of specularity, even though it may be extremely low, so increase the base value here to around 5%. This will also help display the bumps we added earlier.

STEP 60: With the Specularity set, you may notice that the highlights are a little too sharp. This is because we haven't set the Glossiness yet, which is still set to its default of 40%. Again, in the Surface Editor, lower the Glossiness value to around 5%. Low values like this are good for rough surfaces such as concrete, stone, and wood. Now, let's specify the value for the Glossiness texture. Open the Texture Editor for Glossiness and set the Texture Value to 40%. Now, just as with the Specularity channel, our Glossiness transitions from a very wide highlight to a sharp one where the texture will be its wettest. The remaining attributes, since we want the Glossiness to transition with the Specularity, should remain the same.

STEP 61: Our last layer of wetness will be on the Reflection channel, and this will simulate the reflective properties of the surface of water. Click the T button for Reflection and reactivate the texture layer here by rechecking it in the list. This texture will be used to define the actual pooling area of the water, so it should be thinner than the other channels we just textured. To make it thinner, we just increase the Vein Sharpness, as we did with the lightning bolt earlier. Pretty much any number will work here, as long as it's greater than the 2.5 we were using for the other channels. Values around 8 will work great in this case, but the final look is a matter of personal preference. As for the Reflection amount, it should be at least 50%, which will give us some nice reflections.

Note: Real water is not very reflective when viewed straight on, but at glancing angles, where the line of sight is nearly parallel to the water surface, it virtually becomes a mirror, especially when it's motionless. Since we're working with a reflection attribute, its effects will not be visible in the VIPER window, so we'll need to do an actual render. Don't forget to reactivate the second layer of the Diffuse texture, and then press F9. In a minute or so, you should have an image similar to Figure 4-52. This is another case where using the channel visibility of the Display menu comes in handy. By selecting the Reflection channel, you can get a good idea of how much water will appear on the surface. In this mode, the water will appear as the white area in VIPER. The brightness of this white area will match the amount of reflection you will see in the surface.

FIGURE 4-52 The finished puddle effect on a parking lot.

As mentioned before, this scene was already set up with a Sky-Tracer sky, to give this surface something to reflect. You can see that there's more than just a blue sky when you move the camera closer to a puddle. SkyTracer, as its name implies, generates nice sky backdrops, complete with clouds, and is very configurable. Since this plug-in is located on the Effects panel on the Backdrop tab, as an environment shader, it can be seen through windows or in reflections. We'll cover SkyTracer more in another tutorial.

About the only thing we could do to improve this surface is to remove the bumps where the water is most reflective. Unfortunately, at the time of this writing, Marble is one of a few procedurals that doesn't work as an alpha layer in the Bump channel. This could be rectified before this book goes to press, so as an experiment, try copying the texture layer you created in the Reflection channel, paste it into the Bump channel, and set it as an alpha. Since the actual texture of a procedural itself is used to "punch a hole" through the layer below, you'll need to select the Invert Layer check box for the alpha layer. We'll cover an alternative, more advanced method of making puddles a bit later on in the next tutorial. For now, save this object, and then try populating it with some of the various cars in LightWave's Objects > Vehicles directory (Figure 4-53). (Remember to use the Wireframe mode for easy placement.)

FIGURE 4-53 A populated parking lot, just after a small rainstorm.

Tip: For best results, scenes such as this should be rendered with the Ray Trace Reflections check box selected in the Render Options panel. It's the small details, such as the cars being reflected in the puddles in Figure 4-53, that boost the realism of an image. Our eyes are so accustomed to these little details that we come to expect them. If they're missing, our mind quickly registers that there's something wrong, although just exactly what is wrong isn't always as quickly determined. Frequently you'll find yourself working on a project, only to run into a detail that just doesn't look right, but the reason escapes you. When this happens, try rendering with and without shadow, or reflection, or even just work on another project for a while. Many animators run into periods when things just don't seem to look right, and simply taking some time away from one project by working on something else is a great way to let your mind refresh. When you come back at the project later, you might find that it looks better than you remembered, or you have new ideas on how to improve it (or both!).

Project: Raindrops

Well, we've made some puddles (a proud moment, I'm sure), but how did they get there? I'm not talking about the steps we just went through to create them, but rather, why would puddles be there in the first place? Obviously, it rained recently, but why should we stop the rain? Rain itself is a simple effect to create, and LightWave even used to come with a simple rain scene as an example (included on the accompanying CD as **Rain.lws**). However, recreating the effect of rain hitting a surface is a little more involved. Well, at least it seems involved, but there's a deceptively simple trick to simulate it, which we'll cover here.

STEP 62: Rather than continue on the parking lot, let's clear the scene from LightWave and start fresh. Load the **RainTest.lws** scene, which simply consists of a box with three sides removed so we can see inside. Open the Surface Editor and you'll see that this box contains two surfaces: Floor and Sides. The surface we're going to be concerned with is the floor right now, so select that.

The effect we're going to create is the small ripple caused by a raindrop hitting water. While we do have a couple of Ripples textures available to us, they create concentric ripples emanating from fixed locations. Obviously, ripples caused by falling rain are not confined to a few fixed locations, but rather happen in rapidly changing, random locations. We need a texture that has this random attribute to it. If you look back at the Crumple texture, you'll remember that it has a glass bead pattern (Figures 4-45a and 4-45b). Now if we could only separate those beads, we'd have a texture that could resemble rain drops in 3D. Crust just happens to fit this resemblance.

Before we continue, let's get an understanding of this texture. Crust, as well as the Dots texture, creates a series of round dots. While the Dots texture creates a simple, regular array of dots, one per scale unit, Crust randomizes its dots. The number of dots is roughly the same, but their placement is haphazard, as illustrated in Figure 4-54.

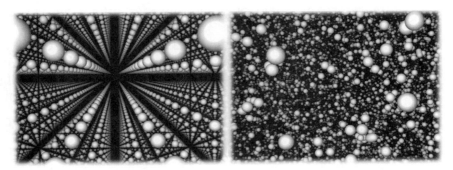

FIGURE 4-54 A 3D representation of the Dots texture, left, and the Crust texture, right, illustrating the arrangement of the texture spheres for both. The actual texture you'd see on a surface would be determined by where the polygons of that surface would intersect these volumes.

Aside from the Color or Value setting for Crust, there are only three parameters to worry about: Coverage, Ledge Level, and Ledge Width.

Coverage defines the size of the dots of this texture. Since this is a procedural, the texture actually occupies 3D space, and each of these dots is actually a spherical volume floating in 3D space. Where a polygon intersects one of these spheres, we see a round dot. All the spheres in the texture are the same size, defined by this coverage value, but they may appear to be a range of sizes up to the size we specify. Where a polygon intersects one of these spheres determines how big the dot will appear. A polygon slicing a sphere through the center will create the largest dot (equal to the Coverage size specified), while a polygon that just clips the edge of a sphere will reveal a much smaller spot. Unlike the Dots texture, the dots in the Crust texture always have a soft edge, which is not adjustable (yet).

Ledge Level defines the size of the center area of each sphere, which will appear flat when the texture is applied as a bump map. A value of 0 will cause a rounded dimple, with no flattening effect visible, while higher values create more of a pancake-shaped bump. Values higher than 1.0 will tend to run all the spheres into one another, eventually creating a continuously flat surface again (all the flat sections blended together into one extremely large flat bump) by the time the value reaches 2. Values between 1.3 and 1.5 create an interesting, randomly scratched surface effect.

Ledge Width defines the width of the sloped edge around the area defined by the Ledge Level. Small values create a sharp edge, much like coins embedded in the surface, while larger values create wider, smoother slopes between the center ledges and the surrounding areas.

It's important to note that Coverage has no effect on the Bump channel, while Ledge Level and Ledge Width affect *only* the Bump channel. Coverage *can* be helpful in setting the Ledge values for the Bump channel, though, which we'll see a bit later.

Note: If you haven't already, this would be a good time to get VIPER going so it can start generating those handy, quick previews again.

STEP 63: We'll start by applying the Crust texture to the Diffuse channel so we can more clearly see what's going on. Open the Texture Editor for the Diffuse channel and select the Crust procedural. Since the base color of the floor is already a light gray, we'll make this texture dark, so turn the Texture Value down to 0%, which will create a series of random black dots on the floor (Figure 4-55). Note that the pattern looks something like a splattering of black paint.

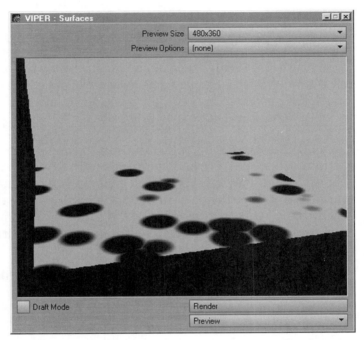

FIGURE 4-55 A random splattering of what resembles black paint.

STEP 64: Remember from the lightning bolt that we can move a procedural texture through a surface, and if you look back at Figure 4-54, you can see that the 3D illustration of Crust resembles water drops suspended in space. So if we move this texture through the floor surface, along the Y axis, we should get a changing pattern that resembles drops hitting the surface. Let's give that a shot. Click the Position tab at the bottom of the Texture Editor and click the E button next to the Y value. (Actually, any of the three E buttons will work, since they all become active when you click on one of them.) The Graph Editor will open, and the three position channels will appear in the channel list in the upper-left section of the window. The Y channel will be selected and ready for editing.

We're going to move this texture down the Y axis, so click the Add Key button (the one with a key and a plus sign) and create a key at frame 10 in the graph. To make the texture move down, we need to specify a negative value, so let's start with a value of −5 m at frame 10. As before, set the Post Behavior to Linear, so the graph continues this motion past frame 10 to infinity and our rain doesn't come to an abrupt halt during the animation.

Tip: When you create a new key, you can drag the new key up and down to select a value. If you accidentally release the mouse button, you can simply click anywhere along that frame again to reposition the key. Effectively, you're just creating a new key there again, and overwriting the old one, so it appears that you're just changing its value.

Now that we have applied motion to the texture, let's see it in action. Click the Preview button on the VIPER window and choose Make Preview. As VIPER generates an animation of this surface, you'll see the pattern of dots changing quite drastically on each frame. This texture looks like it's moving too fast, and playing the preview back after a few frames will confirm this. Let's slow this down a bit.

STEP 65: Click the Move tool on the Graph Editor (first button on the left, just below the graph), and drag that key on frame 10 to −1 m (or simply enter −1 in the Value field on the Curves tab). Generate another VIPER preview and play it back. This time you should see a bunch of random dots, all growing large and shrinking again, at random intervals. We're getting closer now—but before we go any further, let's see what exactly is going on.

STEP 66: To see why these dots are changing size, when they're supposed to be all the same, we'll render a cross-section of the texture to see it as it moves down the Y axis. In the Surface Editor, right-click the Floor surface in the surface list and choose Copy. This will copy every texture attribute for this surface (including any shader plug-ins that might be applied, which we'll get to later), allowing us to easily copy surface settings from one surface to any other. Now, click the Sides surface to select it, then right-click it and choose Paste. Now, generate another preview and play it back. You'll see a series of random dots moving down the walls, and when they reach the floor, they'll momentarily spill out onto the floor and recede again as each dot disappears below it (Figure 4-56).

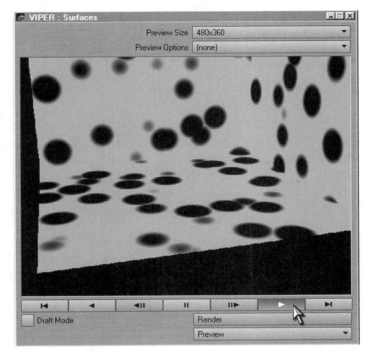

FIGURE 4-56 When a dot appears near a corner, you can see its 3D nature by the fact that it also appears on the adjacent wall. As the dot moves down the wall, its appearance on the floor changes size, constantly matching the pattern along the bottom of the wall.

This animation illustrates that the dots on the floor are seen to grow as a sphere of the texture approaches the surface from above. As the dot passes through the polygon and begins to move away, the dot it creates begins to shrink again. This is a clear example of how the patterns we see are simply slices of a three-dimensional texture.

Note: The Copy or Paste function will be applied to whatever surface is currently selected, so even though the menu may appear over the surface you want, and the surface becomes selected after performing a Copy or Paste, it will actually remain unaffected if it was not highlighted before you accessed the menu. Make sure you select the surface first, or you could find that you've copied the wrong surface, or worse, pasted into the wrong surface.

We have the beginnings of a raindrop pattern, but the ripples created by real rain are ring-shaped. Ours are simply a series of expanding and contracting dots so far.

In the last two projects, we've seen that we can layer textures over one another, and that the top layer always renders on top of what's underneath, only revealing details through the transparent parts of the texture. In this case, the transparent part of the Crust texture is the space between the spheres. If we were to add a second layer of Crust, but with a lighter value, and smaller coverage, we should get rings, so let's try that.

STEP 67: Let's continue using both the Floor and the Sides surfaces so we can see what the texture's doing as we continue to adjust it. Rather than constantly adjust one surface, then copy it to the other, let's work on both of them at the same time. In the Surface Editor, click one of the surfaces, and then, while holding down the Ctrl key, click the other one. Much as you would use the Shift or Ctrl keys to select multiple files in Windows, you can select multiple surfaces (or objects) in LightWave. You'll also see that the Texture button for the Diffuse channel now has a different appearance (Figure 4-57). This signifies that the textures for these two surfaces may be different from one another, or simply that they've been created at different times. Click the Texture button again to make sure that the Texture Editor is updated with the knowledge that it's now working on two separate surfaces. Now copy this current texture layer and paste it back using the Add To Layers command. We've just added a new layer to two surfaces.

Note: When you are editing multiple surfaces, if the Texture Editor is open while multiple surfaces are selected, it will remain locked to the single texture it was originally opened with. You will have to click the Texture button again to update it with the additional surface's textures. Otherwise, any edits you make will be applied only to the surface attribute you had opened the editor for.

STEP 68: Now that we have two layers, we need to make the top one cancel out the effects of the bottom one, so raise its Value setting to 100%. This will replace the 0% Value setting for all the dots of the bottom texture with 100% again, which theoretically should erase the bottom layer. However, as mentioned earlier, these dots all have a thin soft edge, so while the centers of the dots will be completely erased, you will still see a bit of the soft edge of each black dot showing through the soft edges of each light dot. Now this looks more like a ripple pattern (Figure 4-58).

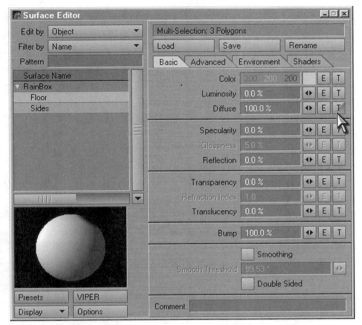

FIGURE 4-57 Two surfaces selected and ready to be edited as one. The small diagonal mark on the Texture button warns that the textures for these surfaces may be different.

Well, we're almost there. Generate another preview to see how it looks in action. It'll be close, but we need to do something about the way those rings contract again. If they didn't do that, the texture would look great. We need a way of erasing the trailing edge of the spheres, without erasing the rest of them. A slight offset to the second layer, placing it slightly higher on the Y axis, should do the trick.

STEP 69: Click the E button for this layer's Y field to load the graph for it. Next, holding down the Shift key, select both keys in this graph. Now, while watching VIPER update, slowly move these two keys up (Figure 4-59). This will move the upper texture layer's position so it's located slightly higher than the first layer. Since we're moving both keys that make up this graph, we've effectively moved the layer's entire motion, so the top layer is always the same distance above the lower layer. Move the layer until the

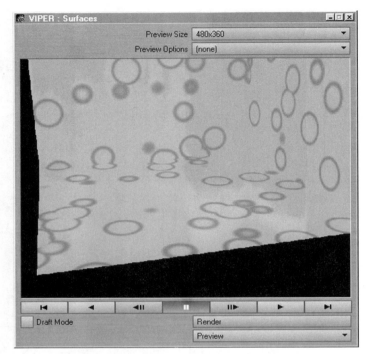

FIGURE 4-58 Soft-edged white dots over soft-edged black dots results in a soft ring pattern.

image in VIPER resembles a series of dark crescent shapes like those in Figure 4-60. This should happen when the first key is positioned near the 10 cm mark on the graph.

STEP 70: Generate another preview in VIPER and watch the effect closely. As the new crescent shapes reach the floor, they start to reveal the first dark layer of dots. Then as the second layer approaches, it begins to overwrite the dark dots. Then as the dark dots pass through the floor and begin to contract, the light dots are still moving closer, and still expanding, effectively erasing the trailing half of the darker spheres. The result on the floor is that of an expanding ring that then fades into oblivion rather than contracting again. Even the texture on the walls looks like raindrops.

Now, experiment with the Coverage value for different looks. Lower values will make smaller dots, which would be ideal for a light drizzle effect, while a larger value would be good for a downpour. If you give the top layer a higher coverage than the bottom

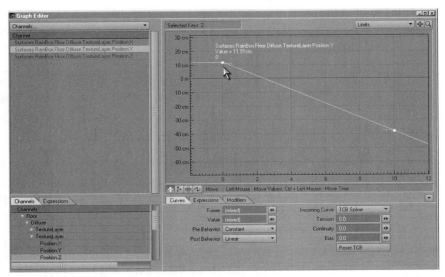

FIGURE 4-59 By selecting multiple keys, you can offset an entire envelope, without changing its shape.

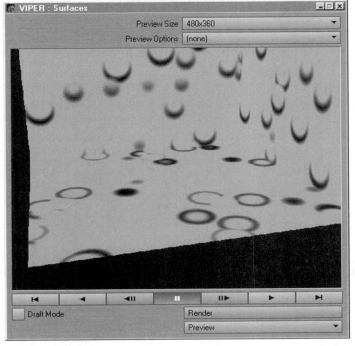

FIGURE 4-60 While moving the top layer's Y motion upward, the texture takes on a new pattern, looking rather driplike on the walls, while the floor retains its ringlike appearance.

layer, the result will be thinner rings that fade faster. That would work well for a surface that's not very wet, like a car or statue in the rain.

Tip: When you're finished with this project, try expanding on it to create water drops running down a window. We'll revisit this project later to reveal more tricks that can be used to make each drop move with random squiggles, as you'd expect from real drops.

Now that we have the texture effect working, let's get the texture to look right. Ripples are really just bumps on a surface, so let's convert this texture to a bump map. As previously mentioned, the Coverage value has no effect on bumps, so we'll need to learn the two Ledge values.

STEP 71: So we don't get confused, deactivate both of these layers by unchecking them in the Texture Editor. Now, Copy All Layers and then open the Bump channel's Texture Editor by clicking the T button next to it in the Surface Editor. Since we still have both surfaces selected (if you don't, then select them both again), we'll be creating the bumps for both at the same time. Now, paste these textures into the editor using the Replace All Layers command. Finally, activate the lower layer by rechecking it in the list.

Note: When you copy and paste textures, all settings, including whether the layer is active or not, gets copied. In that last step, we just copied two inactive textures. Keep this in mind because it can serve as a handy way to undo a change. If you make a copy of a texture you like, add it to the list, and make it inactive, then you can work on the original all you want. You'll then be able to go back to the old settings at any time since they'll be right there in the list.

STEP 72: Since the bottom layer had a Value setting of 0%, it has no effect on the Bump channel, so VIPER will show a completely untextured object again. Raise the Value setting to 100% and you will see a series of random round bumps (Figure 4-61).

If you were to generate a preview of the surface as it is now, it would almost work, but again, we have that shrinking effect we need to get rid of.

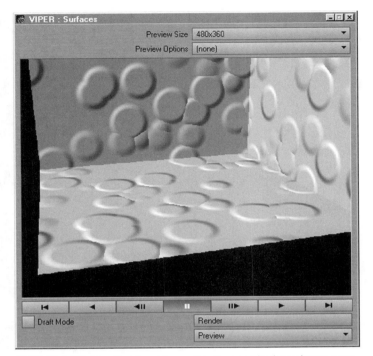

FIGURE 4-61　The first Crust layer, this time applied as a bump map.

Once again, we need to add a second layer to erase the bumps, and this is where things get a bit strange. If we simply activate the second layer as it is, also at 100%, we'll end up with a double set of round bumps. We could set the Texture Value of that second layer to a negative value, so instead of a bump, it creates an impression. However, with the offset we've applied to it, that will create an expanding raised ring, followed by a contracting, impressed one. Figure 4-62 shows this wave reversal.

Note: When applying an image as a bump, using a positive Texture Value and the Subtractive Blending Mode will have the same effect as using a negative value with the Blending Mode set to Additive. This *only* applies to the Bump channel. In other channels, there is a significant difference between inverting a layer and applying it as a subtractive layer!

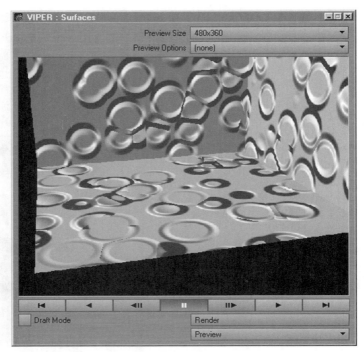

FIGURE 4-62 Inverting the trailing Crust layer causes an unwanted wave reversal, where the ripples contract, but as an impression, rather than a bump. Note the lower raised edge of the bumps on the walls, and the recessed trailing edges.

We need another way to erase that trailing edge. An alpha layer should do the trick. All we need to do is set the second layer to an alpha and away we go. Almost. There is one minor flaw in there, and it's not our logic. Yes, it's a bug!

Normally, we would just apply the alpha to the trailing Crust layer, and set it so the spheres of that layer knock holes in the bottom layer. Unfortunately, this texture suffers from the fact that it *only* works the other way around, where the space around the spheres is what cuts the holes in the layer below. If we try it as is, we'll end up with the exact opposite of what we're trying to get (Figure 4-63).

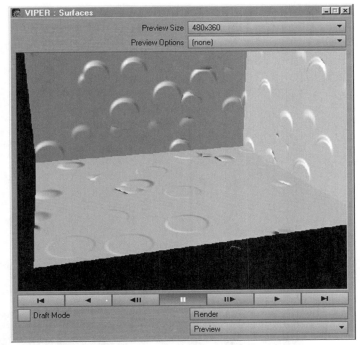

FIGURE 4-63 Setting the second layer to an alpha layer gives us the effect we're after, except it's going the wrong way. The bumps on the walls should look like water drops running down, not up.

Luckily, since it's the exact opposite, it's easy to fix. We just reverse our settings. One way is to simply change the direction the textures are moving. On a flat surface, like our floor, we'll never know which way the texture's moving anyway, since we only see a thin slice of it. However, on any surfaces, like the walls in this scene, that direction will become obvious. So, that means we can't have the trailing layer cutting an alpha on the leading one. But if we swap the layers around . . .

STEP 73: Click the lower layer and drag it up above the upper one, then let go. Now our active layer is the top one. Activate the new lower layer. This will temporarily create a very exaggerated set of bumps in the VIPER preview. Now, select that new top layer, and change its Blending Mode to Alpha. You should now have what appears to be drips running down the walls, rather than up them

(Figure 4-64). We just used the bug to fix itself. Since we couldn't use the actual Dots part of the texture to cut the trailing edge of the first layer, we used the outside area of the leading layer to cut the trailing edge of the second layer.

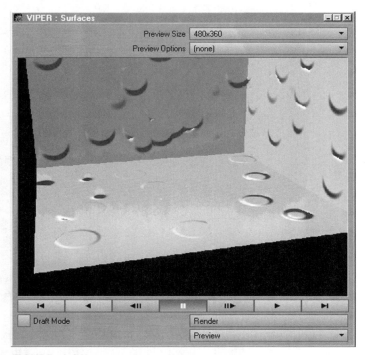

FIGURE 4-64 Reversing the order of the layer solves our little dilemma and our drips are once again going in the right direction.

Note: It's hard to explain, but frequently, when you can't get the effect you're after, swapping layers around like this can usually yield the results you're after. Try playing with the alpha layer on bumps using different procedurals. A good test is to use a base Turbulence texture (since it works quite well for this), and then try the other procedurals as alphas on that. Once you get a feel for what parts of the texture remove the layer below them, you'll be less intimidated by these layers.

You might remember that the Coverage value of this texture has no effect on bumps. It does, however, affect the alpha layer, so increasing or decreasing the Coverage will change how the alpha affects the layer below it. As far as the actual bump-generating layers go, only the two Ledge options have any effect.

You might want to create another preview animation in VIPER to see a much better rain pattern in action.

STEP 74: You'll notice that each bump is flat in the middle, and while this will not normally be noticed in a real animation, it could be detected in any close-up shots. This can actually be fixed very easily, by simply selecting the lower layer, copying it, and then adding it to the top of the list using Add To Layers. Next, either give it a negative Texture Value, or set its Blending Mode to Subtractive. Since this is the same size as the original, it's going to be canceling the first layer out. To use this layer to create a dimple in the center of each bump, reduce the Ledge Level, which works in much the same manner as the Coverage does for the other surface channels. The larger the Ledge Level, the more area the bump will cover. You can leave the Ledge Width as it is, since it's only specifying the extra distance around the dot for the bump to gradually increase its amplitude. The Ledge Width actually gets added to the Ledge Level, increasing the total diameter of the bumps. Figure 4-65 illustrates the two ledge values.

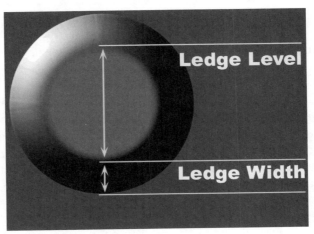

FIGURE 4-65 An illustration showing the areas defined by the two Ledge settings.

STEP 75: All that's needed is to cut the trailing edge of this layer as well, so we don't have any unwanted bump contractions. This is simply another matter of copying the current alpha layer, which is the middle one now, and adding it to the top, so we have one alpha affecting the lowest layer and another identical alpha affecting the upper layer. The final arrangement will go as follows: alpha layer, Subtractive layer (to create the dip in the middle of the bumps), alpha layer, and Additive layer. Figure 4-66 shows the final look of the texture.

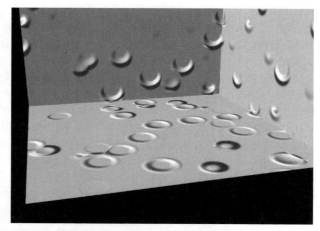

FIGURE 4-66 The final ripple pattern in action.

Note: For best results, the Coverage of the alpha layer should be the same as the Ledge Level of the layer it's affecting.

There's only one thing left to fix on this surface now. The box we've been using is actually 5 meters per side, so these raindrops are quite large. We need to scale these down if we plan on using them in a scene at some point. During a typical rain, raindrops will rarely be closer than a few inches together. In heavier storms, they'll get quite close, but a light shower will have them about a foot apart, or even more. We'll pack ours to simulate a moderate rainstorm.

Note: For the next few steps, it's a good idea to move the camera close to one of the walls and render a frame with the wall filling the frame. This will provide VIPER with new data, so as the next few steps are followed, you'll be better able to make out what's going on. (Or you can just move the frame slider to frame 101, which has the camera in such a position already.)

STEP 76: The first thing we need to do is reduce the texture's scale. Dropping it to 0.1 m (10 cm) will give us a good rain density. Remember to change the scale for all four layers (Figure 4-67).

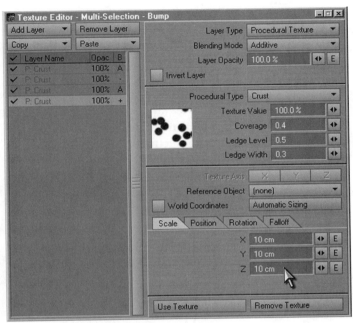

FIGURE 4-67 Remember to change the scale for each layer!

STEP 77: Once that is done, we'll run into another problem. The offset we applied to the two alpha layers is now placing them too far behind the leading layers. Since we scaled the size of the textures to 10%, we'll have to do this to their motions as well. Open the Graph Editor and select all the Y position channels for the Bump texture (one of these will already be highlighted, so just select the other three). Drag these up to the Channel list and then use the Ctrl key to select them all (make sure you select only the Y position channels, just in case there are a couple of strays in the list).

Note: Although there are entries in the Channel list for the four textures for the Floor surface, as well as another four for the Sides surface, you need to select only the remaining three that belong to the surface that the editor already had selected. Since the Texture Editor is working on two surfaces, the second surface will automatically update with the changes we make to the first one.

STEP 78: With all the channels selected, click the top keyframe at frame 0. This would be the graph for the channels that we previously offset. Some text will appear, informing you of that key's value, which should be about 10 cm.

STEP 79: Select all the keys on the graph by using the right mouse button to drag a box around them. Once this is done, click the Stretch button below the graph (third from left) and then place your pointer over the 0 m mark. Then click and drag upward to scale the graphs down until the offset key at frame 0 is approximately $^1/_{10}$ of what it was (approximately 1.3 centimeters should do). This will fix the rest of the texture, bringing the motions back to the same scale as the textures (Figure 4-68).

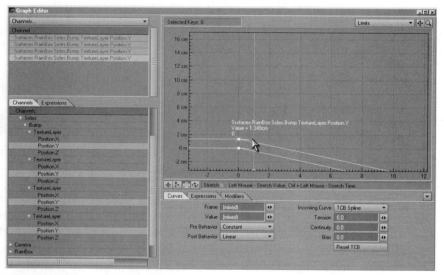

FIGURE 4-68 The Graph Editor showing the four Y position channels we need to select, and their graphs after being stretched with the Stretch tool.

We're done! Save this as a preset by double-clicking either the surface preview or the VIPER window (you might want to save the object as well), and you're ready to load this into your next rainy scene. This is easily accomplished by simply loading this object into the scene, selecting the Bump texture, copying all layers, and then pasting these into the Bump channels of any surfaces you want to have rained on. Just be sure to paste using Add To Layers.

ALPHA BLENDING

Well, we've done a fair amount of texturing so far, and we've started to get into alpha layers a bit. These next two projects will get a little further into alphas to provide some idea of just how powerful they can be. While it's impossible to cover every conceivable use for these layers in any book, we can at least get some basics covered that we can use to further refine our skills later on.

Project: Marble Globe

This project will be a bit quicker and less intensive, but the results are quite nice, especially when you consider that what we're going to create used to take multiple surfaces. In LightWave 6.5, it will require only one.

STEP 80: Load the **BallChex.lws** scene again. Select the Test Ball surface in the Surface Editor, and get VIPER set up again. We're going to use an image to define two separate surface textures on this sphere, and a good example is to make a small globe with different textures for the water and land areas. Figure 4-69 shows the final result we're after.

FIGURE 4-69 The final look of the globe we're after.

Tip: Knowing what the final product is supposed to look like makes creating it in LightWave much easier, which is why you should try to get as much visual reference as you can from a client.

STEP 81: Since we're creating a marble globe here, we should start off by getting that marble look. First, increase the Specularity to 100% and set the Glossiness to around 25–40% to give the ball a polished shine. I mentioned earlier that the Marble procedural is good for almost everything, except marble. It can be done, but other procedurals look better as a marble texture. Let's get started by adding some water to this globe. We'll keep the white base color the ball already has, as this will be seen through the textures we'll apply, keeping things from getting too dark. Later, you can change the base color to anything you want. Open the Texture Editor for the Color channel and select the Procedural Layer Type. We'll use the Turbulence procedural for now, but since we're doing the water section of the globe first, let's give it a blue color.

Turbulence is an excellent texture for creating a marbled surface, as you'll quickly discover. For best results, you'll need to use a Frequencies setting of 5 or higher and a Contrast of at least 25%. The higher the Frequencies, the better, but remember, values over 10 create details so small that they're virtually indistinguishable, and they take much longer to render as well. If the Contrast is too low, there will be very little definition of the texture. A higher contrast will create a sharper transition between the texture color and the underlying color, with 100% contrast creating a solid, hard-edged separation. Values between 25% and 80% work well for creating a marbled look. The Small Power should be between 0.7 and 0.9 for a good, mottled marble look. Anything lower will create a softer, blobby texture, while values higher than 0.9 tend to become too grainy. If you want a really grainy texture, though, try values of 1.0 or higher.

The values I've used for the examples shown are as follows:

Texture Color	20, 20, 200
Frequencies	10
Contrast	50%
Small Power	0.8

Note: Any time you're applying procedurals during these projects, definitely take some time to experiment with the various values to get a feel for them. The instant updating in VIPER will greatly aid you in understanding what each parameter does. I'm frequently asked how I learned my Light-Wave techniques, and my answer is, "Through many hours of experimentation and observation. And innumerable days spent watching it render."

STEP 82: Now that we have a nice blue and white marbled globe (Figure 4-70), it's time to add our land. We'll make the land from the same texture settings, just to make things easy. Copy this current layer and paste it using the Add To Layers command. At the moment, this will appear to simply intensify the blue texture in VIPER. Change the color of this new layer to a deep green. RGB values of 10, 80, and 10 will create a nice dark green.

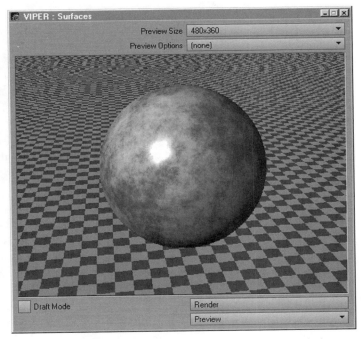

FIGURE 4-70 A blue marbled surface created with Turbulence. Waterworld?

OK, we've just added a land texture, but it's now blended with our water (Figure 4-71). Not exactly what we're after . . . yet. We now need some way to separate these two layers into two defined areas.

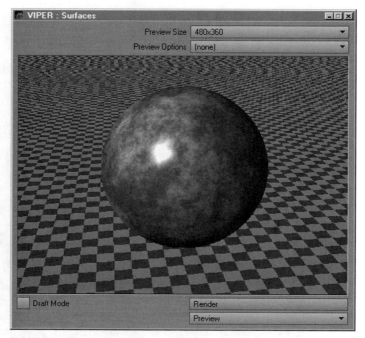

FIGURE 4-71 The blue and green texture layers blended together. Not a bad thing, but not what we're after either. Swampworld?

We could use another procedural to define them, but it's very unlikely we'll find one that looks like an earth map. There is, however, an image on the CD that does. Add a new texture layer and set its Layer Type to Image Map. Since we're going to add an image of a map of the earth, which is a spherical surface, we'll need to change the Projection method to Spherical. Next, we need the actual map, so choose Image > Load Image. Load the **Earth-alpha.iff** image from the CD. This image is a simple black and white image that defines the water and land masses of the earth. Set the Texture Axis to Y and VIPER will show you this image mapped on the ball (Figure 4-72).

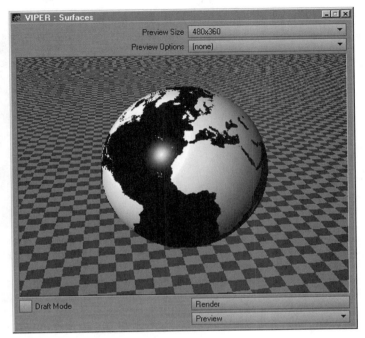

FIGURE 4-72 The two-color earth map applied to the ball.

STEP 83: You'll see in this image that the land areas are white and the black areas are the bodies of water. If we use this as an alpha map, the black areas will cut through the green layer to reveal the blue layer below, so set the Blending Mode to Alpha and watch VIPER.

We're halfway there. The alpha map did what we wanted and cut the holes through the green layer to reveal blue where the water should be. However, we're still getting the blue layer blending with the green in the land areas (Figure 4-73), resulting in flooded lands (must be from all that water we created earlier). We need to also cut out a section of the blue layer to prevent this blending.

STEP 84: Copy this alpha layer, and then deactivate both of the top two layers, so only the blue layer is active. Paste this layer back using Add To Layers. You'll see that suddenly the blue has been affected. Where the water areas would be, we now see only the base color, but the land areas have the blue texture. Click the Invert Layer button to switch this around. Now it's time to reorganize our layers.

FIGURE 4-73 The earth map cuts holes through the green layer as expected, but we still have blue blending with the land areas. Rainy season?

Note: Alpha layers will affect the *first* active layer below them. In this case, we have four layers, with an active alpha at the top, an active texture at the bottom, and two inactive layers between them. Since these are inactive, the top alpha layer ignores them and its effects are applied to the nearest active layer, which is the blue one. If you reactivate the other procedural layer, the alpha will affect that layer instead, resulting in a blended green and blue for the water areas, and blue land.

STEP 85: Drag this active alpha layer down the list so it's second from the bottom (Figure 4-74). We've removed the blue texture from the areas that will be our land, leaving only the white base color. This will let the green layer blend with the same base color that the blue layer does, so we'll have matching patterns, but with different colors.

STEP 86: Remember, alpha layers affect only the first active layer below them, so if we reactivate only the green Turbulence layer, it will actually cover the entire globe again, but blending with the masked blue layer below it. This time the land areas will have only the green texture, but the water areas will be blended. By reactivating the top alpha layer, we'll once again cut holes in that green layer. We now have two distinct textured areas on our globe (Figure 4-75).

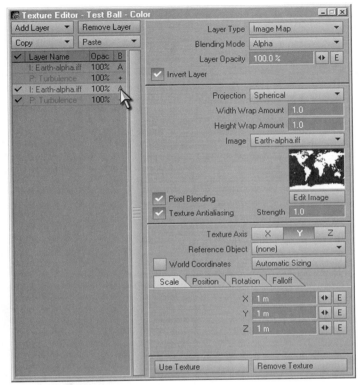

FIGURE 4-74 The new position of the alpha layer we just added.

FIGURE 4-75 The finished color texture for the globe. Previously, layering procedurals like this would require multiple surfaces.

We've seen how we can use a combination of alpha layers to apply different textures to different areas of a surface. Now let's try the same thing on some bumps to make this globe look better.

STEP 87: The first bump we'll add will create an edge along the shorelines, to make the land area look raised. We can use the same earth image we've used as the alpha mask, and since white areas of an image will appear raised when applied as a bump, this will be an easy step. We still have the last alpha layer we copied in memory, so open the Texture Editor for the Bump channel and paste it there, replacing the current layer. Make sure the Blending Mode is set to Additive and we'll have a very thin ledge along the shorelines.

We can increase the Texture Amplitude to make this ledge more prominent (Figure 4-76), but what if we want a gentler slope? Recall from Step 35 that we can use the Texture Antialiasing option to create special texture effects. Here comes one of them.

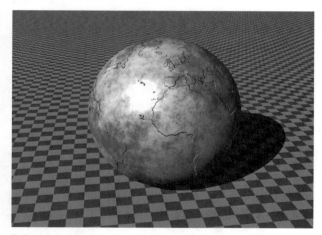

FIGURE 4-76 The same image applied as a bump map creates a thin ledge along all the shorelines.

STEP 88: Increase the Strength of the Texture Antialiasing to 5 or more. You may also want to use a Texture Amplitude of 5 to see the effect easier. Increasing the Strength causes LightWave to force an exaggerated antialiasing procedure on the image for this layer, resulting in the wider slope to the bump (Figure 4-77).

FIGURE 4-77 An exaggerated Texture Antialiasing creates a smoother, wider bump effect.

Note: LightWave uses "MIP Mapping" for its Texture Antialiasing. This basically creates a set of copies of an image in memory, with each copy being scaled to progressively smaller sizes. LightWave then applies one of these images to a surface based on the distance and angle of the surface at any given point. The more distant the surface, the smaller the image LightWave will pick to map on the surface. Rather than trying to use the full-sized image that will end up only being a fraction of the size of the final rendered frame, which can cause a problem known as *chattering* or *moiré,* LightWave will use a smaller image that it has previously scaled internally, much as you would reduce the size of an image in a paint program when you decide to take a large image and place it into a smaller area of another image. LightWave will pick one of the duplicates it created that would best fit the area it's currently rendering. The Strength option can force LightWave to pick these lower-resolution images for closer or more distant surfaces. Higher values will cause LightWave to use more lower-resolution images, while smaller values will force the original image to be used for all but the most distant surfaces. This doesn't actually antialias the image, but it does make it softer—again, just like reducing an image in a paint program. The smaller the image, the less detail it will have, and the more blurred it will look. To see this in better detail, map an image onto a flat polygon, with Pixel Blending turned off. Do several test renders with the Strength set to increasingly higher levels. You'll see that the image gradually becomes more and more pixelated as the strength increases.

Tip: You can use this technique of blurring image maps to "cheat" a beveled edge. Sometimes, rather than actually build an intricate logo or design, you'll want to simply clip map a high-contrast image of it to a polygon. You can then use that same image mapped on the polygon as a bump map, but with a higher Texture Antialiasing strength, to create a fast beveled effect on it (Figure 4-78).

FIGURE 4-78 Exaggerating the Texture Antialiasing on a clip-mapped object is a quick way to simulate a beveled edge. (The grid is another 3D object added for effect.)

STEP 89: Let's add some more bump textures to this globe, starting with the land. We know now that we can apply textures to virtually any area of a surface, without affecting the entire surface, through the use of alpha layers, so we can use the same technique to add some roughness to the land areas on this globe. Add a new layer and make it a procedural layer. We can use pretty much any procedural we like, but we'll stick with Turbulence for now since there are a couple of procedurals in the list we'll be covering in detail later. Enter the following settings to create a simple, rough surface like the one in Figure 4-79.

FIGURE 4-79 A simple rocky look is achieved by applying a Turbulence bump map to the ball.

Texture Value	80%
Frequencies	8
Contrast	0.0%
Small Power	0.5
Scale X	10 cm
Y	10 cm
Z	10 cm

STEP 90: Once the rocky texture has been applied, simply paste the alpha layer we copied earlier to the top of this texture, using the Add To Layers command. This new layer will now remove the Turbulence bumps from the blue areas of the surface (Figure 4-80).

STEP 91: Now for some fun, repeat the process, but this time, we'll apply a Ripples texture to the water areas. Remember, since we want to affect the other half of the surface, the next alpha layer will need to be inverted. Here are some interesting settings for the Ripples texture:

FIGURE 4-80 Applying yet another copy of the alpha layer, this time to the Bump channel, removes the stony bumps from the water areas.

Texture Value	50%
Wave Sources	5
Wavelength	0.02
Wave Speed	0.001
Scale X	30 cm
Y	30 cm
Z	30 cm

Ripples and Ripples 2 are very similar in appearance, and they have the same parameters. The only difference is that Ripples 2 generates waves with sharp crests, while the original Ripples creates smooth waves when used as a bump. Both textures are identical when used in other channels.

Both of these textures actually generate a series of concentric, expanding spheres in their 3D volume. The number of Wave Sources determines how many points these spherical shells will emanate from. These wave sources will always appear within a volume defined by the scale of the texture. If the Scale is set to the default 1 m, then every wave source will be located within a 1-m cube at the texture's center. With Wave Sources set to 1, all the waves will emanate from the very center of the texture. As more wave sources are added, their positions change to keep their spacing relatively even, but they'll always appear within that cubic volume. You have no control where each new wave source will be located within this volume, but you can control their spacing by simply changing the scale of the texture. A larger scale will space them out, while a smaller one will concentrate them toward the center of the texture. Texture scale has no effect on the wavelength or wave speed, both of which are fairly self explanatory.

Note: The Underwater texture is also very similar to the Ripples textures, but the rings it creates *can* be affected by adjusting the texture scale. With more wave sources specified, the rings this texture generates will start to interfere with one another, causing them to warp and twist.

You should now have a surface like the one shown in Figure 4-81. For even more fun, since the Ripples texture has built-in motion, you can render a short animation of this globe. It's not every day you see a marble object rippling like water.

FIGURE 4-81 A Ripples texture, with its own accompanying alpha layer, affects only the water areas, providing us with two separate bump textures on a single surface.

Before we move on, let's cover one more small trick. We can enhance the edge between the two colors on this globe by creating a soft gradient along the shores, reminiscent of those old-style maps. Remember, we can blur an image without resorting to an external image editor by simply adjusting the Texture Antialiasing strength.

STEP 92: Open the Texture Editor for the Diffuse channel. We still have the original earth map texture stored in memory, so we can simply paste that here, then set the Blending Mode to Additive. You'll notice that this has the effect of turning all the water areas black in VIPER (Figure 4-82).

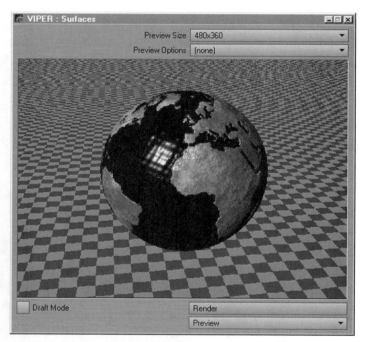

FIGURE 4-82 Adding a copy of the earth image to the Diffuse channel seems to turn the seas to tar.

Note: The water areas did not actually turn black. If we make the surface luminous, or have Color Highlights (on the Advanced tab of the Surface Editor) active, we'll still see the blue/white texture. You can also view the Color channel on its own through VIPER, which will also reveal the blue color, unaffected by any lighting or shading. The Diffuse channel only affects how much diffuse light the surface reflects.

Now add a second copy of that texture to the channel, and leave it as an alpha layer. The surface will appear to revert to what we had before. Let's take a better look at what happened.

STEP 93: Click the Display menu in the lower-left corner of the Surface Editor and choose Diffuse Channel. The small preview above it, as well as VIPER, will now show what appears to be a luminous white ball. What we see now is only the information contained in the Diffuse channel, stripped of any color or lighting influences. You should also see a thin, pencil-like outline of the shores of our earth map (Figure 4-83).

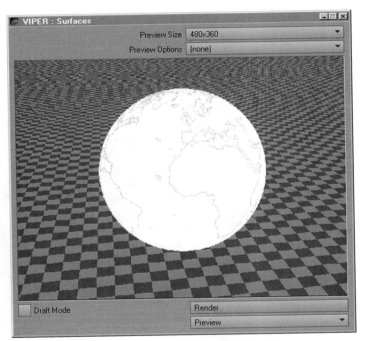

FIGURE 4-83 The ball's Diffuse channel, displayed without any unwanted distractions.

The edges in the **Earth-alpha.iff** images are antialiased, so they have a slight blur to them. When we applied this image to the surface and then added a copy of it as an alpha, the soft edge acted much as the Crust texture did in Figure 4-58, and created a thin outline of the image, looking much like a pencil drawing. You'll also remember that the lines we got with the Crust texture were thicker, because Crust had much softer edges than our image. But, as we've seen when we applied the image as a bump, then raised the Texture Antialiasing strength, the edges became softer.

Note: Texture Antialiasing is partly affected by the output resolution specified in the Camera Properties panel. Low-resolution renders will show more of this exaggerated blurring than high-resolution renders.

STEP 94: Click the lower layer again, and raise the Texture Antialiasing strength to 5 or more. VIPER will update to show a wider line around the shores, with a soft blend toward the land, but with a hard edge bordering on the sea. To better understand what just happened, deactivate the alpha layer and you'll see that the black and white image is quite blurred now. The alpha layer, however, is still sharp, so it still cuts the sea areas out of the lower image. What remains still contains some of this blurring, creating this old-style map effect (Figure 4-84).

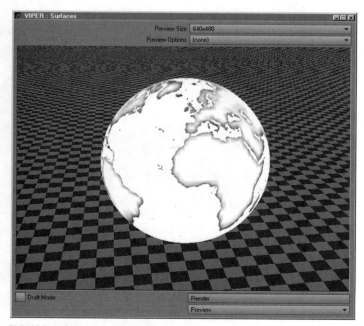

FIGURE 4-84 Blurring the main image and combining it with a crisp alpha layer creates an old-style edging effect.

Now what if we wanted to reverse the direction of this blurring, so our continents are nice and sharp, but the sea has the soft gradient? There are two ways. We could activate Invert Layer for both layers, or we could set the strength for the alpha layer higher and the strength for the main image lower, effectively swapping their strengths.

Note: As mentioned before, inverting a layer and applying it as a subtractive layer are two different things. While they do, in fact, have the same effect in the Bump channel, in other channels they're very different.

So let's get those values swapped so we have a gradient facing the sea (Figure 4-85).

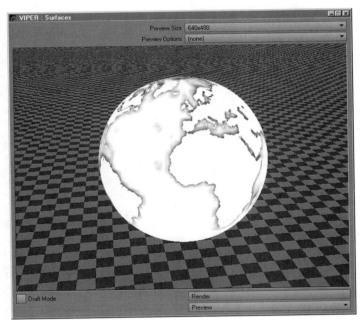

FIGURE 4-85 Swapping the Strength values is one way to reverse the blurring direction.

Note: At higher strength settings (in this case 25 or higher), the blurring becomes more diffused over the surface. As a result, the alpha layer begins having less of an effect on the layer below it, and you see very little of the original image showing through. This is one case where you may prefer to use the Invert Layer command, rather than blur the alpha, which will keep the main image at full intensity. However, in cases where you need to blur the alpha but keep the layer below sharp, you'll need a way to keep the image from fading away. The Texture Opacity value, as mentioned earlier, can be used as an intensity control. Try increasing the lower layer's opacity to 200% or so. This will return the faded image to a much more visible state (Figure 4-86).

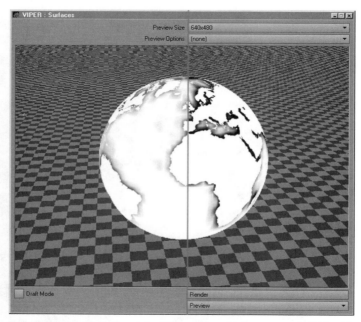

FIGURE 4-86 With the alpha layer set to a higher strength (30 in this image), the lines start to fade (left). When we increase the Layer Opacity of the bottom image to 200%, the lines become darker (right).

STEP 95: Now we have a cool blurring effect, but what do we do with it? Lower the Bump value to 0% in the Surface Editor and we'll see that this serves as a nice edge-enhancement technique. Since the texture is applied to the Diffuse channel, it will darken the shorelines, adding some contrast, which is much needed when no bumps are applied. Figure 4-87 shows a full render of the same surface without bumps.

FIGURE 4-87 The soft edging effect seen on a bumpless globe for clarity, looking somewhat like a drop shadow of the continents.

Note: To quickly turn the bumps on and off without losing the settings used to create them, simply drop the Bump value in the Surface Editor to 0%. This is a global bump control for this surface, allowing you to modify the strength of all the bump layers at once, or even animate them, through the use of the Envelope button and the Graph Editor.

STEP 96: Without bumps, this effect tends to look like a drop shadow effect. Set the Bump value to 100% again, and set the Display mode back to Render Output, or simply render a frame. Now that same drop shadow effect looks more like a weathering or dirt effect along the edges of the bumps. It's shiny dirt at the moment, but that's about to change.

STEP 97: Copy both of these layers using the Copy All Layers command, then open the Texture Editor for the Specularity channel. Paste these layers into that panel using the Replace All Layers command. Since the outline these layers create is dark, when applied as a specularity map, they'll cause highlights in these areas to be diminished. Figure 4-88 shows a globe with this dirtied appearance.

As you can see, several effects are possible using a single image and alpha layers. Adding another alpha layer on top of these, but using a procedural such as Turbulence or Fractal Noise, can further refine this dirt effect. Add this texture to the Reflection channel as well, if you have a reflective surface. Color can also be added to create a rusted or mossy effect if you like, which we'll cover in the next tutorial.

STEP 98: Now that we've gotten used to these alpha layers, try using the techniques from these last few steps to add a glowing effect to the globe, as shown in Figure 4-89. (*Hint:* One of the layers will need to be reversed for this effect.) And as always, experiment with new ideas.

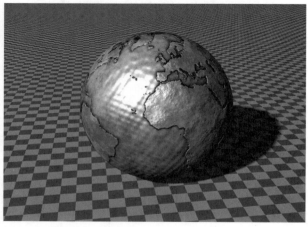

FIGURE 4-88 The soft-edged line, in combination with a bump, creates a nice weathered and worn look to the surface.

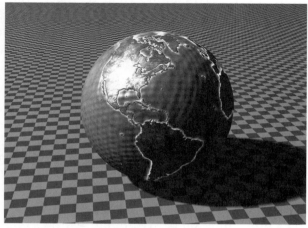

FIGURE 4-89 A backlit or glowing effect is another variation of the technique used to create the dirt look.

Note: Again, a small reminder to frequently save your work is in order (using a new file name!). If you haven't, and everything just vanishes, due to a power failure or a crash, remember to check the **lwhub** folder in your system's Temp folder. A recent version of your object could very well be sitting in there, saving you a bit of time redoing all these steps.

Save surface presets as well. While the surface of this globe might not be all that useful on other objects, other surfaces, such as metals that we'll create later, are. As we'll discover later, many surfaces will start out with very similar settings, so it's a real convenience to not have to recreate these settings. It's much faster to just pull up a preset and then work from there.

Well, that should do for this globe. Now we'll move on to another blending mode we've been neglecting for a while.

TEXTURE DISPLACEMENT

By now you'll have noticed the option at the bottom of the list of blending modes, called Texture Displacement. This mode is quite different from the others in that it does not actually change the value of a surface, but rather moves the values already there. The result is an effect that looks as if the texture has been applied to putty, and then the putty stretched. Usually you'll want to use procedurals for these layers, but images will work as well.

Project: Parking Lot, Part 2

There are several reasons you'll want to use a displacement layer, but most of them are not immediately obvious. Remember the image tiling we did in Steps 40–45, to add the lines to the pavement. We took a small image and tiled it to cover a larger area, which is far easier on memory requirements than using a larger image with each space marked out. However, when was the last time you saw parking lines that were perfectly straight? Sure, our image could have been made with wavy lines, but since we tiled it, that would mean that every space would have the same exact wave to it.

STEP 99: To better understand how displacement layers can be used, let's revisit that parking lot. Load the **ParkingLot.lws** scene again. You should have the surface we set up earlier still applied to the lot. (If not, you can cheat here and use the surface preset on the CD-ROM.)

STEP 100: Move the camera so it's looking down the center of a row of parking spaces (or simply advance to frame 101, which already has the camera positioned in this way), and set a keyframe there. Now open the Surface Editor and get VIPER set up again. Finally, press F9 to render a frame that VIPER will use (Figure 4-90).

FIGURE 4-90 A view down the parking lot, revealing lines that are unnaturally too straight.

Since the parking lot has a large number of procedurals applied, updates will be a bit slow now. You may want to deactivate a few textures by unchecking them in the various texture channels. Make sure you don't remove them!

Since we're also going to be working with the Color channel, you might even want to set the preview display to show the Color channel information only.

STEP 101: Open the Texture Editor for the Color channel, add a new procedural layer, and set the Blending Mode to Texture Displacement. You won't see anything change right away, since this layer will now affect only layers above it. We're going to use it to modify the lines on the pavement, so drag this layer down below the two layers that use the **ParkingLines.iff** image. This will place our displacement layer third from the bottom (Figure 4-91).

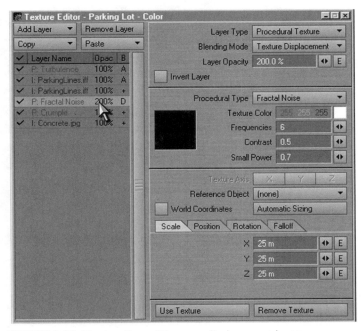

FIGURE 4-91 The location of the new displacement layer.

Note: Unlike alpha layers, which apply their effects directly to the layer below them, displacement layers affect everything that's above them, including alpha layers, which will have no effect on a displacement layer. Because of this nature, displacement layers should be placed carefully, so they don't affect the wrong layers.

You should see some small, but severe, displacement happening to the lines now (Figure 4-92).

We can obviously see the effects of the texture now, but we need to tone it down. The effect we're after is a hand-painted look, as though someone had been trying to get these lines as straight as they could, but wasn't entirely successful.

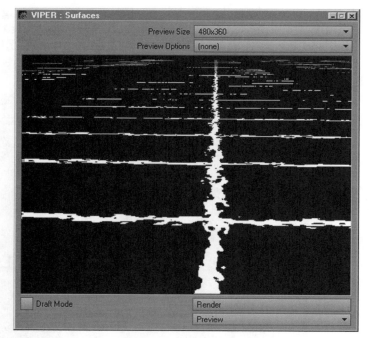

FIGURE 4-92 The default Turbulence texture creates a very watery distortion to the lines.

STEP 102: Change the Procedural Type to Fractal Noise. Right away, you'll notice that the disturbance is much less turbulent than before. We want to create larger waves in these lines, so increase the texture scale to 5 m or so. VIPER will update again, this time showing a more stretched wave in the lines, but not very much deviation.

Note: For displacement layers on the Color channel, the actual color of the texture has no effect. This is not the case for other channels, though! It's generally a good idea to keep the texture value, or color, white for these layers, just to prevent headaches from trying to track down a problem later.

STEP 103: Once again, we'll be using the Layer Opacity as an intensity control. Increase the opacity to 200% and watch VIPER.

Note: Higher opacity values will increase this effect even more, while lower ones will reduce it. However, negative values will not have an inverse effect. In fact, they will have the same effect as a value of 0%.

STEP 104: The lines have larger, random bends to them now, and look a little more natural. However, there's still a bit of a sharpness to the turns, which we can round out a bit more. Increase the Frequencies setting to 6 or higher, and the lines will take on a softer, wavy look (Figure 4-93).

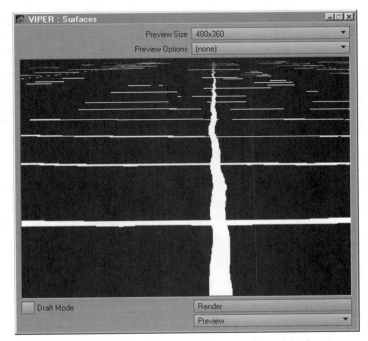

FIGURE 4-93 Fractal Noise set to a larger scale and higher Layer Opacity creates a more gentle randomness to the lines.

Remember, this texture will affect *every* layer above it, so in this channel, it's bending not only the visible lines image, but also the two alpha maps above it.

STEP 105: Play around with a few other procedurals to get the feel for how they work as a displacement. When you have a randomness to the lines that you like, remember to turn on the other texture layers (if you previously deactivated them) and render a frame. Figure 4-94 shows the parking lot with the Fractal Noise displacement we just added.

FIGURE 4-94 The same view down the parking lot, with all the texture layers back in place. Now this is what I'm used to seeing.

This technique is very handy for creating a slight randomness in tiled images, or even repetitive procedural textures, such as brick. It can also be used on moving textures for some liquid effects. And speaking of liquid, let's revisit those raindrops. . . .

Project: Water Drops

You'll recall back in Step 70 that we were going to come back to the raindrops, and add some squiggles to them as they run down a surface. Well, here we are.

STEP 106: Load the **RainTest.lws** scene, which should have that test box surfaced with our rain texture. Once again, get VIPER set up, but this time, advance to frame 101 before pressing F9. This frame provides a close-up view of one of the sides of this box, which is what we'll be working with.

STEP 107: Select the Sides surface in the Surface Editor and then open the Texture Editor for the Bump channel. You should see the four Crust texture layers we created earlier. (If not, now is a good time to either go back and add them, or load the surface preset from the CD-ROM.)

STEP 108: Add a new procedural layer and drag it to the bottom of the layer list. We're going to use the Turbulence procedural since it's conveniently set up for us, though similar results can be achieved with some of the other noise procedurals. We're going to create a displacement that will cause these drops on the walls to move in random directions, and since this procedural is a 3D texture, it will push the spheres of the Crust texture in all directions, as we'll see soon enough. Change the Blending Mode to Texture Displacement and watch VIPER update (Figure 4-95).

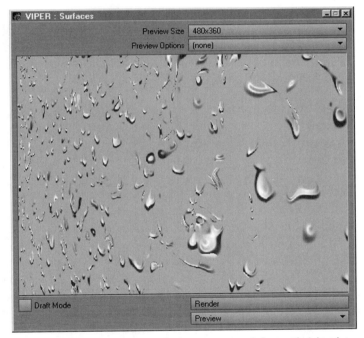

FIGURE 4-95 The default Turbulence texture deforms the droplets too much, causing some of them to break apart.

STEP 109: You'll notice right away that the surface now looks as if it actually has water drops scattered all over it, but they appear to be too deformed. Let's fine-tune that displacement. To see more easily what's going on, let's apply a grid to that wall. Open the Texture Editor for the Diffuse channel, set the Layer Type to Procedural, and then select the Grid texture. Give it a texture size of

0.2 m, so we can see a few more lines from our current vantage point. You may want to make the lines thinner as well. Finally, give this texture a value of 0%, so it creates dark lines on the wall.

Tip: If you apply the grid texture to a flat surface and it appears to become solid, try changing the size or position of the texture slightly. Since this texture is three-dimensional in nature, it's possible for the lines to run along the surface it's applied to. This is particularly true for polygons that are aligned to an axis, and centered on that axis, since this grid texture draws lines going through the center coordinate. Look at the grid on the ball back in Figure 4-9, and imagine if it were sliced in half. A polygon running through the center would fall completely within the volume of one of the grid lines. You may find it useful to use the same guidelines for grid as you would for Marble, and offset the center by half of the scale value, especially when mapping this texture to flat panels.

STEP 110: Switch back to the Bump texture and copy the displacement layer, then deactivate it. Next, add it to the Diffuse texture, dragging it below the grid layer. The grid in VIPER will now become distorted, just as the droplets did.

Note: In LightWave 6.5A, a bug in displacement layers can cause them to affect textures in other channels. This has been fixed in 6.5B. Because of this bug, you may need to create a duplicate surface that is 100% transparent, and apply this rain texture to it. This is easily accomplished by loading the object into Modeler, duplicating it in another layer, smooth-shifting the polygons by a few millimeters, and giving this polygon a new surface name. Even if this bug is fixed in a future update, this layered surfacing technique is actually quite useful, and will be covered in more detail in the next tutorial.

STEP 111: Now we can use this grid to adjust the displacement. Lower the Texture Value to 25% or so, and watch VIPER again. The grid should start to look like it's behind some wet glass, which is the look we're after. Remember, we're looking at this surface close up, so the distortions we're seeing are a bit large. Reduce the texture scale to around 50 cm to tighten it up. Avoid scaling it too small, though, since we don't want the lines of this grid to start to split and break apart. We just want a series of random ripples in them (Figure 4-96).

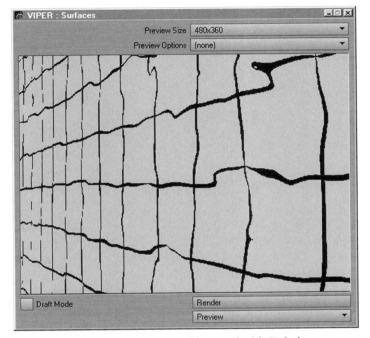

FIGURE 4-96 A watery-looking grid created with Turbulence.

As mentioned earlier, this displacement will affect textures in three dimensions, so you'll notice that the lines of this grid are bent from side to side as well as vertically. Since we're moving a texture down through this displacement, parts of the moving texture will seem to pause and then speed up. This can be tested right now with the grid by applying the same motion to it that the Crust textures have. You can also see these areas in the grid itself. Anywhere one of the horizontal lines dips down indicates an area where the drops will speed up, while a line that swells upward indicates where the texture will slow down. Vertical lines reveal the general path the texture will take as it moves down the Y axis.

STEP 112: Reactivate the displacement layer for the Bump channel. You'll see that some of the drops deform to match the grid lines, as in Figure 4-97. Copy this displacement layer and paste it over the one in the bump channel. Now we can remove that grid reference by holding down the Shift key and clicking the T button for the Diffuse channel.

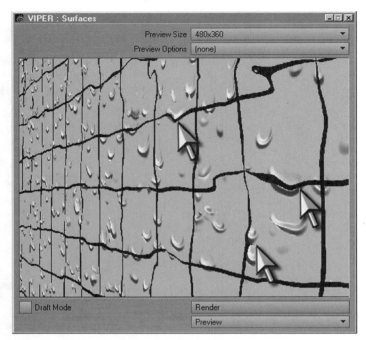

FIGURE 4-97 The Crust bump map applied with the grid reference. Note the shapes of some of the drops, indicated by arrows, conform to the lines of the grid.

STEP 113: Create a preview animation in VIPER to see these drops in action. When the preview plays, you'll see a very wet-looking surface.

You'll also notice that some of the drops seem to vanish for periods of time, while others seem to appear from nowhere. This is because our three-dimensional displacement is pushing parts of the three-dimensional Crust texture through the wall, so spheres that lie just in front or behind it can now occasionally move close enough to it to appear on the surface. This occasional appearance and disappearance is a nice side effect to the technique, which creates the illusion of new drops landing on the surface, and other drops merging together. You'll even notice that the small highlight on the upper side of the bumps resembles the focused light effect, or *caustic,* that would appear inside a water droplet, further

selling the watery effect (Figure 4-98). We don't even need to create actual transparency effects because they've been simulated for
us. And that's exactly what surfacing is about: simulating visual
cues so images will appear to be real.

FIGURE 4-98 A very wet-looking surface.

Well, that was a short project, but an interesting one. Now try
experimenting with this technique on your own. One thing you
might want to try is increasing the size of the Crust texture along
the Y axis, to simulate trails of water. Remember to save presets of
effects you like so you can use them on other surfaces later.

Note: When an image map is used as a displacement layer, the displacement effect is only two-dimensional, as opposed to the three-dimensional
displacement of procedurals. Images will not displace a texture along their
mapping axis—only across it. Figure 4-99 shows a simple grid texture being
displaced by an image mapped on the Y axis. The vertical lines of the grid
are visibly distorted laterally, but the horizontal lines are left flat. There is no
vertical distortion.

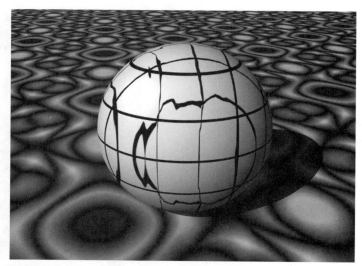

FIGURE 4-99 The effects of an image applied as a displacement layer on a ball. Note that the horizontal lines remain flat. The same image is mapped on the ground for reference.

We'll finish this tutorial with a quick look at a new texture type that would seem useless at first glance, but as we'll see soon, is far from it.

VALUE

Located midway down the procedural list is a very simple texture, simply called Value (Figure 4-100). Even its interface conveys a sense of overwhelming simplicity, with its single texture parameter, simply titled Texture Value or Texture Color, depending on which channel you're editing (Figure 4-101). If you've guessed that all it does is create a solid color or value, you've guessed right. Now the question remains: "Why would anyone need that?"

This texture used on its own isn't very useful. However, when used with another texture layer, an alpha layer, it solves some pretty common problems.

Quite often, animators will need to place text and logos on a surface. Very frequently this artwork is in a black and white for-

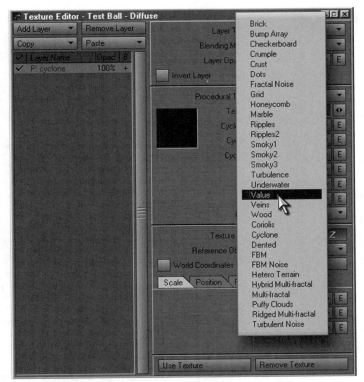

FIGURE 4-100 The Value procedural, nestled between Underwater and Veins.

mat, which is preferred for clip mapping and alpha layers since color images may not create the correct amount of transparency needed. If we need to set up an area of a yellow and blue procedural pattern on a surface that already has another procedural blend, we can now use the Value procedural. The globe in Figure 4-102 is an example. On that globe, a brown base color was applied, with a darker brown wood texture added. Value provided the easiest way to cover the wood textures and provide a clean yellow base, to which was added a green Turbulence noise. When we're finished with the next two projects, try to create a similar effect with your globe.

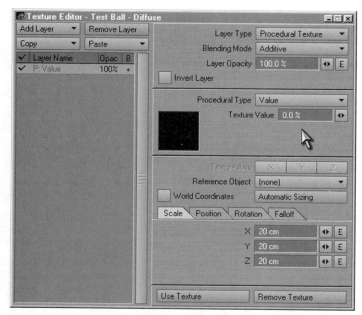

FIGURE 4-101 The true power of the Value texture is concealed behind its single parameter.

FIGURE 4-102 One example showing some of the true potential of the Value texture. Here it was used to create a second base color for the textured green/yellow brass areas on a light brown/dark brown wood texture.

For now, we'll work on a simpler task, which is more representative of the types of uses you'll most likely run into.

Project: Parking Lot, Part 3

No, we're not going to build another parking lot here. We will add some color to the one we already have.

STEP 114: Load the **ParkingLot.lws** scene and once again, get VIPER up and running.

When we first worked on this lot, we used a simple black and white image to paint lines on the pavement. This worked well, especially since we used the same image as an alpha to remove the black parts of the image. But what if we wanted yellow or orange lines on that pavement? We could create a new image of those yellow lines, but remember, every image loaded into Layout eats a certain amount of memory. On small scenes, it's not a big problem, but the more complicated the scene gets, the more memory becomes an issue. We obviously need one copy of the image in order to place the lines, and that one really should be black and white, since it's used as an alpha layer. A color image with yellow lines would not give us the same dynamic range as the black and white version, and the alpha layer would not be as clean.

Previously, we could solve this by simply making a small image, consisting of a single pixel in the color we need. A single pixel would take up almost no memory at all, and in fact, this method has been used quite often over the years. There are only two problems that you can run into with this technique. First, if you need to change the color, you pretty much have to create a new image, which leads us to the second problem—organizing all these single-pixel images that will eventually accumulate.

And this is where we first see the value of Value.

STEP 115: Select the Parking Lot surface in the Surface Editor and open the Texture Editor for the Color channel. Now go through the layer list and select the layer that applies the **ParkingLines.iff** image as an Additive layer. This should be the third layer down, labeled I:ParkingLines.iff followed by a 100% and a plus sign designating it as an additive layer. Change the Layer Type to Procedural and select Value as the Procedural Type. By default, it will have a very light gray color, so you won't see much change in VIPER at this time.

Tip: When working with Color channels on surfaces that have values on the Diffuse channel darkening them, you'll be able to better see what you're doing by switching the preview Display mode to Color Channel. In fact, you'll find surfacing much easier once you get the hang of changing the Display mode to show the channels you're working on. Also, don't forget that you can also temporarily deactivate various textures at any time, so you can restrict the render output to the ones you're adjusting.

STEP 116: Now that we have a Value procedural positioned, change its color to a yellow-orange. RGB values of 210, 150, and 10 will do nicely, but any color will work fine (Figure 4-103).

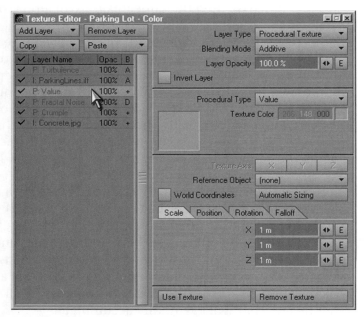

FIGURE 4-103 The location of the Value layer, and a simple orange color applied.

You'll now see that VIPER has updated the lines to the color you specified, and only the lines (Figure 4-104). When we first textured this lot, we used two layers of the ParkingLines image: the first was additive, and the second was applied as an alpha. This alpha layer is still present, and it's now affecting this Value texture, with which we replaced the original lines texture. In fact, a quick glance at the layer list will show that we have two alpha layers above this Value texture, so we still have the weathered appearance on the lines. The only difference is that we can now change their color at will (Figure 4-105).

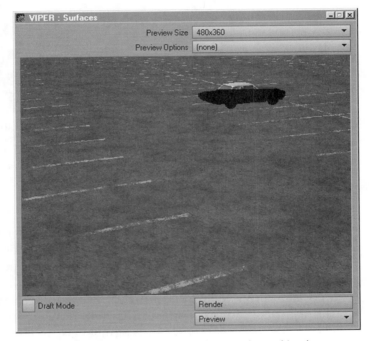

FIGURE 4-104 We now have orange lines in the parking lot.

Value works almost exactly like using a solid-colored image, with one minor exception. Image layers have tiling options, which can be turned off. Value, while it still has Scale and Position values, is actually an infinite texture. In fact, it's the only procedural that is unaffected by its Scale values. Position, Rotation, and Falloff, on the other hand, still work, and as we'll see in this next project, add even more power to the texture.

FIGURE 4-105 A final render of the parking lot. Note that not only do the lines now have an orange color, but they're still weathered-looking and slightly crooked due to the other layers we added in this texture.

Project: Water Attenuation

Anyone familiar with LightWave 5.6 will remember the Natural Shaders plug-in, which included a nice water shader. (If you're familiar with *LightWave Applied 5.6,* you'll remember that the Water Shader was used a couple times there as well.) Now, before you go searching, no, you no longer have it in LightWave 6.5. In fact, the entire Natural Shaders collection has been removed.

This does not mean you can no longer create textured surfaces as before, however. Most of the functionality of those shaders has been duplicated by the new texturing tools of LightWave 6.5. The depth attenuation of the water shader, for example, is easily simulated in the next few steps.

STEP 117: Load the **WaterDepth.lws** scene from the CD. This scene simply contains a single object called **WaterTest.lwo,** consisting of two layers; Water Surface and Lumpy Ground. The surfaces of this object are only "roughed in" at the moment, so don't feel that they shouldn't be modified. The only other special detail about this scene is that SkyTracer has been added (though it's not visible through the camera view), so the water surface will have something to reflect.

Note: When working with water and other transparent or reflective surfaces, the surrounding environment is as important as the actual surface itself. Getting the right look for a reflective surface is extremely difficult without providing something for the surface to reflect. Likewise for transparent surfaces, which really need to have something visible through them.

Before we set up VIPER this time, we need to be aware that we'll be working on the Lumpy Ground layer of this object. A test render will show a rounded, lumpy white surface, partially submerged in water (Figure 4-106). If we supplied this information to VIPER, the water surface layer would appear solid and basically cover the area of the ground that we'll be dealing with.

FIGURE 4-106 A render of the WaterDepth scene, showing a lumpy white landscape surrounded by water.

Note: VIPER displays only the closest polygons to the camera, which means that anything in the scene that's located behind another polygon, even if it's normally visible through a transparent surface, will not be shown in VIPER.

STEP 118: Open the Object Properties panel by clicking the Object button on the bottom menu screen and then pressing P. Select the Water Surface layer, and then click the Rendering tab (Figure 4-107). Raise the Object Dissolve value to 100% so this object will no longer appear in the render.

FIGURE 4-107 The Object Properties panel, showing the Water Surface layer of this object.

Note: When set to a value between 0% and 100%, Object Dissolve basically applies a level of transparency to every polygon on the object. This will cause the object to render in the same way that normal transparent surfaces render, with one difference. While a transparent surface will retain visible reflections and highlights, even at 100% transparency, a dissolved surface will reduce these highlights as well. Also, when an object is 100% dissolved, it's no longer rendered at all, while a 100% transparent surface will still take time to render, because it may still be reflecting or refracting something. On a side note, when you partially dissolve a 100% transparent surface that's tracing refraction, you will end up with a double image of what's visible through the surface: one refracted and one nonrefracted.

Now you can set up VIPER, and you will see the entire lumpy ground surface, which is a consistent white shade. We want to make this surface grow darker as it gets deeper below the water-line. This is where the Value texture comes in handy again.

STEP 119: Open the Texture Editor for the Color channel of the Lumpy Ground surface, and set up a procedural layer with the Value texture. We'll simulate murky greenish-brown water for now, so set the Texture Color to RGB values of 25, 35, and 30. Right away, VIPER will turn the entire surface to a dark, drab green.

STEP 120: Now we need to confine this color to the deepest areas. We can do this by using the Falloff setting. Click the Falloff tab and, since we want the falloff to be vertical, enter a value of 100% for the Y axis. Again, you'll notice that VIPER quickly updates, but rather than a deep green in the depths, we have a bad case of "bathtub ring" (Figure 4-108). While this isn't what we're after, this accident can prove to be quite useful, so let's remember this.

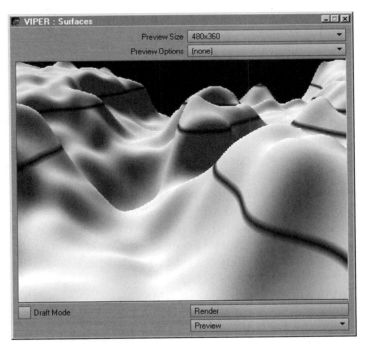

FIGURE 4-108 Not exactly what we wanted, but it could prove useful . . .

STEP 121: We've just caused the opacity of this texture to fall off to a value of 0% over 1 meter along the Y axis. However, this falloff works both ways, above and below the center of the texture on that axis. We just want it to fall off on one side, leaving the other side a solid color. You've probably already noticed the Type menu that's set to Cubic, so click that and select Linear Y.

Unlike the Cubic falloff method that's been around for years, the new Linear falloff settings allow a texture to dissipate in one direction along a single axis. With Value, this results in a nice gradient effect. Since the falloff is applied only toward the positive or negative axis, the solid texture remains on the side opposite the falloff, going on forever in the opposite direction. Once 100% falloff has been reached, the texture is no longer seen in the other direction. As you can see in VIPER, we now have a completely solid green covering the polygons that are below the water level. This green dissolves upward for 1 meter above the water level, until we're left with the original white color. Now we just have to lower this green so it's all below the water level.

Note: For some interesting effects, you can use a displacement layer below a Value layer like this one to distort the area of falloff. This will be handy for adding certain texture effects to a landscape.

STEP 122: Click the Position tab and enter a value of −10 m in the Y field. This will move the center of the texture down 10 m, and VIPER will confirm this (Figure 4-109). This is looking better, but the falloff area is a bit too narrow.

STEP 123: Go back to the Falloff tab and lower the value there (there's only one axis available to edit when using a Linear falloff mode). Since we just lowered the texture by 10 m, we can safely spread the falloff over 10 m without it popping above the waterline. A simple way to figure the correct percentage is to type the expression right into the field. In this case, we want 100% falloff over a span of 10 m, so we can just type *100/10*, which will give us 10% when we press Enter. VIPER should now show a much more gradual effect, like that in Figure 4-110.

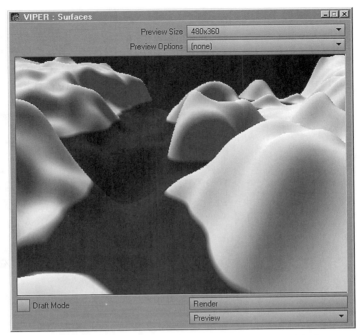

FIGURE 4-109 This is getting better, but the falloff is a bit fast.

FIGURE 4-110 A more gradual falloff creates a more natural effect, looking more like a sediment deposit.

STEP 124: The final step in this project is to activate World Coordinates for this texture, then turn the Object Dissolve off for the Water Surface. Now when you render the scene, you'll see some reflection of the sky in a simple water surface, while everything below the surface turns murky green (Figure 4-111).

FIGURE 4-111 Replacing the Water Surface over the Value texture finishes the effect. The water now seems to get darker as it gets deeper.

Now, what if you want to place other objects in the water? That's not a problem. Remember, we can copy this texture layer and add it to other surfaces. All we need to do is copy it, then paste using the Add To Layers command to put it at the top of any color textures other objects may have. This might seem like a lot of pasting to do, but don't forget, you can edit multiple surfaces at the same time. Simply select all the surfaces of the objects you want to place in the water, and paste this texture into them.

The texture will now make them become dark and greenish as they get deeper into the water. Why? When we activated World Coordinates, we locked this texture to the universe, so it's no longer "stuck" to the polygons it's applied to. If you wanted to move this lumpy ground higher or lower, you could, without worrying about having to reposition the Value textures. As you raise the object, the effects of the texture will seem to lessen, as though you were actually pulling this object out of murky water. With the

World Coordinates activated on this layer, you're free to move objects through the water, and they'll render as if they're actually in a volumetric murk. Figure 4-112 shows a couple of simple objects with this layer added, placed in the water.

FIGURE 4-112 This same Value texture, applied to other objects, will make them appear to fade into the murky depths as well.

While we haven't created any spectacular scenes in this tutorial, we have covered a few good texturing techniques that we can use to improve models and scenes. As always, once you've completed a project, go back and try out your own ideas, using the tricks you've already picked up. Try adding some rain to the parking lot, or this water object we've just been using. But don't throw anything away, because we're going to be using a few of these projects again in the next tutorial.

5

Understanding Textures, Part 2 (Advanced Techniques)

Dave Jerrard

OVERVIEW

In the last tutorial, we learned how procedurals work, and ways we can layer them to both create surfaces and animate surface effects. Now we're going to get into more powerful surfacing techniques.

So far, our surfaces, while looking good, are missing one important attribute. Virtually every physical surface you encounter in day-to-day life has this trait. It's called the *Fresnel effect,* and it causes surfaces to become more or less reflective as your viewing angle changes. If you look over a still pond, even though the water is clear, you won't actually see through it. Instead, you're more likely to see everything on the other side reflected in it. Yet if you stand in it or at its bank and look down, you'll see your reflection, but it will be much less intense, and you'll also be able to see into the water.

In LightWave, we have a couple of methods available to us to duplicate this effect. We'll take a quick look at the older method first.

In this tutorial you will use:

- Image mapping

- Procedural textures

- Gradients

- Graph Editor

- VIPER

- Shader plug-ins

What you will need:

- Texture images included on CD

- Prebuilt objects included on CD

What you will learn:

- Basic to advanced surfacing techniques

- In-depth knowledge of how procedurals and gradients work

- Cross-texture referencing

- Volumetric simulation techniques

- Advanced surface layering methods

- How to use VIPER

FRESNEL

LightWave has a series of shader plug-ins that simulate the Fresnel effect. They include LW_FastFresnel, LW_RealFresnel, LW_ThinFilm, and LW_Interference, and can be found in the Add Shader list on the Shaders tab of the Surface Editor (Figure 5-1). LightWave old-timers will notice that the old Polygon Edge Transparency controls have been replaced by the Edge_Transparency shader, which is another Fresnel effect. The Water Shader mentioned in the previous tutorial also applies a Fresnel effect to the surface, but it's being phased out, and is included with LightWave only as a legacy shader for compatibility with older objects. In fact, there is no interface available for it (or the rest of the Natural Shaders collection) under LightWave 6.5, so we don't have to worry about it.

We'll do a quick and simple project here to get the feel for the Fresnel effect using the LW_FastFresnel shader.

Note: The following projects assume you've already read Tutorial 4.

Project: Fresnel

STEP 1: Load the **BallChex.lws** scene, and get VIPER going. We'll just stick with the default surface on the ball for now, since it'll make the effects of the shader readily apparent. Open the Surface

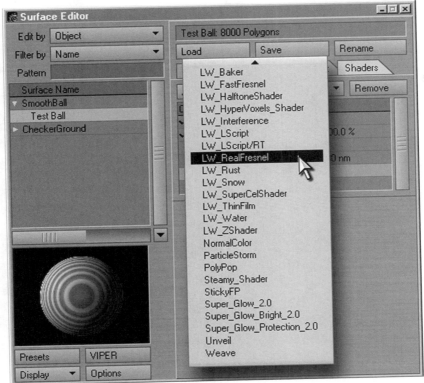

FIGURE 5-1 A portion of the list of LightWave shader plug-ins, showing four different Fresnel-based shaders.

Editor and click the Shaders tab. Click the Add Shader button and select the LW_FastFresnel shader.

If you have VIPER set up correctly, you should see a change in the ball's appearance there (Figure 5-2). If not, you may want to press F9.

Note: Sometimes VIPER refuses to show the effects of LW_FastFresnel, so don't worry. The effects still show up in the smaller surface preview window.

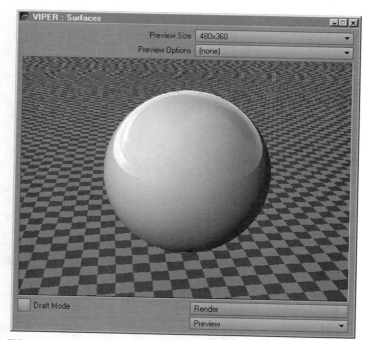

FIGURE 5-2 The ball with the default LW_FastFresnel settings applied.

You will notice that along the edge of the ball, where the surface begins to turn away from us, we can see the sky and ground reflected; but in the center, where the surface is pointed straight at us, we only see the default white color.

STEP 2: Now let's take a look at what this plug-in is really doing. Double-click the LW_FastFresnel entry in the Surface Editor and a small panel will appear (Figure 5-3).

As you can see, this shader can control up to six different texture channels, including the new Translucency channel. The Glancing Angle setting specifies the amount of the effect for that channel this shader will apply to the surface when it's facing 90 degrees away from us. This value blends with whatever values or textures already exist for that channel, and the blending decreases as the surface points more directly at the camera. Thus, in our first exam-

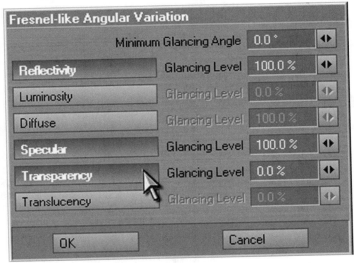

FIGURE 5-3 The Fast Fresnel interface, with its default settings.

ple, we had a ball that had 0% reflectivity applied. When we added this shader, the parts of the surface facing the camera still had zero reflection. But as they turn away, the shader started to add more reflectivity to it, to a maximum of 100%, at which point the polygons were facing as far away from the camera as possible while still being visible.

The Minimum Glancing Angle is just a simple control that specifies how far a polygon has to be turned away from the camera before this effect is applied, and the resulting effect is then spread between this angle and the maximum of 90 degrees. Figure 5-4 illustrates how this setting controls the effect. To better understand the illustration, let's duplicate it in Layout.

STEP 3: Deactivate all the channels in the LW_FastFresnel shader. Activate the Luminosity button and set its value to 100%, which will make our ball 100% luminous along its edge. Click OK to close the panel.

STEP 4: Click the Basic tab and lower the Diffuse value to 0% so the ball will no longer be shaded by the light.

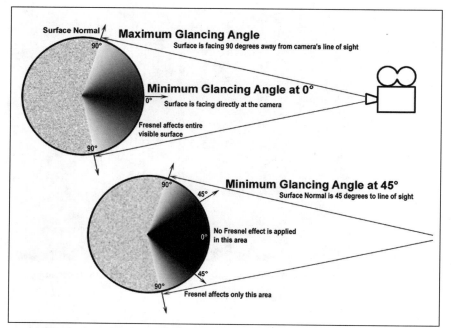

FIGURE 5-4 An illustration of how the Minimum Glancing angle controls the Fresnel effect. Note that the effect is always contained between the minimum and maximum angles. The effect is shown here as a gradient, with black representing 0% and white representing 100%.

Since the base luminosity for our ball is already 0%, we don't need to touch it. VIPER will now show what appears to be a radial gradient going from black in the center to white at the edge, which is quite similar to the illustration.

STEP 5: Now go back to the LW_FastFresnel shader and change the Minimum Glancing Angle to 45 degrees. The dark area in the ball will now appear larger, squeezing the gradient toward the edge—again, as we'd expect from the second part of Figure 5-4. It's easy to see that the higher the Minimum Glancing Angle, the more the effect will be concentrated toward the polygons facing farther away from the camera (Figure 5-5).

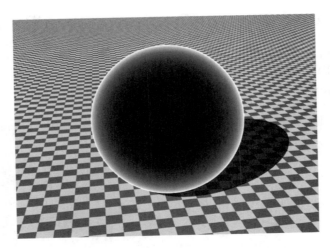

FIGURE 5-5 The Fresnel effect seen in LightWave, showing the same settings from Figure 5-4. At top, the Minimum Glancing Angle is 0 degrees. At bottom, it's 45 degrees.

Play around with various settings, keeping in mind that the value of a channel in the shader only controls the value of the polygons facing away from us, creating a smooth transition to the base value (or texture) of the polygons facing toward us.

It's important to note that the Fresnel effect is based on the angle of the surface normal, an imaginary line extending perpendicular to the plane of a polygon, rather than the actual polygon itself. What's the difference?

STEP 6: Using the luminous ball we just created (if you've changed the surfacing, repeat the last three steps), add a bump map to the ball. Turbulence, Bump Array, or Crumple will work quite well for this example. You will notice that the bumps actually affect the gradient of the Fresnel shader (Figure 5-6).

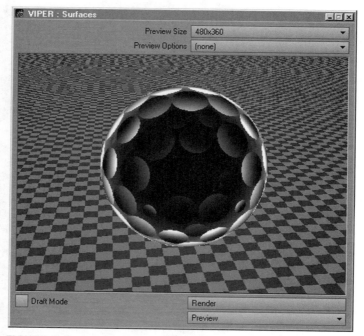

FIGURE 5-6 The effect of a bump map combined with a Fresnel effect.

Fresnel is actually based on the direction of the surface normal at every visible point of the surface. This normal, which would normally just be perpendicular to the polygon it belongs to, can be altered over the entire area of a polygon. When you activate Smoothing, you're actually modifying the normals slightly, causing them to slightly rotate to create the illusion of a smooth, continuous surface. When a bump map is applied, these normals are adjusted again, pointing in various directions, creating the illusion of bumps. Figure 5-7 illustrates how these normals would appear under each situation described, and their effects on a rendered sphere.

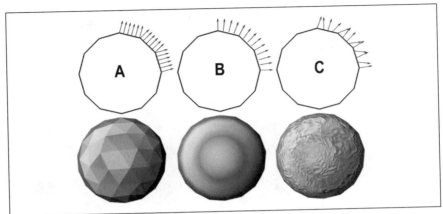

FIGURE 5-7 An illustration showing how surface normals affect the surface. In A, there is no smoothing, so normals for a given polygon are all parallel. With smoothing on in B, the normals are adjusted to blend away corners. In C, a bump map is applied, which perturbs the normals, causing them to point in various directions. The spheres below each diagram show the effects of each. A colored Fresnel shading has been applied to further illustrate the effects.

Note: The colored Fresnel effect in Figure 5-7 was created using the Interference shader, which simply creates a color spectrum between a minimum and maximum angle.

We're not going to get into these shaders too much here, mainly because they're all virtually outdated. In these next few steps you'll understand why.

After seeing the added realism the shader provides in Figure 5-2, when we simply added it to a ball, you might think, "Gee! These are great! I should be using them all the time!" Well, you could, but these shaders do have one small problem. Being a shader, their effects are added last, after textures have already been applied. If you wanted an area of a surface to remain dull while other parts became reflective, well, let's just see the results firsthand.

STEP 7: Reload the **BallChex.lws** scene again, so we're starting with a clean slate here. Select the Test Ball surface and load the Corroded Green preset.

Note: If you haven't added the presets from the CD, click the Load Surface button instead, and select **CorrodedGreen.srf** from the CD. This surface file contains the same settings as the preset.

A render of this surface will reveal a simple shiny green surface, with areas of rough, rustlike patches that have no highlights (Figure 5-8).

FIGURE 5-8 The Corroded Green surface, in all its glory.

STEP 8: Now add the LW_FastFresnel shader and double-click it to open its panel. Deactivate the Transparency channel in the shader, but leave the Specularity and the Reflectivity active. This is where we find the problem with the shader. If you look at the textures applied to the Specularity and Reflectivity, you'll notice that they both apply a Turbulence texture with a 0% value, which normally makes these areas nonreflective, as we saw in Figure 5-8. But now, with the shader applied, these areas become shiny as they face away from us (Figure 5-9). The shader overwrites the textures in the channels it modifies.

Because of this, these Fresnel shaders should really only be used as a quick and dirty solution for those times when you need to slap a surface together fast. The rest of the time, you might find that the next few projects more than fit the bill, and outperform these shaders. In fact, you might never touch these shaders again, since LightWave's newest texturing method, Gradient, virtually makes these shaders obsolete.

FIGURE 5-9 The same corroded surface, but this time with a Fresnel shader added. Note the unwanted reflectivity added over the rusted areas.

GRADIENTS

Gradients are not actually textures themselves, but rather surface modifiers. While it is possible to set the values of surface channels with gradients, it's not a very effective use of them. Gradients are most useful when other factors are involved. Although they're far more powerful, probably the most common use you'll have for Gradients is to re-create the Fresnel effects we've just looked at. To get started, let's revisit that water surface we were working with in the last tutorial.

Project: Water 2

STEP 9: Load the **WaterDepth.lws** scene we used in the last tutorial, and set up VIPER again. Figure 5-10 shows the water surface as it appears now.

STEP 10: Remember that we worked only on the surrounding landscape last time, creating a depth attenuation effect below the water. This time we'll work on the water itself, so select the Water surface in the Surface Editor. Open the Texture Editor for the Reflection channel and set the Layer Type to Gradient.

FIGURE 5-10 The water scene we worked with in Tutorial 4.

You will now be presented with a vertical white bar, with a single yellow arrow across the top of it. This bar represents the value this layer will apply to the channel, based on the input parameter to the right. This will currently be Previous Layer, which we'll get into later. Click that button and select Incidence Angle. The panel will not change much, except now the number at the bottom of the bar simply reads 90 and is dimmed. What this just did was change what this bar represents, which is now a span from 0 degrees at the top to 90 degrees at the bottom, corresponding to the glancing angles we used in the LW_FastFresnel shader. In this case, the angle is the Incidence angle, which is the angle at which our line of sight intersects the surface. This is different from the shader's handling, which used the surface normal. The Maximum Glancing Angle in the shader was 90 degrees, since the normal was pointing 90 degrees away from us, but the Incidence angle with the surface is 0 degrees. Figure 5-11 illustrates the difference between the shader's glancing angle and the gradient's incidence angle.

STEP 11: Click the white bar, about two-thirds of the way down, and another yellow arrow will appear. The Parameter field to the right will change to show the angle this new arrow represents. Click the point of the arrow and drag it up or down until this value reads 60 degrees, or simply type this number into the field.

We've just created a simple gradient, but because the two arrows have the same value, the bar is still a solid white. Lower the Value setting to 25%, and you should have a white to dark-gray gradient like the one in Figure 5-12.

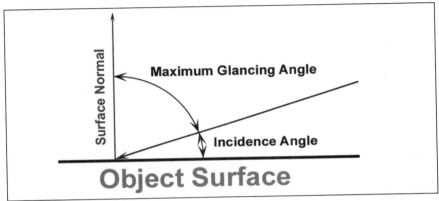

FIGURE 5-11 An illustration showing the difference between the shader's glancing angle and the gradient's incidence angle.

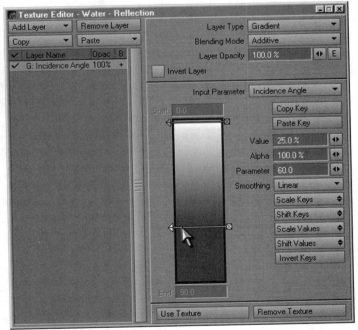

FIGURE 5-12 A very simple gradient setup to apply a Fresnel reflection effect.

This gradient we created controls the reflection of the water surface, making it 100% reflective at extreme glancing angles, while keeping the reflection low when the surface is viewed straight on. We set a "key" on this gradient at 60 degrees in order to force the Fresnel effect further toward the horizon, where water would normally become more reflective.

Note: This value is the equivalent of the default Minimum Reflection Angle used in the old Water Shader.

Generally with water, the surface doesn't start to get more reflective until the incidence angle is less than 60 degrees. However, in LightWave, you can control the look of water all you want with this gradient. Figure 5-13 shows a comparison of this gradient, and one with the second angle set to 30 degrees, applied to the water.

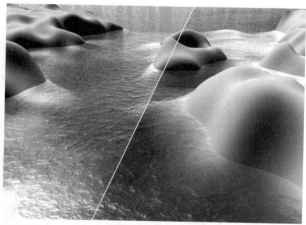

FIGURE 5-13 By modifying the second gradient key from 60 degrees (left) to 30 (right), we can push the higher reflectivity back toward the horizon. Note that in the left half of this image, there is little sky reflected in the water near the bottom of the frame, but toward the top, the reflections are very similar.

Tip: It might be easier to visualize the gradient bar as though it were a strip of land. The top of the bar would be the horizon and the bottom of the bar would be the ground at your feet. When you look down at your feet, you are looking 90 degrees straight down, and as you look further toward the horizon, your incidence angle gradually decreases to 0 degrees at the horizon.

STEP 12: Since Specularity is actually a form of reflection, and thus also affected by the Fresnel effect, it should also have a similar gradient. Open the Texture Editor for the Specularity channel and set another gradient layer there. Once again, set the Input Parameter to Incidence Angle.

There's a little rule of thumb you might find useful here. Specularity should usually be about twice as strong as reflectivity. If you've ever looked into a pool of water and saw the sun reflected in it, you'll probably recall that you could see very little else reflected in the surface. In fact, take a look around you and you'll find a variety of surfaces that are shiny and have specular highlights. But if you look closer at those surfaces, you'll see that they also have varying degrees of reflectivity as well, but much weaker than the specularity.

Keeping this point in mind, create a new key at the bottom of this gradient, at 90 degrees, and set the Value of this key to 50%. This will give the entire surface a minimum 50% specularity that will increase to 100% at the horizon. This will keep the specularity twice as intense as the reflections, up to the point where we have the first key on our reflection gradient. At this point the two values will slowly merge, until they're both 100% at the horizon.

We can optionally control the transparency of the surface as well, by applying another gradient to the Transparency channel. In the real world, when light hits a transparent surface at a low enough incidence angle, it reflects off the surface rather than traveling through it. This tends to happen at higher angles when the light is traveling into a less dense medium, as from water to air. This is what causes air bubbles in water to look silvery, or diamonds to look so brilliant. This is normally called *full internal reflection*, but it's not limited to internal surfaces. Again, using a lake as an example, as you look at the water farther from you, you eventually get to a point where you can no longer see through the water. Our simulation is already pretty much complete, but let's do this optional step.

STEP 13: Create another gradient texture for the Transparency channel. Figure 5-14 shows a sample setup for this gradient. This gradient will cause the water near the horizon, down to a point where the angle of incidence is 5 degrees, to become completely opaque. Then from 5 degrees to 20 degrees, it gradually becomes 100% transparent (Figure 5-15).

FIGURE 5-14 A Transparency gradient set to make the horizon opaque.

FIGURE 5-15 The effect of the Transparency gradient. Note that the water in the distance is now brighter.

Note: This scene file actually contains two keyframes for the light and the camera. The second keyframe is on frame 60, and causes the camera to pan up slightly, and the sun to set. Figure 5-15 is rendered from frame 20 of this scene to get the actual horizon in the frame.

Before we move on to the next project, there is one other thing we can use a gradient for on this surface. Quite often, procedural bumps on surfaces like this water cause a certain amount of flickering or "chatter" in the distance, because the texture is becoming too small in the frame to be accurately rendered (see the tip on antialiasing at the end of this tutorial). Two methods were commonly used to reduce this flickering. One was to add a certain amount of fog to the scene (which is generally a good idea for any outdoor scene, as we'll cover in a later tutorial). The fog would help reduce the contrast in the distance, but some chatter would still remain. The second option was to apply more antialiasing, including motion blur, to help smooth out the grainy look that was causing the flickering. Both of these options worked to a certain degree, but some flickering would usually prevail.

A third option that was used, though less frequently, was to apply a falloff to the bump textures, so their amplitude would decrease gradually over a distance. However, this falloff was linear, and started from the center of the texture itself. This means that for animation where the camera would be moving, it was entirely possible for the camera to actually fly over the area where the bumps were no longer visible. It also meant the texture itself had to be positioned in such a way that its falloff would occur where it was desired.

With a gradient, we finally have the control we want.

STEP 14: Open the Texture Editor for the Bump channel. Notice that there's already a Crumple texture in there, which is a favorite texture for creating waves. We want to fade this texture off in the distance, and we'll use another gradient to do this. Click Add New Layer and select Gradient from the list. Set the Input Parameter to Incidence Angle.

Remember from the last tutorial that we can use any texture to remove parts of a bump map by making it an alpha layer, so let's change this to an alpha. We want only the waves near the horizon to fade out, so let's create our second key near the top of the bar. A key at 15 degrees will do for now, and we can always tweak it later if we're not satisfied. Remember also that the dark areas of an alpha layer punch holes through the layer immediately below the alpha. We want our hole punched on the horizon, so click that top key and set its value to 0%.

Note: No matter how hard you try, you cannot remove that first key at the top of the gradient bar. You can, however, effectively turn it off by setting its alpha value to 0%, but we'll get into that later.

If you press F9 again, you should get a much smoother water surface at the horizon (Figure 5-16). The reason the bumps vanish in this area is that the alpha gradient is making the Crumple texture transparent here. Since there is no texture below the Crumple layer, the base value is seen instead, which is a solid value, making it smooth.

FIGURE 5-16 A gradient alpha layer used to reduce the bump amplitude near the horizon. The advantage of this method is that the bumps will always be visible near the camera, wherever it's placed, and no "bald" spots will appear.

You might want to save the object in this scene again, as well as create a surface preset. These gradient settings for Specularity, Reflection, and Transparency also serve as excellent bases to create other transparent surfaces, such as glass, so feel free to experiment with them.

We've just seen one way these gradients are better than a shader for creating Fresnel effects on a surface. Now we'll see another. Remember that corroded green ball?

Project: Rusted Fresnel

STEP 15: Load the BallChex scene again. Select the TestBall surface and apply the Corroded Green surface to it again, as we did before, and set up VIPER.

Instead of adding the LW_FastFresnel shader, we'll add a gradient. We're just going to make the green areas shiny with the Fresnel effect, as we wanted to earlier, but this time things will work right.

STEP 16: Open the Texture Editor for the Reflection channel and add a new Gradient layer. Set this gradient to Incidence Angle and add a key at the 90-degree point at the bottom of the bar. Give this key a value of 0%.

As this texture stands right now, it suffers from the same problem the shader did—the Fresnel effect coats the entire surface.

STEP 17: Now drag this gradient layer down below the Turbulence layer, and watch VIPER. You will now see the smooth gradient reflectivity on the green surface, but the rusted patches are unaffected and remain dull (Figure 5-17).

FIGURE 5-17 The use of a gradient below the Turbulence texture provides us with a Fresnel effect that is texture-friendly. Note that the rusted areas are not reflective.

Note: Alternatively, the Turbulence layer could be added as an alpha layer over the gradient, with Invert Layer activated. This would remove the gradient and reveal any surface settings below the gradient.

We can further refine this gradient by adding another key at 30 degrees and giving it a value of 25%. This will force the effect toward the edge more, while keeping a smooth transition to the 90-degree point, for a more realistic look. Most surfaces don't exhibit this Fresnel-based reflectivity until the incidence angle is less than 30 degrees, and this gradient is a good approximation of this.

STEP 18: Since we added the Reflection gradient, let's add a matching Specularity gradient. Open the Texture Editor for Specularity and add a new gradient layer to it. Once again, drag this down to the bottom of the texture list, and set its Input Parameter to Incidence Angle. Create a key at 90 degrees and set its Value to 50% (since our Reflection value was 25%). Now, as the light moves behind the ball, its highlight will get brighter, and it will fade as the light moves toward the front. Figure 5-18 shows this scene from a point behind this ball.

FIGURE 5-18 The same ball, when viewed from behind, reveals a brighter highlight and more prominent reflections along the edge.

That's it! We now have a full Fresnel effect added to this ball, which doesn't interfere with the rusted texture that's on it.

As you get used to gradients, you'll find they're a great way to start texturing a surface. We'll create a simple, yet realistic, metal surface, and naturally we'll use gradients to build it.

Project: Ball Bearing

The ball in Figure 5-18 does have a bit of a metallic look to it, especially if we got rid of the middle key on its reflection gradient. But rather than work on this green one any further, let's start fresh and build a better ball. Bearing, that is.

STEP 19: Reload the BallChex scene, so we have a clean surface to start with. Get VIPER started as usual and select the TestBall surface. Metals are actually a dull gray in color, once you get rid of their reflective natures. We'll make our ball a cool gray, so give it RGB values of 245, 250, and 255, which gives us an off-white blue color.

STEP 20: Now we'll apply our first gradient. Open the Texture Editor for the Reflection channel and set up an Incidence Angle gradient layer. Create a key at 90 degrees and give it a Value of 25%. To keep the reflections focused near the edge of the ball, create another key at 30 degrees, and give it a Value of 50%. We'll smooth this key a bit by making it a Spline key. Click the Smoothing button to the right of this key and select Spline from the list. This will cause the grayscale to run smoothly through this key, and you'll notice that the white area pushes up away from it a bit when the mode is selected. We're using the Spline mode here because it creates a more natural-looking effect.

STEP 21: Our second gradient will be on the Specularity channel, and again, we'll keep the specularity approximately double the strength of the Reflection channel. Create an Incidence Angle gradient on the Specularity channel, and create a key at 90 degrees with a Value of 50%. So far, we have what looks more like a very polished cue ball (Figure 5-19). Now we will add the metallic look.

STEP 22: Since metallic surfaces are more reflective than they are diffuse, we'll need to lower the diffuse value. Rather than just lower the base value, we'll use another gradient. Open the Texture Editor for the Diffuse channel and create yet another gradient (don't worry, it's our last one for now). Again, this gradient will be using the Incidence Angle for its Input Parameter. Add a key at 90 degrees again, and set the value to around 20%, which will darken the surface of the ball quite a bit, except around the edge. Now, for the edge, we'll make it less diffuse, since at these angles, the reflections will tend to take over on smooth metals. The ball in VIPER should be starting to look a bit more metallic now (Figure 5-20).

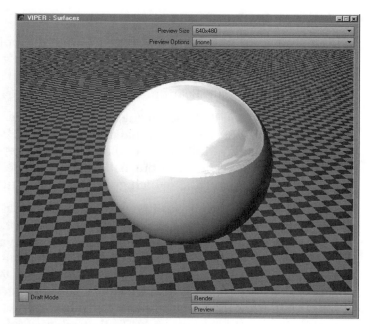

FIGURE 5-19 The first two gradients create a very polished look to the ball.

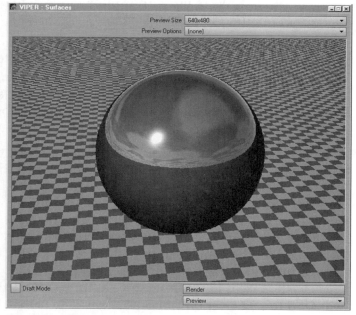

FIGURE 5-20 After adding a Diffuse gradient, the ball is starting to look more metallic.

STEP 23: To add the last missing element for the metallic look, click the Advanced tab in the Surface Editor. In the bottom section is a value called Color Highlights. Bring this up to 50%, which will give us an even blend of the normal light color and the surface color. This feature will actually strip away colors from any reflections or highlights in the surface, based on the surface colors. If we had a red surface, then this would strip away the blue and green elements, leaving us with highlights consisting entirely of red. At 50%, only half of the green and blue would be removed, leaving us with a red-tinted reflection. Metals like gold, brass, and copper all have this trait, which is one of the reasons they're used in so many decorative ways. Our ball is a very light blue, so the effect will be very hard to make out right now, but you should be able to see a slight blue tint to the specular highlight.

This ball is just too perfectly reflective at the moment, so let's add some imperfections to it. If you pick up a shiny metal object, chances are it'll have smudges on it somewhere. These smudges tend to catch the light very well, which gives them a brighter appearance than the metal, especially in darker surroundings. Since they catch the light so well, they must be less glossy than the metal itself. We can simulate this with a texture on the Glossiness channel.

STEP 24: Open the Texture Editor for Glossiness and create a procedural layer. To keep things simple, we'll just use the Turbulence texture—though for this channel, several of the other noisy textures (FBM, Fractal Noise, or any of the hybrids at the bottom of the list) will create similar results. Give this texture a Value of 5%, which, for Glossiness, creates a very wide, diffused highlight. At first, you'll see the highlight in VIPER get a bit wider, but it's too uniform yet. Raise the Frequencies value to 8 or more to add more detail to the texture. To further break it up, increase the Small Power to 0.8 or more, but try to avoid going over 1.0 since that's a little more extreme than we need. Finally, increase the contrast to 50% so the texture stands out more and we can make out those details better.

Note: The specular highlights in VIPER are actually a bit smaller than what you'll see when you actually render the frame. As was mentioned in the last tutorial, VIPER is not a replacement for test renders, but rather an aid. Occasionally you'll still need to do test renders.

Figure 5-21 shows a slightly larger, but messier highlight, as though the surface were scuffed. Without these imperfections, not only does the surface not register as real to our eye, but it also has no sense of presence. A perfectly reflective surface is almost impossible to focus on since our eyes can't tell where the surface actually is. A house of mirrors is a great example of this. If the mirrors and windows are completely free of marks, then we can't rely on our eyes to let us know if we're about to walk into one.

FIGURE 5-21 Adding some noise to the Glossiness really improves the realism of the surface.

Note: Occasionally, VIPER will decide to ignore a gradient placed on a channel after a test render. To reactivate it, temporarily disable the gradient in the channel, re-render, then re-enable the texture. VIPER should snap back to its senses.

STEP 25: We'll add another type of imperfection to the surface now. Again, it's extremely rare to find a ball so perfectly smooth, so we'll ding this one up a bit. Open the Texture Editor for the Bump channel and add a Fractal Noise layer. We want the bumps to be almost imperceptible, so set the Texture Value to around 5%. Raise the Small Power to 1.0 and increase the Frequencies setting a bit. This slight bump texture will give the ball a very slight disturbance across its surface, which will give it the appearance of having a more physical presence (Figure 5-22). These bumps will also enhance the Fresnel reflectance we added earlier.

FIGURE 5-22 A very slight application of fractal bumps.

Note: The Contrast setting in Fractal Noise, when applied as a bump, has no effect.

STEP 26: Finally, we need one last application of noise to break up those clear reflections. This time, we'll bring the Diffuse values up in areas, so we'll see what appears to be more scuff marks, even in areas away from the specular highlight. Add another layer to the Diffuse channel, and make it a procedural layer. We'll use Turbulence again, but let's make the texture a bit smaller by lowering the Scale to 50 cm. Raise the Frequencies setting to around 6 or more, the Contrast to around 50%, and the Small Power to around 0.8. Finally, lower the Texture Value to 25%.

This texture, since it's applied on top of a gradient, will simply apply a uniform 25% texture over the entire surface. However, since our base gradient has a value of 25% at a 90-degree incidence angle, this procedural will be virtually invisible at this angle. But as the surface turns away from us and the gradient makes the diffuse level drop, the texture will become more obvious.

Scratches, dust, and other marks on metal are often more visible at these sharper angles, and this texture will help simulate them (Figure 5-23). These marks we just added will not be immediately obvious in a still image, but as soon as motion is applied, they'll define exactly where the surface of this sphere is.

FIGURE 5-23. A slight Diffuse texture helps define the rest of the reflective surface.

Well, we now have a fairly realistic-looking ball bearing. Still too clean for my tastes, so let's age this thing. We'll add a bit of rust to it, so the first thing we need to do is add some rust color.

STEP 27: Open the Texture Editor for Color and change the Layer Type to Procedural. We'll use the Turbulence texture again, mainly because it has a very nice contrast control we can use to create a hard edge between the texture and the underlying layers. Raise the Frequencies setting to 8 or more, and increase the Small Power to 0.8 to break the texture up even more. Next, increase the Contrast to 90%, which will create a hard edge around the texture. Finally, we need to give this a rust color. Try RGB values of 80, 60, and 30, which creates a set of dark, reddish-brown blotches.

You'll notice that the reflections and highlights still cover this rust area, and are actually colored by it also. We're going to need to mask these reflections so they don't occur in this rusted area.

STEP 28: Copy this texture, since we'll be using similar settings on a few other channels. The first channel we'll add it to is the Diffuse, so open the Diffuse textures and paste this one in, using the Add To Layers command. This layer will be used to raise the Diffuse value for this rusted area so it will be illuminated by lights better. Increase the Texture Value to 100% and raise the Contrast to 95%. This will tighten the edges more, so we don't inadvertently cause the metallic area outside the rust to lighten as well. Figure 5-24 shows a full render of the sphere at this point. The rust areas still have reflections over them, so let's get rid of those next.

FIGURE 5-24 A matching Color and Diffuse texture adds the first signs of rust to our ball.

STEP 29: Copy this layer again and paste it into the Reflection channel, again using the Add To Layers command. We'll keep all the settings the same here, except the Texture Value. Since we don't want any reflection in this area, set this value to 0%. Since we also don't want any specular highlights in this area, copy this texture again, and paste it into the Specularity channel the same way. This just applied the same texture settings to both Specularity and Reflection. A new render will show a much more intense rust look (Figure 5-25). All that's left is to make this smooth rust bumpy.

FIGURE 5-25 Another pair of matching textures applied to Specularity and Reflection.

STEP 30: Paste this same texture into the Bump channel, adding it on top of the fractal bumps we placed there earlier. Increase the Texture Value to 100% so this layer actually applies some bumps (it was 0% when we last copied it from the Reflection channel). Also, increase the Contrast to 100% so the texture has an extremely hard edge. Most other procedurals will apply bumps over the entire surface, requiring an additional alpha layer to isolate a few areas so they'll remain flat. Turbulence with a 100% contrast would provide an excellent alpha layer for this, but in this case we don't even need one. Because of this extreme edge the Contrast creates, only the area of the texture that originally applied the rust coloring actually exhibits bumps. The surrounding area remains bump-free, just the way we want. However, if we wanted to smooth those bumps out by reducing the contrast, we'd need to add that alpha layer to keep the sharp separation. One more render will show us the finished rusted ball bearing.

Note: We can have the rust appear raised, as if it's about to flake off, or pitted, as though some of the metal has eroded away. A negative Texture Value for the Bump channel will push the bumps into the surface, creating the pitted look (Figure 5-26).

FIGURE 5-26 Two rusted looks. A bump value of 100% at left and −100% at right.

If you want, you can change the base color of this sphere to simulate gold, brass, or whatever metal you like. And for a small challenge, use the methods in this project to create an oxidized copper ball (Figure 5-27). (*Hint:* It's really little more than a couple of color changes.)

Now, for a small change, let's take a look at a few special effects that you can create with a gradient based on Incidence Angle.

FIGURE 5-27 With a couple of simple color variations, an oxidized copper ball is quickly created with the same techniques.

Project: X-Ray

So far we've seen how we can use a gradient to control reflections and bumps. With a little imagination and some playing around, we can create other effects. One of these is an X-ray effect.

STEP 31: Clear the scene and load the **FootBones.lwo** object. Position and rotate it so we see it from the side, as in Figure 5-28.

Note: This is the same object that appears on your LightWave installation CD.

STEP 32: Open the Surface Editor and set up VIPER again. Next, give this object a faded gray-green color. X-ray film is actually monochrome, but a little color here won't hurt. Finally, select the Double Sided check box, which will allow us to see all the polygons in this object when Transparency is applied.

Now that we have the base color set up, let's create that X-ray effect. X-rays are actually negative images on film, where the black area has been fully exposed to X-rays, but white areas have not. Bones and other bits of anatomy have blocked the X-rays to some extent, and the image you see on film is actually a recording of their X-ray shadow. Different tissues of the body block different amounts of X-rays, with bones blocking them the most. X-rays still pass through them, but not as well, which gives these photographs

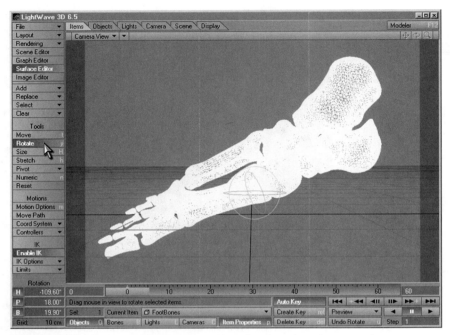

FIGURE 5-28 The FootBones object positioned and ready to be X-rayed.

their distinctive look. More rays will pass through thin bones than through thick ones, and you can in fact see bones through other bones. Where the bones overlap in the image, they block even more rays, creating a lighter, less exposed area on the film. In effect, the lightness on the film adds up as the bones overlap.

STEP 33: We can simulate the additive effect in LightWave by clicking the Advanced tab and increasing the Additive Transparency. Set this to 50%, which will give us the effect, but without getting too blown out.

Note: Since we're working with an additive transparency, VIPER will tell us very little about its effects on the final render. We're going to have to do things the old-fashioned way again here, and press F9 a few times.

STEP 34: We don't want this object to be affected by any lighting since that would ruin the effect, so lower the Diffuse value to 0% and raise the Luminosity to 100%. This will now give us a very flat-looking white silhouette image of the bones in a render, but the VIPER preview will still show them as green. This white coloring is caused by the fact that both the front-facing and rear-facing polygons are rendering, and their colors are being added together due to the Additive Transparency. Now let's tone that down a bit.

STEP 35: We'll start by making the edges of these bones more transparent, to simulate the fact that there's less bone for X-rays to pass through there than through the centers. Open the Texture Editor for the Transparency Channel and create a Gradient layer. Set it to Incidence Angle and create a key at 90 degrees. Next, lower the Value of this key to 25%, so this entire surface is at least 25% transparent. This will reduce the effect of the Additive Transparency, especially at the edges, where the normal transparency will be 100%. VIPER will immediately show what appears to be a simple shaded view of the foot (Figure 5-29). However, if you do a test render now, you'll see something that looks much more like an X-ray (Figure 5-30).

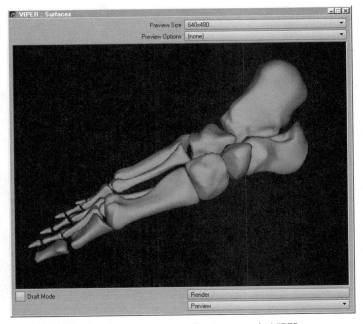

FIGURE 5-29 The Transparency gradient as seen in VIPER.

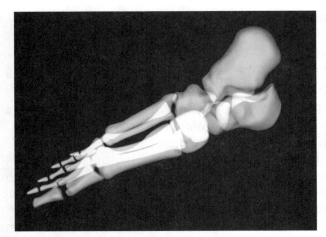

FIGURE 5-30 The same surface as it appears when actually rendered. The additive effects are visible here, creating the whiter areas where the bones overlap.

STEP 36: Now we'll fine-tune this effect. Create another key at 60 degrees and give it a Value of 75% with Smoothing set to Spline. This will force more transparency over a greater area, and will help bring out more detail in the object (Figure 5-31).

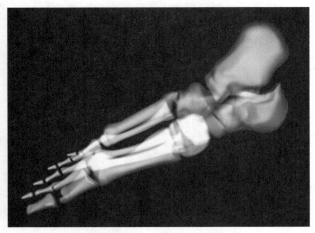

FIGURE 5-31 An additional key to force more transparency toward the edges to help reveal more detail.

STEP 37: Optionally, we can finish this effect off by adding a bit of grain to it. An easy way to do this is to add a small procedural bumpiness to the bones, so open the Texture Editor for the Bump channel, and select a procedural layer. Again, we'll use Turbulence here, but most of the noise procedurals will create similar effects. To keep the bumps small, lower the texture Scale to 10 cm. Next, increase the Frequencies setting to 8, Small Power to 0.8, and Contrast to 25%. Finally, give this texture a Value of 50%. This will create a small, uniform coating of grainy bumps to the entire surface. Since bumps do affect gradients, they'll show up in a render, even without any light (Figure 5-32).

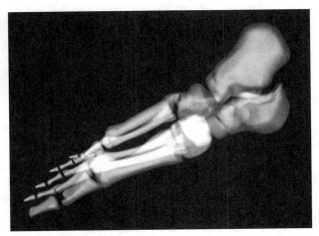

FIGURE 5-32 A small bump map adds a graininess to the image.

That was another quick effect to create. Now let's move on to another one. We've used LightWave to see with X-ray vision, so how about thermal vision?

Project: Thermal Vision

In this project, we'll create an effect similar to the false-color, alien point of view that was used so much in the two *Predator* movies. And just to keep the mood, we'll use a spooky critter as our test subject.

STEP 38: Clear the scene in Layout and load **LizardMonster.lwo** from the CD. Position the camera so you have an interesting view of him, then get VIPER running again (Figure 5-33).

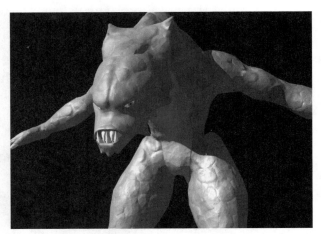

FIGURE 5-33 Back away slowly.

Note: **LizardMonster.lwo** is also included on the LightWave installation CD.

STEP 39: Notice that this character has six different surfaces on him. Since we want to apply this thermal vision effect to all of them, we could just work on one, then copy it to all the other surfaces, but in this case, we'll just work on all six surfaces at once. Click the top surface, then hold down the Shift key and click the last surface to select all six (Figure 5-34).

STEP 40: The first thing we need to do is get rid of the textures that are already on this guy, so again, holding down the Shift key, click each of the T buttons to deactivate them, except for the Bump channel. We'll leave the bumps for now. You'll also want to clear the Double Sided check box and drop the Specularity value to 0% while we're at it. Now, let's get this effect under way.

STEP 41: Since we're going to simulate the effect of seeing heat radiating off this creature, we don't need any external light shading it, so drop the Diffuse value to 0%. Raise the Luminosity to 100%, which will make the creature appear to glow.

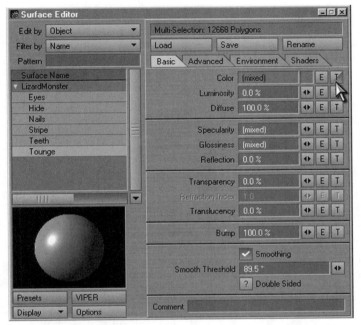

FIGURE 5-34 Deactivating all the Texture channels. With multiple surfaces selected, a diagonal will appear on the T button if any of the surfaces has a texture on that channel.

STEP 42: Open the Texture Editor for the Color channel and create a Gradient layer using the Incidence Angle. This should temporarily turn our beast into a flat white silhouette.

We'll design our effect so that "warm" areas will be red, and will cycle through yellow, green, and finally to blue for the "cooler" areas.

STEP 43: Our cool areas will actually be the areas where the incidence angle is near 0 degrees, so give the key at the top of this bar a deep blue color (0, 0, 120). VIPER will now have a solid blue image of the creature. Now add a key at 90 degrees and make this bright red. Suddenly detail will reappear in VIPER, where we have a vibrant red and blue duotone image of the lizard.

STEP 44: You can probably see how the rest of this project will go now. Let's add a few more colors. To speed things up, just create four new keys. 75, 60, 45, and 30 degrees will do just fine and give us a series of evenly spaced keys. Now set the colors as follows:

Key	RGB Color
30	0, 0, 255
45	0, 255, 255
60	0, 255, 0
75	255, 255, 0
90	255, 0, 0

This will give us a smooth spectrum going from red at the bottom to yellow, green, cyan, and finally blue (Figure 5-35). Our creature, on the other hand, now looks more as if he's been caught on a thermal imaging camera. Figure 5-36 shows our creature in thermal vision. (Bonus points if you know where the quote comes from.)

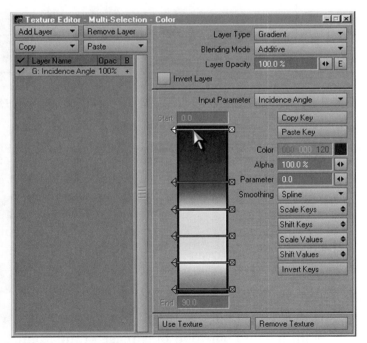

FIGURE 5-35 A series of six keys on the gradient creates a smooth color spectrum.

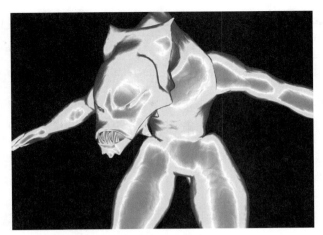

FIGURE 5-36 "The snake does not like what it sees."

Now you can adjust the bump level in the Surface Editor to adjust the intensity of the bumps to your liking, since their current level may seem a bit too harsh. Feel free to slide the keys around and try other colors (even try inverting the layer and inverting the keys for more fun).

Now let's move on to the next simple project, which also has something to do with heat.

Project: Heat Exhaust

In this project, we'll simulate an effect you see quite often. Whenever two volumes of air of different temperatures combine, we get a shimmering effect, where light is bent, causing a rippling effect in the air. Exhaust spewing from the business end of a jet engine is a perfect example of this.

Unfortunately, in LightWave, when we apply refraction to a transparent surface, it always looks like glass because we can never get rid of that hard edge, which we'll see shortly. There were a couple of third-party plug-ins that could do this, but now we can do it right out of the box.

STEP 45: Load the BallChex scene again and set up VIPER.

STEP 46: The first thing we need to do is make this ball transparent, so increase the Transparency to 100%. Next, to have this ball actually start to refract, increase the Refraction Index to something higher than 1. For convenience, we'll simply use a value of 2.

Note: For the rest of this project, you should change the background of the preview to a checkerboard. Click the Options button below the surface preview, and then click Checkerboard in the panel that opens. This checkerboard will appear behind the surface ball, allowing you to see how transparent it is. The pattern will also appear on reflections on this sample sphere, if reflections are active for the surface. In addition, a larger version of the checkerboard will also appear in VIPER, being visible through transparent surfaces as well as reflected on reflective surfaces. If a surface has refraction applied, the checkerboard will appear refracted in the preview, so it's a great way to set refractive surfaces.

As soon as we added refraction, our otherwise invisible ball suddenly reappeared, distorting the ground behind it (Figure 5-37). Now our task is to get rid of the hard edge between the ball and the background.

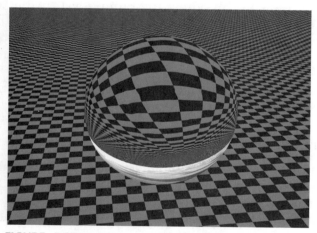

FIGURE 5-37 A 100% transparent ball, with refraction applied, suddenly becomes visible again.

STEP 47: We'll create a gradient to control the amount of refraction, since we already know that the ball is completely invisible when the Refraction Index is 1. Create a Gradient layer and create a key at 90 degrees. While you're doing this, pay close attention to the small surface preview.

STEP 48: With both keys set to 100%, the sphere in the preview is completely invisible against the checkerboard. However, watch what happens when you set the value of the second key to something other than 100%. Even the slightest deviation creates a visible edge. Values higher than 100% will also cause the checkerboard to appear to be sucked into a smaller area while values lower than 100% make it bulge and expand.

Now set this second key to 200% and do a test render. Watch the render preview as the frame renders, and pay attention to the order in which things are rendered.

Figure 5-38 shows how this gradient affects the refraction. You notice that the very center of this ball has the same effect as it did in Figure 5-37, but the refraction changes toward the edge of the ball. This is because the 200% value we gave the gradient is identical to just giving the ball a Refraction Index of 2. Basically, on a gradient, we simply multiply the Refraction Index we want to apply by 100, and we have the value we need to put on the gradient for the same results. Try it! Pick a number and apply it to the Refraction Index, and disable the gradient. Then apply this same number, times 100, to the gradient (be sure to do it for both keys, or get rid of the second one), and then reactivate the layer. The effect in both the preview and VIPER will be identical.

FIGURE 5-38 Refraction controlled by a gradient.

Note: This is different from how it used to work in LightWave 6.0! Previously, the Gradient would modify the base Refraction Index, and changing this value would have drastic effects on the results. Now, the gradient completely overrides the base value, making our lives much easier.

Now drop the base Refraction Index back down to 1.0 and do another render, again, paying close attention to how LightWave renders the frame. You will probably notice that the first time, when the RI (Refraction Index) was 2, the ball rendered before the background. However, when we dropped it back to 1, even though the gradient was still applying refraction to the surface, it rendered after the background. It also took longer. You might think this is a little timesaving tip. When using a refractive surface, make sure the base RI is not 1.0, and the surface will render along with the nontransparent polygons, rather than over the top of previously rendered stuff. This method can save time, but it does have its problems, which we'll see soon.

STEP 49: Now that we understand how the numbers in the refraction gradient work, let's get rid of that hard edge. In Figure 5-38, we actually already have eliminated it, but it's right on the edge of the sphere. We need to pull it in a bit. Add another key to the middle of the gradient, and give it a Value of 100% as well, so our first two keys are 100% and the last one is 200%. The sphere in the small preview will seem to shrink a bit, but the one in VIPER will seem to have a flat ring around it where the checkerboard is unaffected (Figure 5-39). However, a render will show something else (Figure 5-40).

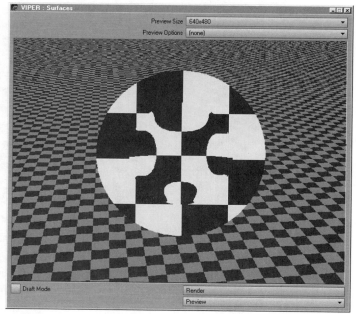

FIGURE 5-39 A three-key gradient's effect on the VIPER preview.

FIGURE 5-40 The same three-key gradient as it affects a render. Enter the BROD!

Luckily, we have a few ways to get around this big black ring. First, it occurs only when we have the base RI set to anything other than 1.0, so you can see why that apparent timesaving tip isn't always a good one. Second, it occurs only when we have more than two keys on a gradient and the first two are both 100%. Third, it occurs only if the second key has Linear or Step Smoothing.

If all three of these conditions are met, we'll get this big ugly Black Ring Of Death (BROD). It's pretty obvious now that the BROD is easy to avoid.

STEP 50: Select the second key and set its Smoothing mode to Spline. This way, we can still use the time savings of the rendering order we discovered, and avoid the BROD. There is another benefit to using the Spline mode as well, which we'll see after pressing F9. Also, to make the refraction less severe, lower the value of the bottom key to 120%, then press F9.

Figure 5-41 shows the effect we were after. You'll notice that the checkerboard ground has a smooth curve to it as it enlarges in the middle, rather than a harder edge as we would have had. The actual edge of the sphere applies no refraction at all, and thus it blends in perfectly with the background. As the surface curves toward us, the amount of refraction slowly increases, leaving us with an effect that looks as if we simply warped an image of the ground in some paint program.

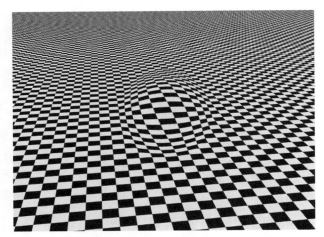

FIGURE 5-41 The effect we were after, without the BROD gracing our presence. Note that the actual edge of the sphere is completely invisible against the background.

STEP 51: Now that we have the gradient working, let's set up a good hot gaseous effect. Add another key at 75 degrees and give it a Value of 105%. Move the second key to 60 degrees, and finally lower the bottom key's Value to 110%, which is the equivalent of a 1.1 RI. A render of this will reveal a very slight bulge in the image.

Now it's time to add some disturbance to this texture, to simulate the turbulence in the air that causes the rippling effect we're used to.

STEP 52: Open the Texture Editor for the Bump channel and create a procedural layer. Select one of the noisy textures, such as Fractal Noise or Smoky, and adjust it to create some random distortions in the surface. For the figures here, Fractal Noise was used, with the Frequencies value set to 8 and both Contrast and Small Power set to 0.9. The scale was set to 10 cm.

Simply by adding this bump map, we've revealed the edge of the sphere again. Bumps affect incidence angles, so now that we have bumps in the area that previously had no RI applied, we also have refraction happening again (Figure 5-42).

We've done it before with the water, so we can do it again. We'll add another gradient layer, this time as an alpha, to reduce the bumps near the edge of the sphere.

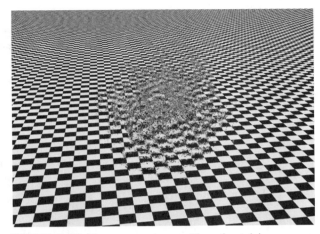

FIGURE 5-42 The same sphere with a fractal bump map applied.

Note: At this point you may find it helpful to switch the preview display mode to Diffuse Reflection, which will show a solid grayscale version of the sphere without transparency. This mode will show the bumps as they would appear if the ball were not transparent, making them much easier to work with (Figure 5-43).

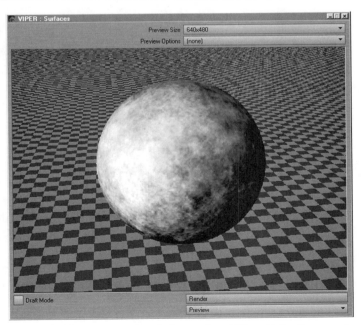

FIGURE 5-43 Changing the Display mode to Diffuse Reflection reveals the bumps as they would appear on an opaque surface in VIPER.

STEP 53: Add a new Gradient layer, once again set to Incidence Angle, and set a key at 45 degrees and 90 degrees. Next, set the Values of the top two keys to 0%, making them black. Black in alpha layers punches holes in the layer below. Finally set the Blending Mode to Alpha (Figure 5-44). Figure 5-45 shows the ball with the alpha gradient applied. Note that a few smaller bumps that were near the edge are now flattened.

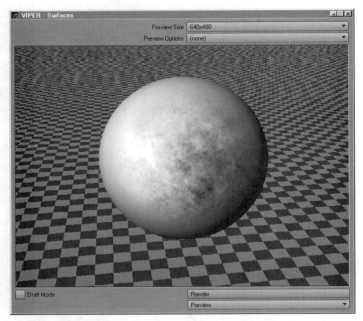

FIGURE 5-44 The addition of a gradient alpha layer removes bumps from the surface near the edge of the sphere.

You're probably wondering why this works. Why would a gradient that's based on Incidence Angle affect bumps, which in turn affect the Incidence Angle the gradient is using? Wouldn't the gradient affect only the back sides of these bumps? The answer is in the way LightWave works with layers. LightWave calculates alpha layers before the layer they're applied to. This means it figures out the area the gradient will affect, before it calculates how the bumps will affect that area. In effect, the bumps in that area never had a chance to do anything before the alpha layer squashed them.

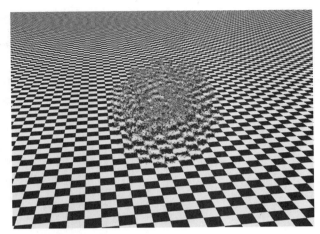

FIGURE 5-45 A render of the sphere now that we've got the bumps under control.

STEP 54: We can finish off this effect by making the center of the ball a little less transparent. Normally, exhaust is dark, so give this ball a dark gray-black color. Next, open the Texture Editor for the Transparency channel and create yet another gradient layer. Set the Input Parameter to Incidence Angle, then create a key at 45 degrees. Set it to Spline smoothing, then create another key at 90 degrees and lower its Value to 75%. You will now have a slightly darker center to this ball.

A surface like this can be used several ways. You could leave it as a ball, modify the color and the bumps, and create a steam effect over a pot. Or you could just take the bumps off again, and move the ball over an image to magnify an area for a special effect, or just to simulate one of those screen blankers. Or, apply it to a tapered cylinder and place that behind a jet engine (Figure 5-46). In fact, there's a scene set up on the CD that will allow you to do just that.

STEP 55: Save this surface as a preset, then load the **JetExhaust.lws** scene. Select the Exhaust surface and reload that preset you just saved.

Now for this object, there's one last gradient we should add. Right now the black coloring will stretch the entire length of the object, but we really want it to fade toward the end. The center, or pivot point, of this object is located at the front, where it's butted against the engines. We're not using a Value shader for the black, so we can't use the falloff trick. But there is another way to do it.

FIGURE 5-46 The heat effect applied to some tapered cylinders and placed on a familiar object.

STEP 56: Open the Transparency texture, add a new layer, and set it to Alpha mode. We could use a gradient on this, based on distance from object, but we'd need to specify an object. We have four of these exhaust objects, all using the same surface, so the gradient on all four would be locked to the same object. We could struggle and try to make it work, or take the easy way out. Since this layer is currently an Image layer, set it to Cylindrical image map, and then click the Image button. Select (load image) and load the **Corona.iff** image. This is a vertical grayscale image with streaks.

A nice thing about the normal textures is that if you don't use an external reference object, they will lock themselves to the object they're applied to. You could have millions of clones of this object scattered everywhere, and each one will have its textures locked to it, with no influences from the other objects. These textures are self-contained, unless, as mentioned before, they use a reference object or have World Coordinates (which is like using a reference object that never moves from its origin).

Set the Texture Axis to Z and click the Automatic Sizing button. Now since the top of this image is black, and the object is built on the negative side of the Z axis, the black area of this image will be at the front of the object, where it's attached to the jet. This is where the alpha will have the most effect, but it's where we want the least effect. You can either click the Invert Layer button, or go down to the Scale section and change the Z value to a negative, which will flip the image around.

That should do for this effect. I'll leave you to try a few of your own ideas for this now. One thing you might try is a larger bump map, and adding some motion to it.

PREVIOUS LAYER

You'll have noticed this option by now, since we've repeatedly changed it to Incidence Angle over the past few projects. What is it?

When you apply a texture, it creates a range of values from 0% to 100% over the surface. Usually it's a simple blend, like what you get with Marble, Dots, Grid, and so on, but as textures become more convoluted, the gradient is more and more distorted, and harder to recognize as a gradient between two values. Marble, for example, with no turbulence, is a simple set of parallel lines that fade from 100% at the center of each vein to 0% at a point midway between them. The Previous Layer option allows us to redefine that gradient and replace the values of that texture with new ones. To get a good understanding of this, let's revisit that lightning bolt.

Project: Lightning Bolt

STEP 57: Clear the scene and load the lightning bolt object we created in the last tutorial. Open the Surface Editor and activate VIPER.

STEP 58: Open the Texture Editor for the Color channel, where we originally created the three Marble layers that generated a white-blue-purple glow effect on our bolt. Deactivate the first two layers, so only the dark purple one is active. We'll use this one because it's the widest vein, and gives us more of an area to work with.

STEP 59: Add a new Gradient layer, and add a key at the bottom of the bar, which now has a Value of 1.0 instead of the 90 we're used to. This 1.0 equates to the areas of the layer below where the texture value is 100%. Note this does not mean that the actual visible texture is 100%. It refers only to the maximum part of that texture. In this case, the brightest part of the marble texture we have has RGB color values of 100, 0, and 150. This is the color we've given the maximum point of the Marble texture. Now we're going to strip this color definition from the texture and see it for what it really is.

Change the color for the top key to black. You will now have a white version of the marble vein, which used to be a dark purple (Figure 5-47). This is what the texture looks like internally, before the range of grays in it are converted to colors. And we're about to change the way it's converted to colors.

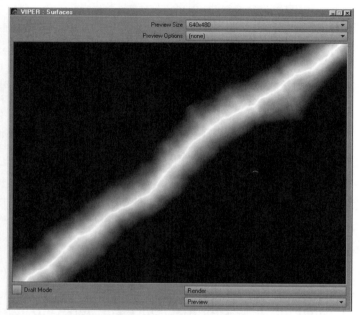

FIGURE 5-47 A previous layer gradient applied to the lightning bolt strips it of its color.

STEP 60: We'll try to duplicate the original lightning bolt, so set the color of the bottom key to 255, 240, and 255, which is the same color we used for the thin, top layer of Marble. Now, add two more keys to the bar, relatively evenly spaced. Color these two new keys using the same colors as the two other Marble layers, so we have a gradient going from black at the top, to purple, blue, then white.

VIPER will now show you a new bolt that's quite close to the one we had before (Figure 5-48). Now it's simply a matter of sliding those keys around until the image in VIPER matches the original render, or until you're satisfied.

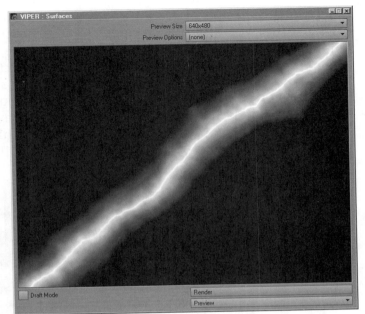

FIGURE 5-48 Adding two colored keys to the gradient remaps it so it's now very similar to the original.

Note: When a gradient like this is applied, the color or value of the layer it's referencing is unimportant, unless the gradient layer is less than 100% opaque.

Note: Since the original effect had three layers overlapping, some color blending occurred. Using the exact same colors on the gradient will get us close to the original effect, but not an exact match. The colors used on the Marble are what actually appears in the center of each vein. This color then blends with the layer below it as it expands away from the vein center. For example, the bottom purple layer used to add a slight amount of red to the blue layer above it, but this red isn't present in the color we gave the blue key. Adding a small amount of red will help get rid of that dark area that forms between the blue and purple keys. Also, you may want to darken the purple key since the original purple was blending with the black base.

There are a couple of benefits to using a gradient for stuff like this. The first is control. You can quickly and easily change a color and redefine the entire look with a few quick mouse clicks, rather than delve into a stack of textures and try to predict how they'll blend. The other benefit is speed. Procedurals take some time to calculate, and as we increase the number of procedurals, we also increase the amount of time it takes to generate them. Figure 5-49 shows the bolt done with three layers of marble, which took 128 seconds to render, and a similar bolt done with this gradient, which took only 59 seconds.

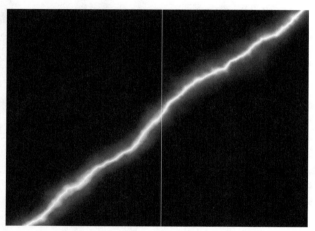

FIGURE 5-49 A split view of the original three-vein bolt on the left, and the new gradient-controlled bolt on the right. While they're virtually identical, the one on the right renders in less than half the time.

Now, if you're feeling adventurous, try using this technique on those puddles in the parking lot to give them a harder edge (Figure 5-50). (*Hint:* Just play with the Reflection channel.) This technique can be used on any type of texture (excluding Displacement layers), and on certain procedurals, it has some nice effects that would come in handy for space scenes.

FIGURE 5-50 A gradient applied to the parking lot puddles, giving them a sharper edge.

Project: Planets

If you've ever looked closely at color maps of the earth, you'll notice they tend to follow a certain pattern. They normally have a thin tan line for the shorelines, and then graduate through shades of green for higher land masses, then to dark browns and grays for mountains, and finally to white, for the tallest, snow-capped mountains. Sounds like a gradient to me.

STEP 61: Clear the scene and load **SmoothBall.lwo** from the CD. Now add one of the noisy procedurals to the color channel. Again, Turbulence works well, but feel free to experiment.

Note: You might find it helpful to make the base color of the sphere blue, just as a visual aid to help picture what the ball will look like with areas of land and water.

We're going to create a fractal landscape on this ball, and several textures can be used. The gradient we apply here will need to be tweaked differently for each landscape, and it's entirely a matter of personal taste. For best results, though, the procedural you use should have a lot of detail, so a higher Frequencies setting, around 8, is preferred, as well as a Small Power of 0.8 to 1.0. For the FBM, hybrids, and multifractals at the bottom of the procedural list, usually increasing the Lacunarity will add detail, but again, play around to best learn how these settings affect each texture.

Note: FBM noise, Hetero Terrain, Hybrid MultiFractal, MultiFractal, Ridged MultiFractal, Turbulent Noise, and Puffy Clouds all share the same general pattern, but have different noises applied to them. For example, the default Puffy Clouds texture can be closely approximated using the Hetero Terrain texture with its Offset and Increment lowered.

STEP 62: Once you have a nicely detailed sphere, such as the one in Figure 5-51, add a Gradient layer, based on the previous layer, and create a series of keys, preferably evenly spaced. Following is a good set for creating a mountainous green landscape with water:

RGB Color	Smoothing
50, 60, 130	—
180, 180, 120	Step
90, 150, 60	Linear/Spline
130, 100, 80	Linear/Spline
50, 60, 30	Linear/Spline
70, 50, 40	Linear/Spline
30, 20, 20	Step
240, 240, 240	Step

The actual positions of these keys doesn't matter at this time, since they'll be manually adjusted to fit the particular fractal pattern you have. Three of these keys use the Step smoothing, which simply makes the gradient jump to the new values, without any transition. The first step key creates a hard edge between the blue and the first green, which will create our shorelines. The next one is a dark brown, which will create sharp definition around our mountain ranges. Finally, the last one creates our snowcapped mountains.

After setting up these keys, you will probably have a bit of a messy-looking ball (Figure 5-52). With luck, you might already have something that looks planetlike.

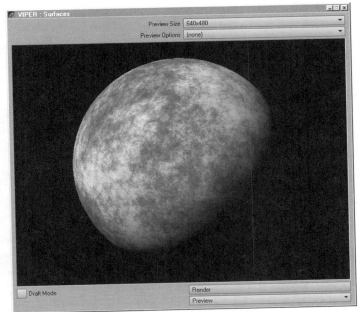

FIGURE 5-51 A noise procedural applied to a simple blue ball. It already looks like cloud cover on some blue world.

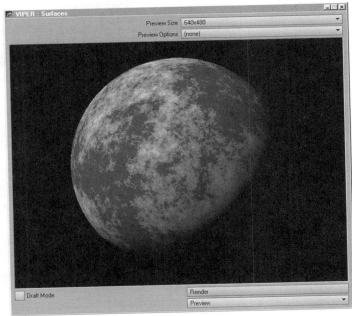

FIGURE 5-52 A previous layer gradient recolors the planet, turning it into some desert/jungle world.

STEP 63: Now comes the task of tweaking these keys. It's best to just move them all down near the bottom, but be careful not to pile them over one another (Figure 5-53). Then drag the second key, which creates our shorelines, until you get a balance of water and land masses you like in VIPER.

FIGURE 5-53 A landscape gradient with several of the keys sitting out of the way near the bottom and the shoreline key adjusted.

Note: If the shorelines always appear dithered or too broken up, you can always select the procedural and adjust it, or even change the procedural texture itself. (The joys of terraforming!) When you have the shorelines the way you like them, then start moving the next key in toward the shore, and then the next, until you have a land texture you like (Figure 5-54). Since an infinite variety of patterns are possible, it's beyond the scope of this tutorial (and the entire book, for that matter) to cover them all. My best advice is, as usual, "Play with it." Also, don't feel locked into using the colors, or even the same number of keys, listed. This is your world, so it can look any way you want it to look.

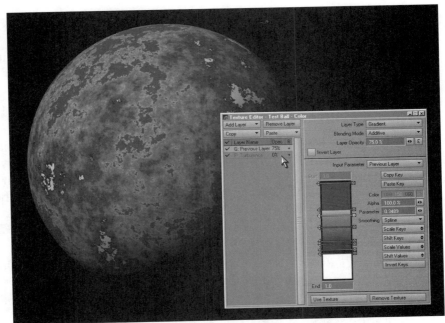

FIGURE 5-54 A full-color procedural planet, using a single procedural texture.

Tip: One of the most common errors people make with 3D imagery is making colors too vibrant. This same error was made here, although intentionally in order to make the positioning of the keys easier. Once the keys are positioned, rather than go through and desaturate each one, we can use the base value of the sphere, which is blue. And since this *is* a planet, when seen from space, all those colors that make up the surface will tend to turn slightly blue from the atmosphere. But as mentioned before, the color of the procedural is unimportant, unless we blend the gradient layer. We could make the procedural the same color as the base, and this would leave us with a solid blue ball that our gradient is painting over. Then we could set the Layer Opacity for the gradient to around 75% to let some of that blue show through—in effect, desaturating the colors slightly. Another trick is to simply lower the opacity of the procedural layer to 1% or less, but *not* zero. As long as the opacity is greater than zero, the procedural is feeding the gradient the information it needs (Figure 5-54). If you want, you can give the procedural an opacity of 0.00001%, and the landscape will still appear. I'd recommend not going more than four decimal places, though, since Light-Wave will round the number off in the display, making it look like 0.0%.

Well, we have an interesting-looking planet, but that surface looks a bit flat.

STEP 64: Since we just used the amplitude of a procedural to define the landscape colors, we can easily do the same to create bumps. Copy the procedural layer and paste it into the Bump channel. Set the Texture Value to 100% and the surface of this planet will now look a little rougher (Figure 5-55).

STEP 65: Depending on the procedural you used, you may see bumps appearing in the water areas. To remove these, simply paste this procedural into the Bump channel again, but make it an alpha layer. When this is done, increase the Contrast to 100%; if the procedural doesn't have this setting, adjust the Offset and Increment values slightly until the small texture preview in the Texture Editor develops sharp edges. Some procedurals work better than others here, but you never know what you'll find by experimenting.

FIGURE 5-55 The same world, this time using bump elevations to define the land masses.

Now we have three procedurals on this ball, but we can actually get rid of one. Since the same texture is being used to define both the colors and the bumps, why can't we just use the bumps?

STEP 66: Open the Texture Editor for Color again, and select the gradient. Copy this layer and paste it back, adding it to the list, then deactivate the first layer. The planet will temporarily lose its texture. Click the Input Parameter button and select Bump, and you should see the planet revert back to the texture it had before (or something very close). Now you can deactivate the other layers in this channel, or delete them, and just use the Bump channel to define the landscape. In fact, you can even mix procedurals on the Bump channel, using one to create a series of bumps and the other as an alpha to keep the water flat. Again, the variations are endless.

Save this planet, since we'll be using it later, then clear the scene. We're going to visit that monster again.

LIGHT INCIDENCE

This time, we'll use gradients to create a different look. We've already seen how we can use them with the camera, bumps, or surface color to create various effects. Well, we can also use a light to change the color, and this next project will show an interesting trick with them.

Project: *Cel Look*

One of LightWave's regular uses, particularly in Japan, is for creating animation that looks hand-drawn. This is actually seen quite frequently on TV, in such cartoons as *Nascar Racers,* or even in big-budget anime films. Normally this is done using a shader like the SuperCelShader, which will be covered in detail later, but there's no reason we can't do something similar with a gradient. After all, we've already seen that we can create hard-edged color transitions when we created that shoreline.

STEP 67: Load the LizardMonster again and position the camera so you have a good view of him, and set up VIPER.

Probably the main thing about celshading is the fact that it consists of areas of solid color, and you might remember from the last time we used this guy that for a short time, we did have a solid-color version of him at one point. This was because we made the surface luminous and nondiffuse, so let's do that again here.

STEP 68: Select the Hide surface and lower the Diffuse value to 0% and raise the Luminosity to 100%. Also make sure the Specularity is 0% and that textures for these channels are removed as well, so we have no shading happening on this surface. You can leave the bumps, though, but turn them down to 10% so they don't interfere with the gradient. Don't worry about the other surfaces on him just yet. We'll get this one out of the way and the rest will be little more than a simple matter of copying and pasting.

STEP 69: On the Color channel, create a gradient layer and set it to Light Incidence. A new button will appear below this, asking for a light to use. Click this and select the only light we have in the scene. This beast will once again turn solid white.

STEP 70: Cel drawings rarely have color blends, except for backgrounds, so we'll do the same for this guy. Rather than constantly setting each key to Step mode, let's set the key at the top to Step. Now every new key we add will also be set to Step mode.

Tip: When you add a key to a gradient, the Smoothing mode for the new key will be identical to the key above it.

This type of gradient might seem confusing at first; it's just like using the Incidence Angle, but this time the gradient is responding to a light's point of view, not the camera's. Colors at the top of the bar correspond to surfaces where the light is hitting at a small angle. The bottom of the bar represents the color of surfaces that are pointed directly at the light. With this in mind, let's create our first key.

STEP 71: Create a key near the bottom of the bar, around 85 degrees. This area will be the highlight color of our character. Now, lower the color of the top key to a dark gray. This will be our shadow color for now. He may look a bit weird at this point (Figure 5-56), but that will change now.

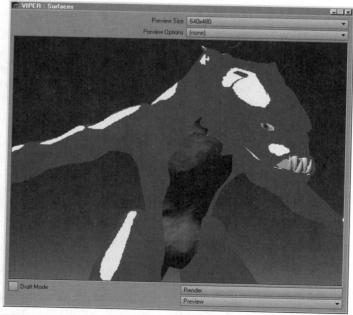

FIGURE 5-56 A quick two-color gradient applied to the creature's hide.

STEP 72: Add another key near the top of this bar, around 5 degrees. Now make this green, making sure it's a bit lighter than the gray above it. Now our monster is starting to take shape. Add one more key near the middle now, and make this an even lighter green. That should do for now. You should have something similar to Figure 5-57.

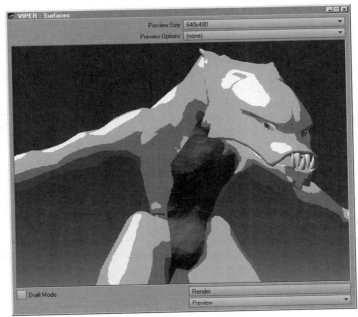

FIGURE 5-57 Now we're getting the toon look!

STEP 73: Now that we have a rough gradient set up, let's fine-tune it. First of all, let's tone that highlight color down. The highlight should be a lighter version of the body color, which we've just made green, so make this a very light green. We'll do something similar for the dark gray. Change this to a dark blue-green color, to simulate cool shadows.

STEP 74: All we have left is a bit of tweaking to get this right. First of all, let's reduce the amount of shadow color by dragging that second key up closer to the top, around 2 degrees. Finally, drag that middle key up or down, watching the results in VIPER, until you get a look you like. This is a matter of taste, so there's no real correct setting.

Note: Since this gradient is based on the incidence angle of light, everything facing away from the light will have the same shade.

STEP 75: Now that we have a gradient set up that we like, let's copy it to the other channels. Right-click the Hide surface and select Copy. This model has a separate surface for the chest and stomach, called Stripe, so select that and right-click it, this time selecting Paste. His chest should now match the rest of him. Now do the same for the other surfaces, but as you paste into each one, set the colors of the gradient to something similar to the colors that were used there before. The tongue, for instance, should be made of shades of red or pink.

The only surface that doesn't need a gradient is the eyes. Rather than copy the gradient here, simply make this surface luminous and nondiffuse.

Note: There is no rule that says you must use four colors for each surface. In fact, for the tongue, nails, and teeth, two colors are plenty.

STEP 76: Now all that needs to be done to finish the look of this guy is to add the ink lines. We won't get into the details about ink lines here, since these will be covered in greater detail later. We'll just add some quick and dirty lines to help sell the look (or should I say, cel the look?).

Click the Objects button on the bottom menu and press P to open the Object Properties panel. Click the Edges tab and select the Silhouette Edges check box. This will now draw a fine black line around our character, making it look as if we just colored in a line drawing. Figure 5-58 shows a final render of the lizard guy against a cloudy backdrop.

Note: That cloudy backdrop is also a gradient texture with Turbulence clouds on top of it. Another variation of this backdrop is visible behind the jet airliner in Figure 5-46. The backdrop was created procedurally using the LW_TextureEnvironment plug-in on the Backdrop tab in the Effects panel. There's a scene file on the CD called BG-Sky that has this texture all set up. We'll cover this in more detail later.

FIGURE 5-58 A simple celshaded look to a character you'd rather not meet in a dark alley.

There's currently a big debate in the anime industry about celshading, and what's right and what's not, and 3D celshading is one of the hot points. Purists don't like the idea of using Fresnel-based celshading techniques like this, but it really boils down to a matter of personal taste. After all, one of the most popular cartoons on TV today isn't even done in the typical cel-drawn cartoon style. *South Park,* which was originally done with paper cutouts and stop motion, is definitely not celshaded. But it *is* done on computers now, to simulate that original paper cut-out look.

It should be noted that this lizard monster was originally built for normal shading, and not with celshading in mind. Models that are not designed for celshading run the risk of appearing posterized when they're animated (or even in still images), or even rotoscoped to look celshaded. This isn't always a bad thing. Ralph Bakshi seemed to do all right for himself with that look. For a more serious celshading treatment, the Celshader Goddess herself takes you through the process of creating a celshaded character, designed from the ground up, in Tutorial 9.

Let's move on to another project now—one that will interest the space buffs out there.

Project: Earth

Since I've already covered the details on building an earth in the previous *LightWave Applied* book, I'll shorten this project by supplying a prefabricated earth. We could actually call this Prefab Earth 2 since it does use some of the new features of LightWave 6.5, so I strongly recommend you take a look at the texturing that's set up in it. One good way to see what's going on is to get VIPER going and then look at each channel separately using the Display mode. In fact, let's just take a quick run through and see what's going on.

STEP 77: Clear the scene and load the **Earth.lwo** object. To get the full space feeling, open the Light Properties panel and click the Global Illumination button. Turn the Ambient light to somewhere between 0 and 5%. In space, there is no real ambient light, since there's very little out there for light to come from or bounce off.

Note: You might find it useful to turn the globe so you're facing your favorite continent.

Now, get VIPER going and let's look through those channels.

Color: This is little more than a simple earth map wrapped around the globe. Nothing special going on here.

Luminosity: There is no luminosity . . . yet.

Diffuse: You should see a flat white disc, which means that the entire surface has a uniform diffuse level. This makes sense since there's no texture applied here.

Specularity: There are two layers here. The top is a simple black and white image like the one we used before, which is used as an alpha on the gradient layer below. This reveals the gradient in place of the oceans. The gradient layer is providing a small amount of Fresnel for the specularity, making the oceans more specular as the light moves behind the planet (Figure 5-59). Note that the base Specularity value is 0%, otherwise our land would be slightly specular. (Try adjusting it and you'll see.)

Glossiness: This is virtually the same setup as the Specularity channel, but with a more shallow gradient. This one simply tightens the specular highlight slightly at the horizon.

FIGURE 5-59 A view of the Specularity channel for the earth, showing the gradient applied to the oceans.

Note: For shiny surfaces, you might want to create these gradients to make the surface more glossy at glancing angles, but for rough surfaces, such as stone, you might find it useful to make the gradient work the other way, and make the highlights wider to emphasize the effects of backlighting. This would be handy for skin.

Reflection, Transparency, and Reflectivity: These are all set to 0% and untextured, since they're not necessary for this surface.

Bump: This is simply a grayscale image spherically mapped on the sphere to create bumps for the land. Again, there's nothing special here. The amplitude is lowered to 0.5 to keep the bumps from becoming too prominent, but you might want to lower it even more since bumps on the earth's surface, when seen from space, are very hard to see unless you're in low orbit.

Note: Although there is no way to view the Bump channel in VIPER, you can usually see its effects in channels that have a Fresnel-simulating gradient applied. It's also visible in the Diffuse Reflection, Specular Reflection, and Mirror Reflection display modes. In our current case, though, due to the various maps on the other channels, the bumps will not be visible. Don't worry. They are there!

STEP 78: Well, we've toured the earth, but found no signs of intelligent life. Maybe there is life, but it comes out only at night. Rotate the light so that it's lighting the back side of the planet, and we see mainly the dark side. You should see a nice crescent earth in VIPER now.

But no signs of life. Where is everyone? Don't they have electricity or lights yet? We'll give them some.

Open the Luminosity channel and select Spherical as the Projection method. Now click the Image button and load the **Earth-lights.iff** image from the CD. Set the Texture Axis to Y. Finally, change the Display mode to Luminosity Channel, and you should see a splattering of white dots over the land areas of the globe (Figure 5-60).

FIGURE 5-60 The city lights added to the globe. They've been brightened for better visibility in this image.

STEP 79: Since this image is merely brightening the colors that are already on the surface, the lights will most likely seem a bit dim. If we wanted to be more accurate with this planet, then technically, they should be much dimmer, and in fact, virtually invisible in a frame where the lit side of the earth is also visible. But we'll skip accuracy for now and continue with our bright lights.

Tip: To control the brightness of the lights, use the Layer Opacity. A setting above 100% will make them brighter, and lowering it will dim them.

Looking at Figure 5-60 again, you can see that the lights are on, even in the daytime. We're trying to convey the sense of intelligent life here, so why are they leaving the lights on? A better question is, how do we turn them off on one side of the globe, but leave them on the other side?

Previously we could try to use an image map, with white on one side and black on the other, as an alpha, but that would mean the alpha was locked to the lights image. We could do it now, but then we'd also have to mess around with it to get it to show only the image on the dark side of the planet, and turn the lights off where the planet's facing the sun. Do you see where this is going?

STEP 80: Add another layer to this texture, and make it a gradient. Set the Input parameter to Light Incidence and select the light we have in the scene.

Note: You might want to rename that light to something like Sun, since this surface will look for a matching light when it's loaded into a scene. By default, you have a light simply named Light in Layout. If you load this object as it is, this gradient will use that light for reference, and it's entirely possible that it won't be the correct light to use. If you name the light Sun, then the gradient will look for that. If it doesn't find it, it will leave the Light button blank. You can always fix it later. It's usually easier to catch something that's not set up at all than it is to catch something that's set up wrong.

We've already seen with our cartoon effect that a gradient using the Light Incidence will be visible only on the lit side, and the value of the key at 0 degrees completely fills the dark side. This actually creates an automatic terminator for us.

Note: The *terminator* (before it became known as a shiny, high-tech, evil cyborg out to destroy humanity, or those little electronic parts) is the point along the earth's surface where day turns into night.

STEP 81: To see this terminator, create a key at 1 degree and give it a value of 0%. You should now see half of the globe lit up. To be more precise, you should see the dark side of the globe lit up (Figure 5-61).

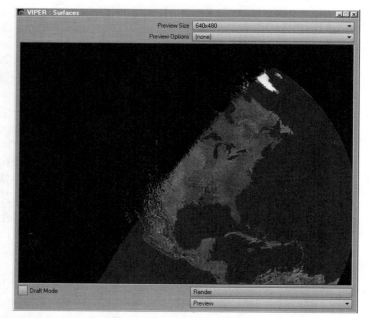

FIGURE 5-61 Adding a gradient manages to light up the night side of the world.

Now we will apply this gradient to the lights.

STEP 82: There are actually two ways we can do this, but we'll cover the ones that are easiest to do right now.

Change the gradient's Blending Mode to Alpha. That was the easy way. You should now see some lights in VIPER, but only where the gradient used to make the surface bright. Change the Display mode back to Render Output and you'll see both the daylit side and the lights on the night side (Figure 5-62).

The other way to do this would be to drag the gradient layer below the image and then set the image as an alpha. Then you can control the brightness of the lights by adjusting the value of the top key in the gradient. With the gradient on top, you can still control the brightness of the lights by adjusting the image layer's opacity. Higher is brighter.

FIGURE 5-62 Changing the gradient to an alpha layer turns the city lights on, but only on the side facing away from the sun.

With this setup, you can position the earth anywhere and rotate it any way you like, and the city lights will turn on only when they've crossed over into darkness. As they come back toward the daylight, they'll turn off again. Now you might want to adjust the second key of the gradient to allow for more of a transition, since city lights do start to turn on before it's completely dark. I wouldn't recommend moving the key beyond 10 degrees, though.

The map for this earth was designed with an atmosphere in mind, which is why it's so dark. Adding the atmospheric haze over the planet will make the colors appear as they would from space. And that's what we'll do next.

LAYERING SURFACES

Layering surfaces should not be confused with layering textures. Texture layering is done within a single surface, but surface layering requires another surface, usually at a slight offset. This second surface is generally transparent or has some transparency in its textures. We'll look at a few uses for surface layering in this last set of projects.

Project: Atmosphere

Don't clear the scene just yet! We still have work to do with this planet.

Note: If the Hub is running, you should have a Modeler button in the upper-right corner of the main Layout screen. Click it or simply press F12 to load Modeler. Occasionally, when you start LightWave, it might finish loading before the Hub is fully loaded and the button will not appear. Quitting Layout when this happens, and running it again, will usually fix this.

Here's an interesting thing about the Hub. You can edit the **Lwhub.cfg** file (something I do not recommend for beginners) and manually add other software to the list. If you have Aura, you can add that, and when you right-click the Hub and select Launch Process, you will see Layout, Modeler, and Aura! And you will be able to launch Aura from that icon (although it will complain about a missing file). It's entirely possible that at some future date, Aura will be able to be fully integrated into the LightWave pipeline (and possibly even other software), and in fact, NewTek has been hinting at this for some time now.

STEP 83: The first thing we need to do if we're going to give our world an atmosphere is to actually create it. Start Modeler and we'll begin.

Note: If the Modeler button is present but doesn't work, it's probably because you just installed LightWave. When LightWave is first installed, there are no configuration files to tell the Hub where anything is. If you run the Hub after freshly installing the software (or after deleting any current configuration files), before you run Layout or Modeler, it will not have them listed in its Launch Process section. Before the Hub can share data, it needs to know where both programs are. This is a simple matter of running each program from its icon, then quitting again. This will update the configuration files, and the Hub will see each program from that point on. If you open the Hub and look for the Launch Process section, you should see a 2 in front of it. If it's a 1 or a No, then either the installation is fresh and configs haven't been created yet, or they've been misplaced and the Hub can't find them. If you expand the section by clicking on the small triangle, you will see a list of the programs the Hub currently knows about—in this case, Modeler and Layout. If one's missing, just run it normally and it will be added to the list.

STEP 84: Modeler should already have the **Earth.lwo** object loaded and ready to go, thanks to the Hub. Press C to copy this object and then switch to the second layer. Paste the ball here by pressing V, then set the first layer as a background layer.

STEP 85: This new layer will be our atmosphere surface, so let's give it a new surface name. Press Q to open the Change Surface panel and call this surface Atmosphere.

We're almost there. All that's left to do is give this atmosphere some depth, since right now it's the same size as the planet, and if we put both objects in the same place in Layout, we could easily be facing weird render errors.

STEP 86: Click the Size button under the Modify tab, or just press Shift+H. We need to make this sphere slightly larger than the planet, since this is supposed to be the atmosphere that covers it. You could do this interactively, but for now, let's work numerically so we have the same results as shown in the figures. Press N to open the Numeric panel, enter a Scale value of 104%, then click the Apply button. You should now have a sphere in the foreground layer that's approximately 20 millimeters bigger than the planet in the background (Figure 5-63).

Now we'll take advantage of a new feature of the new object format. Rather than cluttering the drive with multiple spheres for a planet, we can keep them all in one handy file. If you were to save this object, you would not be saving just this layer (which is what would happen in pre-6.0 LightWave), but *both* layers. In fact, if you switch back over to Layout, you should see both spheres in there now. Don't be fooled by the fact that two objects are listed in Layout, either. LightWave has only one object loaded, but it consists of two layers, which will appear to be separate objects in Layout. These layers appear with the object name, followed by the layer name. Since we haven't named any layers yet, they simply appear as Earth:Layer1 and Earth:Layer2. Other than that, these

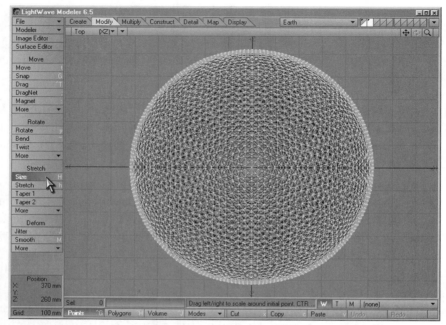

FIGURE 5-63 A duplicate sphere in the second object layer, scaled slightly larger than the main planet.

layers work just as though they were separate objects, meaning you can move them independently, deform them, parent them to other objects, or even remove them from the scene. The only place where layers appear as a single object is in the Surface Editor, where we now have the earth surface and the new Atmosphere surface that we just created.

STEP 87: Before we jump back into Layout, let's do one more thing to make our lives easier. Click the Modeler button in the upper left corner of Modeler, and choose Windows > Layer Browser Open/Close . . . (Figure 5-64), or just type Shift+Y. A small window will appear with the Earth object listed and a small triangular arrow to the side. This browser lists all the objects currently available in Modeler, which in our case is simply this earth object. Clicking the arrow will expand the list to show all the layers for the object. We have two layers in ours, and they're both currently unnamed. Double-click the top layer, which will be numbered 1, and a small panel will appear. Give this layer a name by simply typing one in the field, then clicking OK. In this case, let's call ours Surface, since in Layout, the object name is already visible. This will make it appear as Earth:Surface.

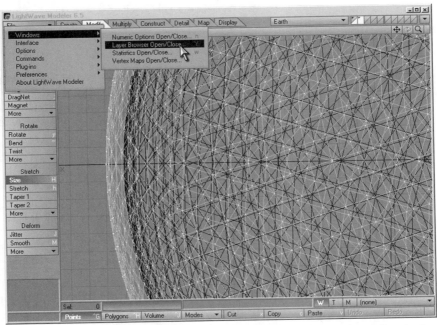

FIGURE 5-64 The location of the Layer Browser Open/Close command. Remembering the keyboard shortcut of Shift+Y will get you there faster.

STEP 88: Double-click the second layer and call this layer Atmosphere. Before you close this panel, notice the button labeled Parent. Click that and you will see the first layer listed (Figure 5-65). Select that, then close the window.

What we've just done is parented this second layer to the first layer of the object. Now whatever we do with the first layer, the second layer will do too, just as if we had parented them together in Layout. In fact, switch back to Layout now.

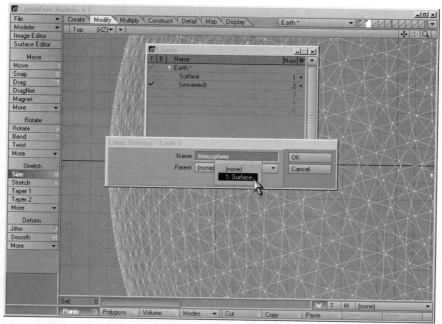

FIGURE 5-65 The Layers Browser and its settings options.

If you open the Scene Editor, you will see that the atmosphere appears parented to the Surface layer (Figure 5-66). Layered objects like this are extremely handy, since you can create objects that have moving parts and include those parts, and the entire hierarchy, all in one object file. This will greatly reduce the need to set up special assembly, or "loader," scenes that you use with the Load Items From Scene command. Again, these layers behave exactly like regular objects, and even though they're parented in the actual object file itself, you can still change the parenting in Layout.

Note: Sometimes Layout can get stuck and refuse to update this parenting information. If this happens, simply clear both layers from Layout, then go back to Modeler and click the small button in the top right corner and choose Send Object to Layout. This should update the object parenting.

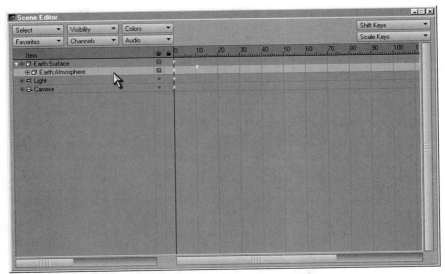

FIGURE 5-66 The Scene Editor, showing that the Atmosphere layer of the object is now parented to the planet part.

Now that we've made sure our planet layers will act as one object, let's get that atmosphere to look right. The earth's atmosphere has an additive effect in that the blue light that it scatters is added to whatever we see above it, which is generally just black with some stars and the occasional moon. This additive effect works both ways, and can also be seen from space. When you see a picture of the earth from space you'll notice that everything has a slight blue tinge to it, and this blue tint gets more pronounced at the edge of the planet. This is due to the fact that near the horizon, we're not just looking straight down through the atmosphere, where it would appear it's thinnest. Instead, we're looking further across the surface near the edge, and we're seeing through more atmosphere. The more air we look through, the brighter it becomes—that is, until our line of sight leaves the planet and is just glancing through the upper atmosphere, where the air gets much thinner again. Thin, thick, thin again . . . sounds like a gradient.

STEP 89: Open the Surface Editor and select the Atmosphere surface. The first thing we'll do is make it a light sky blue, so give this a very light blue color for now.

You won't see anything happen in VIPER at the moment because we've just changed the object on it. It currently has no idea that there's a sky object to worry about, so we'll have to do another render to let it know. Press F9, and you should see a simple blue ball.

STEP 90: Click the Advanced tab and increase the Additive Transparency to 100%. Also increase the Diffuse Sharpness to 25% to help spread the light over the entire lit side of the atmosphere. This will help simulate the way light scatters through the air and make the atmosphere work more like it should. If you do another render, you'll see the earth's surface through the blue (Figure 5-67). You will not see it in VIPER, though, because VIPER shows only the closest polygon to the camera for any pixel. However, you can see the backdrop through this surface, as you'll see soon enough.

FIGURE 5-67 The outer blue ball is starting to look more like an atmosphere. Just a little more tweaking to go.

Note: Usually for additive surfaces, we would use Luminosity and lower the Diffuse level. In this case, we want the atmosphere to get its light from the sun. Otherwise, we would have a bright blue sky over the entire planet, including the night side. We could use another gradient using Light Incidence to control it, but we can save ourselves that hassle and just use the light the way it was originally intended.

STEP 91: Now it's time to control that transparency a bit. Open the Texture Editor for the Transparency channel and create a gradient layer based on Incidence Angle. Add two keys for now, one at 25 degrees and another at 90. Set the value of the key at 25 degrees to 0%. This will make the sphere completely opaque, except for its additive nature, near the horizon of the planet. The key at the top of the bar will make the atmosphere become fully transparent right at the edge. The bottom key will have the same effect, which is close to what we want. In fact, it should look pretty good already (Figure 5-68). You should also see that the ball in VIPER also has a soft edge.

FIGURE 5-68 This is looking much better, but still needs some work.

Note: Depending on the distance from the camera to the planet, this key at 25 degrees may need to be moved up or down the gradient slightly.

STEP 92: Let's give this gradient one last tweak for now. Since we're supposed to be looking down through the atmosphere in the middle of this ball, we should still see some blue added. Lower the value for the bottom key to 75%. Also, change each of these keys so they're using Spline smoothing, to help prevent any unwanted banding from occurring. Now add two more keys, one at 15 degrees and the other at 30 degrees. These two keys will be used to adjust the curve of our gradient at the horizon. As it is now, our atmosphere still appears too thick and evenly distributed at the horizon. It should actually appear much thinner there, but with a very faint hazy glow above that slowly transitions to black. Set the Value for the key at 15 degrees to 75%. This will ramp the transparency up more sharply from the 0% on the key below it, but still allows the gradient to smoothly flow to 100% at the top. Basically it will stretch the more transparent area to cover more space above the ground.

Tip: When setting up gradients like this, you can more easily see the effects of each key if you set the key to Step smoothing. This way you'll see a hard edge that will reveal exactly where along the surface of the object that specific key applies. Then you can move it where you want, and return it to Linear or Spline smoothing.

The other key we added will basically do the same thing, but in this case we'll use it to push the less-transparent areas of the atmosphere out toward the edge of the planet, spreading the more-transparent area over more of the planet. Set this key to 25%. VIPER will show these changes, which will make the ball seem a little smaller, and more transparent in the center. Figure 5-69 shows the results on the rendered sphere.

FIGURE 5-69 A slight change, but we're not done yet.

The transparency of this atmosphere now looks pretty good. The atmosphere may still appear a little thick, but that will change. Aside from the amount of transparency the atmosphere has when seen from space, it also has a slight color change. Looking straight down through it, we see a simple blue color. As we look through more of it toward the horizon, it becomes whiter, and then fades to a deep bluish-purple glow, then blackness. You guessed it—another gradient.

STEP 93: Open the Texture Editor for the Color channel, and once again, set up a gradient based on Incidence Angle. Create keys at 25 degrees and 90 degrees, just like last time, and set them to Spline smoothing. Now, make the very top key black, since this is where the atmosphere dissolves into space. Give the bottom key a nice light blue color. RGB values of 200, 210, and 255 work well. Finally, give the middle key another shade of blue, but slightly darker. RGB values of 150, 190, and 255 will do nicely.

This will give us a very slight color change over the surface of the planet, and a slightly thinner-looking atmosphere at the edge (Figure 5-70). All we need now is a little more control over the gradient at the edge, and to see more purple in that thin region.

FIGURE 5-70 One more slight change, but this time to the color. The atmosphere at the horizon is a little thinner now.

Tip: You may find it easier to work with this gradient if you think of the gradient bar as a cross-section of the atmosphere. The top of the bar would be the top of the ionosphere, where the sky is black, and then as we go further down through the atmosphere, the sky continues to get brighter. The earth's surface in this bar would actually be around the 25-degree mark, since that's the angle of the atmosphere at the point where we can see the edge of the globe through it.

STEP 94: Add a new key at 10 degrees and change its color to a darker blue-purple. RGB values of 50, 20, and 100 will do nicely. Add a second key at 22 degrees, which we'll use to further pinch this gradient toward the ground. Give this one a lighter color, such as 80, 120, and 210, which will finish our horizon transition from light blue to deep blue-purple to space (Figure 5-71).

FIGURE 5-71 The finished atmosphere, ready to be populated with clouds—after one or two optional improvements.

The effect is subtle (virtually invisible in black and white), but if you flip through previous renders in the Image Viewer, you can see the improvements (or you can flip through Figures 5-68 to 5-72 on the CD).

We could call this atmosphere finished now, but there's always room for improvement. For example, there are two light effects that we can simulate yet, and both are actually quite simple. They are related as well, and have to do with how light scatters through the atmosphere. Where the sun is shining more directly onto the surface of the earth, the atmosphere is much brighter, creating a nearly white sliver of atmosphere around that section of the edge of the earth. But near the terminator, where the earth would be experiencing sunrise or sunset, the scattering is more attenuated, shifting the color from blue to red, as the light has to travel through much more air. Since this second effect is another color change, we'll cover it first.

STEP 95: Add a new layer to the Color texture, and make it another gradient. This time, set the Input parameter to Light Incidence, and use the sun as the light source. Now, give the gradient a red color by setting the initial key to red. RGB values of 255, 55, and 55 give a good red that's not too saturated.

Note: Again, one of the most common mistakes when starting out in 3D is making surface colors too saturated. Try to keep the saturation below 200 (240 tops, unless you require a specific color for some special effect) both to keep the colors within legal video and printing limits, and to keep the image from looking artificial. Very few colors in the real world are very saturated, with the exceptions of some fluorescent colors, certain flowers, and some colored lights. Aside from these, most colors, while appearing bright under sunlight, are actually more muted when seen printed. A red tulip, for example, may seem like a very bright red, but when compared to RGB values, would be more around 150, 40, and 40, which is a color saturation value of 187.

Create a second key at 10 degrees. This will default to the same color as the initial key, and we won't change that. This time, we'll use the Alpha value below the Color field. Lower this to 0% and you should see a short gradient that goes from red to fully transparent, revealing a checkerboard pattern. This is just like the transparent areas of procedurals, which reveal the texture values below the current layer. In this case, we just added a small red gradient at the terminator, creating a blend with the base blue gradient (Figure 5-72). Since this is a Light Incidence gradient, the color of the key at 0 degrees is actually applied to all the polygons that face away from the light. In other words, we just made the dark side of the sky red, with a short gradient to blue on the day side. (You can see this if you increase the luminosity of the surface.)

FIGURE 5-72 A second color gradient adds a slight reddening to the atmosphere at the terminator. The light was rotated in this image to bring the terminator into view. Note the slightly more intense specular highlight in the water at this angle.

Note: You could also assign this gradient layer to the surface of the planet if you wish. This would intensify the effect and also make the surface look as if it's being affected by the light in the atmosphere. You should lower the texture opacity to 50%, or drop the Alpha value of the top key to 50% so there's still some detail on the dark side of the globe. This will also turn the city lights to a red color as well, so by adding this blend, we won't end up with cities bathed in deep red light.

STEP 96: Now we'll add that other lighting effect. Open the Texture Editor for the Diffuse channel and create another gradient based on Incidence Angle. Create three keys as follows:

Key	Value
0	100%
20	100%
25	120%
45	100%

This will cause our gradient to reflect more light at 25 degrees, which is where the edge of the globe is located. VIPER will show a slight brightening on the side facing the sun, but very little change elsewhere. Figure 5-73 shows our final atmosphere.

FIGURE 5-73 At long last, the atmosphere is done.

Note: To make the atmosphere appear more hazy, try lowering the Additive Transparency. This will cause the normal transparency's blending to take over, and more of the surface colors will appear over the earth surface, creating a more dense effect. Unfortunately, due to the loss of Steamer, the atmosphere method covered in *LightWave Applied 5.6* cannot be duplicated in LightWave 6.5. HyperVoxels 3 can come close, but it lacks the edge softness that Steamer had. It can, however, create very nice volumetric clouds, if you can accept the longer render times involved.

Now that we've finished the atmosphere, let's add some clouds.

Project: Clouds

STEP 97: Switch back to Modeler now. You'll notice that the object there automatically updates with the new surfacing we just added. We're going to create another sphere that we'll use as our cloud layer, so copy the Earth layer and paste it into the third layer.

STEP 98: Press Shift+H to activate the Scale tool, then press N to open the Numeric panel. Clouds appear very close to the surface, so we'll need to scale this object very slightly. Enter a value of 100.1%, then click the Apply button. If you have the original layer in the background, you'll see that an almost imperceptible shift has occurred in the polygons in the third layer (Figure 5-74).

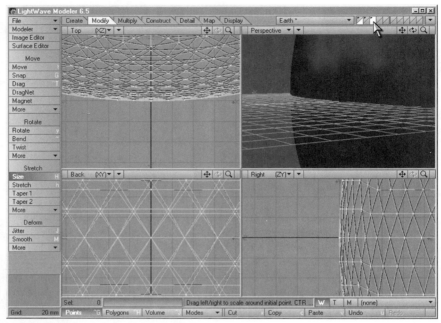

FIGURE 5-74 Scaling the third layer by a very small amount to create a cloud layer.

STEP 99: Now that we have a cloud layer of polygons, we need to create a new surface for them. Press Q and give this surface a creative new name, such as Clouds, then click OK. We're almost done here.

While we're naming things, let's name this layer as well. Press Shift+Y to open the Layers Browser, if it's not already open from when we created the atmosphere layer. Double-click the third layer, which should be labeled (unnamed). Again, create a new name for this layer, something like Clouds, and parent this layer to the Surface layer.

STEP 100: Switch back to Layout now. You should now have three object layers visible if you click the Current Item button (Figure 5-75).

There are three ways we can set up this Cloud layer. The first is simply to treat it as a separate object, texture it, and rotate it to position the clouds the way we want them. This has one drawback: since this object has such a small gap between it and the Surface layer, the corners of the Surface layer run the risk of poking through the centers of the polygons in the Cloud layer when it's rotated at certain angles. Another option is to actually move these polygons into the same layer as the Surface polygons, where they can't be rotated independently of the surface, and then use the atmosphere as a texture reference to rotate the cloud texture. This would resolve the problem of poking polygons. The third option is to leave the clouds as a separate layer, but still use the atmosphere layer as the texture reference. This is the method we'll use, since it provides the solution we need, but also allows us more control over the cloud polygons. We can scale, dissolve, duplicate, or even remove them from a scene if necessary this way.

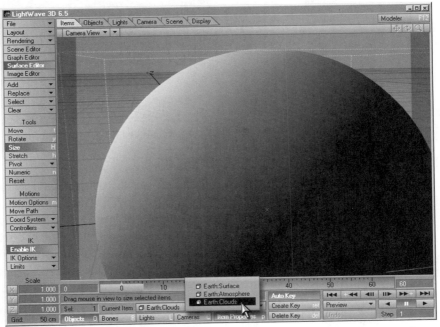

FIGURE 5-75 Switching back to Layout automatically updates the object there, adding the new Cloud layer.

Note: To prevent any unwanted motion, simply turn off the various motion channels for the Cloud object by clicking the small X, Y, Z, H, P, and B buttons in the lower-left corner of the Layout screen (Figure 5-76). This is not the same as locking the channels in the Graph Editor. Locking a channel on the main screen prevents you from dragging it around in the Layout view, but you can still modify it through the Graph Editor. The inverse is also true; locking a channel in the Graph Editor still allows you to move it in Layout (at least at the time of this writing). To fully lock an object down, you would need to lock it in both the Graph Editor and in the main Layout window.

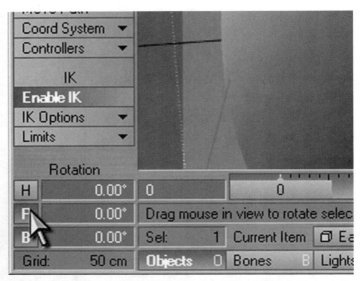

FIGURE 5-76 Deactivating these buttons will prevent you from accidentally moving an object.

Before we can see what we're doing on this surface, we have to do something about the outer atmosphere layer we've already surfaced. Currently, since it's the nearest polygon source to the camera, it will be the one we see in VIPER, completely obscuring the cloud layer we want to see there. There are several ways to prevent this object layer from rendering. We can scale it so it's smaller than the other objects, hiding it neatly inside; we can move it away from the other objects, out of the camera's view; we can make it unseen by camera, or 100% dissolved, or give it a polygon size of 0%.

STEP 101: To make things simple, we'll just scale this object because we can do that directly from the Layout screen without having to go into any other panels to reach those controls. Select the Atmosphere layer, then press Shift+H to activate the Size tool (just as in Modeler), or click the Size button on the Items tab. Next, drag in Layout view to interactively scale the object until it disappears inside the other object layers, then keyframe it there by pressing the Enter key twice (once to open the Create Motion Key panel and the second time to accept the default settings and actually create the key).

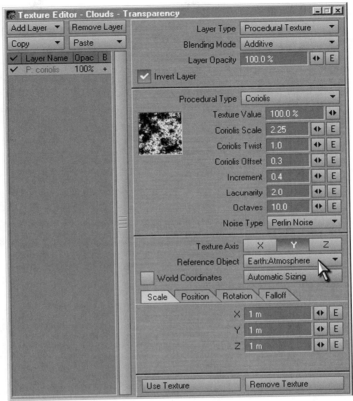

FIGURE 5-77 The settings for the Coriolis procedural that were used to create the cloud patterns in Figure 5-78.

Note: If you have Auto Key active (on the bottom menu, above the Create Key and Delete Key buttons), then there's no need to create a key, since it will be automatically updated.

STEP 102: Open the Surface Editor and select the Clouds surface. Set the color of this surface to a bright white, but slightly below the maximum white in order to allow for some shading. A white level of 240–250 should do nicely. Since Smoothing is not automatically updated in VIPER as are other surface settings, let's activate that first. Now we can get VIPER going again by pressing F9 to feed it the information it needs.

STEP 103: Since clouds are very effective at catching and reflecting light, increase the Diffuse Sharpness to 50% in the Advanced tab.

Note: We could go higher, but higher values tend to wash out bump maps, except at the most extreme lighting angles. Anything over 50% makes bumps hard to see, and tends to make the surface very flat. The terminator at this point also begins to take on a harsh appearance. Values over 100% are allowed, but create some pretty strange effects.

STEP 104: Clouds also cast shadows on the planet, but our polygons are currently all facing away from it. Polygons in LightWave will cast shadows only on their visible side, requiring the light to be coming from their invisible side in order for any shadows to be created. To fix this, simply select the Double Sided check box in the Surface Editor. This will cause the polygons to have two surfaces, facing opposite directions, so no matter where the light is, the polygon can cast a shadow.

We have a couple of ways to create the clouds. One is to use procedural textures, and we have a few that will create some cloudy textures. Turbulence is good for creating fluffy clouds for backgrounds, as can be seen in Figures 5-46 and 5-58, but for a cloud map as seen from space, it's not quite as effective. Coriolis is a good one, and is actually designed for this sort of thing. In fact, the name Coriolis refers to the twisting of the clouds in the atmosphere due to different areas of the atmosphere moving at different speeds, like the jet streams on earth. The default settings for this texture are very similar in appearance to the cloud patterns on Venus.

Note: To get a feel for many of these textures, simply play with them a bit. Modify each parameter, one at a time, and observe how that value affects the look of the texture. Don't be afraid to try negative values, since some parameters do allow them.

This texture has the most settings of all the procedurals, and would take pages to fully explain. Instead, we'll just use the set of values used for the following figures, and save a tree or two in the process.

STEP 105: Open the Texture Editor for the Transparency channel and set the Layer Type to Procedural. Select the Coriolis procedural and set the values as shown in Figure 5-77. If you've copied the settings exactly as shown, you should have a cloud pattern similar to Figure 5-78.

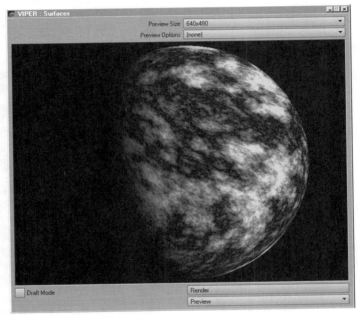

FIGURE 5-78 The cloud patterns created by the Coriolis texture, as seen in VIPER.

STEP 106: Now that we have the transparency map for the clouds, let's add some bumps to them. Copy this texture layer and then open the Texture Editor for the Bump channel. Paste the texture using the Replace Current Layer command, then lower the Texture Value to 10% so the bumps aren't too severe. This effect will be fairly subtle, but it will be most apparent near the terminator, where the light is angled enough to highlight the bumps the most.

STEP 107: Finally, reset the size of the Atmosphere layer by selecting the layer, then clicking the Size button, followed by clicking the Reset button below it. Before we do the final render, choose Rendering > Ray Trace Shadows. (Or just open the Render Options panel and select the Ray Trace Shadows check box there.)

Now that we have everything in place, position the camera and light the way you like and render a nice earth-from-space image (Figure 5-79). You will notice that the addition of the cloud layer will lighten the look of the atmosphere quite a bit, which is quite normal. Water vapor in our atmosphere does the same thing, though it's usually just called haze when it's not thick enough to look like clouds or fog. A planet that's 67% covered in water tends to have a large source for this haze, and it's quite common.

FIGURE 5-79 The fully rendered planet showing the reddish terminator, a few city lights, and the illusion of depth that the layered surfaces create.

Tip: You can set up the scene much easier by using the textured mode of OpenGL to see where the continents are on this planet. However, the atmosphere and cloud layers will obscure the surface map. You might find it useful to change the display mode for these two layers to wireframe, or even show them as vertices only. You can still see where these two layers are as points, but they still show the planet surface below, as seen in Figure 5-80. You can also set the base transparency of surfaces that use a gradient on the Transparency channel to something higher than 0% and the OpenGL display will show it as transparent. Note that if you're using a procedural or image map as the main texture layer, modifying the base transparency could adversely affect the texture and is not recommended.

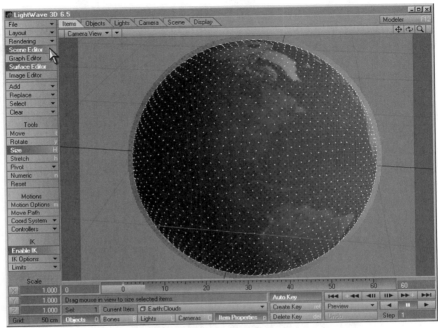

FIGURE 5-80 A handy way to view an object that has transparency layers in Layout.

These procedurals can create some very detailed clouds, but they still don't quite match the look of real cloud images. One of the nice things about the way textures can be layered in Light-Wave is that you can apply multiple textures to a surface and switch between them. And that's exactly what we'll do now.

STEP 108: Open the Transparency channel's texture and uncheck the Coriolis layer, then add a new Image Map layer. Set this one to Spherical projection, load the **Cloudmap1.iff** image, and then set the Texture Axis to Y. Finally, since this image has the clouds as white, which makes the surface transparent, we'll need to invert the layer so the cloud area remains visible while the rest of the image makes the surface transparent.

Note: This image is a composite of several weather satellite photographs, with a good deal of retouching added to increase the cloud cover as well as to add detail, since the original satellite images were much smaller. It's highly unlikely that the earth ever had this exact cloud pattern over its surface.

STEP 109: Copy this layer and paste it into the Bump channel, using the Add To Layers command. Clear the Invert Layer check box and lower the Texture Amplitude to 0.1. Finally, deactivate the Coriolis texture that's already there. We've now just added an actual image map of clouds to the cloud layer, without losing the Coriolis procedural we had before. A new render will show some more realistic clouds, but at the expense of smaller details that we had with the procedural (Figure 5-81).

FIGURE 5-81 An image map of clouds provides a more accurate result, but not always quite the way we'd like it to look.

Since we have two texture layers in the Transparency channel, there's really no reason we can't just combine them to get both the natural patterns of the image map and the finer details of the procedural. To do this, we'll need to make a couple of changes on the Transparency channel.

STEP 110: The first change is to swap the layers around. Drag the Coriolis texture up above the image map. Since this layer is applying levels of transparency, we need to stop it from applying transparent holes to our image. Set the Texture Value to 0%, which will cause this texture to apply areas of zero transparency—in other words, fully opaque areas—to the already partially transparent surface. Finally, to get the same cloud pattern we had before, clear the Invert Layer check box.

Note: Applying a Transparency texture with a value of 0% will actually cause the surface to become opaque again. In fact, adding a 0% texture to a 100% base transparency will look the same as applying the same texture, but inverted with a value of 100%, on top of a fully opaque surface. Normally, the first texture layer in the Transparency channel will be used to create the initial areas of transparency. Further layers will then be used to add or subtract from this transparency texture.

STEP 111: Finally, go back to the Bump channel and reactivate the Coriolis layer there. Since there are no alpha layers to worry about, the bumps these two layers create will blend together the same way, regardless of which layer is on top. A new render will show a more natural-looking cloud pattern (Figure 5-82).

FIGURE 5-82 A combination of the procedural and the image map create a very nice cloud layer to finish off our planet.

We've spent enough time with this planet now. This would be a good time to save the object so we can move on to something completely different.

Project: Lacquer

Another common use of layered surfaces is to create multiple specular highlights that just can't be done any other way. We do have the BRDF shader plug-in, which can give us up to three different colored highlights, but the shapes of these highlights will all be similar. Some materials have both smooth highlights and distorted ones. A good example can be found in virtually any musical instrument shop, where these surfaces abound. Guitar bodies frequently have sparkly coatings and rich lacquer finishes, which create a smooth highlight over a surface that also has a distorted highlight. Wood grain itself, due to its fibrous nature, can have a very rippled highlight. The lacquer finish is also usually quite thick, and frequently adds color of its own to the surface it's applied to, leading to some very striking effects.

This isn't restricted to just musical instruments. Paint jobs on automobiles frequently employ a "clear coat," which gives the surface a deep shine created by the combination of the underlying paint's highlight and the tighter highlight on the glasslike coating. For now, we'll just worry about the lacquer look. The clear-coat effect will be covered later, and a few variations also appear on the CD.

STEP 112: Clear the scene and load the **Stratocaster.lwo** object from the CD. (Alternatively, you can load the **GuitarTest.lws** scene, which has the lighting used in the accompanying figures.) The object has a simple shiny red body, which doesn't look too bad (Figure 5-83). However, we're going to give it a makeover here.

FIGURE 5-83 The Flomder Guitarworks limited-edition red body Stratocaster.

Note: This is a modified version of Erik Flom's original model that was included with LightWave for the past several years. The main modification is that it is now a layered object, rather than the original five pieces it comprised before, in order to make it LightWave 6.5–friendly. Some new surfacing has been applied as well, but feel free to experiment with it.

STEP 113: Since we're going to add a nice wood lacquer to this guitar, we should first strip that red stuff off and get down to the bare wood—or in our case, create the wood surface. Open the Surface Editor and select the Stratbody surface. Open the Texture Editor for the Color channel and start an Image Map layer. Leave the Projection set to Planar, click the Image button, load the **Pinewood-vert.iff** image from the CD, then click the Automatic Sizing button. This will stretch the image to fit the body of the guitar. All the other settings will work fine as they are.

Before we move on, let's copy this layer, since we'll be using a copy of it soon. Click the Copy button and choose Current Layer. If you've set up VIPER, you should see a shiny wood surface applied to the body (Figure 5-84). It's nice, but looks a bit plastic yet.

FIGURE 5-84 A simple image-mapped wood surface, but a bit on the plastic side.

STEP 114: First of all, unfinished wood is not very shiny, so we need to dull this surface a bit. Remove the reflectivity from this surface, then lower the Specularity to 50%, and set the Glossiness to 5%. This will give it a very soft, wide highlight.

STEP 115: Wood, being a very porous material, also has a very diffuse surface, like rock, and thus it lights up fairly evenly. Click the Advanced tab and increase the Diffuse Sharpness to 50%. We could go higher, but we'll be adding some bumps, and higher values tend to wash bumps out.

Finally, since wood is also a fibrous material, a good portion of the light reflected from the surface actually reflects from inside the surface, either from between fibers or even from within the fibers themselves. This light will be colored slightly, and to simulate that, let's increase the Color Highlights to 100%.

We're almost there. As soon as we added the increased Diffuse Sharpness, the highlights on the surface started to get a bit hot and blown out. To fix this, we'll add another texture.

STEP 116: Open the Texture Editor for the Diffuse channel and paste the layer we copied earlier into this channel. This will add a little more contrast to the texture, as well as darken it a bit. To darken it even more, lower the Layer Opacity to 75%.

This will appear to make the surface brighter, but we're not done. Go back to the Surface Editor and lower the base Diffuse value to 0%. This just blended the texture we just created with a base value of 0%, or black, which had the effect of dimming the entire texture by 25% (the inverse of the 75% opacity we gave it). It should now look more like wood than the plastic we had earlier.

We have one final thing to do before we move on. You'll be very hard-pressed to find a piece of lumber that is made up of perfectly straight wood fibers. These fibers, if you look closely, all have what appear to be ripples running through them, as the fibers twist and turn through the length of the wood. This twisting causes the wood to reflect light in various directions, and focuses the highlights in the areas where the fibers curve. This is very similar to how light reflects off shiny hair. If you could split wood apart between the fibers without damaging them, you would end up with a smooth, rippled surface. This is what we're going to simulate now.

STEP 117: Open the Texture Editor for the Bump channel and paste that texture we copied earlier. This is just a lazy cheat to set up this texture with the settings we want. Now, click the Image button and load the **LightOakSm-Hor.iff** image from the CD. Notice that this image has the wood grain going horizontally, which will create bumps across the grain in our other image layers. This is intentional. Rather than use a procedural to create the rippling effect, we can just use a wood texture to create the rippling wood effect for us. Finally, lower the Texture Amplitude to 0.75 so the bumps aren't overpowering. You should now see a wood surface that has a few irregular highlights on it (Figure 5-85).

FIGURE 5-85 A rougher, unfinished-looking wood surface, ready to be lacquered.

OK, so we have a dull wood guitar now, but how do we get that shiny coat of lacquer? Model it, of course!

STEP 118: Click the Modeler button and the guitar will now appear in Modeler, filling the first four layers. We're interested in only the first layer for now, so select it by clicking the top of the layer 1 button in the upper-right corner.

We're going to create another set of polygons that cover the Stratbody surface, but rather than try to model the new surface, we'll simply duplicate an existing one, and save a lot of time.

STEP 119: Click the Polygons button on the bottom menu to switch to Polygons selection mode, then press W to open the Polygon Statistics panel. This panel will show a list of the various types of polygons that are in the scene. Second from the bottom of this list is an entry starting with Surf:. Click this to see a list of all the surfaces in this layer (Figure 5-86). Select the Stratbody surface, then click the small white plus sign to the left. All the polygons that make up the Stratbody surface will be highlighted. Copy these by pressing C (or clicking the Copy button on the bottom menu), then click the top of one of the empty layer buttons to move to a new layer. Layer 5 will do nicely.

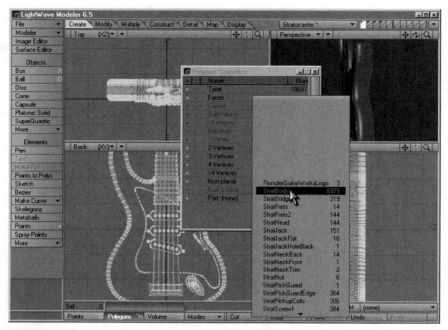

FIGURE 5-86 These Stratbody polygons will be used to create a lacquer surface.

STEP 120: Paste these polygons into this new layer by pressing V. These polygons will be our lacquer surface, so the first thing we need to do is create a new surface. Press Q to open the Change Surface panel, and create a new surface called Lacquer.

STEP 121: Now that we have our surface, we need to adjust the polygons slightly so they don't end up right on top of the original polygons. Before we do that, though, let's Merge Points by pressing M. You should get a message saying that 367 points have been removed. The original body of this guitar had separate front and back polygons that were not connected with the rounded sides. This separation stopped these two polygons from developing smoothing errors that would normally occur if these polygons were merged.

Note: Quite frequently, modelers will split polygons apart by cutting and pasting them, without merging points, in order to stop their surfaces from smoothing across certain areas. This is a simple cheat to avoid creating a new, nonsmoothing surface, or extra geometry to control it. While this method works well, disconnected polygons can cause all kinds of trouble for various modeling tools, especially for Boolean operations.

Another handy trick to avoid smoothing over corners, but without affecting modeling operations at all, is to simply set the Max Smoothing Angle for the surface to something lower than 45 degrees. This is great for beveled text, since it will stop the sides and front faces from smoothing into a 45-degree bevel, yet allow the polygons of the bevel to smooth themselves without affecting anything else. The side polygons will also have the same benefit.

STEP 122: Now that we've merged points to avoid any problems, click the Modify tab at the top of the screen. We have a handy tool called Smooth Scale, which we'll use to push all these polygons outward slightly. Click the More button in the Stretch area on the main toolbar and select the Smooth Scale tool (Figure 5-87). In the panel that opens, enter a value of 2 mm, which is the equivalent of a good thick layer of lacquer, then press Enter. The polygons will all be shifted 2 mm in the direction they're facing, giving us a copy of this guitar body that's an even 2 mm thicker all over.

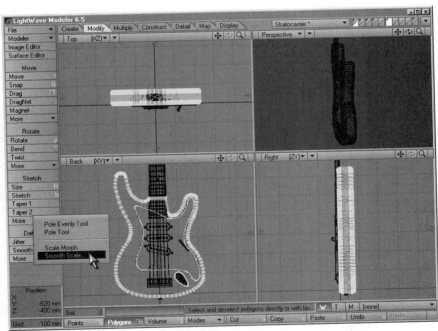

FIGURE 5-87 Smooth Scale will give our lacquer coating its thickness.

Now we need to do a small amount of cleanup. Since each polygon moved 2 mm in the direction it's facing, the edges had to be stretched slightly to keep them attached. For most of the polygons, this isn't a big problem, but we do have two big polygons here that will now have slightly crooked edges because of this.

STEP 123: Select these two large polygons, as shown in Figure 5-88. The first one can be selected easily in the Front view window by clicking one of the edges that cross the inner area. The second is more easily selected by clicking on the back in the Perspective view window. For now, just select the front polygon, since we can work on only one at a time. When the polygon's selected, press H to activate the Stretch tool, then place the cursor on the highlighted polygon in the Right view window. Make sure the small cross is directly on top of the yellow line, then hold down the Ctrl key and sharply drag left until the top value in the lower-left corner is 0%. This will scale the polygon down on the Z axis, centered on the point where you clicked. Since we're constraining the scaling to one axis by using the Ctrl key, the polygon will keep its shape. All we're doing is making it flat again (Figure 5-89). Once this polygon is flattened, do the same to the back polygon, again making sure the pointer is directly on the edge of the polygon.

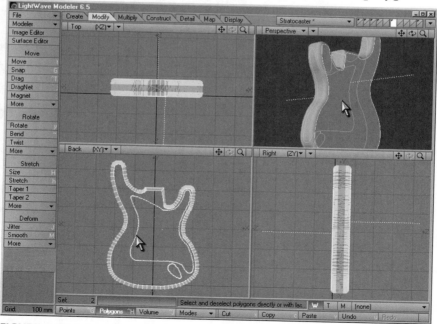

FIGURE 5-88 Select these two polygons that will need to be reflattened.

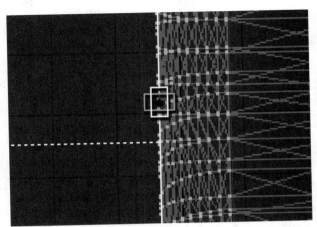

FIGURE 5-89 A close-up of the cursor position needed to flatten the polygon.

We're almost done now. We have only one small smoothing issue to worry about. If we apply smoothing to this surface, those two large polygons are going to try to smooth into the sides, which is why they were separated in the first place. Rather than using the cut and paste method of smoothing control, we'll use some extra geometry to solve the problem this time.

STEP 124: Select both of those two large polygons again, and then press B to activate the Bevel tool. Since we're going to add a very small bevel amount, it will be easier to do it numerically, so press N to open the Numeric panel. Click the Actions button at the top and choose Activate, then enter an Inset value of 2 mm, leaving everything else at 0. This will create a small strip of polygons around these large polygons, but sharing the same plane (Figure 5-90). Now these large polygons will smooth into the new polygons, which won't affect the shading since they're on the same plane. The new polygons, however, will smooth into the side polygons, and since they're so small, the smoothing effect they have will be constrained to the thin strips they occupy.

STEP 125: Before we can apply this lacquer surface to the body, we must triple all the polygons in this layer. Since we did a Smooth Scale operation that changed the geometry of this layer, we're going to have several nonflat polygons, which can cause trouble during rendering. Since we have the two large polygons still selected, and we know they're flat, we don't have to worry about them. It's the others

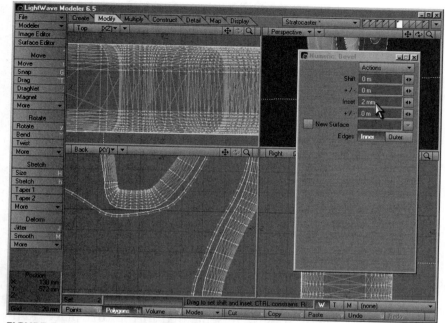

FIGURE 5-90 Adding a slight bevel with no shift value adds a small amount of geometry between the two large flat polygons and the surrounding curved edge, resulting in an "edgeless" smooth blend with the side polygons.

we need to work on. Press Shfit+' (the double quote key) to invert the polygon selection. Now press Shift+T to triple these polygons.

STEP 126: Finally, deselect everything by clicking in the gray area on the left side of the Modeler window, then press X to cut these polygons from this layer. Now go back to layer 1 and paste them there. We now have our lacquer surface built, and we're ready to move back to Layout.

Switch back to Layout, and the guitar should be updated with the new version we just worked on in Modeler (Figure 5-91). At first it may seem to have lost the wood texture we gave it earlier, but it's in there. To find it, let's start surfacing again.

STEP 127: Select the Lacquer surface in the Surface Editor and set the Transparency to 100%. Also set the Refraction Index to about 1.3 just to give it some refractive quality if you feel like using refraction in your renders. Finally, lower the Diffuse value to 0%. This will have very little effect on the surface since it's transparent, but the Diffuse level does affect specular highlights slightly.

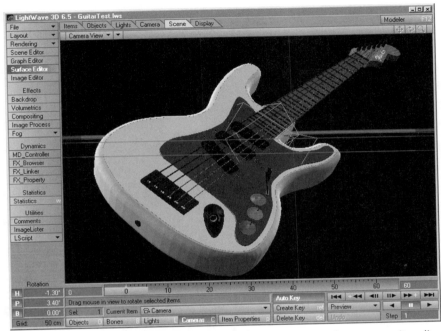

FIGURE 5-91 The updated guitar, seemingly without its wood surface we gave it earlier.

Note: The Refraction Index will have no effect if the Ray Trace Refraction check box is not selected in the Render Options panel, so setting a value here is a harmless action. Just be sure you're applying it only to surfaces that you would really want to refract in a scene, and only those surfaces. Otherwise, you could be in for some mighty long renders if you activate refraction in a scene that just happens to have an object with a large area of refracting polygons you set up before, but forgot about.

STEP 128: Activate Smoothing, and then set up a couple of Incidence Angle gradients for Specularity and Reflection. The following settings will give a good Lacquer look:

Specularity		Reflection	
Key	**Value**	**Key**	**Value**
0	100%	0	100%
90	50%	15	50% (Spline)
		90	0%

Finally, set the Glossiness to 20% to create a strong but soft high-light. Figure 5-92 shows the guitar with this clear lacquer finish so far.

FIGURE 5-92 The same wooden guitar, this time with a clear coat of lacquer. This would look better with a darker wood, or some color in the lacquer. . . .

You can see that we not only have the rippling effect visible on the wood surface, creating a few irregularly shaped highlights, but we also have smooth, bump-free highlights on the lacquer surface. Now, let's make this guitar look a little more classy.

STEP 129: Open the Texture Editor for the Color channel and apply an Image layer. Load one of the StratoLacquer images from the CD (**StratoLacquer5.iff** is a personal favorite) and click Automatic Sizing. These images create the classic deep red and orange gradients seen on many lacquered guitars. To finish the effect here, we need to do one last thing. Click the Advanced tab and increase the Color Filter value to 100%. A new render will show that not only does the surface look like real lacquered wood, but it also starts to bring out that natural glow that we're used to seeing in real wood, but rarely ever in computer graphics (Figure 5-93).

The quality of this glow depends on the wood images used, and these images aren't that special. In fact, you could use the Wood procedural to create a wood look and get similar results. Of course, lacquered wood isn't the only effect we can create. We can create an endless variety of surface effects with this technique. Different textures can be applied to both the lacquer surface or the underlying base surface. Replacing the StratoLacquer image with the **TigerStripes.iff** image, for instance, gives a new look to Erik's original Stratocaster design (Figure 5-94).

FIGURE 5-93 A little color in the lacquer brings out the wood nicely, and gives the guitar a real sense of elegance.

FIGURE 5-94 The original tiger-striped model, and the new version, updated for the new millennium.

Well, this should get you well on your way to feeling at ease with the new Surface Editor. It's really not that scary once you learn to break surfaces down into smaller chunks and work on them one layer at a time. And don't forget that Display option. Being able to view different channels independently of one another is a real treat.

Tip: All rendered images in these tutorials have been rendered using Enhanced Low Antialiasing with Adaptive Sampling turned off. If fine lines in your images seem to break up, it's probably due to either not having antialiasing turned on or not having Adaptive Sampling turned off.

Adaptive Sampling is a method in which LightWave looks at the rendered image it created on the first render pass and searches for pixels that are brighter/darker than their neighboring pixels by a given amount, which is specified in the Threshold setting. Unfortunately, it sees only the details that were seen on that first render pass. If LightWave was rendering a scene that had some very fine details, such as a chain-link fence or parking lot lines, far in the distance, those details will frequently fall between the pixels of the rendered image. A very thin line on a slight diagonal, for instance, when rendered normally, will appear to vanish in some areas as it crosses one row of pixels to another. This is because it's falling between the rays that LightWave shoots out from the camera, to see what's visible. On a standard video frame, LightWave is shooting out 640 × 480 rays, and the farther they travel, the farther they diverge, until they hit a surface. At that point, Light-Wave sees a surface, and generated a color for that pixel. Obviously, the further the rays diverge, the more space there is between them, meaning there's a lot more room for error. Objects can be completely missed if they're small enough, and not show up in the frame. Usually, some of the rays will hit the object, while others will miss it. In the case of textures, they'll start to appear to break up in the distance because the rays that see them are seeing parts of the texture that are actually quite distant from one another. During an animation, this can cause effects called chatter, moiré, or texture crawling.

When LightWave renders its antialiasing passes, it applies a slight offset to the data the camera sees, so in effect, it shoots out those same rays again, but this time they hit slightly different areas. When Adaptive Sampling is active, only the pixels that LightWave has considered to be an edge get rendered again. Pixels that LightWave considers safe are frequently the ones that have just missed a polygon on the first render pass. With our diagonal line, two adjacent pixels may have missed the line, each firing a ray to either side of it, and hitting the sky behind it. In the rendered image for that area, it would appear to be a solid sky, and thus, those pixels are virtually identical and don't need to be rendered again.

By turning Adaptive Sampling off, you force LightWave to resample every pixel on the frame. Each pixel then has a much greater chance of hitting anything that might be trying to hide between them. Fine details that were missed the first time will be seen on one of the subsequent render passes, and the data collected for all the passes is then blended together, to get an average value for each pixel. The result is a much more accurate image, with smoother fine lines and cleaner textures. Animations will look cleaner, and fine textures in the distance will look more natural and will suffer much less from chatter or noise. Full-frame antialiasing like this does take a bit longer to render, but unless you're animating scenes composed only of large, smooth colored objects, the results are usually worth the time.

6

Lighting and Atmospherics

Dave Jerrard

OVERVIEW

In this tutorial, we'll take a small break from the Surface Editor and take a look at lighting. Since there's so much ground that can be covered here (pun intended), rather than go through another long series of projects, we'll just note some of the many aspects of lighting and atmospheric effects in LightWave and how we can use them.

In this tutorial you will use:

- Light and shadow options

- Sky Tracer

- Fog

What you will need:

- Prebuilt objects and scenes included on CD

- Spare time

What you will learn:

- An understanding of LightWave's different light types

- How to correctly place a moon in the sky

- Backdrop shader usage

- SkyBall use

LIGHT TYPES

LightWave currently has five different light types that you can use to light a scene. While these are covered quite well in the manuals, there are a few points to be aware of. The first three types—Point, Spotlight, and Distant—all create relatively even lighting; when shadows are traced, these lights create razor-sharp shadows. Unlike a real physical light, these shadows are always sharp, no matter how distant the light source may be. To combat this, two newer light types were added: Linear and Area.

Linear is best thought of as a fluorescent tube that you can also scale. Light from this type of light radiates from a line segment, rather than from a point, like the Point and Spotlight types. Just as with a real fluorescent light, the shadows cast by this light are soft-edged. The softness of these shadows is determined by the length of the light, the proximity of the object it's shining on, and the surface receiving the shadow. It's important to note that the softness of this shadow is directional, based on the rotation of the light itself. Shadows will appear softer along the same direction as the length of the light. A horizontal light pointing down the Z axis will cause objects around it to have some softness to their shadows along the Z axis, but on the X and Y axis, the shadows will still appear sharp. Figure 6-1 shows (1) the familiar BallChex scene as seen in Layout with a single linear light over the ball and (2) the rendered frame. Since the light is aligned with the X axis, the shadow of the ball is softened in that direction, but it still becomes sharper near the bottom of the frame.

The amount of light hitting a surface from a linear light is based on how much of the linear light is visible to any given point. Since this light has some length, it's now possible for an object to eclipse only a part of it, unlike the other light types, which, since they're actually a nondimensional point in space, are either visible or not. Basically, with this type of light, the more of the length that's visible, the brighter the light. This also explains the dark areas at the tips of this light. Since this light has only length, but no thickness, if you look straight at the end of it, it will vanish. Since the light itself is invisible from this angle, there's no visible source of light either, so anything that falls in this area will render dark. Figure 6-2 shows the lighting pattern of this type of light.

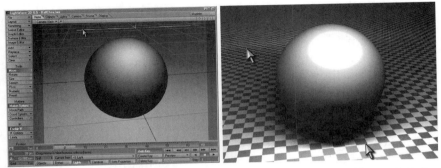

FIGURE 6-1 The position of a Linear light and its effect in a rendered frame. Note the two linear shadow artifacts designated by the arrows in the rendered frame, which match the angle of the light in Layout.

FIGURE 6-2 The lighting pattern of the Linear light. The line in the center is the size of the light, and is located a couple of centimeters in front of the white wall. Note the darkening at the ends, as well as the area near the light itself. This indicates that placing the light close to objects should be avoided.

Unfortunately, the way this light type is aligned, a dark end of it is pointing in the same direction the light is facing. This means that if you're trying to set the light up by looking through it, what you see from its point of view will get very little light at all. The Linear light casts most of its light to the sides, so setting one of these up using the target will rarely be useful. Linear lights are fantastic for creating the ambient glow from effects elements such as lasers and rocket thrust. Place one of these lights inside one of these elements and scale the light to fit it, and the laser beam or flame will appear to actually cast light onto surfaces nearby, complete with the appropriate shadow softness.

Area lights, on the other hand, do cast light in the direction they're facing. Area lights take a little longer to render than Linear lights but are more versatile. Since they're basically light-emitting flat panels that can be stretched vertically and horizontally, they can be used like Linear lights. Also like Linear lights, though, they have a dark region. This region is larger than you get with a Linear light, since it occurs in a full 360-degree arc around the light's edge, where it has no thickness. Most of the light from this model shines forward and behind the light. Figure 6-3 shows the pattern of light created by an Area light. Since Area lights cast light in the direction they're facing, they can be targeted to other objects, or positioned while you are looking through them.

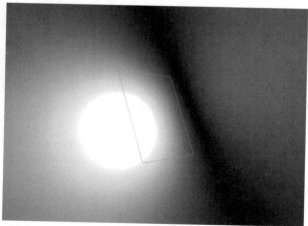

FIGURE 6-3 The purple outline shows the orientation of an Area light, and the vertical wall behind it reveals a similar lighting pattern to the Linear light. Note the absence of light along the edge of the Area light, where it would be seen edge-on.

Both of these lights create much more realistic-looking shadows than the first three types, but at a significant cost in render times. Shadows from an Area light take roughly seven times longer to calculate than a regular shadow, depending on the Area light's quality setting. A lower quality takes less time, but results in a grainier shadow. Currently LightWave has Area light quality settings ranging from 1 to 5, with 1 creating a very harsh, dithered shadow, and 5 creating an exceptionally smooth shadow. The render times between these two extremes can range from seconds to hours, depending on the scene. Generally, a quality of 5 takes roughly 10 times longer than a quality of 1. Figure 6-4 shows a comparison using the BallChex scene lit by an Area light at different quality settings, and the render times involved for each.

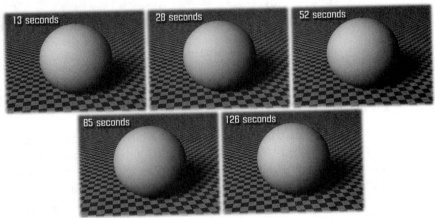

FIGURE 6-4 A comparison of the five Area light quality settings and their respective render times. Without any antialiasing, grain can be seen in all five shadows, but is most apparent in the first two images.

However, rendering with Antialiasing turned on and Adaptive Sampling turned off will clean this shadow up quite nicely, so you can actually get acceptable results with lower-quality lights. Figure 6-5 shows the same setups rendered with antialiasing. Note that a light quality of 2 looks better with antialiasing than a non-antialiased frame with a quality of 3.

Note: 6.5B introduces a new feature called shading noise reduction, which smoothes the grain caused by area lights. This can be found in the global illumination panel.

FIGURE 6-5 The same setup, but with Low Enhanced antialiasing applied. Note that the quality of the shadows actually surpasses that of a higher light quality seen in the previous images. The last image shows a standard Spotlight's shadow map with Fuzziness set to 5, just for comparison. While the effects are very similar, the shadow map has a uniform soft edge, while the Area light becomes softer with distance.

Aside from their superior shadow rendering, Linear and Area lights also surpass the other lights in general surface shading, particularly when surfaces have bump maps applied. This is because the light rays coming from these lights are hitting a point on the surface from several different directions at the same time. Surfaces using a higher Diffuse Sharpness setting, whose bumps would normally be washed out under normal lights, will look much better under an Area light. Area lights are also exceptional at duplicating sunlight for both their shading and the shadows they create. Their higher intensity compared to other lights is also a benefit, since a scene can be set up using the faster Spot or Distant lights, and then simply switched to an Area light for final rendering.

Note: One other important thing to keep in mind with Linear and Area lights is their intensity. Due to the nature of their lighting models, these lights tend to be twice as bright as normal lights. This is important to keep in mind for those times you might want to do test renders with normal lights as stand-ins, and then switch to Area lights for a final render. It takes only one extra bright Area light to wash out a scene.

Setting up an Area light in a scene requires a little more planning than normal lights due to the fact that their size is now a consideration. The effects of Area lights are best when there's some space between them and the objects they're shining on. This distance between the light and the object should generally be at least half the Area light's size. The following tutorial will illustrate the effective use of an Area light.

Area Light Setup

We'll use the old BallChex scene as our test subject again, though the technique here works anywhere.

STEP 1: Load the **BallChex.lws** scene and then press 4 to enter Perspective view. Next, click the small double-curved-arrow button in the upper-right corner (Figure 6-6) to rotate the view. This allows us to see the scene from an external vantage point, without adjusting anything in the scene itself.

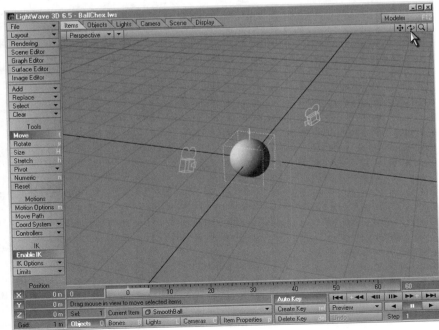

FIGURE 6-6 Viewing the scene in Perspective view allows us to look down on everything in the scene without affecting anything. Here we see the BallChex scene and the two cameras that are set up in it.

STEP 2: Select the light in the scene and press P to open the Light Properties panel. Change the light to an Area light, then lower the intensity to 50% to compensate for the extra brightness this light type has.

This light is already placed a fair distance away from the rest of the scene, which you'll be able to see by pressing 5 to look through the light (Figure 6-7). However, looking through the light doesn't tell us anything other than what the light is shining on. In fact, without actually doing a test render, it's difficult, especially with area lights, to tell just what the shadows will look like. VIPER can give us a good indication of what the shading will be like, but as we've discovered earlier, it also doesn't handle shadows. So just how do we know how to set up an Area light?

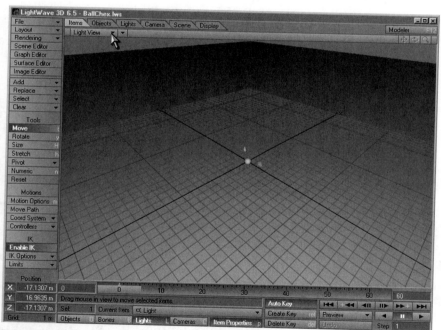

FIGURE 6-7 The scene as seen from the light's point of view.

STEP 3: Press 4 again to enter Perspective view. Then click the View Rotate button in the upper-right corner again and rotate the view so your position is actually below the ground plane, looking up at the ball. Keep rotating until the light becomes visible in the frame.

You should now see the Area light just behind the ball, as in Figure 6-8. Now, pay close attention to the grid, and rotate the view very slightly, so the Area light moves back and forth across the edge of the ball. The part of the grid that is always in front of the Area light, while the light is still eclipsing the edge of the ball, is the part that is going to be receiving some amount of shadow (Figure 6-9). The intensity of the shadow in this area depends on how much of the light is behind the ball for any given point. If the light is smaller, or more distant so it appears smaller from this angle, the shadow will appear sharper.

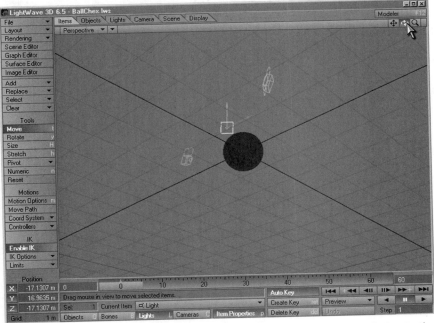

FIGURE 6-8 Rotating the Perspective view allows us to see the light in relation to the objects in the scene.

Figure 6-10 illustrates how the size and position of an area light affect its shadows. The wider the triangle the edge of the object and the width of the light create, the softer the shadow will be. This area of partial shadow is called the *penumbra,* and its angle is an exact opposite to the one created by the width of the light and the edge of the object.

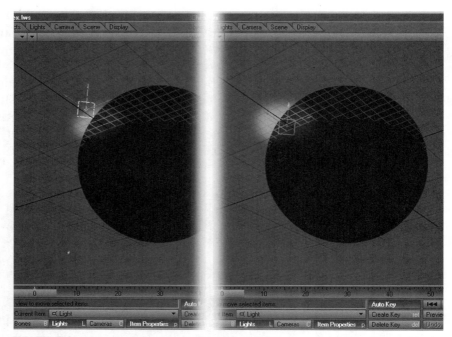

FIGURE 6-9 By rotating the view back and forth, you can get an idea of how wide the penumbra of the shadow will be.

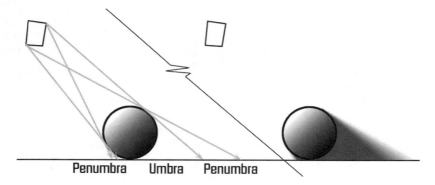

FIGURE 6-10 An illustration showing the umbra, or solid shadow area, and the penumbra created by an Area light shining on a ball.

By using this trick of looking up at the light, we can not only position the light and get an idea of the shadow it will create, but also set the size of the light. The light is currently fairly large, and generates a nice soft shadow. If we want it to look more like sunlight, we'll need to sharpen the angle of the penumbra. We can do that either by moving the light further away, or by simply scaling it down. Sunlight on earth comes from the sun, a huge ball of gas over 860,000 miles in diameter, which is 93 million miles away. At this distance, all the light rays hitting the earth are virtually traveling in the same direction, which is why the Distant light is so commonly used for outdoor scenes. Yet when you look at the sun, even from this distance, it still appears to have some thickness to it. This thickness is enough that the light rays hitting the earth actually have up to a half a degree of variation in their direction. This means that the angle of the penumbra of a shadow on earth is 0.5 degrees, which doesn't sound like much, but it is enough to cause the shadow of your head to becomes nothing more than a blurry blob when it's only a few meters away.

Fact: The sun and the moon both appear about the same size in the sky. They fill an area of the sky, measured in *arc angles,* of 1,800 *arc seconds,* which can also be stated as 30 *arc minutes*. There are 60 arc seconds in an arc minute, and 60 arc minutes in an arc degree, just like the measurements used to find locations on earth using latitude and longitude. The arc size of the moon and sun is actually about the same as an aspirin held out at arm's length.

To duplicate this in LightWave, we need to make the light fill the same arc angle. If we size the light to fill it, we run the risk of the light appearing only in a small area, as you would get from a normal light bulb a few meters away. Another solution is to simply duplicate the sun's actual size and distance, but this is overkill, and LightWave's math precision isn't quite up to that challenge. We can however, compromise, and place the light very far away, and get good results.

STEP 4: Select the light and activate the Move tool, and then choose Coord System > Coordinate System: Local on the main toolbar for the Items tab (Figure 6-11). This will have the immediate effect of causing the handles of the light (if they are visible) to match their orientation to that of the light itself, rather than the grid in Layout. The blue Z axis handle will now be pointing straight out through the front of the light.

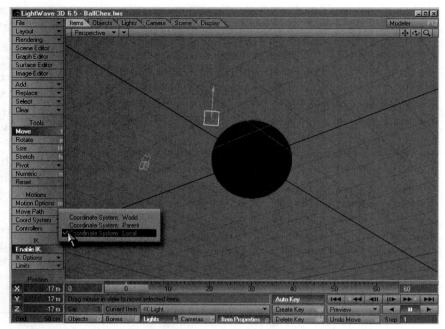

FIGURE 6-11 By setting the Coordinate System to Local, we can move the light in a straight line in whatever direction it's facing.

Deactivate the X and Y buttons at the lower-left corner, leaving the Z button active. Now we'll be able to move the light only along the Z axis, but due to the change in the coordinate system we just made, the light will actually be able to be moved only along its own Z axis.

While staying in Perspective view, drag back and the light will begin to recede into the distance, in a straight line. If the light is near the center of the Layout window, it will appear to simply shrink.

Note: We can also temporarily switch to Local Coordinates by simply holding down the Ctrl key while we move or rotate something.

We could spend all day slowly moving that light farther and farther until it's a small point in the sky, but let's speed things up a bit. Press the right square bracket key ( ]) a few times to increase the grid size and make everything in Perspective view move farther away from us. To counter that, press the period key the same number of times, and the view will zoom in, virtually countering the side effect of the grid size change.

Tip: The left square bracket key ([) and the comma key work together the same way.

Now when you move the mouse, the light will move through the scene much faster. We'll just move it back until the coordinate readout in the lower left corner reads −200 meters for the Z axis.

Note: Even though we're using the light's Local Coordinates, the values listed in the position readout are still using the normal (Parent) coordinate system.

The light should appear quite small in Perspective view now (Figure 6-12). We have a good distance between the light and the objects so the light will bathe the scene in a nice, even illumination, but at this distance, the 1-meter-square light fills less than the half-degree arc angle we'd like.

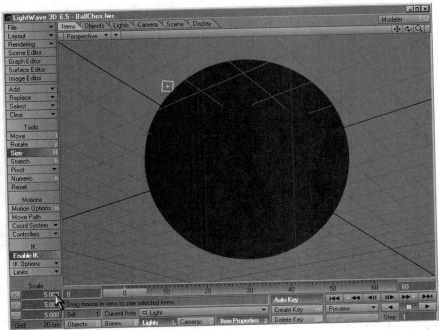

FIGURE 6-12 After we move the light 200 meters away, it appears much smaller in the sky.

Unfortunately, LightWave doesn't provide us with direct information such as arc angles; we must actually do the math ourselves. We can cheat, though, and use a temporary Spotlight for reference.

STEP 5: Click the Add button and choose Lights > Add Spotlight from the menu. Don't worry about the name, since we won't be keeping this light for long. This light will appear in the middle of the scene, at the 0, 0, 0 location. This puts it inside the ball object. Press 5 to switch to Light View and then rotate the light up and to the right until the upper left rear corner of the ball's bounding box becomes visible, as in Figure 6-13. The Area light will actually be hiding near that corner, but is so distant that it can't be seen with the light's current view angle.

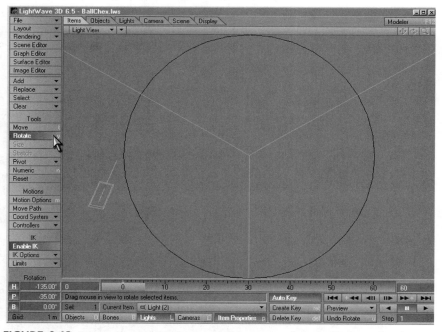

FIGURE 6-13 Rotate the Spotlight toward this corner of the ball's bounding box to find the other light, which is just distant enough to be hiding against the thin lines in this view.

STEP 6: Open the Light Properties panel and lower the Spotlight Cone Angle using the small slider button. As the cone angle narrows, the Area light will start to come into view. When the Cone Angle reaches 0.5 degrees, the Area light will be quite visible (Figure 6-14).

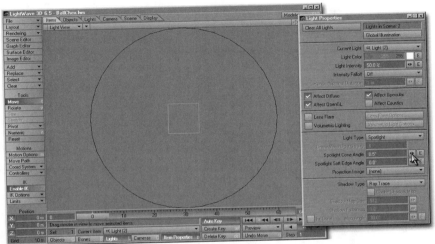

FIGURE 6-14 The Spotlight Cone Angle can also be used as a zoom feature when looking through the light. Here, the Cone Angle is lowered to 0.5 degrees, and the Area light is plainly visible.

Note: The Spotlight Cone Angle measures how far the edge of the cone is angled away from the centerline of the light. At 90 degrees, the cone would appear flat, and the light, if placed in the center of an inward facing sphere, would illuminate exactly one half of the sphere. At 180 degrees, the light would behave just like a Point light, radiating light in all directions.

Since we want our Area light to match the size of the sun, we want it to cover a half degree of arc. We can use this Spotlight to show us exactly what that amount of arc looks like by simply setting its cone angle. Enter a Cone Angle of 0.25 degrees (remember, the cone angle is only the measurement from the center of the cone, not the opposite side, so we need to use half the amount), and the view through the light will show us a full half degree of arc. The Area light will be approximately one-third the width of this view now.

Note: The actual area of the spotlight cone, as seen through the light, is a square that's the same width as the circle we see. If we were to project a white image through the light, we would actually have a square beam of light, whose corners would extend outside this circular area.

STEP 7: Now that we know how big the sun would appear (if we did actually place a full-sized sun 93 million miles away, it should fill the circle of this view almost exactly—almost, because the sun's actually wider at its equator), we can size the Area light to match. But there is a trick. If we simply select the Area light, our view will switch to its point of view, looking back down at the spotlight. We have to be tricky here. Open the Scene Editor and select the Area light, which will be the first light in the list. Now click the Size button in the Layout window. Next, hold down the Ctrl key and click the Spotlight in the Scene Editor. The view will switch back to the Spotlight, and we'll see the Area light also selected. Now we can change the size of the light to fit the Spotlight's view (Figure 6-15).

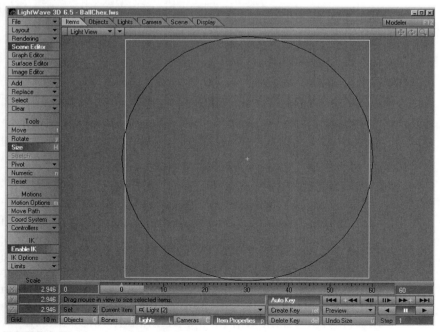

FIGURE 6-15 The view through the spotlight, showing the area light filling the field of view.

We just tricked LightWave into allowing us to select an option that wasn't normally available. If we selected the lights in the reverse order, we would be looking down at the Spotlight and resizing that instead. The options that we can adjust are the ones available to the last item we select. However, we also got around that by selecting one that wouldn't be available for the last item. The Size tool is normally unavailable for Spotlights, so the only way to activate it is by switching to the Area light. When we selected the Size tool, we forced it to stay active while we selected the Spotlight. At the same time, the view mode switched to the Spotlight's view. Now we have both lights selected, and the Size tool is actually scaling both of them. However, the only real effect it has is on the Area light. The Spotlight will change size only in Layout, but this has no effect during rendering.

If we render this scene now, we'll get a very accurate shadow, which will match what we get from real sunlight (Figure 6-16).

FIGURE 6-16 The Area light now creates a shadow that accurately simulates real sunlight.

Note: For a more detailed treatment on shadow types, as well as the technique that has become known as the "Spinning Light Trick," check out the bonus tutorial "A New Spin on Lighting" on the CD, which was originally published in NewTekniques but is included here, updated for LightWave 6.5.

OK, that's enough about shadows. A couple other settings for lights can be a bit tricky to understand. You may have noticed that we now have two new falloff modes in addition to the familiar Linear falloff that's been in LightWave for a long time. The Intensity Falloff menu now includes Inverse Distance and Inverse Distance^2. Inverse Distance^2 uses the actual falloff properties of physical lights in the real world. The old falloff was a nice general method for 3D, but it falls quite short of the real thing, especially when you're trying to match the lighting of a live-action image, or even worse, trying to combine 3D with one. If something gets too close to a light in the real world, aside from getting a little toasty, the object will be very difficult to photograph, since it will tend to be overexposed near the light and underexposed a very short distance away from it. This is due to the way real light fades off sharply near the source; as the distance from the light increases, the rate of falloff decreases.

This is the main reason photography and film studios need to use such bright lights. To get smooth, even lighting over everything, several very bright lights have to be placed far enough away that their falloff effect is minimized. But placing them so far away also means that the intensity of the light hitting the scene has already decreased quite a bit over that distance. The farther the subject is from the light, the more evenly lit it will be. Sunlight, coming from 93 million miles away, has already lost a great deal of intensity by the time it reaches earth, and it basically illuminates everything on the surface with equal intensity. The top of a skyscraper receives just as much sunlight as the bottom. This same type of lighting indoors would be virtually impossible to achieve, since we'd have to place an impossibly bright light a million miles out into space, just to achieve the same kind of falloff for a city model. Hollywood hasn't reached that kind of movie budget yet.

If we tried to use a normal LightWave light, the contrast would just never match the real world. Near the light's source, the falloff would be too gradual, and farther out, it would be too sharp. Not anymore!

We won't get into the technicalities of these lights or how to use them, but we will look at how the falloff works for them. The Linear falloff mode has a falloff range attached to it. This range is the maximum distance the light will reach to. A value of 1 m means the light will illuminate objects within this range. The light intensity falls off in a linear fashion between the light itself and this maximum range. A light with 100% intensity will light objects half a meter away with only 50% intensity, and objects 25 centimeters away would receive 75% intensity. Objects at the maximum range would receive virtually no light at all.

With the inverse modes, the range is now called Nominal Distance. This is very different from the linear range. The intensity of the light at this nominal distance is *equal* to the light's Intensity setting. The intensity of the light then increases progressively as the distance to the light decreases. This means that objects within this nominal range will be receiving much more light than the Intensity value would suggest. Objects outside this range will get slightly less light, and the falloff effect will continue far beyond this point.

Figure 6-17 illustrates the different falloff modes clearly. The balls in the scene are all half a meter in diameter and positioned at 1-meter intervals. The light has a Range/Nominal Distance of 2 m, and is placed exactly 1 m from the front of the first ball. As you can see with the Linear falloff, there is no light beyond 2 m, so the second ball is completely dark. However, the second ball with the two Inverse modes receives as much light as it did when there was no falloff. The first ball is getting a much harsher light with the Inverse Distance than it did before, while the rest of the balls all receive slightly less light beyond the 2-meter range. With Inverse Distance^2, the first ball is so overexposed at 1 m that there's very little gradation left in the shading. The remaining ball outside the nominal distance proceeds to get darker faster than with the Inverse Distance mode. You can also see that the lighting on the ground is much more evenly distributed in the distance than it is near the light source for both of the inverse modes.

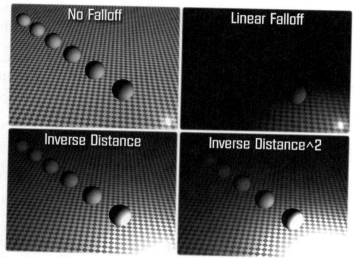

FIGURE 6-17 A comparison of the four different falloff modes.

The Inverse Distance^2 mode is best suited for scenes where you're trying to simulate lighting from standard light sources, such as table lamps or candle flames. As you can see from the figure, it gives a nice sense of intimacy to the image. The Inverse Distance mode, due to its smoother, longer-reaching falloff, is a better choice for focused lights, such as spotlights, headlights, and other lights that shine in one general direction.

Linear is a good, quick-and-dirty mode that works well for most 3D scenes, as it has for the past several years. Since its range can be explicitly defined, it is also ideal for controlling lights used to fill in shadow areas. Since there are no lighting effects outside the range, these lights can be used quite liberally without casting unwanted shadows. They can also be safely used without shadows, since their lighting range can be so strictly limited.

Let's discuss one last note about Inverse lights before we move on. Since the Nominal Distance is the point where the light's Intensity value is actually applied, changing it can seriously change the overall intensity of the light. In Figure 6-17, the light in each case was 100% intense with a Range/Nominal Distance of 2 m. Figure 6-18 shows the same light, using the Inverse Distance^2 falloff, with the Nominal Range increased to 4 m. The light's Intensity value is still 100%, but the greater nominal range places this illumination value further from the light source. The result is that the intensity of the light's effect is increased dramatically, severely overexposing the first ball. When using these modes, you'll generally want to keep the Nominal Distance value low since it's quite easy to overexpose a scene, even with a light that has a low intensity.

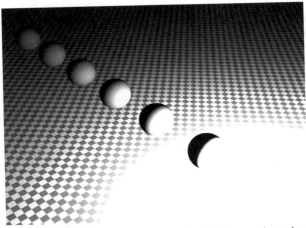

FIGURE 6-18 Increasing the Nominal Distance has the effect of making the light brighter.

ENVIRONMENTS

OK, so we've looked at some of the main differences in lights and learned how to re-create sunlight. Now let's take a look at the sky this sunlight usually comes through.

Some of the most common settings for scenes in LightWave, next to the popular space scenes, are outdoor scenes. These usually require some sort of a sky since they're outdoors, and there's no ceiling to cover up that empty black backdrop color. The simplest way to add a sky to a scene is to use the Gradient Backdrop in the Effects panel. This simply creates two vertical color gradients instead of the default black. The first two colors are generally used to create the sky, and the default colors work well for this. The second two create an artificial ground, which can be confusing to most newcomers because it's not actually an object in the scene, and thus will not receive shadows. The gradients are not the same as those found in the Surface Editor, and the only control we have over them is with the Squeeze setting. This is simply a bias control that will push the midpoint of the gradient closer to or farther from the horizon. Higher values move it closer, which is usually the direction you'll want it to move.

Figure 6-19 shows the default sky gradient and the same gradient with a higher Sky Squeeze. As you can imagine, a higher Sky Squeeze would be good for creating a sunset or sunrise. Unfortunately, this gradient is applied around the entire scene, as though it were mapped on the inside of a giant sphere. The horizon you see facing north (or facing straight down the Z axis, which most people would equate with north in LightWave) is the same as any other direction. Sunsets don't work that way. On earth, a sunset tends to affect only the sky around the sun, which for sunset is the western part of the sky. The eastern horizon is generally darker and still quite blue, providing there aren't many clouds in the sky. This is one of the areas where the Gradient Backdrop falls short.

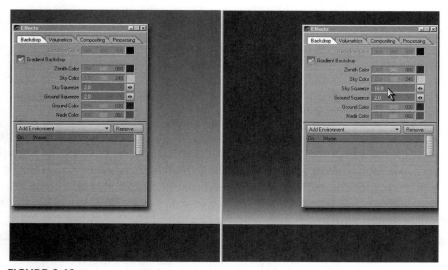

FIGURE 6-19 Two versions of the same sky gradient and their respective settings.

This is not to say it's completely useless. With the right colors, the gradient is still quite adept at creating a sky, as evidenced in the Blade Runner scene, **Blade.lws**, located in the Space directory that comes with LightWave. Figure 6-20 shows a clear blue sky over a mountain scene that uses the Gradient Backdrop.

FIGURE 6-20 The gradient backdrop used in a mountain scene creates a very clear sky effect.

Note: The Ground and Nadir colors don't have to be ground colors. Setting the Ground color to the same color as the Horizon will create a smooth three-color gradient. One good use of a three-color gradient is underwater scenes, where you would have a lighter blue color above and a darker blue below the camera. Adding some fog using the Backdrop Fog option would finish the effect. This is actually used in another sample scene included with LightWave—**UnderwaterShip.lws**.

While this backdrop is handy for nice clear skies, it does prove to be less interesting than if it had clouds. However, there is no option to add clouds to the backdrop. We do have a few ways to add them, though. The first is to simply create a cloud texture on a transparent surface.

Every Cloud Has a Polygonal Lining

Probably the easiest way to create clouds is to simply use the "cloudball" or hemisphere object.

STEP 8: Start Modeler and select the Ball tool. Press N to open the Numeric panel and create a ball using the values shown in Figure 6-21. This will give us a squashed ball that we'll use for our clouds.

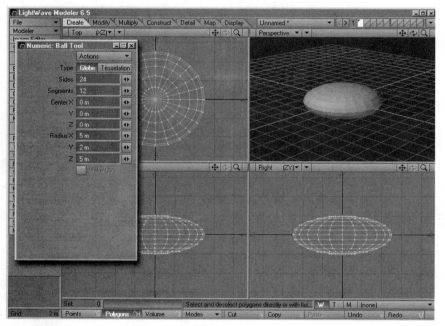

FIGURE 6-21 The beginnings of a cloudy sky.

STEP 9: Since this object will be placed around the scene, we don't need the polygons on the bottom. Use the right mouse button to lasso all the polygons of the bottom half of the sphere, as shown in Figure 6-22, and then press Delete to remove them. Finally, press F to flip the polygons around so they're facing inward. This will make them visible to the camera, which will be located inside this object when we use it in Layout.

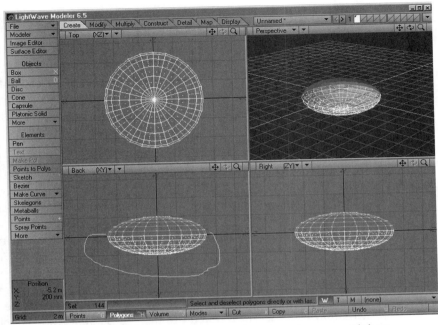

FIGURE 6-22 Select these lower polygons by dragging a lasso around them.

STEP 10: Save this object as **CloudBall.lwo** and send it over to Layout using the small menu in the upper-right corner. Switch back to Layout, since we're done with Modeler for a while.

STEP 11: When you switch over to Layout, the camera will automatically move itself back to a point where the CloudBall object will fit in the camera view. Select the Camera, and click the Move button. Next, click the Reset button and the camera will snap to the center of the object. Rotate the camera up slightly so the CloudBall fills most of the view.

Note: The camera will automatically reposition itself to fit objects inside its view as they're loaded. This will happen only if the camera has not been given any keyframes. As soon as a keyframe has been set, the camera will no longer change position to fit any new objects that are loaded.

Open the Effects panel and select the Gradient Backdrop check box so we have our sky colors.

STEP 12: Open the Surface Editor and select the Smoothing check box. Since the polygons are all facing down, they're unlikely to receive any light, so we can lower the Diffuse value to 0% and raise the Luminosity to 100% so the surface has an even illumination to it. Increase the color to 240, 240, and 240 to make it a brighter white. So far, we simply have a white surface, which is just what we want for the clouds. Now we just need to form the shapes of the clouds.

STEP 13: Open the Texture Editor for the Transparency channel and select Procedural Texture for the Layer Type. We'll use the Turbulence texture, since it does a wonderful job at creating fluffy clouds. In fact, if you have VIPER running, you should already see a cloudlike pattern in it.

Raise the Texture Value to 100%, which will increase the transparency of the texture, and then raise the Contrast to 50% or more.

Note: The VIPER preview will show a slight gray edge around the clouds. This is simply because VIPER doesn't display transparency, and is only "faking it" with the backdrop colors. The clouds will lose this gray color when they're actually rendered.

STEP 14: Increase the Frequencies setting to 5 to add some finer detail to the clouds. Finally, lower the Y scale of the texture to 0.2 so the clouds flatten out a little. A test render will show some nice fluffy-looking clouds, like the ones in Figure 6-23.

To break up the clouds more, increase the Small Power slightly. Increasing the Contrast will create a harder edge to the clouds and clear up the sky between them more as well.

If you want less cloud cover, add a second texture layer and offset its position. Since this texture is actually making areas of the surface transparent, duplicating it will increase the area of transparency, resulting in less cloud cover (Figure 6-24).

Other textures can be used to create the clouds as well, so don't be afraid to try other ideas. If you give the texture a slight amount of motion, not only will the clouds move across the sky, but because they're moving through a curved surface, they'll actually change shape as they move.

FIGURE 6-23 The cloud texture rendered against a gradient backdrop creates an impressively realistic sky.

FIGURE 6-24 The same sky, with a duplicate cloud layer added with a 1-meter offset on the Y axis, creates a less cloud-covered sky.

The main benefit from this technique is that not only do you have the full arsenal of the Surface Editor at your disposal, but the clouds created can also cast shadows on the other objects in the scene. Figure 6-25 shows the mountain scene again, this time with this CloudBall added.

FIGURE 6-25 The same mountain scene, this time with our CloudBall added. Note the shadow of the clouds across the mountain face.

Note that the object, as we built it, is a bit small to cover a landscape. By keeping the object within a few meters, we don't have to worry about having to use large values for the texture scales. The object itself, on the other hand, is easily scaled up in Layout. For the mountain scene, it was simply scaled to 1,000 times its normal size.

Placing clouds on polygons isn't the only way to add clouds to a scene. There are three other methods, but we'll just cover two of them here. The third method, which uses HyperVoxels, is very time-consuming. While it can work quite well, it also tends to be overkill in most cases, and the polygonal method we just described can serve just as well.

The other two ways we can add clouds are through the use of environment shaders. The first one is Sky Tracer, which we've already seen a couple of times in the previous tutorials. This shader is applied through the Add Environment menu in the Effects panel, right below the Backdrop options. This shader, when it's applied here, will appear through transparent surfaces and in reflections, unlike its Pixel Filter version. Generally, you'll be using it as an environment shader, since it's more useful this way.

This shader works by calculating a volumetric cloud pattern and then applying the results to the backdrop (Figure 6-26). The clouds actually respond to the angle of the light, and the light itself can even be seen in the sky as a sun or moon, but there is a catch. The position of the sun or moon in the sky is not related to the direction the light is facing. Instead, much like lens flares, the sun appears in a straight line with the light's position and the camera. If the light is visible in the frame, the sun will appear in the sky at that same spot. Normally, the position of a Distant light is unimportant, but when using Sky Tracer, position does matter. It's possible to have a Distant light off to the left side of the screen, pointing left, which would light everything in the scene from the right side. However, the sun it creates in Sky Tracer would appear on the left, and in fact, would be lighting the clouds from the left as well (Figure 6-27).

Since this shader is applied to the backdrop, it doesn't react with objects in the scene. No matter how far an object is, it won't go through the clouds, and the clouds won't cast shadows on objects.

FIGURE 6-26 The same mountain again, this time with a SkyTracer sky, creating a dark, stormy look in the distance.

FIGURE 6-27 An example of incorrect lighting. Although the light used to illuminate the ball is pointing to the left, its position in Layout dictates the location of the sun it creates in SkyTracer.

We won't get into the various options of this shader here, since they can easily take up an entire tutorial of their own. However, the shader does have a handy preview option, which makes tweaking the settings much more interactive. Again, the best way to learn this shader is by playing with it.

The second method of adding clouds to the sky is another environment shader called LW_TextureEnvironment. This shader allows us to apply textures to the backdrop, as though it were a sphere placed around the entire scene. Images, procedurals, and even gradients can be used to create an infinite variety of textured backdrops. However, this shader supplies two new gradient types: Pitch and Heading. Pitch works in a similar fashion to the Gradient Backdrop, creating a gradient that starts at a point 90 degrees above us, and continues down to a point 90 degrees below us. The middle of this gradient is at 0 degrees pitch, and this is where the horizon would appear. By placing a key at this point and using the Stepped smoothing method, we can create a hard-edged horizon line.

The Heading parameter works in a similar fashion, with the center of the gradient located at the positive end of the Z axis and the two ends of the gradient meeting at the negative end.

Textures can also be layered here as well, allowing us to create virtually any kind of backdrop we could want. Just for fun, let's re-create those clouds we made earlier with this shader.

STEP 15: Clear the scene, since we don't need anything loaded for this. Open the Effects panel and click the Add Environment menu. Choose the LW_TextureEnvironment shader and then double-click its entry in the list below. A set of controls will appear in the Effects panel. These controls basically set the size of an imaginary sphere on which the texture will be mapped. No matter what the size is here, the shader will always appear in the background. In most cases, you won't need to adjust anything here. The only control you'll usually use is the Texture button, so click that.

STEP 16: In the Texture Editor, select a Gradient layer and set its Input Parameter to Pitch. First we'll re-create the familiar Gradient Backdrop default colors. Change the color of the top key to 0, 40, and 80, which is the color of the zenith. Add a new key at −1 degrees (keys can't be placed much closer together than about 1 degree on this gradient) and give it a color of 120, 180, and 240. That's the color of the sky at the horizon. Now create another key just below this one, and set its smoothing mode to Stepped. This will create the hard edge of the Gradient Backdrop at the horizon. Give this key a color of 50, 40, and 30 and set its Parameter to 0 degrees. Finally, add one last key at the bottom and make its color 100, 80, and 60.

We've just recreated the default Gradient Backdrop. Now let's add those clouds.

STEP 17: Add a new Procedural layer and set it up the same way we did in Step 14, but set the color to 240, 240, and 240. Press F9 and you should see a familiar-looking sky (Figure 6-28).

FIGURE 6-28 A new set of clouds created by the LW_ TextureEnvironment shader.

Figures 5-46 and 5-58 in the last tutorial used this shader to create their skies. The **BG-Sky.lws** scene was used to create Figure 5-58, and is included on the CD.

There is one unfortunate problem that all these methods of sky creation suffer from, though, and I've seen it pop up quite often in movies and on TV. Since these skies are backdrop elements, they're rendered behind everything else in the scene. This is usually what we want, but every once in a while, it's nice to have something behind that sky, like a planet or moon. Scenes like this are quite popular in science fiction, and they make for some fantastic scenery. The movie *Pitch Black* used one such shot in one of its most dramatic scenes, but unfortunately, got it all wrong. In that scene, the ringed planet appeared in a way that would not be possible (aside from it having two sets of rings in the impossible arrangement of one above the other). It was darker than the sky!

The atmosphere of a planet is an additive effect. You can see this quite easily by just looking up at a clear sky during the day. In space, the sky is completely black, except for the tiny specks of light we know as stars. Between the stars, there's really not much out there for light to come from, so most of space is completely black. At night, the sun no longer illuminates the sky, so the additive effect is reduced considerably, and we see the stars against this blackness. During the day, the sun lights up the atmosphere, and the blue scattering of light through it is added to that blackness beyond.

In additive color, black, which is RGB values of 0, 0, and 0, added to blue, say, 20, 180, and 255, results in blue! This makes the sky blue, and all that blackness behind is unseen. Since you can't get any blacker than pure black, nothing out there would be able to make the sky darker. Even the half moon, when seen during the day, is bright on one side, but the dark side is replaced by the sky color because it's black. The atmosphere will always add its color to whatever is out in space.

Fact: Stars still shine during the day, but only the brightest can actually be discerned against the surrounding blue sky since it's so bright. If you track Venus, Jupiter, or Sirius, three of the brightest objects in the sky (aside from the sun and moon), with a telescope through sunrise, you'll be able to see them faintly against the surrounding blue haze of the atmosphere for most of the day. You'll need extremely good color perception though.

In fact, the atmosphere even adds color to objects on the ground, but to a lesser extent. Generally, this effect is called haze, or in some areas, smog. The atmosphere is a large volume of gas, with a bit of moisture and dust added in, and when you look through it for a great enough distance, it gets pretty hard to see through.

This haze isn't all bad, though. For outdoor scenes, it's almost essential to add some amount of haze to relate a sense of scale. Even on a clear day on earth, objects in the distance, most notably mountains, all become slightly bluer as their distance from the camera increases. We'll duplicate that effect in the next few steps.

The Good Old Haze

STEP 18: Clear LightWave and load the **Mountains.lws** scene. This scene contains three copies of a mountain object, each scaled and positioned differently to create a small mountain range.

Press F9 to do a test render and study the resulting frame (Figure 6-29). You'll notice that even though there are three mountains in the scene, they tend to blend together and appear as one. There's no contrast between the mountains, except for a small amount of greenery on the lower portion of the foreground mountain. The edges of the mountains, except along the skyline, are very difficult to distinguish. If this were an airless planet, then these mountains would actually look like this. However, we have that nice blue sky in the background, so there's an atmosphere here, and these mountains are in it. They should be slightly affected by it at this distance, so let's fix the scene.

FIGURE 6-29 The mountains.lws scene rendered without any atmospheric haze. Note that the lack of contrast between the three mountains makes them appear as one large one. There is virtually no sense of depth.

STEP 19: Open the Effects panel and click the Volumetrics tab. The top section of this tab is LightWave's Fog. We have three fog types available to us: Linear, Nonlinear 1, and Nonlinear 2. All three work equally well for fog, and the one to use is really a matter of personal choice most of the time. Sometimes you'll want to use the Linear mode, and other times you'll want a nonlinear one, even on the same scene with just a minor camera change. Select the Non-linear 1 for now, since it was used for the following figures.

If we were to render now, we would have a nice blue sky, but the landscape would suddenly appear as a flat dull gray silhouette. That's because the default Max Distance is only 1 m, so anything beyond that will have the maximum fog level applied to it. Since we're simulating a thin haze that gradually builds up over a distance of several kilometers, and is not readily apparent over short distances, let's increase the Max Distance to 20 kilometers. Now everything beyond this distance from the camera will be affected equally by the fog. Everything within this distance will be partially affected, with objects nearest the camera affected the least. We're not using the fog to make this a completely foggy planet, however, so let's reduce the Max Amount to 75%, so even objects beyond 20 kilometers away will still have visible details.

Note: If you run into a situation where your objects are all rendering in a solid color, don't panic. It's quite likely that fog was applied and that the objects are all outside the maximum distance. Simply increase the Max Distance (or lower the Max Amount, or just turn fog off) and the objects will return to normal.

The next thing we need to do is set the fog color. This should be similar to the sky color, since the fog and the sky are both part of the same atmospheric effect. The color of the fog should actually match the color of the sky the mountains cover. If we were using a solid backdrop, we would know exactly what this color was. Similarly, we can get the exact color of the sky from the Gradient Backdrop's Sky color, but we want the color at a point somewhere between the two gradient colors. This is actually much easier than it sounds, and it can be done without using some other image processing software.

STEP 20: Go to the Image Viewer, where you should have a full-sized render of the image we just created in Step 18. Click the sky just over the tops of the mountains and the pointer will turn into a small magnifying glass. As you drag this magnifying glass around, you'll notice that some numbers appear in the title bar and constantly change as the pointer moves (Figure 6-30). These numbers show the X and Y coordinates of the image, followed by their RGB values. The final digit is the alpha value, which represents the transparency of that point.

FIGURE 6-30 By clicking the image in the Image Viewer, we can find the RGB values of any pixel in the image.

Note: The alpha value shows only the transparency value of the first surface at any given point in the frame, or the alpha value that surface has been given. Switching the Image Viewer to Alpha by clicking the button in the upper-right corner will show a grayscale version of the frame, representing the transparency information, much as the Display button does for VIPER and the Surface Preview.

Note: There are two versions of the image viewer, the regular one (pictured here), and the full precision one, image viewer FP, available in the Render panel. The full precision version shows colors using percentages. If you use this version, you'll need to change the color format to percentage as well (options panel). For these tutorials, the regular viewer is recommended.

By dragging this pointer around, we can get the exact RGB values of any point in the frame, and we can then use those to set the color of the fog (or any other attribute in LightWave that we want to match to a specific color). Select a point near the tops of the mountains in this image and then use those values for the Fog Color. Figure 6-31 shows the fog settings used for the accompanying figures.

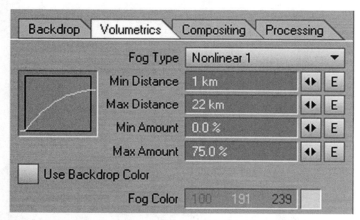

FIGURE 6-31 A good set of fog values to add some atmospheric haze to our mountain scene.

Note: Fog replaces the surface values of an object with its own color, based on distance. The farther away the object is, the more the fog will color it. This goes for shadow areas as well, which will lighten (or darken, depending on the fog color) to the value of the fog over distance. This results in the object rendering with less and less contrast as the distance increases. However, the contrast between near and far objects will also increase, with farther objects being lighter than foreground objects.

Press F9 again, and this time you will see a more natural-looking mountainscape. Note how the background mountains now appear more distant and are beginning to blend with the sky, while the small foreground mountain is only slightly affected by the haze. The mountains now appear as three separate mountains, rather than one large one (Figure 6-32).

FIGURE 6-32 The same scene, but with some aerial perspective added. Note how the three mountains now appear separate due to the presence of some haze between them.

Note: We could use the Background Fog option, which will use the colors of the background for the fog, but it has some side effects that are usually undesirable. Background Fog is basically fog, but with a Front Project Map of the background applied to it. This means it is possible to apply an image to the fog and have that image gradually apply itself to every object in the scene as fog. However, for landscapes, this creates an unwanted artifact. When using a gradient backdrop, the horizon line that's usually formed by the gradient also gets applied to the scene. The result looks as if objects are becoming more and more transparent with distance, with a hard horizontal color change occurring through them where the horizon would be (Figure 6-33). This artifact can be reduced by using the same color for the ground and the sky, creating that three-color gradient mentioned earlier. For seascape scenes, this works very well, and is further improved by using the zenith color for the nadir color as well, effectively mirroring the sky gradient in the ground gradient. For scenes where the backdrop is not creating the sky, this method will fail, so it's generally a good idea to explicitly specify a fog color.

FIGURE 6-33 The drawback of using Background Fog on a landscape. Note the dark bar near the bottom of the frame, where the fog colors change from the sky blues to the browns of the gradient backdrop.

You'll also notice that the darker shadow region of the foreground mountain is not as dark as it was earlier. If we increased the amount of fog, or simply increased the distance between the camera and this mountain, it would become even lighter, until very little surface detail remained (Figure 6-34). Areas of shadow will gradually be lightened by the atmosphere, up to a certain maximum. That maximum is the point where the atmosphere can no longer apply any additional effect, which is basically the same point where the atmosphere comes to an end . . . outer space. At this point and beyond, the atmosphere's effect is at its maximum.

So in order for that planet, or moon, or asteroid to appear darker than the sky, it would actually have to be *inside* the atmosphere! That's not a very good place for one of these to be.

FIGURE 6-34 An increased amount of haze further reduces the contrast of the surface details on each mountain. Note that the dark shadow area on the foreground mountain is becoming lighter, and there are no longer any really dark areas visible in the distance at all.

Hanging a Moon . . . Properly

Let's just take a quick look at the main error made with moons and planets in the sky by making the error ourselves.

STEP 21: Load the **SmallMoon.lwo** object from the CD into the scene. This moon is 8 km in diameter, so it will need to be moved quite a distance for it to fit into the sky behind those mountains. It will also need to be scaled up to be more easily visible at a distance at which a moon would typically orbit. Move this moon to 300 Mm (megameters) on the Y axis and 700 Mm on the Z axis, and then scale it to 10,000 times. This will place it far out into space and make it large enough to fill the sky above the mountains.

Note: This distance is more extreme than would normally be used, and is mainly for illustrative purposes here.

Press F9 to see how it appears in a final render (Figure 6-35). Notice that even though it's affected by fog, the moon appears darker than the surrounding sky. This is because our fog will apply only up to 75% of its color to anything beyond its Max Distance. Also notice that the moon is entirely made of shades of blue in this frame. Even though you would never see a moon like this in the real world, this image does show some amount of correctness. But it's still wrong. Currently, it looks more like a giant ball approximately the same distance away as that mountain in the background, since it has about the same amount of surface contrast.

FIGURE 6-35 A moon affected by fog looks very wrong in the sky.

Let's get rid of the fog's effect on the moon, since if we tried to increase it in order to make the dark areas even lighter, we would simply end up with a solid, fog-colored disc. Again, not what we want.

STEP 22: Open the Object Properties panel for the moon and click the Rendering tab. Select the Unaffected by Fog check box and then render again. This time we'll have a nice full-color moon in the sky, complete with a very dark "night" side (Figure 6-36). This is basically the same effect that appeared in *Pitch Black,* as well as several other science fiction shows. The moon, even though it is over 700,000 kilometers away, now appears to be a small ball suspended a very short distance from the camera, or even just pasted onto the mountain image, since its dark features are darker than those of the mountains in the distance.

FIGURE 6-36 The same moon, unaffected by fog here, still looks out of place. Although it's much farther away than the mountains, it appears to be much closer and smaller.

Remember, the atmosphere makes objects become lighter with distance. The visible atmosphere of earth also does not extend quite as far as 700,000 kilometers into space, so we need a way to create an atmosphere that will affect our moon, without the moon appearing to be inside it. Our problem here is that we're using that Gradient Backdrop, which, because it's a simple backdrop, is rendered behind everything in the scene, no matter how distant the objects are. So let's get rid of it.

STEP 23: Open the Effects panel again, switch back to the normal Solid Backdrop, and make sure it's set to black. Next, since there's no ambient light in space as there is in an atmosphere, open the Global Illumination panel and lower the Ambient Light to 0%. Press F9 again, and in a few minutes you should have what appears to be a night scene with a nice moon in the sky (Figure 6-37). As far as the sky is concerned, this is correctly rendered (aside from a technical lighting inaccuracy). The only thing that spoils it is the extra-bright haze on those mountains. Since we're dealing with the sky at this point, we'll let those mountains slide for now.

FIGURE 6-37 Removing the gradient backdrop results in a better-looking night sky. A lighting change would fix the rest of the image.

Note: A moon will never appear in the night sky lit like this. Light coming from above can only happen during the day, since that same light would be above us as well.

So we know we can get the night sky to render correctly. Now we just need to be able to put a bright sky between the moon and us. And that's the secret.

STEP 24: Launch Modeler and press Shift+N to create a new object. Select the Ball tool and drag out a ball like the one in Figure 6-38, approximately 100 kilometers wide and 80 kilometers high. Select the bottom half of the sphere as we did with the CloudBall, and delete those polygons. Finally, press F to flip the remaining polygons and then press Q to open the Change Surface panel. Call this surface Sky, and then save the object itself as **SkyBall.lwo.**

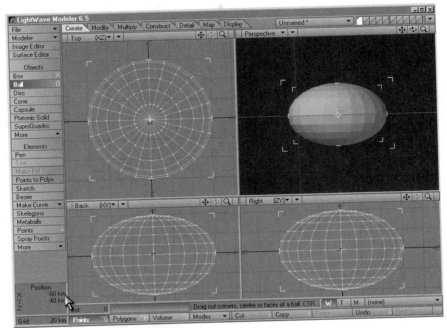

FIGURE 6-38 A simple sphere works well as a SkyBall.

STEP 25: Send this object to Layout and open the Surface Editor. Select the Sky surface and open the Texture Editor for the Color channel. Create a Gradient layer based on Y Distance to Object, and use the SkyBall object as the reference object. We're going to create a sky color gradient here, going from light blue at the bottom, which is the horizon, to a deeper sky blue at the top. For the horizon, give the first key a color of 210, 240, and 255. Expand the gradient by entering 40,000 into the End field at the bottom of the color bar.

Next, create a second key at 30,000 meters, and make its color something like 100, 190, and 240. Finally, set the Smoothing of these keys to Spline and click the Use Texture button.

STEP 26: Now that we have our colors for the sky, let's make it a little more skylike. Lower the Diffuse value to 0% and increase the Luminosity to 100%. Select the Smoothing check box and then click the Advanced tab.

This is where we'll make this Sky object do its magic. Remember that the atmosphere is an additive effect, which we've simulated not only with fog, but also as a surface in the previous tutorial when we created the atmosphere for our earth. The same thing applies here. Set the Additive Transparency to 100% so the sky adds its color to everything we see through it.

Our atmosphere is almost ready to go. Since we have fog in the scene yet, we don't want the sky to be affected by it, so open the Object Properties panel and click the Rendering tab. Select the Unaffected by Fog check box here, just as we did for the moon. Also deactivate the shadow options for the sky, since we don't want it trying to cast shadows. Now it's ready to go. Press F9 again and you should get an accurate image of a moon in the sky during the day (Figure 6-39).

FIGURE 6-39 The same moon, placed outside the SkyBall, finally looks as if it belongs there. Note that no point on the moon appears darker than the sky.

We've re-created the entire atmosphere setup of the earth, where everything inside the atmosphere, in this case our SkyBall, is affected by it. In this scene, the fog is doing the atmospheric effects. We created a Sky object that gives us the actual sky color, and also serves as a boundary for the sky, separating the atmosphere from space. Beyond the SkyBall is blackness and whatever celestial bodies we want to place out there.

Note: Anything placed outside the SkyBall should be Unaffected by Fog. We can only specify the minimum and maximum fog distances, but we can't change the amount of fog outside those limits. Thus, if anything outside the SkyBall does not have Unaffected by Fog active, it will be colorized and the effect will be ruined.

With this setup it's possible to also add clouds, as we did earlier. The only thing to remember is that they should also be Unaffected by Fog, and should be inside the SkyBall, just where you'd expect real clouds to be. If they were outside the SkyBall, the additive nature of it would make the clouds too bright, and again, the sky effect would be ruined.

There is one last thing to be aware of. For the effect to work right, the Ambient Light must be set to 0% to avoid illuminating the dark side of the moon. This means that you must be careful when lighting a scene. Since the moon is so far behind the main scene, spotlights can be used to create the Ambient Light without affecting the moon in the background. The sunlight, on the other hand, should be created with a Distant light, so the lighting on the moon matches that of the planet.

This common mistake pops up quite frequently in film and CG art in general. If it's daylight on the planet, then any moons in the sky will be lit from above, since the planet we're on is being lit from above. Chances are, the moon is being lit by the same light source . . . the sun. During the day, you will never see a crescent moon with the lit crescent on the lower side. The lit side of the moon is always going to be facing the light source, so if the lit side is facing down, then the light source must be below it somewhere. If you see a crescent moon like this, then it's night where you are. After all, the sun would have to be below you to light the moon like that, and that means it's lighting the planet you're on from below as well.

So we've done a daytime scene, but what about a night scene? There's very little difference involved in setup, actually. All you need to do is point the sun up instead of down. This will automatically change the lighting on the moon in the sky, and the surface of the planet will also be in shade. However, depending on how the landscape is modeled, some sunlight may leak through and cast unwanted light in some areas. To prevent this, it's a good idea to place a single large polygon below the landscape that will act as a huge sun block. This will prevent unwanted light from creeping into the landscape, but will not prevent the sun from lighting the moon correctly (Figure 6-40).

FIGURE 6-40 Placing a large shadow-casting polygon below the ground will prevent any stray sunlight from lighting the landscape, without affecting the way it lights the moon.

The only other difference is that you'll want to use much darker blues for the SkyBall. Keep the color values all below 50 and your night skies will allow the color of the moon or planets to show through better. Figures 6-41a and 6-41b show a full mountain scene with both day lighting and night lighting.

This should get you well on your way to creating some nice outdoor scenes. And again, feel free to experiment. After all, to use a pun . . . the sky's the limit!

FIGURE 6-41A A finished mountain scene on some distant world. Note that the direction of light on the planet and the moon matches the lighting on the mountain.

FIGURE 6-41B. A night version of the same scene. Note that the planets are now lit from below. You would never see a moon lit like this during the day. Also note the coloration that is visible on the ringed planet due to the darker sky affecting it less.

7

Automotive Effects

Dave Jerrard

OVERVIEW

Now let's put some of these techniques to work on a larger project. In this tutorial, we'll take a car and set it up for animation. We'll also do a little body work and lighting as well. The first thing we'll need is the car.

In this tutorial you will use:

- Object layers and parenting

- Graph Editor Motion and Envelope plug-ins

- Master Channel plug-in

- BRDF shader

What you will need:

- Texture images included on CD

- Prebuilt objects included on CD

What you will learn:

- Techniques to create realistic headlight assemblies

- Use of nulls as animation controls

- Automotive studio lighting

- How to create and use layered objects

- Hierarchy construction for animation

- Linking graphs to one another

THE CAR

STEP 1: Load **LW-Classic.lwo** into Layout. Before we get too far, we'll take a closer look at this object to see what needs to be done.

First of all, you'll see that the car is only partially surfaced. We'll be getting to that a bit later. We're more interested in the actual setup of the car at this point.

If you open the Scene Editor, the first thing you will notice is that we have four object layers loaded (Figure 7-1). These layers are currently not connected to each other, so if you move one layer, the others will remain where they are. If we wanted to animate this car the way it is, we'd have our hands full just trying to keep everything together. We could just put everything into one layer, but that would cause problems with the wheels, since they'd no longer be able to rotate independently of the rest of the object. Previously, objects like wheels were separate objects and were parented to the car body in Layout. This worked well for years, but had the side effect of requiring a special assembly scene to be made. The car, and all its hierarchy, would then be loaded into other scenes using the Load Items From Scene option. The layered object format allows us to clean things up a bit by keeping all the parts of an object together in a single file, just like this current car is. The file format also allows us to set up some basic hierarchies as well, so let's do that now.

Setting Up the Hierarchy

STEP 2: Launch Modeler, and the car layers should appear in the first four layers (Figure 7-2). The first thing we want to do is fix the wheels, since they're actually modeled in their correct position relative to the car body. This means that when you try to rotate them, they'll rotate around the center of the car itself, and not on their axes. We could move the pivot point in Layout, but we can also do it in Modeler, and keep this information intact in the object itself as well. In fact, we can pretty much do away with the whole assembly scene now, and do all the hierarchy setup in the object file, so let's do that.

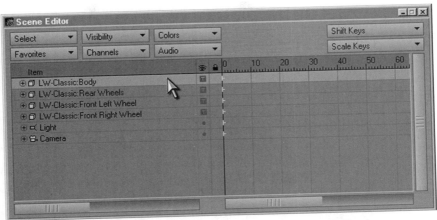

FIGURE 7-1 The Scene Editor showing the four layers of the car object.

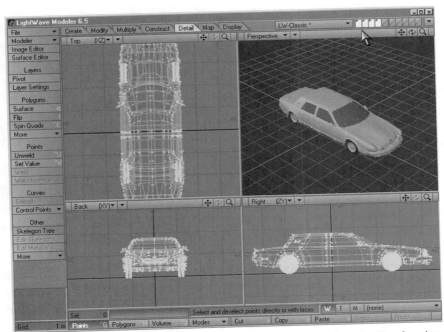

FIGURE 7-2 The car as it appears when loaded into Modeler, filling the first four layers. Note also that the body is using subdivision surfaces.

Select layer 2, which contains the two rear wheels. Move the pointer over the Side view and press 0 on the numeric keypad to zoom that window to full screen. Press A to fit the wheels to this view.

Next, click the Detail tab and select the Pivot tool. Now, click the wheel's center and a blue crosshair will appear. Drag this crosshair until it's perfectly centered on the wheels. The coordinates at the lower left corner should have a value of 410 mm on the Y axis and −1.88 m on the Z axis, as shown in Figure 7-3. We've just changed the pivot point for this wheel, so now if you rotated it in Layout, it'll rotate around its center as a real wheel would.

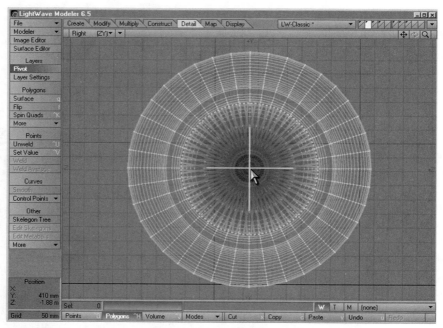

FIGURE 7-3 Drag the crosshair to the center of the wheel to change the pivot point of the object layer.

Note: When this object is loaded into Layout next, you will see that this layer no longer loads with a position of 0, 0, and 0. Instead, since the pivot point has been changed, this layer now loads with the object's position offset by this same amount. Avoid clicking the Reset button for this layer's position, or the wheels will snap to the center of the car!

STEP 3: Now let's do the same thing for the two front wheels. Since the front wheels of a car are placed on separate axles, allowing the wheels not only to roll along the ground, but also to change heading in order to turn the car, it's necessary to separate them into their own layers as well. Select the third layer, which contains the front left wheel, and press A to automatically fit it to the view. The Pivot tool should still be active, so simply click in the view window again and position the crosshair in the center of the wheel. The position of this crosshair should be −1.14 m on the X axis, 410 mm on the Y axis, and 2.62 m on the Z axis.

Note: The crosshair really only needs to be centered on the wheel's axis and not actually the wheel itself. The pivot point should be centered on the X axis for these wheels, but since these layers will eventually be rolling only on their pitch, only the Y and Z positions are important. The X position could be anywhere, though it's generally a good idea to keep the pivot points centered in the object's geometry. This isn't only a matter of neatness, but convenience as well. If at some point in time, you decide to have a wheel fly off the car, bounce across traffic, and smash through a windshield of another vehicle in oncoming traffic, you'll find it much easier to animate if the pivot is in the center of the wheel, rather than off to the side.

STEP 4: Once this wheel's pivot is set, do the same for the fourth layer, but make the X position of the pivot 1.14 m. Send this object back to Layout by clicking the small arrow button in the top right corner, and then switch over to Layout again.

Note: Object geometry and surfacing information will normally be updated in Layout automatically when the Hub is running, but the pivot information is not. To get the new pivot position into Layout, we need to actually reload the object, which is what the Send Object to Layout command just did.

You will now have two copies of the car in Layout, so let's get rid of that first one since it has the old pivot information. Open the Scene Editor and select the top four object layers. These will all be followed by a number 1 in parentheses (Figure 7-4). Simply click the top layer and then hold down the Shift key while you click layer 4. Next, press the minus key to remove the object. A small panel will appear to confirm the delete operation; just click Yes to All. The car that remains will have the new pivot information we wanted, and if you select any of the wheel layers, you'll see that the wheel's handles now appear centered between the wheels (Figure 7-5).

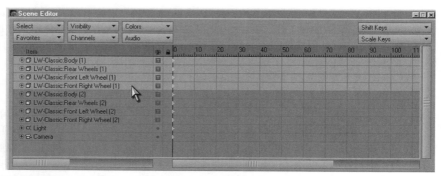

FIGURE 7-4 The original car layers selected in the Scene Editor, ready to be removed.

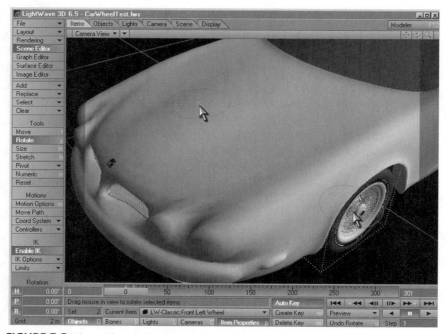

FIGURE 7-5 The updated pivot points for the front wheels can be seen floating inside them.

Note: If you don't see any of these arrows, press D to open the Display Options panel and then select the Show Handles check box. If this check box is not available, then you'll see a small yellow X that designates the object's pivot location. Showing the object handles isn't necessary here, but it does make the location of the pivot much easier to see in Layout.

Now that we have the pivots set up, we can start assembling the car. Most people would start by parenting the wheels to the car, but this doesn't lend itself to very accurate animation afterward. Real cars have springs and shock absorbers between them and their wheels, and this suspension allows the car to bounce and tilt while the wheels stay on the ground. Parenting the wheels to the body of this car would mean that if we tried to tilt the body, the wheels would tilt as well, and in all likelihood, they'd either sink through the ground or lift off it. Manually moving the wheels to compensate later simply adds more work than is necessary.

We really want to parent the wheels to something else that will keep them together, and allow the body of the car to float with them. In fact, we can parent the body and the wheels to the same object.

STEP 5: Click the Add button and choose Object > Add Null. Give this null a name, such as ++++ *Car Suspension* ++++, and click OK. Next, go to the Scene Editor and parent all the object layers to this null by selecting them all, then dragging them onto the suspension null (Figure 7-6).

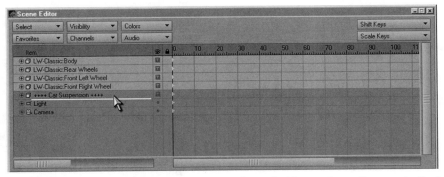

FIGURE 7-6 Dragging the four objects onto the null object to instantly parent all of them at the same time.

Note: The plus signs in the name are simply one way to mark this null as a type of control null, making it easy to find in the object list. When you get into large hierarchies in complicated scenes, making these various nulls easier to find can save a lot of time, especially when you start working with larger and more complex scenes. Some studios use color coding to make the nulls easier to find in the main Layout window (red for the right side of characters and green for the left, for example), and frequently use special characters in the names of nulls, though there are no standards for this. I use square brackets to designate a *handle null,* which is simply a null to which all the parts of an object assembly are parented for easier scene management. Pluses refer to a pivot or control null, and stars mark a target or reference null. When you get in the habit of marking nulls like this, finding object assemblies in large scenes becomes much easier.

Now that we have the wheels and the car attached to a single null, we can simply move the null to move everything. In fact, let's do a quick little animation to show what we can do with this very simple setup.

Test Drive 1

STEP 6: Select the null object, and move the frame slider to frame 100. Now move the null down the Z axis a short distance, say about a car length or two, and create a keyframe for it there by pressing Enter twice. This will create a simple motion of the car moving forward. However, the car will start moving immediately, but we want to have it appear to start moving forward from a full stop, so we need to have it gradually accelerate. To set this up, open the Graph Editor and select the ++++ Car Suspension ++++ Position.Z channel, which will be the third channel in the Channel list.

The blue graph should now be visible in the Graph Editor with two small keys applied to it. Click the first key, then right-click it and a small menu will appear (Figure 7-7). Choose Ease In/Out and the first key will now create a smooth curve up to the second key (Figure 7-8). This option is simply a fast way to toggle the Tension value for the key between 0 and 1 and back again. We've just created a simple two-keyframe animation of the car starting to move with a gentle acceleration. If you click the Play button in the lower-right corner, you'll see this car gently start to move. It doesn't quite look right, though. When a real car starts to move, it tends to tilt back slightly for a moment or two as the body of the car lags a bit. With the setup we have now, we can create this rocking effect easily.

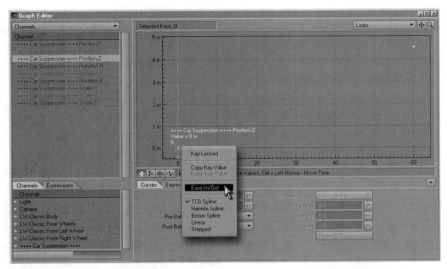

FIGURE 7-7 Selecting the quick Ease In option to set the tension for the first key.

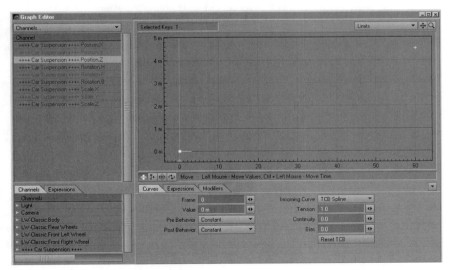

FIGURE 7-8 The shape of the motion curve after applying the Ease In command.

STEP 7: Expand the channels for the LW_Classic:Body layer in the Graph Editor and double-click the Rotation.P channel. This will place it up in the Channel list as well as in the graph. Click the small Create Key button (the one with a key icon and a plus sign) under the graph and then click the graph at frame 10 and frame 30 to add two new keys. Set the value of the key at frame 10 at −1 degree and the value of frame 30 back to 0 again. Finally, set the tension of the first and last frames to 1 (Figure 7-9). This motion will cause the car body to rock back slightly as the car starts to move, then gently return to its horizontal state again. Since the pivot point of this object layer is actually centered at ground level below the car body, the entire body will also move back and forth very slightly, giving it the illusion of having mass.

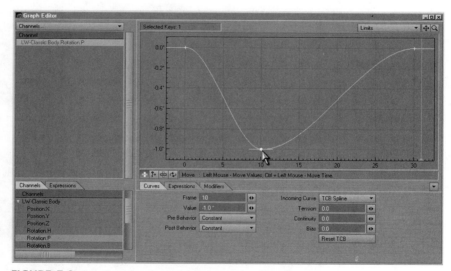

FIGURE 7-9 Another simple graph creates the illusion of the car having mass as it starts to move.

To see this in action, create a preview animation by clicking the Preview button in the lower-right corner and choosing Make Preview. If you set the view to either Left or Right, you'll see this slight pitching easier. It's a subtle motion, but it's one your eyes have come to expect.

Tip: Since the Body layer is composed of Subpatches, you can speed up the screen refresh rate by lowering the Display Subpatch Level in the Object Properties panel. This will affect only how the object appears in Layout and will not change the object file in any way.

It was mentioned earlier that we could set up all of the hierarchy for this car within the object file itself, yet we just added a null. OK, let's incorporate some nulls into the object, then. There's only one problem. What exactly is a null? There are no null object tools in Modeler, and you can't save one from Layout.

Longtime users of LightWave will remember a time when you had to actually load a null object (**nullobject.lwo**) from disk. This object was nothing more than a single point, with no polygons attached. And if you open the Object Properties panel for the Car Suspension null, you'll see that it's composed of a single point and no polygons. That's the secret!

Note: You can save a single-point/zero-polygon object from Modeler and load it into Layout. However, previous versions of LightWave used to recognize this special object case. When you saved a scene that had any of these objects, LightWave would automatically write a different command into the scene file: "AddNullObject null" rather than "LoadObject Objects/NullObject.lwo." This is no longer the case. LightWave now remembers where the null object came from and will write this path into the scene file, just as with any other object.

The Tune Up

STEP 8: Go back to Modeler and select layer 6. Click the Create tab, and then click the Points button on the bottom menu. Next, press A to center the view, then click in the middle of one of the view windows to create a point in the center (Figure 7-10). We've essentially just created a null object in this layer.

Note: Actually, even an empty layer can be loaded into Layout and appear as a null, but only if another layer is parented to it. Also, if a layer is empty, the pivot point for that layer, while seemingly able to be adjusted in Modeler, will always load into Layout centered at 0, 0, and 0. The pivot can still be adjusted within Layout, however, but by adding a single point to a layer, you'll have some reference for where the pivot should be if that information somehow gets lost, since you can position the point where the pivot will be.

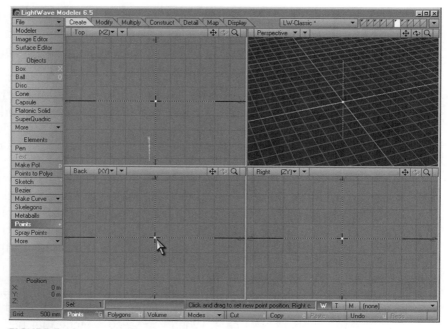

FIGURE 7-10 Create a single point to duplicate a null object in the form of an object layer.

STEP 9: Now we need to parent the other layers to this one. Press Shift+Y to open the Layers Browser and then click the small triangle to expand the list of layers for this object. Double-click each of the four layers and assign this sixth layer as the parent for each. When this is done, double-click layer 6 and give it a new name. ++++ *Car Mover* ++++ or something similar will do.

While we're here, let's set up another couple of null layers so we can turn the front wheels in order to steer the car. Select layer 7 and create another point. This time we'll create a point by clicking the Points button and then pressing N to open the Numeric panel. Click the Actions menu and choose Activate, then enter the following values:

X   −700 mm

Y   410 mm

Z   2.62 m

This will create a point just a short distance from the inner-facing side of the front left wheel, which we'll use as the pivot for steering that wheel.

STEP 10: Select layer 8 and create another point there, but this time on the other side of the X axis, at 700 mm. This one will serve as the pivot for the front right wheel.

STEP 11: Now that we have our pivot locations designated by points, let's set up the actual pivots themselves. Click the Detail tab again and click the Pivot button. Position the blue crosshair over the point in this current layer. To make things easier, press N to open the Numeric panel, and enter the same values you used for the point in this layer (Figure 7-11). Once this is done, go back to layer 7 and position another pivot over the point there. We have set up the two pivots that our front wheels will rotate around to steer the car.

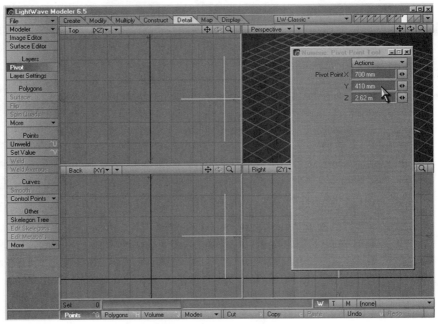

FIGURE 7-11 Use the Numeric panel to position the pivot in the same place as the point in each layer.

Now that we've added two more layers, let's go back to the Layers Browser and get things rearranged.

STEP 12: Double-click layer 7 and name it Front Left Wheel Axis or something similar. Next, select the Car Mover layer as this layer's parent. Rename layer 8 to Front Right Wheel Axis, and set its parent to Car Mover as well (Figure 7-12). Now the pivots are set up and attached to everything else. We just need to update those two front wheels now, since we parented them to the Car Mover layer as well.

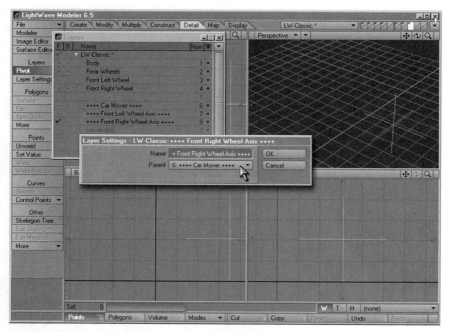

FIGURE 7-12 The Layer settings for the new null layers we just created, showing the new names and their parent layer.

STEP 13: Double-click the two front wheel layers, and parent them to their respective axis layers (that is, left to left and right to right). Our general car assembly is now complete.

Note: Another way of setting these front wheels up is to simply move the pivot of each wheel to 700 mm (or −700 mm, depending the wheel) on the X axis, rather than use the intermediate null layer. However, using nulls as pivot controls is good practice with mechanical objects, since they can help prevent unwanted motion problems from occurring. The front wheels would work without these null layers, but if you were to apply motion modifiers to the wheels later, they could interfere with the rolling motion of the wheels, so we're just playing it safe here.

Now we need to send this object back to Layout. We've just done two things to the object that can't be updated automatically in Layout. We already know that pivots need to be explicitly loaded. The same is true for parenting information. Any time either of these is changed, you'll need to manually reload the object into Layout for it to recognize the changes.

Test Drive 2

STEP 14: Click the small arrow in the upper-right corner and choose Send Object to Layout, then switch to Layout.

Once again, we'll have two copies of the car loaded, so select the first set of layers and delete them by pressing the minus key. You should be left with seven car layers, starting with the Car Mover layer at the top (Figure 7-13). This would be a good time to save the object to disk so we don't lose this hierarchy.

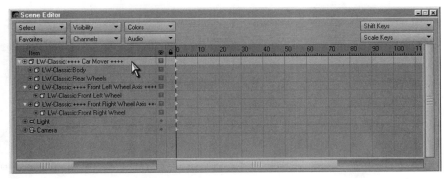

FIGURE 7-13 The car's new layer hierarchy as it should appear in the Scene Editor.

Now that we have this setup, let's take a look at how we can animate it. We've already done a quick test using the null to move the car, and that's what we'll be using the Car Mover null for. This null will be the main object we animate in order to drive the car around.

The car body, as we've already seen, is free to rock back and forth, to give a sense of mass for the car. As the car accelerates, we simply tilt the body back slightly. When it decelerates, we pitch it forward slightly. We can also bank the body as the car turns, so we don't need to do much with this object.

As for the wheels, we want them to turn as the car moves, and there's a handy way to automate this.

STEP 15: Open the Graph Editor and expand the three wheel object layers in the lower Channels list. Select all the channels that are currently in the upper Channel list and remove them by right-clicking and choosing Remove From Bin, or by pressing Shift+D. Now drag the Rotation:P channels for each of the three wheel objects up into this area. Select all three, since we're going to give them all the same motion (Figure 7-14).

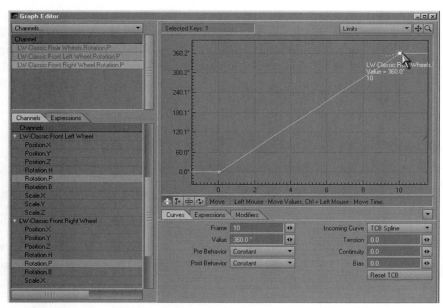

FIGURE 7-14 The Graph Editor, showing the three pitch channels for the wheels being edited to rotate 360 degrees over a span of 10 frames.

STEP 16: Now that we've got the three channels selected, click the Create Key button below the graph, create a key at frame 10, and give it a value of 360 degrees, as shown in Figure 7-14. This motion will cause the wheels to rotate forward one full revolution over the course of 10 frames. Don't worry about the length of this motion being so short, since it's only going to be used as reference in the next step.

STEP 17: We'll start with the rear wheels, since these are the simplest to set up. On the main Layout screen, select the LW-Classic: Rear Wheels object layer, and press M to open the Motion Options panel. Click the IK and Modifiers tab, then click the Add Modifier menu near the bottom. Choose LW_Cyclist and then double-click its entry in the area below (Figure 7-15).

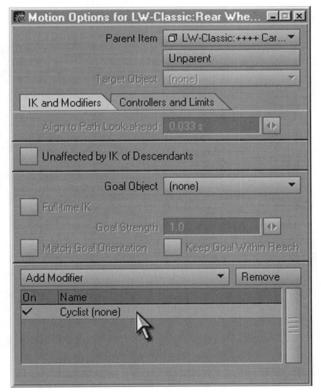

FIGURE 7-15 The Motion Options panel, showing the LW_Cyclist plug-in that's just been added.

This plug-in will probably seem a bit scary at first, but like the Surface Editor, it's friendlier than it first appears. We want to set these wheels up so that they'll rotate on their own as the car moves, without needing us to keyframe them manually. We've already set up the basic motion for the wheels, to make them roll along the ground, by rotating them on their pitch. That's our motion cycle that we'll be controlling in Cyclist.

STEP 18: Since we're rotating the wheels on their pitch, that's the only channel we need to worry about, so deselect all the channel buttons at the top of the Cyclist panel except for the P channel, as shown in Figure 7-16. Next, in the Cycle Frames fields, we need to specify the same range we just gave the wheels, so set this to a range of 0 to 10. This part tells Cyclist how much of the reference motion is going to be used, and since we set it with a 10-frame sequence, we'll get the whole thing here.

FIGURE 7-16 The Cyclist plug-in interface, with everything set up to make the wheels roll as the car moves.

STEP 19: Next, we need to specify an object that will be used to control this motion. We have a few choices here, since all the objects that make up this car will all be moving together. That means they're also moving at the same speed. However, only one of them is actually going to have keyframes defining its motion, so we'll use that one. Select the Car Mover object as the Cycle Controller. Now the rotation of the wheels is linked to this object, but we still have to define how this object affects the wheels.

STEP 20: Obviously, we want the wheels to roll along the ground under the car, without sliding, so we'll need to figure out how far they would travel along the ground if they were rolled one complete rotation. Yes, this means math. Luckily, we're using computers, and they're relatively good at this sort of thing. First, we need to figure out the diameter of these wheels. We could bring one into

Modeler and measure it, but there's a faster way, right here in Layout. Close the Cyclist plug-in for now and open the Surface Editor. Select one of the Tire surfaces (one of the Tire Rear or Tire Front surfaces), and then open the Texture Editor for one of the untextured channels.

Note: The tires have already been surfaced using a couple images for treads and labels. A gradient has been used to apply a dusty look to them. Since dust becomes more apparent at glancing angles, a gradient for the Diffuse channel has been used to brighten the surface slightly, while another gradient on the Color channel defines the color of this dust. In this case, it's a slight orange-brown color, as you would find in some of the desert areas of California. These tire surfaces are good examples of other ways to use various textures, so definitely feel free to study them.

We'll just use the default Image Map texture that pops up, since all we want is a single little feature. Click the Automatic Sizing button (don't worry about selecting an image, since we'll just be removing this texture again anyway) and then read the Scale values at the bottom of the panel. The X and Y values should both be 83.9864 cm. There's the diameter of the tire! Now we just need to get the circumference.

STEP 21: Click the Remove Texture button at the bottom of the Texture Editor and then go back to the Motion Options panel. The circumference of a circle, in this case, our tire, is 2*Pi*Radius, or Pi*Diameter. Don't go running for the calculator yet. Reopen the Cyclist panel and, in the Controller Range To: field, type *3.14159 *83.9864* and then press Enter. The field will update to show 2.6385, which is the circumference of our tires. We've now told Cyclist that the controller object has to go through a range from 0 to 2.6385 in order to make the wheels rotate a full 360 degrees.
But 0 to 2.6385 of what?
Since we want the wheels to rotate as the car moves either forward or backward, we want to use the motion of the car in this direction. The button to the right of the Controller Object lists several channels that can be used for reference, but only three of them—Position Z, Path Length, and Forward Progress—fit our needs. Position Z would work, but only if we don't plan to turn the car, so we can count that one out. This leaves Path Length and Forward Progress. Both of these will work for the back wheels, but

they start to show differences when objects are located deeper into hierarchies, as we'll see shortly. For now, we'll use the Forward Progress option for the back wheels.

Now, as we move this car forward and back, the rear wheels will rotate appropriately, with very little sliding.

Note: Some sliding will be present since this car has a virtual fixed differential, so both wheels will rotate the same amount, even during a turn. This is different from most cars today, which allow the rear wheels to rotate independently of one another. The wheels on the side of the car that's facing outward from a turn will rotate faster than the wheels on the inside of the turn. If you want, feel free to split these wheels apart so they can turn independently, but not until you've finished with the front wheels, since they'll be using the correct setup for this.

Now we need to do the same for the front wheels. The front wheels will be a slightly different matter since they're separate from one another. They're also buried deeper into the car's hierarchy.

STEP 22: Select the front left wheel and add Cyclist to the Motion Options panel for it, and then open Cyclist. The main difference for this wheel is that it will reference itself as the Control Object. Since this wheel is isolated from the others, and its center is near the side of the car, where it can be affected by speed changes due to turns, it makes sense to use its location as the control source. After all, this tire is touching the ground immediately below the center of this wheel. Select this wheel as the Control Object, and set the other values as shown in Figure 7-17.

FIGURE 7-17 The Cyclist setup for the front wheels. Note the use of Path Length instead of Forward Progress, as well as the activation of World Coordinates.

Notice that we're also using the Path Length option instead of Forward Progress. Since this object is self-referencing, using Forward Progress can cause it to rotate back and forth, as though it were loose and about to fall off. This is mainly because the wheel is trying to base its pitch amount on how far it has traveled down its Z axis. However, the wheel isn't always facing down that axis due to the pitch rotation, so Cyclist would just get confused and the wheel would occasionally just spin loosely. Using Path Length avoids this by using the actual distance traveled along the motion path, which is completely independent of heading.

Finally, the World Coordinates check box has been selected since the wheel is parented to a null, which is in turn parented to the Car Mover null. The wheel itself has no actual motion other than its rotation, so according to its local coordinates, it's not moving at all. Neither is the Axis null it's parented to. To get the actual motion data of these objects, we need to provide their world coordinates to Cyclist so it can tell how far they're moving.

Do the same setup for the right wheel, and use it as its own reference as well.

STEP 23: Now create a 300-frame motion for the Car Mover, making it turn slightly as it travels (Figure 7-18).

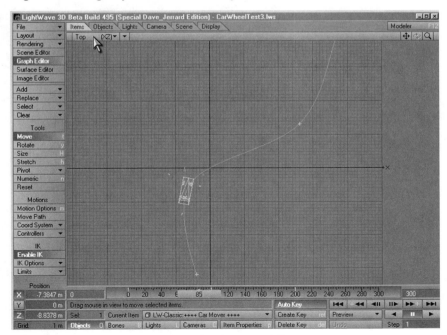

FIGURE 7-18 A sample, curved path for the car to follow.

Change the display mode to Bounding Box by clicking the small triangle in the upper-left corner of the Layout window, so we can more easily see the wheel rotation. Next, parent a Camera to the Car Mover null as well, and aim it so it looks toward both front wheels, as in Figure 7-19.

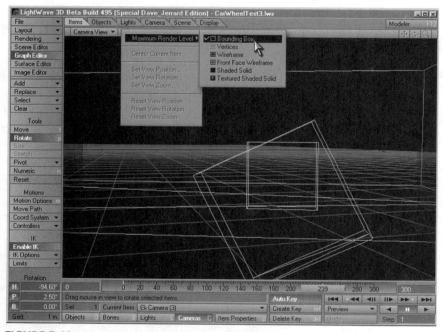

FIGURE 7-19 Changing the display to Bounding Box by clicking the small arrow in the upper-left corner of the Layout window.

Now play the animation using the playback controls in the lower-right corner, or make a preview animation. Watch the two front wheels closely. They'll start out rotating the same speed, but as the car starts to turn, the wheel on the outside of the turn will start to rotate faster, taking them out of sync with one another (Figure 7-19).

Now let's get these front wheels to steer. We're not going to use any fancy plug-ins or expressions to get the wheels to automatically steer as the car turns. In real life, the front wheels are often turned in a direction other than the one the car is moving in. This happens during skids, but most often during short, abrupt turns, such as those made when parking. Instead, we'll do the steering the old-fashioned way: manually. Well, almost . . .

STEP 24: Open the Plug-in Options panel by choosing Layout > Plug-ins > Plug-in Options. Click the Add Layout Or Scene Master button and choose Master Channel. This plug-in will create a generic envelope that will appear in the Graph Editor. Rather than using a null to add reference channels for various effects, and being forced to try to remember which of its motion channels were for what, we can now simply add a single channel and give it a meaningful name. Double-click the Master Channel entry in the list it was just added to, and a small panel will open, with a whopping two options (Figure 7-20).

FIGURE 7-20 No fluid required. The Master Channel interface, set up to give our car a steering assembly.

We'll call this channel Steering, so type that into the text field, and then change the Type to Angle. Click OK and we're done. You should now see Channel: Steering listed in the Plug-in Options panel. This new channel also appears in the Graph Editor as well, listed as an object called MC with a single channel attached, called Steering (Figure 7-21).

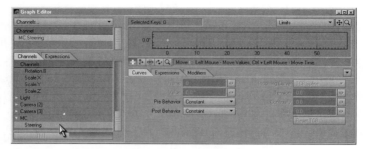

FIGURE 7-21 The new Master Channel we just created now appears in the Graph Editor.

STEP 25: Select the Front Left Wheel Axis null and open the Graph Editor. Select the Rotation:H channel for this object and place it in the upper Channel list. Click the Modifiers tab and then choose Add Modifier > Channel Follower (Figure 7-22).

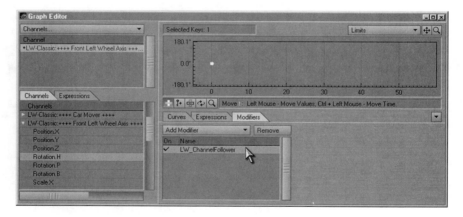

FIGURE 7-22 Adding the Channel Follower plug-in to the axis null.

Tip: If the Graph Editor is open and you're trying to find a channel for an object you have selected in Layout, simply close the editor and re-open it. The channels for the selected object will be in the Channel list ready to be edited.

STEP 26: Double-click the plug-in's entry in the list and its small interface will open (Figure 7-23). In its simplest form, the Channel Follower (a.k.a. Set Driven Key, which is the same plug-in but under a different name) simply reads the information from one graph and feeds it to another graph, duplicating its effects. However, it can add to the effects of the first graph by scaling the values, offsetting them in time, adding a delay, or making things happen sooner. In this case, we'll be using it for its duplication ability.

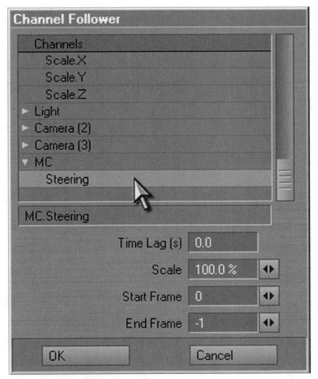

FIGURE 7-23 Selecting the Master Channel's Steering channel as the reference for the Channel Follower plug-in.

Scroll down the list of channels in the top half of this plug-in and double-click the MC: Steering channel at the very bottom, so it appears in the small line below the list (Figure 7-23). The rest of the settings are exactly what we want, so don't bother with them.

We've just locked the rotation of the wheel axis null to the value of this Steering channel. Now, whatever values we give this steering channel, the null will duplicate. This might seem a bit silly right now, since we could just rotate the null itself. There's nothing wrong with that either, except that we have two of these axis nulls, and they should rotate together. Now we could link one to the other and keyframe one of the nulls for steering, but if we use the Master Channel, the graph controlling the steering will be much easier to find. It's also labeled more appropriately.

STEP 27: Now select the Rotation:H channel for the other axis null and do the same for it. It's time to try driving the car.

STEP 28: Select the Steering channel in the Graph Editor and create a keyframe at frame 300. Simply create a key anywhere in the graph and then use the Frame and Value fields on the Curves tab to position the key at frame 300. Now, move the Graph Editor so it won't block the Layout screen, since we're going to be working in one while watching the other. Select the Car Mover null so we can see the motion path it's following. We're going to need this as reference for aligning the wheels.

Tip: You might want to parent a camera to the car and position it above the front wheels, so we can see both of them and the motion path for the Car Mover null. Simply add a new camera for this so you don't mess up any motions you have set up for the main camera. There's really no limit to the number of cameras you can have in Layout, and you'll quickly find that they're extremely handy to have since you can now set up predefined vantage points throughout the scene to check on things.

Now drag the Frame Slider in Layout until the car comes to a turn in the motion path. When the path turns enough that it's no longer parallel to the front wheel, go over to the Graph Editor. You will see a line through the graph indicating the current frame. Create a key on this line, and move it up or down until the wheels are aligned with the path that's between them (Figure 7-24).

Continue scrubbing through the animation with the Frame Slider, and create new keys in the Graph Editor whenever there's a sharp turn in the motion path. Play the animation once in a while as well to check the motion of those wheels.

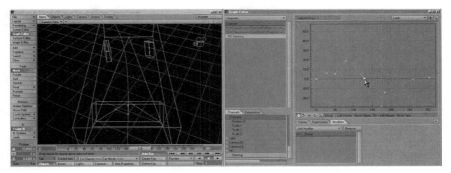

FIGURE 7-24 When you adjust the graph of the Steering channel while watching the wheels in Layout, you can easily steer the car, just as if you were driving it.

Note: Try to keep the values of this Steering channel in the range of −20 to 20 degrees. Anything more than this can cause the wheels to pass into the body of the car.

Tip: To see the effects of a key change immediately in Layout, without having to scrub through a frame or two, press O while you have the Graph Editor selected. An Options panel will open where you can select the Maximum Interactivity check box. This will cause Layout to update as soon as a change is made in the Graph Editor.

In a short time, the car should be steering right along that motion path, while the wheels all rotate accurately. For a final touch, we'll bank the Car Body slightly as the car turns.

STEP 29: Since we already know when the car is going to turn, and which way, thanks to this Master Channel, we can use it to automatically bank the car into turns. Select the Car Body's Rotation:B channel in the Graph Editor. Add the Channel Follower plug-in and select the Steering channel as the reference. This time, since we don't want the car to tip 20 degrees to either side, we'll need to modify the amount of influence the Steering channel has on this one. Earlier, we pitched the body 1 degree to give it a slight lag as the car accelerated, which looked good. Since the body is not as wide as it is long, we can afford to tilt it a little further. If we use the Steering channel as it is, the body will tilt up to 20 degrees. We want only about 2–3 degrees, which works out to roughly 10% of 20. So, change the Scale factor to somewhere between 5 and 15%. I'd recommend using values of 8 to 10% to avoid too much tilting.

Also, since the car would normally have to get into the turn a bit before the body actually tilts into it, we should have a slight delay. About half a second should do, so enter 0.5 into the Time Lag field. Now when you play the animation, the car will rock side to side slightly as it turns.

While we're at it, we can also give this car a slight vibration as it drives. Again, this will be added to the Car Body's bank channel.

STEP 30: Add another modifier to the Rotation:B channel and this time select Noisy Channel. Double-click it to open its interface, which will appear to the right, right on the Graph Editor itself (Figure 7-25). Give this modifier a Scale of 0.01 and a speed of 0.5, which will give a very slight gentle vibration to the car.

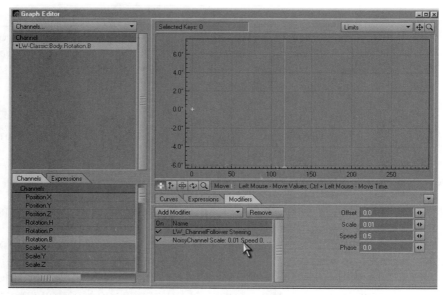

FIGURE 7-25 Adding Channel Follower and Noisy Channel to the car body gives it a much more realistic motion.

Tip: This modifier is great for making motions look more natural by adding a random wobble to them. Camera motions in particular will benefit greatly by the addition of this plug-in, as will character motions.

Create and play back another preview and you'll see a much more realistic-looking motion as the car drives around. Now we just need to make the car itself more realistic.

STEP 31: By now you're probably tired of this dull white car. Let's give it some color. First, open the Surface Editor and select the Paint surface. We'll start off by making this a classic black car, so change the color to a near black. RGB values of 20, 20, and 20 will give a nice black color, and still allow for shading.

Tip: Much as it's a good idea to avoid pure white colors, it's also good practice to avoid pure blacks as well. If a surface is made completely black, the subtle shading that occurs in shadow areas will be greatly reduced. Try to keep RGB values approximately 20 away from the minimum and maximum, or in the range of 20 to 240. Pure black surfaces should be reserved for special cases, such as seams between panels, the gaps around doors, or anywhere you absolutely need a pure black.

STEP 32: Now that we have the color set, let's give this car some shine. We'll do this with a couple of gradients set to Incidence Angle. Set the first gradient on the Specularity channel and create a key at 60 degrees with a value of 75%. Create the second gradient on the Reflection channel, with its second key at 45 degrees and 25%. Figure 7-26 shows the new and improved black car.

FIGURE 7-26 A quick application of gradients dresses the car up very nicely.

Note: These are just quick-and-dirty gradients to set up some simple Fresnel effects. They are completely open to modification to fit your personal tastes.

Tip: To best show off the reflection gradient, select the Gradient Backdrop check box in the Effects panel. Figure 7-27 shows the same image rendered with this backdrop reflecting in the surface. We won't worry too much about how the model is lit right now, but you will probably want to have two Distant lights shining on it from different directions just to get some good specular highlights. Later on, we'll set up some nice studio lighting. If you want a little more detail in the reflections, you can click the Add Environment button and add Sky Tracer. This will quickly add some clouds to the reflections, without having to set up anything fancy in the scene.

FIGURE 7-27 Same surface, different environment. This image shows the kind of impact the environment can have on the surface of a car.

Now that we have a basic black car, let's give it a little more depth. Right now we have the equivalent to simple glossy black enamel on this car, but we're going to dress this car up a little more and give it a more metallic finish. To do this, we need to understand just what makes a metallic finish look metallic. Basically, real metallic car paint is little more than fine metal flakes suspended in transparent enamel. These small flakes all have flat reflective surfaces, and are facing in all directions, so no matter where you view the paint from, some of these flakes are reflecting light straight at you. The closer the flakes are to where the normal specular highlight is, the more likely they are to reflect the light in your direction. This results in what appears to be a very soft, wide highlight. The actual transparent enamel these flakes are suspended in creates its own highlight, which is much sharper, like what you would get from glass. In effect, you actually see two different highlights, one sharp, and one wide and usually colored. We could do the same thing we did for the guitar in Tutorial 5 and create a second layer of polygons, but there's a simpler solution for just adding a second, or even a third colored highlight.

STEP 33: Click the Shaders tab in the Surface Editor and then add the BRDF shader. Double-click the entry in the shader list to open the shader's interface. You will see four main sections to the shader. The left side is simply a list of all the lights in the scene, and the other three sections are separate specularity controls (Figure 7-28).

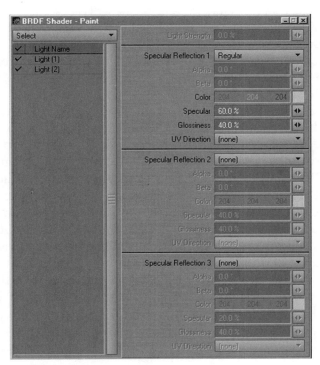

FIGURE 7-28 The BRDF shader, which is very well suited for automobile finishing.

With this shader, we can define up to three different specular highlights, and even select which lights in the scene will affect this surface (much as with the Light Exclusion list in the Object Properties panel). Normally, you'll just leave the lights as they are, since you'll most often use this shader for what we're about to do.

If you have VIPER running, you may have noticed that the specularity changed slightly as soon as we added this shader. The main drawback of using this shader is that it overrides the Specularity and Glossiness channels. The car surface will now have a constant Specularity value of 60% and a Glossiness of 40% thanks to the shader; however, the Reflection gradient will remain unaffected.

Note: When you are using the BRDF shader, the base Glossiness setting can cause some unpredictable results. For example, base values of 0% and 100% both create the same size specular highlight when BRDF is applied, while values of 1% and 99% are very different. A 50% base value tends to lock the highlight to a large size, and the shader's Glossiness setting has virtually no effect. You might find it helpful to simply set the value to 100%, which allows the values in the shader to work the way they're expected. A base value of 0% would work as well, but the specular highlight shown in Layout will tend to be quite large if you're using one of the OpenGL modes.

STEP 34: The first thing we should do is get that sharp glossy highlight back, so increase the first Specularity value to 100% and raise the Glossiness to 50%, just to make it a bit sharper than before. Also, make the specular color a bright white by raising all three RGB values to 255. This will look nice in the Surface Preview and VIPER, but since the base Glossiness is 40%, the highlight will become quite large in the actual render (Figure 7-29). Go back to the Basic tab of the Surface Editor and lower the Glossiness to 0% so it doesn't interfere with the shader. (You don't have to close the shader to do this.)

Now when you render, you should get a nice sharp highlight, as shown in Figure 7-30.

FIGURE 7-29 The strange effects of a Glossiness setting between 0% and 100% combined with the BRDF shader.

FIGURE 7-30 Setting Glossiness to 0% solves the super-bright highlight problem, returning the surface to its sharp glossy appearance again.

Note: Since the car body is a subdivision surface, you can improve its smoothness for rendering by raising the Render Subpatch Level in its Object Properties panel. A level of 6 will create a very nice, rounded surface without getting too heavy on the geometry. Although objects now have virtually no point limits, it's still a good idea to try to keep the point counts low. In the case of this car, you could easily leave the Subpatch level at 3 for moderately distant shots, or even lower it more if it only appears in the background. Increase the geometry only for scenes where the car, or any other subpatch object, will be seen clearly up close.

Now let's add that metallic look. We already have a shiny black car, so let's start with a darker metallic color first. A dark metallic bronze should look quite nice.

STEP 35: Activate the second specular section in the BRDF shader by clicking the button labeled Specular Reflection 2 and choosing Anisotropic. Set the color of this highlight to RGB values of 240, 170, and 40, and increase the Specularity to 100%. Finally, since we want this metallic highlight to be much wider, lower the Glossiness to 30. You should now have a dark, shiny metallic bronze finish on the car (Figure 7-31).

FIGURE 7-31 A second, colored highlight with a lower Glossiness creates a nice metallic bronze effect.

Note: The Anisotropic setting with both angle values set to 0 degrees creates a very soft-edged highlight, which makes it ideal for a metallic surface.

Generally, for metallic finishes like this, you'll want to use Glossiness values of 30% or less. Another rule of thumb for these surfaces is to keep the base color half as bright as the specular color, if not darker. In this case, we used a black base color and used the BRDF shader to provide the only color seen in the surface. If we want a metallic red or blue, the process is very similar, as we'll see.

STEP 36: Go back to the Surface Editor and change the base color to a dark red. RGB values of 80, 40, and 40 will do nicely, but any shade of red should do; for best results, keep the values below 100. Now go back to the BRDF shader and change the color of the second specular highlight to 250, 20, and 20. You may also want to lower the Glossiness of this highlight to widen the metallic look even more. Figure 7-32 shows the same car, but this time as a dark metallic blue, created by simply swapping the red and blue values from this step.

FIGURE 7-32 A metallic blue finish is as easy to create as a metallic red one. Or green, or yellow, or purple, and so on . . .

Note: These colors are kept slightly desaturated by keeping all three values above 20 and below 240. While very saturated colors may look nice, again, they rarely ever occur in the real world. No matter how intense a car's paint job may appear, it will not look as intense when compared with an oversaturated render. Again, the base color is kept quite dark so the BRDF shader's effect is more prominent.

Try out other color combinations of your own. As another rule of thumb, when you create the base color, use the same RGB values and then increase the value of the color by switching to the

HSV color model (achieved by simply right-clicking the RGB values in the panel or by using the Color panel). However, don't feel you must always use lighter versions of the same color for the highlights. There's nothing wrong with using a red highlight on a blue base coat. With a little tweaking, this would create an attractive iridescent finish. Adding a third highlight with another color is not out of the question either. Again, there's nothing like experimentation when it comes to surfacing (Figure 7-33).

FIGURE 7-33 Another variation, this time recreating a metallic silver finish. Now if we could just spice up those headlights.

Note: You can create a second surface layer for the car if you want. This would have the benefit of allowing gradients to adjust the highlights, or even allow you to create other, more psychedelic effects. Simply select the Paint surface in Modeler, copy it to another layer, rename it, then Smooth Scale it by approximately 1 mm. Then just copy it back to the original layer and you're ready to surface it.

Now that we've painted the car, we really should do something about those ugly white wheel rims and lights. We've already covered metal surfacing in Tutorials 4 and 5, so you should be well-armed for making the wheels and grille a nice chrome finish. The lights, on the other hand, will require a little work.

Tip: The CD contains several surface files that can be used to texture this car to match the image on the cover, as well as a few others to play with.

INSTALLING THE HEADLIGHTS

If you've looked at the modeling and surfacing of headlights on some of the other 3D models out there, including the ones that come with LightWave, you've quickly noticed that they're very bland-looking. They have either a simple luminous surface, or even just a default dull white surface, as is present on the '64 Thunderbird model (Figure 7-34). While this will work in a pinch, it does tend to kill the realism of the car when seen head-on.

FIGURE 7-34 The '64 T-bird with its dead-looking white headlights.

Adding actual lights to these headlights also reveals some nasty limitations. Since the light lenses are rarely ever transparent, they tend to block the beam of a spotlight if one is placed behind them. And if the light is placed in front, if you're using a volumetric beam, then you end up with a light cone that comes from some minuscule point (Figure 7-35).

FIGURE 7-35 Simple white headlight lenses don't allow for realistic volumetric light beams. Here, the source of the light is slightly in front of the headlight, and results in a light beam emanating from a small point, rather than from the full headlight lens itself.

What makes headlights look the way they do is a complex series of refractions and reflections that take place inside, in much the same way as the various internal light paths of a diamond give it its bright shine. This effect cannot be done easily with a single surface. It can be cheated with an image map of real headlights, which looks good from a distance, but tends to look flat when viewed close up. Some techniques use a series of photographs of real headlights, taken from various angles and mapped onto the 3D ones, using the incidence angle to determine which image is seen for that particular viewing angle. These techniques are not exactly commonplace, nor are they well suited for casual use.

To simulate the internal reflections of a real headlight assembly, we'll need to actually build a headlight, complete with the internal details, and duplicate the reflections going on in there—or at least a simplified version of them. Figure 7-36 illustrates the basic assembly we're going to create, so let's get started.

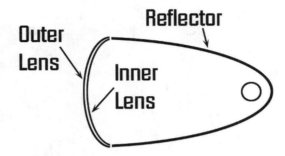

FIGURE 7-36 A simple diagram of the three main surfaces we'll need to create for a realistic light assembly.

STEP 37: Load the **LW-Classic.lwo** object into Modeler and select layer 1. In order for us to create the internal parts of the headlights, we'll need to create some new geometry. We already know where the headlights are, and they've already been given surface names (which is why they've remained white while we surfaced the rest of the car), so open the Polygon Statistics panel and select the surfaces called Lens-Headlight.

STEP 38: Cut these surfaces and then press Shift+Y to open the Layers Browser. Select layer 10 and paste these lens surfaces there. Now, select layer 11 and paste them there too. We're going to use the second copy of these lenses as the source for the internal geometry. First, though, we need to add some space between the outer lens surface and the internal surfaces. Between these, we'll need a "spacer" surface, or a seal that will cover the edges of the headlight lens where it contacts the rest of the car.

STEP 39: We have four separate lenses in this layer, two for each side of the car. To make things a bit easier, we'll use the Symmetry mode, which will allow us to focus on the lights of just one side. The lights on the other side will be edited automatically, following the same steps we will perform on the first side, without having to repeat steps or mirror the first set of lights. Click the Modes button on the bottom menu (Figure 7-37) and select the Symmetry mode.

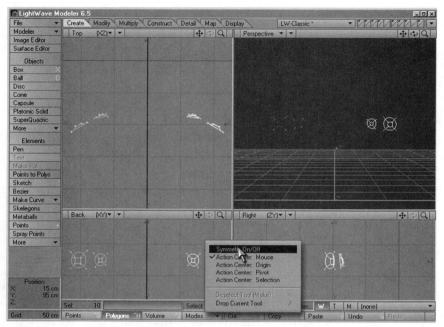

FIGURE 7-37 The Symmetry tool has been moved to the bottom of the screen in the new LightWave 6.5 menu configuration.

Note: With Symmetry on, every action on one side of the car will be mirrored on the other side, but only if there's a matching set of points on that side. Whether or not there is a matching set of points on either side, any actions performed on the negative side of the X axis, along the X axis, will actually work in reverse. Trying to drag a point on the negative side to the right by moving the mouse to the right will actually move it to the left, and vice versa. Points on the positive side will behave as expected. Points that are centered on the X axis cannot be moved on the X axis at all while Symmetry is active. Also note that trying to rotate anything will cause points on the positive side to rotate normally, but points on the negative side to rotate in the opposite direction. The points on the positive side will rotate around the rotation's center as expected, but the points on the opposite side will use a mirrored rotation axis. This makes it fairly important to remember to turn Symmetry off when you don't need it, or to modify only selected points and polygons to avoid accidentally mangling your models.

Hint: Since Symmetry is active, you can press Shift+A to automatically fit the lenses to the view. This will fit only the lenses on the right side of the car, even though the lenses on the other side are also selected. With Symmetry active, we really don't need to see what the other side is doing, so we can zoom in on the half of the object we're working with, and not worry about the other half since it'll be a perfect mirror of what we're doing.

Press Q to open the Change Surface panel and create a new surface called Lens Seal. Now select the patches on the positive side of the X axis in this layer and press Shift+F to Smooth Shift them. Drag slightly to the left until the readout in the lower-left corner reads −1 cm (or −10 mm). This will give us a second, inner surface that's 1 cm from the headlight surface in the previous layer.

STEP 40: Everything in this layer is currently using the seal surface, which we want only for the very edge of the headlight lens. Since we selected some patches before we used the Smooth Shift tool, those original patches are still selected. These selected patches will become the inner surface of the lenses, to which we will apply an "air" surface. Open the Change Surface panel again, and give these patches a surface name of Lens-Headlight Air.

Since we renamed only the selected patches, the new ones that were created during the Smooth Shift operation still have the Lens Seal surface. This means we have the inner lens and seal surfaces in this layer, and the outer lens surface in the previous layer. All that remains for us to create is the reflector.

We'll create that reflector using this existing geometry again, but we need to be aware of one thing. Since we're using sub-patches, the shapes they create are influenced by the surrounding geometry they're attached to. Right now, as you can see in Figure 7-38, the seal and air patches flow together in a smooth curve. If these patches were returned to the car layer, and their points merged, the shapes they form would be modified by the surrounding geometry of the car. Likewise, the lenses will also modify the geometry of the car itself. Figure 7-39 shows one possible unwanted result of keeping the lens patches merged with the rest of the car.

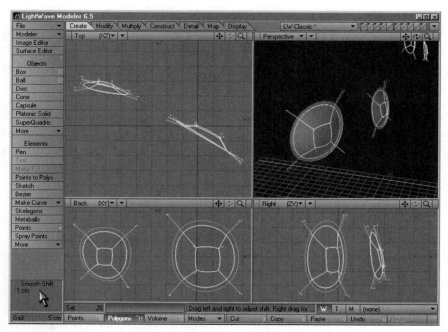

FIGURE 7-38 Smooth Shifting the patch inward by 1 centimeter gives us the thickness of the headlight lenses, as well as the width of the headlight seal surface.

STEP 41: Cut these selected patches and paste them back into this layer, without merging the points. You will now have a sharp corner where the two surfaces meet, as in Figure 7-40. This completes the modeling of the actual lenses themselves. We also have the geometry that will become the reflectors stored in memory as well.

STEP 42: Select layer 12 and press V to paste the air surface here. Now select the two very center patches of these lenses, and then press T to activate the Move tool. Drag these patches back −15 to −20 centimeters along the Z axis. This will cause each lens to form a sort of hyperbolic cone, which will be our reflector (Figure 7-41).

Hint: You may want to place the lens or car layers into the background to better see how these reflectors look against the surrounding geometry.

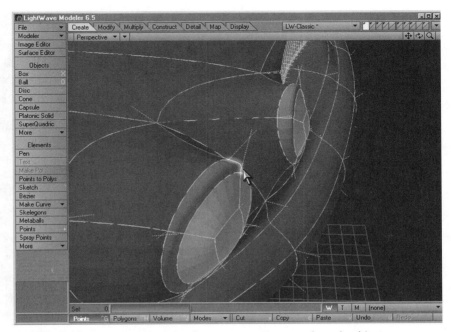

FIGURE 7-39 Merging points in the wrong areas on subpatch objects can cause unwanted curves and stretched surfaces. Here we see the seal surface, which should be a thin strip at the edge of the lens surface, being stretched back toward the main body of the car.

Note: This is one big, gas-guzzling monster of a luxury car, which could give any Hummer a run for its money. This car was originally built as a limousine for a *Max Steel* episode, and required enough room inside to stage a fight scene. As such, the car's dimensions were slightly exaggerated, which explains why these headlights have such deep reflectors. If you try this procedure with other vehicles, you can reduce the depth of the reflectors. In fact, it's a good idea to create the reflector for each light independently, just so the shapes can be fine-tuned to the size of each light. We're doing both the low- and high-beam lights simultaneously just for expedience here.

STEP 43: Deselect everything and open the Change Surface panel again. Create another new surface with the name Reflectors, and we're done. Now all we have to do is assemble these three layers together.

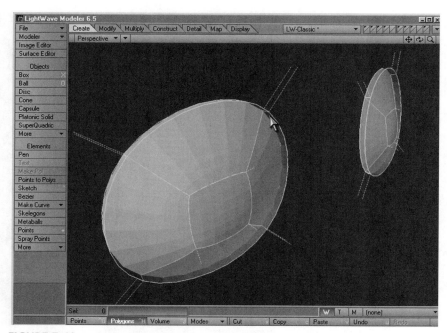

FIGURE 7-40 Cutting and pasting patches back into a layer without merging will create a break in their continuity, allowing for sharp edges between adjoining patches.

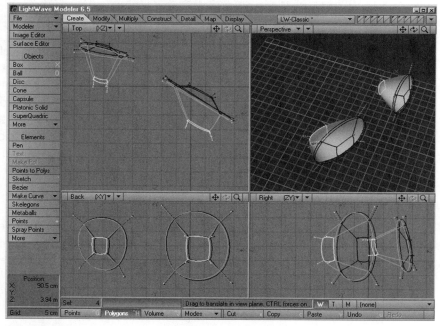

FIGURE 7-41 Dragging the middle patch of the air surfaces back creates a smooth, conical surface that will work well as a light reflector.

Before you start to copy all these layers and paste them into the first layer with the rest of the car, let's think about how the lighting will work with them. Obviously, the air and the lens surfaces will have some transparency so we can see the reflector behind them. However, if we try to use a shadow-mapped spotlight with them, they'll cast a solid shadow, even if they're 100% transparent. This would prevent light from spotlights pointed at the car from lighting up the interiors, and would also block the beam of a spotlight if we use one inside as the light source, which we will be doing shortly. If we use normal ray-traced shadows, this light-blocking effect can be avoided, but then we run into the big render hit that tracing shadows of transparent surfaces causes. We could turn the shadow options off, but that means that the car itself would no longer cast shadows. We need a way to turn the shadows off for just these transparent surfaces.

And we have one staring right at us. These object layers each load into Layout as if they were separate objects, complete with their own object properties. This means we can set shadow options for each object layer, as well as light exclusions and so on for each layer of this object.

STEP 44: Hold down the Shift key and select the three layers (10, 11, and 12) that contain the headlight surfaces (Figure 7-42). Press X to cut all the patches in these layers, then select layer 5, which is currently empty. Paste the headlight surfaces into this layer by pressing V, and make sure you don't merge anything.

STEP 45: Double-click layer 5 in the Layers Browser to open the Layer Settings panel. Set the parent for this layer to layer 1, and name this layer Light Lenses (Figure 7-43).

STEP 46: Now that we have the light assemblies in their own special layer, let's separate them further. We want only the transparent surfaces in their own layer, so the reflector and seal surfaces, since they won't be transparent and should cast shadows, can be safely moved back to the car's main layer. Using the Polygon Statistics panel, select the reflector and the seal surfaces and then cut them by pressing X again. Select layer 1 and paste them here by once again pressing V (Figure 7-44).

Send this object to Layout now, where we'll finish the setup for these headlights. The first thing we should surface should probably be the two transparent surfaces. Let's start with the outer one.

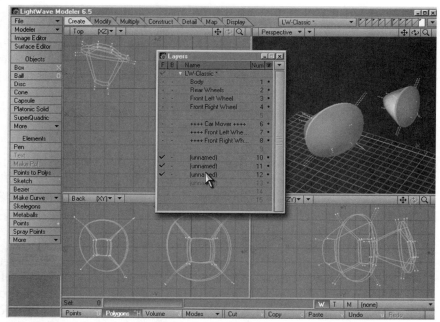

FIGURE 7-42 Selecting multiple object layers using the Layers Browser and the Shift key.

FIGURE 7-43 The Layer Settings panel, showing the parent layer and the name of the new lens layer.

STEP 47: The outer surface will be a smooth shiny glass surface, which is found on virtually all cars today. Open the Surface Editor and select the Lens-Headlight surface. Let's start off by activating Smoothing, and then adding a couple of gradients for Specularity and Reflection. Again, make sure the Reflection gradient starts at half the intensity of the Specularity gradient. Glossiness can be left at 40%, but you may want to make it higher. Also, increase the Transparency to 95% and set the Refraction index to 1.35 or so. Figure 7-45 shows a good set of surface attributes for these headlights. Note that Translucency is applied. This is intentional, and will be covered shortly.

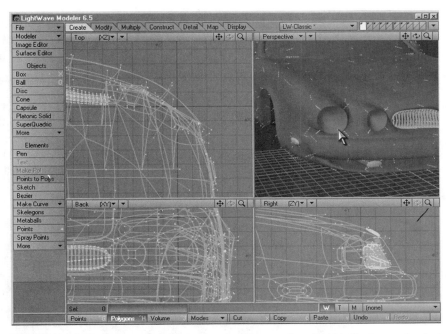

FIGURE 7-44 The updated car body, showing the new headlight reflectors we've just installed.

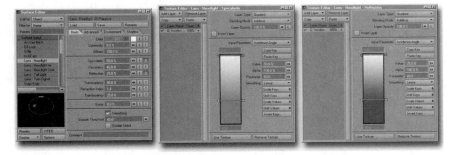

FIGURE 7-45 Some good surface values to create a glassy headlight lens surface. Note the presence of Translucency, which will play an important role later.

Finally, click the Environment tab and set both Reflection and Refraction Options to Ray Tracing + Backdrop.

Tip: As we learned in Tutorials 4 and 5, VIPER will be of very limited use with these transparent surfaces. To see what's really going on, we'll need to do real test renders again. For best results, you should have all three ray-tracing check boxes selected in the Render Options panel.

Note: Since the geometry of the lens layer was derived from the original body layer, these two object layers should use the same subpatch levels. Otherwise, a visible gap could appear between the lenses and the body of the car where the geometry doesn't line up due to differing values.

STEP 48: Next, select the Air surface and select the Smoothing check box for it as well. This surface will also have a special little trick up its sleeve, which will require the use of the Double Sided option, so select that check box as well. Figure 7-46 shows the surface settings for this surface. Use the same Environment settings for this surface as we just set up for the glass.

FIGURE 7-46 The Surface Editor showing the simple setup for an air surface.

Now let's look at what these two surfaces are doing so far. The first surface is our glass surface, and this has a refraction index to simulate the qualities of glass. As a ray enters, it becomes refracted when it hits the surface, and then continues in a new direction.

The ray then hits the second surface, which has a Refraction Index of 1, which is the value of air. This second surface causes the ray to become unrefracted and changes course again, continuing on until it hits the reflector. These two surfaces combined give the lens its thickness and glassy look that slightly distorts the view of the reflector inside (Figure 7-47). So far, there's nothing really special going on. That's going to change.

FIGURE 7-47 An early test of the two transparent lens surfaces. They look slightly better than before, and a small amount of distortion is visible in the unsurfaced reflectors.

STEP 49: Select the Reflector surface and give it a highly reflective surface. Set the Reflection and Specularity values to 100% and reduce the Diffuse level to 25% or lower so it is not affected by shading very much. Select the Smoothing check box and then set the Reflection Options for this surface to Ray Tracing + Backdrop.

Tip: For best results you should select the Gradient Backdrop check box in the Effects panel, or load Sky Tracer so this surface has something to reflect.

Do a test render of the headlights now, and you'll see that they're much more impressive-looking (Figure 7-48).

FIGURE 7-48 A close-up of the headlights, showing their much more believable surface details.

Optional: Many newer cars have thinner, untextured headlight lenses these days, but many still use a gridded bump texture to help diffuse the beam of light they produce. This pattern of ridges was normally placed on the inside of the lens while the outside was left smooth. To add a similar bump to these lights, select the Air surface again and then open the Texture Editor for the Bump channel. Select Planar Image Map, using the Z axis, and load the **DiamondChecks.iff** image. Set the texture Scale to 10 mm, 10 cm, and 1 m, and increase the Texture Amplitude to 5. This will keep the front surface of the lenses smooth while the bumps on this surface will create a patterned distortion in the refraction.

Note: As a small homework assignment, set the turn signals and the brake lights up the same way. The same procedures can be used to create similar light setups for these. The only differences are that the Smooth Shift amount should be smaller, such as 2–3 mm, and the names for the lens and air surfaces should be different to allow them to be surfaced differently. The reflectors for all lights can use the same surface name, since they'll all be the same. The bump maps, as with the headlights, should be placed on the Air surface, but the outer lens surfaces should be colored and have their Color Filter value set to 100% so they color the reflections behind them. These transparent surfaces should also be placed in layer 5, while their reflectors are added to the car's body. There are a couple of surface files on the CD that can be used for the different lenses, but just giving them the same surface values as the headlights and then changing the colors to red or orange is really all that's needed for these.

Note: The seal surface, since it's not seen very well, doesn't require any special treatment. Generally, you'll just want to make it a dull gray and leave it at that. All it really does is prevent light from leaking between the lenses and the car body.

So far, there's still nothing really special going on, except now we have some internal reflections visible through the lenses. So what's the big deal? The big deal becomes apparent when we actually place a light inside these headlights, so let's do that.

STEP 50: Add a Spotlight to the scene and parent it to the car's Body layer. This light should already be facing in the same direction as the car, so simply move it into position inside the front left headlight. The actual position of the light depends on how deep you made your reflectors. Just make sure it's not falling somewhere behind the reflector. Note that the light does not need to be perfectly centered in the reflector itself. It should be positioned slightly ahead of the center patch, and set up in such a way that the cone of the light just fills the headlight lens (Figure 7-49). It should also be angled downward one or two degrees.

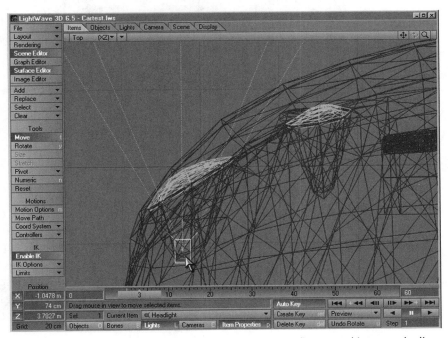

FIGURE 7-49 Position a spotlight near the back of the reflector, making sure the lines of its cone just cover the lens.

Tip: For placing lights in an object like this, you may find it useful to use the Wireframe view mode and use the light's point of view to make sure the lens fills the light's cone.

STEP 51: Once the light is in position, open its Light Properties panel and set its Intensity to 100%. Set the falloff to Inverse Distance, which will give it a very intense light near its source, and set the Nominal Distance to 10 meters. Remember, this forces the light to be 100% intense at a distance of 10 meters, unlike the Linear mode, which would have the light fade to 0% at this distance. The Inverse Distance mode is well suited for focused lights such as headlights and flood lamps.

Pressing F9 now will show our fully functional headlight assembly that actually fills with light when a light source is active inside it (Figure 7-50).

FIGURE 7-50 With all raytracing options turned on, a light inside the reflector assembly creates both internal highlights and an even surface glow. Note the bright reflection of the lens in the bumper.

Normally, a light is not visible through a transparent surface. Its effects are, but the light source itself is actually invisible. Using Radiosity can make the light appear slightly through transparent surfaces, but at an extreme cost in render time. Lens flares only place a glow over the actual position of a light as seen through the camera, but don't take into account the apparent shift of a light due to refraction or reflections. Volumetrics are the closest we can get to showing the source of a light, but even these can fail, especially when seen through a surface with Additive Transparency, or nonrefracting surfaces, in which case they, too, disappear.

So how are we getting all these internal reflections to show up? Especially since the light itself is not shining on the reflector, and no lens flares are involved?

Two things are going on here. The first has to do with the Translucency setting on the glass surface. When this is applied, light hitting the back side of the surface will cause it to light up, almost as if the light were shining on the front. As long as the surface is either less than 100% transparent or more than 0% diffuse, Translucency will lighten a surface when it's backlit. Since we have a very intense Spotlight pointed directly at the back of this glass surface, it affects the translucency enough to make the entire surface brighten up, as illustrated in Figure 7-51. This glowing effect fills the headlight's surface with light, duplicating the look of headlights as they would appear on film or video. Of course, a lens flare can be used to add some glare and lens reflections.

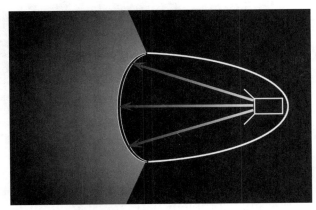

FIGURE 7-51 The light shining on the back of the glass surface affects its translucency, and the surface becomes lighter.

The second thing that's happening, which causes the multiple highlights inside the light, has to do with the air surface. This surface is not reflective, which wouldn't have any effect on lights anyway, but it does have some specularity. Reflection sees only other surfaces or the backdrop colors, and lights, no matter how bright, are ignored in reflections. However, the specular highlights of a light in a surface *can* be seen in reflections, and this is what's happening here. The air surface, which is double-sided, is creating a very bright specular highlight on the inside surface. This highlight is then reflected in the Reflector's surface a few times (Figure 7-52). This has the effect of creating lots of bright hot spots inside the assembly, which change based on our viewing angle. With the addition of some bumps on the air surface, the effect becomes quite sparkly, just as a real headlight would be.

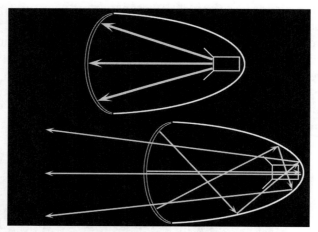

FIGURE 7-52 The light hitting the air surface (top) creates a bright specular highlight that's invisible from the outside. However, this highlight is then reflected in the reflector surface, where it can be seen through the lens surfaces (bottom).

STEP 52: We can speed up the rendering of this light by using a Shadow Map instead of raytracing the shadows. However, we do have the small problem with transparent surfaces casting solid shadows. Since we've already separated the lenses into their own object layer, this is easily fixed. Change the Shadow Type to Shadow Map and then open the Object Properties panel and select the lenses layer. On the Rendering tab, clear the Self Shadow and Cast Shadow check boxes.

Now we can render with faster shadow maps and still be able to light the road in front of us.

THE BEAUTY SHOT

Well, we now have an elegant-looking car, so let's finish this tutorial by showing it off. You'll notice in many automobile ads, both in print and on TV, that the car is lit and photographed in such a way as to show off its curves and shine. The trick is not so much in the lighting, but in the reflections. Frequently ads, and even posters, have the car lit so that you see only a thin white highlight that traces the profile of the car, while the rest of the frame is generally black. In some cases, the only visible detail is this highlight, but how is it created?

If we try to use any of the lights in LightWave, we always get small highlights or wide, soft-edged ones. We can never get those long, sharp-edged ones we're used to seeing in photographs. However, it's not the lights we need to worry about. If we were doing a shot of a car as it would appear on a showroom floor or at a convention, with all those harsh mercury lamps blazing down, then the LightWave lights would be ideal. But we're going for the classic, elegant look of a studio shoot. For this, we really don't even need a light!

Photographers use special devices they can attach to their assortments of lights. These come in several forms, including "snoots," "gobboes," "cookies," white and gray bounce boards and reflectors, tinfoil, and soft boxes, among others. However, it's the soft box that makes that classic highlight.

These come in all sizes, from small handheld devices to several meters in length. They're little more than a thin white fabric stretched over a wire frame and sealed with a light-tight black fabric. Many of these resemble tents with a white base and black sides, and are light enough to be attached to most studio lights. The white fabric is lit from the inside by a light, and then diffuses this light over an even area, eliminating hard shadows and creating a very soft lighting effect—thus the term *soft box*.

For automobiles, large soft boxes are used, generally suspended above the car in such a way that the illuminated white area of the box is visible in the reflections on the car's surface. The edges of this reflected box create the sharp contrast between highlight and darkness in these studio shots.

We could actually build a soft box in LightWave, by making a large box with one white translucent side and placing a light inside it, but this is a little overkill. All we need is the actual white surface, which we can easily make luminous.

STEP 53: Launch Modeler and create a new object. Select the Box tool and create a box using the following values in the Numeric panel:

Low X	−5 m
Y	0 m
Z	−10 m
High X	5 m
Y	0 m
Z	0 m

Press Q to open the Change Surface panel and give this polygon a surface name of Softbox. Save this object as **Softbox.lwo** and then switch to Layout.

Tip: You might want to start with a fresh scene now.

STEP 54: Load the car, and then load the Softbox object. Move the Softbox 5 m above the car, and keyframe it there.

STEP 55: Open the Surface Editor and select the Softbox surface. Give it a bright white color, and make it 200% luminous and 0% diffuse.

Note: While a white surface that's 200% diffuse will render as white as one that's 100%, or 500%, the appearance of the surface when seen in reflections can vary greatly. The brighter the luminosity, the brighter the reflection will appear in surfaces that are less than 100% reflective.

Next, open the Object Properties panel and select the Softbox object. Select the Rendering tab and select the Unseen by Camera check box. This will prevent this white box from rendering above the car if it happens to creep into the frame, but will still allow it to be visible in reflections. While we're here, increase the Subpatch levels for the car body and lens layers of the car to 6 or so. Also, deactivate the shadow options for the lens layer.

STEP 56: Open the Light Properties panel and set the Intensity of the light to 0%. Next, click the Global Illumination button, and lower the Ambient Light to 0% as well. (Alternatively, you could just lower the Global Light Intensity to 0%.) We've now just shut off all the lights in Layout.

STEP 57: Open the Render Options panel and select all the ray-tracing check boxes.

STEP 58: Finally, position the camera to the side of the car, as in Figure 7-53. Don't worry if the Softbox is visible in the frame, since we've already told it not to render. Press F9 and you should get a nice black car rendered against a black backdrop, but nicely highlighted with a glossy sheen (Figure 7-54).

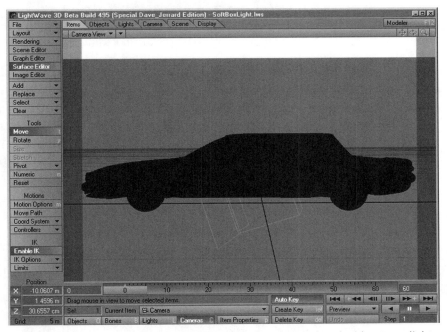

FIGURE 7-53 The view of the car in Layout, ready to be rendered without any lights.

Notice that even though we made the Softbox 200% luminous, we still have some gradation in the reflection. This is due to the gradient we placed on the car earlier, making the reflection more intense at the edge and more subtle on surfaces facing the camera. You'll also notice that the frame rendered quite quickly—not surprising, considering we don't have any lights on to cast shadows.

FIGURE 7-54 A very elegant image created without a single light.

Try rendering the car from a few other angles and moving the Softbox around slightly. You'll find that the angled shots generally provide a much nicer effect. Of course, there's no reason not to use lights. If the car's using the BRDF shader, you'll definitely want to add a light or two to bring out that secondary highlight (Figure 7-55).

FIGURE 7-55 A nice angled view of the car, showing off a couple of colorful specular highlights created by the addition of two Distant lights.

Tip: Try to make sure you have a Softbox visible to silver and chrome areas. A large white highlight is ideal for setting these surfaces off. Also, try to make sure the edge of the Softbox is visible in the reflections. It's this edge that makes the highlights so attractive.

As you can see, some very beautiful imagery can be created in LightWave, even without lights!

8

From Molehills to Mountains

Dave Jerrard

OVERVIEW

We've already dealt with atmospherics and planets, and taken a good look at parking lots and water, but now we'll take a look at the land itself. There are several ways to create landscapes, from simple image-mapped planes to USGS digital elevation maps that accurately recreate real-world locales. Every landscape will pose its own unique set of modeling and surfacing challenges, so it's impossible to cover every possibility in a single book. Instead, we'll cover a few techniques to get you over some of the bumps.

In this tutorial you will use:

■ Subdivision Surfaces

■ Procedural Textures

■ Displacement mapping

What you will need:

■ Prebuilt objects and surfaces included on CD

■ Spare time

What you will learn:

■ Procedural object creation

■ Deformation techniques

■ More surfacing techniques

543

Subpatch modeling is much like working with clay, and it lends itself very well to creating lumpy, organic shapes. Rolling hills, beaches, and other well-worn landscapes can be created quite quickly with subpatches. Terrain like this is very easy to achieve by simply dragging a few points up or down on a large, subdivided mesh. This will create the smooth rolling hills effect quite quickly, but getting the finer details requires breaking the mesh down even more. It would be nice if we could create landscapes with the same kind of detail we had in Tutorial 5, when we used procedurals to create the surface of a planet, which worked well. After all, if they can be used to make bump maps, why not actual bumps?

They can!

MODELING WITH TEXTURES

STEP 1: Launch Modeler and use the comma key to zoom the view to a grid size of 500 m, as in Figure 8-1. Select the Box tool and drag out a box in the Top view window from 3 km on the X and Z axes to −3 km. While the cursor is over the Top view window, press the up and left cursor keys three times each, which will subdivide this box into sixteen sections. This will simply add a small amount of detail that we can use as visual reference in Layout for the next few steps, as well as help the object keep its square shape.

Finally, press the Tab key to turn this object into a subpatched surface (Figure 8-2).

STEP 2: Save this object as **ProceduralMountain.lwo,** and then switch to Layout.

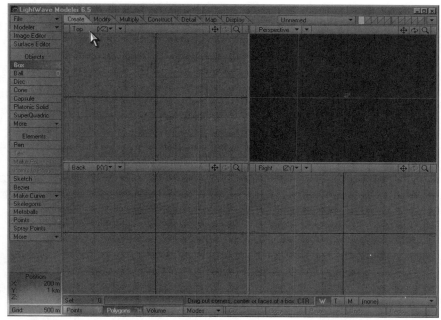

FIGURE 8-1 Zoom out until the grid size in the lower-left corner reads 500 m.

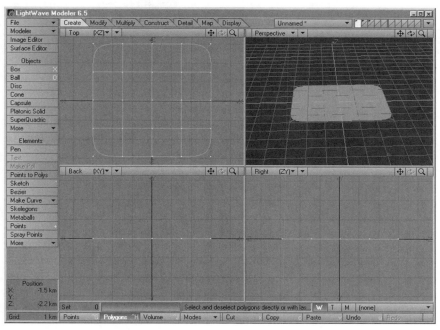

FIGURE 8-2 The subdivided and subpatched box, showing rounded corners.

Move the camera so it's looking at this object from above (Figure 8-3), and then open the Object Properties panel. Click the Deformations tab and then click the Displacement Map button. The familiar Texture Editor will open, but with one small difference. There will now be three additional axis buttons, labeled Displacement Axis (Figure 8-4), near the top of the panel. These will constrain the direction of displacement for some of the textures to one of the three axes. For image maps, this will affect only the Cubic Mapping method, but several procedurals use these as well as all the gradients. For a landscape, these are particularly useful since you'll generally want the points of the object to be moved only up or down, not to the side, where they can cross over other points, resulting in a horrible mess of crossed polygons.

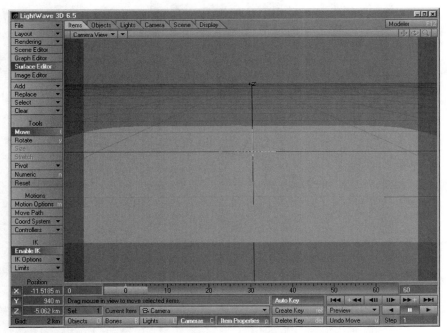

FIGURE 8-3 A good vantage point for surveying the landscape as we work on it.

Note: For best results, you may want to activate Smoothing for this surface.

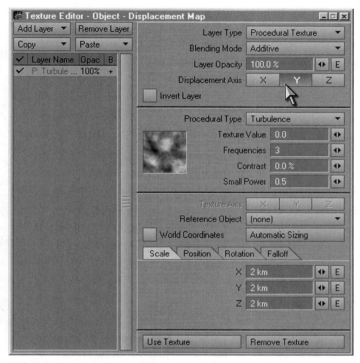

FIGURE 8-4 The Texture Editor for Displacement maps has three additional buttons.

Let's make that landscape now. Switch the Layer Type to Procedural and you'll notice that those Displacement Axis buttons become active for the Turbulence texture. We'll leave them alone, since they've defaulted to the Y axis, which is the direction we want the points to move.

However, nothing seems to have moved in Layout, even though we have a texture applied now. Since the object is 6 kilometers wide, it's a large object, and the default Texture Value for Turbulence is only 0.8. This value, for displacement maps, is a distance value now, meaning that points can be displaced up to 0.8 meters. This is a very small displacement in comparison to an object this large. Increase this value to 500 and the ground will update with some obvious displacement (Figure 8-5).

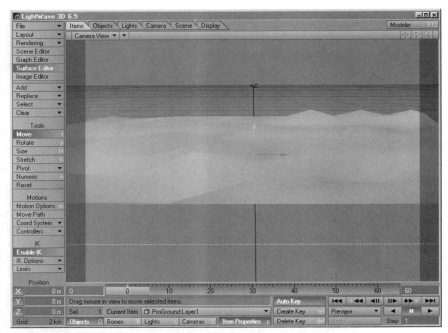

FIGURE 8-5 The landscape after applying the default Turbulence texture with a Texture Value of 500.

Note: The points of an object will always be displaced toward the positive end of the Displacement Axis, unless a negative Texture Value is used. In that case, the points will be pushed to the negative end. For textures that don't use the Displacement Axis buttons, such as Fractal Noise, the direction is random, but using a negative value will cause the points to move in the reverse of their individual random paths.

This might look OK for a starting point for a landscape, but we have to remember the scale of this object. We're applying a texture with a small, 1-meter scale to it. The points in this object are spaced much farther apart than that.

STEP 3: Click the Geometry tab of the Object Properties panel and increase the Display Subpatch Level to 50. This will update the object by subdividing it into a much finer mesh. When that's done, you should see something that resembles a bed of nails (Figure 8-6). This brings us to one rule of thumb about displacements: The Texture Value of a displacement map should be less than the Texture Scale in order to avoid harsh, jagged displacements.

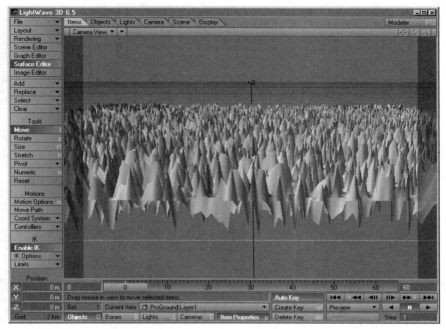

FIGURE 8-6 Increasing the resolution of the mesh reveals the texture as a jagged bed of nails.

To see how this rule works in action, simply increase the texture Scale to 500 m on each axis. The landscape will now appear more rounded and actually start to resemble some park areas of Yosemite or the Grand Canyon (Figure 8-7). If we increase the scale even more, for example, to 2,000 meters, the landscape will smooth out even more, and in Layout view it will begin to resemble the surface of the moon (Figure 8-8). While each procedural texture has its own set of parameters that affect its appearance, this rule of thumb applies to all of them, although each will follow it with slightly different results.

Textures whose level of detail is independent of texture scale, such as Ripples and Underwater, will not be as affected by the scale as the noise textures such as Turbulence or Fractal Noise. Try out a few of the other procedurals to see just how they affect the shape of the surface.

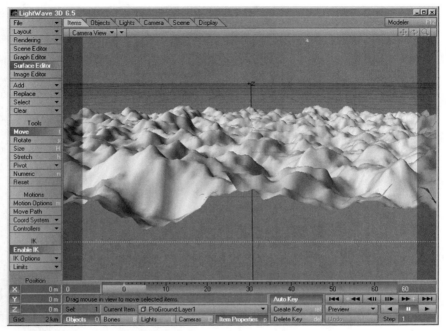

FIGURE 8-7 Increasing the texture scale smoothes out the spiked appearance, resulting in a more rounded landscape.

Note: The Crumple texture works well for making waves on the ocean when used as a bump map, and it works just as well as a displacement map.

GROWING A MOUNTAIN

Now that we've experimented with these procedurals, let's build a mountain.

STEP 4: Remove any additional texture layers you might have and select the Dented procedural. If you've experimented with Dented before, you'll remember that it has small, isolated areas that are more intense than the rest of the texture, creating a mottled look. As a displacement, those isolated areas can become nice craggy, isolated lumps. If we make one of these lumps big enough, we'll have a mountain. All we need to do is find a lump that looks promising.

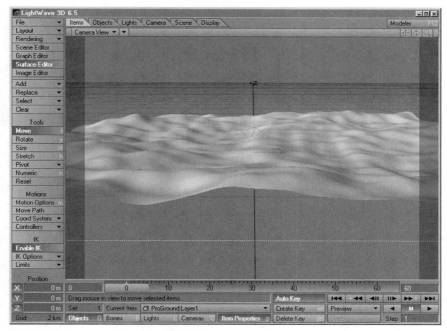

FIGURE 8-8 Increasing the scale further creates a landscape reminiscent of the lunar surface.

Increase the Texture Value to 200 and then increase the texture Scale to 2,000 m. In the Layout window over to the right, we can see a very good-looking candidate (Figure 8-9). Now all we need to do is bring that mountain toward the center of the landscape object.

STEP 5: We could click the Position tab in the Texture Editor and change the position numerically, but this can be tedious. Instead, let's move that mountain visually. To do this, click the Add button on the main toolbar and choose Objects > Add Null. Go back to the Object Properties panel, and select the mountain object again, and lower the Display Subpatch Level to 3. Next, open the Display Options panel (File > Options > Display Options) and set the Bounding Box Threshold to 1,000 or higher (but try to keep it below 10,000 or the refresh rates can get pretty slow).

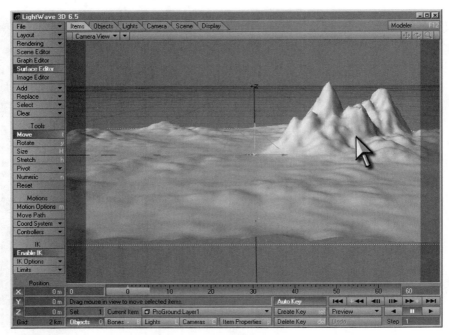

FIGURE 8-9 The dented texture has this nice-looking mountain hidden inside it.

Go back to the Texture Editor, click the Reference Object button, and select the null we just added. Now, when you move the null in Layout, the displacement texture will follow in real time. Move the null to the left and back a bit to position the mountain near the center rear edge of the landscape. You might find it helpful to use the Top view window to see exactly how close the mountain is to the rear edge (Figure 8-10).

Note: Not only can you move the texture, but you can also rotate and scale it with this null. Rotating the null on its pitch and bank will have the effect of changing the landscape, since you'll actually be moving the texture through the surface. Moving the null up or down will have a similar effect. The points of the object are displaced based on the value of this 3D texture at the point where it intersects the original object. By moving the texture, we actually change the value that occurs at the point of intersection, and the distance each point is displaced changes.

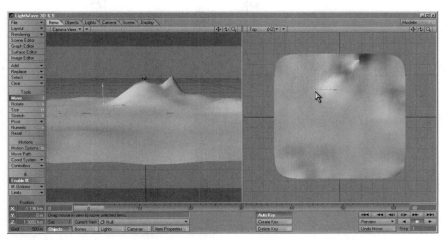

FIGURE 8-10 Using a null to position the texture exactly where we want it.

Once the texture is positioned, click the Reference Object button again and select (none). A panel will ask whether you want to keep the item's parameters. Click Yes to apply the null's position to the texture's position values. We can now safely remove the null from the scene again. We can also increase the Display Subpatch Level to 20–50 again as well.

While we're at it, increase the Render Subpatch level to 100, since we're going to want more detail in the render than we see in Layout. Now let's fine-tune that mountain.

STEP 6: First, we should add a little more detail to this mountain. With this texture, the Octaves is the main parameter that controls the level of detail. Increase this to 10; smaller bumps will appear on the object. The Scale value is almost identical to the Texture Value in that it controls the height of the bumps. Power is much like a contrast control in that higher values increase the spikiness of the landscape, while lower values make it more rounded and bumpier. Frequency controls the size of a portion of the texture, and can be used to make the mountain jagged and sheer with a lower value, or more rounded and more detailed with higher values. The default of 0.8 works well here. Good values for our mountain are shown in Figure 8-11. Figure 8-12 shows a test render of the mountain as it appears with these settings.

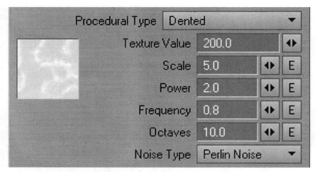

FIGURE 8-11 The values for the Dented texture, which will fine-tune our mountain.

FIGURE 8-12 The same mountain, but with better detail.

We can add a little more detail to this mountain by adding a second texture layer, so let's do that.

STEP 7: Add a new Procedural layer to the texture. You'll notice right away that the landscape flattened out again. This is normal; this new layer is applying a very small amount of displacement again, and is overwriting the previous layer with its 100% opacity.

Note: Unlike bump maps, which add themselves to previous layers, displacement maps tend to overwrite previous texture layers, so adjusting the Layer Opacity, and frequently the Texture Value, of the layers will become necessary to get the desired amount of blending.

To fix this, lower the Texture Opacity of this new layer to 50%. The two layers will now blend evenly. This also means that both are now having only a 50% effect on the displacement.

We'll stick with the Turbulence texture here, so give it the settings shown in Figure 8-13. We're using a negative Texture Value here in order to push some areas of land down below the grid in the Layout window. This will allow us to place some water in the scene, and have the water surface at 0 m on the Y axis. Now, since this texture is actually reducing the amount of displacement of the Dented texture by 50%, we need to compensate for this to get the mountain back to its full height again. Go back to the Dented texture and increase the Texture Value to 400, and the mountain should return to its full height in Layout (Figure 8-14).

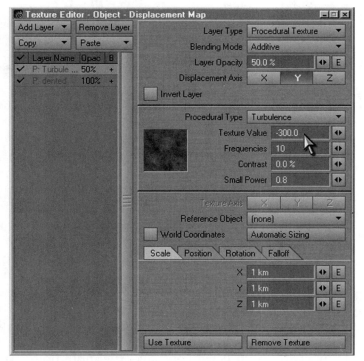

FIGURE 8-13 A second texture layer that will add even more detail to the mountain. Note the negative Texture Value and the 50% Texture Opacity.

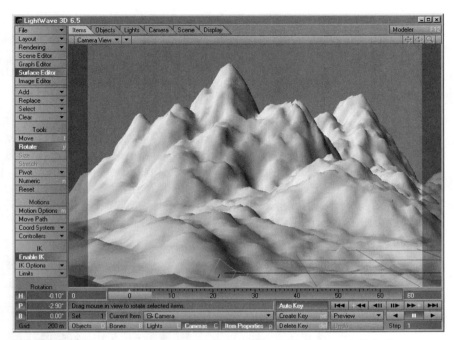

FIGURE 8-14 The same mountain with the additional displacement. Note the appearance of the Layout grid in the lower-right corner, where we can easily create a small lake or river.

STEP 8: Let's save this object so we don't lose the shape. Since these displacement textures are actually a part of the scene, simply saving the object will result in us saving a flat subpatch object consisting of 16 patches, just the way we saved it from Modeler. This means that if we want to load this mountain into another scene, we'll have to first save this scene, and then do a Load From Scene. This will work, but it's a bit clumsy. Instead, we can use Save Transformed to save the object as it appears in Layout, complete with the deformations and the subpatched detail intact. Click the File button, choose Save > Save Transformed, and then give this object a new name. Be aware that the object will save with as many points and polygons as it currently has in Layout, so the larger the Display Subpatch Level you have, the more points the object will have. This also means the object's file size will be larger as well.

Note: To see how many points and polygons an object will have at any given subpatch level, simply enter the value into the Display Subpatch Level and wait for LightWave to update the object. At the top of the Object Properties panel, the current number of points and polygons will be displayed.

You can easily see that creating a landscape like this can add detail that would take a great deal of time dragging points. By simply moving a few textures around, you can create a variety of landscapes, all using the same basic object. In fact, you can move the displacement texture around and save multiple transformed objects that can then be loaded into a scene later, and assemble them into a larger continuous landscape.

Now that we have an interesting mountain, let's give it some texture.

PAINTING BY NUMBERS

This mountain could actually be made of any material we want it to be. With its relatively spiky appearance, it could be crystalline, or ice, or just very dark and rocky. For convenience, we'll just use a texture similar to the one that was on the mountains in Tutorial 6, and take a peek at how they work.

STEP 9: Open the Surface Editor and click the Load Surface button. Select the **Mountain.srf** file and do a test render. You should see something similar to Figure 8-15.

Now let's take a look at what's going on in the surface we just loaded. First, we'll look at the bumps. There are two layers here: one that applies the Crumple texture, and a gradient applied as an alpha. This gradient uses the slope of the surface as its input parameter, and is used to reduce the effect of the Crumple texture on the more level areas of the mountain, while keeping it intense on vertical areas. This creates the jagged-looking cliff faces.

The Color channel has a lot going on, but as we learned in Tutorials 4 and 5, it's easy to figure out when you break it down into smaller sections (Figure 8-16).

FIGURE 8-15 A fully rendered version of the mountain we've created, using the textures contained in the **Mountain.srf** file.

Snow Layers
Slope based gradient alpha
Value supplies color and falloff
Displacement layer distorts snow line

Grass Colors
Based on Y distance
Gradient limits color to level areas

Cliff Colors
Based on slope

Striation Color
Rotated Procedural

Rock Colors
Color based on Bump level

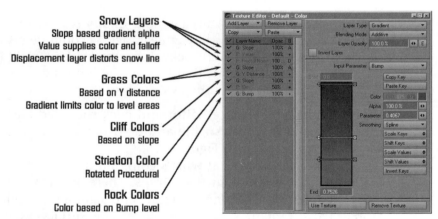

FIGURE 8-16 A breakdown of the various texture layers that create the colors of the mountain.

Let's start with the bottom layer. This is a simple gradient based on the Bump channel, which makes deep areas of the bumps a darker color than the higher areas. Basically, it creates a simulated eroded look.

The FBM procedural above that adds a blue-gray striation effect to the surface. The texture is rotated 20 degrees on its bank to simulate the way mountains are pushed up from below the ground due to tectonics.

The third layer up adds a darker gray to vertical surfaces.

The next two layers combine to add green to the surface, simulating vegetation. The first gradient limits the green colors based on the Y distance. The second gradient is an alpha that prevents the green color from occurring on vertical areas.

Finally, the last three layers combine to add the snow caps. The middle of these layers uses the Value procedural, with a Linear Y falloff to add the snow color to the tops of the mountains. This texture is centered at 700 m on the Y axis to allow the falloff to work downward. The alpha gradient above it prevents the white color from occurring on vertical surfaces, since snow would not be able to accumulate on these. The Texture Displacement layer affects the Value layer above it and adds some irregularity to the snow line created by Value's falloff.

If you check and uncheck the various layers, you can see exactly how each one affects the surface. It's not really that difficult once it's broken down. As before, I urge you to experiment. Don't like the colors I used? Change them! Don't like the snow? Well, you know the layers that create it, so you can remove them.

Now that we've created this landscape, let's have some fun with it. We've already covered a huge variety of techniques in the last few tutorials, and they can all be put to good use here. Remember that small area that was mentioned in Step 7? Since we've already worked with water in Tutorial 4, try using that Depth Attenuation effect here and add some small bodies of water to this scene.

While you're at it, a SkyBall and clouds can be added as well. A few other techniques from the CD can be added too. Basically, everything you need to turn this simple mountain into a fullfledged work of art has been dealt with in one form or another. And this is where I'll turn you loose to create. There are worlds out there to conquer. All you need to do is create them.

9

Character Setup

Jennifer Hachigian

OVERVIEW

The best character setups do not get in the way of the animator. The character's joints must keep their volume when bent, and the animator should have little trouble posing the character.

In this tutorial, we will build a skeleton for the elf-girl on the CD-ROM. We will also write simple expressions and use inverse kinematics to make her easier to pose.

In this tutorial you will use:

■ Skelegons

■ Bones

■ Creating a "null" weight map

■ Weight Map Assignment

■ Expressions

■ Inverse Kinematics (IK)

What you will need:

■ The Kara model from the CD-ROM

■ Spare time

What you will learn:

■ Basic character setup

LightWave's bones act nothing like real bones.

If you've ever handled a raw chicken for cooking, you know how real bones work. The hard bones form a frame for soft tissue. Ligaments, cartilage, tendons, and muscle hook the bones together. The bones themselves do not move—the muscles and tendons form a pulley system, tugging the bones this way and that. The skin stretches over this system like a sock, attached here and there to underlying structures. The shape of the skin changes with what takes place underneath, forming most of what one sees on the living animal.

A real creature derives its shape from the system of bones and muscles underneath the skin. Yet the elf-girl on the CD-ROM, Kara, has only an empty "skin" of polygons to call her own. She has no rib cage or skull, no calcium frame or meaty stuffing. Just skin.

Somehow, we must distort this hollow shell of polygons so that it acts solid. LightWave's bones will let us easily distort Kara's shell, but maintaining her volume could get tricky.

LightWave's bones act as "magnets" for points. When an active LightWave bone has the same position and rotation as its "rest" position and "rest" rotation, it has no visible effect on the points surrounding it. Once moved or rotated, however, an active Light-Wave Bone of more than 0% strength will drag as many points as it can along with it, distorting the shape of the object.

Unfortunately, a LightWave bone doesn't know which points it should grab (it's an artist's tool, not an artist!). An active, non–0% Strength, non–Limited Range bone will affect all points in the object that uses it. As the artist, you must make it clear to each bone which points it can and cannot influence.

Artists working in LightWave 5.6 sometimes resorted to the brute-force method of turning on Limited Range for a given bone. A bone with a Limited Range cannot influence points that lie more than a specified maximum distance away from the bone in its rest position. Even using Limited Range, however, it could get tough to make the bones grab specific points without using (too) many bones.

Happily, LightWave artists now have the luxury of weight maps. On a weight map, each point of an object has a weight value, which consists of a percentage (such as 100.0%). When assigned to a bone, a weight map restricts its influence to only those points weighted as something other than 0.0% on the map. For example, a weight map named "Left Hand" might mark all points that form the left hand of a humanoid model with weight values of 0.0%, and leave all other points with values of 0.0%. A bone told to obey the "Left Hand" weight map would not be able to drag any points marked with weight values of 0.0%. It would, however, influence all points marked with values of 100.0%. When that bone moves and rotates, it would affect only the points of the left hand—those points weighted with values other than 0.0%.

Think of a weight map as an "alpha map" for the effect of a bone (and other deformation tools). An object can have as many weight maps as the artist likes, and the same weight map can be applied to more than one bone. Each bone, however, can only have one weight map assigned to it.

ABOUT SKELEGONS

Skelegons do not deform an object. Bones deform an object. Skelegons just describe an arrangement (or "skeleton") of bones. Because you can use Modeler tools on Skelegons (such as Mirror, Drag, Move, Rotate, Set Value, Copy, and Paste), you can use Skelegons to set up bones faster than you might by using Layout alone.

Skelegon information also gets saved with the object file, making most of the bone setup information part of the object itself (instead of requiring a separate scene file for all of the bone information, as with LightWave 5.6 and earlier).

Once loaded into Layout, the object containing the Skelegons is made the current item. Then choosing Add > Bones > Convert Skelegons into Bones adds a bone for each Skelegon, creating a skeleton nearly instantly. From that point on, the settings of each bone may be tweaked to taste. Bones may be deleted, and even more bones might be added (using the list of tools found under Add > Bones). (The Skelegons may even be ignored entirely, and not converted into bones at all. Skelegons are just a tool—they don't care if they get used or not. It all hinges on what the artist wants to do).

Note: Skelegons are not bones, nor are they truly "converted" in Layout. Even when "converted," the Skelegon information itself remains unchanged. One could keep "converting" Skelegons forever, until the object contained endless copies of the bone skeleton described by the Skelegons.

Skelegons contain information for bone position, rotation, parenting/hierarchy, and weight map assignment (if any). They do not contain information for Falloff Type, Joint Compensation, Muscle Flexing, Strength, and Bone Active. Before we start working with Skelegons, let's take a look at what each of these settings does in Layout.

About Falloff Type

Found only in Layout, the Falloff Type setting affects the way an object's points react to its bones. The higher the rate of falloff, the more a point will "stick" with the closest available bone. A high rate of falloff means less "interference" between bones and more clearly defined joints (such as an elbow). The lower the rate of falloff, the softer the bend of the joints will look (like a ponytail of hair). Figure 9-1 shows what happens between two bones with different Falloff Type settings.

About Joint Compensation

One of the bone settings available only in Layout, Joint Compensation tries to maintain the volume of an object around the pivot point of a bone as that bone rotates on its pitch. Joint Compensation for Parent attempts the same thing, but uses the influence of the bone's parent rather than the influence of the bone itself. Figure 9-2 shows what happens between two bones when the child bone has different Joint Compensation settings.

Joint Compensation, while useful, can happen only when the bone rotates on its pitch.

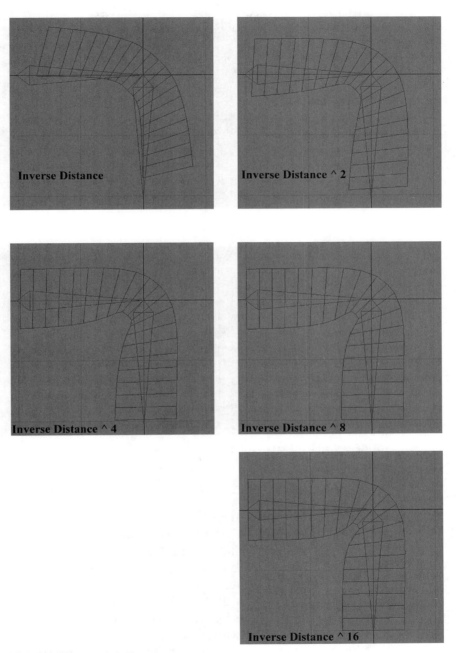

FIGURE 9-1 Five falloff types.

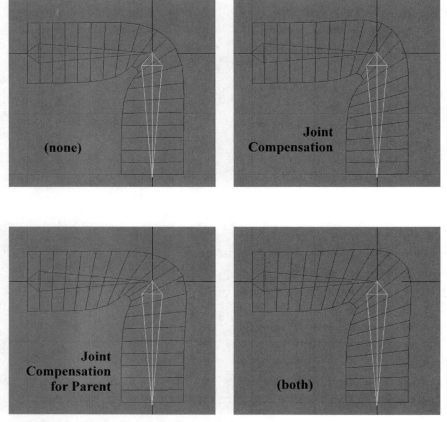

FIGURE 9-2 The effects of Joint Compensation.

About Muscle Flexing

Another bone setting available only in Layout, Muscle Flexing "puffs out" the points that run along one side of a bone as that bone rotates on its pitch. Muscle Flexing for Parent does the same thing, but uses the influence of the bone's parent to "puff out" the points that run alongside one edge of the parent. The edge that gets puffed out is always the "inner" edge of the bent joint. Figure 9-3 shows what happens between two bones when the child bone has different Muscle Flexing settings.

Muscle Flexing, while potentially useful, can happen only when the bone rotates on its pitch.

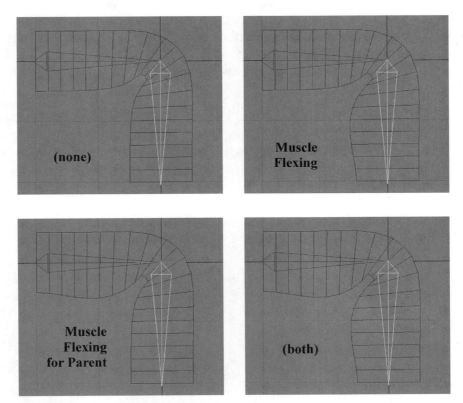

FIGURE 9-3 The effects of muscle flexing.

About Strength

If an object has only a single active bone, and that bone has a Strength greater than 0.0%, all points of the object will move along with that bone's motion, as though the points of the object were "parented" to the bone. The behavior of the points would not change no matter what the Strength of the single active bone, as long as that bone's Strength was greater than 0.0%. If the bone's Strength was set to 0.0%, the points would ignore the motion of the bone entirely.

Strength matters when the object contains more than one active bone. The Strength of a bone affects how that bone relates to other bones in the grand tug-of-war over points. The joints between bones would look the same if every bone had the same higher-than-0.0% Strength setting, whether that setting is 100.0% or 10.0%. However, when the Strength settings among the bones are unequal, the points of the object will "stick" more to those bones with higher Strength settings.

Figure 9-4 shows what happens when one bone has a Strength of 10.0% while the other has a Strength of 100.0%. Figure 9-5 shows what happens when the child bone has a Strength of 0.0%, and the even more interesting situation that happens when the child bone has a Strength of 0.0%, but with Joint Compensation for Parent turned on.

Every bone generated by Skelegon information is initially made active and set to 100.0% Strength.

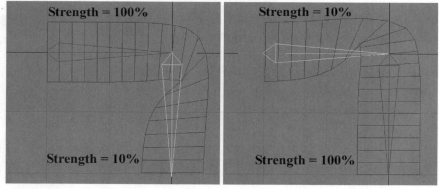

FIGURE 9-4 The stronger bone influences more of the points in the joint area.

About Bone Active

As you might have guessed from the previous paragraphs, Bone Active just means that the bone can affect the points of an object. When Bone Active has been turned off, the bone acts as though it has 0.0% Strength. (Joint Compensation for Parent and Muscle Flexing for Parent would still work, though, as long as the parent bone was active with a Strength greater than 0.0%.)

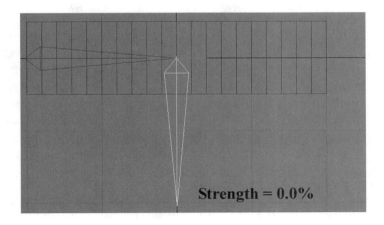

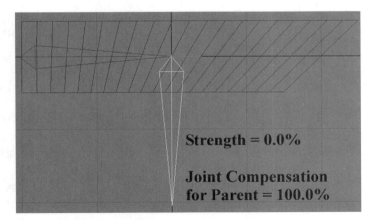

FIGURE 9-5 The parent bone has a strength of 100%.

Tip: Skelegons do not allow you to set Strength or Bone Active status directly, but you can still create Skelegons that will not affect the points of an object when converted to bones. To do this, create a weight map where all points of the object have weight values of 0.0%, and assign this weight map to those Skelegons that should not distort the object. An appropriate name for this zeroed-out weight map might be "(null)." Bones will not touch the points on a weight map with weight values of 0.0%, which means that the bones assigned to the "(null)" weight map will not touch *any* points on the object, no matter what their Strength or Bone Active status.

Load **bonedemo.lws** from the CD. It consists of a plane of 20 polygons and two Skelegons that have been converted to bones.

The child bone has been rotated 90 degrees on its pitch from frame 0 to frame 60. Go to frame 60, select the child bone, and press P to access the Properties panel for the bones of that object. Play with the different Strength, Falloff Type, Bone Active, Joint Compensation, and Muscle Flexing settings to see how the polygons deform with each setting. Some settings might seem more appropriate for a character's body; others may be more appropriate for a character's ponytail (if that ponytail had enough sections in it).

ABOUT SKELEGON CREATION

Each Skelegon you create will have three control circles—two surrounding its end points and a mysterious circle attached to a dotted line extending from the base point of the Skelegon. Clicking and dragging inside the circles surrounding a Skelegon's end points will let you adjust the placement of those points. Clicking outside those circles when the Skelegons button is active will create a new Skelegon, with the base of the new Skelegon attached to the tip of the last Skelegon in the chain.

Clicking inside the third circle (the one attached to the dotted line) will control the initial bank rotation of the bone described by the Skelegon. Because the bank of the parent affects the pitch of the child, we will tweak these handles to make sure that the elbows and fingers of the elf-girl rotate on pitch. Elbows and finger joints that bend on pitch will let us exploit Joint Compensation for Parent to maintain the volumes of these particular joints.

Skelegon Creation Applied

STEP 1: Load **kara04.lwo** into Modeler (if you did not complete the web tutorials and just want to learn Skelegons, you may load **kara04.lwo** from the CD). Go to the nearest empty layer, and make the layer containing the geometry for the body the background layer. Zoom in on the area representing the waist and the head (Figure 9-6).

STEP 2: Click the Skelegons button (Create > Elements > Skelegons) to activate the Skelegons tool. Then, in the Back view, click seven times on the following seven spots along the spine, in the order given:

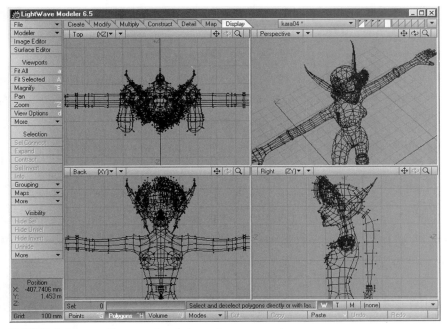

FIGURE 9-6 We will create the skeleton in an empty layer.

1. The center of Kara's waist

2. Slightly above the center of Kara's waist

3. The center of the bottom of where the rib cage would be

4. The part of the spine to which Kara's clavicles would point

5. The bottom of the neck

6. The top of the neck

7. The top of the head

The arrangement of Skelegons should look like the one shown in Figure 9-7 (which has been set to a single window for the purpose of clarity).

Note: The initial bank of a Skelegon, when created, will point along the axis not represented by the view in which you created the Skelegon. Because you created these Skelegons in the Back view (which does not represent the Z axis), their bank currently points to the end of the Z axis.

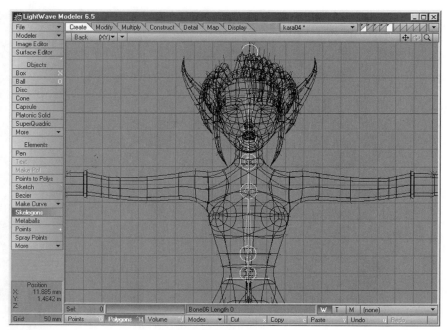

FIGURE 9-7 Getting the skelegons of the spine in place.

STEP 3: Let's make sure these bones are perfectly centered in the Back view. Press Ctrl+V to open the Set Value panel and enter a value of 0 m on the X axis. All of the points will snap to 0 m on the X axis (Figure 9-8).

STEP 4: In the Right view, press Ctrl+T to activate the Drag tool. With the exception of two points, drag each point to where you want the joints to pivot (Figure 9-9). These exceptions are the point second from the bottom and the point fourth from the bottom. The bone at the root of the chain will be an anti-gimbal-lock bone, so make it as tiny as possible by moving the point second from the bottom (the point representing the end of the root bone and the start of the next bone) as close as possible to this bone. The point fourth from the bottom will form a convenient spot at which to connect the chain of bones representing the shoulder and arm, so center it as much as possible within the circles of points representing the arm in the Right view.

Note: Rotating an item 90 degrees on its pitch will cause the functional loss of the Heading channel. This loss (where heading behaves like bank) is called "gimbal lock."

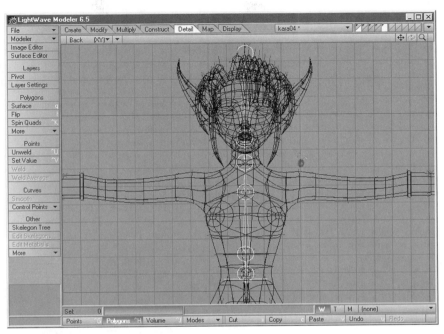

FIGURE 9-8 The spine is straightened after using Set Value.

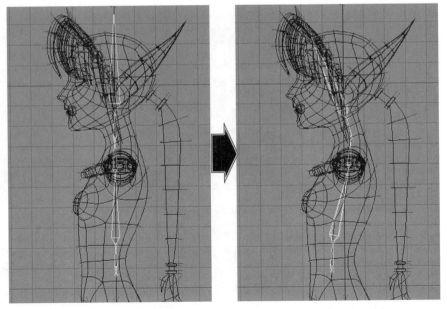

FIGURE 9-9 Skelegons before and after their points are moved into position.

STEP 5: Let's start giving these Skelegons names. Open the Skelegon Tree by clicking the Skelegon Tree button (Detail > Other > Skelegon Tree). The Skelegon Tree window has two columns: Skelegons and Weight Map. Under Skelegons, you should see a hierarchy made up of the names Bone01, Bone02, and so on. ("Bone" is the default name when creating new Skelegons, unless one uses the Numeric panel to change it to some other name.) Double-clicking any of the names in the Skelegon Tree will open the Rename Skelegon panel. Double-click the name Bone01 and give it the new name of KARA_Waist_(anti-gimbal-lock). Do the same for each of the other bones, as follows:

1. Rename Bone01 as KARA_Waist_(anti-gimbal-lock)

2. Rename Bone02 as KARA_Waist

3. Rename Bone03 as KARA_Torso

4. Rename Bone04 as KARA_Upper Torso

5. Rename Bone05 as KARA_Neck

6. Rename Bone06 as KARA_Head

The Skelegon Tree should now look like the right panel of Figure 9-10. Exit the Skelegon Tree for now.

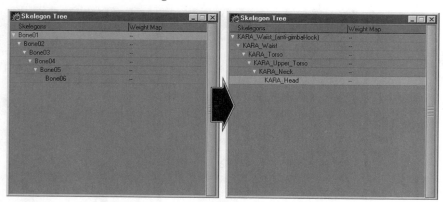

FIGURE 9-10 Renaming Skelegons with the Skelegon Tree.

Tip: If you are uncertain whether the right Skelegons got the right names, select each Skelegon you are uncertain of and click Rename Skelegon (Detail > More > Rename Skelegon) . . . to check its name. If the name in the Rename Skelegon panel matches the name that you want, click Cancel to leave the Skelegon's name unchanged. If the wrong name appears, type in the correct name and click OK to change the name of the Skelegon.

STEP 6: At the time of this writing, Modeler has the strange habit of rotating the bank of the root Skelegon of a Skelegon chain by 90 degrees when enough Skelegons have been added to the chain. Select the root Skelegon (KARA_Waist_(anti-gimbal-lock)) and Zoom in on it in the Top view. Click Edit Skelegons (Detail > Other > Edit Skelegons) and check to see whether the bank handle of the root Skelegon lines up with the Z axis. If it does not (Figure 9-11), hold down the Ctrl key, click within the circle at the end of the bank handle, and drag it up so that it does line up with the Z axis (Figure 9-12).

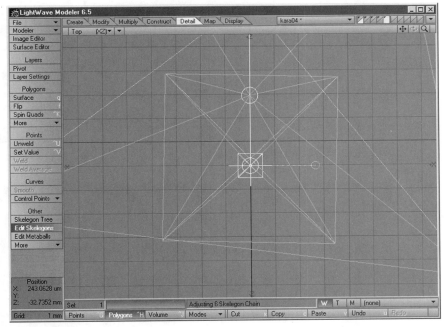

FIGURE 9-11 If you see this . . .

Note: All the bank handles of the spine should point along the Z axis, as shown in Figure 9-13. This way, the pitch of all the spine bones will line up with each other, and rotating the pitch of each spine bone will make Kara bend predictably forward or backward (rotating the heading will make Kara predictably bend from side to side). This makes more "sense" than a spine where the heading and pitch of each spine bone makes the character bend in unpredictable directions. A good character setup should not get in the way of the animator.

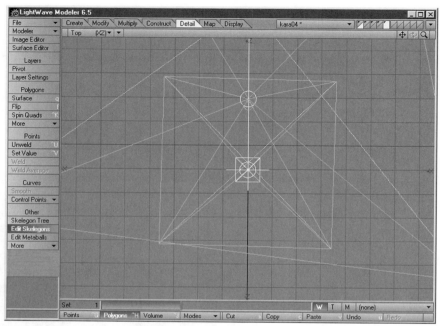

FIGURE 9-12 . . . make it look like this.

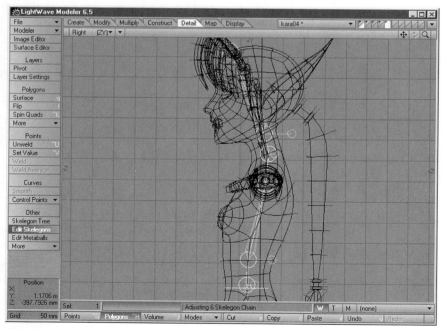

FIGURE 9-13 Aligned bank handles.

STEP 7: Now for the arm. Go to a new empty layer, with the body mesh still in the background layer. Zoom in on the left arm in the Top view. Create a chain of 13 Skelegons, starting from near the center of the spine and ending at the fingertip. Press Ctrl+V to open the Set Value panel, and set the value of these points to 0 m on the Z axis to "flatten" the chain.

Figure 9-14 shows where most of the pivots go. The section of the Skelegon chain between the spine and the root of the shoulder should have three Skelegons—two for the clavicle and a tiny, tiny bone at the root of the chain. Two Skelegons form the section between the shoulder and the elbow. Three Skelegons form the section between the elbow and the wrist. Two Skelegons form the section between the wrist and the root of the middle finger, and three Skelegons form the section between the root of the middle finger and the middle finger tip.

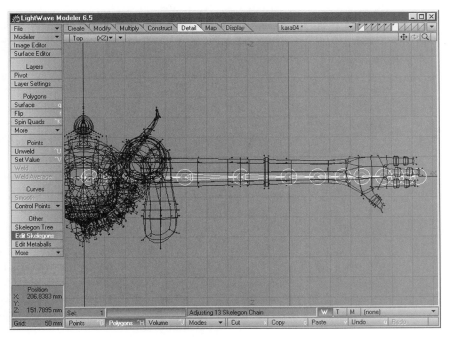

FIGURE 9-14 The pivot placements of the arm chain.

A real humanoid has fewer joints (shoulder, elbow, wrist, finger joints). Why all these extra bones?

Consider how the skin of a real arm behaves. Bend your own arm at the elbow. Rotate your wrist so that your palm faces up. Then rotate your wrist so that the palm faces down. Keep rotating your wrist back and forth . . . and note that this twist happens not just at the wrist, but also all the way up your forearm. The twist fades as it gets closer to the elbow, which itself remains fixed. The three bones in the forearm will help us recreate this twisting effect (also known as *torsion*).

Also remember that LightWave bones do not act like real bones, and that this model has only skin, with no underlying structures. Bones moving on their heading and pitch may not hurt the volume of the figure all that much, but bones twisting too much on their bank may cause an ugly distortion at the joint. A real-world example might be a drinking straw or a sock—hollow structures with nothing underneath. When you bend them, they may crimp, but they maintain their diameter. When you twist them, however, they lose the width of their diameter, and start to resemble a bow tie.

Distributing the bank rotation among many bones can produce a softer, more natural twist. (Unless Kara breaks her arm, these extra bones are not meant to be rotated on their heading or pitch.) Instead of rotating the hand bone 90 degrees on its bank, for example, it might be banked 30 degrees, and the two bones closest to it in the forearm might also be banked 30 degrees. The total rotation is the same (90 degrees), and the palm would face the same direction as it would if the hand bone alone rotated 90 degrees, but less distortion would occur at the wrist joint.

STEP 8: Press T to activate the Move tool. Move this Skelegon chain up in the Top view until it looks centered in the arm and in the middle finger. Then, in the Back view, Move the Skelegon chain until it looks centered vertically between the shoulder and the elbow, as shown in Figure 9-15.

STEP 9: The bones past the elbow may not be perfectly centered in the forearm and hand. Select all of the Skelegons from the elbow to the fingertip. Press the left square bracket key ([ ) to activate the Shear tool (Modify > Move > More > Shear Tool). Right-click the outer side of the elbow in the Back view, and drag the

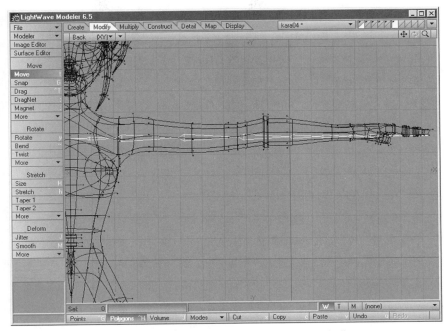

FIGURE 9-15 Centering the arm chain within the shoulder and elbow.

falloff triangle out until its wide end touches the end of the wrist bone (if your falloff triangle looks curved, tap the up arrow key until the triangle looks perfectly straight). Holding down the Ctrl key to restrict movement to one axis, click and drag up until the Skelegons look centered within the wrist (Figure 9-16).

STEP 10: Zoom in on the hand. In the Top view, use the Drag tool to place the pivot points of the finger (Figure 9-17). Select the three finger bones and Move them until they look centered in the middle finger. In the Back view, move the pivot points of the finger up and down until they follow the slant of the finger (Figure 9-18).

STEP 11: Zoom in on the clavicle/shoulder region. In the Back view, use the Drag tool to make the root bone of the arm chain ultratiny. Make the other two bones about the same size as each other (Figure 9-19).

STEP 12: Select the root bone. Click the Edit Skelegons button and check the bank handles of each bone. Because you created these bones in Top view, their bank handles should be aligned with the Y axis. If not, raise their handles now.

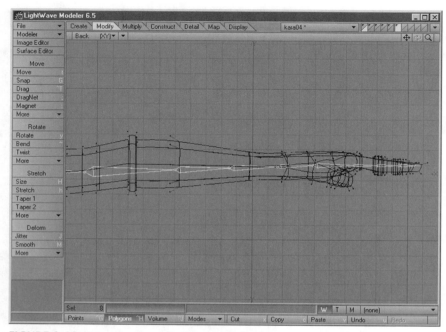

FIGURE 9-16 Using the Shear tool to center the forearm section of the chain.

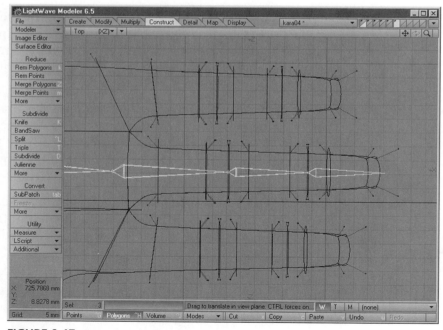

FIGURE 9-17 Centering the finger bones.

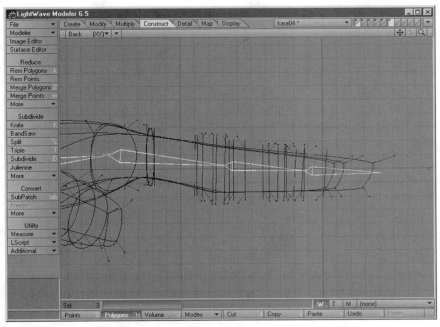

FIGURE 9-18 Adjusting the pivot points of the finger.

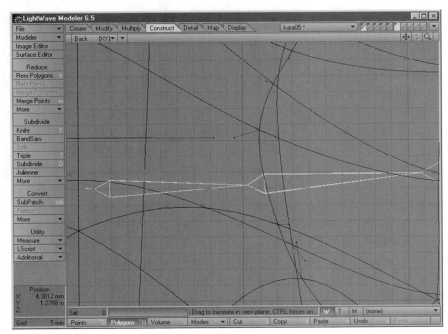

FIGURE 9-19 The first three Skelegons of the arm chain. Note the tiny Skelegon on the left.

STEP 13: Right now the shoulder bends downward on its pitch, and the wrist and fingers bend down on their pitch. This will let them take advantage of Joint Compensation. Let's edit the bank of the two upper-arm Skelegons so that the elbow bends forward on its pitch, so that it, too, can take advantage of Joint Compensation. Select the two Skelegons between the shoulder and the elbow of the model, and press the equals key (=) to Hide all the other unselected Skelegons. Click the Edit Skelegons button. Holding down the Ctrl key to rotate the bank handles in increments of 90 degrees, click the circles of the bank handles of the two Skelegons, and in the Right view drag them forward until they point straight forward. Press the backslash key (\) to Unhide hidden geometry. Deactivate Edit Skelegons. Your screen should look like Figure 9-20, with every other Skelegon's bank handle pointing straight up.

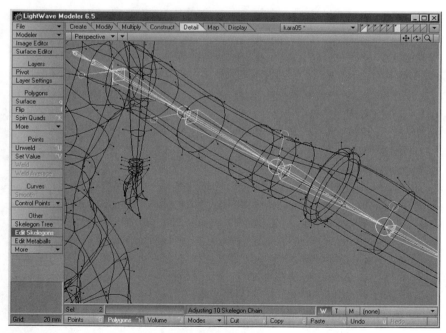

FIGURE 9-20 Adjusting the bank handles of the arm chain.

Note: Only the bone that connects to the elbow needs to have its bank handle twisted forward so that the elbow bends on its pitch. As it stands, not only does the elbow now bend on its pitch, but the upper arm bone connected to the elbow also has a bank of 0.0 (since its bank handle is aligned with that of its parent). This might make it easier to write an expression for the outer arm bone so that it follows the bank of its parent. (Or not. Past a certain point, everything depends on the personal preference of the character setup artist.)

STEP 14: Either using the Skelegon Tree or directly selecting each Skelegon and using Rename Skelegon, rename each skelegon in this arm chain as follows:

1. Rename Bone01 as KARA_L_Arm_root_(orientation-bone)

2. Rename Bone02 as KARA_L_inner_clavicle

3. Rename Bone03 as KARA_L_outer_clavicle

4. Rename Bone04 as KARA_L_Arm

5. Rename Bone05 as KARA_L_Arm_(bank-follower)

6. Rename Bone06 as KARA_L_Forearm

7. Rename Bone07 as KARA_L_Forearm_(center)

8. Rename Bone08 as KARA_L_Forearm_(outer)

9. Rename Bone09 as KARA_L_Wrist

10. Rename Bone10 as KARA_L_Mid_root

11. Rename Bone11 as KARA_L_Arm_Mid_base

12. Rename Bone12 as KARA_L_Mid_mid

13. Rename Bone13 as KARA_L_Mid_tip

When finished, the Skelegon Tree for this layer should look like Figure 9-21.

STEP 15: Let's use copies of the Skelegons for the middle finger to make Skelegons for the thumb, index, and pinky fingers. Zoom in on the hand in the Top view. Select the four bones at the end of

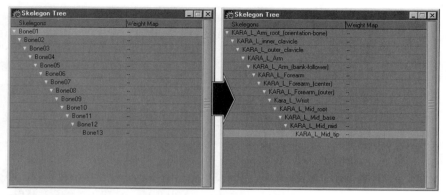

FIGURE 9-21 Renaming the Skelegons of the arm chain.

the chain. Press C to Copy them, then press the minus key (−) to Hide them. With the originals safely hidden, press V to Paste a copy of the Skelegons for the middle finger into the layer. Press M to Merge Points on the root point of this finger chain. (It should overlap with the end point of the KARA_L_Wrist Skelegon, and you should see "1 point eliminated" in the Merge Points panel. If not, select the two points and press Ctrl+W to Weld them together.) Select the three Skelegons at the end of the chain, and use the Move tool to Move them into the center of the pinky finger. Then press H to activate the Stretch tool, and Stretch the Skelegons to fit the length of the pinky finger. If their pivot points don't line up with the joints, make them line up with the Drag tool. Your screen should look like Figure 9-22. Do not Unhide the original Skelegons for the middle finger—we still need to use two more copies of the original for the index and thumb.

STEP 16: Repeat the technique of the last step to create Skelegons for the index finger and thumb (Paste, Merge Points or Weld, Select, Move, Stretch, Drag). After the index and thumb have their Skelegons in place, press the backslash key (\) to Unhide the original middle finger Skelegons. Your screen should look like Figure 9-23.

STEP 17: Select the three Skelegons that form the end of the thumb. Rotate them at their base so that they lie centered in the thumb. (*Hint:* Use the Perspective view.) Your screen should look like Figure 9-24.

STEP 18: In the Top view, drag the end point of the wrist bone back until it looks like Figure 9-25.

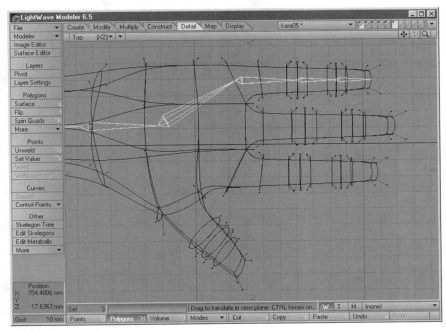

FIGURE 9-22 The pinky uses a copy of the middle finger's Skelegons.

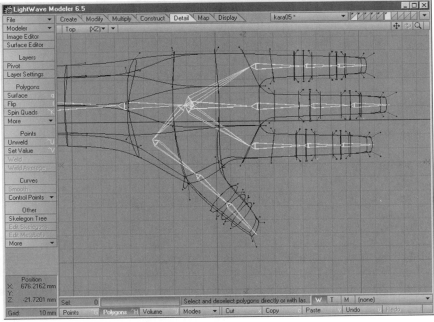

FIGURE 9-23 Copies of the middle finger's Skelegon chain give us Skelegons for the index and thumb.

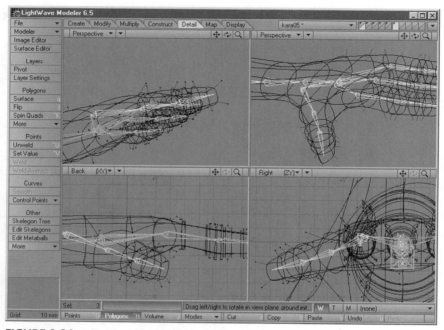

FIGURE 9-24 Adjusting the Skelegons of the thumb.

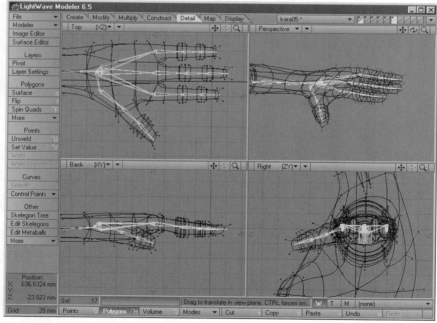

FIGURE 9-25 Adjusting the Skelegon of the wrist.

STEP 19: Select the root bone of the thumb, and click the Edit Skelegons button. Twist all the bank handles of the thumb bones until they face in the same direction—specifically, the direction in which the thumb will bend. Their handles should look like the ones in Figure 9-26 (in which we have hidden the other bones for the sake of clarity).

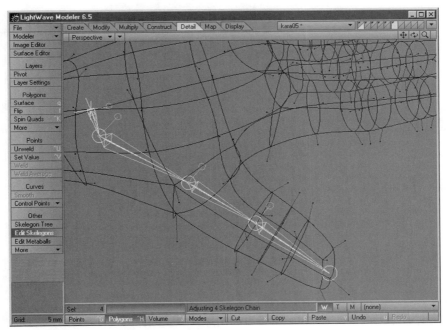

FIGURE 9-26 Adjusting the bank handles of the thumb.

STEP 20: Let's rename these new Skelegons. They all show up as KARA_ L_Mid . . . bones in the Skelegon Tree, so it'll be easier this time around to just select them and rename them directly. In the Top view, select the root bone of the pinky Skelegon chain, and use Rename Skelegon to name it KARA_L_Pinky_root (replacing the "Mid" part of the name with "Pinky"). Click OK, deselect this Skelegon, and select the base bone of the pinky Skelegon chain. Use Rename Skelegon to name it KARA_L_Pinky_base. Keep going until all of the pinky, index, and thumb Skelegons have been renamed. When finished, the Skelegon Tree for this layer should look similar to Figure 9-27.

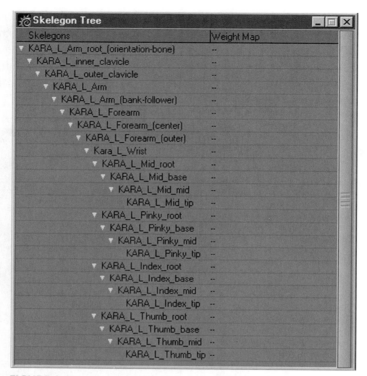

FIGURE 9-27 Renaming the Skelegons of the hand.

STEP 21: In the Back view, the Skelegons for the left arm should look like Figure 9-28. If not, use whatever tools you like to move their points into place.

STEP 22: That's it for the arm Skelegons right now. Let's create the Skelegons for the hip. In the Back view, in a new empty layer, create two Skelegons for the hip—a tiny Skelegon for anti-gimbal-lock purposes, and a big Skelegon to represent the pelvis. Use Set Value to make them snap to 0 m on the X axis (Figure 9-29). Rename the tiny root Skelegon as KARA_Hips_(anti-gimbal-lock) and the big child Skelegon as KARA_Hips. In the Right view, move the root bone so that it lies underneath the root of the spine (Figure 9-30).

That's it for the hips right now. On to the leg.

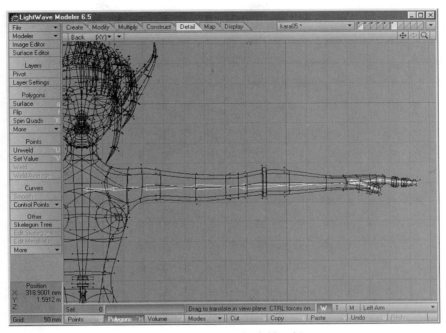

FIGURE 9-28 The arm Skelegons should now look like this.

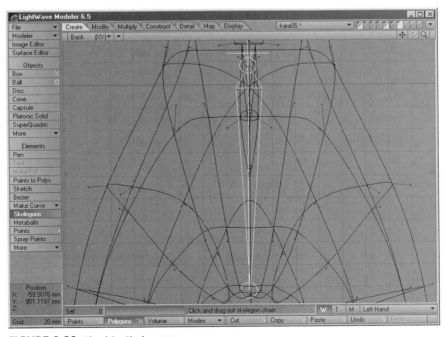

FIGURE 9-29 The hip Skelegons.

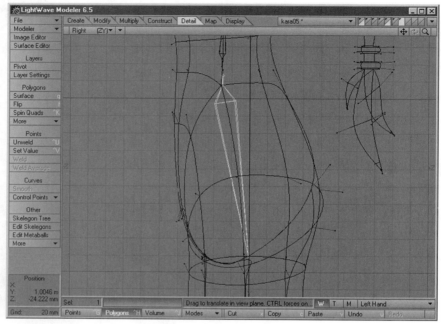

FIGURE 9-30 Align the root of the hip with the spine.

STEP 23: In a new empty layer, with the body mesh in the background, Zoom in on the left leg in the Back view. Click the Skelegons button, and click five times in the spots shown in Figure 9-31 to create Skelegons for the leg, shin, foot, and toe. Keeping your clicks in Back view ensures that all of the bank handles align themselves with the Z axis. (If any handles inexplicably pop out of place, click within the circles for their bank handles and drag them back into alignment with the Z axis.)

STEP 24: Use the Drag tool to move the pivot points of these Skelegons into place. Think about where the joints should rotate, and drag the pivot points to those spots. If you're using the model from the CD, your leg setup will probably look like Figure 9-32.

STEP 25: Rename each of these Skelegons as KARA_L_Leg, KARA_L_Shin, KARA_L_Foot, and KARA_L_Toe. The Skelegon Tree for this layer should look like Figure 9-33.

Now for the ponytail.

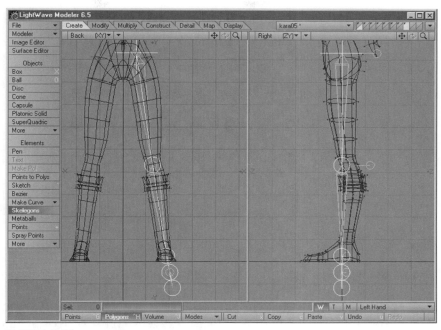

FIGURE 9-31 Create Skelegons for the leg.

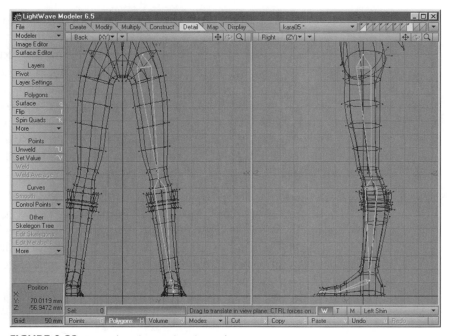

FIGURE 9-32 Drag the pivot points into place.

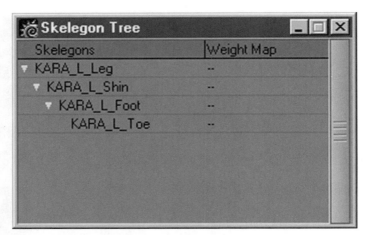

FIGURE 9-33 Renaming the Skelegons of the leg.

STEP 26: In yet another empty layer, with the body mesh in the background, Zoom in on the ponytail region in the Back view. Click the Skelegons button. In the Back view, click six times in the spots shown in Figure 9-34 to create a chain of five Skelegons— one for the upper ponytail holder, three between the upper and lower ponytail holders, and one for the hair tuft at the end. Before you deactivate the Skelegons tool, press N to activate the Numeric panel. Change the Name from Bone to KARA_Ponytail, leave Part Tag and Digits activated, and leave Start At set to 0. Exit the Numeric panel. If any bank handles do not point along the Z axis, set them straight now. Use Set Value to make all points snap to 0 m on the X axis. In the Right view, use the Drag tool to move the points into place, as shown in Figure 9-35. (If you opened up the Skelegon Tree right now, you'd see that the Skelegons have already been named KARA_Ponytail . . ., as specified in the Numeric panel for the Skelegons tool.)

STEP 27: Let's assign some weight maps to these ponytail Skelegons. Open the Skelegon Tree. Note again that two columns exist—Skelegons and Weight Map. Double-clicking Skelegon names in the Skelegons column lets you rename Skelegons; double-clicking to the right of a Skelegon name in the Weight Map column lets you assign a weight map to that Skelegon. Try it now— double-click to the right of the name KARA_Ponytail01 in the Weight Map column (aim for the dashes that currently occupy

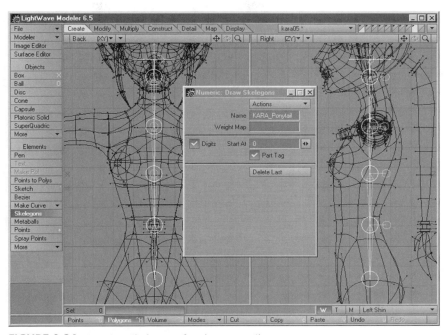

FIGURE 9-34 Creating Skelegons for the pontyail.

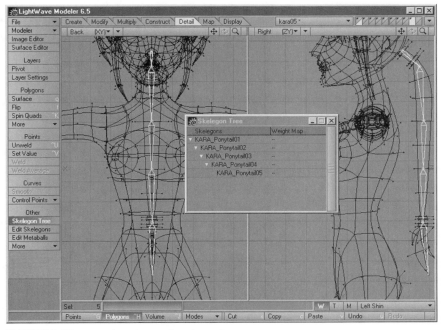

FIGURE 9-35 Drag the pivot points into place.

that space in the column). The Select Weight Map panel will appear. Select Ponytail from the list and click OK. Repeat this for each of the other KARA_Ponytail . . . Skelegons, so that they all have the Ponytail weight map assigned to them. When finished, the Skelegon Tree for this layer should look like Figure 9-36.

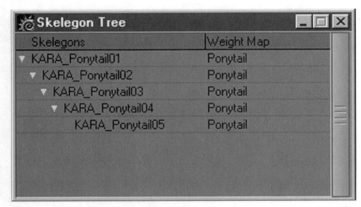

FIGURE 9-36 Assigning weight maps with the Skelegon Tree.

STEP 28: Let's assign some weight maps to the spine Skelegons. Go to the layer containing the six head, neck, torso, and waist bones, and open the Skelegon Tree. Assign the Waist weight map to KARA_Waist, the Torso weight map to both KARA_Torso and KARA_Upper_Torso, the Neck weight map to KARA_Neck, and the Head and Bangs weight map to KARA_Head.

As for KARA_Waist_(anti-gimbal-lock) . . . exit the Skelegon Tree for a moment. We're going to create a new weight map—a "null" weight map in which everything is marked at 0.0%. Look at the lower-right corner of Modeler. Of the three buttons marked W, T, and M (for the three kinds of vertex maps: Weight, Texture, and Morph), click the W button (make sure that the W button is active). Then click the menu of weight maps found to the right of the three vertex map buttons. Select "(new)" to activate the Create Weight Map panel. Type *(null)* for the name, set its initial value to 0.0%, and click OK. You have just created a new weight map called (null).

Open up the Skelegon Tree again. Assign the (null) weight map to KARA_Waist_(anti-gimbal-lock). Now this little bone won't touch a thing in Layout—it's been assigned to a weight map where all points have been marked as "off-limits" (with that 0.0% value). The Skelegon Tree for this layer should look like Figure 9-37.

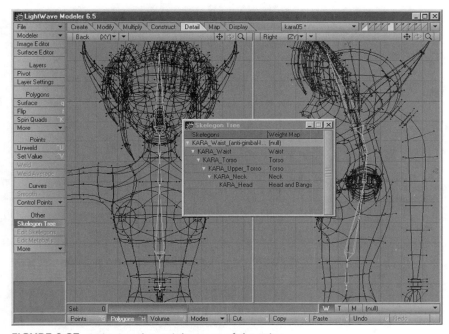

FIGURE 9-37 Assigning the weight maps of the spine.

STEP 29: Let's join the ponytail Skelegons to the spine Skelegons. Go to the layer containing the ponytail Skelegons and press X to Cut them out. Then go to the layer containing the spine Skelegons, and press V to Paste the ponytail Skelegons into that layer (Figure 9-38).

STEP 30: Next, click the Skelegons button. In the Right view, draw a Skelegon from the top of the head to the base of the ponytail. In the Back view, grab the bank handle for this new Skelegon and drag it so that it points straight up (Figure 9-39).

STEP 31: Rename this Skelegon as KARA_Head-Ponytail-Bridge. Weld its base point to the tip point of the KARA_Head Skelegon. You have just made this Skelegon a child of the KARA_Head Skelegon. Weld the tip point of KARA_Head-Ponytail-Bridge to the base

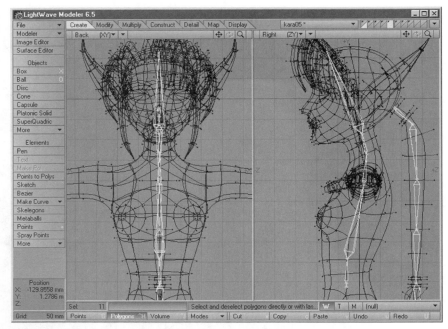

FIGURE 9-38 Cut and paste the ponytail chain into the spine layer.

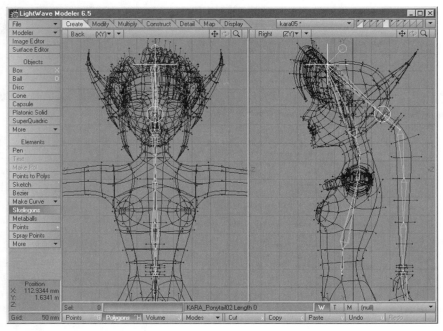

FIGURE 9-39 A new Skelegon connects the two chains.

point of the KARA_Ponytail01 Skelegon. The chain of ponytail Skelegons is now parented to the chain of spine Skelegons. Open the Skelegon Tree and assign the (null) weight map to KARA_Head-Ponytail-Bridge. Your screen should now look like Figure 9-40.

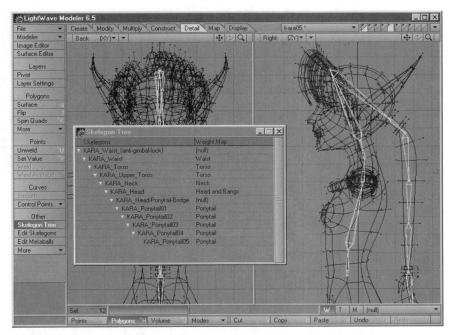

FIGURE 9-40 Assigning the "(null)" weight map to non-animation Skelegons.

STEP 32: Go to the layer containing the hip bones. Open the Skelegon Tree. Assign the (null) weight map to the KARA_Hips_(anti-gimbal-lock) Skelegon. Then assign the Hips weight map to the KARA_ Hips Skelegon. Your screen should look like Figure 9-41.

STEP 33: In the layer containing the leg bones, open the Skelegon Tree. Assign the Left Leg weight map to the KARA_L_Leg Skelegon and the Left Shin weight map to the other three Skelegons. The Skelegon Tree for this layer should look like Figure 9-42.

STEP 34: Cut these leg Skelegons out of this layer and Paste them into the layer containing the hip bones. In the Back view, Zoom in on the area between the end of the hip bone and the beginning

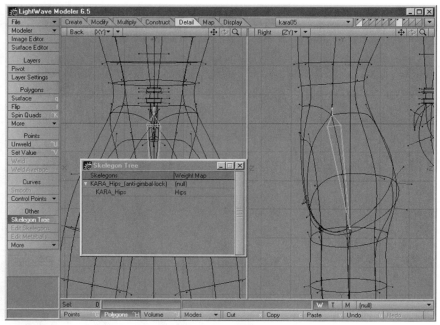

FIGURE 9-41 Assigning weight maps to the hip Skelegons.

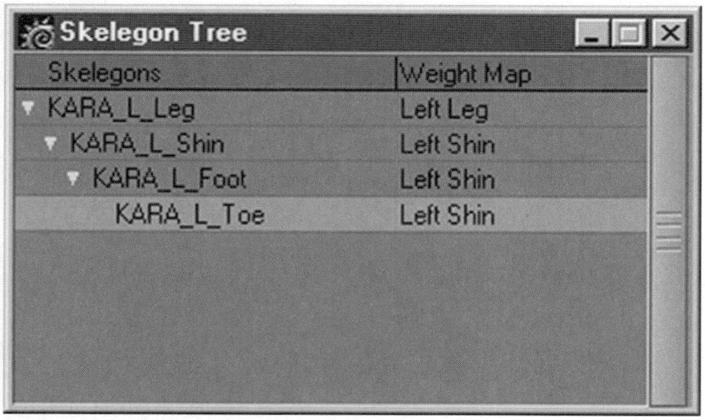

FIGURE 9-42 Assigning weight maps to the leg Skelegons.

of the leg bone. Draw a Skelegon between them (Figure 9-43) and name this Skelegon KARA_Hip-L-Leg-Bridge. Weld its base point to the end point of the hip Skelegon chain, then Weld its tip point to the base point of the leg Skelegon chain. In the Skelegon Tree, assign the (null) weight map to KARA_Hip-L-Leg-Bridge. Your screen should look like Figure 9-44.

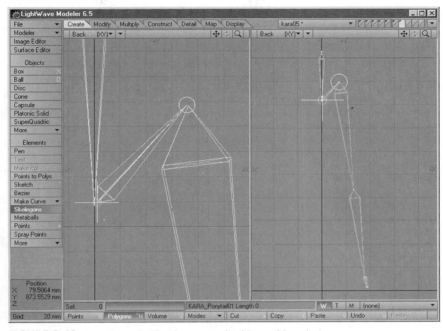

FIGURE 9-43 Creating a bridge between the hip and leg chains.

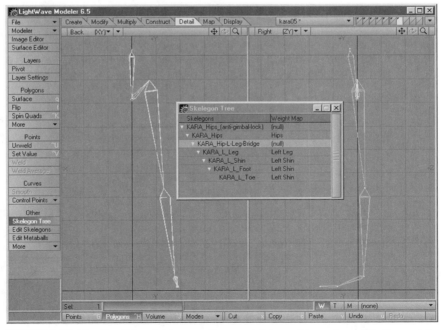

FIGURE 9-44 The "(null)" weight map will prevent this small bone from affecting points.

STEP 35: Deselect everything. Select the four leg Skelegons and the "bridge" Skelegon, press Shift+V to activate the Mirror tool, and mirror these five Skelegons across the X axis (Figure 9-45). If the points at the tip of the hip Skelegon chain failed to merge together, select them and press Ctrl+W to Weld them.

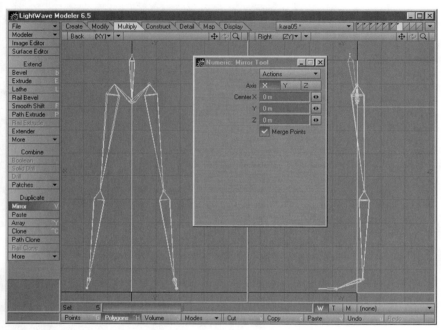

FIGURE 9-45 Mirroring Skelegons across the X axis.

STEP 36: Select each of the Skelegons that make up the right leg and rename them so that their names (mirrored along with every other attribute from their counterparts on the left side) use R instead of L. For example, the right leg Skelegon that is currently named KARA_L_Leg (just like its counterpart on the left side) should be named KARA_R_Leg.

STEP 37: When each of the leg bones on the right side has been renamed, open the Skelegon Tree. The right leg Skelegons currently use the weight maps assigned to the left leg Skelegons. Let's fix this now. Assign the Right Leg weight map to KARA_R_Leg and the Right Shin weight map to KARA_R_Shin, KARA_R_Foot, and KARA_R_Toe. (Leave the KARA_Hip-R-Leg-Bridge Skelegon set to the (null) weight map.) The Skelegon Tree for this layer should now look like Figure 9-46.

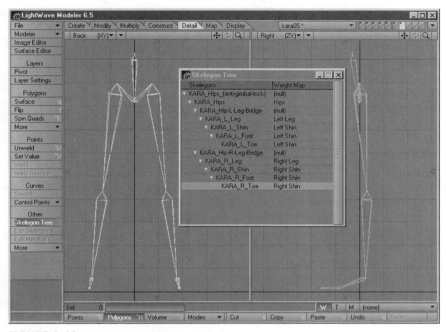

FIGURE 9-46 Renaming the mirrored Skelegons.

STEP 38: Cut these leg and hip Skelegons out of this layer, and into the layer containing the spine and ponytail Skelegons (Figure 9-47).

STEP 39: Now for the arms. Go to the layer containing the Skelegons for the left arm, open the Skelegon Tree, and assign the following weight maps to the following Skelegons:

Left Clavicle—the two clavicle Skelegons

Left Arm—KARA_L_Arm and KARA_L_Arm_(bank-follower)

Left Forearm—the three left forearm Skelegons

Left Hand—the wrist, thumb root, and finger root Skelegons

Left Pinky—the three Skelegons at the end of the pinky chain

Left Mid Finger—the three Skelegons at the end of the mid finger chain

Left Index Finger—the three Skelegons at the end of the index finger chain

Left Thumb—the three Skelegons at the end of the thumb chain

When finished, your Skelegon Tree should look like Figure 9-48 for this layer.

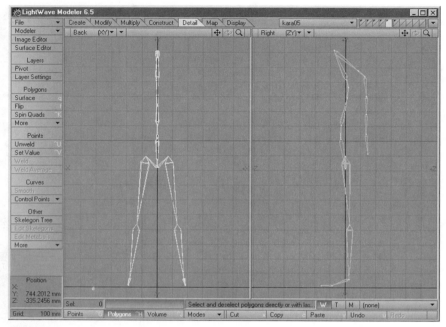

FIGURE 9-47 Cut and paste the hip and leg Skelegons into the spine layer.

Skelegons	Weight Map
▼ KARA_L_Arm_root_(orientation-bone)	(null)
▼ KARA_L_inner_clavicle	Left Clavicle
▼ KARA_L_outer_clavicle	Left Clavicle
▼ KARA_L_Arm	Left Arm
▼ KARA_L_Arm_(bank-follower)	Left Arm
▼ KARA_L_Forearm	Left Forearm
▼ KARA_L_Forearm_(center)	Left Forearm
▼ KARA_L_Forearm_(outer)	Left Forearm
▼ Kara_L_Wrist	Left Hand
▼ KARA_L_Mid_root	Left Hand
▼ KARA_L_Mid_base	Left Mid Finger
▼ KARA_L_Mid_mid	Left Mid Finger
KARA_L_Mid_tip	Left Mid Finger
▼ KARA_L_Pinky_root	Left Hand
▼ KARA_L_Pinky_base	Left Pinky
▼ KARA_L_Pinky_mid	Left Pinky
KARA_L_Pinky_tip	Left Pinky
▼ KARA_L_Index_root	Left Hand
▼ KARA_L_Index_base	Left Index Finger
▼ KARA_L_Index_mid	Left Index Finger
KARA_L_Index_tip	Left Index Finger
▼ KARA_L_Thumb_root	Left Hand
▼ KARA_L_Thumb_base	Left Thumb
▼ KARA_L_Thumb_mid	Left Thumb
KARA_L_Thumb_tip	Left Thumb

FIGURE 9-48 Assigning weight maps to the arm Skelegons.

STEP 40: Mirror all the arm Skelegons across the X axis. Select all of the mirrored arm bones on the right side of the body, Cut them out of this layer, and Paste them into an empty layer. With so many Skelegons in the arm, the last thing we want to do is rename the wrong bone or assign the wrong weight map. Isolating the mirrored arm in its own layer will help us keep better track of it.

Open the Skelegon Tree for this layer. Rename every bone so that their names use R instead of L. (*Hint:* You don't have to retype the entire name. Just replace each L with an R.) Then assign the correct weight maps by swapping out the Left versions for the Right ones. When finished, the Skelegon Tree for this layer should look like Figure 9-49.

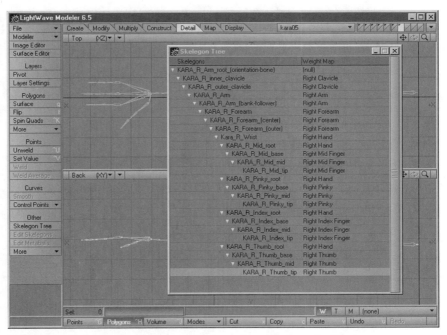

FIGURE 9-49 Renaming the arm Skelegons mirrored across the X axis.

STEP 41: Cut the Skelegons for the left and right arms out of their respective layers, and Paste them into the layer containing the spine, ponytail, hip, and leg Skelegon chains. Select the three points shown in Figure 9-50 and Weld them together. Move the single point up or down until the clavicle orientation bones level out, as shown in Figure 9-51. The skeleton should now look like Figure 9-52.

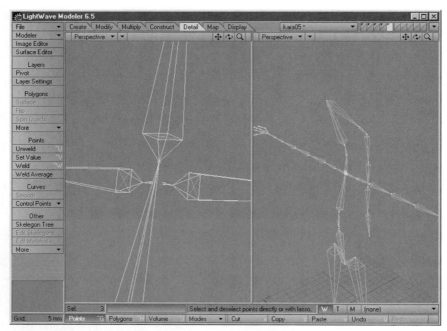

FIGURE 9-50 Joining the arm chains to the spine chain.

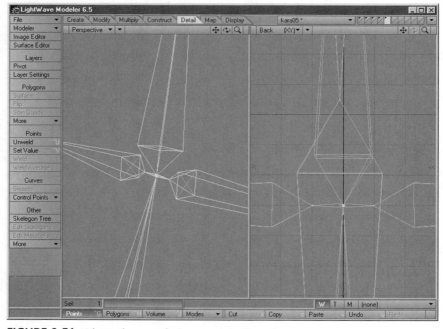

FIGURE 9-51 Where the arm chains now join the spine.

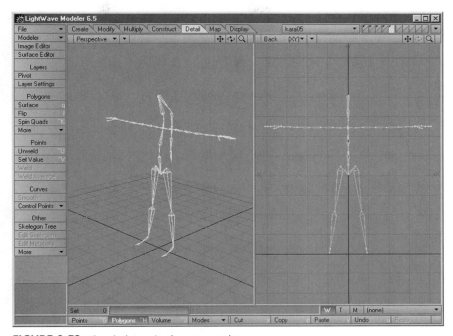

FIGURE 9-52 The skeleton is almost complete.

STEP 42: Let's not forget about the eyes. We can use bones to rotate the eyes, along with everything else. Go to an empty layer and make the layer containing the geometry for the elf-girl's left eye a background layer. Click the Skelegons button, hold down the Ctrl key to make sure that the first Skelegon you draw will be perfectly straight, and (in the Top view) draw a chain of two Skelegons, as shown in Figure 9-53. Make sure that the chain begins at the center of the hemisphere.

STEP 43: In the Back view, use the Move tool (and hold down the Ctrl key, to restrict movement to one axis) to move this new chain of Skelegons vertically, until it looks centered vertically in the eye in Back view (Figure 9-54).

Note: Don't worry about how odd this looks. The eye needs to pivot from its physical center, which is why this Skelegon chain must have its base pivot point centered in the hemisphere, as shown in Figure 9-55. Also, though the geometry seems to face outward, this cartoon eye actually faces "forward." The direction of the Skelegons should reflect this.

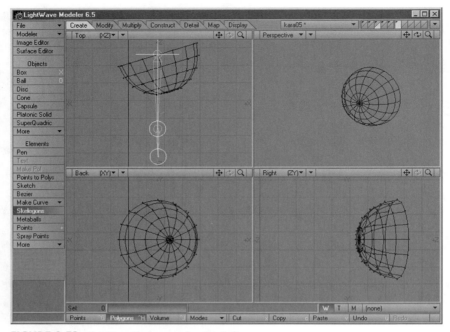

FIGURE 9-53 Creating Skelegons for the left eye.

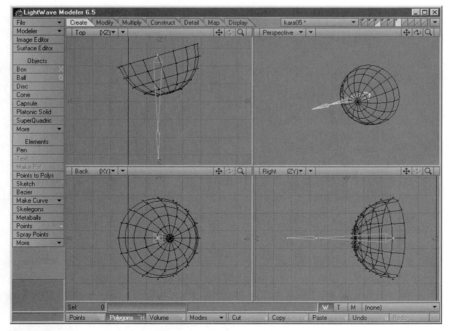

FIGURE 9-54 Place the root at the center of the hemisphere.

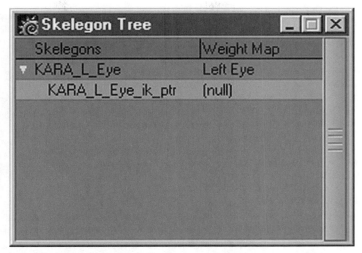

FIGURE 9-55 Renaming Skelegons and assigning weight maps.

STEP 44: Open the Skelegon Tree. Rename the base Skelegon as KARA_ L_Eye and assign the Left Eye weight map to it. Rename the little child Skelegon as KARA_L_Eye_ik_ptr and assign the (null) weight map to it. When finished, the Skelegon Tree should resemble Figure 9-55.

STEP 45: Mirror these Skelegons across the X axis. Rename the Skelegons in this new Skelegon chain on the right side as KARA _R_Eye (for the base Skelegon) and KARA_R_Eye_ik_ptr (for the child Skelegon). Open the Skelegon Tree and assign the Right Eye weight map to KARA_R_Eye. KARA_R_Eye_ik_ptr, taking its cue from the original Skelegon from which it was mirrored, should already have the (null) weight map assigned to it. If not, assign it now. The Skelegon Tree should look like Figure 9-56.

Note: You might want to make the geometry of the right eye a background layer, to double-check on whether the Skelegons for the right eye look centered in the correct place.

STEP 46: Copy all four of these Skelegons and Paste them into a new empty layer. Make the layer containing the original four eye Skelegons a background layer. Activate the Move tool. Holding down the Ctrl key to restrict movement to one axis, Move the

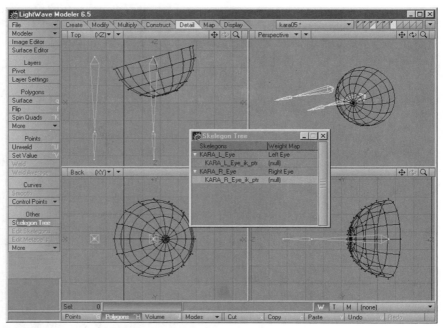

FIGURE 9-56 Skelegons for the right eye.

copied Skelegons directly behind the original Skelegons. Rename the little Skelegons on the elf-girl's right and left sides as KARA_R_Eye_orientation and KARA_L_Eye_orientation, respectively. Rename the big Skelegons as KARA_R_Eye_Bridge and KARA_L_Eye_Bridge. Open the Skelegon Tree and assign the (null) weight map to all four Skelegons. Your screen should look like Figure 9-57.

STEP 47: Cut these Skelegons out of this layer. Go to the layer containing the original eye Skelegons, and Paste the "orientation" and "Bridge" Skelegons into that layer (Figure 9-58).

STEP 48: Now let's join these four separate chains into two chains. In Top view, Zoom in on where the base of the left eye Skelegon and the tip of the left eye orientation Skelegon almost meet. Select the point at the tip of the orientation chain, then the point at the base of the eye/ik chain, and press Ctrl+W to Weld the tip point to the base point, making the two separate chains a single chain. Repeat this for the right side, Welding the tip of the bridge/orientation chain to the base of the eye/ik chain. When you open the Skelegon Tree, it should look like Figure 9-59.

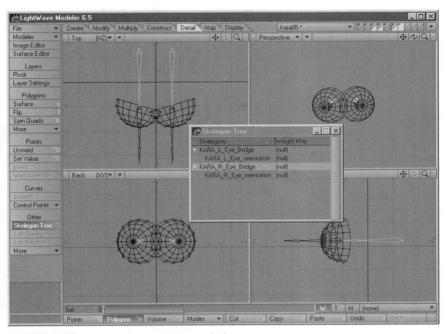

FIGURE 9-57 Creating more "bridge" Skelegons.

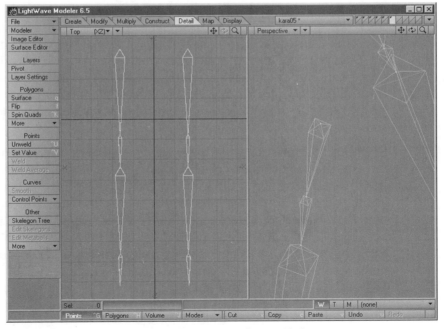

FIGURE 9-58 Joining the bridge Skelegons to the eye Skelegons.

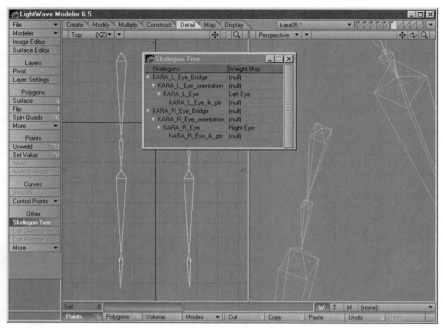

FIGURE 9-59 The eye hierarchy should look like this.

STEP 49: Cut all eight of these Skelegons out of this layer and Paste them into the layer containing the rest of the skeleton. Weld the base point of each eye chain to the tip point of the head Skelegon. (Remember that Weld snaps all selected points to the position of the last point you selected and then merges them into a single point, so select the tip point of the head Skelegon last.) Your screen should look like Figure 9-60.

STEP 50: We must deal with one last detail. The Skelegons representing the upper half of the body and the Skelegons representing the lower half of the body are not connected to each other. Some animators like to move the character by moving the bone to which all bones are parented, rather than moving the object itself. Yet the rotation of the waist should not affect the rotation of the hips (during a walk cycle, for example) and vice versa (during a belly dance or an Elvis impersonation, for example).

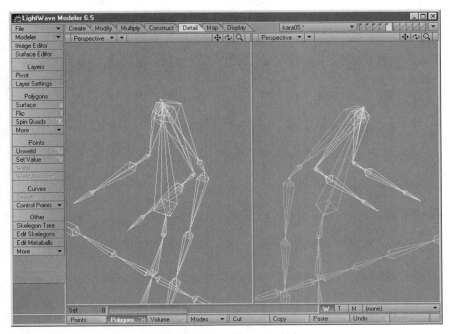

FIGURE 9-60 The eye Skelegons joined to the main skeleton.

The waist chain should therefore not be parented to the hip chain, or the other way around. We need an impartial parent Skelegon here, so let's create one. Zoom in where the waist should meet the hip. Draw a Skelegon in front of them that points toward the positive Z axis. Weld the base points of the hip and waist chains to the tip of this new Skelegon (Figure 9-61). Rename the new Skelegon as KARA_Skeleton_Master. We don't want this bone's influence fighting with any of the other bones, so in the Skelegon Tree, assign the (null) weight map to KARA_Skeleton_Master.

Note: If you want to move *and rotate* this character with KARA_Skeleton_ Master (during backflips, for example), move the base point of KARA_Skele-ton_Master as close to its tip point (and thus, as close to the true center of the body) as possible. Bones rotate about their base points, not their tip points, so the entire skeleton will rotate around the base point of KARA_Skelegon_Master (if you choose to rotate that bone).

The skeleton should now look like Figure 9-62.

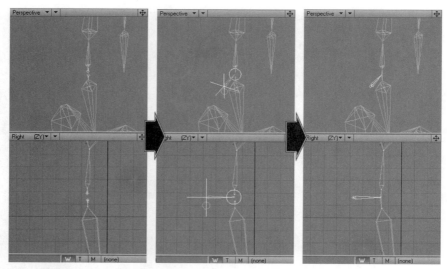

FIGURE 9-61 Creating the skeleton master.

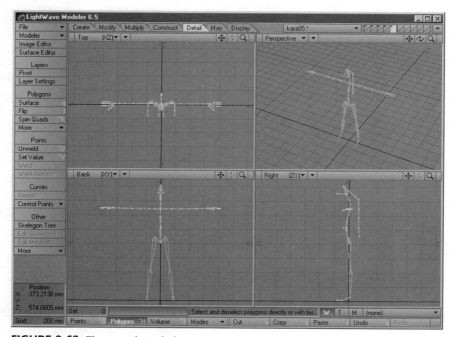

FIGURE 9-62 The complete skeleton.

STEP 51: Press Ctrl-F5 to open the Layers Browser. Name this layer Skelegons and remove its dot from the column on the right, so that it will not load into Layout (Figure 9-63).

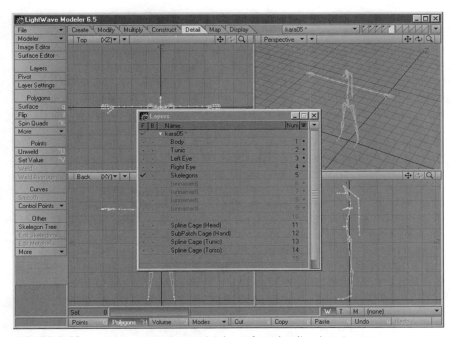

FIGURE 9-63 Removing a dot keeps this layer from loading into Layout.

STEP 52: Let's make the ponytail a separate layer from the body. With the ponytail as a separate object, we'll be able to use a different bone falloff setting for the ponytail geometry.

Go to the layer containing the body. Select all of the geometry that represents the ponytail, and press X to Cut it. Go to a new empty layer and press V to Paste the ponytail geometry into that layer. Press Ctrl-F5 to open the Layers Browser, and name this layer Ponytail (Figure 9-64).

STEP 53: Return to the layer containing the Skelegons. Press C to Copy all of the Skelegons from this layer. Go to the layer containing the body geometry and press V to Paste a copy of the skeleton into the body (Figure 9-65).

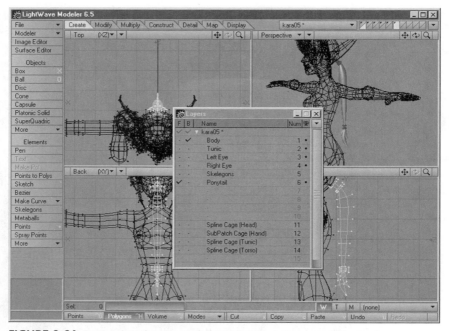

FIGURE 9-64 Separating the ponytail geometry from the rest of the body.

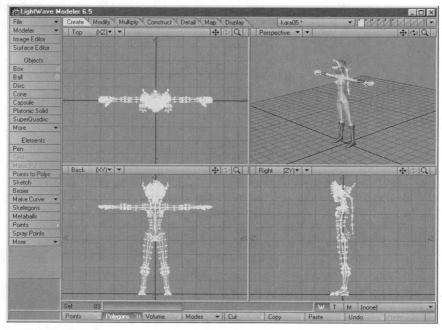

FIGURE 9-65 Pasting a copy of the skeleton into the body.

STEP 54: Go to the Layers Browser again. We can use this to provide parenting information to Layout. In this case, we should parent the tunic and eye layers to the body layer. Double-click the name representing the Tunic layer to open the Layer Settings panel. From the menu next to Parent, select the body layer (Figure 9-66). When you next load this object into Layout, the tunic will automatically be parented to the body. Repeat this for the ponytail and the left and right eye layers, so that they, too, get parented to the body layer.

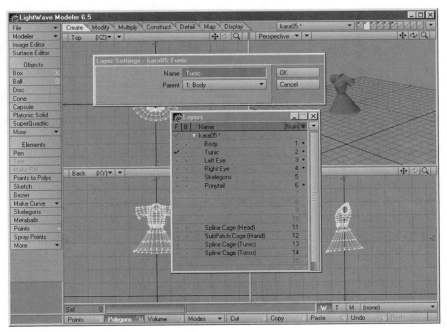

FIGURE 9-66 Parenting through the Layers Browser.

STEP 55: Return to the layer containing the body. Activate the Pivot tool. In the Right view, click where the tip of KARA_Skeleton_Master meets the hip and waist Skelegon chains (Figure 9-67). Now, when you load this object into Layout, the body will rotate about the point you just specified with the Pivot tool in Modeler. (Precision fanatics can even press N to open the Pivot tool's Numeric panel, to enter the exact XYZ coordinates that they want for the pivot point.) Deactivate the Pivot tool by clicking its button again, so that it keeps the settings that you just entered.

STEP 56: Save this object as **kara05.lwo.**

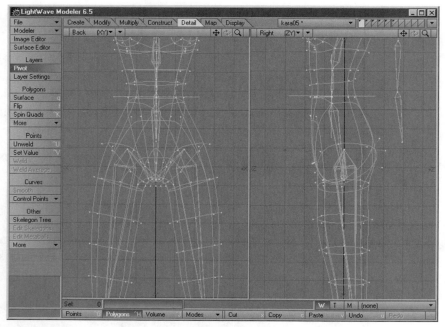

FIGURE 9-67 Setting the pivot point in Modeler.

SKELEGON CONVERSION

STEP 57: Load **kara05.lwo** into Layout. (If you did not follow the previous steps and just want to learn how to fine-tune bone settings, you may load **kara05.lwo** from the CD.) To make everything easier to see, set the Maximum Render Level to Front Face Wireframe.

STEP 58: By default, everything loads with its Display SubPatch Level set to 3. This may make the display match the final renders more closely, but right now it gets in the way of our view of the elf-girl's interior (where the bones will be). Press Shift+O to make Layout look at the objects in the scene, then press P to open the Object Properties panel. On the Geometry tab, set each object's Display SubPatch Level to 1 (Figure 9-68). For the body, ponytail, and tunic, set the Subdivision Order to Last. (This way, the smoothing effect of subdividing will happen *after* the bones have distorted the object, making the joints look softer, smoother, and more natural. It doesn't matter for the eyes, which will not get distorted by their bones.)

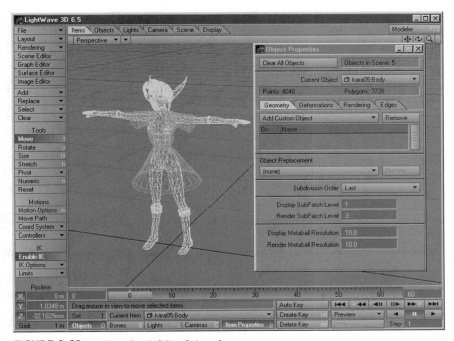

FIGURE 9-68 Setting the SubPatch Levels.

STEP 59: The body geometry contains the Skelegon information, so make the body the current object. Convert the Skelegon information into true bones by choosing Add > Bones > Convert Skelegons into Bones on the Items tab. If you're using the object from the CD, you should see a message that "83 bones were created."

STEP 60: Press D to open the Display Options panel (Display > Options > Display Options). From the menu next to Viewport Layout, choose Double Vertical. Exit the Display Options panel and set the left view window to Perspective view and the right view window to the Schematic view (Figure 9-69).

STEP 61: The Schematic view offers a visual representation of the elements in a scene, but we must first move the nodes into a chart that we like. Press A to Autosize the Schematic view (Figure 9-70). As you can see, it needs a bit of organization.

STEP 62: Click the Scene Editor button to open the Scene Editor panel. Clicking the triangle next to an item will toggle on or off a display of all the names of its children (collapsing and expanding one's

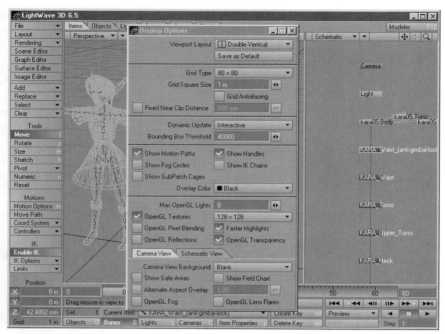

FIGURE 9-69 Setting up the viewports.

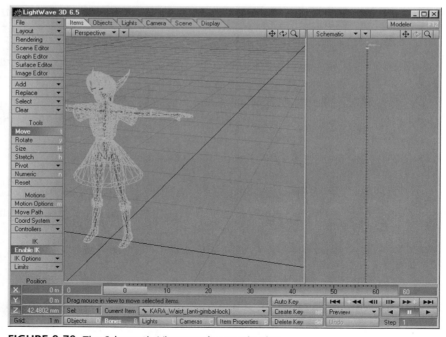

FIGURE 9-70 The Schematic View needs organization.

view of the hierarchy). Click the triangle next to KARA_
Waist_(anti-gimbal-lock) to hide your view of all its children.
Then click the triangle next to KARA_Hips_(anti-gimbal-lock) to
hide your view of all its children. Your screen should look like Figure 9-71.

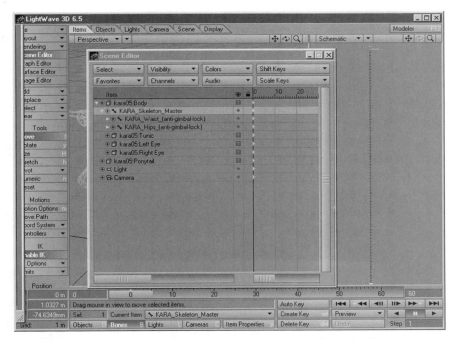

FIGURE 9-71 The Scene Editor can help one organize the Schematic View.

STEP 63: Click the name KARA_Skeleton_Master in the Scene Editor to highlight it. You have just selected this bone and have made
it the current item. Not only has it been selected in the Perspective view, but the node representing it in the Schematic view has
also been selected. In the Schematic View, click anywhere in the
gray area and drag upward to move the node representing
KARA_Skeleton_Master close to the light blue nodes representing
the objects in the scene. Note that all of the dark blue nodes representing the child bones of KARA_Skeleton_Master have moved
along with their parent.

　　Now, in the Scene Editor, click the name KARA_Waist_(anti-
gimbal- lock) to select the bone that carries that name. In the
Schematic view, click anywhere in the gray area and drag downward

to move the node representing that bone down and to the left of its parent node, KARA_Skeleton_Master. Note again that all of the nodes representing the children of KARA_Waist_(anti-gimbal-lock) have followed their parent.

Return to the Scene Editor. Select KARA_Hips_(anti-gimbal-lock). In the Schematic view, drag its node down until it goes underneath the node representing its parent, KARA_Skeleton_Master. Again, all of its children will follow their parent node. The child nodes will always follow their parent node, unless otherwise specified in the Display Options.

STEP 64: In the Scene Editor, click the triangle next to KARA_Hips _(anti-gimbal-lock) to expand the smaller of the two chief hierarchies (the upper and lower body). Select KARA_Hip-L-Leg-Bridge in the Scene Editor. In the Schematic view, move its selected node up and to the right of its parent. Return to the Scene Editor and select KARA_L_Leg. Move its node in the Schematic view down and underneath its parent node. Repeat this for KARA_Hip-R-Leg-Bridge and its immediate child, KARA_R_Leg, but move the node representing the "bridge" bone on the right side to the left of its parent node, instead of to the right (Figure 9-72).

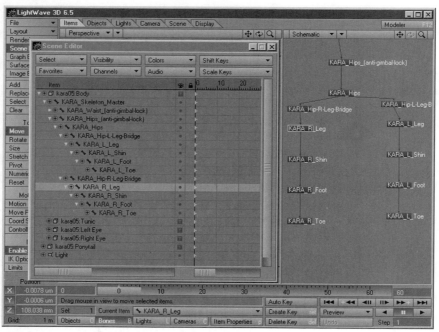

FIGURE 9-72 Organizing the Schematic view representation of the legs.

Tip: When your mouse pointer hovers over the Schematic view, holding down the Alt key and the left mouse button will let you navigate the Schematic view by dragging the mouse pointer around. Pressing A will Autosize the view so that all nodes in the view are visible. Pressing Shift+A will Autosize the view so that it zooms in on only the selected nodes. As in Modeler, pressing the comma key will Zoom out; pressing the period key will Zoom in.

STEP 65: In the Scene Editor, click the triangle next to KARA_Waist _(anti-gimbal-lock) to expand your view of its children. Collapse the major hierarchies in the Scene Editor, as shown in Figure 9-73. Move the node for KARA_L_Arm_root_(orientation-bone) to the right of its parent; move the node for KARA_R_Arm_root_(orientation-bone) to the left of its parent. Select the bones themselves in the Scene Editor to select their nodes in the Schematic view, then move the nodes into place in the Schematic view.

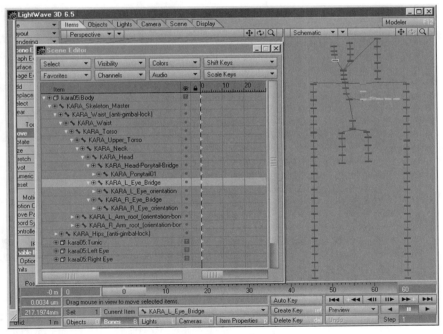

FIGURE 9-73 Organizing the spine and eye nodes.

Invert the vertical order of the nodes representing the spine bones, as follows. Move the node representing KARA_Waist above its parent node; move the node representing KARA_Torso above its parent node, and so on, until the top node is the head node. Move the chains of nodes representing the eye bone chains and the ponytail chain above the head node, and move the nodes representing the eye bone chains closer together.

STEP 66: Keep moving the nodes until they resemble a stick figure that makes sense to you (Figure 9-74). Use the Scene Editor to select the roots of the chains of bones for the fingers, and move those root nodes apart and close to their parent node. When all of the node chains have been made visible, you may close the Scene Editor and start selecting and moving nodes directly, by clicking the nodes that you want to select.

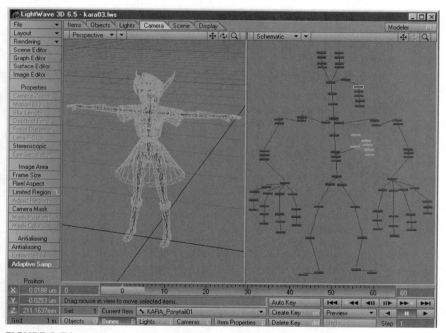

FIGURE 9-74 This is not the only way to organize a Schematic View.

STEP 67: Right-clicking a node will let you set its color. Change the color of all the bridge and orientation bones to a different color (such as gray). Give the nodes representing the roots of the fingers and the "extra" arm bones the same color (Figure 9-75). This will make key bones, such as those in the joints, easier to see and select.

STEP 68: Now we'll fine-tune some of these bones. Select the bone called KARA_L_Forearm. Go to frame 60, rotate it 90 degrees forward on its pitch, and set a key for that frame (Figure 9-76). It seems to

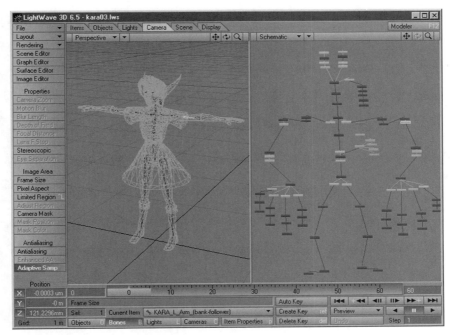

FIGURE 9-75 Designate important nodes with color.

lose some of its volume at that joint. Press P to open up the Item Properties panel. First, set the Falloff Type to Inverse Distance^16—this will affect the entire object. Then, since the current bone is still KARA_L_Forearm, select the Joint Comp for Parent check box, and set the value for Joint Comp for Parent to 200.0% (Figure 9-77). The joint now has more of a "corner." Select the bone called KARA_R_Forearm, select the Joint Comp for Parent check box, and give it the same setting of 200.0%.

STEP 69: Open the Scene Editor and set the Visibility of the tunic object to Hidden. Now we can see more of what's going on with the body (Figure 9-78).

STEP 70: Set the body's Display SubPatch Level to 3. Select KARA _L_Arm and Zoom in on the left shoulder. Rotate it on its pitch by 90 degrees, and set a key for it at frame 60. It might look OK at first, but if you scrubbed through the time slider, you might notice that it doesn't fold naturally (Figure 9-79). It may not matter much, since her tunic will cover up this joint, but let's see how far we can get with the bone settings alone without having to go into Modeler and adjust her weight maps.

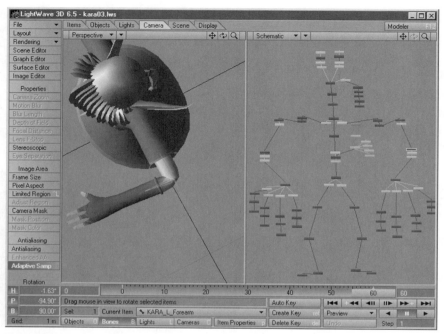

FIGURE 9-76 The elbow currently loses its volume when bent.

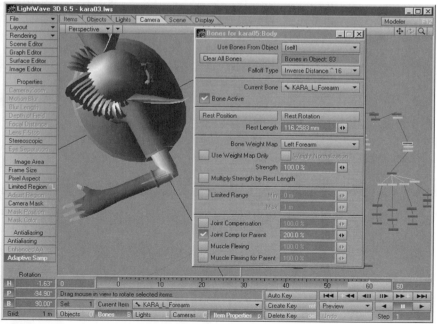

FIGURE 9-77 Joint Compensation for Parent fixes the problem.

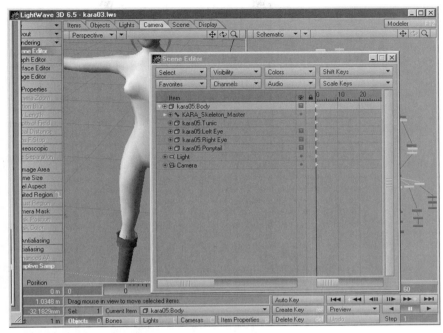

FIGURE 9-78 Hide the tunic to focus on the body.

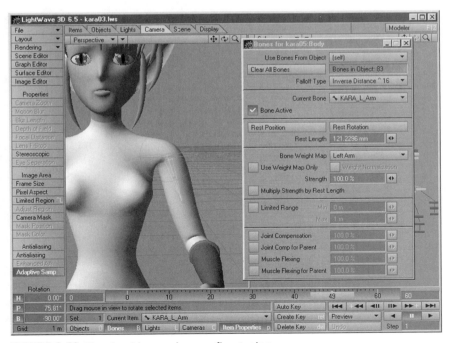

FIGURE 9-79 The shoulder needs some fine-tuning.

STEP 71: Press P to open the Item Properties panel for KARA _L_Arm. Select the Joint Compensation check box and set a value of −200.0%. This setting appears to pull down the crease and give more volume to the joint. Select KARA_R_Arm, select its Joint Compensation check box, and give it a setting of −200.0% as well (Figure 9-80).

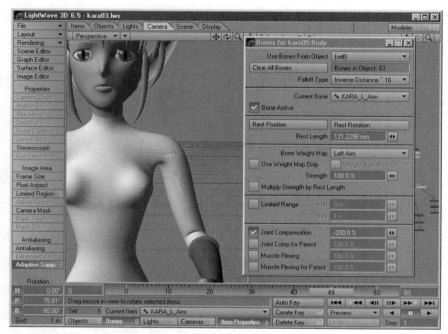

FIGURE 9-80 Joint Compensation appears to fix the problem.

STEP 72: Select KARA_R_Shin. Rotate it backward 90 degrees on its pitch and set a key for it at frame 60 to see how it looks. Chances are, it doesn't look all that good (Figure 9-81). Press P to open the Item Properties panel, select the Joint Comp for Parent check box, and give that setting a value of 200.0%. It should look better (Figure 9-82). Select KARA_L_Shin and give it the same settings—with Joint Comp for Parent selected and set to 200.0%.

STEP 73: Try rotating the KARA_R_Toe bone on its pitch. It's currently duking it out with two other bones over the points marked on the Right Shin weight map—the shin bone and the foot bone. It appears to be losing the fight, as it loses its volume at the joint whenever it bends on its pitch. Help it out by giving this bone

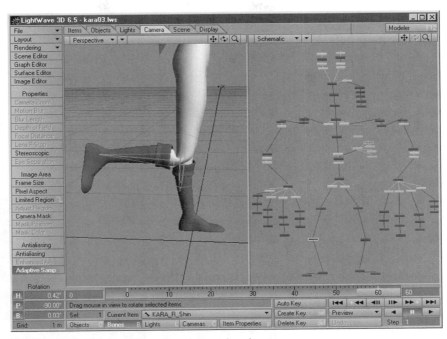

FIGURE 9-81 This knee loses its volume when bent.

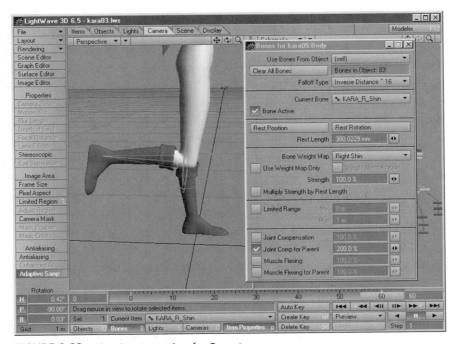

FIGURE 9-82 Joint Compensation for Parent.

both a Joint Compensation of 200.0% and a Joint Comp for Parent of 200.0%. Give these same settings to its counterpart, the bone called KARA_L_Toe.

STEP 74: Rotate KARA_R_Leg forward on its pitch by 90 degrees. That joint is definitely losing some volume there (Figure 9-83). Technically, it doesn't matter since the skirt will cover up this joint, but that doesn't mean we can't try to fix it. Give this bone a Joint Compensation of 150.0%. It should fill out a bit better (Figure 9-84). Give the same settings to KARA_L_Leg.

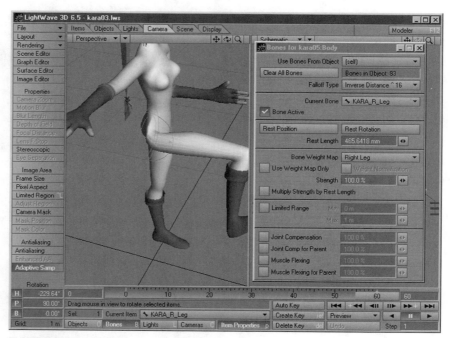

FIGURE 9-83 Although the skirt will hide this . . .

STEP 75: Rotate all three of the index finger bones inward on their pitch by 90 degrees. The Falloff rate doesn't seem to be working too well here. These bones all share the same weight map, so they're fighting over the same points (Figure 9-85). Set the Falloff Type to Inverse Distance^4. That's a little bit better, but they could use some "fattening up" (Figure 9-86). Try these settings for these bones:

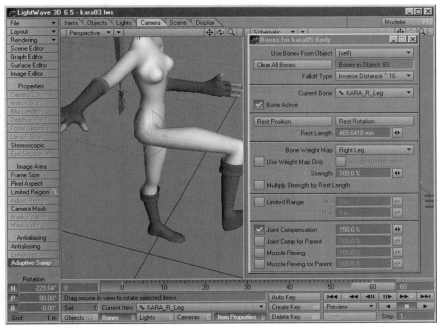

FIGURE 9-84 . . . use Joint Compensation to improve it.

KARA_R_Index_base—Joint Comp for Parent at 300%; Muscle Flexing at 100%

KARA_R_Index_mid—100% Joint Compensation; 100% Joint Comp for Parent; 300% Muscle Flexing for Parent

KARA_R_Index_tip—50% Joint Comp for Parent; 500% Muscle Flexing; 500% Muscle Flexing for Parent

Your screen should now look like Figure 9-87.

Note: Changing the Falloff Type affects the entire skeleton, not just one or two bones. Fortunately, only the ankles, toes, and hip joints share enough points between bones for Falloff Type to matter. The ankle and toe joints still seem OK under Inverse Distance^4 falloff; the hip joint, however, has lost a bit more of its volume. Because the hip joint will be hidden under a skirt (and thus never seen), this flaw may be overlooked this time. In the future, experiment with different weight maps and bone settings to see which gives you the exact results that you want.

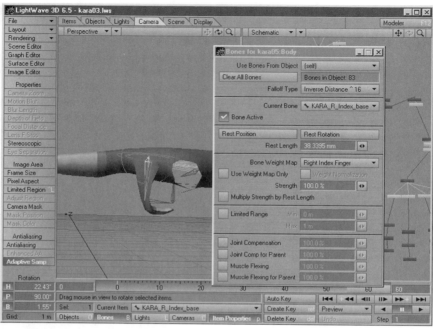

FIGURE 9-85 Inverse Distance^16.

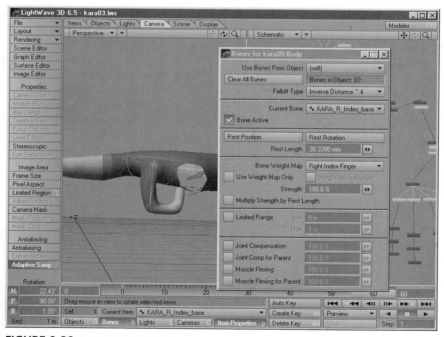

FIGURE 9-86 Inverse Distance^4.

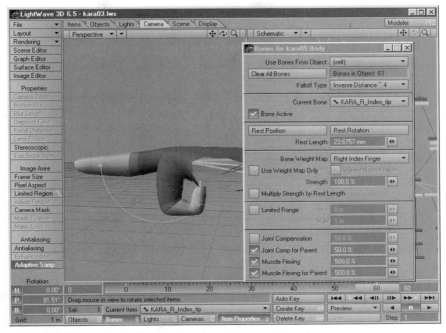

FIGURE 9-87 Tweaking the bone settings improves the volume.

STEP 76: Give all base finger bones the same Joint Comp for Parent and Muscle Flexing settings as KARA_R_Index_base. Give all mid finger bones the same Joint Compensation, Joint Comp for Parent, and Muscle Flexing for Parent settings as KARA_R_Index _mid. Give all tip finger bones the same Joint Comp for Parent, Muscle Flexing, and Muscle Flexing for Parent settings as KARA _R_Index_tip. Try selecting these bones through the Schematic view—you may find it quicker than selecting them in the Scene Editor, the Perspective view, or the Current Item list.

Note: There's no harm in tweaking and experimenting. Test each finger, and experiment with the settings to see what looks best.

STEP 77: Right now, the ponytail, tunic, and eyes don't "see" the bones, since these bones belong to another object. If you were to rotate the waist bone, for example, these objects would not move with the bones; they would stay in place. In the Scene Editor, unhide the tunic object. Its sleeves stay in place, rather than moving with the arms.

Let's make the tunic move with the skeleton of the body. Make the tunic object the current object. Press Shift+B, then P to open the Bones panel for the current object (in this case, the tunic). Right now, Use Bones From Object is set to (self), but the tunic has no bones of its own. Select the body object from the menu instead (Figure 9-88). It's as though the tunic now has an exact copy of the body skeleton, with all its motions and settings. It even respects the weight maps of the tunic—the leg bone will not take the tunic's skirt geometry with it, because the skirt has no weight values marked as Right Leg. (The skirt is meant to be animated with Motion Designer.)

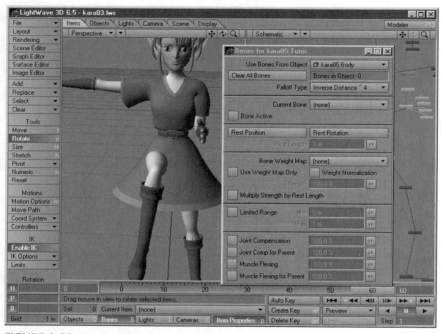

FIGURE 9-88 The tunic uses the same skeleton as the body.

STEP 78: Go to the Bones panels for the eyes and ponytail, and in each panel select the body object for the Use Bones from Object setting so that the eyes and ponytail will also use the body's skeleton. In the case of the ponytail, set the Falloff Type to Inverse Distance^2 so that it has a softer bend at its joints.

STEP 79: Now we'll add one last touch. Set the Joint Compensation of the wrist bones (Kara_L_Wrist and Kara_R_Wrist) to 1000.0%, so that they keep their volume when rotated on their pitch.

STEP 80: As far as bone settings are concerned, we're done. Delete the keys you made at frame 60, and save this scene as **kara03.lws**.

EXPRESSION SETUP

Face it, we all know how cool expressions can get. Mathematical expressions, that is. Anything you can express mathematically, LightWave can do for you. Let's put some expressions in these arms.

STEP 81: Load **kara03.lws** into Layout. (If you did not follow the previous section and just want experience with expressions, you may load **kara03.lws** from the CD.)

STEP 82: Zoom in on the left arm in the Perspective view. Try rotating Kara_L_Wrist on its bank by 90 degrees (Figure 9-89). It doesn't look too bad, but it's still losing some of its volume.

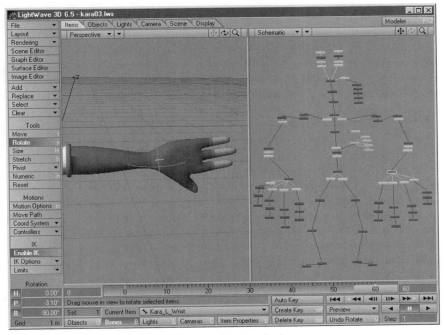

FIGURE 9-89 The wrist loses its volume when banked.

STEP 83: Set the Maximum Render Level of Perspective view to Bounding Box. Note the two forearm bones behind the wrist bone that could help out with the Bank of the wrist. Hold down the Shift key and click each bone to select both bones, and open the Graph Editor. Press Shift+G to load the channels for all selected items into the Graph Editor. Press W to open the Filter Channels panel (the command is also found on the Channels . . . Menu in the Graph Editor). Enter *.B* for the Pattern and click OK to remove all channels that do not have *.B in them. You should be left with only the Bank channels for KARA_L_Forearm_(outer) and KARA_L_Forearm_(center), as shown in Figure 9-90.

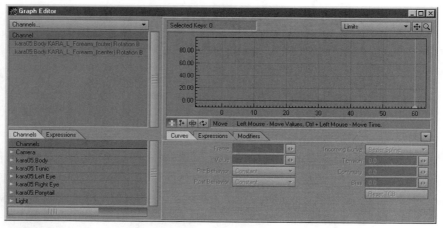

FIGURE 9-90 The Graph Editor.

Note: At the time of this writing, Shift+G will not load all channels into the Graph Editor in some betas of the next version of LightWave 6.5. In these beta versions, Shift+G will load only those channels that have more keys than a single key at frame 0. If Shift+G does not load the channels for KARA_L_Forearm_(outer) and KARA_L_Forearm_(center), you can load their Bank channels into the Graph Editor directly. Go to the Channels tab in the lower-left corner of the Graph Editor. Click the triangle next to kara05:Body to expand its hierarchy, scroll down until you see KARA_L_Forearm_(outer), and click its triangle to expand its hierarchy. Select Rotation.B and drag it into the Channel window in the upper-left corner of the Graph Editor. Repeat this technique to drag the Bank channel for KARA_L_Forearm_(center) into the Channel window as well.

STEP 84: In the section of the Graph Editor containing the Curves, Expressions, and Modifiers tabs, click the Expressions tab. On this tab, click New to cook up a new expression. Enter *KARA_L_Wrist_Torsion* for the name. We want these bones to have the same Bank as the wrist at all times, so replace Value with Kara_L_Wrist.rotation(Time).b. (The expressions engine is case-sensitive, so make sure you type in the correct item name. The wrist bones in the CD version of the scene file use Kara instead of KARA in their names.)

Press Enter to enter the expression. If you typed in the correct item name, nothing will happen when you press Enter. If anything is amiss, a warning will appear, and the expression will not work. Check to see if you misspelled the name of the item, or if you used the wrong case for any part of the rest of the expression.

STEP 85: We have an expression; we just need to apply it. Hold down the Shift key and click both of the Bank channels listed in the Channel window (in the upper-left corner of the Graph Editor). The Apply button on the Expressions tab will now be available, so click it to apply the expression to the selected channels. Asterisks will appear to the left of these channels, marking them as expression-controlled (Figure 9-91).

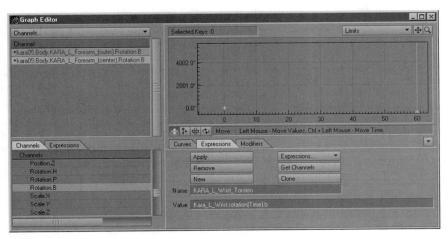

FIGURE 9-91

Those who are unfamiliar with expressions may wonder what the heck Kara_L_Wrist.rotation(Time).b means. Well, Kara_L_Wrist is the *exact* name of the left wrist bone that we want the forearm bones to follow.

The "rotation" function returns the Heading, Pitch, and Bank values of the object at a given point in time. For example, "rotation(0)" would always return the rotation values at frame 0. Also, "rotation(1.0)" would return the rotation values that happened one second into an animation (the exact frame number depending on the frames-per-second setting of the scene). The "rotation(Time)" statement returns the rotation values of the current time (whether it's 2 seconds or 200 seconds into an animation).

The "rotation(Time)" function could return a Heading, Pitch, or Bank value, but we just wanted the Bank value. Kara_L_Wrist .rotation(Time).b returns the Bank value of Kara_L_Wrist. Substituting "h" for "b" would have returned the Heading value of Kara_L_Wrist instead; substituting "p" for "b" would have made the expression return the Pitch value.

The value itself is just a number. When Kara_L_Wrist has a Bank of 30 degrees, Kara_L_Wrist.rotation(Time).b equals 30. When Kara_L_Wrist has a Bank of 15 degrees, Kara_L_Wrist.rotation (Time).b equals 15. You could have applied this expression to *any* motion or envelope graph available in the Graph Editor. Light-Wave is an artist's tool, not an artist—it wouldn't care. Or stop you.

Applied specifically to the Bank channels of the forearm bones, however, the numbers generated by Kara_L_Wrist.rotation(Time).b at every moment will cause the forearm bones to perfectly match the Bank of Kara_L_Wrist at every moment.

STEP 86: Try rotating the Kara_L_Wrist bone on its bank now. With the two forearm bones mimicking it, it should not only take less bank to get to a 90-degree angle, but it should also look much softer (Figure 9-92).

STEP 87: Let's set up the right forearm the same way. Load the Bank channels of KARA_R_Forearm_(center) and KARA_R_Forearm_ (outer) into the Graph Editor. In the lower-right corner of the Graph Editor, click the Expressions tab to see a list of all the expressions in this scene. Select KARA_L_Wrist_Torsion from the list to load it.

We can use a modified copy of this expression on the bones of the right forearm. Click the Clone button to make a copy of this expression. Your screen should look like Figure 9-93. Name this expression KARA_R_Wrist_Torsion. Enter *Kara_R_Wrist.rotation (Time).b* for the Value and press Enter. If all goes well, your screen should look like Figure 9-94.

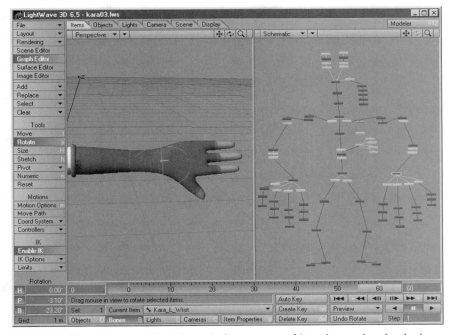

FIGURE 9-92 With expressions, the wrist keeps more of its volume when banked.

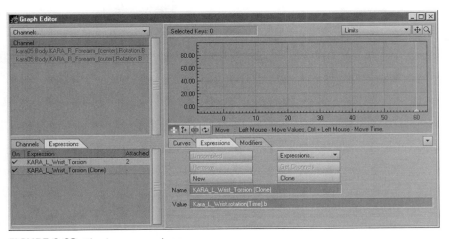

FIGURE 9-93 Cloning expressions.

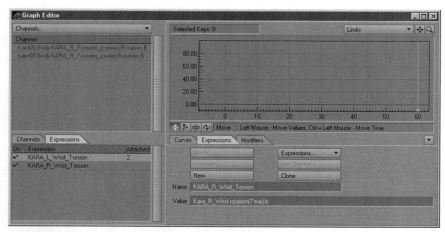

FIGURE 9-94 Renaming and modifying the cloned expression.

Apply this expression to the two channels in the Channel window. Your screen should look like Figure 9-95. Now the Bank of the two outermost right forearm bones will match the Bank of the right wrist.

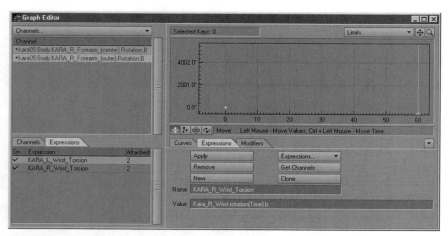

FIGURE 9-95 Applying the newly modified expression.

STEP 88: Let's try to write an expression so that KARA_R_Arm _(bank-follower) matches the Bank of its parent, KARA_R_Arm. Here the potentially tricky part is that their Bank settings are different—when not rotated at all, the child has a Bank of 0, while the parent has a bank of 90. A straightforward KARA_R_Arm.rotation (Time).b would return 90 when the child needs to be set to 0.

Well . . . 90 minus 90 equals 0.

STEP 89: On the Expressions tab of the Graph Editor, click New to create a new expression. Call this expression KARA_R_Arm_Torsion. Enter *KARA_R_Arm.rotation(Time).b − 90* for the Value and press Enter. Apply this new expression to the Bank channel of KARA_R_Arm _(bank-follower). Your screen should look like Figure 9-96.

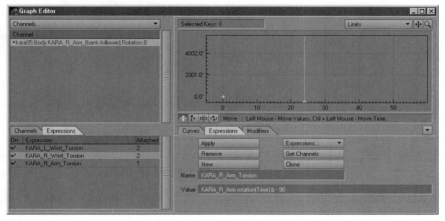

FIGURE 9-96 Creating a new expression.

Try rotating KARA_R_Arm on its bank. Its child bone, KARA_R_Arm_(bank-follower), should now match its bank at all times.

Note: The −90 part of this equation keeps KARA_R_Arm_(bank-follower) 90 degrees behind its parent's bank (represented by KARA_R_Arm.rotation (Time).b) at all times . . . which is what we want.

STEP 90: Now let's do the same for the left arm. Here the parent has a Bank of −90 while its child has a Bank of 0, so the child should be 90 degrees ahead of its parent at all times. Create a new expression, call it KARA_L_Arm_Torsion, and enter a Value of *KARA_L_ Arm.rotation(Time).b+90.* Apply this expression to the Bank channel of KARA_L_Arm_(bank-follower) (Figure 9-97). The bank of this bone will now match the bank of its parent.

STEP 91: Save this scene as **kara04.lws.**

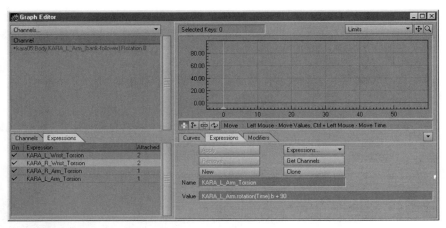

FIGURE 9-97 Expressions for the upper arms.

INVERSE KINEMATICS SETUP

Inverse kinematics, like everything else in LightWave, can help the animator, but it cannot replace the animator. By keeping feet, hands, and eyes locked in place or aimed at specific spots while the rest of the body independently moves and rotates, inverse kinematics can make animation easier, but it cannot animate for you. (Cheer up, now. If a software program alone could replace the animator, we'd *all* be out of a job.)

A character animator is both artist and actor. For specifics on the art of character animation, check out books on the subject from your local library (Preston Blair's wonderful *Cartoon Animation* comes to mind). Page through them and you may notice a common theme: Poses. Poses for walk cycles and run cycles. Poses for laughing and crying. Poses for falling and flying. Every "key" frame of a specific character action has a specific pose.

The best character setups are easy to pose. The best character setups, like the best 3D animation programs, do not get in the animator's way. Time spent on fighting a poorly designed character setup to get the "right" pose for a given frame is time wasted, time that the animator could have better spent . . . well, *animating,* instead of struggling.

Let's see if we can make Kara easier to pose.

STEP 92: Load **kara04.lws** into Layout. (If you just want practice setting up inverse kinematics, you may load **kara04.lws** from the CD.)

STEP 93: Choose Items > Add > Add Null to add a null called KARA_L_Wrist_Goal. Move its node in the Schematic view close to the node that represents the wrist bone of the left arm. In the Perspective view window, move this null so that it lies inside the wrist of the character, and set a key for its position at frame 0 (Figure 9-98).

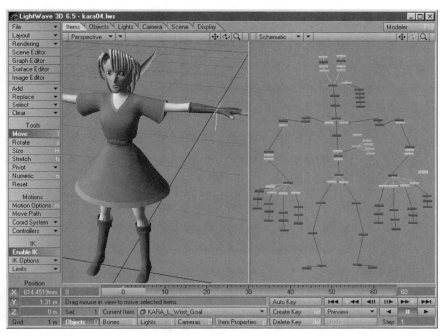

FIGURE 9-98 Creating the IK goal for the left arm.

STEP 94: Select the wrist bone (Kara_L_Wrist) and press M to open the Motion Options panel for that bone. Select KARA_L _Wrist_ Goal from the menu next to Goal Object, select the Full-time IK check box, and set the Goal Strength to 100 (Figure 9-99). In the Schematic view, a dotted line should now connect the node representing the goal null to the node representing the wrist bone.

STEP 95: Now let's tell LightWave which channels we trust it to automate with inverse kinematics. Select the bone whose pivot point represents the left elbow joint (KARA_L_Forearm). Press M to open the Motion Options panel. On the Controllers and Limits tab, click the menu next to Pitch Controller and select Inverse Kinematics (Figure 9-100).

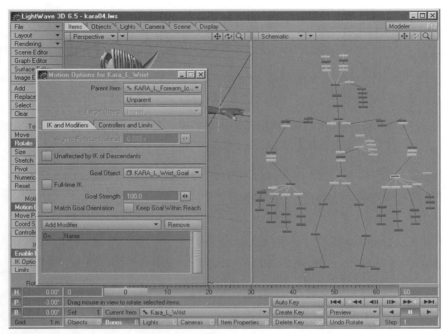

FIGURE 9-99 Setting up the IK target for the wrist bone.

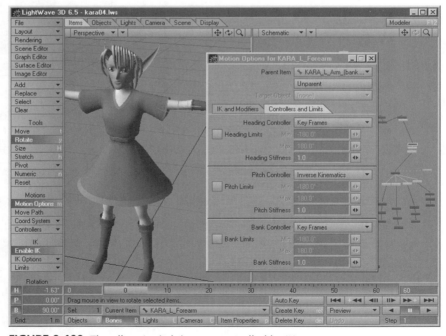

FIGURE 9-100 The elbow's pitch is now controlled by IK.

STEP 96: Now open the Motion Options panel for KARA_L _Arm (the pivot point of which represents the shoulder joint) and set both its Heading Controller and Pitch Controller settings to Inverse Kinematics (Figure 9-101).

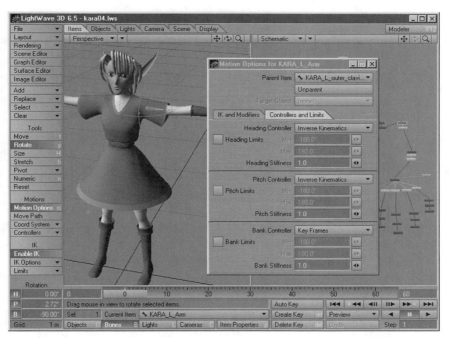

FIGURE 9-101 The heading and bank of the shoulder are now IK-controlled.

STEP 97: Select KARA_L_Wrist_Goal and start moving it around. The arm should do its best to match the goal and—oh dear . . . (Figure 9-102). LightWave sees nothing wrong with this—it used each of the channels it could to make the pivot point of the wrist bone touch the pivot point of the goal.

STEP 98: Let's make it clear to LightWave as to how the elbow should bend at all times. Click the Enable IK button (Items > IK > Enable IK) to disable Inverse Kinematics, so that we can have access to the pitch of KARA_L_Forearm again. Rotate KARA_L _Forearm forward 120 degrees on its pitch (−120 degrees, specifically, if you're using the scene file from the CD), so that the elbow bends naturally as far as it can go, and set a key at frame 0. Click the Enable IK button again to enable Inverse Kinematics again.

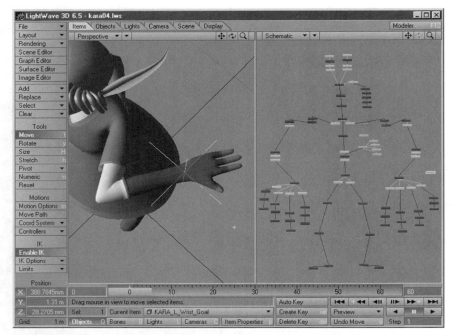

FIGURE 9-102 Proof that computers, by themselves, are stupid.

When you move KARA_L _Wrist_Goal around this time, the elbow will not bend backward. The shoulder might act up, though, if the goal gets too close to the shoulder. Again, let's make it clear to LightWave as to how the shoulder should bend in such a situation. Disable Inverse Kinematics, rotate KARA_L_Arm backward on its heading by 60 degrees (−60 degrees if you're using the CD scene file), and set a key for this at frame 0. When you enable IK again, the shoulder should not act as confused as it did before.

Note: Though we have just "trained" LightWave as to how it should behave on the left arm's IK, LightWave still sees this as one big game of tag. It will try to touch the goal with the pivot point of the wrist bone. At the same time, though, it always tries to maintain the earliest pose of the arm before IK was turned on. When the arm had little to no rotation before the IK was turned on, the IK did its best to maintain the pose of the perfectly straight arm (and when the goal got close to the body, IK saw no difference between a correctly bent elbow and an elbow bent backward).

IK may make it easier to pose an arm quickly, but without a way to control the direction of the elbow, this IK setup will get in the animator's way. Happily, the direction of the elbow can be controlled easily . . . from the last place one might expect.

STEP 99: Move the goal closer to the elf-girl's body and set a key for it at frame 10. At frame 10, select KARA_L_Arm and see what happens when you rotate it on its bank. The Bank channel of this bone is not controlled by Inverse Kinematics, so it can be keyframed at any time to fine-tune the direction of the elbow on any given frame.

Note: To get an idea of why this actually works, disable IK and rotate KARA_L_Arm on its bank. By itself, this rotation does not raise or lower the elbow—it just raises and lowers the wrist. Yet the heading and pitch of KARA_L_Arm have their IK orders to make that wrist touch the goal, no matter what. If the bank lowers the wrist, the IK-controlled heading and pitch will adjust themselves so that the wrist is raised enough to touch the goal. If the bank raises the wrist above the goal, the IK-controlled heading and pitch will adjust themselves so that the wrist drops enough to touch the goal. The elbow winds up getting carried along for the ride.

STEP 100: Let's set up IK for the right hand. Add a null called KARA_R_ Wrist_Goal to the scene. Move its node near the node representing the right wrist in the Schematic view. Move its position until it lies inside Kara's right wrist in the Perspective view window, and set a key for it at frame 0.

Pose the right arm so that its elbow joint (represented by KARA_R_Forearm) bends forward on its pitch at a 120-degree angle, set its shoulder joint (represented by KARA_R_Arm) to bend backward on its heading at a 60-degree angle, and set keys for both bones at frame 0.

Select the wrist bone (Kara_R_Wrist) and press M to open the Motion Options panel. Set the Goal Object to KARA_R_Wrist _Goal, select the Full-time IK check box, and set the Goal Strength to 100.0.

Select KARA_R_Forearm and press M to open the Motion Options panel. On the Controllers and Limits tab, set the Pitch Controller to Inverse Kinematics.

Select KARA_R_Arm and press M to open the Motion Options panel. On the Controllers and Limits tab, set both the Heading Controller and the Pitch Controller to Inverse Kinematics.

The right arm now behaves like the left arm—move the goal object to position the wrist, and rotate KARA_R_Arm on its bank to fine-tune the pose of the arm and the direction of the right elbow.

That's it for the arms. Let's try something more complicated for the eyes.

STEP 101: Zoom in on the eyes. Before we set up their IK, we should set up some rotation limits. Select KARA_R_Eye and press M to open the Motion Options panel. Rotate it on its heading toward Kara's left side. Stop when it reaches as far as you want it to go in that direction. On the Controllers and Limits tab in the Motion Options panel, select the Heading Limits check box and enter the current Heading value of the bone into the Min setting (about −13 or −14 degrees). Now the eye cannot be rotated on its heading past that minimum—try it and see (Figure 9-103).

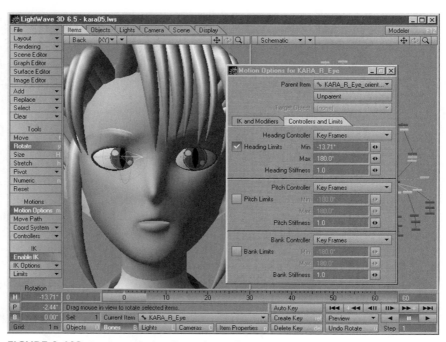

FIGURE 9-103 Setting rotation limits for each eye.

STEP 102: Rotate the eye in the other direction as far as you want it to go. Input this maximum Heading value (about 20 or 21 degrees) into the Max setting for the Heading Limits of this bone in the Motion Options panel (Figure 9-104).

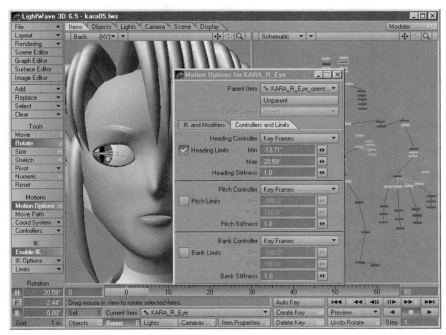

FIGURE 9-104 Limits prevent the eye from rotating too far.

STEP 103: Repeat this for the left eye—select KARA_L_Eye, press M to open the Motion Options panel, figure out what the minimum and maximum Heading rotations should be, select the Heading Limits check box, and enter the values into the Min and Max fields. You might end up with something like Figure 9-105.

STEP 104: Use the same technique to figure out what the Pitch Limits should be for each eye, and enter those values into the Motion Options panel for each eye. (−8.5 for the Min and 4.5 for the Max might work, but try these Pitch settings out for yourself first to see if you like them.)

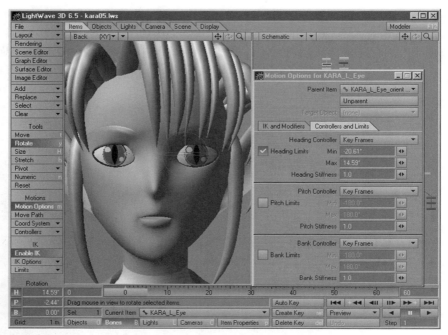

FIGURE 9-105 The rotational limits for the left eye.

Note: These settings can get in an animator's way, if the animator wants Kara's eyes to roll back into her head. Since rotational limits can be activated or deactivated on a scene-by-scene basis, this may not matter all that much. Still, if you're going to hand this character setup over to a friend who has not yet had a chance to learn about character setup in LightWave, show him or her how to activate and deactivate the rotational limits on the eyes. (Select the eye bone, press M to open the Motion Options panel, and activate or deactivate the Heading and Pitch Limits check boxes. Simple, but frustrating for the animator who doesn't know where to find these control options.)

STEP 105: Add three new nulls to this scene. Name them KARA _Eye_Ctrl, KARA_Left_Eye_Goal and KARA_Right_Eye_Goal. Parent KARA_L_ Eye_Goal and KARA_R_Eye_Goal to KARA_Eye_Ctrl. Move KARA_Eye_Ctrl up on the Y axis until it lies on the same level as the eye bones. Move it on the Z axis until it lies in front of Kara's face, and set a key for it here at frame 0. Move KARA _L_Eye_Goal on its X axis until it lies right over the KARA_L_Eye bone in the Back view, and set a key for it there at frame 0. Move KARA_R_Eye_Goal on the X axis until it lies right over the KARA _R_Eye_Goal in the Back view, and set a key for it there at frame 0. In the Schematic view, arrange the nodes representing these three nulls so that they hover over the top of the nodes representing the eye bones. Your screen should look like Figure 9-106.

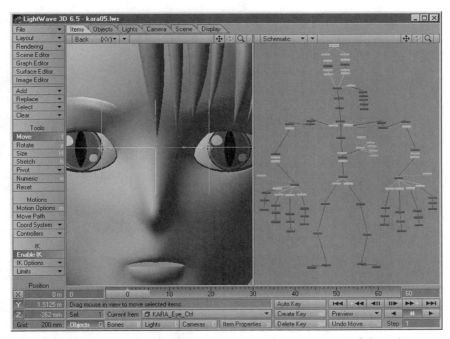

FIGURE 9-106 The goal nulls should stick close to the pivot points of the IK bones.

STEP 106: Open the Motion Options panel for KARA_R_Eye_ik _ptr and make its Goal Object KARA_R_Eye_Goal. Select the Fulltime IK check box and leave the Goal Strength at 1.0 (Figure 9-107).

STEP 107: Now go to the Motion Options panel for KARA_L_ Eye_ ik_ptr. Set its Goal Object to KARA_L_Eye_Goal, select the Fulltime IK check box, and leave the Goal Strength set to 1.0.

STEP 108: Select the KARA_L_Eye bone and open the Motion Options panel. On the Controllers and Limits tab, set both the Heading and Pitch Controllers to Inverse Kinematics. Repeat this for the KARA_R_Eye bone. Now the eyes will track the two nulls parented to KARA_Eye_Ctrl. Move KARA_Eye_Ctrl about to see for yourself (Figure 9-108).

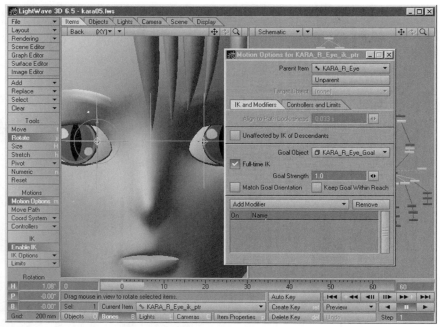

FIGURE 9-107 Activating IK.

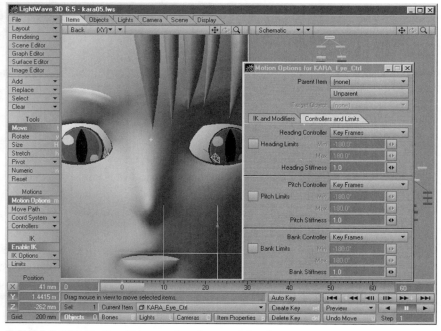

FIGURE 9-108 Testing IK by moving the control null.

Tip: One neat thing about having two eye IK goals parented to KARA_Eye_ Ctrl is being able to get lots of eye poses quickly by animating one null instead of two. Try stretching KARA_Eye_Ctrl on its X axis to move its child nulls closer to or farther away from its center (resulting in the character looking cross-eyed or spaced out). Try rotating KARA_Eye_Ctrl on its bank to make one null move up while the other moves down, for a delirious look.

That's it for the eyes. Let's try tackling the legs.

STEP 109: Add four nulls (count 'em—four) to this scene: KARA_R _Foot_Ctrl, KARA_R_Heel_Lift_Ctrl, KARA_R_Heel_Goal, and KARA_R_ Toe_Lock. Parent them as follows:

Parent KARA_R_Heel_Goal to KARA_R_Heel_Lift_Ctrl.

Parent KARA_R_Heel_Lift_Ctrl to KARA_R_Foot_Ctrl.

Parent KARA_R_Toe_Lock to KARA_R_Foot_Ctrl.

In the Schematic view, set the color of the node representing KARA_R_Foot_Ctrl to a dark cyan. Move this null underneath Kara's right heel, and set a key for it at frame 0. Move KARA_R_ Toe_Lock to the front of Kara's right foot, and set a key for it at frame 0. Move KARA_R_Heel_Lift_Ctrl to the pivot point of the right toe bone, and set a key for it at frame 0. Finally, move its child, KARA_R_Heel_Goal, to the pivot point of the right foot bone, and set a key for it at frame 0.

In the Schematic view, move the nodes representing these four nulls close to the nodes representing the foot bones. You should have a null setup that looks like Figure 9-109.

STEP 110: Open the Motion Options panel for the KARA_R _Toe bone. Set its Goal Object to KARA_R_Toe_Lock, but do not turn on Full-time IK. Instead, select the Match Goal Orientation check box. Scrub through the time slider to see what happens. The toe should promptly collapse, as the toe bone snaps to the direction in which KARA_R_Toe_Lock is facing (in this case, the wrong way) (Figure 9-110). Select KARA_R_Toe_Lock and rotate it until the toe bone points the right way again (Figure 9-111). A Heading of −180 and a Bank of −90 should do it, but use the rotation settings that look best to you. Set a key for KARA_R_Toe_Lock at frame 0, so that it stays in place.

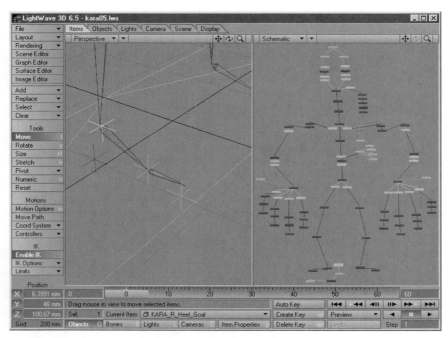

FIGURE 9-109 The null setup for the right leg.

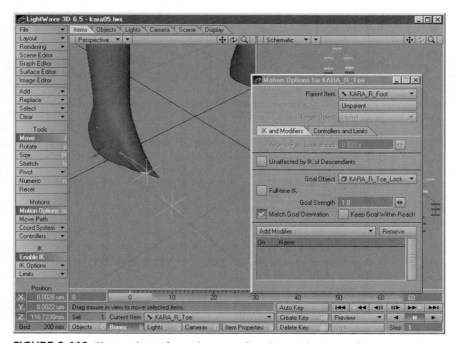

FIGURE 9-110 The toe bone faces the same direction as the toe null.

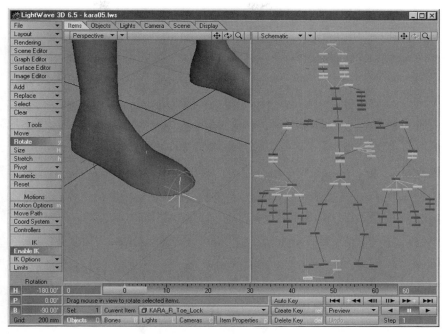

FIGURE 9-111 Rotating the toe null corrects the orientation of the toe bone.

STEP 111: Open the Motion Options panel for KARA_R _Foot. Set its Goal Object to KARA_R_Heel_Goal, select the Full-time IK and Match Goal Orientation check boxes, and set the Goal Strength to 100.0. The foot should lose its volume as the bone matches the direction that KARA_R_Heel_Goal faces (again, the wrong way) (Figure 9-112). Select KARA_R_Heel_Goal and rotate it until the foot bone points toward KARA_R_Heel_Lift _Ctrl. A pitch of about −159 should do it (but, again, use your judgment). Set a key for KARA_R_Heel_Goal at frame 0, so that it stays in place (Figure 9-113).

STEP 112: Before turning on IK for the knee and hip, we should give LightWave a hint as to which direction they should bend. Rotate KARA_R_Leg 90 degrees, and set a key for it in this rotation at frame 0. Then rotate KARA_R_Shin −135 degrees, and set a key for it in this rotation at frame 0 (Figure 9-114).

STEP 113: Open the Motion Options panel for KARA_R_Shin and set its Pitch Controller to Inverse Kinematics. Open the Motion Options panel for KARA_R_Leg and set its Heading and Pitch Controllers to Inverse Kinematics. Your screen should look like Figure 9-115.

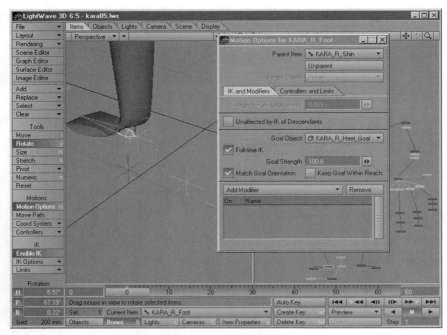

FIGURE 9-112 The bone matches the goal's orientation, but . . .

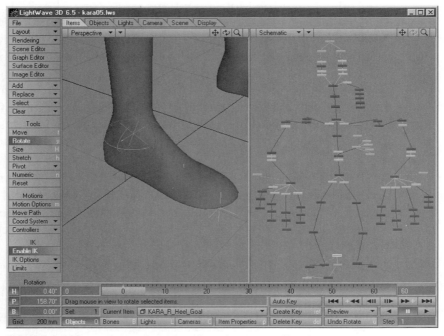

FIGURE 9-113 . . . the goal needs to face the correct direction.

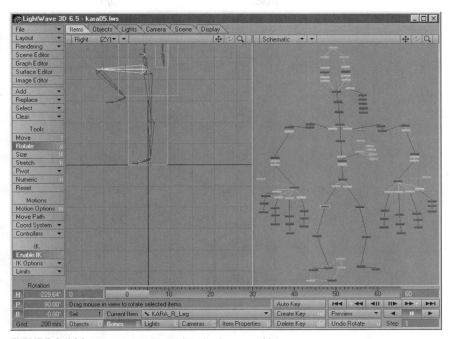

FIGURE 9-114 "Training" the IK for the knee and hip.

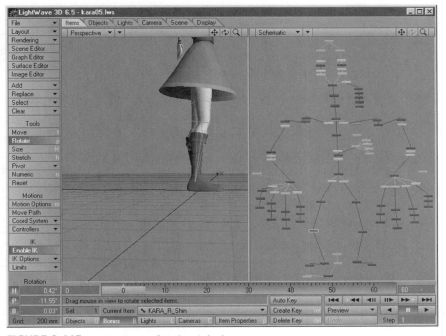

FIGURE 9-115 Activating IK for the right leg.

STEP 114: To get a feel for how to operate this IK setup, select KARA_R_ Foot_Ctrl and move it up and forward. Rotating it will rotate the foot at the heel. (When animating the leg, you should always animate this null first before animating its children.) Set a key for it at frame 10 (Figure 9-116).

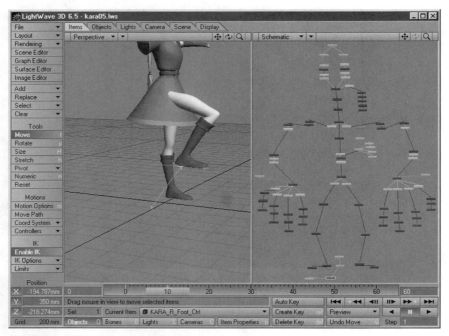

FIGURE 9-116 Use Motion Designer for the skirt.

STEP 115: Select KARA_R_Heel_Lift_Ctrl and rotate it on its pitch. It will lift its child null, KARA_R_Heel_Goal, up and around in an arc, simulating what happens when the toe stays put and the heel lifts up off the ground. KARA_R_Toe_Lock forces the toe to stay put (Figure 9-117). When animating, use KARA_R_Foot_Ctrl to position the foot first, then rotate KARA_R_Heel_Lift_Ctrl to tweak the lift of the heel.

STEP 116: The direction of the knee has the same type of control as the direction of the elbow. Rotate and keyframe the Bank of KARA_R_ Leg to control the direction of the knee after the foot has been keyframed into place (Figure 9-118).

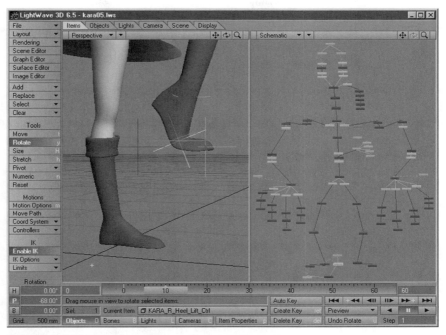

FIGURE 9-117 The toe goal forces the toe to stay put.

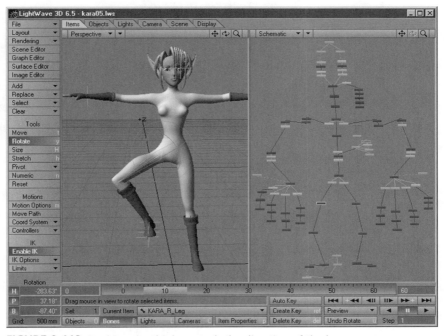

FIGURE 9-118 Banking the thigh controls the direction of the knee.

STEP 117: Now that you know a bit about IK, try your hand at setting up the IK for the left leg. Make it as simple (such as the IK used on the arms) or as complex (such as the IK used on the right leg) as you like.

STEP 118: When finished, delete any keys at frame 10. Add a new null called KARA_Master_Null and parent the body, arm goals, eye control null, and left and right foot control nulls to it. When you move this null, everything will move with it. Give it a black color in the Schematic view (Figure 9-119).

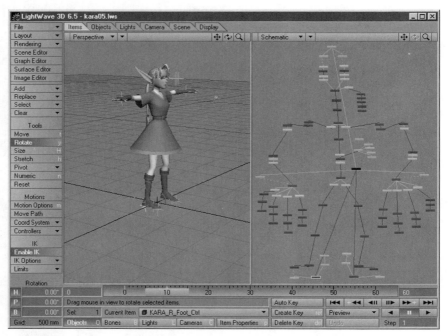

FIGURE 9-119 Make the master null stand out with a unique color.

One last touch. Even though only a few bones have their rotation channels controlled by IK, all of the bones shiver (however slightly) whenever you move the IK goals. Perhaps they're uncertain as to whether they should move. We can clear up this mystery for them in no uncertain terms.

STEP 119: Open the Motion Options panel for the bone called KARA_Hips. Select the Unaffected by IK of Descendants check box (Figure 9-120). Now KARA_Hips and the bones above it will ignore the IK of the children of KARA_Hips. Repeat this for KARA_Head and KARA_Torso—select the Unaffected by IK of Descendants check box in their Motion Options panels as well. Now the bones above them will ignore the IK of their children.

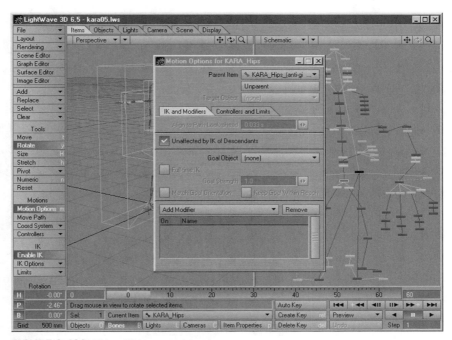

FIGURE 9-120 This will prevent shivering.

STEP 120: Save this scene as **kara05.lws.**

For the adventurous, the website contains in-depth tutorials for building and surfacing Kara from start to finish.

Happy animating!

10

Building an Animation Business

Joe Tracy

Many people enjoy making careers out of fun hobbies, which is how many animation companies begin. While starting an animation business may seem like a quick and easy task, in reality the path to success will be a bit turbulent. If you're willing to weather through a few storms, however, I'm prepared to give you some initial guidance in your quest.

In the mid 1990s, I was a high school teacher contracted to teach specialty courses such as journalism, photography, drama, and video productions. In my third year of teaching, I started teaching an animation course. At the time, NewTek's LightWave 3D was available only on the Amiga, as part of a bundle with the revolutionary Video Toaster. This was fine with me, since the Video Toaster was the focus of my video production courses.

Teaching video productions and animation was like a dream job for me because I was getting paid to do something I was passionate about. What made it different from running an animation business, however, is that I was guaranteed a regular salary for teaching animation. When you run your own business, all bets are off.

The first rule you must follow when exploring the possibility of turning your passion into a business is this: *don't give up your day job*. I have known too many budding animators and video producers who have quit their jobs and taken out loans to finance their business. This type of cold-turkey action will often lead to failure because *new business owners often overestimate the amount of money they will make while thinking they are underestimating it!*

As a teacher, I had the luxury of summers off (while still getting a paycheck). Sure, the teacher salary was pretty pitiful, but the summer vacation was nice! After my third year of teaching, my wife and I decided to start a small video production and animation business, deciding to take a cautious approach. Here were the three basic ground rules we set:

RULE 1: Both of us would continue our full-time jobs for the first year.

RULE 2: We would begin small and grow until we could determine whether the business could support one of us leaving our full-time job.

RULE 3: We would build referrals from the jobs we did during the experimental year so that we had a strong base should we go into the business full-time.

With the rules in place, we began preparations.

FROM RULES TO REALITY

When looking to start a business the first things you need are the following:

1. *A name for your business.* The name should be professional and also be one that is available online (as a .com) that you can register. Also keep in mind that there are probably state laws you must follow in registering your business name with the state. Check with your local county clerk's office information on applying for a business name and for forms that you must fill out.

2. *A location.* Where will your business be located? Is there enough room for you to have a workspace and meeting place (to meet with clients)? Does the rent cost take up too much of your overhead? Is the price reasonable? Do the exterior and interior appear professional and in good shape?

3. *An identity.* Creating your business identity means creating a logo, slogan, stationery, business cards, branded contracts, and so on. Branding will become a vital part of your business efforts, and it is important that the identity you present is both professional and consistent.

4. *A business plan.* The single most important document for your business will be the business plan. Yet amazingly nearly 75% of animation companies I know do not have a business plan! *The business plan is the foundation of your company.* It helps give your company direction, purpose, and reason. There are hundreds of books dedicated to creating business plans, and dozens of software programs such as Business Plan Pro for the PC or Business Plan Toolkit for the Macintosh that you can use for assistance. Your plan must cover operations, finances, marketing, an analysis of your competitors, mission statements, projections, and so on. If you do not wish to use software or a

book to help you, then at least go online for assistance or to the library. Most important is that you *do it*. Once your business plan is done, refer to it often and update it as needed.

5. *Equipment.* It is likely that you already have LightWave 3D or a similar animation program, and because of your enjoyment in using the program you've decided to turn your hobby into a career. That will call for a big investment up front. There are a lot of costs associated with owning an animation business, most which go into the hardware and software. Make a detailed list of every single thing you will need, even down to items such as DVD recorders and CD recorders. Also add in costs of all your identity material, such as stationery and business cards. What about tape stock for your demo video? And what about your entire overhead such as electricity, water, and Internet connection? Every single possible cost must be figured into your financial analysis. Once you've completed your detailed financial analysis, add a few thousand dollars to a Misc. column, as you may come across many more expenses once you get up and running that you didn't originally count on.

6. *Finances.* How will you fund the start of your business and pay for all the equipment? Will you take out a loan and start your business already in debt? Have you been saving up for the venture so that you start with a clean slate? If you decide to apply for a bank loan or Small Business Administration loan, you must be well prepared for your interview. It is vital that you have a realistic business plan, marketing plan, outline of all expenses, and so on. Your presentation at the loan meeting is one of the determining factors as to whether you will get the loan. Always be overprepared for such a meeting. Part of handling your beginning finances is opening up bank accounts under your business name that must first be registered with the state.

PROCEED WITH CAUTION

My wife and I spent a year sampling the waters before running an animation business full-time. We took on some small projects, analyzed the marketplace, started to build a portfolio, and did some minor advertising. Because of our full-time jobs, our business work was confined to nights and weekends. We also made a determination that you will have to make: Is an animation business enough?

Is there enough work in your community for a solo animation business? In our case, we determined that there wasn't and that the animation business would have to be combined with another business to be successful. The natural progression for us was a full-fledged video production company with a strong animation division. This would allow us to create videos for clients that also featured animation. It was a natural combination.

Now you may be only interested in animation, and if you are, that's not a problem. Just make sure the community you live in is ripe for a solo animation services business, or be prepared to do a lot of networking with other companies (and possibly even studios) to keep your business in demand.

More and more bigger Hollywood animation studios are beginning to contract out work to smaller animation companies or talented individuals. That's how Blue Dream Studios conducts its business (there's more on Blue Dream Studios later in this tutorial). Contact some bigger studios and offer your services. A phone call won't do, however. You must create a stunning videotape that properly showcases your talents. The demo tape should focus most on your strengths. For example, if you are a great character modeler but a lousy spaceship animator, then keep the focus of your demo on your character modeling skills. Companies will call on you specifically for these types of skills. Show your strengths and continue to work on your weak areas in order to better round out your skill base.

A year after we began testing the waters, we determined that I could successfully leave my full-time teaching job to pursue a full-time animation and video production business. That year is of the utmost importance because it gives you the chance to save money for your venture and to build a few clients so that you have work to show others. The year also gives you time to properly fill out all the business paperwork and check into all the legalities of running a business in your state. A good starting point for this type of legal information is http://www.nolo.com/.

One aspect of running your own business will determine whether you fail or succeed. It will determine whether you make money or lose money. It will determine whether customers return to you or leave you. I'm talking about *marketing*.

MASTER MARKETING

In order to succeed in starting a business, you must become marketing-savvy. Marketing is the single most important element for the sale of your services. Marketing isn't just about advertising, however. It is about products, communication, effort, and your own personal integrity. It is an exploration into the question of what kind of person you are and how much a customer really means to you.

My wife and I successfully ran our animation and video production company in Oregon for seven years, leaving it only because of my calling to California to become the founding editor of *NewTekniques* magazine. During that time we watched other animation and video production businesses open and close—usually within a year.

So why did our company succeed where others failed? The answer is that we knew how to market and we knew how to treat a customer.

Learning valuable marketing techniques is mandatory to your success in running an animation business. By learning to master ethical marketing, you will be able to help your company grow while creating customers who will forever remain loyal to you. You must be genuine in this quest; if you are not, the customer will see right through you.

Learn Strategic Marketing Techniques

Remember the saying that selling a product is 80% marketing and 20% product? That saying is true. Strategic marketing will be the single most important factor that will determine whether people come to you for animation work or to your competitor.

First, you must do your homework. This will take an entire day. First, purchase a brand-new notebook and a nice pen. Now head to your local library or bookstore and spend the entire day going through marketing books and taking notes on the techniques you feel will work best for your business. Follow this simple three-step process: Learn. Review. Implement.

Here are some marketing strategies I implemented that resulted in a high success in recruiting business:

1. *Have a fair booth.* The most profitable marketing tool I ever used was having a booth at the local county fair every year.

But any old booth won't do. You must be able to grab people's attention to attract them to your booth. Once there, they will pick up your brochures, newsletters, demo videos, and other promotional material. Our approach was to bring our whole studio to the fair and do editing of TV commercials right there with a big monitor that people could preview and a sign explaining the project. In another part of our booth, we played a strong fast-paced demo video that contained a lot of impressive LightWave scenes. Then we had an attractive display of brochures and newsletters and even a sign-up sheet for people who wanted to audition with the potential of being in a future commercial. While we didn't make any money at the fair, the business we generated afterward as a direct result of the fair was astronomical (at least 50 times the cost of our booth). We even received business from other fair exhibitors. Our biggest contract came from a company in Los Angeles that tours fairs across the United States selling products. They had come by our booth, saw our demo video, and were so impressed that they hired us to work on one of their national infomercials!

2. *Exhibit at business fairs.* Setting up displays at local business fairs was almost as profitable for us as the county fair. As with our fair booth, we would bring our studio and edit TV commercials live. We had demo videos, brochures, and newsletters available for people to take. At business fairs, we also would have a drawing in which businesspeople could drop their business cards in a jar for the chance to win a free animated logo for their business. We used the business cards to build an excellent direct mailing list of businesses that had dropped by our booth.

3. *Attend career days.* Career days not only have been profitable for us, but the events are free for us to attend. Students not only learn all about our business, but they also learn that we rent studio time at special "student discounts." When doing a career day event, it is important to have a catchy demo video playing that grabs not only the students' eyes, but also the eyes of other exhibitors when they wander around on their breaks. We received quite a bit of business from other people who were exhibiting at the career day event.

4. *Collect data on your clients.* It is vital that you keep track of every one of your clients. By collecting and organizing data from every account, you are building a priceless mailing list to target for repeat business. It is also important to find out exactly how every single client heard about you. This will help you track what methods of marketing are most successful for you so that you can focus more time and money on those efforts.

5. *Publish a newsletter.* Every quarter we would send a newsletter to our clients and other "select" people we wanted as new clients. The newsletter was four pages each issue, containing news, features, and even business tips. It was also a great way for us to share with our clients what projects we were working on and what TV projects they could watch for to see our work in action.

6. *Maintain a Web site.* These days it is vital that you have a Web site. Your Web site should have its own URL and a professional design, and should make it easy for people to learn about your services, with the ability to view samples of your work. Since the quality of your Web site will reflect the quality of your work in some people's eyes, it is vital that the design is appealing without being overwhelming. Besides services and work samples, your Web site should contain your contact information, client list, mission statement, image gallery, information on obtaining a demo video, and a newsletter sign-up list. You may also want to archive the newsletters you mail your clients on the Web site so that future clients can access back issues. Read my *Web Marketing Applied* book for hundreds of tips on marketing your Web site and services.

7. *Give the client more.* When your clients expect a certain amount of work by a certain time, try to deliver more work at an earlier time and it will skyrocket your credibility. You always want your clients to know that they received more for their money. Do high-quality work, throw in a few surprises, and always be pleasant even when the client is not.

8. *Collect testimonials.* When you complete a project and your client is pleased, ask your client to write a short testimonial for

you based on their experience. Collect these testimonials and begin to build a "testimonial book." You can show this book to prospective clients, as it speaks directly to the quality of your work.

Consistency, Chambers, and News

The key to succeeding in marketing your business is *consistency*. You must be consistent in all your marketing efforts and you must always keep your company's name in the public eye. When you take out a fair booth, don't do it for just one year, but do it every year in the same location. After about three years, people will expect to see you there.

For many years we consistently set up a booth in the same spot at the local fair. When I was hired as editor of *Video Toaster User* magazine, however, I was told that they would be flying me to SIGGRAPH to meet with readers, advertisers, and other industry professionals. SIGGRAPH fell on the same week as the fair where we had consistently exhibited. Our only choice was to cancel our fair booth. When I returned from SIGGRAPH, our clients and people we knew from the local chamber of commerce would say, "We didn't see you at the fair this year," or, "I looked for your booth at the fair and couldn't find you." We had become part of the local fair and people expected us to be there—to the point that when we weren't there, we were actually missed.

One of the most important things you can do to improve your status in the community is to join the local chamber of commerce and attend all the chamber meetings. Be sure to always have business cards with you and consider sponsoring some chamber events if you have the money. If there are subcommittees within the chamber of commerce that need help, consider becoming a part of a subcommittee. Having this interaction with your local chamber of commerce allows you to network with a lot of important people who in return may bring you future business. At the least, it will improve your status over your competitors if you are a member and they are not. Many chamber members tend to support each other. Set your standards high and make sure that your marketing campaign makes you a very influential part of your community for years to come.

Once you are well established within your community, you will want to seek opportunities to gain news coverage. Write a letter to your local newspaper's business editor letting him or her know about your business and some of the unique things you do. Enter national animation competitions frequently and be sure to submit press releases to local news media when you win a big prize or have your animation featured at an international event (such as a film festival). Coverage in your local newspaper is essential to keeping your name in the forefront of the business minds in your community. You must be established as a leader in animation so that people will think of you first when they need an animation project completed.

Besides marketing to your community, you must also market to your clients. This comes not only in the form of a quarterly newsletter, but also in the form of "gift certificates." When you conclude a big job, consider sending a special thank-you note and discount certificate—with an expiration date—to your client.

Always have demo videos available to give to prospective clients. Make sure the videos are on high-quality VHS tape (or even DVD). Make sure each tape is professionally labeled with your contact information. Also, consider differentiating your tape by using tapes with a colored shell (preferably blue, which color analysts state usually signifies importance).

Spending Advertising Dollars

A lot of media will be happy to take your advertising money, including the Yellow Pages, radio, TV, and newspapers. So which should you use and what do you do when you can't afford an advertisement?

First, it's a given that you need to be in the your local phone directory. The local phone directory is still usually the first place a person turns when he or she needs a service. Make sure a portion of your advertising allowance goes toward a decent ad that can lead a customer to you.

With other advertising media, you need to "test the waters" and do bartering. Testing the waters means that you find out from every potential client how he or she heard about you, and use this knowledge to build your future advertising base. You'll never know how effective an ad or advertising medium will be unless you measure the result and determine what your cost per lead is and whether that particular advertising medium is paying for itself.

When you don't have any money, bartering becomes an option. Radio stations often advertise on TV (particularly during "sweeps" periods) and they are always looking for something snazzy to draw attention to their commercial. This is where you come in. You can provide your services at no cost to a radio station in exchange for free radio commercials. We aired hundreds of radio commercials for our business for free by striking a trade agreement with the top local radio station, where we simply exchanged services.

Always be creative in your approach for gaining advertising at a limited cost, and remember to keep careful track of every inquiry and where it came from so that you can find out what type of advertising is working best for you.

Know Your Competitors

Part of building a strong marketing campaign is knowing who your competitors are, what they are doing, how they are advertising, and how they run their company. By knowing your competitor in depth, you not only can see how your standards measure up to them, but you can also map out potential opportunities of your own.

So how do you get to know a company? Have one of your relatives become a "potential customer" or conduct your own inquiries by phone. You want to gather as much data as you can on your competitor from their prices to how professional they are on the phone. Is your experience a pleasant one when dealing with them? When you called, did you get a live person or an answering machine? How clean are their offices? How well are they dressed? What type of atmosphere did you walk into when entering their offices? How was the production quality? Did they have a demo video? Did they conduct a follow-up with you?

Come up with a list of questions to help you know your competitor better. When you are done, ask yourself the same questions. In doing so, you will discover what opportunities you have to improve your own business. You may even want to hire a friend to find someone you don't know to conduct this same experience on your business "within the next six months" so that you can receive an evaluation of what someone else really thinks about your business and your manners.

Part of marketing is making the customer feel comfortable and confident while building loyalty through the way you treat him or her. You must always treat a customer—even mean ones—with the ultimate respect and professionalism.

Avoid Marketing Deception

Nothing turns off a potential client more than deception in marketing, which I call the "Deceptive Marketing Syndrome." Unfortunately there are ignorant marketers in our society that help give marketing a bad name with their marketing deceptions. Some business owners even say, "Well, everyone else is being deceptive, so why not us?" Why not you? *Because you are different.* You are going to build your business on honor, not deception. Your word will be your bond.

Deceptive marketing occurs when you mislead the public in order to gain business. Sometimes this appears in the form of exaggerations; at other times it appears as outright lies. You must avoid it at all costs. When you start using deceptive practices in your marketing, you will begin to lose the trust of your customer and potential clients. While some will put profits ahead of trust, you should always put trust ahead of profits because it is the only way that you can win as a businessperson and as a respected individual.

A company that was once a competitor to NewTek products used deceptive advertising to try to get business, and they quickly lost respect because of it. This company would advertise that you could buy their product for $4,995 COMPLETE in all of its advertising. The key emphasis in the ads was "complete," indicating that everything you needed was included for $4,995 to successfully use the product.

This wasn't the case. The company failed to state in its advertising that there were certain *modules* you needed that didn't come with the package. You had to pay nearly $1,000 for each module. How long did this company think it would take customers to realize that they couldn't buy the product for $4,995 complete? This type of advertising not only was clearly deceptive, but it also caused customers to lose trust in the company.

Another deceptive marketing practice you must avoid is known as "bait and switch." In this practice, a company advertises a product or service and when you go to buy it, you are told that it is "no longer available" but there is a "much better one" at a higher price. You are then subjected to a sales pitch and pressure to buy this "much better" product or service.

Deceptive marketing practices are a good way to lose customers forever. At all costs always strive to be honorable, informative, and 100% honest when marketing and advertising. The trust you will receive as a company will be priceless.

In the days of old, the word of a man or woman was gold, and honor was taken very seriously. Therefore, you should develop your own code of honor that you will stick to at all costs and that you will uphold as a pledge to your family, friends, customers, and society.

HOW MUCH ARE YOU WORTH?

As an entrepreneur, how much is your time worth? Is it worth $10 an hour, or more like $175 an hour? Is all your money going toward debts, or are you making a hefty profit? These are things that you need to analyze when starting a company. The simple fact is that most LightWave animation companies are not charging enough money for their services, and the result is continued debt and longer hours.

In the second year of running our animation business, we determined that we simply weren't making enough money. But we were afraid that a steep rise in our prices would result in less business. However, knowing the importance of marketing and the loyalty of our clients, we went ahead with a 50% price increase. To help "cushion" the news to our current clients, we wrote them a polite letter indicating the price increase "to better meet their needs and improve the services offered" and we included certificates for our clients to still get their next project completed at the old prices. We continued our strong marketing and the most amazing thing happened. Our business grew. When we increased our prices, our business grew. As a result we made more money, had more money for advertising, and were able to upgrade our equipment. All around, we became a better company because we were finally charging what we felt we were worth and the clients knew they were getting a top-quality job for the price.

How much you charge in your business will reflect how much you are worth. Don't undercharge, as you may simply become known as the "cheap alternative" and you'll never make the money you need to expand your operations.

Contracts and Payments

Based on my personal experience, I highly recommend that you always have clients sign a contract and always get 20–50% payment in advance. I further recommend that you never let a final project leave your hands without 100% payment. If the person wants to take an animation to "show to partners" before approving it, make sure the animation contains writing over it such as "SAMPLE" or "DEMO" so that the client can't use it without paying you.

Be careful also about bending your payment rules, even for loyal clients. A local TV station once hired us to do all their TV commercial work (animation, video, and so on). The TV station's payments were consistent for the first three months, so at their request we extended to them a 30-day credit. Within a couple of months they missed a payment. After a reminder, they gave us a partial payment. Because they had been a faithful client, we accepted the partial payment and continued to do work for them until their payments were three months past due with a bill well over $5,000. We gave them a two-week deadline in which we would stop production if we didn't receive payment. The payment never arrived, so we stopped production. We never received the money and ended up losing over $7,500. We also lost a lot of potential clients because we had spent the majority of our time working for the TV station and had to turn down other work. The result was a major blow to the success of our company, almost causing us to go under.

Here are three basic rules:

1. *Never put all your eggs into one basket.* I've seen many major animation studios shut down because their whole staff was put to work on a lengthy animation project that went over budget and over time, and didn't pay off in the end.

2. *Collect partial payment in advance.* Make sure you receive a down payment for your services.

3. *Never release any final production without full payment.* You can't go to a gas station and say, "I'll pay you in 30 days for gas today." Neither should you allow your clients to say they'll pay you later for a job you've completed.

Efficiency

Once your business is up and running you must consistently ask yourself the following question: "What can I do to become more time efficient while making more money?" You must look for ways of increasing the profitability of your company without sacrificing quality and without increasing costs.

In my upcoming *Achieving Web Profits* book, I dissect exactly what the problem is with many Internet ventures, and I present tips on how to make a Web site profitable in a short amount of time. In closely examining hundreds of Internet businesses, I began to see the same failure similarities as I've seen in most offline businesses. Companies would get money and from the beginning they would spend, spend, spend. Their goal was to become a multimillion-dollar company overnight. It doesn't work that way.

As I teach my consulting clients, it is vital to apply a "ramp up to profitability" model to your business. This means that from the first time you touch money that is not yours (loan, venture capital, and so on), you apply that money only to elements that will help grow your business slowly, while making it profitable from the beginning. Hiring 70 employees and moving into a state-of-the-art building with new office furniture is not a smart way to start a new business. Rather, you begin slowly with a few people and start to master the elements of your business by building a client base. You work out a business model that will make your company profitable in two months, rather than five years from now.

Control your spending from day one and work to maximize profits. As part of your business model you may want to incorporate a "percentage spending" model. This type of model takes money you earn and distributes that money after taxes into separate elements of your business. For example, 20% of all our business income may go to future marketing expenses; 10% may go to future upgrades; and so on. This allows your income to help determine your spending without you getting further into debt. It's always better to pay with cash than a credit card. You get more value for your purchase.

Consider the following simple equation I created:

Price determines your value

Value determines your worth

And now add this to the equation:

Spending determines your costs

Costs determine your debt

And now for the final part of the equation:

Marketing determines your business

Business determines your success

May your business be of the utmost success and may you see much profit from your venture.

ANOTHER VIEW: BLUE DREAM STUDIOS

In March 2001 I interviewed Scott Sava of Blue Dream Studios (http://www.bluedreamstudios.com/) for *Digital Media FX* magazine (http://www.digitalmediafx.com/). Knowing that Scott and his wife, Donna, have good business skills and run a successful animation production company (at the time of this writing, using LightWave), I asked if they'd be willing to share some thoughts for those thinking about starting their own animation company. Here are Scott's comments:

Blue Dream Studios has been several years in the making. There are several steps we would recommend to someone starting out in the animation field. First you must build your client base. We've spent several years working on large- and small-scale projects with sometimes little to no pay. By doing work for free, sometimes you can gain so much more than a paying job. Starting your own business means taking risks and if you *love* money, I wouldn't recommend starting your own company. I'd have to say that if you don't lose too much money in the first year, it was successful. If you break *even* the next year, you've been successful. And if you start to show a profit the third year, you're on your way!

If you want to start your own company, plan for it. Save up your money and be prepared to *not* have any work for months at a time. But in that time, work on your own properties or take on work for free that would help your studio. Never underestimate the value of unpaid projects. If you can work with someone you respect and you have to do it on your own dime, it's worth it! If you can afford it, take time away from paying jobs so you can develop your skills and your portfolio.

Learn about the companies that are out there and what types of software they are using for various projects. We have done a lot of networking with other professionals in our field as well. In addition, we've spoken with other animators and modelers, compositors, and texture artists. This is how we were able to broaden our talent base and be able to offer all of these services to our clients.

Of course you need to deal with the typical things to start up a business, such as equipment, business licenses, bank accounts, and so on. But in reality, the most important asset you will have is the contacts you meet.

Another important aspect of starting a business is to find a partner who will complement your talents. That way you aren't stepping on each other's toes! I handle all of the creative work, animation storytelling, and so on while my wife, Donna, handles the day-to-day operations as well as business development and publicity. We each bring our unique talents to the table and can just run with what needs to be done. Here's a checklist that I had in mind when planning my studio:

1. *Clients.* Do you have enough clients to count on for work? I built up my client base originally from contacts when working on movies and by approaching people I wanted to work with and doing side projects with those people for free. Now they all love my work and call me whenever there's a project they need character animation for, because they've worked with me and they know my work ethics.

2. *Savings.* You have to assume the worst. Get yourself set up with at least six months of savings *before* you quit your job and start your own studio. This way there's no pressure to take on jobs that aren't in your studio's interest.

3. *Contacts/Freelancers.* Do you know everyone you need to know? If you are a great modeler but don't animate that well, why would you take on an animation-intensive project by yourself?

Get on some mailing lists; go to meetings and conventions. Network! Before you start your studio, make sure you have people you can rely on in case you get a big project. You may need compositors, character animators, texture artists, storyboard artists, musicians, and others. Make a contact list so you know you're covered!

4. *Software.* Can your software handle the projects you'll be asked to do? Photoshop for textures, After Effects for compositing, and so on? Do you own everything? You can't go into business for yourself with cracked [pirated] software; it's unethical and your clients will assume you're a thief and you don't want that. If you're making money with your software, *purchase it!*

5. *Hardware.* Can your computer handle a big project? Do you need a render farm? In my case, I have companies that will allow me to use their 60-plus-CPU render farms whenever I need them, for a nominal cost or a called favor. If you get a really render-intensive job, make sure you can get it to your client on time. Also, do you have the latest drivers and video cards? How will you transfer files? Can you output to tape? Burn CDs?

ANOTHER VIEW: VIP 3D

Through Scott and Donna, you've learned some important firsthand-experience tips in starting your own animation business. Now let's switch gears a little and take a look at someone who has run his own animation business for several years. As you'll discover, running your own animation business may not always be as glamorous or profitable as you hope, but there are still many additional rewards. I'd like to introduce you to Tom Kubat, who has run his own animation business, VIP 3D (http://www.vip3d.com/), for many years.

The way I figure it, this body is going to experience its last breath at some point, and in that moment I'll remember all the times I thought I had to worry about losing something, or failing, or for that matter, succeeding . . . and I am going to laugh. I am going to laugh like there's no tomorrow, and that laugh will carry me to whatever this mystery has in store next. In the mean time, I am going to live life like there's no tomorrow and that means that when I am lucky enough to find a dream or a vision, there will be no logic or belief system that could persuade me not to follow it. What do you have to lose anyway?

In the end you are going to lose everything that isn't permanent, so you might as well go for it.

I remember when I started this business—it was after 25 years of dreaming of being an animator. I followed the industry, attended every NAB and SIGGRAPH, knowing that there was no way I could afford to learn enough to be hired by one of the few companies who needed that talent. I figured the only way was to start my own business. Of course, with equipment and software costs in the millions, that was out of reach . . . until NewTek showed up with the Toaster and Light-Wave. I borrowed every penny I could, bought one of the first Toasters released, and started the business on a shoestring with fabulous visions of the great animation I would be able to sell. As it turned out, in upstate New York there weren't a lot of clients clamoring for my services. So, inadvertently, I became a video producer because editing was all anyone wanted from me. Still, I spent every free minute practicing and learning, and eventually I began selling logo animations for $100 to $300 (my "big" clients). It was awful, but I was happy because I was following my dream and somehow I knew that by doing that, I could not fail, no matter how hard it would be at times.

Sometimes people say that to make it in business you have to be lucky. The thing you have to realize is that you are already unbelievably lucky. Of the six billion people in the world today, how many start an animation business each year, or even have such a ridiculous thought? It cannot be more than a handful, and that makes you as rare as Walt Disney. During his early years only a handful of animation companies were started—far fewer than today, but there were far fewer people back then. The ratio is about the same . . . one in 10 million or 100 million perhaps. It doesn't matter, of course, but what does matter is that this inspiration doesn't just come to everybody. You are rare, and you are lucky because you actually have the means to put such a business together. Believe me, you can trust this. It wouldn't come to you if you didn't have the ability to pull it off.

What all of this leads up to is that it isn't really luck that makes a business work, it's more fundamental than that. It's the love of the art and the deep desire to be involved in this kind of creative work. It's the recognition that you are destined to do this or you wouldn't have the burning desire in the first place . . . in other words, believing in yourself is the most critically important element. Fortunately it'll be easy and natural for you because you are following your dream. Don't worry about failing . . . you can't fail. Just worry about how to get through the tough moments without quitting. Trust me, your mettle will be tested.

You will experience several common emotional states. On the one hand there will be the elation of having landed a job. Then comes the "Wait a minute, how will I accomplish that effect?" Then you'll get the answer in 10 minutes in the LightWave newsletter and you'll be filled with wonder and gratitude. Then you'll sink into a deep depression as you realize you're getting paid half of minimum wage because this job is going to take double or triple the time and resources you thought in order to get the high-end look that you want for your reel. And to make matters worse, the client will come in and want changes that make it look awful in your opinion. Then you'll begin to wonder why you are bothering with this business in the first place. After all, this isn't the kind of animation you'd always dreamed of doing anyway, and who needs all the stress? But through it all, maybe deeply buried at times but present nonetheless, is recognition that this is all much bigger than any of these temporary states. It springs from your heart, where you know that truth and permanence reside and the very experience of living through it somehow makes you brighter, stronger, and more in touch with the creative essence that is more you than even those imaginary dreams of animated glory that got you started on this path in the first place.

Eventually the client will shower you with praise for such a fine job, and it will somehow make up for all the pain you had to endure; but deep down you know that the praise and the good feelings it triggers are just like the stress you are still reeling from. It feels great, of course, but it is just another emotional state that won't last; in this recognition, you will find that what makes it all worth it is the experience of growing something more permanent, namely your business.

Starting your business is like bringing a child into the world, and you have to look at it with that kind of commitment. It will take nurturing and love and lots of attention (sleepless nights and all the rest). It will delight you and torture you and it will grow toward independence much more slowly than you would like (and at times, seemingly much too fast). It will be a source of joy at times, but often it will not behave itself like the other good little companies down the block. Finally, because you've done your job so well, it will grow up and leave home and survive your little ego and all its fantasies by a long shot. And if you are really lucky (and here's where true "luck" comes in), it will reveal something to you about your own eternal permanence through all the thick and thin of such a fabulous adventure.

Or, maybe nothing like all this will happen to you, but the point is still the same. Perseverance is your friend! I've been in this business for 11 years now, and this year for the first time I *might* take a salary at half what average animators get paid, and the business *might* finally show a profit, but even if I don't and even if it doesn't, I will still be in business five years from now because I deeply honor the friendship I have found in perseverance. If I had to boil it all down to two principles for success in business, I'd choose *"Carpe Diem!"* ("Seize the day!," "Go for it!," "Be willing to live on the edge.") and "Never give up!"

Of course, you need a few other things, such as capitalization and clients and talent, but it is my experience that if you are "married" to these two principles, the money will come from somewhere to get the equipment and the training you need; the clients will come from the most unsuspected places simply because you happened to show up; and the resources and help will be available when you need them. Knowing this is all a part of trusting yourself, which you already know will come easy for you . . . except for one thing. You also have to be willing to be humbled.

The only way your business will have long-term viability is if you are able to bring in people with talents greater than your own. I will never forget how it felt when I trained an intern named John Watson in LightWave (working for no money because he wanted so badly to learn animation) and within six months he proved to be faster than I was at modeling; better and quicker at lighting, surfacing, and animating; and a far better technician at keeping these damnable computers working. At first I felt displaced, as if I wasn't sure where I fit any more. But it doesn't take long to realize how incredible it is to have someone on the team that you can just hand a job to and know that it will be done better and faster than you could have done it yourself. Since then, I have nothing but respect for great talent and am convinced that the business must grow into a community or wither and die. My role has become more administrative than I'd like. I'd rather animate than go out on sales calls and handle customer concerns, but I am willing to do whatever it takes to get the job done and make sure everyone gets paid on payday. You cannot run a business by being a specialist. You have to remove the ego and do whatever needs to be done to keep the baby alive till it can take care of itself.

Finally, there are no prerequisites for this business other than the two I've mentioned. I have degrees in psychology, philosophy, and religious studies, and my former career was as director of quality for a manufacturing company. That's not much of a preparation for art, or graphics, or entertainment, or for building a business. I remember that my favorite teacher in graduate school was focused on getting the job done. His office had nothing on the walls . . . no distractions or frill at all, but he had one 8-×-10 framed card on his door at eye level that had a simple quote typed on it. I don't remember who said it but it read:

> **Doubt a man and he will fail.**
>
> **Believe in him and he will be a stunning success.**

As you read this, you may think I don't know who you are, but I do know that you have discovered at least a spark of the fire for animation. Believe me, I know you well enough. So I would like to end with the last words that my teacher said to me:

> **"I expect great things from you now . . . "**

BUILDING AN ANIMATION BUSINESS STEP BY STEP

Throughout this tutorial you have learned valuable insights into building your own local animation business. I leave you with a step-by-step summary and with wishes that you have much success should this be the direction in which you take your life.

STEP 1: Make sure that you're ready to start your own business. It's an expensive and time-consuming proposition. Proceed only if you have a passion for the work and the desire to stick it out long-term.

STEP 2: Contact the nearest Small Business Administration office and ask them for a complimentary "Free Startup Kit." The kit contains important information on most aspects of starting a business including the business type (sole proprietorship, partnership, and so on) and how to finance your business venture. If you would rather view the kit online, go to http://www.sba.gov/starting/indexstartup.html. Also, learn your local business laws. If you go to one of the bigger local bookstores you should be able to find a series of books that deal with starting a business in your state (for example, *Starting and Operating a Business in California*). Familiarize yourself with state laws.

STEP 3: Determine your business name and also register the Internet URL so that you own the Web site by the same name. Register your name with the state and make sure your business meets state regulations. Check with your local county clerk's office for details.

STEP 4: Decide upon a location. Your business is not dependent on location (as is a fast-food restaurant); therefore, you may want to consider something in a less expensive but well-maintained area.

STEP 5: Create an identity for your new company (*Note:* some aspects of this will have to wait until you have a physical address). Put together a slogan, business cards, stationery, branded contracts, and so on.

STEP 6: Create a business plan and make a detailed list of all your needs and expenses for starting a business, including equipment, overhead, marketing, advertising, office supplies, and contracts. Gather the supplies you need.

STEP 7: Determine your equipment needs and costs. Be careful with spending.

STEP 8: Determine how you are going to pay for everything. Will you save money before opening your business or will you take out a loan? Calculate all your costs and always overestimate. Be sure to add several thousand dollars to a "Misc." category.

STEP 9: Determine whether your services should be more than animation in order to reach a wider audience. If not, consider networking with complementary businesses to help supplement your business income.

STEP 10: Master marketing. Marketing will be the single most important aspect of your business. You must spend a considerable amount of time marketing your services. You'll also need to put considerable time into advertising, evaluating effectiveness, and gaining news publicity. Become an important part of your community and never deceive potential clients.

STEP 11: Learn from other animators. Become a frequent participant in online animation mailing lists and interact with other animation business owners. Share and learn what works best for you.

STEP 12: Set your prices so that you get paid what you're worth, and always collect full payment before releasing a final product into the hands of your client.

> **Note:** Make sure your business is following all the legal and tax standards required by your state and that the name of your company is properly filed with the state. For more information on covering the legal bases of your new business, visit http://www.nolo.com/.

MAKE YOUR DREAMS A REALITY

Walt Disney was a strong believer in making his dreams into a reality. He was constantly hit with obstacles while growing up. He had to declare bankruptcy once, many of his animators betrayed him for other companies, and some of his business associates kept money hidden from him. Yet through all the pain, Disney was able to keep focused by realizing that obstacles are what you see when you take your eyes off the goal.

Keep your eyes on the goal, give it your best work every day, and get paid what you're worth. Have fun at what you do, and most important . . . *make your dreams a reality.*

11

Seventh Heaven—
Experiencing LightWave 7

Dave Jerrard

OVERVIEW

Software development is one of those things that never seems to end. From its introduction more than 10 years ago as a supplemental application for Video Toaster, LightWave is no exception. On average, one major upgrade has been available every year since it first hit the streets, and its feature list has grown in leaps and bounds, quickly bringing it to the attention of Hollywood.

With this growth in the software, particularly the complete rewrite of the entire program for its 6.x incarnations, many things have been added. In fact, since work began on this book, LightWave has gone from version 6.0 to 6.5a to 6.5b and finally, version 7 which we'll look at here.

In this tutorial you will use:

■ SasLite

■ SkyTracer2

■ SunSpot

What you will need:

■ Prebuilt objects included on CD

■ Spare time

What you will learn:

■ Differences between LightWave 6.5 and 7.0

■ Cloud texturing through SkyTracer2 and the Texture Editor

■ Fur layering

With these additions, changes had to be made that required a new interface to allow easy access. The new plug-in architecture required that the interface be in constant flux as new features were added, and thus a customizable interface was designed and default configurations were created. LightWave 6.0 had the simplest configuration, with only three tabs on the Layout window. LightWave 6.5 changed these and added three more. LightWave 7 changes things again by adding one more tab to the top for easier access to LScript functions. Figure 11-1 shows LightWave's progression from 6.0 to 7.

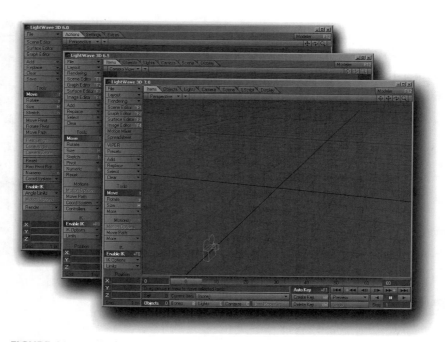

FIGURE 11-1 LightWave 7 adds yet another tab to the top of Layout, as well as a few other additional buttons. Note the addition of the Motion Mixer and Spreadsheet buttons on the main toolbar.

You'll also notice in that figure that some buttons have been moved, and there are a few other additional buttons as well. Changes like these mean that some of our workflow will have to be changed as well. For example, to access VIPER, you no longer have to go through the Surface Editor, since it's right there on the main screen.

So, what else has changed? In one word, lots—far more than can be covered in one tutorial. We'll start by looking at some of the other changes you should be aware of.

CHANGES IN WORKFLOW

Luckily, most of the techniques that worked in LightWave 6.5 still apply to LightWave 7. However, a few new added features have bumped things around that could cause problems. The first one we'll cover is the new Surface Editor. The functionality has not been changed much, but the interface has. The new Surface Editor is now taller than before, and the Surface Preview area has been moved above the texture attributes.

This allows for a longer surface list down the left side. The panel can be collapsed into a more compact size by clicking the small arrow button at the top of the window (Figure 11-2) to remove the surface list from the side. In the collapsed mode, a new menu appears above the preview area, allowing you to select surfaces without using extra screen space.

You should keep a couple of things in mind when using this collapsed state, however. First, if you're using any surface filtering, that filter will remain active in the collapsed state, so to get the entire surface list, you'll need to expand the editor and change the filtering options. Second, editing multiple surfaces simultaneously is not available in this collapsed mode.

Another change that will improve workflow can be seen on the Shaders tab in the Surface Editor. Shaders, as well as any other plug-ins, can be copied and pasted from one item to another via the new Edit menu, as shown in Figure 11-3. Note that plug-ins can be transferred only within their own classes. You cannot, for example, copy a shader from the Surface Editor and paste it into the Image Filter or Deformations areas in other panels. You can, however, have multiple plug-in classes copied in memory at the same time, meaning you can copy the BRDF shader, then go to the Image Filters and copy the blur plug-in, then copy a motion plug-in, and then go back to the surfaces and paste the BRDF shader into a new surface. Each plug-in class has its own copy buffer.

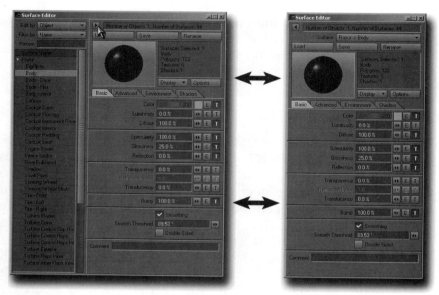

FIGURE 11-2 The new Surface Editor, in both expanded and collapsed states.

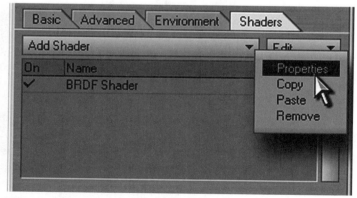

FIGURE 11-3 Plug-ins can now be copied and pasted from one item to another.

The Texture Editor has remained virtually untouched since LightWave 6.5, except for one change that will prove to be confusing at first. In previous tutorials, when you added a texture, you used the Additive Blending Mode. This mode is now called Normal, and texture layers that use it are marked with an N in the Texture List (Figure 11-4). Additive blending is still present, but it now works in a true additive fashion, much like the Additive Transparency mode (or the Screen mode that Photoshop users will be familiar with). This means that the RGB values of the color of the texture layer are added to the values of the underlying layers, making the additive layer appear brighter. Thus, placing a green procedural texture on a red surface will cause the texture to appear yellow, since red and green combine to make yellow when added together. Surfaces created in previous versions will still render correctly, but all old texture layers that were created as additive layers will show up in LightWave 7 as a Normal layer.

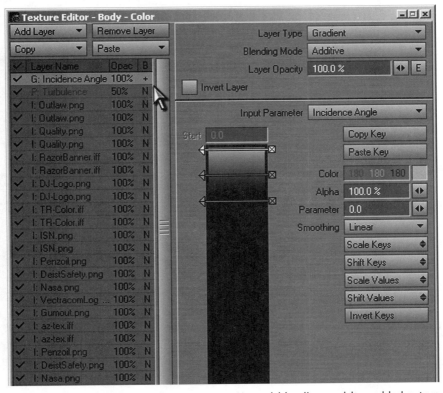

FIGURE 11-4 The Texture Editor now uses Normal blending and has added a true Additive blending mode.

VIPER is now easier to use than before since it's now a single-click operation from the main Layout interface that immediately opens the VIPER window, without an intermediate confirmation requester. Viper is also used by more functions now, including volumetric ground fog and the new SkyTracer2, which we'll get into a bit later.

One of the other things you will notice is the new method LightWave 7 uses when Show Render in Progress is active. Previously this was a real-time update, but now the render preview is updated only twice per second, resulting in a sporadic-looking preview. This is normal, so don't worry that something's gone horribly wrong. With fewer updates per second, using Show Render in Progress will no longer slow the render down as much as it used to. It will also now display the render in progress when multiple threads are used.

A few other features have been added to Layout as well, such as the new Squash tool. This is much like the old Stretch tool, but with constraints that keep the object's volume constant (Figure 11-5).

FIGURE 11-5 The new Squash tool will stretch an object while retaining its volume in one easy step.

The Graph Editor has also undergone some new design work, and is much cleaner-looking and faster. A menu appears across the top of the window, and the editor itself is much more customizable (Figure 11-6). The channel lists on the left can also be collapsed, just like the surface list in the Surface Editor.

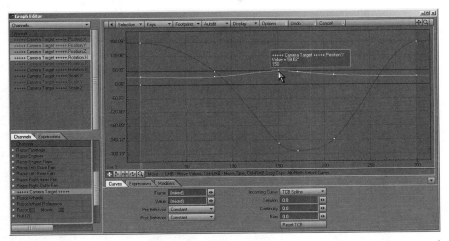

FIGURE 11-6 The new look of the Graph Editor, showing the menu across the top and the new, cleaner look of the graphs.

It's also now possible to load and replace individual object layers, so you'll no longer have to do the object shuffling that was required with the car in Tutorial 7.

In the Render Options panel a new option is present: Ray Trace Transparency. This might seem a bit redundant with the presence of Ray Trace Refraction, but it is different. Its main purpose is to be a one-step solution to allow volumetric effects to be seen through transparent surfaces. Previously, to see volumetrics like this, you had to set the transparent surface's Refraction Index to something higher than 1 and then activate Ray Trace Refraction. Ray Trace Transparency will allow all transparent surfaces to be raytraced, no matter what their refraction values are. With this on, transparent surfaces will render along with regular opaque surfaces, rather than after them. A side benefit to this is that you won't be faced with the message "Rendering transparent polygons" at the end of each render pass. This is of particular interest to people who use Screamernet and don't know what pass a given frame is rendering, since while this message is displayed, no information about render passes or segments is displayed. These two raytracing options can be used together freely.

Probably the most powerful addition to LightWave 7 that will make life so much easier for everyone is the new Spreadsheet (Figure 11-7). This highly configurable Layout tool will probably replace the old Scene Editor for most people, but for the die-hards, the Scene Editor is still present. Spreadsheet allows you to edit virtually everything in a scene, but much faster than ever before. Every item in the scene is listed, and every attribute for each item can also be seen at a glance and edited simultaneously. Need to change the brightness or color of 100 lights? Previously, this was a tedious task, or one better suited to a text editor. Now it's as simple as selecting the appropriate lights and supplying the new value. Item types, falloffs, colors, display levels, IK, parenting, targeting, timelines, and so on can all be edited for multiple items, simultaneously. You might want to open the Spreadsheet while going through some of the other projects in this book.

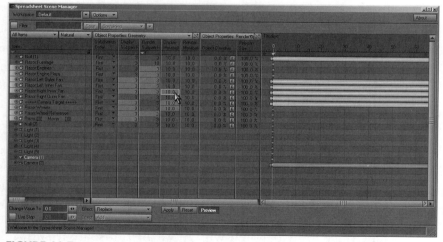

FIGURE 11-7 The spreadsheet allows virtually unlimited, at-a-glance control of everything in the scene. Here, the Subpatch levels of several objects are being edited together.

Modeler has also undergone a few changes, though not quite as drastically as Layout. The one change that would be the biggest concern here is that of the Z key. It has reverted, by default, to the Airbrush tool again. In 6.5b and all pre-6 releases, the Z key has been the delete key, so be aware that if you're trying to delete something in Modeler, you'll have to use the Delete key (or change your configs so the Z key is Delete again).

The interactive Bevel tool now works backward from the way it used to. Dragging up and down affects the Shift amount while dragging from side to side affects the Inset amount.

Generally speaking, though, workflow in Modeler is basically untouched, aside from these changes.

OK, enough of the feature list. Let's use some of these new goodies.

SKYWRITING MADE EASY

We played a bit with skies in Tutorial 6, using textures on a sphere to create clouds. We touched on using SkyTracer, but there's a new SkyTracer in town. SkyTracer2 takes the atmospheric engine of the original and combines it with the Texture Editor, providing us with an unlimited range of cloud effects. Any texture type can be used, just as with regular surfacing, but in SkyTracer, the textures are used to create areas of clouds. Let's take a quick look at what we can do with this.

STEP 1: Load Layout and tilt the camera up so the grid is near the bottom of the frame. A pitch of −15 degrees should do nicely. While we're here, let's turn the camera to the left to a heading of −70 degrees. Don't worry about not having anything else in the scene, since we're just going to focus on the clouds.

STEP 2: Press Ctrl+F5 to open the Effects panel and select the Backdrop tab. Click the Add Environment button near the bottom and select SkyTracer2 from the list.

STEP 3: SkyTracer is now active, but in order to see what we're doing, we need to activate VIPER. Click the VIPER button on the main toolbar. You should now see a gradient blue sky (Figure 11-8).

If you've used the original SkyTracer, one of the first things you'll notice, aside from the completely different interface of the plug-in itself, is that there is no longer a black horizon. The sky blends into a thick haze color at the horizon now, which continues downward, avoiding the much maligned black line that frequently appeared at the horizon in old SkyTracer scenes.

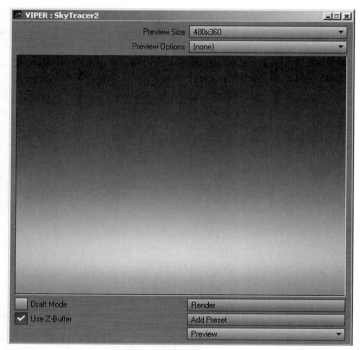

FIGURE 11-8 SkyTracer2's improved sky rendering eliminates the old black horizon and creates a much nicer backdrop.

You might also have noticed that a new light has been added to the scene, called SKT_Sun. This isn't the only thing that was added. If you select this light and open the Motion Options panel by pressing M, you see that it has a motion Modifier called SunSpot applied. This plug-in allows us to simulate sunlight for any place on earth, at any time, simply by telling it where we are and the time and date. The light will then be moved to where the sun would be in the sky at that time. Let's position the sun in the west, just a couple of hours before sunset, which will give us some nice angled lighting to work with on our clouds.

OK, so where's west? In Lightwave, when you start with a fresh scene, by default the camera is pointing toward the positive Z axis. This equates to north in SunSpot. West would then be negative X, east would be positive X, and south would be negative Z. If you ever feel lost, just switch to Top view and imagine the four compass points aligned with the sides of the screen, like a map.

STEP 4: Now that we know where west is, let's move the sun that way. Double-click the SunSpot plug-in entry to open its interface. Since the sun sets in the west at night, we should set the time to early evening. SunSpot uses 24-hour mode, or military time, so any times after noon will have 12 hours added to them. We'll set the time to 5:30 P.M., so add 12 to that to get 17:30. Set the Hour to 17 and the Minute to 30. The position and angle of the SKT_Sun will immediately update.

Note: The SKT_Sun is a distant light by default, and SunSpot modifies both its position and its angle. While the location of a distant light has no effect on how it illuminates a scene, it does affect how SkyTracer2 will display it in the sky. Much like a lens flare, the glare of the sun will appear only if the light used as the sun is visible within the frame. The angle of the light is unimportant for this. This is why the light is also moved back 1 km by default when SunSpot is first set up. If you would like to use an Area light to create accurate shadowing, as we've done in Tutorial 6, you may want to move the light back even farther. This is easily accomplished by simply increasing the Distance value in SunSpot. It's also important to note that SunSpot will keep the light pointing toward the center of the scene, so the objects in the scene will be lit appropriately to match the sky (remember the incorrect lighting in Figure 6-27 in Tutorial 6).

All that's left now is to select a date and location. Let's set the date to August 6th, 2001, and choose Los Angeles for our location. You should now be able to see the light in the camera's view. If you refresh VIPER, you should also see a bright sun in the sky (Figure 11-9).

Note: You can access SunSpot more easily right from SkyTracer2's interface. Click the Suns tab and then click the big Sun Position button at the bottom of the panel.

Now it's time to add some clouds.

STEP 5: Go back to SkyTracer2 and click the Clouds tab. You'll see two new tabs appear below, where we can edit two different cloud layers, much as in the original SkyTracer. We'll just deal with the Low Altitude Clouds for now. Click the Enable Clouds button and you should see a few bright clouds appear in the sky. These are not the same clouds we had in the original SkyTracer. Click the Texture button and you'll see that these are being generated by the Turbulence texture.

Turbulence worked well for clouds in Tutorial 6, and it does an excellent job here as well. In fact, it's better since it's creating a volumetric texture here. As with all volumetrics, it will take a little longer to render, so let's speed things up a bit.

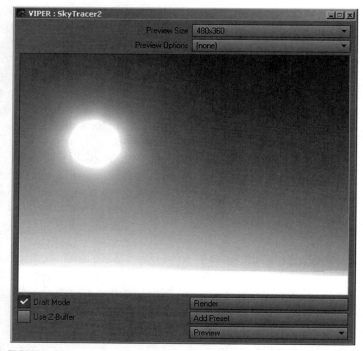

FIGURE 11-9 When you supply a date, time, and location, the sun appears in the sky just as it should.

STEP 6: Click the Volumetric Rendering button in the middle of the panel to turn it off. The cloud pattern will change its appearance slightly in VIPER (Figure 11-10). We've just turned the clouds into a two-dimensional texture, much like mapping a normal texture on a transparent polygon. The texture is the same, which is why the clouds in the distance have the same pattern. But why did the foreground cloud in front of the sun vanish?

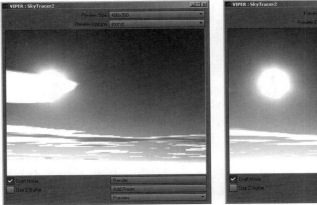

FIGURE 11-10 The same cloud texture shown with volumetric and two-dimensional rendering.

The Turbulence texture has a soft edge to it, as we've seen in previous tutorials. This soft edge is still present in SkyTracer, but is handled slightly differently when rendered volumetrically. When LightWave renders a volumetric object, it samples a number of evenly spaced points along a ray from the camera that passes through the volumetric area. These points are spaced evenly between the closest and farthest ends of the volumetric area. You can think of each of these points as a polygon with a transparency texture applied. As a ray from the camera passes through each polygon, it sees another part of the volumetric texture. Each polygon then adds its particular slice of the texture to the ones before and after it, resulting in a gradual buildup. Normally-imperceptible changes in transparency, such as those over 95% transparent, become more obvious as they start to overlap. In the case of our clouds, this overlapping tends to spread their edges out more and adds a little more contrast in the process, since completely transparent areas will not add up (there's nothing in these regions to add). If you compare the two renders more closely, you'll notice that the clouds in the distance are slightly thicker-looking when rendered volumetrically. (You'll also be able to see a very small portion of cloud to the left of the sun in the nonvolumetric image.) Since they're farther away, the change is scaled down by perspective.

To show that the cloud in front of the sun is actually still there, lower the Contrast setting in SkyTracer to 100%. You'll notice that the foreground cloud becomes more visible (Figure 11-11). Increasing the Luminosity of the cloud will brighten it up even more. In most cases you can get very useful clouds using this nonvolumetric method, and it's much faster to render. Another thing you might notice when switching Volumetric Rendering on and off is that the volumetric clouds tend to thicken upward from the nonvolumetric version. This thickening is controlled by the Cloud Height value. Higher values here will make the clouds thicker, but will also increase render times. Basically, Cloud Height is how much higher the cloud tops are from their Altitude. Generally, you can get excellent results with a Cloud Height of 50 m without spending too much time on rendering.

FIGURE 11-11 A change in contrast spreads the clouds a bit, revealing the same detail that was present in the volumetric version.

Note: The old SkyTracer cloud textures are still available. In the Texture Editor, you'll find a new procedural called STClouds. This texture brings back the familiar Cumulus, Cirrus, and Jet Streams cloud textures.

Tip: The Jet Streams option of STClouds, when used as a bump map, can create a nice scratched appearance on a surface.

Since we're using the Texture Editor for clouds, we're not limited to just using procedurals. Images and gradients can also be used and layered any way you like. Since we can use images, we can put whatever we want, wherever we want it, in the sky.

STEP 7: Add a new Image Map texture layer and click the Image button. Load the **SkyWrite.jpg** image from the CD (Figure 11-12) and set the Texture Axis to Y. Set the tiling options to Reset and then click the Position tab at the bottom. Change the X value to −1 m and the Z value to 0.4 m (40 cm). You should now have a message written in the clouds (Figure 11-13). It's easy to see that you could take an animated write-off as an image sequence and use that in place of a still image to create the illusion of a plane drawing each stroke of the letters in the sky.

You've probably noticed that SkyTracer2 isn't exactly a speed demon, particularly when using the volumetric options. Making the clouds thinner helps, but if you really need to have the thicker volumetric clouds, you're not going to want to have to render them for every frame of an animation. Well, you've probably noticed the Sky Baker button at the top of the panel by now.

FIGURE 11-12 Any image can be used to create clouds now. For example, skywriting is as simple as taking an image like this . . .

FIGURE 11-13 . . . and mapping it in the sky like this.

STEP 8: Click the Sky Baker button to open the Sky Baker panel (Figure 11-14). Sky Baker is like the older Render Warp Images, but with more control over the images it creates. Where the old Sky-Tracer was limited to creating five separate images that you would later map on the inside of a "sky-box," Sky Baker also allows the creation of Cylindrical and Spherical projection images. Spherical is probably the most convenient of the three. First, it creates a single image, and second, since it's designed to be mapped on a sphere, there will be no distortion as you'd see with images mapped on a cube.

FIGURE 11-14 Like the old Render Warp Images, Sky Baker allows you to pre-render a sky image, but in a variety of ways.

All the images that Sky Baker creates are square, and the Resolution value represents both the width and height of the image in pixels. We'll use the default of 512 for now, since it won't take too long to generate.

Normally for most video work, you'll want to use a higher value, such as 1,000 or higher, since the camera will only be able to fit a small portion of this image in its field of view, resulting in a more pixelated sky. A good rule of thumb is to make the Sky Baker image at least two times your frame resolution.

Select a place to save your Sky Baker image and select a file format. Finally, select the Spherical mapping method and then click OK. Sky Baker will immediately open a new window that shows its baking progress.

In a couple of minutes, the window will vanish and you have an image similar to the one in Figure 11-15. If you look closely, you can also see that our skywriting has been reversed (Figure 11-16). This is normal. Since this image is designed to be mapped on a sphere, the writing will appear correct when viewed on the inside of a ball. For fun, try using this image for the sky in Tutorial 6.

FIGURE 11-15 Our "sky writing" sky rendered out as a spherical projection.

FIGURE 11-16 On closer inspection, you can see that our sky writing is in reverse.

Note: Since this is a spherical Projection image, it's best to use a round sphere, rather than a squashed one like we used in Tutorial 6, for the sky-ball. This will prevent the sky image from becoming distorted. Also, if you're using only the top half of a sphere for the sky, be sure to center the image at 0, 0, 0 or the sky will become distorted again.

Well, it was nice to feel the sun on our face. Now how about the wind in our . . .

HAIR!

That's right! LightWave 7 has hair! The kind folks at Worley Laboratories have provided us with SasLite, a lite version of their extremely popular fur shader, Sasquatch.

Fur and hair, as well as grass, have always been a bit of a modeling problem. For realistic-looking hair and grass effects, you had to either model (and occasionally animate) many thousands of strands or blades, or use many image-mapped panels. This much geometry can really bring LightWave to a crawl, even on the fastest machines. Sasquatch and SasLite use a technique known as *instancing,* where the geometry for the strands is created only when it's needed, where it's needed, so that at any one time, only a few strands are in memory. The strands are actually a volumetric effect with an extremely specialized procedural texture applied. Unlike other volumetrics, though, SasLite is added through the Pixel Filter list on the Processing tab of the Effects panel. This is where the actual fur rendering takes place. However, SasLite needs to know where the surface of the object is in order to apply the fur to it. This is done, much as with HyperVoxels, by also applying a displacement plug-in to the object. This displacement plug-in provides us with all the settings for controlling the look of the fur. Let's take a closer look at this process.

STEP 9: Clear the scene and load the **Lizardmonster.lwo** object from the CD. Open the Object Properties panel and click the Deformations tab. At the bottom of this tab, click the Add Displacement button and select SasLite from the list. Next, double-click the SasLite entry in the displacement list.

In the panel that opens (Figure 11-17), you see a couple of columns of settings. The top section of the left column is the first thing we need to worry about, since this is how we tell SasLite where to put the fur. By default, it's set to all surfaces.

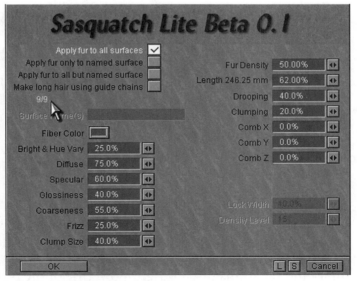

FIGURE 11-17 The SasLite displacement plug-in interface is a very simplified version of Sasquatch, yet still very powerful.

This Lizardmonster has six different surfaces on him, as we noticed when we played with him in Tutorial 5. Obviously, things like eyeballs should not have fur on them, so we don't want to use this setting. The next two options allow us to specify surfaces to apply SasLite to and surfaces to exclude. Either of these options will activate the text field below them, where you can specify the surfaces to affect. You can select multiple surfaces by entering their names here, separated by commas. An asterisk can also be used as a wildcard for fast multiple selection of surfaces. For example, to apply fur to all surfaces that start with "hair," you could enter "hair*" and SasLite will look through the entire list of surfaces for this object and find everything that has "hair" at the beginning of the name. The fourth method to place hair, "Make long hair using guide chains," allows us to sculpt the hair any way we want by adding some special geometry to the object, which we'll get into later.

Note: The green numbers immediately below these four options tell you how many surfaces SasLite is affecting in the object. The number before the slash is the number of surfaces that SasLite is actually applying fur to; the number after the slash is the total number of surfaces in the object.

STEP 10: For now, we'll just use the default settings to see what we get. Since we're done with this panel for now, let's set up the second part of SasLite. Press Ctrl+F8 to open the Effects panel and select the Processing tab.

Click the Add Pixel Filter button and select SasLite from the list. Open this plug-in's interface and activate both shadowing options, since fur looks best when it's receiving shadows. Also, increase the Render Backside Fur to 100%. We'll be adding some longer hair to this guy soon, and by increasing this value, we'll be able to see the hair on the side of the lizardmonster that's facing away from the camera. Everything else can be left alone here, so click OK to close the panel.

STEP 11: We've set up both panels for SasLite now, so let's see what we've got. Press F9 to do a render, and in a few moments you'll see something like Figure 11-18. OK, so it's a bit hard to make out what this thing is right now. One of the problems is that there's not enough shading to tell us the shape of the object under all that fur. Even though we've set up the shadowing options for SasLite, we're still not seeing them. SasLite only uses shadow maps, and those are available only with Spotlights. Our default light is a Distant one, which doesn't support these. Open the Light Properties panel and click the Light Type button to select Spotlight. Now, change the Shadow Type to Shadow Map and press F9 again. This time this mess of fur will have more depth (Figure 11-19).

OK, now that we have the fur working, let's give this guy a trim.

FIGURE 11-18 The default settings give us a very hairy-looking . . . something.

FIGURE 11-19 When we use a Spotlight, this mess of fur starts to take on some depth.

Tip: When applying fur to an object, you will find it handy to have the Surface Editor open with its surface list expanded. This will eliminate the guesswork in adding surfaces to affect, since you'll be able to see all the surface names listed for the object. This is even more useful when you consider the fact that SasLite is case-sensitive. If the spelling is not exact (excluding the use of the wildcard option), SasLite will ignore the surface name. Another helpful tip is to keep an eye on the numbers above this area. When you press Enter or Tab after adding a surface name, the number to the left of the slash should change. If it doesn't, then you probably spelled the surface name incorrectly, or you may have forgotten to add a comma between names. If it's zero, then no fur will be applied to the object. This number will be updated only when you press Enter or Tab, or click the OK button. Simply clicking elsewhere in the panel will not update it.

STEP 12: Go back to the Object Properties panel and open the SasLite displacement plug-in again. We'll cut back on the number of surfaces this is applied to now, so select the "Apply fur only to named surface" check box. Next, we'll specify a surface to use. The main surface on this object is called Hide, so enter that in the Surface Name(s) field. Also, we'll shorten the hair a bit, since this guy looks like a dust brush on steroids. In the right column, lower the Length to 25%. While we're here, let's make that fur a bit easier to see by clicking the Fiber Color and selecting a brighter color. Something close to white will do nicely. Close the panel and press F9 again.

Note: Length is set using a percentage value, which sets the length of the hair in relation to the size of the object. Thus, a length of 50% on a large object will result in longer hair than the same value on a smaller object. This allows us to change the scale of an object without having to worry about adjusting the length of the hair to compensate. SasLite does show the actual current length of the hair to the left of the Length field to help you set things up when you know how big the object is. For our lizardmonster, who is almost 2 meters tall, to have 10-cm-long fur, we can simply adjust the percentage value with the slider button until we see 100 mm in the readout (approximately 39%).

Figure 11-20 shows a better-looking coat of fur, though it could be thicker.

FIGURE 11-20 After a small trim and color treatment, we can see that this guy's fur coat is a bit thin in places.

STEP 13: Open SasLite again, and this time increase the Fur Density to 100%. Do another render and you'll see a much thicker coat of fur (Figure 11-21). It's still a bit patchy, though, so let's smooth it out a bit.

FIGURE 11-21 A little more hair care helps improve the thickness of his coat. Now he needs a little grooming.

Note: Fur Density and Length are the two options that will have the greatest impact on rendering times. The higher their values, the longer the render times. If you're adding long fur to an object, you might want to keep the density lower to compensate. Not only will this help reduce render times, but it will also help keep the fur from looking like a solid mass.

STEP 14: The patchiness of the fur coat is caused by the Clumping value. Higher values will make the hair tips try to clump together more, while lower values will tend to keep them more evenly spaced. Lower the Clumping value to 10% or less to create a softer, healthier-looking fur coat. A value of 5% was used for Figure 11-22.

FIGURE 11-22 After we brush out the clumps, our lizard-monster is looking almost cuddly.

Now we've seen that we can get a variety of looks with SasLite, what if we want our fur to be different lengths? At least with the color of the fur, we can add some variation by adjusting the Bright & Hue Vary value, but there's no variance option for length. Well, not directly at least.

SasLite is a pixel filter that gets information objects from the displacement plug-in. Multiple objects can all be handled by this one pixel filter, which means this filter can read more than one instance of its displacement plug-in. There's really no reason we can't add more than one instance of the plug-in to the same object, then. Many animals have two types of fur: the regular coarse hair that is normally exposed, and the shorter, much softer, very fine downy fur that is hidden beneath. This could easily be simulated by two copies of SasLite.

STEP 15: We'll start off by creating this guy's downy fur first. Down is generally a lighter color, so let's make this first layer almost white. RGB values of 250, 245, and 235 will do nicely. Figure 11-23 shows the other settings for a nice fine-haired downy coat. Note that the Comb Z value is increased to 200%. This sweeps the fur back toward the positive Z axis, giving the fur some natural direction. This layer of fur is also applied to both the Hide surface and the Stripe surface, which is the creature's chest. Figure 11-24 shows the results of these values.

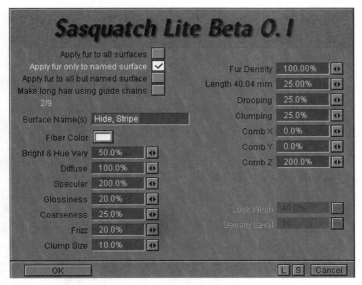

FIGURE 11-23 A set of values for a fine downy coat.

FIGURE 11-24 The first layer of fur is added to our lizardmonster.

STEP 16: Add another instance of SasLite and make this one a darker tan color. RGB values of 230, 205, and 265 were used with the settings in Figure 11-25. Again, combing has been used to sweep the hair back. This layer is also much longer and less dense, and is applied only to the Hide surface, leaving the chest area covered only in the down layer. Figure 11-26 shows these two layers combined.

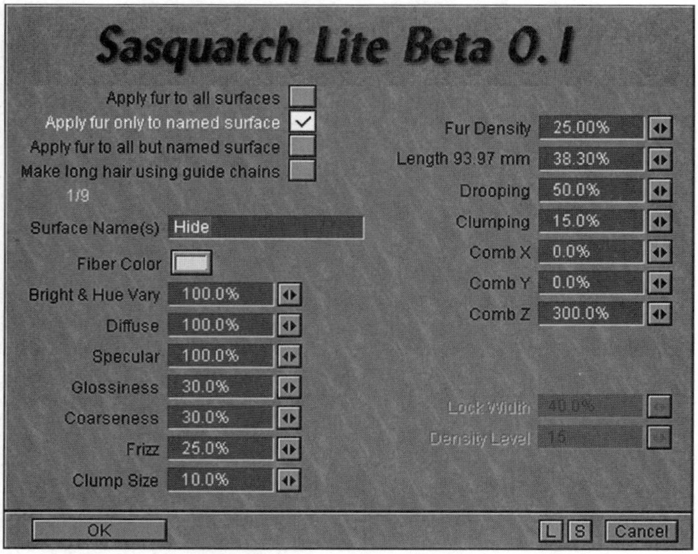

Sasquatch Lite Beta 0.1

Apply fur to all surfaces ☐
Apply fur only to named surface ☑
Apply fur to all but named surface ☐
Make long hair using guide chains ☐
1/9

Surface Name(s) Hide

Fiber Color ☐
Bright & Hue Vary 100.0% ◀▶
Diffuse 100.0% ◀▶
Specular 100.0% ◀▶
Glossiness 30.0% ◀▶
Coarseness 30.0% ◀▶
Frizz 25.0% ◀▶
Clump Size 10.0% ◀▶

Fur Density 25.00% ◀▶
Length 93.97 mm 38.30% ◀▶
Drooping 50.0% ◀▶
Clumping 15.0% ◀▶
Comb X 0.0% ◀▶
Comb Y 0.0% ◀▶
Comb Z 300.0% ◀▶

Lock Width 40.0% ☐
Density Level 15 ☐

OK   L S Cancel

FIGURE 11-25 The settings for a second layer of longer, more coarse fur.

FIGURE 11-26 A second, longer and less dense fur layer combined with the first.

Tip: When adding multiple layers of fur, start with the short fur first. This way you'll be able to see the longer fur when you add it. If you start with the long fur, then it will hide the shorter fur, unless you only have one layer activated at a time. By starting with the short fur, you can keep all the fur layers active and still see what you're doing.

Now that we have a couple of lengths of fur on this guy, let's dress him up a bit. What he really needs is a nice long white mane running down his back. The only problem is, we don't have a separate surface that we can use for that. If we changed the surface name of the polygons down the back, we could do it, but there's a better way that gives us more control. The fourth option for hair placement lets us use "guide chains" to shape the way the hair flows, and is designed for very long hair effects. It also requires adding some detail to the model.

STEP 17: Load Modeler and load **Lizardmonster.lwo** into it. Switch to the second object layer and place the lizardmonster in the background. Zoom in on the side view and press the plus key (+) to activate the Add Points tool. Now add a few points along the spine of the back, as shown in Figure 11-27. We don't need a lot, just 10 or so. These points will serve as the roots for our guide chains, but to do that, they need to have a surface name. This means we need to turn each of them into a polygon.

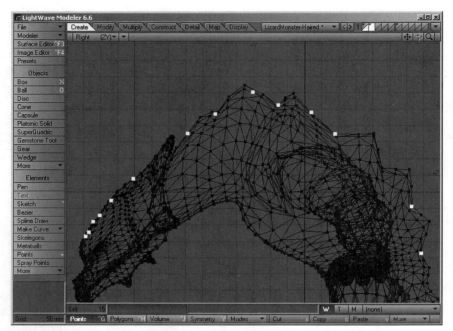

FIGURE 11-27 A few points are created along the spine of the beast.

STEP 18: Make sure all these points are selected and then click the More button in the Elements area on the main toolbar for the Create tab. Choose Make 1-Point Polygons and each of the points will now have a polygon attached to it.

Note: If the Modeler window is large enough, this More button will disappear, and in its place will be purple buttons for all the functions that would normally be menu items under the More button. There will be a button labeled Points to Polys, which is the one we want.

These points will be the roots of the guide chains we'll create. Guide chains are simply chains of two-point polygons, or "polylines" that are connected end to end, that we can twist and bend, much like a spline curve, into a shape that SasLite can use to shape its hair strands. SasLite needs these chains to have a root or base polygon that uses a different surface name from the rest of the chain. This root surface tells SasLite which way to grow the hair around the chain. These surface names can be anything, but you can only have two surfaces per any given chain, and one of them must be only at the base.

The chain itself must not have any breaks in it, and must be another surface name. SasLite will use this surface to guide the hair. While the root surface can actually be any number of polygons, or any number of points, the chain itself must be made of two-point polygons, and one end of this chain must be attached to a polygon of another surface.

Note: We could just copy some points from the original model and extrude these into chains, but this could be very limiting in the case of very-low-detail models. These chains don't have to be attached to the body of the model; they just need a polygon with a different surface name at one end. By using a single-point polygon as the root, we can easily extrude it into a chain, and use the Polygon Stats window to select the chain or the root for surface naming.

STEP 19: Select all these polygons and press Q to open the Change Surface panel. Call this surface Root and click OK. Now we're ready to make the chains. This is as simple as extruding these single-point polygons, but there is a catch. If we did extrude these polygons, they would be changed to two-point polygons. While this isn't necessarily a bad thing, it will create some extra geometry that we don't need. It will also mean that our chains will start somewhere away from the surface due to the fact that the root polygons will suddenly have length. To prevent this, press C to copy these single-point polygons into memory.

STEP 20: Now that we have a copy of these polygons in memory, we can change their surface again, without affecting the copy we just made. Press Q again and create a new surface called Hair. Now we're ready to create the strands. Click the Multiply tab and select Extrude (Shift+E). Now click in the Right view window and drag up to the side. Each point will now have a line extending from it. This will be fine for a punk rocker's spiked hairstyle, but if we want to add some curves to the hair, we're going to need to subdivide these guides. Press N to open the Numeric panel for the Extrude tool. Increase the Sides value to 5, and each of these strands will now have five segments (Figure 11-28).

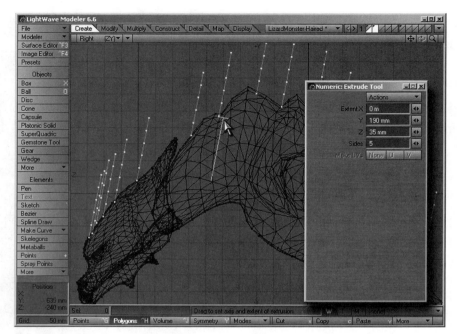

FIGURE 11-28 The chains are subdivided using the Extrude tool's Numeric panel.

Note: You can use any number of segments you like. Five was chosen here for simplicity.

STEP 21: Now we can paste the original polygons we just copied back into place. Press V and then follow that by merging points. Remember, if the chains are not connected to a second surface, they will not work. What you should have in this layer now is a handful of single-point polygons with the Root surface, and several two-point polygons with the Hair surface.

Now we can start sculpting these chains into shape.

STEP 22: Press Ctrl+T to activate the Drag tool. Now it's just a matter of dragging points around. Just place the pointer over a point, then click and drag to move that point around. Just try to avoid moving the root polygons so they don't inadvertently get pulled away from the surface of the lizardmonster. You can shape these chains any way you like, and Figure 11-29 shows one example.

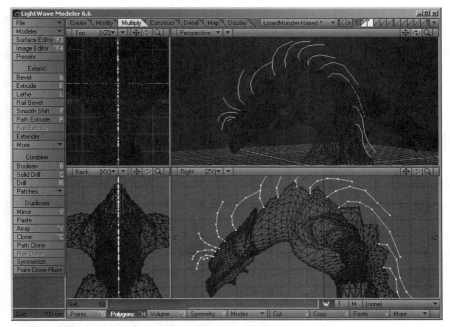

FIGURE 11-29 After a small amount of point dragging, we have the chains roughing out the lizardmonster's hairstyle.

STEP 23: Once you have the guide chains sculpted the way you like, cut them from this layer and paste them into the first layer. They will not work if they're not in the same object layer that SasLite is applied to in Layout. Save this guy as **Harry.lwo** and switch back to Layout. Replace the current lizardmonster with Harry and open the Object Properties panel for him. Add a third SasLite to the Deformations plug-in list and open its interface. Make the hair in this one bright white and then select the "Make long hair using guide chains" check box. This will deactivate most of the options down the right side of the panel and activate two new ones at bottom right (Figure 11-30).

Density Level is self-explanatory, and Lock Width is simply another percentage value that controls how much of the area around each guide chain will grow long hair. Again, since this is a percentage, the amount of hair will vary with each chain. Larger chains will have more hair than smaller ones. You'll have to experiment with these yourself to get a look that's pleasing to you, since the results are based on the shapes of these guides. Figure 11-31 has one example.

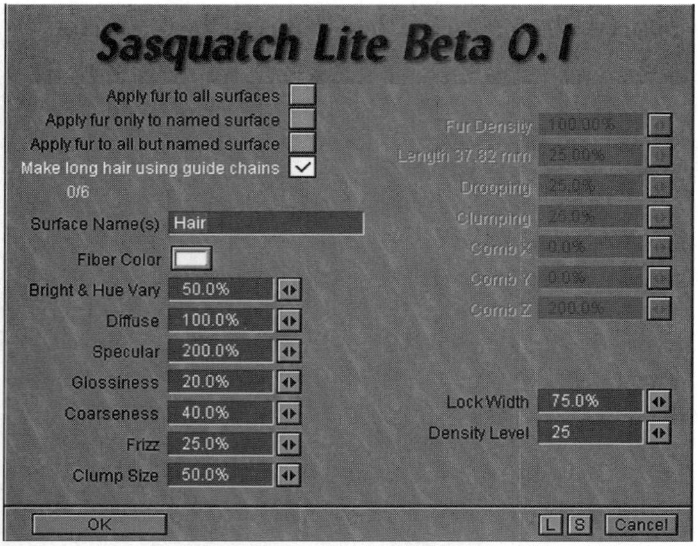

FIGURE 11-30 Guide chains deactivate half of the options in SasLite, but offers two new ones.

FIGURE 11-31 The results of the guide chains. In this image, the guide chains are visible and are casting large shadows. However, you can see how they guide the hair around them.

Tip: You'll notice that we can actually see the guide chains against the fur, even if they're completely transparent. This is just normal behavior for transparent surfaces and volumetrics. Volumetrics need to be raytraced through a transparent surface in order to be seen through it, which is why the new

Ray Trace Transparency option was added in the Render Options panel. However, SasLite does not currently show up the same way, so wherever we have a transparent surface in front of the fur, the fur is not rendered, leaving these gaps where the guide chains are. There is another solution, though. In the Object Properties panel, on the Rendering tab, there's a Particle/Line Thickness value. This is used to define how thick single-point and two-point polygons will render, and it also affects the thickness of lines when rendering wireframe as well. By setting this to zero, we tell LightWave that these lines will have no thickness whatsoever, and the result is that they are no longer visible. This also means that they'll no longer interfere with SasLite's fur (Figure 11-32).

FIGURE 11-32 After we change the Particle/Line Thickness to 0, the guides disappear from the final render.

Now, if anyone needs a hairy-looking lizardmonster, you're just the one to do it! Of course, this is just a small sampling of what the full Sasquatch is capable of. For more information you'll want to visit http://www.worley.com/, and be sure to check out their user gallery for inspiration.

Enjoy these, and the several other new tools that have been added to LightWave 7 that are sure to make the lives of animators so much easier.

Index